Peter Galloway

THE MOST ILLUSTRIOUS ORDER

*The Order of St Patrick
and its Knights*

Peter Galloway

THE MOST ILLUSTRIOUS ORDER

The Order of St Patrick and its Knights

We are but dust and a shadow.
HORACE

UNICORN PRESS

LONDON

To
MY MOTHER
AND IN MEMORY
OF MY FATHER

UNICORN PRESS
21 Afghan Road
London SW11 0QD

Published by Unicorn Press 1999
Copyright © Peter Galloway 1998

The moral right of Peter Galloway to be identified as the
author of this work has been asserted in accordance
with the Copyright, Designs and Patents Acts of 1988

A catalogue record for this book is available
from the British Library

ISBN 0 906290 23 6

Designed and produced by
Pardoe Blacker Publishing Limited
Lingfield · Surrey

Printed under the supervision of Midas UK
by HBM Print Ltd, Singapore

Contents

Foreword

HIS ROYAL HIGHNESS THE DUKE OF GLOUCESTER KG GCVO

=====

A NATIONAL ORDER OF CHIVALRY was an English invention of 1348, enabling the King to single out those individuals who had most contributed to the national well being, and as a spur to the ambition of those whose existing power and influence could be helping or hindering the purposes of the King. Other Orders of Chivalry such as the Knights of St John of Jerusalem and the Knights Templars were supra-national organisations with quite different intentions.

Scotland's Order of the Thistle was created in 1687 for a similar purpose to acknowledge the role of the sixteen Scotsmen whose contribution was most appreciated.

It was therefore of no surprise that Ireland should have its own Order of Chivalry, giving both extra powers to the Government and a further opportunity for pomp and circumstances to the vice-regal court in Dublin.

Further Orders were created – in 1815 of the Royal Guelphic Order for those Hanoverians who had fought so effectively in the British Army against Napoleon; and in 1861 the Star of India for those whose support had proved vital in preserving the British Empire during the Indian Mutiny, both in due course to be overtaken by events.

The history of Ireland is with the benefit of hindsight full of decisions that turned out to be counter productive. The Order of St Patrick was not a consequence of a wrong decision but its demise was inevitable with the advance of the democratic process set against Ireland's turbulent history.

My father was the last member of the Order and there were only a few occasions he could wear it: as Honorary Colonel of the Inniskillings when taking a Parade or as Earl of Ulster when visiting Northern Ireland.

This book gives us an insight into the workings of the vice-regal court in Dublin before the Union and subsequently a rare opportunity for the pomp and pageantry of an investiture in a capital city, but recently deprived of such indulgences.

That such an institution failed to live up to its motto is part of a much wider story but it is interesting to read of what the Order collectively achieved, and of the nature of its individual members.

Peter Galloway has set both the Order and its individual members in the historical context and explains the decisions that caused its inception, its years of glory and its demise.

Richard.

Acknowledgements

WITH ONE OR TWO EXCEPTIONS, I have not reproduced the acknowledgements that appeared in *The Order of St Patrick 1783–1983*, though my gratitude to those individuals, some of whom have died in the past fifteen years, still remains. The following list is pertinent to the present publication.

I acknowledge the gracious permission of Her Majesty The Queen to quote from material in the Royal Archives, to illustrate items of insignia in the Royal Collection and for allowing the mantle of His late Majesty King George VI to be photographed and reproduced; and to Oliver Everett, CVO, and Lady de Bellaigue, MVO, of the Royal Archives, for their help.

I would also record my thanks to the following: Sir Robert Balchin, for reading and correcting the text in proof stage; Elwyn Blacker of Pardoe Blacker Publishing, and Hugh Tempest-Radford, of Unicorn Press, for arranging the publication of a book on a subject as specialised as a dormant Order of Knighthood; Alan Boyd of St Anne's Cathedral, Belfast, for searching the cathedral archives; Ruth Gardner, LVO, OBE, former Assistant Ceremonial Officer in the Cabinet Office, for willingly encouraging and sharing my enthusiasm for rewriting the history of the Order of St Patrick; Fergus Gillespie, Deputy Chief Herald of Ireland, for kindly making available the volumes of correspondence of successive Ulster Kings of Arms, and other records in the Genealogical Office of Ireland; Charles Green, for photographing the mantle of King George VI; Robert Heslip of the Ulster Museum, for help with the insignia of the Order held by the Museum; Lieutenant Colonel Anthony Mather, CVO, OBE, Secretary of the Central Chancery of the Orders of Knighthood, for permission to photograph the insignia of the Knights and Officers of the Order, and for generally supporting and encouraging this project; Michael Murphy and his family, for warmly welcoming me to Kilmorna in County Kerry, and showing me around the site of Kilmorna House, where Sir Arthur Vicars was murdered in 1921; reproduction of *The Knights of the Most Illustrious Order of St Patrick* by John Keyse Sherwin, is courtesy of the National Gallery of Ireland; the Duke of Norfolk, for permission to reproduce Oswald Birley's portrait of Viscount FitzAlan of Derwent; Dr Frederick O'Dwyer of the Office of Public Works, for helping me with aspects of the history and decoration of St Patrick's Hall, Dublin Castle; the Office of Public Works, for permission to include an illustration of the interior of St Patrick's Hall; Doris Pierce, who kindly transferred the text of *The Order of St Patrick 1783–1983* to disk; Charles Reede, for his help in identifying and re-ordering the crests, banners and hatchments in St Patrick's Cathedral, Dublin; Lieutenant Commander James Risk, CVO, FSA, for his seminal work on the history of the Order of the Bath, which first inspired me to work on the Order of St Patrick; Richard Roscoe, Honours Secretary, 10 Downing Street; Randal Sadleir, for allowing me to consult and use the papers of his father, the late Thomas Ulick Sadleir, and for recalling his own memories of the Office of Arms in Dublin Castle in the days before the Second World War; Richard Sands of the Foreign and Commonwealth Office; Jonathan Shackleton, for information on the life of his cousin, Francis Richard Shackleton; Kirsten Stadelhofer for information about the present state of Titania's Palace, now in Denmark, and once the pride and joy of Sir Nevile Wilkinson; David Stanley, for the photograph of Sir Arthur Vicars, and also for alerting me to the existence of the mantle of King George VI; Michael Turner, for patiently driving me around Dublin and Ireland, and for willingly reading and correcting the proofs while on vacation in the Pocono mountains of Pennsylvania. Thomas Woodcock, LVO, FSA, Norroy and Ulster King of Arms, for arranging for the crown and badge of Ulster King of Arms, and the baton and badge of Dublin Herald to be photographed, and Janet Grant, his secretary, for carrying the crown and insignia back and forth across London; Patricia Woods, Head Guide of the State Apartments, Dublin Castle, for allowing me to spend a delightful two hours alone in St Patrick's Hall, examining and recording the banners and hatchments of the Knights; Robert Yorke, Archivist of the College of Arms; and lastly the staff of the British Library, the Irish National Archives, and the Public Record Office, although their names are unknown to me, because their assistance has been invaluable.

Preface

ACOMPANY OF SIXTEEN 'NOBLE AND WORTHY KNIGHTS', was founded in 1783 during the reign of King George III, 'for the dignity and honour of Our Realm of Ireland'. During its flourishing days, from the late eighteenth to the early twentieth centuries, the Order of St Patrick, as it was to be called, was well known as the national honour of Ireland, but radical changes in the Irish political landscape during the twentieth century, encapsulated in the formulaical trinity of 'time, circumstance and parliamentary enactment', have consigned the Order to dormancy, and no new Knight of St Patrick has been appointed since 1936. As there is no prospect that one will be made in the future, the usefulness of the Order is now probably finished, and its story is concluded.

My first attempt to record the history of the Order, was published in 1983, under the title of *The Order of St Patrick 1783–1983*. It was my first book, and represented an attempt to tell the story of an Order which had fascinated me for more than ten years. In the fifteen years since its publication, I have come to realise that it could and should be re-written. Quite apart from the obvious need to correct mistakes that found their way into the original work, the more open attitude of recent years towards access to records, has opened a number of files which were closed to public access at the time, and afforded me an opportunity for more detailed research into the history of the Order than was then possible. In those primitive days, the text was hammered out on a manual typewiter, but now, with the benefit of a word processor and other advances in information technology, it has become possible with less manual effort, to write a new history of the Order of St Patrick.

The decision to accord this history of the Order a new title – *The Most Illustrious Order* – was influenced by the fact that the text of the original publication has been so completely revised and extended, as to be altered beyond recognition, and the result is the emergence of a very different publication. This is not a second edition of *The Order of St Patrick 1783–1983*, which in retrospect can be seen as an introductory monograph, but a new work containing substantial areas of new information and interpretation.

The decision to write this new history was partly inspired, as was its predecessor, by Mr Joseph Cooper Walker, of whom I know very little, beyond a letter written on 5 May 1788, to James Caulfeild, 1st Earl of Charlemont, and one of the founder Knights of St Patrick. Cooper self-deprecatingly declared that he was thinking of embarking on a new literary project. 'I hope your lordship will pardon the liberty I have taken in giving to the public my essay on the Irish dress, in its original epistolary form, and honour with a place in your lordship's library the copy which accompanies this.[1] Having made two feeble attempts to elucidate the antiquities of my country, I am now about to abandon the subject. Indeed, I doubt if I shall ever resume it again, unless it be for the purpose of doing what the herald of the Order of St Patrick (if there be such an officer) ought to do, that is, to collect materials for an historical memoir on knighthood in Ireland, chiefly with a view of preserving from oblivion the several circumstances attending the institution of that Order.'[2]

A search of the catalogues of the British Library failed to reveal any trace of Mr Walker's proposed memoir on Irish knighthood, and I concluded that he did abandon his attempts further to 'elucidate the antiquities' of Ireland. In his 1842 study of the history of the United Kingdom Orders of Knighthood, Sir Harris Nicolas did not cite Joseph Cooper Walker as an authority on the Order of St Patrick, and Walker's thought of becoming the first historian of the Order probably never came to fruition.

I remember discovering his letter to the Earl of Charlemont when my interest in the Order was passing through a transitional phase from acquisitive curiosity to serious research, and the inspiration that it provided at that time and subsequently, proved to be a silent but continuous encouragement, which has now borne fruit for a second time. I would like to think that I have succeeded in achieving his aim of 'preserving from oblivion', not only the circumstances surrounding the institution of the Order of Saint Patrick but also its history as the national honour of Ireland.

In the years since 1983, my research interests have extended to other honours and other fields, but I have never lost my affection for this Irish Order, and I am pleased to have an opportunity of presenting a much fuller account of a comparatively unknown aspect of Irish history, in the hope that what follows, will be the final and definitive record of The Most Illustrious Order of St Patrick.

CHAPTER ONE

THE POLITICS OF AN HONOUR

The eighteenth-century origins of the Order

===

Pray let me have my Order of Knighthood
as it is necessary for our House of Peers.
LORD TEMPLE, November 1782

THE HISTORY of the Order of St Patrick can be written entirely in the past tense, because it no longer has any meaningful existence. Although the Order has never been formally abolished, Prince Henry, Duke of Gloucester, the last Knight of St Patrick, died in 1974, and this Order of Knighthood now has no more than a wraith-like existence in the shadows of twilight. It stood at the centre of Irish ceremonial life for more than one hundred and forty years as the national honour of Ireland. But like so much beautiful ceremonial icing, it looked enchanting, but had very little substance and no existence independent of the Irish viceregal court of which it was but a decorative feature. It outlived its usefulness and was consigned to oblivion. It was born from the turmoil of Irish politics in the eighteenth century, and it died from the turmoil of Irish politics in the twentieth century.

The Order of St Patrick was formally instituted on 5 February 1783, when Letters Patent passed the Great Seal of Ireland, creating a new Order of Knighthood for that kingdom, and so the Order of St Patrick (of Ireland) joined the Order of the Garter (of England) and the Order of the Thistle (of Scotland) as the third of the three 'national' honours of the United Kingdom. It was the first Order to be founded in Britain or Ireland since the Order of the Bath in 1725, and the reason for doing so was displayed in the lofty language of royal formality: 'Whereas Our loving Subjects of Our Kingdom of Ireland have approved themselves steadily attached to Our Royal Person and Government, and affectionately disposed to maintain and promote the Welfare and Prosperity of the Whole Empire; And We being willing to confer upon Our Subjects of Our Said Kingdom a testimony of Our sincere love and affectionate regard, by creating an Order of Knighthood in Our Said Kingdom ... This is Our Royal Will and Pleasure and We do hereby Authorize and Require You upon Receipt hereof forthwith to cause Letters Patent to be passed Under the Great Seal ... for creating a Society or Brotherhood to be called Knights of the Most Illustrious Order of St Patrick'.[1]

These are formal, stylised documents which reveal nothing of reality, and that which created the Order of St Patrick in 1783 is typical of the genre. Such documents need to be read with circumspection, and rarely if ever do the archaic forms of their language give even the vaguest hint of what personalities and situations lie behind an occurrence as rare as the foundation of a new Order of Knighthood. If the courtly language of the Warrant is taken at its face value, the reader would believe that a scene of peace and harmony reigned in late eighteenth century Ireland, and that its relations with England were nothing but cordial. Consequently, King George III had been moved to institute this Order as a means of recognising the loyal service of his Irish subjects, all of whom were mindful of their duty to him and to the empire. Nothing could be further from the truth. Irish political life in 1782–3 was marked by restlessness and turbulence, and an increasingly clamorous protest against the tight political control exercised by the government in London, and the Order of St Patrick arose from a serious political crisis.

The history of the Order is inseparable from the history of Ireland. Only by disregarding the wording of the Royal Warrant, and examining the events, the political temperature, and the mood of opinion in Ireland in the twenty years preceding 1783, can the true reason for the institution of the Order of St Patrick be discerned. The creation of the Order needs to be set not within the chronological history of the development of honours, but firmly in the context of Irish politics in the late eighteenth century.

The government of the kingdom of Ireland (it was theoretically a separate kingdom from Great Britain until the union of 1801) was nominally headed by a representative of the Crown and the British government, styled the Lord Lieutenant. His formal designation was 'Lord Lieutenant General and General Governor', but the shorter form of 'Lord Lieutenant' was commonly in use. In 1782 a house in Phoenix Park, Dublin, was purchased for the residence of the Lord Lieutenant; it was styled the 'viceregal lodge', and, verbally and unofficially, the Lord Lieutenant was sometimes referred to as the 'viceroy'.

The Lord Lieutenant of Ireland was customarily a peer, appointed by the government of the day, and changing with each administration. His wealth and status had to be such that he could be seen to be the personal representative of the King in Ireland. Nominally he ruled Ireland in the name of the King, maintaining a smaller version of the royal court and household, and he represented in Ireland the authority and the pageantry of the monarchy. Until the middle of the eighteenth century, the appointment was an honour that rarely involved a visit to Ireland, let alone residence there. The Lord Lieutenant's power of actively governing Ireland in the name of the King, was effectively delegated to deputies known as Lords Justices. There were customarily three Lords Justices, one of whom was usually, though not invariably the Archbishop of Armagh; the others were Irish peers.

The office of Chief Secretary, theoretically subordinate to the Lord Lieutenant, had emerged by 1566, and the holder performed in Ireland a function analogous to that of the Prime Minister in London. He represented government administration and policy in Ireland, especially in the Irish House of Commons, and was also a political appointee, who changed with each British administration. The office grew more important and powerful in the second half of the eighteenth century, with the increasing residence in Ireland of the Lord Lieutenant.

Among the Chief Secretary's responsibilities was the conduct of government business in the House of Commons of the Irish Parliament. This body, in theory the legislature of Ireland, had emerged in the Middle Ages, and from 1729 its sessions were held in the impressive classical colonnaded building which can still be seen in Dublin, on College Green opposite Trinity College. The Irish Parliament was superficially similar to the British Parliament, being a bicameral legislature with a House of Commons and a House of Lords; but there the similarity ended. By successive pieces of legislation, beginning with Poyning's Law in 1494 and ending with the Irish Parliament Act of 1720, the freedom of the Irish Parliament to legislate, was substantially curtailed. The head of any bill arising in either chamber of the Irish Parliament was first passed to the Irish Privy Council, that could either suppress or amend it as it pleased. If the proposed legislation passed this first test, it was then formally drafted and sent to the British Privy Council, which also had unlimited power of suppression or alteration. If this second ordeal was passed, the bill was returned, with such changes as both privy councils had made, to whichever chamber of parliament in which it had originated, and then passed to the other chamber. Neither the Irish House of Commons nor the Irish House of Lords had the power to alter the bill; they could only accept it as it had been returned from London, or reject it altogether and start again. By these measures, the Irish Parliament was essentially powerless, and the humiliation was deepened by the fact that acts of the British Parliament in London were binding in Ireland, and the supreme court of appeal was the House of Lords in London. There was no Habeas Corpus Act for Ireland, nor was there any legislation obliging members of parliament to resign their seats when accepting places of profit, or pensions from the Crown. There was no national militia, no security of tenure for judges, and two-thirds of the country's revenue was outside the control of the Irish Parliament.

There was little objection to this state of affairs during the climate of civil war and unrest in the years after the civil war in 1689–90 between factions loyal either to the deposed King James II or to his successor King William III, but from about the middle of the eighteenth century there was an increasingly vociferous demand for change, and this new atmosphere began to pervade the debates of the Irish Parliament. The growth of a middle class, the calming of the passions of the seventeenth century civil war, the decline of religious intolerance, and the sudden rise of a free press were significant factors; another was the decision of the Chatham administration in 1765 requiring the Lord Lieutenant to be resident in Ireland during his term of office. Hitherto, each holder of the office had spent, at the most, only six months of every two years in the country, and the government was 'undertaken' by a few important Irish peers with considerable parliamentary influence, on the condition of obtaining a large share of the disposal of the Lord Lieutenant's powers of patronage. The arrival of a succession of residential Lord Lieutenants inevitably brought an increased sense of conflict between this imported British peer and the Irish peers.

In October 1767, Viscount Townshend arrived in Dublin as the first resident Lord Lieutenant, charged with restoring power to the British administration. Townshend was a tactless and impatient man, and he tried to assert his authority by attempting to break the power of the Irish 'undertaker' peers, complaining that the Lord Lieutenant had been reduced to a mere 'pageant of state'. Within Ireland, the 'under-takers' were a force to be reckoned with, and Townshend rightly estimated that they were the effective rulers of Ireland. If their power was not formally checked, the authority of the British government would gradually weaken, and the dependence of Ireland on Great Britain would be jeopardised. In 1767–9 Townshend attempted to navigate through the Irish Parliament a bill to increase the size of the Irish standing army from 12,000 to 15,000 men. Twice it was brought before the Irish House of Commons, and twice it was rejected. Though a third bill, initiated by the Parliament itself, did pass, it is significant that at this point we find the first mention of an Irish Order of Knighthood. On 17 August 1769 Townshend wrote to Viscount Weymouth, the Secretary of State for the South, urging the propriety of creating an Irish Order. 'Before I conclude, I must request Your Lordship to lay before His Majesty my humble opinion, that the establishment of an Order of the nation of that of the Thistle or the Bath, would be received with greatest gratitude and pleasure by the nobility and gentry of this kingdom, and would facilitate His Majesty's affairs in the highest degree, particularly at this junction.'[2] Weymouth may or may not have submitted Townshend's request to the King, but the fact that there is no mention of an Irish Order in Weymouth's reply indicates that if he did, the King was not disposed to agree with the proposal.

The Irish Parliament was not divided into clearly identifiable political groupings. Settled political parties had not yet developed, due to the nature of constituencies which gave a predominating influence to a few personal interests. The electoral system that sent members to the Irish House of Commons, was as corrupt and decayed in Ireland as it was in Britain. Some of the numerous small boroughs were held by men who had purchased their seats; some were attached to the properties of moderately wealthy gentry who effectively nominated the member; some were under the direct influence of the government, and some were connected to the Church of Ireland. But the majority of seats in the House of Commons belonged to a few wealthy members of the House of Lords, and it was considered a point of honour that, on important questions, the member should vote in accordance with the wishes of his patron. On ordinary non-controversial matters, the government could usually be sure of a sizeable majority, but there could be issues on which the strongest government saw its majority vanish overnight. Finance bills, for example, which either originated, or were substantially modified in London, were almost always rejected. It was quite common for paid servants of the Crown, while in general supporting the government, to go into strong opposition on certain questions, and for others, who had been the most active opponents of the government, to pass suddenly into its ranks. There was a rapid fluctuation of politicians between government and opposition and, in such a situation, it was almost inevitable that bribery and corruption became legitimate and accepted parts of government. Every kind of ecclesiastical, official, legal and civic office was shamelessly used as a bribe to gain support for the government in parliament. Peerages, baronetcies, knighthoods and pensions were widely distributed, and the most archaic sinecures, if they carried an income, were widely coveted. The peerage in particular was grossly devalued by the large number of Irish peerages created from 1760 onwards, much to the considerable annoyance of King George III, who rightly believed that they devalued the peerage in general. In 1766 eighteen commoners were ennobled on eighteen consecutive days, and twelve peers were promoted to higher peerages. In most cases the terms of the bargain were well known to be a reward for supporting the government by their votes in the House of Lords, and by their nominees in the House of Commons. Horace Walpole, that shrewd observer of eighteenth-century life, assessed their true worth. 'Thirty creations at once was more than had ever been made, even at the beginning of a reign. It was a mob of nobility. The King in private laughed much at the eagerness for such insignificant honours.'[3]

In 1780, the Earl of Buckinghamshire (Lord Lieutenant 1776–80) wrote to the Prime Minister recommending eight commoners for peerages, thirteen peers for advancement in the peerage, five appointments to the Privy Council, seventeen persons for civil pensions, and several others for varying favours, adding that he had been driven to it by not having any other means of rewarding government supporters at his disposal. The Irish peerage was systematically degraded by these profuse creations which grew more frequent as the century drew on, and reached a peak during the debate on dissolving the Irish Parliament in 1800–1.

As Townshend had pressed for an Irish Order of Knighthood in 1769, so did Buckinghamshire in 1777: 'I wish our gracious master would institute an Irish Order of Knighthood ... for Irishmen only. They certainly without invidious comparisons have as good a right as others who enjoy those marks of distinction. The establishment should not be too numerous, and, bestowed with propriety, would occasionally be received in lieu of emoluments and lessen the necessity of lavishing those hereditary honours which ultimately become burthensome to a country and essentially weaken and embarrass government'.[4] Buckinghamshire's view was sensible and practical, but his wish went unheeded, and no action was taken until Lord Temple arrived as Lord Lieutenant, in September 1782, in a very different political climate.

The period from 1760 to 1782 saw a gathering campaign by virtually all sections of Irish opinion to free the Irish Parliament from all legislative restrictions. Attempts by successive Lord Lieutenants from 1765 onwards to break the power of the 'undertakers' and reassert viceregal authority, only served to throw those who had previously supported the government into the opposition camp. Viscount Townshend (1767–72), the Earl of Harcourt (1772–6) and the Earl of Buckinghamshire (1776–80) spent thousands of pounds creating new offices or annexing salaries to old ones, in their effort to maintain their extensive patronage, and therefore their power.

In 1778 the position grew more serious with the appearance of the Volunteers, a largely Protestant armed militia dedicated to the Irish national interest. War with France was beginning to appear inevitable at that time and, with an empty treasury, the government found itself totally unable to raise a militia of 12,000 men needed to defend Ireland against possible invasion. Lord Buckinghamshire therefore recommended that several companies of volunteers should be raised as a kind of home guard or part-time militia, and he received a response that was more overwhelming than he would have liked. Within a short time the Volunteer force numbered some 42,000 men, and the government looked with some concern on this massive army, rising up independently of its control at a time when discontent was simmering. With the army occupied in America, the Volunteers had to be treated with great care. The doctrine that no laws were valid in Ireland that had not been made by the King, Lords and Commons of Ireland, was rapidly becoming the dominant slogan in the country. The army had notably failed to suppress the rebellion in the American colonies, and news of the surrender at Yorktown in October 1781 spurred Irish demands for total legislative independence. Speaking in the Irish House of Commons, Henry Grattan (1746–1820), Member of Parliament for Charlemont, made a passionate declaration that while the crown of Ireland was inseparably united to that of England, Ireland was by right a distinct kingdom. Grattan epitomised the patriot and nationalist aspect of the Protestant ascendancy, which saw itself as fundamentally Irish, and therefore concerned to place the well-being of Ireland before that of Great Britain. In April 1782 the Duke of Portland, newly-arrived as Lord Lieutenant, wrote that the government could no longer exist in its present form, and the sooner England recalled the Lord Lieutenant, and renounced all claims to Ireland, the better. If, on the contrary, concessions were made, then the union of the two countries might be saved.

Faced with a serious and deteriorating situation, the Government introduced a resolution in the British Parliament stating that it was indispensable to the interest and happiness of both kingdoms that the connection between them should be established by mutual consent upon a solid and permanent footing. The Declaratory Act of 1720 was repealed on 21 June 1782, and the Irish Parliament was accordingly freed from all legislative restrictions. The constitution of Ireland was changed with virtually no disorder or violence. Edmund Burke (1729–97), the Irish-born statesman and orator, rightly described the events of 1782 as the Irish analogue of the British revolution of 1688.

In July 1782, the government of Lord North, discredited by the failure of the North American campaigns, resigned, and a new administration was formed under the premiership of the Earl of Shelburne. After only four months as Lord Lieutenant (April–August), the Duke of Portland was replaced by Earl Temple who was appointed Lord Lieutenant in September 1782 and, for the third time, the institution of an Irish Order of Knighthood was debated.

During the 1780s the spirit of Irish political life was completely opposed to anything which might lessen the distinctive dignity of Ireland. As a result of the independence campaign, a new pride in things Irish began to develop, and an Irish Order of Knighthood might have appeared to Shelburne and Temple as a natural corollary, quite apart from political considerations. England had the Order of the Garter, and Scotland, with an insignificant degree of independence since the abolition of the Scottish Parliament in 1707, had the Order of the Thistle. A curious parallel may be noticed here between the creation of the Thistle in 1687, twenty years before the abolition of the Scottish Parliament, and the creation of the Order of St Patrick, only seventeen years before the abolition of the Irish Parliament. For those who appreciate the worth and status of ceremony and emblems of honour, the foundation of the Order of St Patrick might seem in this light to be a simple case of raising Ireland to the status long enjoyed by England and Scotland, but this was not the prime consideration.

There is no evidence of a demand among the Irish peers for an Irish Order; they would almost certainly have aspired to the ancient and prestigious Order of the Garter (founded in 1348) or to the newer but now well-established Order of the Bath (founded in 1725), rather than to a completely new honour. The concept of the

Order of St Patrick arose not in Ireland but in England; but given that premise, the scene then becomes cloudy, and ascribing the idea to any one individual becomes difficult. Although there is no evidence, it is more than likely that the new Prime Minister, the Earl of Shelburne would have discussed the Irish situation with Earl Temple, the new Lord Lieutenant, before the latter departed for Dublin, and that the proposal to institute a new honour, solely for Ireland, would have been one item among many on the agenda of that meeting.

It is to the person of George Nugent-Temple-Grenville, third Earl Temple, that the detailed formulation of the Order of St Patrick can be ascribed. Temple was hardworking, frugal, easily elated or depressed, had an acute sense of his own dignity and importance, and was alert to see (or imagine) and quickly to resent any slight. His despatches to London often refer to the Order of St Patrick as 'my Order', and his surviving papers provide detailed references to the gradual formation of the Order in the few months preceding the public announcement on 5 February 1783.

In November 1782, two months after he had arrived in Ireland, Temple sent a despatch to Thomas Townshend, the new Home Secretary (and a cousin of Viscount Townshend). In the despatch, he revealed that King George III had asked him, before his departure from England, to raise the question of instituting a new Irish Order of Knighthood and to consult the leading Irish nobility on the subject. This statement would seem to indicate that the Order was the result of the King's initiative, which would support the words of the Royal Warrant; it is more likely that Temple himself raised the subject with the King, to secure the King's agreement in principle.

Temple spoke first to the Duke of Leinster, a haughty young man of thirty-three whose power and influence were out of all proportion to his age and abilities. In March 1774, when only twenty-five years old, he wrote to Lord Harcourt, then Lord Lieutenant: 'I do not expect to be a ruler or adviser; tho' my rank in life does not prohibit me from either, I might say entitles me, yet my age forbids me claiming that right at present. I shall however expect to be informed of intended measures'.[5] In December 1782 Temple described him as, 'this blockhead of a duke'.[6] In May 1784, Temple's successor, the Duke of Rutland, described Leinster as, 'so fickle and unsteady in his opinions and so weak in all his public conduct that I hardly know how I shall be able to dispose of him. There seems to be a perpetual struggle in his mind between avarice, pride and ambition. His consequence is solely confined to his name and situation in this country; and if disappointment should drive him to great hostility, with the rabble of Dublin at his heels, he might be able to create some confusion'.[7]

Leinster was insufferably arrogant, but he could not be avoided. Not only was he head of the prominent Fitzgerald family, he was also the greatest borough owner, and the only Irish duke. There being no Irish marquesses, the next rank of earl was some way below the duke, which only increased his own sense of importance. Leinster was flattered at being consulted and pronounced himself in favour of the creation of an Irish Order, wanting to be assured at the same time that the new Order was to be strictly limited in terms both of rank and numbers, to ensure its exclusiveness.

Satisfied by gaining the approval of one of the more difficult Irish peers, Temple wrote to Townshend outlining his plans: 'This idea will be productive of the best consequences by holding out honourable marks of distinction among the peers of this country who have hardly any objects to which they can look forward. I trust that whenever I may think it most advisable for his service I may be permitted to send over for His Majesty's approbation any number of names not exceeding sixteen and at the same time submit for his consideration such a plan as may best suit the tempers and inclinations of those for whom this dignity must be intended'.[8] Apparently the Government was hesitant, because he wrote again in November 1782: 'Pray let me have my Order of Knighthood as it is necessary for our House of Peers',[9] and again in December 1782, when a name for the new honour first appears: 'Pray likewise press my Order of St Patrick, as it will be very useful'.[10]

By despatch dated 21 December 1782 Temple received the confirmation that he sought. 'The institution of this Order being a measure now determined upon, Your Excellency will be pleased to transmit to me for His Majesty's consideration the names of such persons ... as Your Excellency, after duly weighing their respective pretensions, would recommend to the very high honour of this new investiture – Your Excellency will at the same time transmit your ideas of such a plan for institution as may best suit the inclinations of those for whom the dignity is intended'.[11] On his appointment as Lord Lieutenant, Temple had appointed his brother William Grenville as Chief Secretary for Ireland. Grenville seems to have spent most of his period in office in London, but the two men corresponded frequently on Irish matters, including the Order of St Patrick.

On Christmas Day 1782, the Lord Lieutenant wrote to his brother: 'I will think over the Order again, but my idea is to give it only to peers ... and this was strongly the King's wish. I will look over the list of names and think of limiting the numbers to sixteen: which, considering that we have 157 lay peers, of whom near 100 are resident in Ireland and others occasionally there, will not be more than is absolutely necessary. I shall think myself at liberty to give one to private love and regard, and upon that footing, in confidence, offer one to Lord Nugent as the only testimony I can offer him of my sense of what I owe for him for contributing so largely to my happiness'.[12] Nugent's contribution to Temple's happiness was probably more passive than active; his daughter was Temple's wife, and he himself was a colourful individual, 'a jovial and voluptuous Irishman who left Popery for the Protestant religion, money and widows'.[13]

Temple had drafted a provisional list of the first Knights of the proposed Order by the 28 December, when his brother raised the difficult issue of whether commoners were to be appointed, and therefore whether the number should be raised to more than sixteen. The appointment of commoners had been talked of, but the King had strongly approved the appointment of only sixteen Knights, 'and his very great disinclination ... to increase the number even to eighteen or twenty. I suppose you mean sixteen exclusive of the Sovereign and Grand Master. I apprehend Conolly, Ponsonby, O'Neill and Daly to have been talked of. The difficulty is greater because I understand that the two first have more than once refused peerages. This, however, you will arrange as you think best'.[14] No commoners were in fact appointed to the Order at any time in its history, and in 1783, it would have been difficult to select any without causing irritation to the peers, and reducing the number of stalls available for distribution in the House of Lords. Temple worked quickly to assemble his Knights, because the outline of the Order had been completed within a few days, and on 2 January 1783, he despatched a list of sixteen names to London for the King's approval.

Because of a number of difficulties, outlined below, the list of Knights changed slightly during the period January to March 1783. The decision of King George III to take the first stall himself, reduced the number of Knights from sixteen to fifteen, at which number the Order remained until the appointment of extra Knights in 1821 and 1831, and then the increase of the statutory complement from fifteen to twenty-two in 1833. The following tables show Temple's first despatched list, on 2 January 1783, the formally published list on 5 February, and the final list of founder Knights at the time of the first investiture on 11 March.

Compiling a list of fifteen Irish peers, given that it was now to be limited to members of the Irish House of Lords, was not an easy task. There were those who actively sought the new order; there were those who were quite unsuitable because of their opposition to government policy; and there was the underlying principle that selection should balance reward for the deserving with a care not to alienate the unselected.

2 January 1783	*5 February 1783*	*11 March 1783*
The King	The King	The King
Duke of Leinster	Prince Edward	Prince Edward
Earl of Clanricarde	Duke of Leinster	Duke of Leinster
Earl of Westmeath	Earl of Clanricarde	Earl of Clanricarde
Earl of Inchiquin	Earl of Antrim*	Earl of Westmeath
Earl of Drogheda	Earl of Westmeath	Earl of Inchiquin
Earl of Tyrone	Earl of Inchiquin	Earl of Drogheda
Earl of Shannon	Earl of Drogheda	Earl of Tyrone
Earl of Clanbrassil	Earl of Tyrone	Earl of Shannon
Earl of Charlemont	Earl of Shannon	Earl of Clanbrassil
Earl of Hillsborough*	Earl of Clanbrassil	Earl of Mornington
Earl of Mornington	Earl of Mornington	Earl of Arran
Earl of Bective	Earl of Courtown	Earl of Courtown
Earl of Courtown	Earl of Charlemont	Earl of Charlemont
Earl of Ely	Earl of Bective	Earl of Bective
Earl Nugent*	Earl of Ely	Earl of Ely

*declined nomination

Grenville gave his broad approval to the list, with one exception. 'Your names appear to me to be all unexceptionable, except possibly Lord Bechoe, who you know will give some trouble to the heralds to make out whether his father, who was a grazier, ever had a father of his own. But he is a man of great fortune, and a steady friend of government, and I should think might pass.'[15] Grenville's cautious optimism proved unfounded, and Bechoe's name was removed from the list after objections from the Government,[16] and the name of the Earl of Antrim was subsequently added to the list. The problem is that there is no record of a peer with the title 'Lord Bechoe', leaving the presumption that Grenville was using a pseudonym to refer to an unnamed peer.

Temple formally enquired of each of the intended knights whether they would be prepared publicly to accept the Order if it was offered. He sent a circular letter to each of them, but enclosed a private and personal letter to the Earl of Hillsborough. 'You possibly might wish to decline it, and yet from motives of respect to the King you might have difficulties; and therefore I have wished to give you the means of returning to me the letter, if such should be your determination, and in that case it will not be known that it has ever been offered to you, unless you yourself should divulge it'.[17] Hillsborough did decline the Order, apparently with 'great civility'.[18]

On 28 February, the Earl of Antrim, when informed that he would have to surrender the Order of the Bath, announced his intention of retaining the Bath and surrendering the Patrick. The holding of more than one Order was exceptional in the eighteenth century, and Antrim should have been aware that he would not be allowed to hold both Orders. When the first names for the Patrick were being canvassed in December 1782, Grenville had indicated to his brother that the King expected two Knights of the Bath to be nominated to the Order of St Patrick, thereby creating two vacancies in the Order of Bath. 'The King expects to get two Red Ribands . . . – Lord A. and Lord B. Query the latter.'[19] 'Lord A' was certainly the Earl of Antrim, who had been a Knight of the Bath since 1779, and 'Lord B' was probably the Earl of Bellamont, who had been appointed to the Bath in 1764. The Order of the Bath was well established and prestigious, and Antrim's decision to retain its scarlet riband was not surprising, but he expressed his mortification at having to decline the Patrick. There was a slight difficulty in the fact that Antrim had been publicly named as one of the founder Knights in the Letters Patent of 5 February, and the result was public embarrassment to him rather than to anyone else. His nomination to the Order of St Patrick was revoked by Royal Warrant dated 7 March, 'because he cannot

A silver star with silver pin, c.1800, worn by the 2nd Earl of Arran. (KP 1783)

be allowed to retain the Order of the Bath with which he has already been invested'.[20]

Antrim was quickly replaced by the Earl of Arran, and the two remaining stalls were filled by Prince Edward and the King, fixing the number of Knights at fifteen, excluding the Sovereign. None of the founder Knights, as they became known, was below the rank of earl, and this was Temple's idea, 'because if we go lower, I do not see what line can be drawn between numbers whose pretensions are equal, and the first institution being confined to earls puts it on a higher footing. I mean that the viscounts and barons shall be informed that they will be equally candidates in the future. It is confined to resident earls, except in two instances; Lord Courtown, by which I mean a particular attention to the King, and Lord Nugent, which last needs no comment'.[21]

Nugent also declined the Order. He was almost at the end of his long life (he was about eighty-one, and lived only another five years), and the new Order would have added little to his position and status. He was, 'one of those men of parts whose dawn was the brightest moment of a long life, and who, though possessed of different talents, employed them in depreciating his own fame and destroying all opinion of his judgement, except in the point of raising himself to honours'.[22] Other observers were more blunt in their assessment: 'He changed his politics with every succeeding ministry, his religion at his own convenience'. If one accepts the judgement of the Victorian age that the eighteenth century was broadly immoral, then Nugent was typical of his time. 'The seduction of his cousin Clare Nugent, together with the utter neglect of his child by her, as his political record, show him, alike in public and private life, to have been a thoroughly unprincipled, if amusing, blackguard.'[23]

With Nugent's refusal, Grenville suggested to his brother the name of Viscount Mountgarret, the senior Irish viscount, with the twin motive of honouring the viscount and undermining his popularity. '[This] would show that it [the Order] was not to be exclusively confined to Earls ... Besides this would detach Butler [the Mountgarret family name] of the county of Kilkenny from Flood; and it is surely a great object to cut him off from all hopes of county, as that would give him an appearance of unpopularity, etc. etc. Unless you do something of this sort, shall you not apprehend affronting the lower orders of the peerage.'[24] Temple maintained his opposition to the appointment of any peer below the rank of earl, and the number of Knights was accordingly reduced to fifteen.

An examination of the curriculum vitae of each Knight yields little evidence of why he was chosen and, in any case such a search would be futile. They were either supporters of the Government in Parliament, or they were peers whose power and influence was such that the Government needed their support. For example, the Duke of Leinster and the Earls of Ely, Shannon, and Tyrone between them nominated sixty-two members of the Irish House of Commons, and their support or opposition could make the difference between victory or defeat for the government. 'I have every reason to believe', wrote Temple, 'that the list [of the new Knights] will give real dignity to the Order, and weight to His Majesty's Government.'[25]

True to form, the Duke of Leinster was difficult when first offered the Order and said that he did not regard being placed without distinction in the Order as a sufficient mark of royal favour, and that his birth and rank entitled him to the Garter. Temple managed to soothe him, and assured him that he would be placed first in the list of Knights after Prince Edward, and that acceptance would not prejudice his claims on the Order of the Garter. He was also angling for the vacant Vice-Treasurership of Ireland and was indignant about the Order being a full reward for his services. Temple reported that, 'he rode the high horse so truly for three days, that I doubted his acceptance, however it is now all right'.[26] The duke at first indicated that he would refuse the Order, unless it was accompanied by some other mark of royal favour, 'which I own I have vanity enough to think I deserve'.[27]

The Earl of Bective had three sons in the Irish House of Commons as well as a borough, and had always supported the Government; the Earl of Shannon had a following of about twenty members of the Irish Commons, as well as three peers in the Irish Lords; and after Antrim's refusal, Temple recommended the Earl of Arran, 'whose borough influence is just strengthened by a marriage which gives him two more seats'.[28] Even the otherwise ceremonial officers of the Order were to be exploitable as, 'the honour of wearing a badge in the mode proposed, joined to the fees and to a small allowance upon the establishment would make them eligible, and consequently the disposal of them useful to government'.[29]

At this point, Temple was besieged by Irish peers seeking to be appointed to the new Order. He wrote of being 'plagued' by Lords Arran, Aldborough and Altamont, the last of whom renewed his application on the first occurrence of a vacancy in May 1783.[30] Lords Bellamont, Clermont, Meath and Donegall, also pressed their claims for appointment to the new Order. This grasping for honours, which might seem distasteful to subsequent generations, was both normal and acceptable in the eighteenth century, and it is unwise to judge the morality of one age by the morality of another. Each must be judged by its own standards, as J. C. Risk has indicated in his seminal history of the Order of the Bath. 'It is important to grasp one vitally important fact about the eighteenth-century world. There was nothing in the least reprehensible about the universal scramble for rewards made available for those who were, or who could put themselves, within reach of those prizes. Every man had his price, but also he was convinced that he had a perfectly clear right to it.'[31]

Temple was quite adamant about the criteria for appointment, and his criteria were as equally eighteenth-century as were those of the applicants. 'Lord Bellamont, who ended last session the advocate of Mr Flood [a leader of the opposition], must be objected to till he has expiated his offence.'[32] Bellamont was not minded to accept his exclusion from the list of the first Knights, and Grenville reported on 15 February that the peer was, 'outrageous about the Order, and has been with Townshend about it; but not with me'.[33] Bellamont was still pursuing his claim to the Order after the first investiture on 11 March, and took his case to an audience with the King, who had no time for the peer. 'He believed [Bellamont] was crack-brained, and of whom he told two curious stories of audiences in which he has asked, and in which he at last insisted that, unless the King would make him reparation for the second disgrace he had suffered by the nomination of Lord Arran, by suffering him to kiss hands, on or before St Patrick's Day, for an English baronage, or an Irish marquisate ... he would come no more to Court; which curious condition, you may believe, has not been complied with; and consequently, said the King, I shall be delivered from the trouble of seeing him.'[34]

Grenville tried hard to dissuade Lord Clermont: 'He put in his claim to the Order, to which I gave the answer of non-residence. He said he was always over the parliamentary winter, and had a house and establishment both in Dublin and in the country. I promised to write to you upon it, but gave him little encouragement, nor indeed did he press it much'.[35] Clermont's thirst for the Order rapidly deepened, and on 31 January, Grenville reported that he had had 'daily applications' from the peer.[36] Temple's reasons for rejecting Clermont were more blunt. 'I can have no plea to give the Order to the last upon the earl's bench, who has reached that dignity by an extraordinary exertion of royal favour in five years from the House of Commons'; and Lord Meath declared Temple, 'has almost always opposed.'[37]

Ambition to wear the sky-blue riband was not only confined to Ireland. 'Townshend writes word that many English and Irish peers were competitors. I understand the first to be all but excluded, and that this Order is for Irish government not for English jobs.'[38] In his official despatch to London, Temple remarked rather ambiguously: 'I have endeavoured to select those people whose property and situation seem peculiarly to point them out',[39] but it is clear that he intended the

Order only for those who would guarantee their loyalty to the administration. Lord Bellamont was not without his supporters and admirers, one of whom wrote an ode commemorating the foundation of the Order, doubtless assuming that the peer would be one of the first Knights.

> O may this day, from age to age
> 'Twixt Britain and Ierne prove
> The grave of all domestic rage,
> The bond that seals the sisters love;
> When great ST PATRICK's Knights are nam'd,
> By patriots good and warriors fam'd,
> Then let them say that Order high,
> By princely Brunswick was design'd,
> Like some blest edict of the sky,
> To give two nations but one mind.[40]

The vanity of the Duke of Leinster was almost matched by the pride of the Earl of Charlemont, Commander-in-Chief of the Volunteers. Their numbers had now reached 80,000, and no administration could afford to ignore Charlemont or do without his support. He was leader of the opposition in the Lords, in so far as there was one. Although its numbers fluctuated, he was the leader of a small solid group of about six peers. A leading advocate of legislative independence in 1782, and highly respected by his fellow peers, he was as incorruptible as any Irish peer could be, and his motives for accepting the Order were probably more disinterested than the other Knights. He was still, however, a very vain and pompous man.

Temple wrote to Charlemont, formally offering him the Order, on 6 January 1783. Charlemont's response is best given in the words of his own memoir: 'It seemed to be, and in my opinion really was a proper and honourable distinction to the kingdom, and might be considered as a badge and symbol of her newly-rescued independence. The time also most assuredly was ... peculiarly favourable, since as such institutions usually take place in consequence of some signal success, the present period must be allowed of all others the most proper, as no events could possibly be more worthy of commemoration than those which had lately happened ... As long as this honour was confined to the House of Lords, and more especially to the earls' bench, I must confess that the Crown would not be likely to gain much additional influence by it, as nothing could possibly render my illustrious brethren better courtiers than I knew them already to be. But then, on the other hand, this very argument militated against my acceptance as it could not be very pleasing to me to be one of an Order which must be composed of men who differed so essentially from me in every political principle, and whose association might not be advantageous to me as a public man ... What effect could it have on me? Since I must candidly confess that was His Excellency to suffer me to select fourteen peers from among the earls, I should not be able to find one half of that number with whom I would wish to class myself. This might appear somewhat impertinent, but unfortunately it was but too true. The honour besides would probably descend into the lower ranks of the nobility, and possibly into the commons. Should that ever happen, as in the course of time, and change of government was by no means improbable my former objection would remain in its full force. These inconveniences might, however, perhaps be outweighed by the honourable distinction resulting to Ireland from the institution, and, with regard to my determination the great and capital point was I must confess to discover if possible how the measure would be taken by the people ... My principal objection ... had been lest the people should consider my acceptance of any royal favour as a dereliction of their interests, and should on that account withdraw from me that unbounded confidence by which alone I could be useful. But every such danger was by [his] letter clearly obviated, since both the people and the Volunteers might therein at the first glance perceive that the honour was offered and accepted merely as a regard for services performed, not to the Crown, but to them ... It was certain that, had I refused, the Order would have become unpopular, and possibly might have fallen to the ground; and this was an additional reason for my acceptance, as I did not wish to take upon myself the possible danger of depriving the kingdom of so honourable and so proper a distinction'.[41]

Whatever Charlemont may have thought of the Order, Temple's motives in offering it to him were clearly based on the hope that Charlemont's acceptance would seriously undermine his reputation in the country. 'His Excellency General the Lord Charlemont has accepted the Order, which I shrewdly suspect will be equally unpopular in a very short time; and in this light we shall be masters of our situation, without taking the law of government from one or from the other.'[42] Charlemont was in no hurry to let Temple know that he would accept, and the Lord Lieutenant was obliged to write to him on 13 January saying that the King had required immediate notification of the final list of names, and he could not longer delay in sending it to London. This was not true; Charlemont had signified his acceptance of the Order by 15 January, but the Earl of Clanricarde, the last of the Knights to accept the Order, did not inform Temple until 25 January, when the Lord Lieutenant indicated to his brother that 'the Order is now complete'.[43]

The new Knights of St Patrick were notified of the King's approval of their appointment by a circular letter dated 4 February. 'My Lord Lieutenant has commanded me to acquaint Your Lordship that he has received with very particular pleasure a letter from the Right Honourable Mr Townshend, conveying to His Excellency the King's entire approbation of Your Lordship and the other noblemen whom he has recommended to His Majesty to be created Knights of the Order of St Patrick. His Excellency can not give a more convincing proof of the high estimation in which the King holds the noble persons who are to be companions of this Order, or of His Majesty's desire to gratify the wishes of his nobility of Ireland, than by acquainting Your Lordship that His Majesty has been graciously pleased to take the first stall to himself, and to nominate His Royal Highness Prince Edward to fill the second. His Majesty's letter for carrying the constitution of this Order into execution is expected to arrive very shortly, and Your Lordship will have the earliest notice of the day which shall be appointed for the investiture.'[44]

Temple hoped that the appointment of the young Prince Edward would add to the honour of the Order, by establishing an immediate connection between the royal family and the government of Ireland. The Prince of Wales had desired to be the first royal Knight of St Patrick, but was refused by the King. 'Soon after the Order was determined upon, Lord Mornington, who happened to be at the opera in London, was accosted by the Prince of Wales with warm congratulations upon the honour intended him of being created one of the Knights, adding that the high respect he entertained for the kingdom and people of Ireland, induced him to esteem it an honour indeed of the first magnitude. "At this instant, my lord," said he "there is no nation on earth which so justly claims universal respect; and to show Your Lordship how sincerely I enter into this sentiment, I must inform you that I have this day sent to my father to request that I may be of the Order, and I have nothing more at heart than that my desire should be complied with". The fact was literally true. The prince had desired to be of the Order, and the King was willing to comply, but upon its being intimated that His Royal Highness would expect a permission to go to Ireland to be there installed, those unfortunate jealousies, which have at all times subsisted between the King and the heir apparent, and some other obvious reasons, interfered, and induced His Majesty to refuse his compliance with his son's desire, and, instead of the Prince of Wales, Prince Edward was appointed.'[45] In the tradition of the Hanoverian monarchs, the King was suspicious of the motives of his heir. Grenville confirmed that the Prince of Wales had indeed asked to be appointed to the Order of St Patrick, after the King had approved the list of the first Knights, including Prince Edward. As the Prince of Wales had told everybody that he intended to ask the

The Earl of Charlemont, Commander-in-Chief of the Volunteers. Temple offered him the Order in 1783 in the hope that Charlemont's acceptance would undermine his reputation in the country.

King for the Order, Grenville thought it prudent to wait for a few days to see if the King would agree to the prince's request. He did not, and the formal approval of the agreed list of names was sent to Temple on 31 January or 1 February.[46] The refusal of Earl Nugent and the Earl of Hillsborough reduced the original list from fifteen to thirteen. The inclusion of Prince Edward and the Earl of Antrim returned the number to fifteen, where it remained.

The announcement of the new Order on 5 February 1783 was greeted in Dublin with a high degree of enthusiasm. 'Our Order is wonderfully popular. Lord Charlemont *is convinced* that his taking it has secured its success.'[47] wrote Temple to his brother; and again on 5 February he said: 'half Dublin is mad about the Order'.[48] Some criticism was levelled in England at the Order, notably from Charles James Fox. Fox, joint Secretary of State with the Earl of Shelburne, had left the Government in May 1782 on Shelburne's appointment as Prime Minister. The two men had little liking for each other, and any initiative of the Shelburne administration, including the establishment of the Irish Order, was greeted with ridicule by Fox, as reported by Grenville. 'Fox and his people are very industrious in turning it into ridicule, by which I should think they would not increase their Irish popularity. And what is ridiculous, is that the Duke of Portland is taking pains to persuade all Irishmen that he meant to have done the same if he stayed long enough'.[49] Temple was quite undaunted: 'I am glad Fox abuses it, and I hope he will laugh at it in the House of Commons as it is universally popular with all ranks of people'.[50]

Temple was irritated by the Order being wrongly entitled in the *Dublin Gazette*. 'The gazette writer, in announcing the Illustrious Order of St Patrick has left out the *Most*, which shocks our Irish; and is an omission, as the King has approved the title and Statutes reciting it to be the *Most* Illustrious; enquire if this was a wilful alteration, as I shall announce it with the word *Most*.[51]

Ignoring the fact that Temple was praising his own creation, the Order was, on balance, well received, as newspaper reports bear out. But Dublin newspapers of the time need to be read with as much discrimination and discernment as do Royal Warrants; articles range in content from shrewd perception to total ignorance, and in style from excessive adulation to personal abuse. For example, in the last case, the officers of the Order, particularly the Chancellor, the Secretary and the Usher, came under attack over the large fees they were to receive.

The *Dublin Evening Post*, perhaps typical of the rising independent press of the day, expressed 'apprehension, that the Order of St Patrick ... is not merely intended *honoris causa*; but is a subtle engine of government wherewith to secure the interest of some leading men on questions of consequence that are expected soon to be agitated in parliament. It is a fact too often experienced that the offer of a glittering bauble for personal ornament, has greater influence in subduing patriotic integrity, than any lucrative temptation ... If through the governing miraculous power of St Patrick no venomous animal can live in Ireland, pray heaven that the ribbon of this Order may never be worn by any man who has planted a sting in the bosom of his country'.[52] There was no doubt about that, but the *Post* was still pressing the point a month later. 'The Order of St Patrick is considered by many of the best friends of Ireland only as an additional lure, thrown into the hands of administration, to take off such of our great men, as bare-faced corruption could not render subservient to their every purpose ... The people should carefully watch this accretion of new strength amongst the peerage, and counteract it by that vigour and efficacy, which have rendered them respectable in the eyes of Europe, and emancipated them from a state of Russian vassalage.'[53] At the same time the paper was aware of how much a boost the Order would bring to the depressed Irish economy; remarking that no less than twenty looms were employed making the robes of the Knights, Esquires, and their numerous attendants. Temple had wisely ordered that only Irish materials should be used, as a further gesture to Irish feeling.

The Earl of Antrim was repeatedly lampooned for what the *Post* saw as his unpatriotic decision to retain the Order of the Bath and reject the Order of St Patrick, and in an anonymous letter signed PADDY WHACK and addressed to the Earl of A ..., the author declared himself, 'sick of so scandalous a subject, as your preference of the Lowest Order of England, to the FIRST ORDER of ancient Ierne'.[54] A caricature depicted him trying on the blue riband in front of a mirror, and deciding against it as not suitable to his complexion.[55]

The attitude of the *Post* made little difference to the position of the Order, which was now firmly established in Irish politics as a symbolic adjunct to Irish independence. In 1782–3, Ascendancy Ireland at least, and especially Dublin, was in a state of exhilaration. The kingdom had a fully independent Parliament for the first time since the Middle Ages, and now its own national honour. Loyalty to the Crown seemed to be secure, and the relationship between Britain and Ireland was probably, as far as it ever could be, at a peak of harmony. It seemed as though the institution of the Order was the auspicious ceremonial inauguration of a new golden age in Anglo-Irish relations. In 1782, that exciting year of the declaration of Irish independence, the Order of St Patrick was brought into life. One hundred and forty years later, this time after a bitter and sometimes vicious conflict, a similar declaration of independence ushered in a new age in Irish history; an age in which the colourful ceremonial of the Order of St Patrick became quite irrelevant.

CHAPTER TWO

CONSTITUTIONAL AND CEREMONIAL

The Statutes, the Officers and the inaugural ceremonies

——

Heaven appeared yesterday to beam down a plaudit on the institution of
the Order of St Patrick.
Dublin Evening Post, 18 March 1783

THE ORDER OF ST PATRICK was the product of political need, and the ceremonial that surrounded it, was hardly a principal preoccupation for Lord Temple and his staff. Such things as robes, insignia, rules, rank and precedence, were minor details to the Lord Lieutenant, who put 'his' Order together in the space of only a few weeks, and showed little concern for precision in the intricacies of externals. Temple's prime concerns were to secure the support of the Government in London, and to secure the support of the Irish peerage; if everything was to be ready by St Patrick's Day on 17 March, there was very little time. He dispatched an outline plan of the Order to London on 16 November 1782; the Government communicated its agreement on 21 December; designs for the collars, badges and stars were sent to London on 13 January 1783; the Order was publicly announced on 5 February 1783; the new Knights were invested on 11 March, and then installed on 17 March in St Patrick's Cathedral. The whole process took only four months.

The consequence of Temple's preoccupation with securing the Government's approval for the new Order, and in coping with vain and arrogant Irish peers, and ensuring that everything was ready by St Patrick's Day, can be seen only too clearly in the Statutes of the new Order. Given the limited amount of time available, Temple contented himself by producing a set of Statutes, mostly copied from those of the Order of the Garter, with only the most necessary changes of name and place.[1] Either because of lack of interest, or because of lack of time, or because of sheer ineptitude, no thought was given to writing a set of Statutes relevant to the distinctively Irish situation in which the new Order was to be set, and for more than a century the Order was nominally governed by a set of archaic, anomalous and mostly unworkable rules.

The identity of the individual who formulated the Statutes is unknown. The only reference in Temple's correspondence is a letter to his brother dated 13 January 1783, in which he states, 'I just now learn that the Statutes . . . cannot be prepared in time for this mail';[2] and another dated 17 January. 'Nothing new by this messenger except the mass of nonsense which is put together as Statutes'.[3] By 20 February, Temple was waiting for the Statutes to be returned approved; he was still waiting on 1 March. 'You must enquire why the Statutes, which ought to have been returned a month ago, never have been returned under the sign manual.'[4]

The 'mass of nonsense . . . put together as Statutes' was riddled with anomalies. The Statutes provided a complicated machinery for filling vacancies in the Order by election; the remaining Knights acting as an electoral college. The process appears to have been obsolete before the ink was dry, and it was never implemented. The usual and more practical arrangement was that the Lord Lieutenant would recommend to the King the name of the peer that he thought most suitable for appointment, and the King would usually assent to the nomination; a chapter of the Knights would then be held, and they would formally 'elect' the individual to the Order. A possible exception to the practice of royal nomination may have occurred with the choice of the Earl of Ely in 1794, to succeed to the stall vacant by the death of the Earl of

Westmeath. The Lord Lieutenant, the Earl of Westmorland, appears to have been under the impression that he had the King's approval to nominate Lord Ely, and held a chapter for the purpose of 'electing' the peer as Knight.[5] However in 1795, the death of the Earl of Bective provided another vacancy, which the Lord Lieutenant proposed to fill with the Earl of Clermont. This 'would offer to Your Majesty's consideration the first opportunity of giving effect to the intentions which Your Majesty had signified of conferring the honour of that Order upon the Earl of Clermont, which, Your Majesty will please to recollect, were frustrated by the unexpected election of the Earl of Ely'.[6]

The worst example of lack of thought was Statute XVIII, in which the Chancellor of the Order was charged with the custody of the Seal of the Order, except on occasions when he was more than twenty miles away from the person of Sovereign. At such times, he was to surrender it to a junior officer. It is doubtful if this provision even worked in the case of the Order of the Garter, where the Bishop of Salisbury was Chancellor, but Temple had decided that the Chancellor of the Order of St Patrick was to be the Archbishop of Dublin, who was separated from the King not only by twenty miles, but also by the Irish Sea. The archbishop could not very well comply with the wording of the statute, without either permanently surrendering the Seal, or residing in England.

The 1783 Statutes were never implemented and enforced, because they could not be, and consequently they were mostly treated as a decorative gloss, and ignored. Although additional Statutes were issued throughout the nineteenth century, instituting corrections and additions, as and when it was deemed desirable, the original 'mass of nonsense' remained theoretically in force until the thorough revision of 1905.

With the names of the first Knights finally determined, Temple turned his attention to the Officers of the Order. They were important if only because they could be highly useful additions to the Lord Lieutenant's web of patronage. 'The honour of wearing a badge in the mode proposed, joined to the fees, and to a small allowance upon the establishment would make ... the disposal of them useful to government.'[7] The offices were too valuable to be treated lightly, and careful consideration was given to how they could best be allocated. Temple decided initially that there should be four Officers and two Heralds. Two of the offices were to be allocated for disposal to the vociferous Irish House of Commons, and the other two were assigned to dignitaries of the Church of Ireland, and therefore to the Irish House of Lords. 'I propose to establish two House of Commons offices of Secretary and Registrar with fees, but no salaries; and two bishops as Church officers; and I must likewise be allowed to name two Heralds (of which we have none) with fees but no salaries.'[8] These initially modest proposals quickly succumbed to inflation, partly because of objections from certain quarters within the Church, and partly because of realisation of just how valuable the places could be. Temple's outline proposal on 2 January 1783 for six offices, rose to the unprecedented number of thirteen two months later. No other Order, either then existing or subsequently created, was so well endowed with Officers as the Order of St Patrick. The Grand Master and the fifteen Knights were attended by almost as many officers: a Prelate, a Chancellor, a Registrar, a Secretary, a Genealogist, a King of Arms, an Usher, two Heralds and four Pursuivants.

The proposed fees for the Officers were noted and savaged by the *Dublin Evening Post*. The *Post* accepted what appears to have been a piece of gossip, that the fees of Lord Delvin as Secretary would amount to more than two thousand pounds.[9] But its ire was directed especially at the Chancellor (the Archbishop of Dublin), and John Freemantle, Usher of the Black Rod. 'It is computed that the expence of the Knights of St Patrick will not amount to a less sum than £600 each. The whole of this will be snacked among the Officers of the Order from his sublime holiness the Chancellor to your humble servant the Usher – not bad picking Mr Freemantle.'[10] Initially the three ecclesiastical Officers – Prelate, Chancellor, and Registrar – received no fees, but the rest were handsomely remunerated for their non-existent duties.

	On investiture	On installation
The Secretary	£25	£25
The Genealogist	£25	£25
The Usher	£20	£20
The King of Arms	£15	£15
Dublin Herald	£10	£10
Cork Herald	£10	£10
Athlone Pursuivant	£5	£5
Three Junior Pursuivants	£5 each	£5 each

This brought the cost of becoming a Knight of St Patrick to £250, quite apart from numerous additional expenses. The sum was less than half the cost of becoming a Knight of the Bath, but still a considerable amount of money in late eighteenth-century Ireland. It was a very clever way of endowing ten new disposable offices in the gift of the Lord Lieutenant, without asking the Treasury to provide money for salaries.

The office of Grand Master was the inevitable result of the Irish setting of the Order. No British monarch had visited Ireland since 1690 (and none was to do so until 1821), and so the Grand Master was empowered to 'do all things and enjoy all privileges, rights and prerogatives, and do all manner of things touching the said Most Illustrious Order, in as ample a manner as We ourselves could have done as Sovereign ... if we ourselves had been present'.[11] As the Sovereign's deputy in the affairs of the Order, it was natural that the office should be held by the Lord Lieutenant, his deputy in the affairs of the state; but a striking anomaly emerged. The Grand Master was not a member of the Order over which he presided, and on resigning the office of Lord Lieutenant he ceased to have any connection with the Order. Of the forty Grand Masters appointed between 1783 and 1922, only two were appointed Knights of the Order: Earl Talbot (1817–21) in 1821, and Viscount French (1918–21) in 1917. Although anomalous at first sight, the reason for the exclusion of the Lord Lieutenant from permanent membership of the Order was probably because of the frequency with which the office had changed hands in the eighteenth century.

The appointment of a Prelate to the Order was not originally envisaged by Temple, and was made solely as the result of the Archbishop of Armagh asking Temple, and then the King, to be appointed Prelate of the Order.[12] The first approach was made by the Archbishop to Earl Nugent, shortly after the first list of Knights and Officers was published on 5 February. 'He observed to him that, by the list of Officers of the Order, there was no mention made of any Prelate, although in other respects the Garter was implicitly followed; and he says he thought, by the Primate's manner, that he himself wanted to be that Prelate; as that Officer is, you know, superior in rank to the Chancellor of the Order. If this be the case, I can see no reason why the offer should not be made to him, which might still be done by your writing to say that that office had been omitted, from the impossibility of giving to any other person but himself, and a doubt how far he might like the trouble; but that you had daily expected him in Ireland, and meant to ask him the question; but the time now drawing near, etc. etc.'[13] Temple replied to his brother on 11 February: 'The formal approbation of the Statutes, and the actual notification of the Knights will, I think, put an end to much difficulty. As to the Primate ... you may wait upon him to say that I did not officially offer till I knew whether he wished it, but that if he did, I would still contrive it'.[14]

In a despatch to London, asking for the King's approval, Temple mentions the Archbishop's 'merits and virtues', but a closer look at the hierarchy of the Church of Ireland reveals a picture closer to the truth. The Church of Ireland was the established church of the kingdom of Ireland. It was numerically small (the great majority of the Irish were Roman Catholics), but the fact of its establishment and its considerable endowments, gave it a position of significance far greater than its membership justified. With thirty-eight bishops and four archbishops, its episcopate was excessively numerous. The two senior archbishops, Armagh and Dublin, were styled respectively Primate of All Ireland, and Primate of Ireland, a compromise dating from a time of rivalry between the two for the primacy of the Church. From Temple's correspondence, it appears that a degree of rivalry between the two archbishops flared up again over his decision to appoint the Archbishop of Dublin as Chancellor of the Order. Although the letter has not survived, it may safely be said that the Archbishop of Armagh probably expressed his strong indignation at such an appointment, and pressed his own claims as holder of the senior archbishopric, not only to a position in the Order, but also to one superior to that held by the Archbishop of Dublin. The appointment of the latter as Chancellor was a natural choice, since the headquarters of the Order lay within the province of Dublin, but the Lord Lieutenant stepped on archiepiscopal pride in the process and aroused strong emotions. He described the Archbishop of Dublin as 'outrageous about the Primate's prelacy',[15] and the matter was still simmering a year later when the Duke of Rutland, wrote: 'A dispute has arisen between the Primate and the Archbishop of Dublin with respect to the precedence on the ceremonial of the Order of St Patrick. The Primate claims to walk single. The Archbishop claims to walk at the Primate's left hand. I ask for your opinion and decision as to what was understood and intended as to their particular ranks when you founded the Order. The matter seems trifling but the dispute is conducted with great heat'.[16] Further grief was caused to the Archbishop of Dublin, when the newly-appointed Prelate was also assigned the Chancellor's former duty of administering the oath of new Knights at their investiture.

The Chancellor had the responsibility of keeping the Seal of the Order and of taking the votes at elections of new Knights, which never took place. The office of Registrar was held ex officio by the Dean of St Patrick's Cathedral, Dublin, and it could be assumed that he was to keep a register of the transactions of the Order, though he never appears to have done so. It could be similarly inferred that the Secretary should conduct the correspondence of the Order, though again there is no trace that any holder of the office ever did so. The first holder of the office was the twenty-three year old Lord Delvin, eldest son of the Earl of Westmeath, one of the founder Knights of the Order. Delvin was a member of the Irish House of Commons, and retained the office of Secretary of the Order until succeeding his father in 1792 and moving to the House of Lords.

According to the Statutes, the Genealogist was to have custody of the certificates of the pedigrees of the Knights, and again there is no evidence that he did so. The creation of the office of Genealogist was done at the suggestion of William Grenville. 'Pray oblige me, as a herald, so far as to appoint a Genealogist, and to make the Knights deliver in pedigrees three descents back at least: that is the number in the Garter Statutes, which I send you. The Thistle and the Bath have both Genealogists – the last must be an arduous office.'[17]

No duties at all were assigned to the Usher, who generally led or marshalled processions and acted as a doorkeeper. At least two of the holders of the office between 1783 and 1800 appear to have been also Ushers to the Irish House of Lords, much on the lines of the Usher to the British House of Lords, who was an Officer of the Order of the Garter. Both bore the designation 'Black Rod'. The Irish Usher is mentioned in the first printed journal of the Irish House of Commons in 1634, and it seems that he was intended to be modelled precisely on the British Black Rod. According to the civil list of 1783 his salary was £355 11s 1d, perhaps an indication that his responsibilities were wider than the merely nominal attendance on the Order of St Patrick.

Debate about the nominal function, or lack of function, of the senior officers of the Order of St Patrick in 1783 is of little consequence. They were never intended to be anything more than disposable offices and decorative sinecures. Discussing them in a letter to his brother, Temple wrote, 'the details of these playthings ... is hardly serious'.[18] The offices of Prelate, Chancellor and Registrar were attached ex officio to dignitaries of the Church of Ireland; the office of King of Arms was attached to Ulster King of Arms, and his subordinate Heralds and Pursuivants were within his gift rather than that of the Lord Lieutenant. The Usher of the Black Rod was an official of the Irish House of Lords. The two remaining offices of Secretary and Genealogist were both at first held by members of the Irish House of Commons. Henry Fane (Usher of the Black Rod 1790–6) was probably appointed by his brother the Earl of Westmorland (Lord Lieutenant 1790–5). Lord Forbes (Secretary 1828–36) was appointed by his cousin the Marquess of Anglesey (Lord Lieutenant 1828–9 and 1830–3). Robert Boyle (Secretary 1837–53) was himself a Member of Parliament, as well as being the fourth son of the Earl of Cork (KP 1835).

Throughout the history of the Order, the official who appears to have functioned as the effective officer was the King of Arms. Statute XVII of the 1783 Statutes describes one of the six officers as a 'King at Arms named Ulster'. If this phrase in the 'mass of nonsense' Statutes is taken seriously, then it is clear that, from the beginning, the new King of Arms of the Order of St Patrick was to be identified with the older established office of Ulster King of Arms. The office was analogous to Garter King of Arms in England and Lord Lyon King of Arms in Scotland, in the sense of exercising heraldic jurisdiction throughout Ireland. The office was instituted during the reign of King Edward VI, the first Ulster King of Arms being appointed by Letters Patent dated 1 June 1552.

Now assigned to be King of Arms of the new Order, Ulster King of Arms effectively became the executive officer of the Order, responsible for ceremonies of investiture and installation, preparing the banners and heraldic achievements of the Knights, and the procurement, custody and repair of the insignia. He, rather than the Genealogist, signed the certificates of noblesse of the Knights and their Esquires; he, rather than the Registrar, kept a register of the Order's affairs; and he, rather than the Secretary, conducted all the Order's correspondence. Any decisions about the Order were made either by Ulster or on his advice. In later years, Ulster King of Arms added the title of Knight Attendant to that of King of Arms of the Order. When this was first done is unknown, nor is it known whether the assumption of the title was ever officially sanctioned. It is mentioned in an additional statute dated 1814, and was probably acquired by Sir William Betham (Deputy Ulster King of Arms 1811–20, Ulster King of Arms 1820–53), who described himself in 1831 as 'Knight Attendant upon the Most Illustrious Order of St Patrick'.[19] In his entry in Thom's Directory, Betham was stated to have been knighted in 1812, on his appointment as attendant on the Order of St Patrick.

In 1783, the holder of the office of Ulster King of Arms was William Hawkins, who had been appointed in 1765. A member of the Hawkins dynasty of heralds, of whom five had held the office of Ulster King of Arms. Hawkins was fifty-three at the time of his appointment. Whether or not he was a competent herald, Temple seems to have had a low opinion of Hawkins' abilities, and was reluctant to entrust him with too much responsibility. Admittedly time was short to arrange ceremonial details for the investiture and installation of the new Knights, and Hawkins may not have been up to the task, but Temple had a tendency to underrate the abilities of everybody except himself. 'Our Ulster is not equal to it',[20] he wrote to his brother in London, and requested him to ask Joseph Edmondson, Mowbray Herald Extraordinary, to come over to Dublin and superintend the ceremonies. William Hawkins, incensed at being pushed to one side, made his feelings clear, and a few weeks later Temple cancelled his request: 'Ulster has plagued me so completely, and Edmondson makes so enormous a demand, that I have determined to leave it to this Ulster, particularly as I mean to shorten much of the installation, such as the communion offering'.[21] William Hawkins duly supervised the ceremonial of the installation of the founding Knights of the new Order, and was rewarded by receiving the honour of knighthood on the same day.

Although the wording of the 1783 Statutes implies that Ulster King of Arms was now to be incorporated into the Order of St Patrick as one of its six Officers, it was not entirely clear in those early years whether or not a new office had been created and annexed to the already existing office of Ulster. William Hawkins was King of Arms of the Order for too short a period for any precedent to be established. His successor, Gerald Fortescue, was appointed Principal Herald of the Order of St Patrick on 9 April 1787, and Ulster King of Arms ten days later, on 19 April, implying the existence of two separate offices.[22] His brother and successor, Rear Admiral Chichester Fortescue, was appointed Principal Herald of the Order of St Patrick on 21 February 1788 without any mention of the office of Ulster King of Arms, though that was the position he was deemed to hold. The situation was further confused by the fact that Ulster King of Arms was also styled Principal Herald of All Ireland.

The confusion continued with the junior heraldic officers. Before the foundation of the Order of St Patrick, Ulster had one subordinate officer of arms, styled Athlone Pursuivant, an office also dating from 1552. The Statutes of the new Order added a bevy of Heralds and additional Pursuivants to form a little heraldic court around Ulster. There were to be two Heralds, styled 'Dublin' and 'Cork', and three additional Pursuivants without any particular designation, being known simply as 'Junior Pursuivants'. The confusion at King of Arms level was continued at Pursuivant level; George Twisleton Ridsdale, Athlone Pursuivant 1783–1807, also served as a Junior Pursuivant of the Order of St Patrick 1796–1809.[23]

This confusion of roles in the late eighteenth century continued throughout the history of the Order, and was probably caused by inadequate job descriptions. The heraldic work of the Office of Arms before 1783 was undertaken by Ulster King of Arms and Athlone Pursuivant. In 1783 Dublin Herald, Cork Herald and three Junior Pursuivants were created. Were they additional heraldic experts attached to the Office of Arms? Or were they simply decorative sinecures attached to the Order of St Patrick, with no heraldic knowledge or duty required? The answer is that the position was never made clear. The two Heralds and the three Junior Pursuivants were appointed and used by successive Ulster Kings of Arms for different purposes at different times, and their titles of 'herald' and 'pursuivant' drew the inference that they were primarily working staff of the Office, rather than ceremonial officers of the Order; and the distinction between the two grew blurred from time to time. The Heralds and Pursuivants were listed as members of Ulster's staff, and some occupants of the posts may have engaged in heraldic or genealogical work. James Rock (Dublin Herald 1827–33) was Registrar of the Office of Arms, and was also appointed Rouge Dragon Pursuivant at the College of Arms in London, one month before his death, while continuing as Dublin Herald. Rock was probably an isolated example, and by the middle of the nineteenth century the two Heralds and the Junior Pursuivants were no more than ceremonial officers of the Order of St Patrick.

Considering the extreme youth of some of the Junior Pursuivants at the date of their appointment, it would seem that they were hardly more than page boys or messengers. Although there were now to be three formally attached to the Order of St Patrick, the office was first mentioned in 1623, when there were two Pursuivants in existence. There is no complete list of appointments to that office, and in the early years there were often fewer than the three provided for in the Statutes. In March 1798, Ulster King of Arms wrote to the Lord Lieutenant, seeking permission to appoint two Junior Pursuivants, and complained of difficulties arising in the execution of his duties resulting from the want of necessary aid in issuing and sending forth the orders of the Grand Master.[24] 'Of the four Pursuivants belonging to the Order, the two seniors are, Athlone Pursuivant at Arms, and the Deputy Usher of the Black Rod. And that the two Junior Pursuivants whose province it was to perform the duty of messenger are no longer in existence. Your memorialist therefore prays he may be allowed to appoint proper persons to succeed to the employments of pursuivant messenger to the Order, so that he may thereby be enabled, from their considering themselves under his directions, to execute the duties of his station with more promptitude and punctuality.'[25] There is no reason to doubt that two appointments were made in 1798, but who they were is another matter, and it would seem their names had been lost, when a list of Junior Pursuivants was drafted for inclusion in the revised Statutes of 1905.

The investiture of the Knights of the new Order was originally set for 8 March 1783, but Lord Antrim's refusal caused it to be postponed until 11 March. The place chosen to invest the new Knights was the great ballroom of Dublin Castle. The word 'castle' was as much a misnomer in 1783 as it is today. Anyone with an aerial view of Dublin would be hard pressed to find a castle in the popular conception of that word. Of the square four-towered medieval building, only one tower (the Record Tower) remains intact, although partly rebuilt; the rest of the castle was systematically demolished between 1680 and 1750, and replaced by the present collection of eighteenth-century buildings grouped around two courtyards. Recent excavations have revealed the foundations of the medieval castle, including the foundations of the Cork and Gunpowder Towers.

The great ballroom of the castle is part of the state apartments on the first floor of the range on the south side of the Upper Castle Yard. Built after 1746, and elegantly decorated in blue, white and gold, the hall is an impressive room, and the finest in the castle. The ceiling, supported by richly-gilded Corinthian pillars, is decorated with three paintings. The centrepiece is an allegorical representation of the coronation of King George III. On one side Saint Patrick is shown preaching to the native Irish; and on the other, the Earl of Pembroke receives the homage of the Irish chiefs during the reign of King Henry II. They are the work of Vincent de Waldré, and were executed during Earl Temple's second term as Lord Lieutenant, in 1787–90. In honour of the occasion of the first investiture in 1783, Temple declared that the ballroom would henceforth be known as St Patrick's Hall, and the name remains in use today. Subsequent investitures were not always held in the hall, especially in the first half of the nineteenth century, but it acquired a special relationship with the Order. From 1885 the hall supplanted St Patrick's Cathedral as the location of the banners and hatchments of the Knights.

Twelve of the fifteen Knights were present for the investiture on 11 March, and had Temple not insisted on their presence, there would have been fewer still. 'A circular letter has been sent to all the Knights who are in England; but you may as well send them a line to apprize them of it, and to request that for their own sakes they will attend, as they will lose their precedence if they are absent.'[26] The Earl of Drogheda and the Earl of Clanricarde both wrote asking to be excused from attendance, the latter because of a, 'very precarious and infirm state of health with which I have been afflicted for many years; coinciding with many other material circumstances, would make a journey to Ireland at a season of the year so unfavourable to valetudinarians not less an object of apprehension, and real hazard; than of inconvenience in other respects'.[27] When the Earl of Ely pleaded ill health, he was told that Lords Drogheda and Clanricarde had applied on the same grounds, but on being turned down they went to Dublin, 'with great personal hazard from the singular inclemency of the season'.[28] If Lord Ely were granted a dispensation, they might take offence. Temple's apparent lack of sympathy was only caused by his desire to make a success of the occasion. An investiture with only a few of the Knights present would have been a disappointing inauguration of the new Order. Lord Ely, however, does appear to have been seriously ill. He was not present at either the investiture or the installation, and died at Bath on 8 May, uninvested and uninstalled. There was insufficient time to include the Earl of Arran, who had only been nominated three days previously to replace the Earl of Antrim, and Prince Edward was privately invested by the King in St James's Palace on the 16 March, in view of his youth. Temple sent a badge, riband and star to London on 12 March for the King to give to Prince Edward, 'which you must present to the King in the cabinet ... this will give you an opportunity of talking a little Irish politics if he shall be so inclined'.[29]

The investiture of the twelve Knights with their ribands and badges, although eclipsed in ceremonial by the great spectacle of the installation six days later, was an impressive event. The official account in the *London Gazette* recorded that St Patrick's Hall, 'was elegantly fitted up for the occasion, and the galleries belonging to it were crowded with ladies of the first rank and fashion; and the whole ceremony was conducted with the utmost propriety and with the most splendid magnificence'.[30] The *Dublin Evening Post* reported that several of the Knights appeared at the Theatre Royal, Smock Alley, on the evening of 12 March, wearing their ribands and badges.

The appointment of the Dean of St Patrick's Cathedral as Registrar of the Order, and the use of the cathedral as the chapel of the Order, followed closely on the precedent of the Order of the Garter, where the Dean of St George's Chapel, Windsor Castle – the chapel of the Order – was also Register *(sic)* of the Order of the Garter.

The origin of St Patrick's Cathedral lies with a well at which Saint Patrick was supposed to have baptised converts. A small wooden church was built next to the well, but nothing definite is known of the successive wooden structures until the present cathedral was constructed in the twelfth century. The building has been enlarged and restored on several occasions, including an especially drastic reconstruction in the mid-nineteenth century, and little remains of the original fabric. Since 1872, St Patrick's Cathedral has been styled the National Cathedral of the Church of Ireland, outside the jurisdiction of any bishop, but having a common relationship to all the dioceses of the Church of Ireland, each with canonical representation in the cathedral chapter.

The installation ceremony was appropriately held on St Patrick's Day, 17 March, and it proved to be both very splendid and very expensive. The total cost of the ceremony amounted to £4,419, a substantial sum in the late eighteenth century, which explains the infrequency with which installation ceremonies were held, and why they were formally discontinued in 1833. Only six installations took place before the disestablishment of the Church of Ireland in 1871, which abolished the ceremony and the connection between the Order and the cathedral. The installation

Upper Castle Yard, Dublin Castle. The investiture of the first Knights of the Order took place in the great ballroom, on the south side of the Upper Castle Yard, in 1783.

ceremony was considered to be of great importance, and only on the rarest of occasions, were Knights excused from attendance. Between 1783 and the abandonment of the ceremony only two Knights were given dispensations, and both were installed by proxy: Prince Edward in 1783 (by Lord Muskerry) and the Duke of Cumberland (by Lord Graves) in 1821.

When Temple declared his desire to use the cathedral choir as the chapel of the Order, the Archbishop of Dublin ordered the precincts to be cleaned up in readiness for the event, and provoked a sarcastic comment from the *Dublin Evening Post*: 'Although frequenters of the cathedral may for penance sake, be allowed to wade knee deep in mud to their spiritual exercises, it will be very unworthy for the Knights of St Patrick who are clothed with temporal honour, to soil a single heel-piece'.[31]

The Dean and Chapter were at first delighted by the choice of their cathedral for the ceremony, and expressed their gratitude to the Lord Lieutenant for such a mark of honour. He was given permission to use the cathedral and sixteen stalls on the day, and was permitted to erect scaffolding in the nave, choir and aisles. But their enthusiasm was considerably dampened when Temple informed them that the scaffolding was to be erected at their own expense. The members of the Chapter expressed the hope that, 'should there be a material loss His Excellency will not suffer the Chapter to be essentially injured'.[32] Temple proposed in reply that the Dean and Chapter should pay half the cost, and the Dean as Registrar of the Order should pay the other half. In the same way, profits arising from the sale of tickets for seats should be divided between the Dean and Chapter; this provoked much annoyance. The Chapter replied that each of its members had equal rights and consequently, 'the aggrandizement of one can never with justice be promoted to the prejudice of the rest', and they were, 'concerned and alarmed to find . . . so partial a distribution in favour of the Dean . . . We apprehend that . . . our sentiments of respect and acquiescence to Your Excellency had reference to the necessary preparations within our cathedral and the mode of reimbursement of our several expenses not supposing that those indications of respect could operate to the emolument of one at the expense of 24 . . . We should consider it a breach of trust not to remonstrate upon such a measure as the precedent might be established in the injury of our successors'.[33] Whether or not the Chapter was concerned with its successors, the Dean communicated their decision to Temple on 4 March, reporting that he himself was unable to accept the plan because of, 'jealous murmurings and discontent'.[34] Temple realised that he was in danger of creating a major problem, and agreed to pay the whole cost himself.

On 27 February, the *Dublin Evening Post* reported that the Lord Lieutenant had at first ordered a set of helmets and hauberts (*sic*) of copper double gilt to be erected above the stalls of the Knights, but the project was quickly abandoned on the ground that each one would cost eighteen guineas, and wooden ones, at half the cost, had been ordered in their place. 'Is this beggarly economy suitable to the dignity of a royal order of chivalry?' thundered the *Post*, 'We cannot think that such meanness originates from a Temple, it must be the pitiful offspring of some undertaker'.[35]

No other problem appears to have marred the colourful installation service on 17 March. A series of carriage processions conveyed the Grand Master and the Knights from the castle to the cathedral, through streets lined with cheering spectators and regiments of the army and the Volunteers. Having received the riband and badge at investiture, each Knight was invested in the choir of the cathedral by the Chancellor and the Registrar with the sword, the mantle and the collar, and then conducted to his stall. The Knight's banner was then unfurled by his Esquire, and Ulster King of Arms proclaimed his titles. The *Post* could scarcely contain its excitement: 'Heaven appeared yesterday to beam down a plaudit on the institution of the Order of St Patrick. The sun rose in full splendour, and the whole day was uncommonly bright and serene. The magnificence of the ceremony, the crowds of spectators of the first distinction in the cathedral, and the myriads of all ranks of people in the streets to see the Knights, etc, pass and repass in their carriages to and from the castle, with the animation that lit up the countenances of the public, formed a scene that is indescribable, and which will long be remembered with pride and satisfaction by thousands of the sons and daughters of Hibernia'.[36]

The day was closed with a banquet in St Patrick's Hall for the Grand Master and Knights, and the atmosphere of the occasion was portrayed in 1785 in an oil painting by John Keyse Sherwin. It depicts the Grand Master, Knights and Officers, robed and hatted, standing around the table. The painting still survives, in the National Gallery of Ireland in Dublin. Dinners subsequently took place in 1784 and 1792 on a day close to St Patrick's Day, and it may well have been an annual event. In 1792, 'it was observed as a court phenomenon to see the Duke of Leinster and the Earl of Charlemont at the viceroy's table'.[37]

In November 1785 it was suggested that the Order of St Patrick might follow the example of the Order of the Holy Spirit in France, and commission paintings of each of the Knights. The plan was proposed by the Earl of Orford, to whom the idea had occurred while on a visit to Paris. 'I found in the convent of Les Grands Augustins, three vast chambers filled with the portraits (and their names and titles beneath), of all the Knights of the St Esprit, from the foundation of the Order. Every new knight, with few exceptions, gives his own portrait on his creation. Of the Order of St Patrick, I think but one founder is dead yet, and his picture perhaps may be retrieved.'[38] The interesting proposal was never implemented, and Sherwin's painting of the installation banquet is all that remains.

Lord Temple left Ireland shortly afterwards. He had never relished the duties of the Lord Lieutenant, and had expressed a desire to resign as early as 15 January: 'It would always have been a sacrifice to continue here ... and no temptation shall again draw me from those enjoyments within my reach the value of which I truly know and sacrificed, when I took this splendid plaything'.[39] Only twenty-nine years old at the time of his departure from Ireland, he was a proud young man who knew a great deal and was too fond of communicating the fact. He could be imprudent and headstrong, and the flattering letters he had to write asking Irish peers to accept the Order, some of which bordered on the obsequious, probably caused him great irritation. Writing to Lord Charlemont, he praised that peer's 'public services, so justly distinguished, and of a nature which this kingdom must ever most gratefully remember', adding, 'I cannot hesitate a moment in requesting your lordship's permission to place your name upon the list'.[40] He saw the Order of St Patrick primarily as an extension of the Lord Lieutenant's powers of patronage, a method of easing government business through the Irish Parliament, and he soon tired of the intricate details of setting up an Order of Knighthood. Writing to his brother on 20 February 1783, he said: 'every one is mad about this nonsense, which I am tired to death of',[41] and he greeted the end of the installation with pleasure and relief: 'The parade of our Knights is over much to my satisfaction, but very much I believe to the satisfaction of all Ireland, who seem to have embarked eagerly in the idea'.[42] In February when he was considering a date for the dissolution of Parliament, he wrote: 'our installation will fill the void till the 17th March, and on the 18th I would dissolve if all is safe ... and in the nonsense of the farce of the Order which will be attended from all parts of Ireland, tests will be forgot, and no regular system formed to meet so sudden an event'.[43]

Temple indicated his wish to retire as Lord Lieutenant of Ireland and Grand Master of the Order of St Patrick on 6 April, only a few days after the installation service, handing over both offices to the Earl of Northington. In a rare display of modesty, he did not ask the King for a promotion in the peerage, or for the Order of the Garter; only that he, 'might retain and wear that badge as an honourable distinction to me as having been allowed to found it under his orders and pressing for no further mark of his approbation, till circumstances may enable him to think of me'.[44] He was created Marquess of Buckingham in the following year for his services, and he returned to Ireland for a second term of office in the winter of 1787 which lasted for only a little more than two years. He died in February 1813 at the age of fifty-nine. As befits the founder of the Order of St Patrick, a statue of him, arrayed in the mantle and collar of the Order, stands in the north aisle of St Patrick's Cathedral.

The Order of St Patrick was now set on the course it was to pursue for one hundred and forty years, but despite the euphoria that greeted the new Order in certain quarters, the gaudy installation ceremony was not to everyone's liking, and there were those who saw the new Order for what it was. One contemporary witness of the events of 1783 delivered a fearsome indictment: 'We shall get an ostensible independence, but I firmly believe it never will be a real one, and the collars of the Knights of St Patrick will in time strangle the freedom of the nation'.[45] Voices were being raised from another section of Irish opinion, that the heavy cost of the installation would have been better spent on alleviating poverty, and that the purpose of the Order was less to do with honour than with bribery. 'The giddy and unthinking may cry up the magnificence and finery of Monday last – may say it was an honour to this nation, that the assent of its King has started up a new creation of honour ... But when it is considered that this very Order of Knighthood is putting the means of corruption into the hands of the Crown; that thousands of pounds were lavished, which, if employed to better purposes ... might save many lives and give a spur to agriculture, the natural, but neglected wealth of the kingdom; that £700 was given in the Rotunda for a supper, which sum would have gladdened the hearts of

OPPOSITE: George Nugent-Temple-Grenville, 3rd Earl Temple and 1st Marquess of Buckingham, founder of the Order of St Patrick.

The banquet in St Patrick's Hall, showing the Grand Master, Knights and officers, robed and hatted, standing around the table. Oil painting by John Keyse Sherwin, 1785.

more than 2000 individuals; that a splendid poverty pervades a community in the last stages of bankruptcy. When all this and much more not mentioned is considered, we must consider ourselves in a state of degeneracy and ruin'.[46]

This article in the *Dublin Evening Post* was the angry voice of prophecy that was emerging from another, and discontented, Ireland. It was the voice of an Ireland that was as yet powerless to affect the entrenched position of the ascendancy and its parliament, but it was neither isolated nor unrepresentative, and had it been heeded, the development of the Order of St Patrick in the nineteenth century, and its ultimate fate in the twentieth, might have been very different.

CHAPTER THREE

THE UNION AND AFTER

The Order in the early nineteenth century

━━━

Transporting the imagination to the golden days of chivalry and romance
Irish Times, 29 August 1821

I F TEMPLE or any of his contemporaries, had foreseen that the Irish Parliament was to be abolished seventeen years after the foundation of the Order, he might not have spent so much time and effort in bringing the Order into existence. Nevertheless, for the remainder of the eighteenth century, the Order continued much on the lines envisaged by Temple – a means by which the Irish peers might be thanked for supporting the Government. The Earl of Northington, Temple's immediate successor, was of the opinion that, 'this honour should be bestowed in the channel of great parliamentary weight, or to those who shall shew a disposition to support Government by their activities and abilities in Parliament',[1] and accordingly he recommended Lord Carysfort (later first Earl of Carysfort) to succeed to the stall vacant by the death of the Earl of Ely in May 1783. Carysfort was only thirty-two years old at the time of his appointment, but he was a steady supporter of the Government, and in such circumstances, the age of the recipient was not deemed relevant to the award of an honour. In the opinion of Northington, the Government owed much to Carysfort, 'to whose exertions and steady support in Parliament, my administration has been under great obligation'.[2]

Before acceding to the Lord Lieutenant's request, King George III wanted a promise from the peer of continued support for the government. But on being told that Carysfort had already been informed that he might expect the honour, and was in Huntingdonshire, and that the messenger needed to return to Dublin as soon as possible, the King washed his hands of the business,[3] and Lord Sydney wrote to Carysfort telling him that Carysfort's future support would be expected. The appointment also reveals the considerable influence of the Lord Lieutenant in recommending peers for the Order. In a letter to the King, Sydney urged compliance with Northington's request as it was 'necessary to keep the Lord Lieutenant in tolerably good humour'.[4]

Carysfort's appointment was typical of the pattern of appointments to the Order, until the end of the eighteenth century. Peers were selected either as a reward for their past support, or in return for a promise of future support.

Little is known about the internal organisation of the Order at the time. Sir William Hawkins, the Ulster King of Arms who had so successfully claimed his rights to supervise the ceremonial of the Order in 1783, died on 27 March 1787. He was succeeded briefly by Gerald Fortescue, a cousin of the Earl of Mornington, KP. Mornington wrote to the Lord Lieutenant, then the Duke of Rutland, thanking him, and mentioning that, 'his appointment is understood to be intended as a provision also for Mr Fortescue's brother, the naval officer mentioned in a former letter; and making some suggestions for increasing the value of the office in order more effectually to carry out that intention'.[5] This appears to have been an agreement that Fortescue's brother should have right of succession; and that event occurred perhaps earlier than expected. Gerald Fortescue died in October 1787 at the age of thirty-six, and was succeeded by his elder brother, Captain (later Rear-Admiral Sir) Chichester Fortescue, the first of a series of long-serving Ulster Kings of Arms. Chichester Fortescue may or may not have known anything about heraldry, but the office of

Ulster King of Arms was lucrative and therefore desirable; the salary amounted to £228 9s 9d in 1788. This was especially important to Fortescue, as indicated in a letter in January 1787 from Mornington to Rutland. Fortescue, then a captain, was described as having, 'laid out an investment by an insurance, which had become void by an involuntary misstatement as to the age of the life insured'.[6] Fortescue was short of money and needed the income from the office of Ulster.

After long hours of debate, and the dispensing of considerable amounts of patronage, the Irish Parliament voted itself out of existence in the summer of 1800, and the United Kingdom of Great Britain and Ireland came into being on 1 January 1801. The move towards a union came after the United Irishmen rebellion of 1798, and the case for union was presented to the Irish Parliament as a means of enshrining the Protestant ascendancy in the face of growing demands for emancipation of Roman Catholics. The ascendancy was split in its attitude towards the union, but

The chancel of St Patrick's Cathedral, Dublin. The symbolic swords and helmets of the Knights are still in position above their stalls, as are the banners of the Knights existing at the time of the disestablishment of the Church of Ireland in 1871.

The chancel of St Patrick's Cathedral in the early nineteenth century. The view is from the altar down to the crossing.

Roman Catholics were generally in favour of ridding Ireland of a Parliament of Protestant landowners.

Although succeeding generations came to think of the Irish Parliament with affection, the truth of the matter is that it was corrupt, ineffectual (beyond being a nuisance to the Government in London), and unrepresentative. The Parliament building on College Green was sold to the Bank of Ireland, with the stipulation that the chambers where the two houses had met should be altered beyond recognition to erase any visible relic of Ireland's Parliament. Ireland was not left without representation in a legislative body; one hundred Irish members were added to the House of Commons at Westminster, and twenty-eight Irish peers, elected for life by their fellows, were added to the House of Lords.

After the union, the complexion of appointments to the Order of St Patrick began to change. There was now no longer any necessity of filling the vacancies with those who would guarantee the passage of government legislation in the Irish Parliament, and although the politics of the new Knights were inevitably those of the Government that recommended them, such phrases as 'Lord X looks after his tenantry' or 'Lord X is an excellent Irishman' began to greet appointments. The last two appointments to the Order before the enactment of the Act of Union were, as might be expected, supporters of the union. One of them, the Earl of Altamont, had pressed his claim to the Order as early as 1783. He was also made Marquess of Sligo, and was elected one of the first twenty-eight Irish representative peers to sit in the House of Lords at Westminster. Earl Conyngham was given £15,000 in cash for the loss of his borough influence, and also elected a representative peer. Four other Knights were given United Kingdom baronies, enabling them to sit in the Westminster House of Lords in their own right, and two of them were given Irish marquessates. Sir Chichester Fortescue, Ulster King of Arms since 1788, was not slow in pressing his own claims. The large number of new peerage creations produced a sizeable increase in the amount that he received in fees. Nevertheless, he claimed compensation for the loss of income to his office resulting from the Act of Union, and for the loss of his private apartments and office in the Irish House of Lords.

Among the casualties of the Union was Sir Richard St George, MP for Athlone since 1789, and Secretary of the Order since 1793. He took a firm stand against the Act of Union, to the extent of declining a peerage, and was dismissed from office. He lived on for more than half a century, dying in 1851 at the age of eighty-six, being then one of the few survivors of the Irish Parliament.

The Lord Lieutenant during these proceedings was the distinguished soldier, Marquess Cornwallis, who found himself in the position of having to dispense patronage and shower honours to an extent that no Lord Lieutenant before him had had to do. He regarded the task with great distaste, and reported his feelings with some asperity. In a letter to the Prime Minister he observed: 'The political jobbing of this country gets the better of me. It has ever been the wish of my life to avoid this dirty business, and I am now involved in it beyond all bearing ... How I long to kick those whom my public duty obliges me to court! ... My occupation is now of the most unpleasant nature, negotiating and jobbing with the most corrupt people under heaven. I despise and hate myself every hour, for engaging in such dirty work'.[7] Bishop Thomas Percy of Dromore suspected that the Lord Lieutenant would not enjoy Ireland. Though Cornwallis was, 'very civil and pleasant ... he will not be a favourite here, for he is very sober himself, and does not push the bottle'.[8]

Either to distract himself from his unsavoury tasks, or to distract Ireland from the loss of its Parliament, or perhaps because there were now five uninstalled Knights of the Order, Cornwallis decided to hold an installation ceremony. It was the first installation since that of the founder Knights in 1783, and five new Knights had been appointed since that date, beginning with the Earl of Carysfort in 1784. On the day after the first installation, the *Dublin Evening Post* reported that there would not be another installation service until four Knights were waiting to be installed,[9] and the heavy cost of the installation ceremony appears to have been the principal reason for the infrequency with which they took place. The gap of seventeen years between the first and second installations established the practice of holding the ceremony only after the accumulation of several new Knights. This often resulted in a period of several years elapsing between the appointment of a Knight, and his installation in the cathedral. Were it not for the fact that many Knights were comparatively young at the time of their appointment, several might well have died before being installed. Among the older Knights was the Earl of Clermont, who was appointed and invested in 1795, at the age of seventy-two, but not installed until 1800 at the age of seventy-eight.

Having seen the establishment of the United Kingdom of Great Britain and Ireland on 1 January 1801, Lord Cornwallis departed from Ireland, with relief, a few months later, and was succeeded by the Earl of Hardwicke. Although the union of the two kingdoms was now an accomplished fact, the machinating that accompanied the demise of the Irish Parliament was far from finished, and the new Lord Lieutenant soon discovered the need to quench the thirst of those who had championed the union, for some recognition. Though the nineteenth century had begun, the ways of seeking such refreshment were still those of the eighteenth century, and the two principal figures were the Marquess of Waterford and the Earl of Roden.

There were no vacancies in the Order when Hardwicke arrived in Ireland, but a full complement of Knights of St Patrick was never a bar to those who desired the honour; indeed, it was in their own interests to register their claims at the earliest possible opportunity, and that was either a vacancy, or if there was no vacancy, then the arrival of a new Lord Lieutenant. Hardwicke arrived in Ireland in May 1801, and on 1 July he received the first intimation of the difficult balancing act that he would have to adopt during his lieutenancy; the Earl of Roden quickly pressed his renewed claim to the Order of St Patrick. 'From the various kind expressions Lord Cornwallis was so good to make use of towards me, and his wishes to show regard for my general character, and ... military services during the late unfortunate rebellion in Ireland, on the death of the Lord Marquess of Waterford, I stated to Lord Cornwallis that if he thought any military services of mine had been of use, and that he had the disposal of the Ribbon then vacant, on that ground I should be proud to receive it from his hands. He wrote me a very handsome letter on the subject, and said I should certainly have had it had it not been promised to Lord Conyngham. Though there is none at present vacant, it might happen that one would fall during Your Excellency's residence in Ireland. If that should be the case, I might flatter myself with the hopes of succeeding to it.'[10] Hardwicke returned a courteous but cautious reply. 'Your Lordship will be aware that it would be improper for me at present to make any engagement without being perfectly certain that it would be in my power to fulfil it when the vacancy occurred. But ... I am very sensible of the justice of your claims.'[11]

Roden's longed-for vacancy occurred on 20 October 1804 with the death of the Duke of Leinster. The peer lost no time in reiterating his claim to the Order, and once again, Hardwicke delivered a cautious reply, but perhaps in content, one that was less cautious and more informatory than it should have been, given the subject under discussion. 'Your Lordship is aware', began Hardwicke, 'that I cannot commit myself upon a subject of this nature without a full communication with the King's ministers; nor am I at present able to communicate to you what is likely to be the result of the present vacancy.' Then caution was relaxed and indiscretion took over. 'So far, however, I may venture to assure Your Lordship that there is as much disposition to admit your pretensions in the present, as in the late, administration. Of the claims which have been brought forward upon the present occasion there is only one which appears to be prior in point of time to Your Lordship's, or, in my opinion, equal to it.'[12]

This was a crucial point. Roden now had written evidence that he was within a whisker of gaining his heart's desire; he also had evidence that another was pursuing the same end, and might very well get there before him. So he redoubled his efforts to secure the prize that was now within his grasp, reasserting his claim with renewed vigour, while sensitively acknowledging that he had a competitor. 'I am certain that his pretensions must be superior to mine, as I can never have deserved to claim any merit from any exertion I have made, having merely, as I conceived, endeavoured to perform my duty. But I beg Your Excellency will please to recollect that the ground I

An early nineteenth-century Knight's sword, made by Brady of Dublin.

had for troubling you on the subject was Lord Cornwallis ... having told me, on my application for the Ribbon vacant by the death of Lord Waterford, had it not been given to Lord Conyngham he should have been happy to have given it to me ... Subsequent to the conversation I had the honour of having with Your Excellency, Mr Wickham [Chief Secretary of Ireland] sent to me in London to let me know that His Majesty's ministers were very happy in promising to comply with my former request, namely that I should have the first vacant Ribbon of the Irish Order, which, coming from such authority (considering him as acting Secretary to the Irish Government), I certainly conceived as conclusive, and ever since did consider it in that light.'[13]

Hardwicke was now beginning to drift into trouble. His attitude towards Roden was

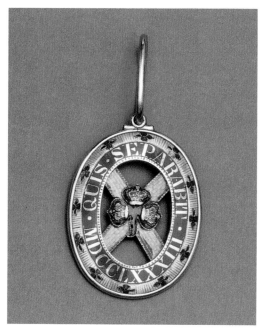

LEFT: a Knight's badge, c.1850.
RIGHT: a late eighteenth-century or early-nineteenth century gold Knight's badge. It is known to have belonged to the Caulfeild family and may have belonged to the 1st Earl of Charlemont.

LEFT: a star, *c.*1840; the reverse engraved *Willm Gray, 13 New Bond Street.*
RIGHT: a star, made by Edmund Johnston, *c.*1860.

impeccably courteous, but somewhat ingratiating, and a firmer line with the insistent peer might have spared him the trouble that was to ensue. In 1801 the Lord Lieutenant had written to Henry Addington, the Prime Minister, supporting Roden's claim to the next vacancy. By the time of the death of the Duke of Leinster in October 1804, there had been a change of Prime Minister. William Pitt had succeeded Addington in May 1804, and the new government was not so well disposed towards Roden as Hardwicke might have hoped. Roden's competitor was revealed as the thirty-two-year-old Marquess of Waterford [Roden was fifty], son of one of the founder Knights of the Order. The marquess, whose father had died in December 1800, duly returned his father's collar to Lord Cornwallis, and pressed his claim to be appointed a Knight at the earliest opportunity. When William Pitt took office as Prime Minister, the marquess again pressed his claim, directly to Pitt himself, who was inclined to favour his claims against those of Roden. Waterford and Roden were both quite convinced that they had a claim on the vacant stall, and Pitt's delay in making a choice between the two peers only served to increase irritation on both sides.

Four months after Leinster's death, Roden wrote again to Hardwicke, this time in slightly stronger language. 'I did not conceive that His Majesty's ministers would have delayed to fulfil a claim made upon so honourable, and, I conceived, so positive a promise. So long a period of time having elapsed since the communication took place, I feel myself absolutely called upon (with all possible respect) to request an answer, one way or the other.'[14] Hardwicke was not in a position to give a conclusive answer, and he had no authority to make any promise as to what the answer was likely to be. Given Roden's insistence that he had been promised the next vacant stall, Hardwicke consulted the Chief Secretary's letter books for the period, and informed Roden that he could not find any documentary evidence of a promise from the Addington government. 'I trust that you will consider me as wishing that the matter may be brought to a satisfactory conclusion, and that you should, at all events, receive an early answer.'[15]

Alas for Roden, he did not receive an early answer, and the matter was not brought to a satisfactory conclusion. More than a year passed by. William Pitt died in January 1806, and on 3 February, Hardwicke was notified that the Marquess of

A star made by West and Son of Dublin, 1846.

Waterford was to be the new Knight of St Patrick. Hardwicke, who clearly favoured the claims of Roden, was both annoyed and embarrassed that his advice as Lord Lieutenant had not been accepted. He tried to prevaricate, by implicitly appealing to the new government to overturn the decision of its predecessor. He stated that the vacancy had lasted since October 1804 because Pitt could not decide between Waterford and Roden, and because Waterford had delayed three weeks in contacting the Lord Lieutenant, after being notified of his nomination, 'I did not choose to take such a step [investing Waterford] without apprising Your Lordship of the circumstances, and requesting you to communicate to me your sentiments, as well as those of Lord Grenville [the new Prime Minister], upon this subject'.[16] Hardwicke's lingering efforts to replace Waterford with Roden met with a firm rebuff from the new Home Secretary. 'As that measure was completely determined upon by the late administration, and the authority was given to Your Excellency by my predecessor in office . . . I apprehend that there can be no doubt of the propriety of Your Excellency carrying the directions . . . into execution.'[17]

Waterford had won, and on 12 March 1806 he wrote to Hardwicke from his Dublin residence informing the Lord Lieutenant of his arrival in town, and asking at what hour the next day it would be convenient to be invested with the ribbon of the Order of St Patrick.[18] There was nothing more that Hardwicke could do except to carry out his instructions, and invest Waterford, which he did on 14 March. If Roden was disappointed, and he must have been, his disappointment lasted only a few months. Another vacancy occurred with the death of the Earl of Clermont on 30 September 1806, and five weeks later Roden was invested with the sky-blue ribbon that he had so ardently felt was his due.

More overtly political considerations can be seen in the debate surrounding the appointment of a new Knight four years later. The vacancy was caused by the resignation of Marquess Wellesley, one of the fifteen founder Knights, on his appointment as a Knight of the Garter. The news of Wellesley's appointment to the Order of the Garter had started discussions in December 1809 as to which Irish peer should replace him in the Order of St Patrick. Correspondence between the Home Secretary and the Lord Lieutenant of Ireland proves that an appointment to the Order was still very much linked to the politics of the new Knight being in harmony with the political hue of the government of the day. The Lord Lieutenant reported that, 'the Marquess of Donegall has constantly asked for the ribbon, but his having it would not be creditable', and although 'the Earls of Enniskillen, Caledon & Longford have not asked for it . . . would [they] be proper persons'.[19] The Government of Spencer Perceval eventually settled on the Marquess of Sligo who was appointed a Knight of St Patrick in March 1810, only ten months after his twenty-first birthday; with the exception of royal princes, he was the youngest appointment to the Order. Age, whether young or old, was no bar to an honour. 'His Lordship is young for that distinction but his rank and his character are in his favour; and it may be the means of fixing him as a friend to the present government. His family are so unquestionably but he has I understand so many intimate acquaintances among the opposition, that they may have shaken his hereditary political attachments.'[20]

Criteria for appointment to the Order included not only the extent to which a peer would guarantee support for the government of the day. In 1783, there was clear evidence that both 'Irishness' and residence in Ireland were firmly established as qualifications for appointment. By the time of the appointment of the Marquess of Sligo in March 1810, 'character' is being mentioned as an additional qualification, and the fact that the Marquess of Donegall, true to the eighteenth-century tradition, had 'constantly asked' for the Order, was not seen as being entirely to his credit. Further discussions in the summer of 1810 were not concerned with filling a vacancy, but with drawing up a short list of the most appropriate candidates to be used whenever a vacancy might occur; and here again the question of 'character' and 'respectability' recur in a letter to the Prime Minister. 'I do not think that there is any

A medallion issued to commemorate the fifth installation of the Order and the visit of King George IV, on the 28 August 1821.

person at present who has an irresistable claim to the Irish ribbon. Of those who may be called purely Irish, Lord Longford appears to be the best entitled on the score of respectability and connection and from the circumstances of his not holding and never having asked for a place. I agree with the Duke of Richmond in thinking he would take it, though he may not be very anxious about it. Lord Courtown's claims are rather his English & Scotch connections than his situation in Ireland. He could hardly expect it so soon after coming to the title. I've, however, no serious objections to his having it now, and should prefer it to any other arrangements, except Lord Longford.'[21] On the death of Viscount Dillon in November 1813, the Earl of Longford was appointed a Knight of St Patrick.

Every new Knight had to be installed in the cathedral, and installation ceremonies were held on 11 August 1800, on 29 June 1809, on 27 May 1819, on 28 August 1821 and, exceptionally, on 18 April 1868. The installation of 1821 marked the occasion of the visit of King George IV to Ireland; and, after a long period of dormancy, the sixth and last installation was held in 1868. Apart from the cost, the ceremony also involved considerable interior reorganisation of the cathedral, which argued against it being a frequent event. The Dean and Chapter, no doubt having consulted the correspondence concerning the dispute in 1783, were careful to state in 1800 that the alterations to the interior should be made by 'the artificers of government ... without any expence whatever to the chapter'.[22] They further stipulated that the Government should restore the cathedral to its original state, immediately after the installation.

With minor amendments, the ceremonial of 1800 followed the pattern set in 1783. A carriage procession conveyed the Grand Master and the Knights from the castle to the cathedral, where they were received by members of the Chapter and the Officers of the Order. The Grand Master was conducted by these officials to the chapter room of the cathedral, and from there a procession made its way to the choir in the following order:

Vergers
Choristers
Prebends
Messengers
Kettle drums
Trumpets
Pursuivants
Pages
Gentlemen at Large
Gentleman of the Bedchamber
Gentlemen of the Horse, Chamberlain and Usher
Steward and Comptroller
Esquires, three by three
Knights elect, two by two
Knights founder, two by two
Ulster King of Arms, Usher of the Black Rod, and Genealogist
Secretary and Registrar
Chancellor
Prelate
A peer carrying the Sword of State
The Grand Master, with Aides-de-Camp on either side, his train carried by pages
Colonel of the Battle Axe Guards
Battle Axe Guards

The Grand Master and the installed Knights wore mantles and collars, the uninstalled Knights wearing surcoats. When the procession had arrived in the choir

of the cathedral, the ceremony began with the singing of *Zadok the Priest*, after which the sword, mantle and collar of each uninstalled Knight were brought in by Ulster King of Arms, and his attendant Heralds and Pursuivants. Each was invested in turn with the insignia by the Chancellor and the Registrar and then conducted to his stall. His titles were then formally proclaimed by Ulster King of Arms, and his banner presented at the altar. After this had been completed, the choir sang an anthem (in 1800, Handel's 'Dettingen' *Te Deum*; in 1809 a *Te Deum* composed by Sir John Stevenson; in 1821, an anthem, *O Lord our governor*; in 1868, Stevenson's *Te Deum* again), and after the Knights returned to the castle for a banquet. As usual, the newspapers were charmed by the colourful spectacles. 'The forms of introduction, splendour of the habits and general pomp accompanying this grand spectacle (of which a description would give but a *maigre* and inadequate idea) rendered it interesting to a vast assemblage of the Nobility and Gentry.'[23]

The installation of 1809 was held at the request of the seven uninstalled Knights, who jointly petitioned the Duke of Richmond, the Lord Lieutenant, requesting that an installation should be held as soon as possible. The duke, not wishing to make a decision on his own, referred the matter to the King. In itself the incident is probably not worth recording since the King readily granted their request, but the significance lies in the fact that this was the only occasion when the Knights, or at least a number of them, acting together, petitioned the Grand Master to uphold their right to be installed. The uninstalled Knights duly gathered at St Patrick's Cathedral on 29 June 1809, accompanied, surprisingly, by only one (the Earl of Arran) of the eight installed Knights.

The conspicuous use of Irish materials for the habits of the Knights, and the dresses of their ladies, provoked a great deal of favourable comment from the press, which saw the occasion as providing much needed employment for the weavers of Dublin. The Duke and Duchess of Richmond had requested that all ladies present in the cathedral should wear only Irish silk or poplin. The Duchess of Richmond was applauded for appearing in a sky blue tabbinet dress and a tiara of Irish diamonds. Even the correspondent of the normally critical *Dublin Evening Post* wrote, 'Nothing in the eyes of the spectators added more effect than the reflexion that all they saw was Irish – they looked upon the duchess as the patroness of the Irish arts, as the benefactor of the decayed artists, as setting a truly patriotic useful example to the higher ranks of this country ... A proud day indeed it was for Ireland – all the rank fashion and beauty of the country were contained within the walls of the cathedral – and all dressed in the manufacture of their country ... about 300 ladies vied each other in displaying the beauties of the Irish loom – never in our eyes did the beauty of our country women appear to greater advantage to give an idea of the benefit conferred on our poor weavers'.[24] The practice was certainly continued in 1819 when Earl Talbot (the Lord Lieutenant) instructed Sir William Betham to ensure that, 'the approaching installation of St Patrick should be as extensively beneficial as possible to the manufacturers of Dublin and of Ireland. Sir William Betham will take care that this object be *strictly* complied to.'[25]

The temporary seating erected for the installation of 1809 so impressed the Dean and Chapter that they resolved that prior to the next installation, the Dean should ask the Government to erect the seating 'in a permanent manner so to remain'.[26] The cathedral chapter minutes record that this cost £446 1s 11d in 1809, with a further charge of £181 15s for replacing the old pews after the ceremony, and the chapter, concerned to save every penny, saw the opportunity to provide the cathedral with new seating at no cost to themselves. Whether the dean did approach the Government in 1819 is not recorded, but it is probable that the request was received favourably. The Government would have been spared an item of heavy expenditure on future occasions, quite apart from the benefit to the cathedral.

Rear-Admiral Sir Chichester Fortescue, Ulster King of Arms from 1788, died in March 1820 at the age of sixty-nine. Despite his long tenure of this executive office,

OPPOSITE: the fourth installation, 27 May 1819 in St Patrick's Cathedral, Dublin.

he does not seem to have been active in the affairs of the Order. In 1788–93 William Bryan (Cork Herald) acted as his deputy, and in 1810–20 William Betham (Athlone Pursuivant from 1807) discharged the same function. In 1812 Fortescue entered into an agreement with Betham by which he bound himself not to interfere with the latter's administration of the Office of Arms. In 1819, presumably at the time of the installation, Betham accused Fortescue of intermeddling, contrary to the terms of their agreement. Records show that it was Betham who supervised the arrangements for the 1819 installation.

William Betham was born in Suffolk in 1779, and began his working life as a printer. He moved to Ireland in 1805, where he distinguished himself in genealogy, the love of which subject he had inherited from his father. He has seventeen publications to his credit, although they were described as, 'works of a somewhat speculative character connected with the study of Irish antiquities'.[27] His greatest work was his index to the names of all persons mentioned in the wills of the Prerogative Office in Dublin, and the task, which he began in 1807, was not completed until 1828; it ran to forty large folio volumes, and Betham was said to spend up to ten hours a day on the labour. In 1807 he was appointed Athlone Pursuivant and Deputy Ulster, beginning a connection between his family and the Order which lasted until 1890. He appointed members of his family to the junior offices of the Order, initiating a policy which was to be continued by his successor, Sir Bernard Burke. His sons, Molyneux and Sheffield, were made Junior Pursuivants, and they rose through the ranks to become Cork Herald and Dublin Herald respectively. Molyneux was appointed a Junior Pursuivant in 1820 at the tender age of seven, and promoted first to Athlone Pursuivant in 1827, and then to Cork Herald in 1829 at the age of sixteen. His younger brother, Sheffield, was appointed a Junior Pursuivant in 1825, at the age of eight, and Dublin Herald in 1833, at the age of sixteen. Betham was not acting entirely without precedent. The first Athlone Pursuivant had been the illegitimate son of the first Ulster King of Arms, and the office of Ulster was virtually a preserve of the Hawkins family for most of the eighteenth century.

At the installation of 1819, the procession went on foot to the cathedral, and neither the Prelate nor Chancellor were present, their places being taken by the Bishop of Down and the Archbishop of Tuam respectively. Archbishop Euseby Cleaver of Dublin was seventy-three and living in Essex. His mind had been impaired for several years before his death, and his functions were discharged by a coadjutor. In the evening, Countess Talbot gave a ball for the Knights, Esquires and Officers of the Order.

The visit of King George IV to Ireland in 1821 provided Betham with the responsibility of organising another installation, only two years since the last; it was to be the only one at which the sovereign of the Order presided in person. Furthermore, it was the first visit to Ireland by a reigning monarch since 1690, and the King's presence provoked great demonstrations of loyalty. The *Dublin Evening Post* recorded that the balconies of houses along the route of the procession to the cathedral, 'were filled with lovely females, in the bright blue costume, one of whom moved a flag as the procession passed, bearing the following inscription in gold letters: The Sons and Daughters of Erin hail their King'.[28]

Nine new Knights were appointed on the occasion of the King's visit; three to fill the existing vacancies, and a further six extra Knights to celebrate the King's visit. The plan was that they should be absorbed into the ranks of the regular Knights as vacancies arose. One of the six was the Lord Lieutenant and Grand Master, Earl Talbot, a rather inept administrator whose service in Ireland from 1817 to 1821 was rendered personally difficult by the deaths of first his son, and then his wife. His sole legacy seems to have been a large stock of Ayrshire cattle, store sheep and horses which were auctioned off in Dublin after his departure. A measure of Talbot's inefficiency can be seen in the fact that Betham had to write to him only ten weeks before the installation, asking who, exactly, was to be installed.[29]

Charles Chetwynd Chetwynd-Talbot, 2nd Earl Talbot (KP 1821) and his Grand Master's badge, in gold set with rubies, emeralds and a pearl, c.1817. An example of the style of Knight's hat in use from 1783 to 1821 can be seen next to Talbot.

Although the installation occurred on 28 August 1821, Talbot had secured the acceptance of least one prospective Knight – the Earl of Courtown – in December 1820.[30] In a language typical of the official hyperbole of the age. Talbot issued a glowing description of the peer: 'A more useful and honourable man than Lord Courtown does not live in Ireland',[31] and 'he is an excellent Irishman'.[32] There was momentary difficulty when it was realised that there were in practice only two vacant stalls. A third had already been promised to the Marquess of Donegall, but because the King had not formally given his approval, the Government regarded it as being technically vacant. One of the two vacant stalls had been allocated to the Earl of Caledon, and King George IV declared his intention to appoint his brother, the Duke of Cumberland, to the other, which was vacant by the death of another of his brothers, the Duke of Kent, in January 1820. This left the Lord Lieutenant in a difficult position, as he had virtually promised a stall to the Earl of Courtown. The Government was sympathetic, but there was nothing that could be done: 'Lord Courtown may wait until the next vacancy, which from Lord Drogheda's very advanced age cannot be very remote'.[33] Drogheda was ninety years old, and died in December 1821. Talbot also reported that he had received letters from the Earls of Ormonde and Mayo, soliciting appointment to the Order. At some point in the summer of 1821, it was decided that the issue was best resolved by dispensing with the statutory limit of fifteen Knights, and appointing a number of extra Knights, who would gradually be absorbed into the ranks of the statutory Knights Companions. The vacant stalls were filled by the Duke of Cumberland, the Marquess of Donegall and the Earl of Caledon, and the procedural farce of an election was held at a chapter of the Order on 12 February 1821, in the presence of the Grand Master, the Chancellor, the Registrar, the Genealogist, Ulster King of Arms, and one Knight of the Order – the Earl of Longford. 'An election was made by command of the Sovereign ... the Grand Master declared the election to have fallen on HRH Prince Ernest Augustus, Duke of Cumberland, the Marquess of Donegall and the Earl of Caledon.' Caledon was present and was then immediately invested by the Grand Master.[34]

Six extra Knights were named. Talbot himself was one of them, the first Grand Master of the Order to be admitted to the ranks of its Knights. 'I had no wish for honours', he wrote, 'but as HM has been graciously pleased to honour me with an Order connecting me for ever with a country to whom I am for ever attached – I cannot but prize this distinction'.[35] The choice of Talbot to be included among the ranks of the Knights was unprecedented, because he was not an Irish peer (although his mother was a daughter of the first Marquess of Downshire who had declined the Order in 1783, and an aunt of the second Duke of Leinster), and none of his predecessors as Lord Lieutenant had been appointed to the Order. The reason for the appointment of Talbot could be purely choreographical. With the presence of the Sovereign in Dublin, there would be no ceremonial role for the Grand Master, who was not a Knight of the Order and would therefore have to fade into the background during the ceremony. For the first time since the foundation of the Order in 1783, the presence of the Grand Master, as the Sovereign's deputy, would not be required. Perhaps to recognise this difficult position, Talbot would temporarily cease to be Grand Master, but become a substantive Knight instead.

Five other new Knights were installed in 1821: the Earl of Courtown, who had been promised the Order; the Marquess of Ormonde, who had asked for it, and had only recently inherited his title; the Earls of Meath and Roden, the latter also recently inheriting his title; and, significantly, the Earl of Fingall, the first Roman Catholic Knight of St Patrick. But the process of gathering the names seems to have been slow; as late as six weeks before the installation on 28 August, Talbot himself did not seem to know who the extra Knights would be.[36] The appointment of the extra Knights should have been covered by the issue of a statute of dispensation, and a document was prepared for the King's signature during his visit to Dublin. It was never laid before the King, 'in consequence of the very full occupation of His Majesty's time during the brief but joyful period of his stay in Ireland',[37] and the extra Knights remained officially unauthorised, until an additional statute of February 1830 recognised their position.

The Duke of Cumberland did not attend the investiture and installation service in Dublin. He had left England in 1818, after just managing to clear his sizeable debts, and he and his wife spent the next ten years as virtual exiles on the Continent. This was of no concern to Betham who had due regard for the technicalities of such matters. 'If it should be the King's pleasure to invest the Duke of Cumberland in England, it will be proper that the Genealogist and King of Arms should attend with the insignia of investiture, to take official cognizance of the ceremony, in order to it being regularly placed on record, in the Books of the Most Illustrious Order.'[38] Being in Europe, Cumberland was invested and installed, not in person, but by proxy, and the collar and badge were not delivered to him until 15 July 1823.

As with preceding installations, the Dean and Chapter formally surrendered the cathedral to Sir William Betham, and the Government defrayed the expense of temporarily adapting the cathedral for the installation service. Although Betham was in charge of the arrangements, the ceremony was marred by one or two upsets, and by the end of the day, his patience had been sorely tried. The Lord Mayor of Dublin wrote to Betham claiming the right to be present ex officio, attended by his Sheriffs and Chaplain, without tickets. He demanded a particular seat – which happened to be the one Betham had assigned to the Lord Chancellor of Ireland, as head of the temporal nobility. The Lord Mayor had consulted the Dean who had evidently given his approval, because Betham maintained later that, 'the Dean had no right whatever to assign places to any one or to give the slightest order on the subject of the preparations further than concerned his own closet'.[39] Betham held that the cathedral was in the county of Dublin, and therefore outside the jurisdiction of the Lord Mayor. On the day before the installation, Ulster King of Arms informed the Lord Mayor that he rejected his claim. The Lord Mayor and the Sheriffs had been sent ordinary tickets of admission and that was that. However, the Lord Mayor seated himself in his desired place. Betham was furious. He was determined that the Lord Mayor's action out of his jurisdiction should not set a precedent. 'I was under the painful necessity', he wrote later, 'of remonstrating on the spot with His Lordship upon his intrusion and to declare to him openly before the whole assemblage there collected that his being there was an intrusion, that he had no right to be in that honourable situation or to take precedence of the peers. His Lordship refused to go away, stating that the liberty of St Patrick's, although in the county was part of the liberties of the city of Dublin'.[40] The Lord Mayor, accompanied by the Sheriffs and the Chaplain, was allowed to remain, and stood at the end of the choir stalls, close to the throne, having declared that nothing but force would remove him from it. 'It is unnecessary to add, that such a measure was not resorted to in a place so sacred.'[41] On the following day, the *Irish Times* revealed that the dispute had been caused by the Lord Mayor having been invited to attend by the Dean and Chapter.

On the morning of the installation the congregation started to arrive at the cathedral before 7am, although the King was not due to arrive until 1.40pm. At 9am, Chief Constable Michael Farrell discovered a man, apparently a bricklayer's labourer, taking two penny pieces to admit a person into the cathedral by a door which was reserved for the King, his household and the Knights. He promptly turned the person so admitted out, and got Mr Maguire, the sexton, to place an authorised person in charge of the gate. With the presence of the conscientious Chief Constable, only those with right of access entered the cathedral. 'One of the first that came was an elderly nobleman in appearance dressed in blue with a star on the breast; him I admitted.'[42]

Surprisingly, a number of Knights asked to be excused attendance; the Earl of Carysfort pleaded, 'very advanced age [he was seventy] and a severe chronic disorder'; the Earl of Shannon was unable to be in Ireland; the Marquess of Ely asked to be excused; the Marquess of Sligo wrote from Paris that he had a 'severe indisposition'; and the Marquess of Waterford was also ill;[43] all were excused attendance.

The ceremony must have been one of the most colourful sights ever to be seen in Dublin. In a gesture, typical of that monarch, King George IV ordered that the Knights should wear an elaborate Tudor-style costume, officially known as an under-habit, beneath their mantles. The King himself wore a richly trimmed silver tissue coat, shoes of white kid skin with large white rosettes and diamond clasps, trunk silk hose and large knee rosettes of light blue ribbon and silver points. He wore a black velvet hat, with a diamond button and loop, and black and white plumes of feathers, and over all this, the collar and the mantle, which the *Dublin Evening Post* reported to be, 'of great extent'.[44] Such was the extent of the train, that six pages were required to carry it.

The Knights wore mantles with large trains, 'which rendered their stepping backward gracefully, and without tripping, a matter of some difficulty',[45] and hats covered with a profusion of crimson, blue and white ostrich feathers. This installation was the last occasion on which the hats and under habits were worn. They were never

worn at investitures and, although still included in the revised statutes of 1905, they passed into oblivion after 1821, never again to be seen at a ceremony of the Order.

Even the stewards were vested in the colours of the Order: blue coat, white waistcoat and breeches, white silk stockings and buckles. They wore white silk sashes, trimmed with blue fringe, and carried wands. The sashes were worn around the waist and were tied at the left side, from which the ends depended. 'The manner of wearing them was novel', reported the *Irish Times*, 'and had a pleasing effect.'[46]

During the installation each uninstalled Knight was brought before a table in the choir, where the Prelate read an admonition. Each then received a sword and a mantle from the two junior uninstalled Knights and a collar from the King, and were conducted to their stalls. The senior Esquire unfurled the banner of the new Knight, and Ulster King of Arms recited the full titles of the Knight. 'The general effect of the spectacle is said to have been most splendid: and the installation of the Knights of St Patrick on that occasion will always form a memorable event in the history of Ireland. While His Majesty remained in Dublin, he constantly wore the star, riband and badge of the Order of St Patrick, and usually appeared with a shamrock in his hat.'[47]

Despite, or perhaps even because of these frills and fripperies, Dublin was generally entranced by the entertainment provided by the whole affair. The presence of the King and his Knights, not to mention the presence of Prince Esterhazy, the Austrian Ambassador, overawed the Dublin newspapers, one of which declared: 'It is impossible to conceive of a more powerfully impressive combination of the religious and state ceremonial than that afforded at this moment. The glitter and variety of rich and splendid dresses – the military uniforms, and various Orders, worn by officers and others – the precious jewels which sparkled in ladies' headdresses, pendant to their ears, and on their snowy necks and bosoms – the glare of the dresses of the Knights and their Esquires – the profusion of feathers to be seen on every side moving in graceful curves, delighted the eye, whilst the pealing of the organ, the finest toned in Europe, mingling celestial sounds with the vocal harmony of the choir, charmed the ear even to satiety. The ceremony was of matchless splendour and magical effect, removing for a moment the curtains of time, and transporting the imagination to the golden days of chivalry and romance.'[48] It was hoped to repeat the pattern of the 1819 installation when the Knights walked from the castle to the cathedral, but heavy rain prevented it.

The King's visit was preceded a few days earlier by the death of his wife Queen Caroline. The history of their unhappy marriage is well known and need not be repeated here, but after the report of her death in black-edged newspapers, the following announcement appeared on 18 August in the *Dublin Evening Post*: 'It is not expected by His Majesty that persons shall appear in mourning on the day of his public entry into Dublin, nor on any of the days of public ceremonials or festivities during the period of His Majesty's residence in Ireland.'[49]

After the conclusion of the installation there was such chaos, that an investigation was ordered into the arrangements made by the police. Sir William Betham complained that the police had neglected the printed regulations, and attributed responsibility for the confusion and disorder to them alone. Alderman Frederick Darnley, the head police officer, replied that the magistrates had not received the printed regulations, and therefore could not give official orders to the police about the arrangements for the car-

riages. 'I am fully aware that the police became unserviceable in consequence of not having a proper understanding with the authorities prior to the installation.'[50] The real cause was identified when the dependable Chief Constable Farrell reported that on the departure of the King from the cathedral, 'all the Knights were anxious to get to their carriages which could not be done readily as every avenue leading to the church was so blocked with carriages and the servants being heated with liquor and anxious to get their families into the coaches that I had a great deal to do to prevent many of the reins being cut.'[51] Thinking it might be needed, Betham had left his carriage at the south entrance to the cathedral during the installation service, only to find that four mounted police had caused mayhem. 'They acted in a most ruffianly manner and not only neglected their duty but brutally attacked my carriage and beat and cut my servants.'[52] It is hardly to be wondered that the Chief Constable added to his report: 'the language of Sir William Betham to me was most abusive and insulting'.[53]

The installation ceremony ended at 3.30pm, and at 6.15pm, an installation dinner was held in St Patrick's Hall. The hall was laid out with three tables: the royal table at which sat the King and the Knights, fully robed and wearing their hats; and two other tables, at which the Lord Mayor of Dublin and the Commander-in-Chief presided. 'St Patrick's Hall ... was fitted up with great magnificence ... The splendour of the scene was truly imposing ... The general effect of this magnificent spectacle almost surpasses the descriptive powers to portray. The rich services of massive gold plate, presented, at various periods, to our Sovereign, by different foreign courts, were displayed on the august occasion; the Hall was lighted by elegant candlestands of exquisite workmanship.'[54] At 7.30pm, after dessert, the King rose, proposed a toast to the corporation of the city of Dublin, and then left for the Viceregal Lodge in Phoenix Park; the excuse given was that he had been fatigued by the laborious duties of the day. The dinner then continued without him until 9pm.

After this great peak in 1821, the Order entered into what can only be described as a period of ceremonial decline, which lasted for more than thirty years. The appointments of the six extra Knights by King George IV, and their gradual absorption into the Order, prevented any further appointments during his ten-year reign, and at the time of the accession of King William IV in 1830, two extra Knights still remained – the Earl of Roden and the Earl of Courtown. With the beginning of a new reign, once again the question of appointments to the Order of St Patrick was considered. The exceeding of the statutory limit on numbers in 1821 had in a sense acquired a statutory permanency of its own, and in 1831, the Government worked on the principle that because there were only two remaining extra Knights, plus the full complement of fifteen Knights Companions, four vacancies therefore existed.[55] Earl Grey proposed to the Lord Lieutenant that they be filled by the Duke of Leinster, the Earl of Charlemont, the Marquess of Downshire and the Marquess of Headfort. Leinster refused the Order, and Grey subsequently felt that Headfort's peerage was a sufficient honour. So Downshire and Charlemont were joined by the Earl of Landaff and the Marquess of Clanricarde to constitute the four new extra Knights appointed on the occasion of the coronation of King William IV, raising the number back to six, and the total number of Knights of the Order to twenty-one.[56] In view of this surfeit of Knights, the probability of a vacancy occurring for several years was remote. Practicality and the need to maintain the flow of disposable honours led to the decision by the Government of Lord Grey, partially to revise the Statutes and to increase the statutory maximum number.

By warrant dated 24 January 1833, the statutory complement was permanently increased from fifteen to twenty-two. One extra Knight having succeeded to a vacancy in 1832, there were now twenty Knights and two vacancies, the latter being filled by the appointments of Marquess Conyngham and the Earl of Leitrim. The same warrant also ordered that Knights might be dispensed from the ceremony of installation, yet wear all the insignia and enjoy all the rights and privileges of installed Knights. What appeared to be optional very quickly became usual. The additional statute was dated 24 January 1833, and the four new Knights were dispensed from being installed six days later, on 30 January. The installation ceremony had been consigned to oblivion.

Responsibility for abandoning the hitherto compulsory installation ceremonies can be ascribed to the prevailing mood of extensive thriftiness that quickly emerged in the years after 1830 with the advent of a new king and a new government. King William IV enjoyed the reputation of being a cost-cutting monarch, anxious to avoid the extravagant behaviour of his brother and predecessor. 'Patriotism and economy were nicely blended in the onslaught which he made on the various royal establishments. He saved £14,000 a year by dismissing George IV's German band ... He sacked the squadron of French cooks who had previously followed the King from residence to residence ... Everywhere pomp was discouraged, the luxurious structure of the late King's way of life was dismantled.'[57] His coronation, costing a fraction (£30,000) of that of King George IV (£240,000), was the most notable example, and the King is known to have wished to do without a coronation altogether. Three weeks before the publication of the additional statute on 24 January 1833, the King had let his decision be known to the Home Secretary. 'In order to avoid the inconvenience of an installation in Dublin which shall confer on any new Knight the right to wear the insignia of the Order, His Majesty is further please to direct that they shall obtain the privilege of so doing by a dispensation as granted with respect to the other Orders, on payment of the customary fees.'[58] The 'inconvenience' was almost certainly financial rather than administrative. Set in the context of the King's philosophy of economy, combined with an identical philosophy of the Whig government, the installation ceremony was a victim of its own expensive elaborateness.

The King's attitude to expenditure was fully in accordance with the pruning instincts of the incoming Whig government of Earl Grey, who was appointed Prime Minister in November 1830. As with so many other opposition parties, the Whig party had fought the election on the ground of reform, retrenchment and economy in public life, and on coming to power, they found the new king not unsympathetic to their views. Savings were to be made everywhere. In 1831 the Government established a House of Commons select committee on civil government charges, with the intention of substantially reducing government expenditure. Among the categories that came under scrutiny was the Irish civil list, which stood at £250,000. The Lord Lieutenant was a viceroy in status; he represented the King in Ireland, and was surrounded by a considerable amount of expensive state ceremonial. His salary was reduced from £30,000 to £20,000, and a large number of viceregal offices and institutions were abolished. Among the casualties were the Battle Axe Guards formed in 1707, a company of fifty foot guards armed with battle axes who guarded the Lord Lieutenant on ceremonial occasions. Another loss was the 'State Music', a foundation of 1662 composed of a kettle drummer, trumpeters, violins, hautboys, a french horn and a dulcimer. The number of aides-de-camp and gentlemen in waiting was also reduced, although the gentlemen in waiting were not finally abolished until 1908. The select committee also proposed to abolish the offices of Athlone Pursuivant, Dublin Herald, Cork Herald and Junior Pursuivant, leaving Ulster King of Arms as a solitary heraldic officer in Ireland, but these recommendations were not accepted.[59]

Although there is no mention of the installation ceremony in the report of the select committee, the reduction in the Irish civil list must have raised a large question mark over the future of the expensive installation services of the Order of St Patrick. No revenues were assigned to the Order at its creation in 1783, and all the expenses of the Order were met from the Civil Contingency Fund. With a reduction in the budget and a reduction in viceregal ceremonial, the installation ceremonies were simply too expensive to continue.

Apart from financial considerations, other factors may have influenced the decision to abandon the installations, including the poor physical condition of St Patrick's Cathedral. By the end of the eighteenth century the fabric of the cathedral was in a terrible state. In 1787 the 'stone arch over the choir' was in a state of decay. In 1792 the south wall was leaning 60cm out of the perpendicular and the nave roof was propped up with wooden scaffolding for a quarter of a century afterwards. The north transept, screened off and used as the parish church of St Nicholas Without from the mid-fourteenth to the early nineteenth centuries, was ruined by 1784, and the south transept, used as the chapter house, was in a dangerous state. The cathedral architect reported to the Lord Lieutenant in 1805 that £16,318 15s 9d would be needed for restoration but suggested that it would be economical to rebuild at a total cost of £81,600. Fortunately the plan never came to fruition. Piecemeal restoration took place during the first half of the nineteenth century: the nave was re-roofed in 1812–14; the north transept was rebuilt in 1821–6; the west door and west Perpendicular window were rebuilt in 1832–4, but when William Makepeace Thackeray visited the cathedral in 1843, he wrote: 'The greater part of the huge old building is suffered to remain in gaunt decay, and with its stalls of sham gothic, and the tawdry old rags and gimcracks of "The Most Illustrious Order of St Patrick" (whose pasteboard helmets, calico banners and lathe swords well characterise the humbug of chivalry which they are made to represent) looks like a theatre behind the scenes'.[60]

Although the language of the 1833 statute allowing the installation to be dispensed with, was permissory, rather than mandatory, the precedent was set, and with the exception of the Prince of Wales in 1868, all further Knights received a dispensation from installation until 1871, when the ceremony was finally abolished. Statute V was amended a few months later to give recognition to the effective desuetude of the installation ceremony, and at the same time, cosmetic changes were made to four other articles relating to the duties of the Grand Master and Genealogist, and the method of electing new Knights. Although regular installation ceremonies were now effectively consigned to history, the cathedral remained the chapel of the Order, and the banners of deceased Knights were removed from the choir, and replaced with the banners of new Knights. In 1838, Sir William Betham reported that he had erected new banners, helmets and swords for the new Sovereign (Queen Victoria) and the King of Hanover (formerly the Duke of Cumberland).[61]

With the disappearance of the installation ceremony, there was now no established method of investing new Knights with the collar. Instead of including this in the ceremony of investiture, the new Knight was simply provided with a collar at a later stage by Ulster King of Arms, and by the warrant dispensing him from installation, he was given permission to wear it. When Betham first enquired how the new Knights were to be invested with the collar, he received a fairly dusty reply from the secretary to Viscount Melbourne, the Home Secretary. 'The collars of the

Orders of the Garter and the Bath are delivered to the respective Knights without any form or ceremonial whatever, by the persons whose duty it is to take charge of the collars, and his lordship sees no reason why a similar mode of proceeding should not be adopted in respect of the collars of the Order of St Patrick.'[62] The seal was set, and for the next twenty years or more, the investiture ceremony was also shorn of something of its grandeur. With rare exceptions, the ceremony was usually held at the more comfortable and intimate surroundings of the Viceregal Lodge in Phoenix Park, or even dispensed with on occasions, and it was not until the popular lieutenancy of the Earl of Carlisle (1855–8), probably at the urging of Sir Bernard Burke, that it was restored to its traditional setting in St Patrick's Hall.

Appointments to the Order were still generally made from among supporters of the government in power, but with the traditional expectation of residence in Ireland. There were two vacancies in March 1833, and, writing to the Lord Lieutenant (the Marquess of Anglesey) the Prime Minister (Lord Grey) remarked: 'I have determined one in favour of Lord Conyngham who will be invested on Wednesday – the other I will take time to consider but I incline to Lord Kenmare. Nothing can be better than Lord Leitrim, but he has lately had an Irish peerage, and we should look to an equal distribution of the good things among our friends'.[63] Grey's statement about Leitrim was inaccurate; he had received a United Kingdom peerage (Baron Clements of Kilmacrenan) in 1831, and he was appointed a Knight of St Patrick in April 1834, on the same day as the third Earl of Donoughmore. Most appointments were greeted favourably and without cynicism. On the appointment of the Earl of Clare and the Marquess of Ormonde in 1845, *The Times* commented that 'both are excellent landlords, and, as far as practicable, constant residents in their native country'.[64]

Although King William IV trimmed as much as possible from the extravagance of the court, he remained generous to a fault in the area of hospitality, and he initiated a custom, which appears to have lapsed at his death in 1837, of entertaining the Knights and Officers of the Order of St Patrick to dinner at St James's Palace, together with the Knights and Officers of the Order of the Thistle. Dinners were held on 8 May 1833, 8 May 1834, 16 May 1835, and 7 May 1836. A further dinner was scheduled for 8 May 1837, and then postponed until 20 May, but the King's illness caused it to be cancelled, and he died on 20 June that year. The King presided at each dinner, wearing the collar and star of each Order. Past Grand Masters of the Order of St Patrick were invited, and in 1834 four of them (Marquess Camden, the Duke of

The investiture of the Earl of Gosford and Lord Cremorne (later Earl of Dartrey) in the Throne Room, Dublin Castle, 22 February 1855.

Bedford, Earl Talbot and Marquess Wellesley) were present. A complicated series of toasts in strict order of precedence was given at the end of each dinner:

The King
The Queen and the royal family
The Duke of Cumberland, KP (senior royal Knight of the Patrick)
The Duke of Sussex, KP (senior royal Knight of the Thistle)
The Knights of the Thistle (drunk by the Knights of St Patrick)
The Knights of St Patrick (drunk by the Knights of the Thistle)
The Grand Master of the Order of St Patrick
The past Grand Masters of the Order of St Patrick
The absent Knights of both Orders
The Prelate, Chancellor and Registrar of the Order of St Patrick
The Earl of Kinnoull, Lord Lyon King of Arms
Ulster King of Arms and Sir William Woods, acting Secretary of the Thistle

No doubt considerable joviality ensued from such an excessive number of toasts.

With the accession of Queen Victoria in 1837, came a request from Archbishop Richard Whateley of Dublin to modify the oaths administered to new Knights. The original oath, described in the statutes of 1783, read, 'I Sir A.B. promise and swear to my true power during my life, and during the time that I shall be Fellow of the Most Illustrious Order of St Patrick, to keep, defend and sustain the honors, rights and privileges of the Sovereign of the said Order, and well and truly I will accomplish all the Statutes, Points and Ordinances of the said Order, as though they were read to me from Point to Point, and from Article to Article, and that wittingly and willingly I will not break any Statutes of the said Order, or any Article in them contained, except insuch as I shall have received a dispensation from the Sovereign, So help me God and the contents of this Book.'

Presumably taking his stand on a literal interpretation of Matthew 5:37 (*Do not swear at all . . .*), the Archbishop objected to the wording of the oath. Although he pleaded only his own personal scruples, and asked for a dispensation for himself alone, his application was favourably received, and by an additional Statute, dated 25 August 1837, a declaration was substituted for the oath. Whateley was delighted. 'I wish Your Lordship to convey to Her Majesty . . . the expression of my sincere gratitude . . . It is a source of additional gratification to me that the relief afforded has come not in the shape of a special Dispensation to myself individually . . . but in a mode which seems more distinctly to recognise the reasonableness of the principle by which I have been actuated.'[65]

Little else of note appears to have taken place in these quiescent years. The register of the Order preserved at the Central Chancery of the Orders of Knighthood has nothing but blank pages for the years from 1821 until 1853, being the period during which Sir William Betham was King of Arms. Each Ulster King of Arms seems to have adopted his own method of recording correspondence, including that relating to the Order, and Betham used a series of letter books and ignored the registers of the Order. Apart from the installations of 1819 and 1821, his letter books record the daily life of the Office of Arms until his death in 1853, including the inevitable series of scandals. In 1848, William Skey, one of the junior pursuivants, was 'removed' from office. Skey had been appointed in 1839, 'to enter upon the general business'[66] as registrar of the Office of Arms at a salary of £100 per annum. He had left the Office of his own free will by August 1847, and Betham had no notion of why or where he had gone, except that he had left the country. 'I regret to say that his health, or wishes, induced him to reside out of Ireland. He said he thought he should go to England, but whether he has or not I do not know. He is not communicative of his motions or intentions. I must however observe that we parted the best of friends.'[67] By the summer of 1848, the truth had emerged, and Betham was feeling less charitable. Despite being a salaried official, Skeys had charged and kept fees without Betham's knowledge. Although it is clear from correspondence that Skeys left the Office of Arms of his own free will, perhaps realising that he was close to being unmasked, Betham subsequently claimed that Skey's behaviour had 'rendered it necessary for me to dispense with his services. I know not where he now is'.[68] Disgruntled clients, claiming that they had paid money to Skeys in good faith, were still surfacing some years later, probably much to Betham's discomfiture. 'Mr Skeys it appears was very fond of sovereigns, but while my clerk he had no authority from me to ask or receive fees.'[69]

The problem with Skeys was difficult enough to explain to clients of the Office seeking Grants of Arms. But an even more serious matter had occurred some ten years earlier in 1838 with the removal of Major the Honourable Sir Francis Stanhope, Gentleman Usher of the Black Rod. Stanhope's crime was so appalling in Betham's eyes that two drafts of a warrant for the Lord Lieutenant appear in his letter books; both are crossed out, indicating that Betham had some difficulty in composing the precise wording. Stanhope's offence was almost eighteenth century in style. He had, in Betham's words, 'feloniously stolen a casket of jewels of great value, and whereas the said Sir Francis has absconded and fled to avoid meeting the said charge, and by such absconding and avoiding to meet the justice of the case, has given strong grounds to conclude that the charge is well founded ... a person lying under an infamous charge and flying from its consequences, is totally unworthy of holding an office of such high honour'.[70] In June 1838, the badge, riband, mantle and rod of the Usher were returned to Betham by Lady Stanhope.[71] Such was the condition of the badge and the rod, that the rod had to be repaired and a new badge ordered in October of the same year.[72]

On a positive note, an interesting entry in the appendices to the 1905 revision of the statutes of the Order records that a certain John O'Flaherty, one of the Junior Pursuivants, was removed from office in 1823, 'having taken holy orders'. Of him and his subsequent ministry, nothing further is known.

Sir William Betham died in October 1853 at the age of seventy-four, and the rule of the Betham family in the world of Irish heraldry came to a close. Sir William's younger son, Sheffield Betham, Dublin Herald, immediately applied to the Lord Lieutenant to succeed his father as Ulster King of Arms,[73] but without success. William Betham was succeeded as Ulster King of Arms and Knight Attendant of the Order of St Patrick by a man whose name was for long synonymous with the compilation of meticulously detailed pedigrees of the nobility of the United Kingdom – John Bernard Burke.

CHAPTER FOUR

THE NEW LOOK

Farewell to the Church of Ireland

———

It is now reconstituted with a more intelligent perception of the great social and political changes which the world has since experienced.
The Times, 4 August 1871

THE APPOINTMENT of Bernard Burke as Ulster King of Arms in 1853 began a connection between the Burke family and the Order of St Patrick, which lasted until the death of his son, Sir Henry Farnham Burke (Genealogist of the Order from 1889) in 1930. Bernard Burke, who was thirty-nine years old at the time of his appointment, was a scion of a family distinguished for its genealogical and heraldic attainments, and probably best remembered for the massive red and gold volume *Burke's Peerage*, which first appeared in 1826, and then, after a few years, annually until the beginning of the Second World War. A companion volume, *Burke's Commoners* (later *Burke's Landed Gentry*) appeared from 1837. The two volumes were founded by John Burke, father of the man who was to become Ulster King of Arms in 1853, and other genealogical works under the name of Burke appeared in succeeding decades.

Bernard Burke had been trained as a barrister and was called to the Bar at Middle Temple. After his appointment as Ulster, he became Keeper of the State Papers of Ireland and a governor and trustee of the National Gallery of Ireland. Apart from being a prolific author on the subjects of genealogy and heraldry, he was a prominent and indispensable figure in the arrangement of the ceremonies and pageants of the viceregal court, and had a grasp of his subject perhaps greater than any of his predecessors. The investiture ceremony which had diminished in dignity and ceremonial since the 1830s was revived and restored to St Patrick's Hall, and a new atmosphere of efficiency began to pervade the office of Ulster King of Arms. There was little that Burke could do to remove the sons of Sir William Betham from their offices in the Order, had he wanted to, and Molyneux and Sheffield Betham continued as Cork and Dublin Heralds until their deaths in 1880 and 1890 respectively. Considering that Sheffield Betham had been an unsuccessful applicant for the post now held by Burke, relations between the two men cannot have been easy.

When the post of Athlone Pursuivant fell vacant in 1883, on the death of the ninety-year-old Captain Robert Smith, Burke appointed his second son, Bernard Louis Burke, to the post. In those days, it was not expected that individuals should resign an office, simply because age or infirmity prevented them from fulfilling their duties. Smith had formally declared in 1874 that he was no longer able to undertake his official duties, 'being incapacitated by old age',[1] and so Joseph Lentaigne was appointed his deputy. Lentaigne resigned in 1882 and was succeeded by Bernard Louis Burke, who succeeded to the substantive office in the following year. When he himself died in July 1892, he was followed by Sir Bernard Burke's youngest son, John Edward Burke. His eldest son, Henry Farnham Burke, already Somerset Herald in the College of Arms in London, was appointed Genealogist of the Order and Deputy Ulster King of Arms in 1889.

This nepotism was not without parallel or precedent. Burke was merely following the practice of his predecessor and, across the water, the Woods family administered the daily affairs of the Order of the Bath for most of the nineteenth century. Burke's nepotistic practices did, however, present difficulties for his successor, Sir Arthur Vicars, who was faced with the difficult task of removing John Edward Burke from office in 1899, on the grounds that he could not be relied upon to attend investitures of the Order, even when summoned.

The two most significant events in the history of the Order during Burke's reign as King of Arms were the installation of the Prince of Wales in 1868, and the secularisation of the Order resulting from the disestablishment of the Church of Ireland in 1871.

Analysing the root causes of the Irish problem in 1844 Benjamin Disraeli, the future Conservative Prime Minister, had defined four areas: 'a starving population, an absentee aristocracy, an alien church, and in addition, the weakest executive in the world'.[2] The position of the Church of Ireland, the 'alien church', was growing steadily weaker. A realistic assessment of the hierarchy of the Church of Ireland caused Parliament to pass controversial legislation in 1833, reducing the number of archbishops by two and the number of bishops by ten. Before many years had passed, the establishment of the Church was being seriously questioned.

An unusually convex star belonging to the Prince Consort (KP 1842). The reverse is engraved *West and Son* and *Belonged to the Prince Consort.*

The Irish administration received a severe battering in terms of publicity from the ill-organised and ill-equipped Fenian rising of March 1867. In 1868, six members of the movement were being tried for murder in connection with the gunpowder explosion at the Clerkenwell House of Detention and, while the Prince of Wales was in Ireland, a Fenian attempted to assassinate his brother, Prince Alfred, Duke of Edinburgh, in Sydney, Australia. The Queen had not visited Ireland since the death of the Prince Consort in 1861, and now something more than another visit was needed to revive the flagging fortunes of the crown in Ireland. There was no question of the Queen herself journeying to Dublin, so a carefully planned, highly visible and ceremonial visit of the heir to the throne was the next choice.

The Marquess of Abercorn (Lord Lieutenant, 1866–8) conceived the idea that the residence of a member of the royal family in Ireland, for at least part of the year, would provoke demonstrations of loyalty; provide a focal point for unity; and give a kind of moral support for the administration in the wake of the Fenian troubles. The only problem standing in the way of this solution was Queen Victoria. The Queen was not well disposed towards Ireland and the Irish and, principally because of her simplistic way of looking at events, she could not understand why they would not behave themselves. Athough the Queen loved Scotland, she was decidedly antipathetic to the question of a royal residence in Ireland and quite intransigent on the subject despite repeated requests. Shortly before the Prince arrived in Dublin, Lady Augusta Stanley wrote from Balmoral to her husband, reporting that the Queen would not, 'hear of anything but flying visits there for herself or any of her family. I believe she is afraid lest any of them should be taken up by, or take up the Irish as to throw Balmoral into the shade, now or later.'[3] There was no question of her visiting Ireland, since the death of the Prince Consort which had sent her into an unpopular seclusion.

A very small badge in gold and enamel which probably belonged to the Prince Consort, 1840–1.

The proposal for an elaborate ceremony for the Prince of Wales in Dublin had to be handled very carefully if the Queen's strong opposition was not to be aroused. Abercorn settled on the plan of inviting the Prince of Wales to Ireland for a week, with the intention of persuading the Queen to allow a longer visit later in the year should it prove successful, and he wisely enlisted the support of Disraeli, to whom the Queen was devoted; and what better a culmination to this visit than the appointment of the Prince as a Knight of St Patrick, and his installation in the newly-restored St Patrick's Cathedral. After years of neglect and decay during which it had fallen into a near ruinous state, the cathedral had been mostly rebuilt in the 1860s at great personal expense, by Sir Benjamin Guinness of the brewing family, and re-opened on 24 February 1865. To appoint the Prince of Wales to Ireland's national Order, and then, with great ceremony, to install him in the cathedral, would prove to be a valuable exercise in public relations. So the sixth and final installation of the Order of St Patrick was held on 18 April 1868, after forty-five years of dispensations.

The first step was to approach the Prince of Wales directly on the subject. Abercorn went to see him and explained his plans: 'I spoke to him very strongly indeed on the good that it would do ... I spoke to him about the Patrick ribbon and the function in the cathedral. He seemed quite pleased with the idea and said he had not got the Patrick, and would like to have it'.[4] The Lord Lieutenant planned to exploit the visit to the full. 'I should think a day's hunting, 2 days racing, the installation, and a review would pretty nearly do him.'[5] With the Prince in favour of a visit, Abercorn wrote to the Queen telling her that an installation in the newly-restored cathedral would give enormous pleasure to the Irish people. Disraeli supported his request, saying that there was, 'a great yearning in Ireland for the occasional presence and inspiration of royalty',[6] adding that the Sovereign had spent only twenty-one days in Ireland in the last two centuries. He ended by cautiously suggesting that the Prince might take up residence in Ireland for a longer period, later in the year, avoiding all mention of a permanent residence.

On the question of a royal residence, the Queen was not to be persuaded. Although she pronounced herself in favour of a week's visit, and the installation, she firmly rejected any idea of a royal residence in Ireland, on the grounds that similar pretensions might be aroused in Wales and even the colonies! Furthermore, she said, no one would dream of going to Ireland for health and relaxation, although thousands went to Scotland. Ever suspicious of the Prince's activities, she cautioned that, 'any encouragement of his constant love of roaming about and not keeping at home or near the Queen, is most honestly and seriously to be deprecated'.[7] When the Prince was unwise enough to mention that his visit coincided with the annual races at

This small collar was made in 1837 for the personal use of Queen Victoria. Of 22 carat gold, it bears the maker's initials 'wc'. The central imperial crown is engraved *Rundell, Bridge and Rundell, Jewellers and Goldsmiths to the Queen.* The collar is 1m 34cm long and the badge measures 23mm by 35mm.

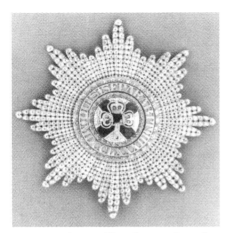

A star in silver, gold and enamel, made by West and Son of Dublin in 1846 for the Duke of Cambridge.

Punchestown, she insisted that he should not be seen to sanction or encourage them as they had, 'ruined so many young men, and broken the hearts thereby of so many kind and fond parents … I have heard of the great wish that you should receive the Order of St Patrick and the wish that you should be installed in Dublin as a Knight. I shall have much pleasure in giving you the Order, and think that your going over to Dublin to be installed there, should be the occasion for your going there, and NOT the races, which should only come in as an incident.'[8]

On 9 March, the Queen eventually gave her approval to the visit, but her initial reservations needed to be carefully handled if the whole project was not to collapse, and for some time, it was uncertain as to whether the visit would go ahead, as the Lord Lieutenant reported to the Earl of Mayo: 'I do not think I shall be able to write to you tomorrow to say that it is settled. If the Prince goes, I think the Duke of Cambridge will come too, and I have asked him to come to us. He is a KP so that will add a good deal to the glories of the installation altogether. I think it will be a splendid success, though I can assure you the whole thing was very near coming to grief.'[9]

The date was set for Saturday, 18 April 1868, and for the sixth and last time, St Patrick's Cathedral was re-arranged for an installation of the Order of St Patrick. Services were held intermittently, and public worship on Easter Day (Sunday 12 April) was limited to a celebration of Holy Communion at 8am. The choir of St Patrick's was temporarily transferred to Christ Church Cathedral, some 200 yards to the north, where sung services were held daily at 3pm. The usual galleries were erected in the choir and the nave to allow greater numbers to attend and, rather theatrically, the west doors of the cathedral were removed and replaced by a scarlet curtain. The disruption to the life and work of the cathedral was considerable, but, as the *Clerical Journal* observed: 'No one, however, grumbles at the Dean of St Patrick's for abdicating his functions temporarily in favour of Sir Bernard Burke. The latter gentleman is well known for his skill and taste and is eminently popular … and the public in general is so rejoiced at the Prince's visit as to wink at any ecclesiastical enormity'.[10]

Not every one was pleased with the venue. The *Daily Telegraph* condescendingly remarked that the restored cathedral looked: 'naked, cold and cheerless. The proportions are good and the nave is long; and when you have said this you have said pretty well all that need be about it. Owing to the recentness of the restoration, the church has no air of antiquity; and the two mouldering banners, which have been carried by British troops in the wars of Marlborough and which floated in their tatters over the north transept, seemed well-nigh the oldest objects in that modernised shrine.'[11] But for the ceremony itself there was fulsome praise on all sides, and it was conducted with as much magnificence as its five predecessors. The Prince was enthusiastically praised for his desire to identify himself with something as, 'truly national, and therefore most highly prized by the Irish people',[12] as the Order of St Patrick.

Of the twenty-two Knights of St Patrick, seventeen (including the Prince of Wales) were present, the senior being the Marquess of Clanricarde, who had been appointed an extra Knight by King William IV in 1831. The five absent Knights were the Earl of Wicklow (who was eighty), the Earl of Fingall (who was seventy-seven), the Marquess of Londonderry (who had long been in seclusion 'in consequence of mental disease'[13]), Viscount Gough (who was eighty-eight) and the Marquess of Donegall (who was seventy-one); all of them were absent on the grounds of ill-health or infirmity.

The train of Lord Abercorn's mantle was borne by young pages, one of whom, Lord Frederic Hamilton (1856–1928), recalled the event in his memoirs published fifty-two years later: 'The cathedral had undergone a complete transformation for the ceremony, and all its ordinary fittings had disappeared. The number of pages had now increased to five, and we were constantly being drilled in the cathedral. We had all five of us to walk backwards down some steps, keeping in line and keeping step. For five small boys to do this neatly, without awkwardness, requires a great deal of practice. The procession to the cathedral was made in full state, the streets being lined with troops, and the carriages, with their escorts of cavalry, going at a foot's pace through the principal thoroughfares of Dublin. I remember it chiefly on account of the bitter north-east wind blowing. The five pages drove together in an open carriage, and received quite an ovation from the crowd, but no one had thought of providing them with overcoats. Silk stockings, satin knee breeches and lace ruffles are very inadequate protection against an Arctic blast and we arrived at the cathedral stiff and torpid with cold ... The ceremony was very gorgeous and imposing, and I trust that the pages were not unduly clumsy. Everyone was amazed at the beauty of the music, sung from the triforium by the combined choirs of St Patrick's and Christ Church Cathedrals, and of the Chapel Royal, with that wonderful musician, Sir Robert Stewart at the organ. I remember well Sir Robert Stewart's novel setting of *God save the Queen*. The men sang it first in unison to the music of the massed military bands outside the cathedral, the boys singing a "Faux Bourdon" above it. Then the organ took it up, the full choir joining in with quite original harmonies.'[14]

On the evening of the same day, the Prince of Wales wrote a letter to the Queen to tell her of the great success of the day. 'We were lucky in having again a very fine day. Lord and Lady Abercorn preceded us in an open carriage from the castle to the cathedral, and we followed in the second carriage, a state one, open, as the people here prefer it so much. Uncle George [the Duke of Cambridge] then followed ... All the streets were lined with troops, and there were thousands of people, who certainly gave us such a reception, that we shall not easily forget it. Ever since our arrival, the cheering and enthusiasm have redoubled ... We reached the cathedral at 3.30, and

The installation of the Prince of Wales as a Knight on the 18 April 1868.

then I walked in procession after all the Knights . . . The ceremony was I think very imposing, and the cathedral looked very well . . . Tonight there is a state dinner . . . and I have to make a short speech as the new Knight of St Patrick.'[15]

The Duke of Cambridge himself remembered the day well. 'The greatest enthusiasm prevailed throughout, not a dissentient voice was heard. We got to St Patrick's by about 3.45, then robed, and then entered the Church in procession, a magnificent sight, all admirably arranged and not a single hitch or confusion of any sort or kind . . . We got back at 5.30 after one of the very greatest successes in point of pageantry and enthusiasm I ever experienced or was present at anywhere.'[16]

The Prince of Wales and the Duke of Cambridge experienced a genuine pleasure at the warmth of their reception in Dublin in April 1868, and there is no doubt that the royal visit did provoke an outpouring of affection and enthusiasm from the crowds of people who turned out to watch the Prince and Princess. But those who lined the streets and cheered the two princes on their way to the cathedral, were only those sections of Irish opinion that were most easily stirred by such things. The harder elements among Irish nationalism were not so easily swayed by the charm and graciousness displayed by the royal couple, and pointed out that life in Ireland had not changed. The nationalist *Nation* gave an alternative and cynical assessment of the worth of the visit. 'The Prince of Wales does not come to our shores as a Messiah of mercy. Did the Government intend anything of the sort, there was no need for all the vain display and grotesque tomfoolery that have characterised the proceedings of the past few days . . . The Prince of Wales, perhaps, has amused himself, the Government have got up such a display in Dublin as every wealthy and strong government, having money to spend and plenty of soldiers, police and detectives, can get up in every large city within their dominions; but for the rest, all things remain as they were.'[17] Such an attitude was to be expected. In the aftermath of the Fenian rising, there was now a harder and more cynical strand in Irish nationalism that was no longer so easily mesmerised by the mystique and the pageantry of the monarchy. Even the Queen was negative about the possible effect of the visit. 'Bertie and Alix's visit to Ireland has gone off well – as ours always did – but like ours, it will be of no real use.'[18]

The installation of the Prince of Wales in 1868 was the last great ceremonial Order occasion to be hosted by the Church of Ireland, and marked the breaking of the link between the Order of St Patrick and the Church of Ireland. Though there is no evidence that the impending legislation caused the desire to hold an installation, the question of the future of the Church of Ireland was beginning to cast a shadow over its relations with the Order. Throughout the 1860s, calls were repeatedly heard for the disestablishment and disendowment of the Church, and the results of the census of 1861 confirmed what many had long suspected. In a population of 5.75 million, members of the Church of Ireland numbered just under 700,000, with the Roman Catholic Church accounting for 4.5 million. The removal of the special privileged status of the Church of Ireland had long been wanted by the Roman Catholic Church and the nonconformist minority, and it was becoming a political issue that could no longer be avoided or deferred. In November 1868 the government of Benjamin Disraeli was defeated on a proposition by William Gladstone to end the privileged state of the Church of Ireland, and the ensuing election was fought on the issue of disestablishment, and won by Gladstone.

The attitude of the Roman Catholic Church to the installation services of the Order of St Patrick was quite pragmatic. The archiepiscopal vicariate of the archdiocese of Dublin issued a statement before the 1868 installation, saying that the diocesan authorities considered the ceremony as purely civil in its character and object, and therefore as not coming within the prohibition against Roman Catholics assisting at acts of religious worship other than those of the Roman Catholic Church. There were

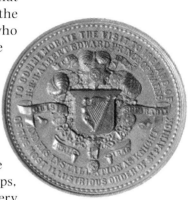

A medallion issued to commemorate the sixth installation of the Order on 18 April 1868.

two Roman Catholic knights in 1868: the ninth Earl of Fingall, and the seventh Earl of Granard, and this interdenominational aspect of the membership of the Order, made the continued presence of the Anglican archbishops of Armagh and Dublin as ex-officio Prelate and Chancellor of the Order, something of an anomaly.

The passing of the Irish Church Act in 1869 disestablished and disendowed the Church of Ireland from 1 January 1871, reducing it to the status of a voluntary body. Within six months of the legislation, Abercorn's successor, Earl Spencer (Lord Lieutenant, 1868–74) wrote to Gladstone proposing the inevitable changes in the constitution of the Order: 'It is clear that for an Irish State Order, these heads of the Protestant Episcopalian Church have no longer any special right to hold office: nor can the Protestant cathedral be the official place for the stalls of the Knights. The difficulties of introducing clerical officers from the different sects in Ireland are so great that the only course to pursue is to follow the precedent of, I think, the Order of the Thistle, and certainly the Star of India, and have only lay officers in the Order ... The rights and privileges of the ecclesiastics now belonging to the Order will be preserved during their lives. I hope that H. M. will consider that the dignity of the Order will be sufficiently maintained under the new warrant.'[19] The logic was faultless and the Queen was satisfied.

The Royal Warrant giving effect to this 'secularisation' of the Order bears the marks of Sir Bernard Burke's desire for efficiency. As well as the removal of the Church of Ireland dignitaries, several other offices were dispensed with or amalgamated on financial grounds. The warrant guaranteed the right of all the existing officers, but decreed the following changes in the event of the death or resignation of the existing holders: the office of Chancellor was to be transferred from the Archbishop of Dublin to the Chief Secretary of Ireland; the office of Registrar, hitherto held by the Dean of St Patrick's Cathedral, was to be amalgamated with the office of Ulster King of Arms; and the offices of Prelate, Genealogist, Cork Herald, Dublin Herald, and Junior Pursuivant were abolished. The ceremony of installation, for long in abeyance, was formally discontinued, though by special desire of the Queen, the banners of the Knights existing at 1 January 1871 were to continue hanging in the cathedral.[20]

One by one the Officers of the Order died, beginning with Sir William Leeson, the Genealogist, in March 1885, and ending with George Frith Barry, the last of the Junior Pursuivants, in 1891. Information relating to the Junior Pursuivants is less than satisfactory. There is no complete list of them, and in several cases their full names and dates of office are unknown. They appear to have been little more than pages or messengers appointed at extremely early ages by Ulster King of Arms, and their disappearance made little difference to the Order. Burke himself felt it to be a nominal and superfluous office: 'It was perfectly useless and very troublesome. No duties were attached and there was no connection whatsoever between it and the heraldic staff in Ireland. In point of fact it had nothing to do with heraldry and genealogy.'[21] Burke no doubt considered the two Heralds to be equally superfluous. In 1865, he referred to them as, 'merely officers of the Order of St Patrick',[22] though the fact that the occupants of the two posts were the sons of his predecessor, might have influenced this dismissive statement. The amalgamation of the office of Registrar with Ulster was only a belated recognition of a situation which had long existed. Why Burke did not recommend the abolition of the office of Secretary when he was cutting out everything else is not clear. Ulster had always conducted the correspondence of the Order, and the post could safely have disappeared without any noticeable loss.

For the rest of the nineteenth century, the abolished offices remained abolished, with the sole exception of the office of Genealogist. In 1889, four years after the death of Sir William Leeson, Burke decided that the office should be reinstated. He was now seventy-five years old, and his argument was based on the need for a second high officer of the Order, who could fill the place of Ulster in case of absence or illness, 'to carry out the requirements of the original statutes, to assist at the investitures and other ceremonials, and to preserve the genealogical records and the sequence of the Knights of the Order'.[23] The office of Genealogist was duly revived and, in 1889, Burke's eldest son, Henry Farnham Burke, was appointed Genealogist and Deputy Ulster. There is no evidence to doubt Sir Bernard Burke's statement that, effectively, he needed an assistant. The slight surprise is the fact that he should have chosen to appoint a person, albeit his son, who was a practising herald at the College of Arms in London.

The abolition of offices in 1871 was accompanied by a sharp reduction in the fees paid by each new Knight, and this appears to have been the reasoning behind the abolition of so many of the lay Officers of the Order. Earl Spencer recommended the necessity of taking some action on the question of the fees paid by Knights on admission to the Order. The cost of appointment as a Knight of St Patrick now amounted to £588 (apart from the cost to each Knight of providing himself with a mantle and a star) and William Gladstone reported to the Queen that there had been, 'difficulties of late in supplying vacancies in the Order of St Patrick on account of the heavy charges attending the admissions'.[24] The fees were distributed as follows:

The Registrar	£25
The Secretary	£25
The Genealogist	£25
The King of Arms	£25
The Usher	£20
Two Heralds	£20 each
Four Pursuivants	£20 each
Similar fees on dispensation	£160
Queen's letter and sign manual, fees of, application for, registration	£21
Certificate of noblesse of blood	£10 10s
Helmet and crest in stall	£8 8s
Sword in stall	£3 13s 6d
Banner over stall	£21
Plate of arms in stall	£6 16s 6d
Fee to Ulster King of Arms, for superintendence	£21
Fees to the officers of arms and his excellency's household on receiving the honour of knighthood	£75
Purse, to the Dean of St Patrick's for the poor	£21

Gladstone's assertion that the heavy fees had deterred some prospective Knights from accepting the honour, is supported by the example of Viscount Lismore, who was nominated a Knight on 14 September 1864, and declined the honour within two weeks. 'Viscount Palmerston presents his humble duty to Your Majesty, and begs to state that he learns from Lord Wodehouse [the Lord Lieutenant] that Lord Lismore ... has now represented that the state of his health makes him unwilling to receive the Order, the probability being that he finds it inconvenient to pay the fees.'[25]

It was decided that, in future, each Knight should pay a flat sum of £300 to the Treasury, who would give yearly allowances to the Officers instead of the individual fees on the appointment of each Knight. The Officers pronounced themselves satisfied with this arrangement, but they claimed that a vacancy in the Order on the death of the Earl of Roden in 1870 had been deliberately left unfilled for nearly eighteen months until after the introduction of the new system. They addressed a petition to the Grand Master, claiming that they were entitled to receive the usual fees on the appointment of Roden's successor, Viscount Powerscourt, in August 1871. Burke was the only officer who did not sign, but he agreed to forward the letter. The Treasury, realising that its position was untenable, agreed to pay the officers their fees, less a 3.5 per cent deduction.

The newspapers were quick to applaud the abolition of the religious side of the

The small oval badge of the Duke of Connaught (KP 1869). Made in 1842 of 18 carat gold; engraved with maker's mark 'WN'. The date of manufacture suggests that the piece may have been acquired by Prince Albert, who was appointed to the Order in that year.

Order. *The Times* remarked, rather pompously, that the original religious foundation had been a 'mistake', and the Order was now placed on a wider and more popular basis, being no longer limited to any sect or creed. The newspaper was incorrect in this assertion. Membership of the Order of St Patrick had not been limited to peers belonging to the Church of Ireland for several decades, the first Roman Catholic peer being admitted in 1821. 'It is now reconstituted with a more intelligent perception of the great social and political changes which the world has since experienced, and is made more in harmony with the liberal spirit of the times.'[26] Perhaps pointedly, one of the first two new Knights appointed after the passage of the legislation – Viscount Southwell – was a Roman Catholic.

The disappearance of the installation and accompanying religious ceremonial left the investiture as the only ceremonial admission of Knights to the Order. For most of the history of the Order, the investiture had been overshadowed by the pomp and circumstance of the installation, and from the 1830s to 1850s it was reduced to a comparatively informal gathering at the Viceregal Lodge in Phoenix Park. Burke had done much to revive its formality, restoring it to its proper setting in St Patrick's Hall, and after 1871, both he and Earl Spencer decided to elevate its status, to the extent that it would replace the installation ceremony in popular esteem.

The first investiture after the passing of the Irish Church Act was held on 2 August 1871, and Burke did his utmost to make the investiture an imposing occasion. The Prince of Wales and Prince Arthur (later Duke of Connaught) were both present, and all the resources of the castle were expended in the production of a brilliant ceremony. The investiture was preceded by a sumptuous banquet, the menu of which has survived. The Knights and their guests were given a choice of stuffed fillets of turbot, boiled salmon with lobster sauce, soufflés of poultry, sweetbread, fillets of duckling, young turkey, venison, mutton, roast beef, quails, hare, artichokes, pineapple, and raspberry meringue glacés.

The investiture then began at the nocturnal hour of 11pm. It was decided to hold the investiture at night, when its pomp and splendour could be displayed to best effect. A large table covered with a blue cloth was placed before the viceregal throne in St Patrick's Hall. Evergreens and flowers were placed at intervals around the walls. Festoons and garlands looped with blue ribbon were suspended along the galleries and from the chandeliers, and a band of the Grenadier Guards, stationed in the gallery,

St Patrick's Hall, Dublin Castle, prepared for an investiture of the Order, c.1871–84.

played a triumphal march as the Knights entered and seated themselves around the table. The new Knights, Viscount Powerscourt and Viscount Southwell, were led in by the Ulster King of Arms, knighted by the Grand Master, and invested with the riband and badge of the Order. The chapter of Knights was then formally dissolved, and the Knights left the hall in procession to the sound of the band playing *St Patrick's Day*.

The investiture of new Knights followed the pattern established by Burke in 1871, up to and including 1911, but seldom with quite the same ceremony. In 1888, with the approaching investiture of the Marquess of Ormonde, Burke remembered with the nostalgia the nocturnal investiture of 1871, and asked that it be repeated. 'The prospect of an investiture always cheers me. Held in the evening in St Patrick's Hall with all knightly pageant, the ceremonial is very brilliant and effective. I remember well the investiture of Lords Powerscourt and Southwell 2nd August 1871. Their Royal Highnesses the Prince of Wales and Prince Arthur attended. When the function ended, the scene changed into a state ball. Do you think Their Excellencies could be induced to follow the precedent?'[27]

After the disestablishment of the Church of Ireland on 1 January 1871, more than ten years passed before the Knights were given a new ceremonial 'home'. The 1783 Statutes had provided for hatchments, swords, helmets and banners to be erected in St Patrick's Cathedral, but this was no longer possible. The centenary of the Order was approaching, and something could surely be done to celebrate the occasion. In August 1881 Sir Bernard Burke secured the agreement of Earl Cowper, the then Lord Lieutenant, for the banners and hatchment plates to be given a new permanent home. 'The banners etc. . . . remain unplaced to the great disappointment of the noblemen invested with the Order ... The Lord Lieutenant has selected St Patrick's Hall.'[28] Burke's proposal was sufficient to cause the Dean and Chapter of St Patrick's to take fright at the prospect of losing the banners of the pre-disestablishment Knights, still in the cathedral. 'The removal of the banners and helmets now in St Patrick's Cathedral has never been contemplated. The proposed placing of insignia in St Patrick's Hall refers only to the banners and helmets of the Knights invested since the disestablishment of the Irish Church. Kindly mention this to the Dean and Chapter.'[29]

The cost of undertaking the work, estimated at 160 guineas, was initially refused by the Treasury. But in November 1881, the Treasury agreed to authorise the sum of £168 in the estimates for 1882–3, and the banners were probably erected in 1885, at the conclusion of a period of renovation. The hall was certainly in a sufficiently dilapidated condition for its state to be condemned by Lord Randolph Churchill in the House of Commons in June 1883. Churchill asked the Financial Secretary to the Treasury whether the attention of the Board of Works had been drawn to the very dilapidated condition of St Patrick's Hall? Was the Government aware that, 'on account of the dilapidated and ruinous condition of the walls of St Patrick's Hall, the Knights of St Patrick created since 1868 have been prevented from having their banners and shields hung up according to ancient custom, although they have been charged and have paid very heavy fees for that purpose?' The Financial Secretary replied that although the hall needed painting and gilding, it was not dilapidated and certainly not ruinous. Provision had been made for repairing the walls to allow for the 'insignia' of the knights to be hung, 'but, in order not to disturb the walls twice, they will not be hung up until the other work is taken in hand'.[30] Churchill's outburst might have been partly motivated by the fact that his father, the Duke of Marlborough, had been Lord Lieutenant of Ireland 1876–80, and his distant cousin, Earl Spencer, was the current Lord Lieutenant. The renovation of the hall was carried out in accordance with the wishes of Countess Spencer who personally inspected the progress.[31] The contract was placed with the Dublin firm of Sibthorpe in June 1884, after the investiture of the Earl of Howth in the previous month, and was probably completed in time for the investitures of Lord Annaly and Lord Monteagle of Brandon in February 1885.

The style of the viceregal courts differed very much from one Lord Lieutenant to the next, and depended partly on the personality of the Lord Lieutenant, partly on his income, and partly on the prevailing political situation. The Marquess of Londonderry (1886–9) hated lengthy dinners and instituted short meals lasting no more than thirty minutes. A footman stood behind nearly every chair, and plates were often whipped away from the guests before they had finished. If guests stopped to talk, there was every chance they would get nothing to eat at all. Lord Houghton (1892–5) was unfortunate enough to be viceroy during the attempted passage of the Home Rule Bill by the Liberal government of William Gladstone. As the Home Rule policy was considered by the Irish unionists to be base desertion by the Government, very few people of wealth and position in Ireland accepted the viceroy's hospitality or attended functions at the castle. Consequently, the viceroy's court was attended by people who had nothing in common with him, and Houghton became a rather melancholy figure. 'His infinite boredom with the dinners and dances and the people he had to entertain he was unable to conceal in spite of his most praiseworthy efforts to do so.'[32] The advent of a Conservative government in 1895, removed any immediate prospect of home rule for Ireland, and with the arrival of Lord Cadogan (1895–1902) the land-owning aristocracy once again happily frequented the viceregal court. Cadogan was a charming and courteous man but, although he had flashes of brilliance, it was difficult to get him to understand the most childishly simple and elementary things. He was not a politician, and it was rumoured that he owed his position more to his wealth and his influence than to his experience.[33]

The Earl of Dudley (1902–5) was rich, and hated any form of economy. He maintained a brilliant and extravagant court, spending £80,000 of his own money during his first year of office. But he was careless and indolent about payments and kept people waiting for their money without realising the inconvenience he was causing. He was also an inconsiderate golfer, and would keep people waiting for a quarter of an hour while he drove off practice shots from the tee. 'On Saturdays and competition days there would be a regular howl of dismay when players saw the viceregal motors drive up to the links.'[34]

Two new Knights of St Patrick were appointed during Dudley's lieutenancy. The Earl of Mayo, founder of the Arts and Crafts Movement in Ireland, was appointed in February 1905, and followed two months later by the great imperialist figure of the Earl of Meath. Mayo's investiture on 3 February was captured in a painting by Count Casimir Dunin Markievicz (1874–1932), and so designed that every person present could be identified (see page 192). The Prince of Wales had travelled to Dublin especially for the investiture, and can be seen sitting to the left of the Lord Lieutenant, close to the head of the table. The Prince was as enchanted by the occasion as he had been by his own investiture eight years earlier. 'We dined at 8.0 a large dinner in full uniform all the Knights of St Patrick and their wives. Dudley made an excellent speech in proposing Mayo's health & he returned thanks. At 10.30 the investiture of Lord Mayo with the Order of St Patrick took place in St Patrick's Hall, it was a very pretty sight, there were 17 Knights present & it was all very well done.'[35]

In December 1905 Dudley was succeeded by John Campbell Hamilton-Gordon, seventh Earl of Aberdeen, the last popular Lord Lieutenant of Ireland. Within eighteen months of his arrival in Dublin, Aberdeen's lieutenancy was overshadowed by an event that was to haunt the remainder of his time in Ireland, and in a sense, worry him for the rest of his life; the theft of the diamond insignia of the Grand Master of the Order of St Patrick in the summer of 1907. Markievicz's 1905 painting depicts a number of the principal figures associated with the event that Aberdeen remembered with a shudder for the rest of his life, and the most prominent, standing to the left of the Lord Lieutenant, and wearing the crimson mantle of his office, was the pivotal figure of Sir Arthur Edward Vicars, Ulster King of Arms.

CHAPTER FIVE

A NEW BROOM

The arrival of Arthur Vicars

═══

I believe I am the only person in Ireland who not being an official
has steadily and most exclusively given his attention to the study of heraldry.
ARTHUR VICARS, 12 July 1890

S IR BERNARD BURKE experienced several years of failing health before his death, and for some time, he was unable to attend to the duties of his office or to take any role in the ceremonies of the viceregal court. He was absent from the investiture of the Earl of Milltown in February 1890, and the ceremony was marked by a number of embarrassing mistakes that would not have occurred had he been present; so much so that the senior Knight, the Marquess of Drogheda angrily laid his concerns before the Lord Lieutenant. 'I think it is my duty to bring before you the very different manner in which these ceremonies are now conducted to what they used to be when Sir Bernard Burke was able to be present. On each succeeding occasion I perceive that the duties of the heraldic department are carried on in an increasingly careless and irregular manner ... In the first procession, that of the Grand Master, the new Knight was allowed to take part & marched into St Patrick's Hall, from whence, of course, he had to be brought back ... The whole business, instead of being an impressive ceremony, has been allowed to become, if I may be allowed to say so, an absurd exhibition.'[1]

Burke could do no more than apologise to the Lord Lieutenant, and promise an improvement in the future. 'My health so shattered of late, is now much improved that I am sanguine enough to expect to be asked to do what it has grieved me sadly to neglect, my personal attendance on Your Excellency.'[2] Further problems were caused by the diminishing numbers of staff of the Office of Arms. The Betham link with the Office ended with the death of Sheffield Betham in 1890, and his office of Dublin Herald was abolished by the terms of the Royal Warrant of 1871. George Barry, senior clerk in the State Paper Department and the last of the Junior Pursuivants, died in 1891, and his office was accordingly abolished. Like Burke, he had been ill for some time, and unable to leave his home. 'His absence', wrote Burke, 'causes me much difficulty.'[3] The series of deaths was completed by his eldest son, Bernard Louis Burke, Athlone Pursuivant, who died in July 1892 at the age of only thirty-one. The loss of his son probably hastened Sir Bernard Burke's own death in December of the same year at the age of seventy-eight.

Two months later, he was succeeded by Arthur Edward Vicars, a comparatively unknown young man of twenty-nine years of age. Vicars, the son of Colonel William Henry Vicars, was born in Warwickshire in 1864. His mother, Jane Gun-Cunninghame (1821–68), a member of the Gun-Cunninghame family of County Wicklow, had previously been married to Peirce K. O'Mahony (1817–50) of County Kerry. She had three sons by this marriage (one of whom died in childhood), and although Arthur Vicars was educated in England, he spent his holidays at the Irish country houses (Grange Con in County Wicklow and Kilmorna in County Kerry) belonging to his older half brothers, George and Peirce, and developed a longing to identify himself with the old Ireland that they represented.

Arthur Vicars' interest in genealogical matters had come to the notice of Sir Bernard Burke in either 1888 or 1889, though how is unknown. In 1888, Vicars had published a fifteen-page pamphlet on the famous mummifying properties of the vaults of St Michan's Church in Dublin,[4] and he may have sent a copy to Burke. His recorded contact with the Office of Arms began in the summer of 1890 with the death of Sheffield Betham, Dublin Herald. Betham, the son of Sir William Betham, who had been appointed Dublin Herald as far back as 1833, died on 2 July 1890, and Vicars was quick to register his interest. On 10 July he wrote to the Lord Lieutenant's private secretary[5] and then, on 12 July, to Arthur Balfour (then Chief Secretary of Ireland and Chancellor of the Order), applying for the office. Despite the fact that the office had been scheduled for abolition by the Royal Warrant of 1871, Vicars breezily and precociously presented his qualifications to Balfour. 'The duties of the office are such as I believe I am competent to discharge, requiring as they do, a knowledge of heraldry and the usages of state ceremonials. To this branch of study I have applied myself for several years and I believe I am the only person in Ireland who not being an official has steadily and most exclusively given his attention to the study of heraldry.'[6]

Vicars was told that the emoluments attached to the office had been discontinued and, in any case, the Royal Warrant of 1871 had specifically abolished the office. A less pertinacious man might well have given up in the face of this official negative, but Arthur Vicars was not to be put off easily, and he pursued the matter over the next three years with a dogged persistence. He wrote back saying that he was quite willing to accept the office without any emolument,[7] and as far as the 1871 warrant was concerned, the discontinued office of Genealogist had been reinstated in 1889, so here was a precedent for reinstating the office of Dublin Herald. Flustered by this unexpected persistence, the Chief Secretary wrote back stating firmly that the Lord Lieutenant could see no grounds for recommending the re-establishment of any of the other offices abolished in 1871.[8]

Sir Arthur Vicars, Ulster King of Arms (1893–1908) in the grounds of Dublin Castle, February 1905.

There the matter rested for eight months until the death of George Frith Barry, the last surviving Junior Pursuivant, in March 1891. Vicars wrote again to Balfour on 4 March, asking to be appointed to the post which he called 'St Patrick Pursuivant of Arms' – an unknown title, probably of his own invention. Again he offered to accept the post without any emolument, and again he quoted the reinstated office of Genealogist in regard to the 1871 warrant.[9] Vicars followed this letter to Balfour with a much longer letter addressed to the Lord Lieutenant. In it, he again asked to be considered for appointment to the office of Dublin Herald, or to that of St Patrick Pursuivant of Arms. He also added that the Office of Arms in Ireland was lacking in 'dignity and efficiency' compared with the considerable number of heraldic officers in England and Scotland, and that two (Ulster King of Arms and Athlone Pursuivant) was an insufficient number to discharge the duties connected with the office. 'I may add', he finished proudly, 'that I am the only professional herald in Ireland not officially connected with Ulster's Office.'[10]

The Chief Secretary was irritated by the fact that Vicars was refusing to take 'no' for an answer, and in his reply he enclosed a memorandum by Burke describing the office of Junior Pursuivant as 'nominal and useless'. Vicars wrote back with an astonishing degree of naivety, bordering on foolhardiness, accepting Burke's opinion, and saying that he could not assume it applied to the post of Dublin Herald as well. 'I scarcely think', wrote Vicars of Burke, 'that he has borne in mind all the considerations which I venture to put forward in the enclosed memorial'.[11] The Chief Secretary replied that since Vicars was so keen to be appointed to one or other of the posts, could he furnish further reasons why the post should be revived. Vicars listed seven: Sir Bernard Burke was an invalid, unable to attend any of the ceremonies connected with his office, and had appointed his eldest son as his deputy; his younger son, Athlone Pursuivant, never attended the investitures of the Order; the Irish heraldic establishment had dwindled to two officers, whereas there were eleven in Scotland and many more in London at the College of Arms, which made the Dublin staff appear insufficient, 'unless the staff of England and Scotland is altogether extravagant'; he was not asking for any emolument so why should there be any objection to revival; the office of Genealogist had been revived, so why not Junior Pursuivant or Dublin Herald, which were more important; Ulster's office was a source of profit to the exchequer and existed of necessity for public convenience; such offices should be maintained to encourage those studying a branch of knowledge as rare as heraldry – 'the state has always recognised its duty to do so'; he had made heraldry and genealogy his profession, and was the only such person in Ireland. Vicars continued on a personal note which, on reflection, he might well have excluded. He had reason to believe that Sir Bernard Burke was antagonistic towards him because he felt that to give Vicars any heraldic appointment would encroach upon the monopoly of the Burke family. It appears that two or three years earlier, Vicars had applied and been accepted for the post of secretary in the Office of Arms. Some days later after his testimonials had arrived, Burke cancelled the appointment saying that he felt they were so extraordinarily high that he did not think he was justified in offering Vicars such a low post, though he did supply a reference on Vicars' behalf to the Duke of Norfolk.[12]

The Government was adamant in its refusal to revive any of the abolished posts, but Vicars was not without influence. He was able to name Lord Rayleigh, the Attorney-General, the Solicitor-General and the Chief Secretary in his letters as referees. The Government must have been impressed by his persistence if by nothing else and on 23 February 1893, two months after Sir Bernard Burke's death, Vicars was appointed Ulster King of Arms, Registrar and Knight Attendant of the Order of St Patrick. His only desire was to make the Office of Arms, which had run down in the last years under Burke, as efficient as possible. He could not remove Henry Farnham Burke from his office as Genealogist of the Order, but his appointment as Deputy Ulster was terminated. He also had to endure John Edward Burke, Sir Bernard's youngest son, as Athlone Pursuivant for the next seven years. John Edward Burke had been appointed to the office in July 1892 at the age of twenty-four, six months before the death of his father. Nothing is known of his relationship with Vicars, if indeed there was one, but it cannot have been easy. Vicars reported to Lord Cadogan that Burke had failed to attend the investiture of Lord Lucan on 2 March 1899, though duly summoned, without giving any reason for his absence, and recommended that he be removed from office. Cadogan supported Vicars' request, and forwarded it to the Home Secretary in London. He reported that Burke, 'cannot be relied upon to efficiently discharge duties in the future [and] I desire that you will submit to the Queen my humble request that Her Majesty will be graciously pleased to revoke the appointment of Mr Burke to the said office'.[13]

The dismissal of John Burke proved to be a forerunner of what was to lie ahead for Arthur Vicars himself. Busy ridding himself of an unwanted colleague on a charge of inefficiency, Vicars could not have foreseen that his own efficiency would be called into question nine years later on a much more serious matter, and that he would be ignominiously dismissed from office amid a blaze of publicity, rumour and innuendo.

One of the high points of those early years of the reign of Arthur Vicars was the visit of the Duke and Duchess of York to Ireland in the summer of 1897. The duke had visited Ireland in 1887 with his elder brother Prince Albert Victor, Duke of Clarence and Avondale. With the death of Prince Albert Victor in 1892, the Duke of York now became heir presumptive to the heir apparent to the throne, and a visit to Ireland was inevitable. Shortly after the celebration of Queen Victoria's Diamond Jubilee, the duke and duchess arrived in Ireland for a three week visit (18 August to 8 September). The Prime Minister [the Marquess of Salisbury] had recommended to the Queen that the duke be appointed a Knight of St Patrick,[14] and the duke was, 'particularly pleased that you should give it me this year, as ten years ago in 1887 I was present in Dublin with dear Eddy when he got it'.[15] On 20 August, with Field Marshal Earl Roberts, he was invested in St Patrick's Hall, in a ceremony that was as colourful and impressive as ever. The Grand Master, eighteen Knights and six Officers [including John Edward

Field Marshal
Earl Roberts (KP 1897)
and his star.

Burke] gathered in the hall to receive the newest addition to their most illustrious company. The occasion was as splendid as it could be, and the duke described it to his grandmother as, 'a very fine sight',[16] and repeated the comment in his diary. 'There were 17 Knights present which was a record, a very fine sight & it went off very well.'[17] The Knights seated on blue and gold chairs around a large table covered with a gold-fringed blue cloth, but *The Times* correspondent thought it, 'a sorry substitute ... for stalls in St Patrick's Cathedral'.[18] The Lord Lieutenant praised the duke's visit as a triumph. 'Not one incident or manifestation of a hostile character occurred', and as the visit was wholly unconnected with party or political considerations, 'much criticism was disarmed and opposition averted by the knowledge this conveyed'.[19]

The duke was deeply impressed by the warmth of the welcome that he received, and urged the Queen to consider the establishment of a permanent royal residence in Ireland. There was no greater chance in 1897 than there had been in 1868 that the Queen would agree, and she refused her consent, but the duke retained very happy memories of his visit. 'It left the Duke of York with a personal affection for Ireland and the conviction (which he never relinquished) that, in spite of the politicians, there existed a sentimental bond of affection between the Irish people and the Crown.'[20] This belief, born of the exhilirating experience of a visit in 1897, at least in part probably contributed towards his belief thirty years later, when he had become King George V, that the Order of St Patrick could and should be preserved. There is no doubt that he retained an affection for Ireland and the Irish until the end of his life, but the reality of his experience of Ireland in 1897 was similar to the experience of the Prince and Princess of Wales in 1868; the royal visitors heard only the vociferous shouts of welcome from the supporters of the union and the crown; hardline Irish nationalists treated the visit as irrelevant to their cause.

With the arrival of the twentieth century came the decision completely to revise the Statutes of the Order. It was the first significant change in the regulations governing the Order since 1871, and the first thorough-going revision and consolidation of the Statutes since they were promulgated in 1783. The first surviving formal record of the process occurs in a handwritten note dated 28 October 1903, from J. B. Dougherty, Under Secretary for Ireland, to the Home Office in London.[21] According to Arthur Vicars, the work of revision was initiated by Lord Cadogan (Lord Lieutenant 1895–1902) about the year 1901.[22] The original Statutes of 1783, copied from the Statutes of the Order of the Garter, contained so many archaic anomalies that they were mostly inoperable from the moment of their publication. Furthermore, they had been subjected to so many amendments over the course of the nineteenth century that they needed to be read, if at all, in conjunction with a large number of amending warrants, ordinances and additional statutes. The 1783 Statutes were hardly fit documents to govern an Order of Knighthood, and they must have irritated a man like Arthur Vicars, preoccupied with tidiness and precision of detail. Given that nobody except Ulster King of Arms was really affected or bothered by the Statutes, it seems possible that Vicars may have prompted Lord Cadogan to issue the directive to revision.

During the course of the revision process, an extraordinary document in the shape of a petition was presented to the Earl of Dudley (Lord Lieutenant 1902–05), and signed by virtually all the Knights of St Patrick, including even the three royal Knights – the Prince of Wales, the Duke of Connaught and the Duke of Cambridge. The petition, drawn up in the summer of 1903, made a single specific request – that St Patrick's Cathedral should once again be used for installation services of the Order. Although acknowledging that the warrant of 1871 was caused by the disestablishment of the Church of Ireland, the petition named the reasons for making such a request: 'That this change has tended to confound two ancient ceremonials [investiture and installation] which in all the other Orders of chivalry are entirely distinct in character and in purpose and is therefore unbecoming the dignity of the Order. That it has also tended to dissociate the present from the past, and to disconnect the Order from the ancient Cathedral Church of St Patrick, a national monument dear to the hearts of all Irishmen. That the banners which now hang in its Choir are those of the Knights who were companions of the Order in one thousand eight hundred and seventy-one, of whom at the present moment only three survive, and those of their successors now displayed in Dublin Castle are seen by comparatively few persons and thus the Order is brought less permanently before the Irish people. That it has tended to dissociate this Order of chivalry from religious sanctions. The name of God is still invoked in the ceremonial of investiture but the Knights of St Patrick have now no connection with any Christian edifice. That the ceremonial of installation could not constitute a grievance in the case of a Knight of St Patrick who did not belong to the Church of Ireland; for the ceremony may be dispensed with at the sovereign's pleasure and has been so dispensed with in the majority of cases in the past, and there is nothing in the ceremonial of installation associating it with any particular religious denomination.'[23]

The petitioners concluded with a 'humble prayer' that the King would direct the Statutes of the Order to be revised, that the banners of Knights should once again hang in St Patrick's Cathedral, and that the Dean of the cathedral should once again be the Registrar of the Order. The petition made no request for the two Church of Ireland prelates, the Archbishop of Armagh and the Archbishop of Dublin, to be again respectively Prelate and Chancellor.

There was never any serious possibility that the requests contained in the petition would be approved. The arguments outlined in the correspondence between Earl Spencer and William Gladstone in 1871 were still valid in 1903. The only serious change envisaged by the petition, and adopted, was the general revision of the Statutes. Initially, Sir Arthur Vicars proposed only a general tidying-up of the Statutes, without any intention of total revision, but he took the precaution of showing his draft to Sir Albert Woods, Garter Principal King of Arms. Woods was an obvious authority to consult; in addition to his work with the Order of the Garter, he was additionally Registrar and Secretary of the Order of the Bath, King of Arms of the Order of St Michael and St George, and Registrar of the Orders of the Star of India, the Indian Empire, the Crown of India, and Victoria and Albert. He had first been appointed to the College of Arms in 1837, at the age of twenty-one, and had been Garter King of Arms since 1869. Although he was eighty-seven years old, physically infirm, and virtually confined to his London house, he had an unrivalled knowledge of ceremonial matters, and was an obvious authority to consult.

Vicars had been in touch with Woods by the autumn of 1903 when the latter, shortly before his death, addressed a long memorandum to Vicars, criticising the working revised draft of the Statutes. 'The draft of the revised Statutes of the Order of St Patrick, which I have attentatively considered, appears to have been hastily put together, and its present shape could do but little in clearing up the obscurity now complained of as attaching to the Statutes. The faults in the Statutes as they now stand [the 1783 Statutes] appear to me to be: (i) a want of plan in drafting; (ii) vague treatment of important matters; (iii) obsolete provisions; and (iv) the use of cumbrous and inexact phraseology; and these faults are largely retained and continued in the new draft. Until a clear decision is arrived at on several important points touching the Order, attempts to settle the wording would be a mere waste of time ... I would recommend that the existing Statutes of the Order should be repealed *in toto* and new Statutes re-enacted, and that the plan and the style and phraseology of the new Statutes should so far as practicable be modelled on the Statutes of the Orders of the Bath and Star of India.'[24]

Vicars travelled to London, and met Woods at his home on 28 November 1903, and the two Kings of Arms examined the Statutes in detail. Vicars was more than prepared to defer to Woods' long experience, and to accept his general opinion that totally new Statutes were required. 'I adopted the phraseology of the original Statutes and only added to or eliminated from them according to the various changes that have been made since they were originally enacted with a view to their consolidation. Garter's remarks on the original Statutes seem to be quite justified ... I decided to re-cast the revised Statutes and base them on those of the Orders of the Bath and the Star of India.'[25] The eighty-seven-year-old Garter probably made many sensible suggestions to the thirty-nine-year-old Ulster, and gave as much help as he could, but it was too late for Woods to play a key role in revising the Statutes of the Order of St Patrick. He was rapidly failing, and died on 7 January 1904.

The new Statutes, essentially the work of Arthur Vicars, were published on 29 July 1905, and generally codified in print what was already happening in practice. The Sovereign was now officially empowered to appoint and nominate Knights to the Order for the first time (Statute VIII), by replacing the obsolete and complicated machinery of election by the other Knights. The Grand Master was now officially allowed to wear the badge of the Order, and his magnificent diamond insignia were fully described in Statute XII. A proposal to end the anomaly of the Grand Master not being a Knight of the Order of which he was Grand Master was vetoed by King Edward VII. The King was prepared to allow former Grand Masters to wear a replica of their badge of office, and the star of the Order, but they should not wear the broad riband, nor should they use the letters KP after their name.[26] Dispensations from investiture were now officially allowed (Statute XVIII), and the Knights were no longer financially penalised for non-attendance at investitures or non-wearing of insignia. Provision was made for the safe storage of insignia, 'in a steel safe in the strong room of the chancery of the Order' (Statute XX), which had caused so much trouble in the early years of the nineteenth century. New Knights were required to sign a receipt for insignia entrusted to their care (Statute XX). Ulster King of Arms was defined as the 'executive officer' of the Order, and the list of his functions (Statute XXVII) made it abundantly clear that he alone was responsible for the care and arrangement of the Order, its insignia and its ceremonies. Only one anomaly was retained: Statute X, dealing with the robes and insignia of the Knights, made brief reference to the hat, the surcoat and under-habit, none of which had seen the light of day since King George IV had prescribed them for the installation in 1821.

Provision was made (Statute V) for the appointment of foreign princes as honorary Knights Companions, although none was ever appointed, and it is unlikely that any would have been, had the Order survived. Foreign heads of state are usually appointed to the Order of the Garter, as the senior of the three 'national' honours. The sole appointment to the Order of the Thistle, was that of King Olav V of Norway in 1962, due to the historic connections between Norway and Scotland. Appointments to the Order of St Patrick would have been highly unlikely, though not impossible. Explicit recognition was given to the possibility that commoners might one day be made Knights of the Order (Statute IX), although again, none was ever appointed. Statute XXIII made provision for the degradation of Knights who were convicted of treason, cowardice or felony or, 'of any crime derogatory to his honour as a knight or a gentleman'.[27] Statute XXIV declared the officers of the Order to be, 'servants of our royal household' and under the protection of the Sovereign. Statute XXVI introduced the right of former Chancellors of the Order to wear a miniature version of the Chancellor's badge after ceasing to hold the office. The right was limited to Chancellors appointed since 1886, who had been cabinet ministers during their time as Chief Secretary of Ireland, and was intended to be no more than a memento of their former association with the Order. Statute XXXVI reduced the sum paid by each Knight on appointment, from £300 to £50. The figure of £300 had been fixed in 1871 when the separate fees payable to each officer were abolished. £300 was still an unwarrantably high figure, and Lord Aberdeen (Grand Master 1905–15) proposed its reduction. The Treasury accepted the Lord Lieutenant's point that the fee was still unduly burdensome and also his proposal of the reduced fee of £50.[28] The fee remained at £50 until 1916 when it was raised to £65, to cover the cost of presenting each Knight with a star, in addition to a collar and badge.[29] Statute XXXIII enshrined the position of St Patrick's Hall in Dublin Castle as the location for investitures, and Statute XXXIV ordered each Knight, 'within a year after [his] investiture' to produce an 'escocheon' of his coat of arms for erection in the hall. Statute XXIV revived the defunct offices of Dublin Herald and Cork Herald. Perhaps Vicars recalled his own efforts to revive the post of Dublin Herald some fifteen years earlier; perhaps he saw them as useful training posts in the world of heraldry and genealogy; or perhaps he simply wanted to increase the size of his little heraldic court, to give it greater dignity. Officially he declared that he needed them because, 'besides assisting Ulster at investitures and ceremonials of the Order it will also assist in the preliminary clerical work of the Order prior to investitures which is very heavy'.[30]

Had Sir Albert Woods survived to read the final draft of the Statutes, he might have noticed an inconsistency in the number of Pursuivants to be attached to the

Order. While there is no doubt that the Statutes of 1905 reinstituted the offices of Dublin Herald and Cork Herald, there is some doubt as to whether the office of Junior Pursuivant was also reinstated. The Letters Patent of 28 July 1905 specifically mention that the Order, 'shall have ... heralds and pursuivants of arms', implying more than one pursuivant. The revised Statutes, published on 29 July, are less clear. Statute XXIV states that, included among the officers of the Order shall be, 'Dublin and Cork Heralds and Athlone Pursuivant of Arms'; but the same Statute also refers to, 'The pursuivants' in the order of precedence among the officers. Statute XXX also speaks of 'pursuivants'. Vicars usefully included as an appendix to the Statutes, a complete list of the Grand Masters, Knights and Officers of the Order, and following the list of Junior Pursuivants is the statement: 'These offices abolished under the Royal Warrant of 14th July, 1871, but revived in 1905'. There is no specific mention of the office of Junior Pursuivant, but the Statutes clearly envisaged the existence of Pursuivants other than Athlone Pursuivant. No appointment seems to have been made until the specifically named 'Cork Pursuivant' in 1921.

Having disposed of John Burke as Athlone Pursuivant in 1899, Vicars continued the nepotistic practices of his predecessors by appointing his nephew, Peirce Gun Mahony, as Cork Herald. For appointment as Dublin Herald, he selected his close friend Francis Richard Shackleton, who had been sharing his house since July or August 1905. Shackleton had first worked at the Office of Arms as an unpaid assistant secretary, from October 1899 to January 1901, and spent some time, without success, seeking an appointment at the College of Arms in London.[31] Neither Herald had regular hours at the Office of Arms, although Mahony later stated that he was usually at the Office from 11am to 6pm, when he was in Dublin; both Heralds were unpaid.[32]

Within two years of the creation of this little court over which Vicars, still only forty-three years old, had confidently expected to preside happily for many years to come, an event occurred which resulted in the abrupt termination of his career, his ignominious dismissal from office, and his death as an embittered recluse. The event passed into history as the disappearance of the Irish Crown Jewels.

CHAPTER SIX

MYSTERIOUS, DETESTABLE AND DISASTROUS

The theft of the Irish Crown Jewels

It is indeed lamentable that such a cloud should have arisen.
MARQUESS OF ABERDEEN
14 October 1907

'WILL ANYONE EVER have the courage to tell the whole truth about this wretched business?' So thundered the *London Mail* five years after the disappearance of the Irish Crown Jewels from Dublin Castle in 1907. Although the incident is now forgotten, it caused a sensation at the time and aroused the fury of King Edward VII. Intimations of scandal, combined with the fact that the castle was the headquarters not only of the Irish government, but also of the Royal Irish Constabulary, only made matters worse. The disappearance of the crown jewels from under the very nose of the Irish police, caused a good deal of humour, embarrassment and anger, depending on the position and political sympathies of the observer. Several months of investigations, concluding with a viceregal commission of enquiry, failed to unearth any hard information on the identity of the thief or the whereabouts of the jewels, and no charges were ever brought. As the days and weeks passed by without any clue to the whereabouts of the missing jewels, rumour and innuendo began to develop, as did the anger of King Edward, which smouldered for several months, as some people found to their cost. But the fog which shrouded the disappearance of the crown jewels, is as impenetrable today as it was then.

Whereas Queen Victoria had visited Ireland on only four occasions in sixty-three years, King Edward VII paid three visits to the country during his nine-year reign; in 1903, 1904 and 1907. The King's attitude towards Ireland was much like that of his mother in her earliest years on the throne. He had a genuine sympathy for the Irish people, and a dislike of the practice of the absentee landlord, and he hoped that simmering popular discontent might be assuaged by agrarian and administrative reforms but, like his mother, he would brook no debate on the union of Britain and Ireland. He would have nothing to do with any proposal for 'home rule' for Ireland, at a time when it was becoming painfully apparent that there was no other choice. The King's last visit to Ireland, in 1907, was overshadowed by the disappearance of the Irish Crown Jewels.

The crown jewels consisted of a jewelled star, a jewelled badge, and a partly jewelled gold and enamel badge of the Order of St Patrick, intended to be worn by the Lord Lieutenant in his role as Grand Master of the Order. The star was made *c.*1830–1, by Rundell, Bridge and Rundell, the Crown Jewellers in London, from Brazilian diamonds, once the property of Queen Charlotte, and given to Lady Conyngham by King George IV. After his death, she returned them to his executors, and King William IV ordered that they should be made into regalia for the Grand Master of the Order of St Patrick. The jewelled star was made from 394 stones taken in part from three bows of brilliants and pearls, which had belonged to Queen Charlotte and from a jewelled badge of the Order of the Bath which had belonged to King George III. The rays of the star were formed from Brazilian diamonds; in the centre a shamrock of emeralds was superimposed on a ruby cross and encircled by the motto of the Order QUIS SEPARABIT and the date of the foundation of the Order in Roman numerals – MDCCLXXXIII – all in rose diamonds. The large jewelled badge,

The Irish Crown Jewels: the Grand Master's badge and star, both composed of rubies, emeralds and Brazilian diamonds, mounted in silver. They were stolen from Dublin Castle in 1907 and never recovered.

which had formerly belonged to King George IV, was a similar composition in Brazilian diamonds, rubies and emeralds, surmounted by a diamond harp and loop. There was also a gold enamelled badge set with emeralds and rubies. All three pieces were contained in a mahogany brass bound case. In the absence of Sir William Betham, they were received in the Office of Arms on 15 March 1831 by James Rock, Dublin Herald.

Described in Statute XII of the Statutes of the Order of St Patrick as 'crown jewels', they quickly acquired the designation of 'the Irish Crown Jewels', rather than 'the diamond insignia of the Grand Master of the Order of St Patrick', and so they have remained. The designation 'crown jewels', implying a fabulous treasury of jewellery, had a much greater appeal and was widely used by the press. Inevitably, exaggerated reports of their value began to circulate. As historic pieces of jewellery their value was put at £50,000 although, as such, they were quite unsaleable and the break-up value of the 'rather old-fashioned stones' was thought to be about £5,000.[1]

The official custodian of the jewels was Sir Arthur Vicars, Ulster King of Arms, and Registrar and Knight Attendant of the Order of St Patrick. He was undoubtedly competent on the subject of genealogy and heraldry but, with hindsight, he might have chosen his friends and colleagues with a little more care, and a contemporary remembered him as, 'a notoriously forgetful, casual sort of creature, nearly always late for his engagements'.[2]

The crown jewels were kept in a safe in the ground floor library of the Office of Arms in the elegant Bedford Tower of Dublin Castle, contrary to the requirements of the Statutes of the Order, which ordered that they should be kept in a steel safe in the strong room of the Office. No one is quite sure when the jewels were stolen. They were last seen on 11 June 1907 when they were shown to a visitor to the office, but the theft was not discovered until 6 July following, because nobody had any reason to open the safe in the intervening weeks. William Stivey, the Office of Arms messenger, was asked by Sir Arthur Vicars to take a collar of a recently deceased Knight of St Patrick and lock it in the safe containing the crown jewels. When Stivey tried to unlock the door of the safe he discovered that it was already unlocked. He called Vicars, who opened the door and examined the contents. To his horror, he discovered that the crown jewels, together with five silver-gilt collars of the Knights of St Patrick, and some personal family jewellery, were all missing from their boxes. The incident attracted widespread coverage in the national press and *The Times* reported that Dublin was 'much excited' over the disappearance.[3]

Four days later, on 10 July, King Edward VII and Queen Alexandra arrived on the royal yacht at Kingstown Harbour (now Dun Laoghaire) for their third visit to Ireland and their first in four years. The visit, which should otherwise have been a great success, was now regarded with great apprehension by the Earl of Aberdeen, Lord Lieutenant of Ireland. 'When we went to Kingstown to receive Their Majesties, as soon as the King had shaken hands, I was conscious that he was scrutinising the badge of the Order of St Patrick which I was wearing. I was afraid it might have been incorrectly placed, and said, "Is it not right, sir?" "Oh, yes," said the King, "but I was thinking of those jewels". Alas! yes, His Majesty was alluding to a very, very sore subject, namely the mysterious, detestable, and disastrous theft of the crown jewels.'[4] Aberdeen remembered that the King, considerately, did not allude to the subject again during that visit, but there was plenty of discussion on the unwelcome topic subsequently.[5]

The King was furious at the theft of the crown jewels and the collars, and his anger did not diminish with the passing of first weeks and then months. He had intended personally to invest Lord Castletown, the newest Knight of St Patrick, during the course of his visit, but there was now no question of the investiture being held. The loss of the crown jewels was bad enough, but the theft of the five Knights' collars would have meant that five of the Knights would not be able to appear correctly dressed. The King was obsessive on the subject of etiquette, and a knowledgeable guide to the protocol of wearing uniforms, orders and medals. Everything had to be exact and correct, and his eyes would notice a medal incorrectly placed or a star incorrectly worn. Had the investiture taken place, the King would also have found himself in close proximity to Sir Arthur Vicars who was, at the least, guilty of negligence in his custody of the jewels. It would not have been a happy experience either for the King or for the King of Arms. So the colourful ceremony of the investiture was postponed and Lord Castletown had to wait until February 1908 to be invested.

The King was outraged by the theft and some of his comments were probably unprintable. His biographer, Sir Sidney Lee, records that when the King learnt the details, 'his language on that occasion was vigorous and forceful, partly for reason that in the particular circumstances he could do nothing and partly because of the feeble efforts that were being made to elucidate the mystery'.[6] The anonymous author of *Kings, courts and society* remembered being told by the King's equerry that, 'he had never seen King Edward so angry ... his rage was something terrible and fearful. At first he would have it that the robbery had been planned as a personal insult, that it was part of a plot to prevent him visiting Ireland and that it might easily be the prelude to an even more serious crime, an attack on his consort and himself ... I am sure the officials he lectured never forgot his words, for His Majesty could be scathingly sarcastic when he wished'.[7] Another individual, who endeavoured to placate the King with helpful comments, was swept aside with a roar: 'I don't want your theories. I want my jewels'.[8]

Whether the King had his own suspicions at this early date is uncertain, nor is it certain whether anyone was whispering accusations into his ear. But if he had been told of the details surrounding the theft, he would have known where to lay the blame for negligence – at the door of Sir Arthur Vicars, the custodian of the jewels. He would have been told something of what was known about Vicars and of the staff of the little heraldic court over which he presided: Peirce Mahony, Cork Herald; Francis Shackleton, Dublin Herald; and Francis Bennett-Goldney, Athlone Pursuivant. Of these three men, attention soon focused on Frank Shackleton, a single and debonair young man with a slightly raffish lifestyle who was known to live beyond his means, and around whom gathered stories of financial impropriety. He was, in fact, an unprincipled con-artist. Younger brother of Sir Ernest Shackleton (1874–1922), the Polar explorer, and uncle of Lord Shackleton (1911–94), Frank Shackleton was widely suspected of being the thief, but nothing was ever proved against him. Suspicion is one thing; evidence and proof are quite another, and no charges were brought.

It has been suggested that, during the course of his visit to Ireland in July 1907, the King was told that Shackleton was suspected of being the thief, that his lifestyle was disreputable and, more significantly, that he was acquainted with the Duke of Argyll, husband of the King's sister Princess Louise.[9] Shackleton was known to be homosexual, and was on friendly terms with the duke's uncle, Lord Ronald Gower, who was also homosexual. The theft of the crown jewels was a favourite topic of conversation in the summer of 1907, and as the time went by, and the culprits remained unidentified, so rumours began to circulate. One of the more preposterous stories was that Lord Ronald and his nephew, the duke, were both involved in the theft, and that both were homosexuals. In fact there is no evidence to show that the duke was so,[10] and the whole story was no more than an exercise in fantasy, created to fill the vacuum caused by the absence of knowledge; a common syndrome. It has also been suggested that the King was sufficiently alarmed by this rumour to do everything in his power to prevent any breath of scandal from touching his brother-in-law.[11] It was a reasonable and understandable theory, but the argument for advancing it must be based at best on possibility rather than fact. Sir Sidney Lee, the King's biographer, postulated the theory that the King's anger was aroused by nothing more than the apparent incompetence and dilatoriness of the Irish Government.[12] If there was any truth in the King's concern to prevent the breath of scandal from touching his brother-in-law, it did not occur to him to dwell upon the fact that perhaps his own lifestyle was a little less than blameless. 'With that excess of righteous indignation which confirmed practitioners of natural vice display so often when unnatural vice is under discussion, King Edward could not wait to find out whether there was any truth in the suppositions ... Vicars must go immediately'.[13] The King was out for blood and by 17 September he was settled in his own mind that Vicars was the person responsible and should be suspended from office.

Whatever the truth of the King's motives it was a fact that his interest in the theft did not wane with the passing weeks. He appears to have been determined that blame should be affixed to someone, and refused to be pacified by letters from Aberdeen assuring him that everything that could be done, was being done. Poor Aberdeen received a frigid letter from Viscount Knollys within a few weeks of the King's return to London. 'He is not I am afraid satisfied with your explanation and he desires me to let you know that there is a mystery and an apparent lukewarmness about the enquiry and in fact the whole proceedings which he does not understand. He says that at the end of nearly 2 months, surely if there is ever to be a clue; it must have been discovered by this time. H. M. also says that somebody must have been careless in their care of the crown jewels, and if so he would be glad to know whom, and whether, whoever it may be, anything in the way of punishment or reprimand has been given to him.'[14] Aberdeen was a kindly man who would have derived no pleasure from administering a punishment or a reprimand, and this intimation of the King's continuing displeasure, and the expectation that a scapegoat would be found, was depressing news. Three weeks later, with Aberdeen still unable to report any encouraging developments, Knollys wrote another stern letter to the Lord Lieutenant. He told Aberdeen that, in the King's opinion, the search for the jewels and the thief was not being prosecuted with sufficient energy. It was His Majesty's wish that Vicars should be suspended from his office. The letter closed with a command that Aberdeen should go to Balmoral on 24 September, so that the King might learn more about 'this disagreeable business'.[15] What passed between the King and the Lord Lieutenant is unknown, but two inferences can be drawn from the preceding correspondence. Firstly, the King wanted action, and quickly. Secondly, the encounter cannot have been a pleasant experience for Lord Aberdeen. Even if the jewels had not yet been found, nor the thief positively identified, some form of action must be taken and be seen to be taken.

If the King thought that nothing was being done, he was mistaken. The theft of the jewels from under the noses of the Irish police was a considerable embarrassment for them, and attempts to solve the mystery were pursued with vigour. Finally, a chief inspector from Scotland Yard was imported to conduct an investigation but with little result. 'Never was there a crime hunt organised with greater efficiency and with less regard to expenditure ... and the result three months afterwards was nothing except a collection of reports which amounted to nothing more than the skimming of the unreliable and misleading gossip of Dublin.'[16]

Lord Aberdeen returned to Ireland with the King's instruction that, if the jewels had not been found within two weeks, heads would have to roll. On 12 October, the unfortunate messenger of the Office of Arms, who had discovered the loss, and who could in no sense have been 'responsible', was dismissed. On 14 October a conference took place between Aberdeen, Augustine Birrell (Chief Secretary of Ireland), Sir James Dougherty (Assistant Under-Secretary), Sir John Ross of Bladensburg (Chief Commissioner of the Dublin Metropolitan Police), and Mr W. V. Harrell (Assistant Commissioner). The meeting agreed that Aberdeen should recommend to the King that the Office of Arms should be reconstituted. All the staff should be requested to resign, and in the event of their refusal, they should be dismissed. Although Vicars was not thought to be personally involved in the theft, he would have to go, the reason being that he was responsible for the custody of the jewels, and that the safe in which the jewels were kept had been opened by a key and not by violence, and therefore there must have been lack of care and vigilance on the part of Ulster King of Arms. There was no doubt about the need to remove Shackleton. 'The fact that he is reported by the police to have visited, recently, various pawn shops in London, for the purpose of raising money, was sufficient to make the retention of his present office unsuitable.' There were political and public difficulties about Bennett-Goldney because he was a former mayor of Canterbury, but if Vicars and Shackleton were to go, he would have to go. There was no doubt about the need to remove these three, but what was to be done with Peirce Mahony, Cork Herald. 'There is no shadow of suspicion of any kind. As however, there would be considerable awkwardness in retaining one of the staff when all others are required to leave, on grounds which ostensibly would seem to apply to all. It is hoped that Your Majesty will approve of Mr Mahony being requested to retire pro-tem, with perhaps a private hint that he may expect to be reinstated after a time.'[17]

The King agreed to the proposals, though Mahony was allowed to remain in office, and on 23 October, Dougherty wrote to Vicars informing him that he would have to go. 'His Majesty had come to the conclusion that he would reconstitute this office, and that his services were no longer in regard.'[18] A few days later, Mahony, Shackleton and Bennett-Goldney were asked to resign.

Aberdeen, however, reckoned without Ulster's tenacity. Vicars had fought hard to get into the Office of Arms and he now fought harder to stay in. Vicars was nothing if not tenacious. He refused to go, and wrote directly to the King asking him to look into the matter personally, presumably quite unaware that the King was doing exactly that. Reminding the King of his hitherto unblemished record in office, Vicars asked for an official inquiry to be held into all the circumstances surrounding the disappearance of the insignia. He received a terse reply from Knollys stating that his appeal should be made to the proper authorities. Vicars duly appealed to Aberdeen, who in turn advised the King to grant the request. The King's reply was brief and to the point. 'I have no alternative', he wrote, 'but to agree to his proposals.'[19]

Sir Arthur Vicars was now becoming something of a *cause célèbre* in Irish society and his case was taken up by a number of individuals, including his redoubtable nationalist elder half-brother, Peirce O'Mahony. O'Mahony was a colourful and adventurous figure who had fought against the Turks in the Bulgarian War of Independence, and he had no liking for the union of Britain and Ireland. He was less than pleased with the pro-union stance of his younger half-brother; but now the situation had changed. His sibling had become a victim, and the fiery O'Mahony was not one to flinch from fighting for the underdog.

O'Mahony related his suspicions to Bulmer Hobson, a journalist of pronounced nationalist sympathies, intent on uncovering anything that might, in his words 'discredit the castle', and his reminiscences of the theft were included in his memoirs, published more than sixty years later. Unfortunately, his account is polemical and riddled with factual inaccuracies of the most elementary kind. He was honest enough to admit, at the start of the chapter, that he relied only on his memory, but a little careful research would have added greater credibility to his account. Hobson was in no doubt that the jewels had been stolen by Shackleton and an accomplice named Richard Howard Gorges, 'a tall, military figure, with a face like Mephistopheles'.[20] He also believed that Shackleton had taken them to Amsterdam and pledged them for £20,000, stipulating that they were not to be broken up for three years. O'Mahony also told Hobson of his belief that King Edward VII was personally responsible for ordering the cloak of secrecy only to shield the Duke of Argyll.[21] A combination of O'Mahony and Hobson would indicate that, whether it was true or not, the story was being used by these two nationalists as a tool with which to

The Earl of Kilmorey (KP 1890), with the obverse and reverse of his mantle star, made by Robinson and Steele of Dublin.

discredit the King. This was the opinion of those involved at the time. 'It is quite clear that O'Mahony was trying to shift the issue to Vicar's private character and to intimidate His Excellency by the fear of a gross scandal being made public.'[22]

O'Mahony urged his brother not to resign under any circumstances and entered into a vigorous correspondence with the Irish government on his behalf, announcing that Vicars was being sacrificed in order to shield those really responsible. Peirce O'Mahony knew that his brother would need supporters more powerful than journalists, and he decided to seek support from the band of individuals that his brother served – the Knights of the Order of St Patrick. He drew up a petition, that urged the King to grant a full public enquiry, and asked each of the Knights to sign it. The petition recorded that Ulster had, 'invariably discharged his functions for the last fifteen years in a manner which has called forth the special approbation of the various Grand Masters of the Order under whom he served',[23] and that an enquiry should be held into all the circumstances of the affair before any steps were taken to dismiss him. Of the twenty-one existing Knights, excluding members of the royal family, sixteen signed the petition; the Marquesses of Ormonde and Waterford, the Earls of Gosford, Carysfort, Bandon, Mayo, Listowel, Dunraven, Rosse, Lucan, Longford, Enniskillen, Meath, and Erne, Earl Roberts, and Lord Monteagle of Brandon. Of the remaining five, the eighty-year old Earl of Howth was too ill to be approached; Viscount Wolseley was abroad; and the Earl of Kilmorey, Lord Clonbrock and Viscount Iveagh declined to add their names. Kilmorey was quietly pursuing Vicars' cause through other channels, and thought it best not to approach the King in such a way. Iveagh had been warned by Knollys that the presentation of the petition would be distasteful to the King, and he refused, adding, 'I am in a different position to that of the other Knights',[24] without elucidating. Of the three, only Lord Clonbrock showed any regard for the internal structure of the Order and its bearing on the affair: 'I am very sorry for poor Ulster and should like to do anything I could to help him, but I think appealing to the King against the decision of the Grand Master of the Order is a very serious matter, and would not tend to his advantage'.[25]

Duly signed, O'Mahony sent the petition to Lord Aberdeen, asking him to forward it to the King. The petition was returned to O'Mahony by the Assistant Under-Secretary with a note saying that the Lord Lieutenant could not see his way to forward it to the King, but there is good reason to believe that the King was apprised of the contents and the names of the signatories. Field Marshal Lord Roberts KP, telegraphed from Windsor on 15 November, ten days after signing the petition, asking for his name to be withdrawn. It is more than likely that the great soldier had been made painfully aware of the King's feelings. The petition was guaranteed to arouse the King's wrath, and it was nonetheless remarkable that so many Irish peers were willing to sign it. It was an act of medieval chivalry for the Knights to take a stand, on the ground of justice, on behalf of an individual for whom the King had developed an intense dislike.

Further delays occurred while Aberdeen continued to seek some face-saving formula by which Vicars might be persuaded to resign and retire. He was sensitive to Vicars' predicament, and tried to shield him from the King's anger. 'He [Aberdeen] was too tender towards Vicars and too anxious to let him down easily.'[26] Aberdeen proposed that Vicars should be allowed to resign, and that the functions hitherto exercised by Ulster King of Arms should be split between two offices. The office of Ulster should continue to exist as before, but its functions should extend only to the fields of heraldry and genealogy. All his duties relating to the Order of St Patrick should be taken over by a new official who was to be styled Registrar of the Order, thus reverting to the position existing before 1890, with the exception that the new Registrar rather than the King of Arms was to be the executive officer of the Order. This would enable Vicars to continue working in the field he loved best, while removing him from all further connection with the Order as a punishment for his negligence in the care of the insignia, which the King had sought.

The plan foundered for four reasons. Firstly, the Statutes would require alteration with the King's personal authority, thereby implying that the King had reasons for making the change. Secondly, altering the Statutes for the benefit of the King of Arms when two subordinate officers had been dismissed (Shackleton and Francis Bennett-Goldney, Athlone Pursuivant, had both resigned on request in November 1907) would be a travesty of justice, and might invite criticism and hostile comment. This would be difficult to answer without involving the King. Thirdly, Vicars's act of gross negligence would be revealed, and condoned by his reappointment. Fourthly, Vicars would occupy a position which would bring him into frequent contact with the Lord Lieutenant and, on more important occasions, the King.

Finally, on 4 December, Knollys wrote to Aberdeen saying that the King was, 'complaining of the affair dragging on for five months', and that he now, 'washed his hands of the whole affair'.[27] If the King had washed his hands several weeks earlier, Vicars might have saved his job and his reputation, but it was now too late. He had become the victim of royal attention and grave royal displeasure, and now that such a juggernaut had come into play, the matter was beyond the control of Aberdeen.

The King was reluctant to deny Vicars the opportunity of an enquiry, and agreed in principle, but made it clear that he would have nothing to do with it. He refused to allow the enquiry to have the status of a royal commission, which would give the appearance by its constitution that he had surrendered,[28] and a compromise was reached in the appointment of a viceregal commission which, as it emanated from the Lord Lieutenant, would free the King from all responsibility. The Government initially decided that the enquiry was to hold its meetings in private, arousing the annoyance of O'Mahony and Vicars, and the surprise of Herbert Gladstone, the Home Secretary. 'All along publicity … was insisted on as essential. For as the Irish government has been pecking in private at this matter for some months, what on earth was the good of more private inquiry by three men of much lower official status than the Lord Lieutenant, the Chief Secretary, the Lord Chancellor and the Attorney-General of Ireland … If there is no publicity you will have to face an awkward position with the King, and a real flare up when the House [of Commons] meets. It may be too late to undo all the mischief. But I think in any case you must make the whole thing public. Publish the evidence already given and admit the press … It's a very ugly business, and you will have, as things are, nationalists and unionists against you.'[29] Gladstone was aware of the rumours of scandal that were circulating, but was insistent that these should form no part of the commission's brief; Vicars was to face a simple charge of negligence.

King Edward himself insisted on full publicity. 'His Majesty must ask you immediately to telegraph to insist on the enquiry being conducted in public without any further delay. The King will be glad to know who is responsible for this disregard of his orders.'[30]

The commission first met on 10 January 1908, and its report was published by command on 25 January. Given the circumstances of the theft and the abounding rumours, publication was the best course, in the opinion of Sir James Dougherty, the Under-Secretary. 'Having regard to all that has taken place, and to the chances of misrepresentation, if anything is omitted from the evidence … it must be published.'[31] The report was essentially a civil enquiry into the conduct of Arthur Vicars as custodian of the jewels and not a criminal investigation into the theft of the jewels. It was given no power to subpoena witnesses, nor to hear evidence on oath, and the outcome was a foregone conclusion. The commission based its judgement largely on the requirements of the Statutes of the Order of St Patrick, and its judgement, pronounced on 25 January, was that Ulster King of Arms, 'did not exercise due vigilance or proper care as the custodian of the regalia',[32] quoting extensively from the Statutes to emphasise Vicars's culpability. Statutes XII and XX stated clearly that the insignia should be deposited in a steel safe in the strong room of the Office of Arms, which had been ignored. When the Office of Arms was transferred to the Bedford Tower in 1903, the safe which housed the crown jewels and some of the insignia was found to be too large to pass through the door of the new strong room, and Vicars agreed to the safe being left in the library, until the Board of Works could provide him with a safe small enough to be admitted to the strong room. It was something of a sadness that the very Statutes that Vicars had himself drafted, were now being used in evidence against him.

The report of the commission confirmed what the Irish government had already decided – that Vicars was guilty of negligence, and that he would have to go. On 30 January he received a letter from Sir James Dougherty, informing him that the Letters Patent appointing him had been revoked, and that his successor had been appointed. The letter came as a shattering blow to Vicars who after an unblemished record of fourteen years in office, was deprived of his job and his career. He never accepted the possibility that he was in any way to blame for the theft and his feelings of hurt and injustice lingered to the end of his life. He referred to his successor, Captain Nevile Wilkinson, as a 'usurper', and that his career had been, 'purposely shattered by a heartless government'.[33] As late as September 1911 he wrote: 'I was simply made a scapegoat to save Ross of Bladensburg and the Board of Works, and Shackleton's wicked threats of a scandal (which were and are all bunkum and lies) were utilised to frighten the late King and make him hush it up'.[34] For a while he nurtured vain hopes that when the home rule Liberal government was replaced by a Conservative and Unionist one, he might be reinstated, but the hope was only a dream, and no Conservative government came to power in his lifetime.

In July 1911 he sent a petition to the new sovereign, King George V, 'praying' that a new enquiry, with power to examine witnesses on oath, should take place under the chairmanship of a judge of the high court of justice, and, in clause after clause, rehearsing the facts of the story once again, each one designed to prove his innocence. King George V was inclined to allow the petition, but the Government advised him that legislation would be required, and that would need parliamentary time. The King took the hint that he should not press the matter, and Vicars was informed at the end of September 1911 that his petition was disallowed.

The tragedy of Arthur Vicars was that he failed to understand the mentality of those who were responsible for his dismissal. Victorian and Edwardian court officials were drawn from the ranks of the armed forces, and the principle of senior responsibility is fundamental to the military machine. If a junior officer fails in his duty, his senior commander is held responsible, even though he may not have been directly involved himself. Vicars was probably innocent of any involvement in the theft of the crown jewels, but it was almost certainly perpetrated by a member of his staff. He was accused, not of being personally guilty, but of being responsible, and for that reason he was dismissed. Not having a military training, the concept of the responsibility of a senior officer was beyond his comprehension. All he could see was that he was the victim of gross injustice. His judges took a different view, understanding him as little as he understood them. Perhaps Arthur Vicars' biggest problem was that he was lamentably naïve, and he could not discern danger. He probably believed the best about everyone, and failed to see the worst in anyone, and his cup of sorrow was still not full. 'His privileged background and the good fortune of his early years probably nurtured Vicars' life-long and almost congenital capacity to ignore unpleasant and inconvenient facts.'[35]

After a hitherto unblemished career, Vicars was shattered by his dismissal. Angry and bitter, he went to live at Kilmorna House in September 1912. The house stood three miles south-east of the town of Listowel in County Kerry, just about as far away from Dublin as it was possible to be in Ireland. The house had belonged to his half-brother George, who had bequeathed it to Vicars' sister, Mrs Edith de Janasz. She allowed Vicars to live there free for the rest of his life. He continued to protest his innocence, certain in his own mind that the King had been frightened by the threat of scandal.

During his last years, he frequently visited Kilmurary House, Castleisland, which belonged to Peirce O'Mahony; there he spent much time in the company of Miss Gertrude Wright, the elder sister of his host's wife. He married her in 1917, and the move may have brought him some comfort in his last years; she did much to erase any residual feelings of bitterness. But for one who had himself already been a victim, his end was sad in the extreme. The Irish Republican Army had initiated a policy of burning the great country houses of Ireland, and occasionally shooting the occupants before the blazing ruins. Arthur Vicars and Kilmorna succunbed.

The first warning came in April 1920 when the house was raided by a group of men. Vicars claimed that they numbered more than one hundred, but there are always two sides to a story, and one of the group claimed in later years that there had only been seven men, and also denied that they ever threatened Vicars' life. After fruitless attempts to break into the strong room, looking for weapons, the raiders left.

The end came a year later when, on the morning of 14 April 1921, Kilmorna House was surrounded by an armed gang of about thirty men (one of the raiders claimed that there were seventeen). They ordered the occupants to leave, and then set fire to the house. Sir Arthur, who had been in bed (he was said not to rise before 2pm), was taken into the garden by three of the men, and shot dead before the blazing house. The Irish Republican Army took the almost unprecedented step of announcing that the murder had not been carried out on their instructions, but the statement amounted to very little, since most acts of violence were organised locally. The death of Vicars was unusual; although the burning of houses was common, the shooting of an owner or occupant was rare. The reasons for his death were believed to have been the fact that he would have been able to identify the men who took part in the raid of April 1920 (two of them took part in the raid that led to his death), and that he was said to be reporting local Sinn Fein activities to the security forces in Dublin. He also regularly entertained British troops whenever they were in the vicinity of Kilmorna, which hardly endeared him to the local population, although they had no other reason to dislike him. The sadness of his death lay in the fact that he was simply naïve; he could not believe that anyone would do anything against him.[36]

The bitterness of the episode of the Irish Crown Jewels, and the tragedy of his death should not obscure the fact that Sir Arthur Vicars was a herald of great attainments, and a worthy successor of Sir Bernard Burke. His whole life had been wrapped up in the maintenance of the efficiency and dignity of his office and, until the disaster of the theft, he had performed his duties impeccably. The plaintive tone of his will shows that he died a confused and unhappy man: 'I might have had more to dispose of had it not been for the outrageous way in which I was treated by the Irish government over the loss of the Irish Crown Jewels in 1907, backed up by the late King Edward VII who I had always loyally and faithfully served, when I was made a scape goat to save other departments responsible and when they shielded the real culprit and thief, Francis R. Shackleton ... My whole life and work was ruined by this cruel misfortune and by the wickedly and blackguardly acts of the Irish government ... I am unconscious of having done anyone wrong and my very misfortune arose from my being unsuspicious and trusting to a one-time friend and official of my former office'.[37] He was laid to rest in the peaceful churchyard at Leckhampton in Gloucestershire.

On 22 April 1921, the following tribute appeared in the *Church of Ireland Gazette*, under the title, *In Memoriam – Arthur Vicars, Knight*:

> Churchman all-knightly, in thy form and mien,
> True fellow with the saintly knights of old,
> Alert and gallant, chivalrous and bold -
> We read it in that brow, those eyes so keen,
> That touch so gentle, that sweet smile serene.
> Thine honour was unsullied, pure as gold;
> Thy courage dauntless, yes, a thousand-fold;
> Thy life, thy worship upright, true and clean.
> And thou wast slain with horror multiplied,
> Like some offending brute led forth and shot
> By ruthless hands, no helper at thy side
> To soothe the anguish of thy soul distraught.
> A land defiled by cruelty and wrong
> Utters its bitter cry: 'Oh, Lord, how long?

Kilmorna House was badly damaged by the fire, and the surveyors and valuers, who visited the house on 7 September 1921, advised Mrs De Janasz and her husband that the remaining walls were too weak to be used in rebuilding, and that the structure would have to be cleared away to allow the construction of a new house. The cost of building a similar house was estimated at £30,300, but the compensation allowed by the Irish Free State government in June 1923 was only £25,000 and Kilmorna House was never rebuilt, and the ruins were cleared away c.1949. All that can be seen today is the pump room, a section of the kitchen garden wall, and three gate houses. Lady Vicars moved to England and died at Clevedon in Somerset in 1946, bequeathing her property to various friends and members of her own family.

When the publication of the report of the viceregal commission was being considered, Shackleton was mentioned in correspondence as someone who might have reason to object; but he had so charmed the commissioners, that it was held to be in his own interest for it to be published. 'It is recognised that Mr Shackleton gave his evidence with much candour, and in view of that fact there was a desire to avoid an exposé of his financial difficulties if possible. But even in Mr Shackleton's own interest, it would seem that, having regard to the charges and imputations made against him, the better course would be to publish the evidence in full.'[38] Candid with the commissioners, he might well have been, but Frank Shackleton's end was entirely predictable, and more pathetic than tragic. Declared bankrupt in 1910 with debts of £85,000, he fled to Portuguese West Africa to avoid his creditors. He was arrested there in October 1912 on a charge of fraud, brought back to London and sentenced to fifteen months imprisonment with hard labour in October 1913. Little is known of his activities after his release from prison. He lived for a while at Paignton in Devon. In the late 1930s, with his unmarried sister, Amy Vibert Shackleton (1875–1953), he ran an antiques shop in Chichester under the name of F. R. S. Mellor. He died on 24 June 1941 at the age of sixty-five, apparently in considerable poverty, in St Richard's Hospital, Chichester, and was buried at Chichester Cemetery as Francis Richard Shackleton Mellor on 27 June 1941.

In the ninety years since the theft of the diamond insignia of the Grand Master of the Order of St Patrick many stories, ranging from the preposterous to the plausible, have surfaced periodically, but all are unsubstantiated. Ireland was delightfully full of rumour and credulity, and the theft of the crown jewels was a favourite subject around which to spin the most amusing yarns. One of the best was related by a Dublin jarvey (cab driver). While driving an official to Harcourt Street railway station about two weeks after the theft, he regaled his passenger with an explanation that might have given King Edward VII a fit of apoplexy, had someone had the courage to tell him.

> The jules, is it? Well! Well! And d'ye say ye never heard tell what way they were took? My Oh my! Whisht now and I'll give ye the word in private, and there's not many in Dublin has it besides meself, but I have it for a fact from a chap in the D Division that's a cousin of me a'nt. Whisper now! Sure it was the King himself took them! He was afther having a great card-playing with the Duke of Devonshire, and he dhropped a power o' money, so he sent round Lord Aberdeen wan night to take them out of the safe and bring them to him and say nothin' at all about it. Sure they were his own, and hadn't he as good a right to take them as he would have to sell his own gould watch and chain? Well, now, what I'm telling ye is a fact, and believe me ye'll never hear tell of them jules again.[39]

Of the diamond star and badge of the Grand Master of the Order of St Patrick, sometimes called the Irish crown jewels, and the five gold Knights' collars, no trace was found, and no further reference to their location of existence was generally known until 1976. In that year, a file of the Irish government was opened to the public for the first time, and contained the following intriguing memorandum, dated 1927:

> IV. The President would not like them to be used as a means of reviving the Order or to pass into any hands other than those of the State.

> V. He understands that the Castle Jewels are for sale and that they could be got for £2,000 or £3,000. He would be prepared to recommend their purchase for the same reason.[40]

Although incomplete, the memorandum is signed by the Assistant Secretary of the Executive Council, Michael McDunphy, and the president referred to is William Cosgrave, President of the Executive Council (Prime Minister) of the Irish Free State 1922–32. There are no subsequent papers on the file relating to the jewels. An unsubstantiated rumour posed the hypothesis that the jewelled insignia had been purchased by the Irish government in 1927, but the rumour was refuted in a letter to the *Daily Telegraph* in 1983 by the late H. Montgomery Hyde. 'As for the theory that the Irish government bought the jewels for a few thousand pounds in 1927, I was personally assured by the late Desmond Fitzgerald, who was Minister of External Affairs at that date ... that a Parisian jeweller offered to sell the regalia to the Irish government and that the offer was refused on the ground that the Government had no interest in these relics of British imperial rule.'[41] Whatever the reliability of this story, the fate of the Irish crown jewels remains a mystery. The mahogany brass bound box which had contained the crown jewels was sent by post to the Office of Arms in the summer of 1928, without any explanation or postmark. It can still be seen on display in the heraldic museum of the Genealogical Office in Kildare Street.

The description of the crown jewels remained in the Statutes of the Order (Statute XII) until 1919, when King George V approved a revision that simply required a departing Lord Lieutenant to return his 'insignia' to Ulster King of Arms.[42]

The investiture of Lord Castletown had been postponed since June 1907, and it was important to fill up the vacant offices as quickly as possible, to enable the Office of Arms to continue functioning. The scandal surrounding the loss of the jewels, and the dismissal of Vicars, made the office of Ulster a rather controversial one. A search was under way in December 1907 to find a suitable successor to Vicars, although he had not yet been removed from office. There was no suitable name among the existing staff. Dublin Herald and Athlone Pursuivant were both tainted by association with Vicars, and had resigned. Cork Herald, although he was allowed to continue in office, because of his innocence, and presumably to provide some degree of continuity, was Arthur Vicars' nephew. News of the theft, and the consequential reconstitution of the Office of Arms, reached as far as Montreal, Canada, and an application for appointment arrived at Dublin Castle in December 1907. The applicant was the thirty-three year old Henry Claude Blake, who had been Athlone Pursuivant and private secretary to Vicars 1899–1907. Blake had resigned in February 1907 having moved to Canada at the end of the previous year, to pursue a career as a solicitor. If the content of his letter is true, Blake's letter of application provides fascinating insight into the world of the Office of Arms under Arthur Vicars, for whom Blake had little liking. 'As to my work in the Office, I know that the Office is not or was not run as a proper office but more as a "private hobby" if I may say so, but *no-one* had a say in this except the head of the department. Often I remonstrated with him [Vicars] but I was always told to mind my own business and that I should remember I was only a clerk in the office ... No one knows the nasty trying times I have gone through in that Office at a meagre pittance of £40–50 a year!'[43] Blake concluded by saying that, although he was doing well in Canada, he wanted to return to Dublin to be with his mother. He was also in communication with Frank Shackleton, and had written to the latter in September 1907 promising, 'to stick to you through the row'.[44] The truth of Blake's relationship with Vicars and Shackleton cannot now be determined, although there is a ring of truth in the content of his letter, but his application to return to the Office of Arms was unsuccessful and he remained in Canada.

So the search was extended into the world of the Anglo-Irish aristocracy. The Honourable Otway Cuffe, a brother of the fifth Earl of Desart (a future Knight of St Patrick), and a gentleman usher to the King, met Lord Aberdeen on 13 December and was asked to accept the office; he declined on the ground that he could not give the time that the job required. Aberdeen then interviewed two more individuals on 18 December, Mr Rolleston and Mr Desmond O'Brien, both of whom also politely but firmly declined the office. Finally, the office was offered to and accepted by Captain Nevile Wilkinson, a son-in-law of the Earl of Pembroke who was himself the largest single landlord in Dublin. Pembroke is said to have suggested the name of his son-in-law at a Privy Council meeting at which the King presided. When another member of the council ventured to enquire whether the candidate was conversant with the subject of heraldry, King Edward VII brushed it aside with the comment: 'that doesn't matter, so long as he's honest'.[45]

Nevile Rodwell Wilkinson was duly appointed Ulster King of Arms, Registrar and Knight Attendant of the Order of St Patrick in place of the disgraced Arthur Vicars. Wilkinson was a splendidly commanding figure; six feet six inches in height, he looked the part of a King of Arms, even if he knew nothing about heraldry. The son of a barrister, and educated at Harrow and Sandhurst, he had been commissioned in the Coldstream Guards in 1890, and retired from active service in March 1907. His interest in art and history led him to heraldry and to study etching at the South Kensington Schools of Design, and his love of heraldry seems to have been purely for its artistic and ceremonial aspects. In some ways he was not a competent successor to Arthur Vicars, and the latter could never reconcile himself to the fact that his successor was virtually destitute of heraldic knowledge. Wilkinson was a very talented artist, rather than an expert on heraldry, and his heart was never really in the heraldic and genealogical work of the Office of Arms. When he received the summons to a meeting at the London office of the Under-Secretary for Ireland, he was occupied with painting the scenery for a performance of a pantomime at Wilton House.[46] [He had already written a guide and a catalogue of the three hundred and twenty paintings at Wilton, the Wiltshire seat of his father-in-law]. Arthur Vicars loved Ireland and Irish heraldry and genealogy and, while Ulster King of Arms, he lived in Dublin. Nevile Wilkinson was a soldier turned courtier; he enjoyed the ceremonial aspects of the viceregal court, but he lived mostly in London, and he regarded the office of Ulster especially, after 1922, as a very part-time occupation.

Captain Guillamore O'Grady was appointed to the vacant office of Dublin Herald. He was generally considered to be a 'safe' appointment. The son of a surgeon, he had a private income, a house in Dublin, and an estate in county Clare. He was a barrister, held a commission in the South of Ireland Yeomanry, and was interested in genealogy and heraldry.[47] George Burtchaell, who had worked in the Office of Arms since 1893, as secretary to Arthur Vicars, was appointed Athlone Pursuivant. Ulster, Dublin and Athlone were invested with their insignia of office on 4 February 1909, at the investiture of Lord Pirrie as a Knight of St Patrick.

Pirrie's appointment to the Order had been met with considerable antipathy by the other Knights who resented his appointment, and declined to take part in his investiture. Born in Quebec of Irish parents, Pirrie joined the Belfast shipbuilding firm of Harland and Wolff at the age of fifteen, and rose to become a partner at the age of twenty-seven. He also pursued a career in local government and was successively Lord Mayor of Belfast, High Sheriff of County Antrim and High Sheriff of County Down. He had been given a barony only three years before his investiture, and that only after objections by King Edward VII. In June 1906 the new Liberal government under Sir Henry Campbell-Bannerman, submitted a list of seven proposed peers for the Birthday Honours List. The King demurred to such a large creation, but took strong exception to the name of William Pirrie. 'He would be glad if some other name could be substituted for that of Mr Pirrie.'[48] His objections to Pirrie were caused by a certain disdain for a way of life and work that was understandably beyond his own experiences. The King, 'does not consider [he] is altogether the stamp of a man who should be created a peer, and as far as His Majesty knows, he has done nothing special to merit the honour. The King does not moreover think he behaved very well or patriotically when an English fleet of steamers, of which he was the part proprieter, was sold to an American company a few years ago'.[49] As the Liberal party had been out of power for ten years and needed to strengthen its representation in the House of Lords, the Prime Minister insisted on the selected names, and the King relented.

When Pirrie was appointed to the Order of St Patrick in 1909, there were further difficulties. As an Ulsterman, Pirrie might have been expected to be a solid unionist;

Major Sir Nevile
Wilkinson, Ulster King
of Arms (1908–40).

in fact he had recently become a Liberal, and spoke in favour of home rule for
Ireland. His defection from the Conservatives to the Liberals had greatly
strengthened nationalism in Ulster, and made Pirrie something of a pariah figure.
Aberdeen suggested that Pirrie's investiture should either be delayed, or that there
should be a public investiture whether the other Knights were present or not. Lord
Aberdeen proposed issuing a warrant dispensing with the statutory requirement that
at least three Knights should be present. Lord Castletown had indicated that he
would be present and that, thought Aberdeen, would be enough. He wrote at length
to the King, urging him to ignore the behaviour of the other Knights, which
Aberdeen clearly thought was childish, and to allow a public investiture for Pirrie,

'So long as there was hope that the Knights of St Patrick would revert to a becoming attitude I did not think it right to send a despairing report to the King. Besides it was only within the past few days that the last of the replies came in. Furthermore, I had sent a strong appeal to Lord Ormonde, who is a senior member of the Order & has much influence with others, & I thought he might change his attitude. But I have now got his reply & it is unsatisfactory ... I am informed ... that the King feels that the course which the Knights have adopted is liable to be for the *discredit of the Order*. That is exactly what I set forth in my letter [to Ormonde]. But I do venture to suggest, or rather, respectfully to beg and urge that His Majesty will allow one more attempt to be made ... namely by postponing the public ceremony for a short time in order to give an opportunity for repentance – or even to allow me to hold the investiture publicly (as at first intended) even if no other Knight than Castletown attends. For the Statutes affecting the Order expressly make provision for holding the full ceremonies without the usual quorum ... To hold the Investiture in *private* would seem to imply a *giving way* to an absurd & most unworthy cabal ... All the provisional arrangements have necessarily been made, & therefore a change to a private ceremony would be marked & I fear it would seem as if the King had been – well I hardly know how to put it – it would seem as if the wishes which His Majesty would naturally have regarding such a matter had been in an extraordinary manner, not been kept in view.'[50]

Aberdeen's embarrassed position was clear, but there was no moving the King, who would not countenance the idea: 'The King considers that to have a public investiture with only one Knight of St Patrick would make the ceremony an absurdity, and he must ask that Lord Pirrie shall be privately invested by you immediately on your return to Ireland. The King feels that he has been placed in a very false position by Lord Pirrie having been recommended to him for the St Patrick when none of the other Knights will meet him in order to be present at his investiture'.[51] Pirrie was a shrewd businessman, and closely identified with all the developments in naval architecture and marine engineering. He transformed Harland and Wolff from a family company into a large industrial organisation in the space of fifty years, and it is doubtful whether he would have taken much notice of the prejudices of his fellow Knights, let alone be affected by them.

On taking office, Nevile Wilkinson, the new Ulster King of Arms, was presented with a problem. Sir Arthur Vicars still smarting from his abrupt dismissal, refused to hand over the keys of the strong room to his successor. Wilkinson tactfully ascribed this to the suddenness of the blow which had deprived Vicars of his career, and thrown him for the moment off his equilibrium, rather than to malice. Apart from the remaining insignia of the Order of St Patrick, the strong room contained the silver maces and the Irish sword of state which were carried before the

The strong room of the Office of Arms in the Bedford Tower of Dublin Castle, in the early twentieth century. On display can be seen the Irish Sword of State, two state maces, the crown, collar and rod of Ulster King of Arms, two collars of the Order of St Patrick, and a former rod of Ulster King of Arms.

The Earl of Iveagh
(KP 1895)

Lord Lieutenant on ceremonial occasions, and all three were needed at a forthcoming levée. There was no option but to force an entry into the strong room, and Wilkinson chose the two hours that guests at the castle spent in assembling and eating dinner on Sunday evening. 'Shortly before the dinner hour, I had collected a select band of conspirators, including a representative each from the Dublin Metropolitan Police, the Board of Works, the office of the Treasury Remembrancer, and the Chief Secretary's Office. This band I admitted into my office under cover of darkness; then, with the assistance of the crowbars wielded by a couple of lusty labourers supplied by the Board of Works, all obstacles were overcome and entrance into the inner sanctuary obtained. Then, my quest accomplished, I quietly joined the guests as they sat over their coffee, and pointed out the recovered symbols of state to His Excellency as we passed through the throne room on our way to join the ladies.'[52]

After his succession to the throne in May 1910 King George V followed the custom of his predecessors, and appointed a number of extra Knights to the Order on the occasion of his coronation, intimating that he would visit Dublin to conduct the investiture in person. The new Knights were Field Marshal Viscount Kitchener of Khartoum, and the ninth Earl of Shaftesbury, Chamberlain to Queen Mary. At the time of his death half a century later, Shaftesbury was the last surviving non-royal Knight of the Order.

The news of the impending royal visit and investiture provoked yet again the suggestion that the Order of St Patrick should once more have a chapel, the obvious choice being St Patrick's Cathedral. The suggestion came from the Earl of Iveagh, KP, third and youngest son of the same Sir Benjamin Guinness who had so carefully restored the cathedral at his own expense in the 1860s. Iveagh discussed the possibility with the Dean of St Patrick's, and proposed the idea directly to the King. He may have been motivated partly by the recent completion of a chapel for the use of the Order of the Thistle, attached to St Giles's Cathedral in Edinburgh, the result of a generous donation from the Earl of Leven and Melville. Lord Knollys, the King's Private Secretary, consulted Augustine Birrell, the Chief Secretary of Ireland, and Chancellor of the Order, who advised strongly against any action. Firstly, any attempt to renew the connection between the Order and the Church of Ireland would provoke objections from the Roman Catholic and Presbyterian churches, and it would in any case be difficult to defend the connection of the Order with one particular religious body out of several, none of which had any connection with the state. Secondly, although Roman Catholic Knights of the Order had attended the installations of 1821 and 1868, the rules of the Roman Catholic Church on the attendance of Catholics at acts of worship in other churches were now much more rigorous, and no Roman Catholic Knight [there was one – the Earl of Granard – in 1911] would be allowed to attend a ceremony in a Protestant Church in Ireland.[53]

The visit of the King and Queen at the beginning of July 1911 was a great success in a country which did not often see its monarch – the last royal visit had been four years earlier. The announced intention of the Liberal government to introduce a Home Rule Bill produced feelings that total independence could not be far off, and enthusiastic demonstrations of loyalty greeted the arrival of the King and Queen. The investiture on 10 July was a brilliant and picturesque affair. All the Knights were present with the exception of the two oldest members – the seventy-eight-year-old Viscount Wolseley, and the eighty-one-year-old Earl of Lucan – for whom the ceremony would have been too exhausting.

The lengthy ceremony was to have been curtailed to save the King and Queen from fatigue but, on the night before it was due to take place, the royal couple were so pleased with the warmth of their reception in Ireland that the King decided that the full ceremony would take place. With the investiture only twenty-four hours away, the official programmes already printed and, on a Sunday evening, no way of summoning the Knights for a further rehearsal, Nevile Wilkinson was faced with a difficult task. 'Fortunately I found the official printers only too ready to help, and by four o'clock the next day the new programme was not only reset, but printed in three colours, dried and ready for issue. The three colours defined the words which were spoken by the Sovereign, which were red, those by the Grand Master and the Chancellor were blue, and the rest black … Then it was that the King's kindliness came to the rescue. I was summoned to St Patrick's Hall, and there, in spite of the heavy programme he had already gone through that day, the Sovereign of the Order rehearsed with me for an hour the whole ceremony word by word, for, as he said, if the two principal performers knew their parts, the others could not go far wrong; and the result fully justified his optimism.'[54]

After a visit to Leopardstown Race Course in the afternoon on 10 July, a banquet was held at 8.15pm, followed by the investiture at 10pm. The King personally invested Lords Kitchener and Shaftesbury with the mantle, collar and badge of the Order, and for the last time, the traditional admonition was heard in public:

> Sir, the loving Company of the Order of St Patrick hath received you as their Brother, Lover, and Fellow, and in token and knowledge of this We give you and present you this Badge, the which God will that you receive and wear from henceforth to His praise and pleasure, and to the exaltation and honour of the said Most Illustrious Order and yourself.

Though none of those present could have imagined such a thing, the days of the Order of St Patrick were numbered, and the investiture of 1911 was to be its last trumpet call. The failure of the Government to implement the provisions of the Home Rule Bill which reached the statute book in 1914, the clumsy mishandling of the Easter Rising of 1916, and the appalling atrocities committed by the Black and Tans after the war, ushered in a new age in which the Order of St Patrick had no role to play. Few could have foreseen in the summer of 1911 that the days of the union were nearly over. When King George V left Dublin Castle at 12.25pm on Wednesday 12 July 1911 on his way to Scotland, he could not have guessed that he was leaving it for the last time, and that neither he nor his successors would ever again ride in state through the streets of Dublin as kings of Ireland. Elisabeth, Countess of Fingall, well-remembered those last days before Ireland changed for ever: 'We did not know those years, that we were riding gaily across the coloured country that was our life, towards a ditch which should engulf many of us; and that those who crossed it would find themselves in another world – a world from which there should be no return ever to life as it had been'.[55]

CHAPTER SEVEN

UNQUIET TIMES

The partition of Ireland

===

Have they any idea in your circles what the future of the Order of St Patrick will be?
SIR NEVILE WILKINSON, 10 January 1922

WHEN THE HOME RULE BILL received the royal assent in 1914, the Liberal government of Herbert Asquith decided that the time had come to make a change in the lord lieutenancy of Ireland. The Earl of Aberdeen, who had enjoyed an unprecedented nine-year term as Lord Lieutenant, accordingly retired in February 1915. He was personally well-liked, even though nationalists were intent on ridding Ireland of the office that he held, and his departure was greeted with genuine regret. The streets of Dublin were crowded for his state departure on 15 February. Lady Aberdeen was a keen amateur photographer, and the volumes of reminiscences that she wrote with her husband, include photographs that she took from the state carriage during their departure from Dublin. The Aberdeens were an earnest, kindly, warm-hearted and well-intentioned couple, and they maintained an unostentatious court, compared with the extravagant Dudleys who had preceded them; and they were not unsympathetic to Irish nationalism: 'but like many people who come over to Ireland imbued with a desire to show their appreciation and sympathy with Irish nationalism, they were more Irish than the Irish themselves, a condition of mind which, when displayed by English people, generally amuses rather than impresses the Irish nationalist'.[1] Lady Aberdeen, who was much the dominant partner in the relationship, set up the Women's National Health Care Association, and a caravan travelled through Ireland, with staff who gave lectures on the prevention and cure of disease. The caravan was rumoured to have had, for demonstration purposes, slides and cultures of bacilli. Consequently certain of the Irish country people became rather wary of the caravan because of the feeling that some of the microbes might escape.

The Aberdeens loved Ireland, and made no secret of their wish to stay on until the implementation of the act, but the Government decided otherwise; after nine years, it was time for them to depart. Ireland was changing rapidly, and a new viceroy was needed to cope with a new situation. On Monday 15 February 1915, preceded by Ulster King of Arms, Lord Aberdeen rode on horseback with his staff, followed by Lady Aberdeen and others in carriages. According to custom, the Lord Lieutenant wore black morning dress with a black silk top hat, the sombre appearance being relieved only by the star of the Order of St Patrick on the left side of his coat. The departure was generally peaceful, but Lord Aberdeen's involvement with the crown jewels affair, and Lady Aberdeen's sincere attempts to improve hygiene, pursued them to the day of their departure. As the cavalcade passed along Nassau Street, an old apple seller was heard to cry out, 'There they go, with their microbes and crown jules an' all!'[2]

Travelling by train from Westland Row Station to Kingstown (now Dun Laoghaire), accompanied by the Lord Mayor of Dublin, the Lord Chancellor of Ireland, and the Commander-in-Chief, Ireland, the Aberdeens set sail for their home in Scotland. It was the last ceremonial departure of a Lord Lieutenant from the shores of Ireland. There were three more Lord Lieutenants of Ireland, but Aberdeen was the last to hold court in Dublin Castle, and the last to ride out of the city in state. In recognition of his long viceroyalty, he was created a marquess in 1916 (taking the title

'Marquess of Aberdeen and Temair'), and died in 1934. With his wife, he published volumes of memoirs in 1925 and 1929, in which he re-told the story of the theft of the Irish Crown Jewels, still, it seemed with a degree of emotion and embarrassment. Lady Aberdeen survived him by five years, dying in April 1939.

With the passage of the Home Rule Bill, Aberdeen had expected that he would be the last Lord Lieutenant of Ireland, but he was not. The outbreak of the First World War in July 1914 caused the Government to decide that the war was a priority, and that implementation of the home rule legislation could justifiably be postponed until more peaceful times. Given the seriousness of the war, and the intensity with which it had to be prosecuted, it was arguably the right decision, but the repercussions in Ireland proved to be serious.

Finding a successor to the popular Aberdeens was not easy. Augustine Birrell, the Chief Secretary, wanted an Irish peer with an historic title, who lived on his Irish estates and had taken no strong line in politics. Someone, 'who was not inimical to the people, and who would be willing to help the Government, so far as in him lay to make the best they could out of the Home Rule Bill when it was launched off the ways'.[3] Sir Henry Robinson, Vice-President of the Local Government Board for Ireland, suggested the name of Viscount Powerscourt, who was thirty-four years old and owned a beautiful house and demesne at Enniskerry, twelve miles south of Dublin. 'Birrell [the Chief Secretary] jumped at the idea and said that he always thought that Powerscourt was a picturesque figure in Irish life, and asked me to find him at once and draw him discreetly, without pledging Birrell to anything. I found Powerscourt at the Kildare Street Club, and put it to him. He promised to think it over, to consult Lady Powerscourt, and to let me know his views by that evening's post. I got his letter the next morning. He said times were bad and looked very threatening for Irish landlords; he had not yet sold his estate, and he feared the expense of the viceroyalty would be more than he could afford. Moreover, he felt that he must consider himself booked for the war, and after full consideration that I must tell Birrell that it would be no use in sending his name forward.'[4]

With Powerscourt's refusal, the concept of appointing a resident Irish peer was abandoned, and the Government selected one of their own to succeed Aberdeen. The new Lord Lieutenant was Ivor Churchill Guest, 2nd Baron (later 1st Viscount) Wimborne, a former Liberal MP (1910–12) and Paymaster-General (1910–12). Wimborne had shown strong nationalist opinions and his appointment was accompanied by the hope that he would be popular with the nationalists. He was a cousin of Winston Churchill, and both he and his attractive wife were young [he was forty-two], smart and extremely rich; but the hope of great things from the Wimborne viceroyalty proved forlorn. One eyewitness to Wimborne's arrival in Dublin, noted that the new Lord Lieutenant was, 'very red in the face, and looked uneasy', and that the welcoming crowd was, 'small and apathetic', though not hostile.[5] Wimborne was an impetuous man with an active mind, who much resented the fact that as Lord Lieutenant he had no real power, except to give effect to the policy of the Government as laid down by the Chief Secretary. Accordingly, he and his wife turned their attention to the ceremonial ways of the viceregal court and adopted an ostentatious style hardly suited to the conditions of the First World War. 'They had gold plate and powdered footmen, and Lady Wimborne tried to introduce the "Spanish curtsy", with a stamp of the heels and a flourish of the fan.'[6]

The desire of the Wimbornes for an increase in ceremonial became apparent over the issue of the next investiture of a Knight of St Patrick. Three months after Wimborne was installed as Lord Lieutenant, the Earl of Bessborough was nominated to fill the vacancy created by the death of the Earl of Lucan in July 1914. Bessborough was a typical representative of the Anglo-Irish ascendancy, equally at home on both sides of the Irish sea. In fact he treated his house in County Kilkenny as a holiday home, staying there for only eight weeks in the summer of each year. As chairman of the London, Brighton and South Coast Railway Company, and of Guest, Keen and Nettlefolds, he was an atypical appointment, and perhaps indicative of a new category of commerce and business that might have penetrated the ranks of the Order of St Patrick in the post-war years.

More interesting than the peer himself was the question of where his investiture was to take place. At the beginning of 1915, the state apartments in Dublin Castle, including St Patrick's Hall, had been converted into a hospital for wounded soldiers, which precluded the hall from being used for ceremonies of the Order for the duration of the war.

During a meeting between the King and Lord Wimborne at Windsor Castle, Wimborne proposed a public investiture for the new Knight, and departed with the firm impression that the King had given his assent.[7] As St Patrick's Hall was unavailable, the Lord Lieutenant proposed that Bessborough's investiture should instead take place at the Royal Hospital, Kilmainham. The hospital, Dublin's equivalent of the Royal Hospital, Chelsea, in London, was founded by King Charles II for veteran and disabled soldiers. The building was constructed in 1680–7 to a Franco-Dutch classical design by Sir William Robinson, and an impressive substitute for St Patrick's Hall. Believing that he had been given formal approval, Wimborne issued summonses to the Knights of St Patrick. In spite of the war conditions, a full public investiture which, 'would furnish me with the opportunity of entertaining as spectators many prominent Dublin people which ... would be in itself desirable ... I may say that all addresses and public utterances since my arrival here have been animated ... by a distinct tendency towards concord which I am anxious to foster and I regard the investiture as offering an opportunity for this purpose'.[8] Wimborne believed that it would be a good opportunity to gather together those, 'who, during the late regime, had studiously absented themselves from the castle'.[9] After the introduction of the Home Rule Bill in 1912, Irish unionists had protested by refusing to attend all Dublin Castle functions. It was a problem faced by successive Lord Lieutenants. If any occupant of the office gave any hint of being sympathetic to nationalism and home rule, he could face a boycott by the unionist community.

The investiture of the Earl of Bessborough would be the first investiture of a Knight of St Patrick in four years, and Wimborne felt sure that a splendid ceremonial occasion and a new Lord Lieutenant would attract both unionists and nationalists. But his hopes of mounting such an occasion were quickly dashed. Whether Wimborne had simply misinterpreted the King's position, or whether the King himself had, on the advice of his senior advisors, changed his mind, the Lord Lieutenant was ordered to cancel his plan for a public investiture at the Royal Hospital. Public attitude towards the war was beginning to change. The use of poisonous gases, the sinking of the Lusitania, and the publication of the report of the Bryce Commission brought a growing realisation that the war was going to last a long time. The original cry of 'business as usual' was being replaced by the view that the country was not taking the war sufficiently seriously, and Wimborne was informed that his proposed public investiture should not take place.

This negative must have caused Wimborne acute embarrassment; arrangements, including the despatch of invitations, were already well advanced. 'I have already issued invitations to the Knights of the Order for the 28th inst. and several have already intimated their intention to attend, including Ormonde, Kilmorey and Mayo, and I doubt not that there will be other acceptances ... I am loath to put them off now ... should the King adhere to his disinclination to sanction a public investiture I would still plead that the ceremony should be performed at the ViceRegal [Lodge] and be limited to the Knights themselves and their wives.'[10] Wimborne's appeal was dismissed by Lord Stamfordham, the King's Private Secretary, almost by return of post. 'His Majesty has abolished for the time all state ceremonies here, and his investitures are done privately ... His Majesty, therefore, thinks that it would be incongruous to summon the Knights of St Patrick, many of whom are engaged in matters connected with the war, to Dublin, to be arrayed in their full dress robes and to assist in a function, which, even held privately at the Viceregal Lodge, would be of a distinctly ceremonial character ... Whenever the war comes to an end His Majesty feels you will have ample opportunity to hold a State Investiture, and he hopes by that time in St Patrick's Hall.'[11] The royal command was quite explicit, and Bessborough was invested privately at viceregal lodge by the Lord Lieutenant, with only George Burtchaell, Athlone Pursuivant and Deputy Ulster King of Arms, and Augustine Birrell, the Chancellor, being present.

The King's decision ended all possibility of any more formal investitures while the war continued, and though Wimborne persisted and again wrote to the King in February 1916 with regard to the forthcoming investiture of Lords Donoughmore, Midleton and Powerscourt, he again received a firm negative. 'As long as the war lasts, the King does not wish state investitures to be held, and this applies to Dublin as well as to London'.[12] As with Lord Bessborough in 1915, the three peers were invested privately at the Viceregal Lodge on 18 April 1916, with only the Lord Lieutenant, Sir Matthew Nathan (Under Secretary, representing the Chief Secretary and Chancellor), and Athlone Pursuivant being present. The pattern of dispensing with the statutory requirement for holding a Chapter with at least three Knights being present, now became normal, and all subsequent Knights of the Order, French (1917), Oranmore and Browne (1918), Desart (1919), Abercorn (1922), Wales (1927), Gloucester (1934), and York (1936), were invested privately by the King.

Of the three Knights appointed in 1916, Viscount Powerscourt was a liberal and humane landowner who blamed the Easter Rising that year on a tendency among the Irish upper classes to despise and resist nationalism. Although only thirty-four years old at the time of the departure of the Aberdeens in 1915, Powerscourt's broad sympathies would have made him an excellent Irish Lord Lieutenant, and more preferable to the imperious Wimborne. Viscount Midleton was a former Secretary of State for War and for India (1900–05) in the Conservative governments of Lord Salisbury and Arthur Balfour. The Earl of Donoughmore, chairman of committees in the House of Lords, had been a junior minister in the Arthur Balfour administration (1902–5), and was grand master of the freemasons of Ireland.

The informality of the 1916 investiture was emphasised rather than alleviated when Wimborne forgot his words. After it was over, he invited the three new Knights into his private room, 'where he made us a set speech, on the success with which he was governing Ireland – without, he said, unnecessary severity, but also without undue laxity. As he developed the latter point, Donoughmore, who was standing behind his chair, winked at me over his head: we had both had circumstantial accounts of the "trial" attack by Sinn Feiners on Dublin Castle, which had gone unpunished'.[13] Wimborne's pompous and self-congratulatory speech showed how little he understood the Irish situation. Considering that the Easter Rising was only a few weeks away, the speech indicated how little he understood the mood of Irish opinion, and with hindsight he may

Viscount Powerscourt
(KP 1916)

have regretted delivering it. The rising marked a watershed in the relations between Britain and Ireland, and a rise in the political temperature within Ireland. The Lord Lieutenant, the Chief Secretary and the Under Secretary all accepted ultimate responsibility and duly resigned. Although the resignations of Birrell and Nathan were accepted, Wimborne was deemed to have no responsibility and was re-appointed.

The officers of the Order suffered a similar fate to the Knights. Henry Duke, who succeeded Augustine Birrell as Chief Secretary in 1916, was never invested with his badge as Chancellor, nor was Sir John Olphert, who was appointed Usher of the Black Rod in May 1915, more than eighteen months after the death of his predecessor. When Olphert died on 11 March 1917, George Burtchaell, acting as Ulster King of Arms in the stead of Nevile Wilkinson who was away on active service, wrote to Samuel Power, Private Secretary to the Lord Lieutenant, on the day after Olphert's death. 'You could I suppose get this office if you cared to. You are the man I should like to see there as you have been at most of the investitures, and have taken part in them on several occasions. It is more satisfactory that the Officers of the Order should have some knowledge of what their duties are.'[14] Power did get the appointment, but not until October 1918, the Government deciding that, as no public ceremonies were to be held until after the war, there was no urgency in filling the mostly ceremonial office.[15]

The end of the war in November 1918 did not bring a revival of the old ceremonies, customs and traditions of the viceregal court. Life was changing in Ireland, and not only because of the First World War. A rising tide of militant nationalism, under the banner of Sinn Fein, had effectively swept aside the old Irish Home Rule Party. The Easter Rising of April 1916, and the insensitive way in which it was handled, swung moderate Irish public opinion against the Government and led to a sharp upturn in civil disturbance. Wimborne was not held responsible for the rising – he would have had the good answer that he was never given the opportunity of exercising any authority – and although he resigned in the wake of the Easter rising, he was re-appointed three months later, having been exonerated from any responsibility. Recent evidence has shown that the leaders of the 1916 rising were not so unshakeably committed to the ideal of a republic, as previously thought. Patrick Pearse, who was named first president of the republic, and Joseph Plunkett, seriously considered the possibility of inviting a German prince to be installed as king of Ireland in the event of Germany winning the war, and they went so far as to name Prince Joachim, one of the Kaiser's sons, as a possible candidate.[16] The concept was vague and visionary, and the eventual outcome of the war ended all thoughts of a German monarchy in Ireland.

Wimborne left Ireland, unlamented, in May 1918. Although he lived until 1939, he refused offers to return to political activity, and never again held public office.

The Government initially proposed Viscount Midleton as successor to Wimborne. In some ways he was an ideal candidate: an Irish landowner and well-known in Ireland (although he lived principally in England); a former cabinet minister (1900–05) who was influential in British government circles; a prominent southern unionist who had opposed home rule for Ireland; and also a Knight of St Patrick (appointed in 1916). But Midleton had a notorious reputation for obstinacy and tactlessness, and refused the lord lieutenancy because of a disagreement with the Government of David Lloyd George. The Prime Minister wished to introduce conscription and home rule in Ireland simultaneously. Midleton refused to accept this policy, declined the lieutenancy, and so Wimborne was replaced by Field Marshal Viscount French.

In different times, French would have made an excellent Lord Lieutenant. He was Irish and he loved Ireland, and on his arrival as Lord Lieutenant, there was a clear indication that he felt he was 'coming home'. He had an estate at Drumdoe, on the shores of Loch Key in County Roscommon, on the refurbishment of which he proceeded to spend a good deal of money. Had Ireland been other than it was at the end of his viceroyalty, he would probably have been happy to retire to County Roscommon. Because of his Irish ancestry, he had been made a Knight of St Patrick in June 1917 in recognition of his services, first as Commander-in-Chief of the British Expeditionary Force in France, and subsequently as Commander-in-Chief of the Home Forces. As an Irishman with a considerable military reputation, he might have won the respect of the Irish, but any such hopes were disappointed.

French was principally a soldier, less of a ceremonial Lord Lieutenant and more of a military governor, and the wisdom of appointing him at such a difficult point in Irish history, is questionable. Events in Ireland had, in any case, moved too far. An increasing polarisation between the people and the Government negated the effect that the appointment of an Irish Lord Lieutenant might have had in earlier years. French was a soldier, straight from the battlefields of the First World War, and his attempts to enforce the law produced a mood of dangerous irritation. Matters went from bad to worse; the struggle degenerated into a campaign of aggression and punishment, of outrages and reprisals, and his position only grew more unsatisfactory with the passage of time. The arrival of the 'Black and Tans' at the beginning of 1920, an auxiliary force to aid the Royal Irish Constabulary, introduced a group that became infamous for their brutality. They were mostly young ex-soldiers who found it difficult to settle down after the brutalising effect of four years of trench warfare. They acquired a reputation for ruthlessness and contempt for life and property, partly from the intense strain imposed on them by service in Ireland, surrounded by enemies who could not easily be identified.

The Order of St Patrick continued on its way. Two Knights were appointed during French's viceroyalty: Lord Oranmore and Browne in 1918, and the Earl of Desart in 1919 – the last two appointments before the constitutional changes of 1921–2 – both of whom were prominent southern unionists. Oranmore was a representative peer for Ireland, and had been a member of the ill-fated Irish Convention in 1917–18. The convention was a gathering of ninety-five representatives from across Ireland, charged with attempting to find a peaceful settlement to the problem of how Ireland should be governed. Every political party was represented, with the sole and significant exception of Sinn Fein. The Earl of Desart was also a member of the convention, and supplied the tact and conciliation that Viscount Midleton often lacked. Desart was seventy-one at the time of his appointment as a Knight of St Patrick. He had been called to the Bar in 1872, and spent his working life as a distinguished lawyer. He was Director of Public Prosecutions 1894–1909, and a Judge of the International Court of Arbitration 1910–15. Although the war was over, there was no return to the pre-war state ceremonial, and Desart was privately invested by King George V on 18 December 1919.[17]

Despite the presence of Desart, the 1917–18 convention was doomed not only by the absence of Sinn Fein, but by the intransigence of the northern unionists, who were determined to stay out of a Home Rule Ireland. The eleven southern unionists, including Desart and Midleton, found themselves increasingly irritated by their northern colleagues, and more in sympathy with southern nationalists. Ten years earlier, the convention might have succeeded in bringing diverse political groups and regions together; but the situation was changing rapidly and it was now too late. By 1921, it was clear that coercive force could no longer control the deteriorating situation in Ireland, and with the passing of the Government of Ireland Act 1920, a new type of Lord Lieutenant was needed. It was a sad end to the distinguished career of French, who had been the wrong person at the wrong time, and the pathos of his departure from Ireland on 30 April 1921 was not lost on observers. 'He nearly broke down at the finish. He is a terribly pathetic figure – such a little while ago the hero of England and now goes out to nothing – a lonely little gentleman.'[18]

Having tried a Lord Lieutenant with nationalist sympathies (Wimborne), then a military Lord Lieutenant of Irish ancestry (French), the Government now tried a

Viscount FitzAlan of Derwent, last Lord Lieutenant of Ireland and last Grand Master of the Order of St Patrick (1921–2). In addition to the mantle, collar and badge of the Order of the Garter, he is wearing at his neck, a Grand Master's badge of the Order of St Patrick.

Roman Catholic Lord Lieutenant. French was replaced by Lord Edmund Talbot, who reverted to his patronymic of 'Fitzalan-Howard', was given a peerage, and took the title Viscount FitzAlan of Derwent. He could have been an ideal compromise candidate for the post of Lord Lieutenant, in the changed Ireland envisaged by the Government of Ireland Act 1920, because he was both a unionist and a Roman Catholic. He was a long-serving member of the House of Commons, having been Conservative Unionist Member of Parliament for Chichester since 1894, chief unionist whip since 1913, and Joint Parliamentary Secretary to the Treasury since 1916; he had also been private secretary to Viscount Midleton KP 1896–1900.

He was a member of the Fitzalan-Howard family, the senior Roman Catholic family of England, and was uncle to the sixteenth Duke of Norfolk, the head of the family. As a conservative unionist, it was hoped that he would appeal to the unionist north, and as a Roman Catholic, it was hoped that he would appeal to the nationalist south. In earlier times, he would have been an excellent and popular choice. But the Ireland to which he went in May 1921, had moved far beyond the time when a Roman Catholic Lord Lieutenant might have been able to calm nationalist protest. 'As a leading Roman Catholic, noted for his calm temper of mind, he was regarded as particularly suitable for this post, but it seems probable that the Government were over-sanguine in their estimate of the sympathy with which Irishmen at that period regarded their co-religionists.'[19] FitzAlan's appointment was greeted dismissively by Irish newspapers. 'That he is a Catholic is outweighed in their view that he is an Englishman, and a Tory politician, and Irish RCs dislike English RCs anyway'.[20]

Under the provisions of the Government of Ireland Act 1920, the Lord Lieutenant would relate to the Parliament of the north in Belfast, and to the Parliament of the south in Dublin. His duties were to appoint government ministers; to summon, prorogue and dissolve the two Irish Parliaments; to give and withhold the royal assent to bills; to appoint county court judges; to remove certain specified officers; and to represent certain constitutional matters to the King in Council. Although the title of Lord Lieutenant was retained, FitzAlan was in effect the constitutional governor-general of a dominion; except that his dominion was divided into two parts. The Parliament of Northern Ireland was duly opened, by King George V, on 22 June 1921, but the Parliament of Southern Ireland was stillborn. It was boycotted by all but six of the members of its lower house, who had no option but to adjourn at its first session.

When it became clear that the provisions of the Government of Ireland Act could not be implemented in the south, FitzAlan was faced with a task which required very little initiative, simply the oversight of the partition of Ireland and the transfer of power to the new provisional government in the south. He was criticised by Lloyd George's private secretary as, 'a viceroy ... who did nothing',[21] but then there was little for him to do, and little that he could do. FitzAlan performed his duties with tact and prudence. He had a reputation of being, 'a very nice man',[22] and Timothy Healy, the first Governor-General of the Irish Free State recalled FitzAlan's, 'accustomed phlegm and courtesy',[23] but his lord lieutenancy lasted only until December 1922, and by then his position was mostly titular. The impossibility of implementing the legislature designed for southern Ireland, was a clear indication that even the amended style of the lord lieutenancy had no future, and FitzAlan rapidly became a nominal viceroy with hardly any duties. Towards the end of his lieutenancy, he did not even reside in Ireland, and lived mostly at his London home in Buckingham Palace Gardens. 'My plans for the winter are quite vague', he wrote to Sir Nevile Wilkinson, 'I am going to unveil a war memorial at Enniskillen towards the end of October and then propose to return to the Vice Regal [Lodge] for a bit.'[24]

As the last Lord Lieutenant, FitzAlan was the last Grand Master of the Order of St Patrick. He made no state entry into Dublin in 1921, but then neither had Lord French in 1918. Historic precedent was followed in detail, but the whole ceremony was of a semi-private nature. He arrived at Dublin Castle on 2 May 1921, to be greeted by the Dublin Metropolitan Band playing suitable airs in the Upper Castle Yard, and a large group of officials. He was received by Ulster King of Arms and Athlone Pursuivant, and conducted by them to the Presence Chamber, where he was received by the Lords Justices. From there, the Lords Justices conducted him to the council chamber, where the Privy Council of Ireland was assembled. After FitzAlan had taken the oath of allegiance and the oath of office, the sword of state of state was delivered to him, and he acknowledged this merely by touching it. Then he was invested with the insignia of the Grand Master of the Order of St Patrick. The investiture was conducted in the same way as the reception of the sword of state; the new Lord Lieutenant merely laying

The last Lord Lieutenant of Ireland leaves Dublin Castle for the last time, 16 January 1922.

his hand upon the insignia. Eight months later, on 16 January 1922, FitzAlan transferred control of the castle to the Irish provisional government, and the last Lord Lieutenant of Ireland left Dublin Castle for the last time. Eleven months later, the lord lieutenancy ceased to exist.

After a protracted period of negotiation with representatives of the Irish provisional government, a new constitution was agreed on 1 April 1922, and enshrined in the Irish Free State (Agreement) Act 1922. The act recognised that the Irish provisional government was now *the* Government in southern Ireland. The office of Lord Lieutenant lingered until the end of the year when, by the terms of the Irish Free State Constitution Act, which came into force on 6 December 1922, it ceased to exist in southern Ireland, and a crown representative styled 'governor-general' was appointed for the twenty-six counties of the Irish Free State. As the six counties of Northern Ireland would have internal self-government, but not dominion status, the crown representative there was styled 'governor'. The office of Lord Lieutenant of Ireland ceased to exist when Lord FitzAlan's viceregal successors were appointed. Timothy Healy, Governor-General of the Irish Free State, was sworn in on 6 December and received by the King on 16 December. The office of Governor of Northern Ireland was created on 9 December; the Duke of Abercorn was sworn in on 12 December and received by the King on 21 December.

Although the office of Lord Lieutenant had been abolished by statute, the office of Grand Master of the Order of St Patrick had not. But who was to suceed Lord FitzAlan as Grand Master? Ireland was now divided into two parts, and there was no longer a Lord Lieutenant for the whole country. In the name of the King, a Governor-General presided over a dominion status Irish Free State, from Dublin; and in the name of the King, a Governor presided over an autonomous part of the United Kingdom, known as Northern Ireland, from Belfast. Which of the two new viceregal representatives was to be the new Grand Master, and what was to be the future of the Order and its chancery in Dublin Castle?

The Ireland of 1922 was very different from the Ireland of 1783. The partition of the island created a situation in which the future of the Order of St Patrick could not be guaranteed, and the uncertainty was not lost on Ulster King of Arms. On 10 January 1922 Sir Nevile Wilkinson wrote to Colonel George Crichton at the Central Chancery of the Orders of Knighthood in London regarding the vacant post of Athlone Pursuivant. 'I have advised His Excellency to offer it to Mr Sadleir, but so far he has very wisely taken no steps, as the future of the entire office is in the melting pot ... Have they any idea in your circles what the future of the Order of St Patrick will be?'[25]

Unknown to Wilkinson, the Order of St Patrick was briefly mentioned during a discussion between the United Kingdom and Irish delegates on 10 June 1922. The debate that day centred on the question of the distribution of honours, and during the debate both Winston Churchill and David Lloyd George spoke their minds. 'Mr Churchill said that the Irish Free State could not stop the grant of honours by the British Crown any more than the British government could prevent Portugal or other foreign countries from conferring honours on British subjects. They could only prevent British subjects from wearing foreign decorations at Court. Take, for instance, the Order of St Patrick. This was a Grand Order of Chivalry and of Christendom. A short time ago it seemed likely that these ancient Orders and Decorations would be swept away as so much rubbish, but things had changed since then and they were now regarded as objects of ambition. Mr Lloyd George said that the Order of St Patrick would be conferred in respect of service in Ireland and that the British government could not confer it.'[26] Ignoring the flamboyant piece of Churchillian hyperbole, Lloyd George had effectively handed the Order of St Patrick over to the Irish Free State, although he probably did not realise it at the time. It was probably typical of the many expansive gestures and meaningless statements made by Lloyd George, and need not be taken as an indication of any firm policy at that date.

On 11 September 1922, Wilkinson raised the question of the future of the Order again, this time with the Lord Lieutenant's secretary. 'I presume that some policy regarding the future of the Order of St Patrick will be arrived at in time; but I should think that the less it is brought into prominence during the present crisis, the more chance there is of its escaping being thrown as a sop, to the extremists.'[27] FitzAlan agreed: 'the less said the better at the moment'.[28]

With hindsight, the attitude of the Government of the Irish Free State to the Order of St Patrick, that was codified in May 1928, could have been predicted by reading the text of Article 5 of the new Free State constitution. The article specifically barred the conferment of any 'title of honour' on any Free State citizen, without the approval of the Executive Council of the Irish Free State; this article was cited by William Cosgrave, president of the Irish Provisional Government in 1928. During the 1922 discussions between the Government and the Irish representatives, an article on titles of honour was specifically inserted in the new Irish Free State constitution. The Irish delegation reported that there was a very strong feeling against the grant of honours by the Government, to citizens of the Irish Free State.[29] Arthur Griffith, leader of the Irish delegation, was informed that the British government could not allow itself to be excluded from the right of granting honours to Irishmen, for services rendered outside Ireland,[30] but the article was nevertheless inserted into the new constitution.

On 19 October 1922, David Lloyd George resigned as Prime Minister after six years in office, and the question of a resignation honours list arose. The 'settlement' of the Irish question was now only six weeks away, and thought was given to the inclusion of the many men and women who had served in the administration of Ireland before the establishment of the Irish Free State. The news had reached Cosgrave, who fired a warning shot across the bows. 'A rumour has got abroad that titles are about to be distributed in this country on the change of government ... I think it right to let you know that the conferring of titles, on what I may describe as our nationals – people, who, on the final passing of the constitution, will be citizens of the Irish Free State – will embarrass us very much indeed. We cannot recommend any such persons at present for titles and it would be said that the thing was being done over our heads and in the face of the clause in our constitution. I hope there is no truth in the matter to complicate matters further.'[31] A few weeks later, he reiterated his position in a letter to the Duke of Devonshire, Colonial Secretary in the new Conservative government of Andrew Bonar Law. 'We had already written ... pointing out the national objections which for many years have been held in this country to honours lists. It was so strong that a special article was inserted in the constitution ... we do feel that the granting of honours to our nationals would not help but might seriously impair the cordial relations we are so desirous of establishing between our two countries.'[32] Here was the first implicit statement that the Order of St Patrick was finished in the Irish Free State.

Cosgrave's letter did not prevent a good deal of debate on the Order of St Patrick throughout the 1920s, and one key figure to emerge in that debate after 1922 was King George V, and the King was not slow in making clear his feelings. On 12 December 1922, he discussed the Order with Viscount FitzAlan, suggesting that it would be advisable to appoint the Duke of Abercorn, the new Governor of Northern Ireland, as a Knight of St Patrick. FitzAlan concurred: 'I told him I thought so too, especially on his being appointed Governor to the north. You will remember it was contemplated long ago to make him one, only LG [Lloyd George] kept it back as he intended giving it to somebody else, and then, when this became impossible, we never could get him to fill the vacancy'. On the subject of appointments in the Irish Free State, FitzAlan urged caution. 'There are two vacancies now. I think it would be a mistake, at any rate at present, to give any in the south, and also wiser not to give two in the north; so a vacancy will still have to exist. Perhaps it may be found

The Duke of Abercorn (KP 1922) and his star. The duke was the first Governor of Northern Ireland, 1922–45.

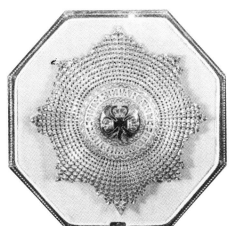

possible in the future to give one in the south.'[33] Lloyd George's successor as Prime Minister, Andrew Bonar Law, agreed with FitzAlan and submitted a recommendation to the King on 13 December, that the Duke of Abercorn should be appointed to the Order. Abercorn was duly received in audience by the King on 21 December 1922 and invested with the insignia of a Knight of the Order of St Patrick.

Abercorn was a symbol of the Anglo-Irish ascendancy and an appropriately eminent figure to preside in the north. Timothy Healy, the new Governor-General of the Irish Free State was of very different stock, but no less eminent; he was also a echo from the past. Sixteen years earlier, then a distinguished Irish barrister, Healy had defended Sir Arthur Vicars in front of the viceregal commission of enquiry into the circumstances surrounding the loss of the Irish Crown Jewels. Healy was an independent-minded figure of somewhat erratic views who was inclined to make unpredictable and unconstitutional statements, and his retirement as Governor-General in 1928, was greeted with a degree of relief by the Irish government. He had no interest in the ways of the viceregal court which preceded him, let alone the Order of St Patrick. Given the great controversy surrounding his office, as around the very dominion status of the Irish Free State, Healy could not risk the adoption of any viceregal state, which might lay him open to the charge of reviving the ceremonial of the lord lieutenancy. Even an attempt to have the Governor-General address the opening of a new session of the Irish Free State parliament, had to be abandoned after two years because of hostility from certain members. Healy's own position towards ceremonial was expressed in an interview with a journalist from *The Times*.

Q. Will there be any Viceregal State?
A. I hope not.
Q. Any Court?
A. That is the last thing I should think of.
Q. You will still be Mr Tim Healy?
A. I hope so – to my friends at all events (*laughing*).
Q. Are you likely to take any other rank?
A. Never.
Q. It will be usual to address you as 'Your Excellency'?
A. I hope not, but I cannot prevent any man from being courteous.
Q. How would you dress for State functions?
A. As I am now.
Q. The old State ceremonial goes, as far as you are concerned?
A. That will be a matter for the Irish Cabinet to determine. In that respect I am entirely in their hands, but my own wish would be simplicity itself.[34]

There was no possibility that Timothy Healy would be the new Grand Master of the Order of St Patrick.

Within five weeks of the partition of Ireland in December 1922, the future of the Order came under scrutiny in the Irish Office in London. Obviously, it could not continue in the new Ireland as though nothing had changed; so much of its contextual support had disappeared. The lord lieutenancy was now abolished, so the office of Grand Master was now constitutionally vacant. Should it be similarly abolished, or continued under a new system? With the disappearance of the office of Chief Secretary (it was vacant from 19 October and abolished on 6 December), what was to become of the office of Chancellor of the Order? Was it necessary to retain both offices? Should (or indeed could) the chancery of the Order remain at the Office of Arms in Dublin Castle, and if so could the status of St Patrick's Hall as the 'Knights' hall' be maintained?

Discussions in the early months of 1923 concluded that, 'nothing ought to be done publicly for a bit, but that there ought to be a preliminary conference'.[35] Almost certainly in response to a request from Sir Nevile Wilkinson, Thomas Sadleir, Deputy Ulster King of Arms notified Ulster in February 1923 that he would, 'make out a list of the volumes connected with the Order of St. Patrick'.[36] A few days later he sent the list to Wilkinson, but reported that he could not make a list of insignia because he had failed to find the keys to some of the boxes.[37] The list was subsequently sent over to London on 1 March. Sir Nevile Wilkinson was clearly involved in these preliminary consultations, and reported that he had been, 'privately notified that it would be injudicious at the present time to raise any questions regarding the property and status of the Order'.[38] Despite Wilkinson urging caution and delay, the future of the Order had to be seriously considered, though the result of such considerations need not be yet published. 'I forget whether I told you that the decision after all those long minutes about the Order of St Patrick was that nothing had better be done publicly for a bit, but that there ought to be a preliminary conference.'[39] The conference was assembled at the Home Office on 30 April 1923 to discuss the Order, and it proved to be the first of many conferences and meetings held in the twenty-year period from 1923 to 1943. The subject of debate was the same in 1943 as it was in 1923; what was to be done with the Order of St Patrick?

Those present in April 1923 included Sir Douglas Dawson (State Chamberlain), Sir James Masterton-Smith (Under Secretary for the Colonies), Sir Mark Grant-Sturgis (Assistant Under Secretary for Irish Affairs), and Sir Nevile Wilkinson. The presence of Wilkinson proved to be crucial to the fate of the Order of St Patrick, because he advised the conference that the Irish Free State government had intimated that nothing should be done which might draw public attention to the existence of his office and the Order, which they were anxious should continue in due time. Considering the strong opposition to the Order expressed by the Irish government in the late 1920s, this is a very curious statement, and highly questionable. Throughout the 1920s, Wilkinson consistently clung to the belief that the Irish Free State government was not anti-British, and that the passions aroused by events of 1921–2 would soon be forgotten. In a display of incomprehensible naiveté, he sincerely believed that this was only a passing phase, and that life would soon get back to 'normal'. Quite how he managed to discern the feelings of the provisional government is unclear, as he did not visit Dublin at all between April 1922 and August 1923. Whatever the rights or wrongs of Wilkinson's assumptions, he wrote to Grant-Sturgis saying that it would be injudicious to raise any questions regarding the property and status of the Order.

Wilkinson's views probably influenced the seven conclusions reached by the conference of April 1923: it was agreed that it would be best to proceed on the assumption that the Irish Free State would in time come to regard the Order with the same respect in which it had been held in the past; if this came about, then the Order could prove to be a valuable link between Ireland and the crown; subject to the safeguarding of the records and insignia, no change should be made at the present, and certainly that no step should be taken which might imply that the Order was to be transferred to Northern Ireland at some future date; the United Kingdom Prime Minister would continue to be responsible for all appointments to the Order; although the Statutes were obsolete in several respects, there was no pressing need to alter them for the time being; Wilkinson should be asked to arrange the transfer of the regalia, insignia and the most important records to London for safety; and finally, that the chancery should remain in the Office of Arms in Dublin Castle, and that no action should be taken with regard to the banners, hatchments, swords and crests in St Patrick's Hall. In short, everything was to be left alone except for the cautious removal of the insignia. Dawson raised the question of the probable attitude of other dominions towards the retention of the Order as an all-Ireland Order, but no difficulty was anticipated in this respect.[40]

Sadleir duly provided Wilkinson with an inventory of all the properties of the Order,[41] but in spite of Wilkinson's emphatic insistence that the insignia and records were probably far safer where they were, the King insisted that they should be transferred to London for safe custody. Wilkinson warned that the danger of them being stolen in transit was far greater, and that, 'Ireland being what it is, any attempt to move them would almost certainly get known and would cause protest, and in a word bring upon the whole question the attention which the Free State government and everybody else wishes at the present time to avoid'.[42] When asked whether he could bring over the Irish Sword of State, he replied that it would be extremely difficult as it was nearly four feet long and it would be a tragedy or a farce or both, if he were caught trying to smuggle it through customs. Cosgrave (President of the Executive Council of the Irish Free State) would have no choice but to intervene and claim it for the Dublin Museum rather than allow it to be carried off to London.[43]

On 25 May 1923, Grant-Sturgis held a meeting with Wilkinson and communicated the King's definite wish that the regalia should be transferred to London. Wilkinson's reply was that it 'could be arranged', but he desired to have a meeting first with Lord Stamfordham, the King's Private Secretary. No such meeting between the two men took place, and by April 1926, complaints were made that the regalia had still not been transferred to London. Geoffrey Whiskard, Assistant Secretary at the Dominions Office was unconcerned. 'The interval of three years which has elapsed since then seems to me to make something of a difference. I do not think any serious question as to the safety of these articles now arises; and I should have thought that so long as the office of Ulster survives we might well leave them where they are until (if ever) a decision as to the Order itself is reached.'[44] The Home Office was more concerned and Wilkinson was summoned to a meeting with the Permanent Secretary on 8 April 1926. He reported that, with the exception of two collars, everything connected with the Order of St Patrick had indeed been transferred and was now safely deposited in his bank in London. Two maces and the Irish Sword of State were still at his office in Dublin, but he promised to do what he could to arrange their transfer to London. 'Wilkinson is crossing to Dublin this week-end and while he is there he will endeavour to make arrangements for bringing the maces and the sword over without attracting notice. He has promised to let me know what he can arrange. It is conceivable that the Free State government might claim these things as their property but such a claim would not be well founded and, as the articles have considerable historical as well as intrinsic value, their proper place is here.'[45] It would seem that, carefully and cautiously, piece by piece, Wilkinson gradually removed everything to London in the years 1923–6. The decision of the meeting of April 1923 was followed faithfully. Nothing was done to draw attention to the Order and no further appointments were made for some years. The posts of Athlone Pursuivant and Secretary of the Order, were left unfilled when they fell vacant in 1921 and 1926 respectively, and the Office of Arms continued to function quietly in Dublin Castle in the presence though not under the jurisdiction of the Free State government.

The new government of Northern Ireland was not slow in registering its own claim to the Order. In July 1924, Sir James Craig, the first Prime Minister of Northern Ireland (1921–40), wrote to Ramsay MacDonald, the Prime Minister of the United Kingdom with a proposal. 'Lord Stamfordham in correspondence with the Duke of Abercorn has intimated that the question of the Order of St Patrick is engaging your attention and he suggests that I should communicate to you direct information that the Primate of All Ireland intimated to me some considerable time ago, that he would be most willing to allocate St Patrick's Chapel to the Order of St Patrick, to which he holds it rightfully belongs. At the same time he intimated that, as there was a strong Presbyterian element in Northern Ireland, he would be willing to make whatever adaptations were considered necessary by the Moderator of the General Assembly, and I for my part undertook on behalf of the Government to bear whatever cost was necessary in regard to adaptation of the stalls, the screen, and minor additions to make the chapel fit for the Order. All this being satisfactorily arranged, I hope you will be able to recommend His Majesty to confer the Order upon the Prince of Wales and the Duke of York prior to the visit of the latter to Northern Ireland next week [the Duke and Duchess of York visited Northern Ireland in July 1924]. It would be a great compliment to the whole of Ireland, and to Ulster in particular.'[46]

Although there is no evidence in surviving files that Ramsay MacDonald, head of the first Labour government in British history, and a minority government at that, was personally engaged in considering the question of the Order of St Patrick in July 1924, it is more than likely that the matter of appointments was exercising the mind of King George V. In the three months period from April to June 1924, four Knights of the Order had died: the Earl of Enniskillen in April, the Earl of Bandon in May, and the Earl of Listowel (at the age of ninety-two, and one of the few remaining survivors of the Crimean War) and Viscount Pirrie in June. There were four vacancies in the Order, vacancies which the King was certainly anxious to fill.

Craig's letter in July 1924 is revealing of the role of Lord Stamfordham. His belief that Ramsay MacDonald was engaged in considering the future of the Order, was based on an 'intimation' from Lord Stamfordham, to the Duke of Abercorn. As will become clear, in the events of 1927–30, Stamfordham pressed successive United Kingdom Prime Ministers to consider reviving the Order of St Patrick, and there is no doubt that he did so, not *motu proprio*, but with the knowledge and support, and probably at the direction of the King. It seems unlikely that, on a matter of potential controversy, Stamfordham would have acted on his own initiative, and the conclusion is that a clear but circuitous line of approach can be detected, from King George V to Lord Stamfordham to the Duke of Abercorn to Sir James Craig to Ramsay MacDonald. The King was using the Northern Ireland Prime Minister to put gentle pressure on the United Kingdom Prime Minister to do something about the future of the Order of St Patrick. From 1922 until his death in 1936 King George V made repeated efforts to keep the Order of St Patrick alive, and his approach to the Prime Minister of Northern Ireland was to be the first of many attempts. In this respect he would certainly have been knocking at an open door; the new Northern Ireland government would have been very happy indeed to have given the Order of St Patrick a home in the north of Ireland.

That the Primate of All Ireland was prepared to offer St Patrick's Cathedral in Armagh, speaks for itself. Charles Frederick D'Arcy (1859–1938), Archbishop of Armagh 1920–38 had raised the offer in February 1923, in a letter to S. G. Tallents, private secretary to the last Lord Lieutenant of Ireland, and imperial secretary to the first Governor of Northern Ireland. The archbishop's letter demonstrates that he knew very little about the Order of St Patrick; he seems to have imagined that it had something to do with the saint, and was working on the belief that, 'Armagh was the real original cathedral of Saint Patrick'. 'If the Order were *for the future* seated at Armagh, it would be more than a restoration of the original intention: it would give the Order a historical standing which it has never yet possessed. We could, I believe, find space for the banners; and we would gladly offer the cathedral for installations, which would, of course, in such a case, revert to the religious character which they had formerly. In former times there were prelates of the Order as well as Knights. If this element were restored, I would suggest that it should include some representative, or representatives, of the Presbyterian Church. I have reason to think that the R. C. Church would not co-operate.'[47] The archbishop had been staying for a week at Stormont Castle, to meet the new Governor of Northern Ireland, and the Duchess of Abercorn, and it is reasonably certain that the archbishop's letter was prompted by the Duke of Abercorn. 'The Duchess told me on Tuesday night that they and he [the archbishop] had been talking over the possibility of making the Cathedral of St Patrick at Armagh the future religious centre of the Order ... This idea seems to me good, and I hope you will try to work it into your Patrick proposals.'[48]

Ramsay MacDonald asked the Home Office and Colonial Office to consider Craig's request, and their opinion was firmly against any action. The result indicates that the Government knew the precise source of the pressure to keep the Order alive. Sir James Craig received a polite and courteous reply; but the letter to Lord Stamfordham was a firm warning. 'At the request of the Prime Minister I have consulted both the Home Office and the Colonial Office, who are both very strongly of the opinion that it would be most inopportune at the present time to make any change in the constitution or administration of the Order or any additional appointments to it, and that in particular to make the proposed appointments on the occasion of the Duke of York's visit, which, as I think you know, was arranged without consultation with either department and at a time when it was known that the boundary crisis must be acute, would be a most serious mistake ... the Prime Minister proposes to reply to Sir James Craig that he cannot regard the present moment as being opportune for the making of any change in the constitution or administration of the Order or any fresh appointments to it.'[49]

This was a clear rebuff to the Prime Minister of Northern Ireland, but it was only the end of the first round, not the end of the fight, and it proved to be a testing of the temperature for a much more lengthy and serious debate that began two years later.

King George V, when
Duke of York, (KP 1897),
wearing the robes of a
Knight of St Patrick.

CHAPTER EIGHT

DIVERGING OPINIONS

The King, the Home Office and the Dominions Office

─────

I feel strongly that it would be far better that no new appointments should be made to the Order
at all unless and until a change of feeling arises in the Irish Free State.
SIR CHARLES DAVIS, 30 July 1926

It is very difficult to go on leaving the Order in suspense
merely to avoid raising troublesome questions with the Free State.
SIR JOHN ANDERSON, 1 March 1927

BY THE SPRING OF 1926, it was clear that a decision on the future of the Order of St Patrick could not long be delayed. Four Knights had died between April and June 1924, followed by the Earl of Ypres in May 1925, and the Earl of Dunraven and Mountearl in June 1926. There were now sixteen Knights remaining from a statutory complement of twenty-two. Never before had there been so many vacancies at any one time, and the longer they were left unfilled, the more difficult it would be to make new appointments to an Order which many now considered to be defunct. In July 1926 it was noted in the Home Office that 'various discussions'[1] had taken place in the years 1922–5 on the future of the Order, but no substantial work had been done. King George V maintained an active interest in the Order, and wore the breast star at the wedding of his son, the Duke of York, in 1923, and it was later to be claimed by the Earl of Granard that the king was being pressed by peers resident in Northern Ireland, to fill the vacancies and save the Order from extinction, though there is no evidence for this, apart from the case of the Duke of Abercorn.

Debate began again in March 1926 with another letter from the royal household; not, on this occasion, from Lord Stamfordham, but from the more innocuous figure of the Earl of Cromer, Lord Chamberlain of the household. The Lord Chamberlain was the head of the King's domestic household but not, unlike the Private Secretary, a confidential conduit between the King and the Prime Minister. Cromer in fact did address his letter to Sir Ronald Waterhouse, private secretary to the Prime Minister. 'As the Central Chancery of the Orders of Knighthood comes within my province as Lord Chamberlain, I think it right to raise for the Prime Minister's consideration, and for whatever directions he may wish to give in the matter, the question of the Order of St Patrick ... Please understand that I have received no directions from His Majesty, and that my sole reason for raising the question is that there are now six vacancies in the Order, and that the Duke of Connaught is the only royal member of the Order.'[2] This is a curious letter, which is probably a good deal less innocent than it appears on first reading. Why should the six vacancies in the Order of St Patrick be of any concern to the Lord Chamberlain of the King's household – unless it was first of concern to the King? The Lord Chamberlain was the head of the royal household, but there was no reason to concern himself with appointments to an Order that was, at this date, within the jurisdiction of the Prime Minister. It is possible but unlikely that the senior member of the royal household would have addressed a letter to the Prime Minister's office, on his own initiative. The fact that this solitary letter is all that is known of Cromer's involvement might, by itself, indicate that the Lord Chamberlain himself was not much interested in the Order of St Patrick, and was acting at the suggestion of others. Despite Cromer's assertion to the contrary, it is not unreasonable to presume that his letter would have been written with at least the knowledge and the support of Lord Stamfordham, if not of the King.

Cromer's letter was followed three months later by one from Stamfordham to Stanley Baldwin, the Prime Minister, in which the position of King George V becomes more clear: 'The King desires me to ask you whether the time has not arrived when the question of the future of the Order of St Patrick should be considered. His Majesty contemplates conferring this Order on the Prince of Wales ... But, before doing so, the King thinks that the further question of filling up the vacancies among the 22 Knights of the Order should be gone into.'[3] Stamfordham's letter produced a flurry of meetings and memoranda in the summer of 1926, debating the possibility of reviving the Order, though the question for discussion at this stage was still largely one of filling the vacancies. Before many months had passed, the question became one, not of revival, but of reconstitution. The closer one looked at the Order of St Patrick against the background of post-partition Ireland, the clearer it became that the clock could not be turned back; the Order could not be revived by filling the vacancies, it had to be completely reconstituted.

The Prime Minister's private secretary referred Stamfordham's letter to the Home Office, with an accompanying memorandum stating that the Prime Minister could see no objection to the King's wish to appoint members of his own family to the Order, and that the Statutes should now be amended. Nobody at the time believed that the obsolete Statutes represented anything more than a minor difficulty; they had been ignored at the time of the appointment of the Duke of Abercorn in 1922, and there was no reason why they should not continue to be ignored, at least in the short term. The fundamental difficulty was, as it was always to be, the attitude of the Government of the Irish Free State, and here, as in every other debate on the Order between 1926 and 1946, the views of two government departments in the United Kingdom, the Home Office and the Dominions Office, sharply diverged. 'Mr Whiskard [Dominions Office] expressed the view that it would be very undesirable to reconstitute the Order as we owed it to the Free State to refrain from any action in the matter which would be likely to cause them embarrassment ... He thought that if it could be put to the Free State that the only sort of appointments contemplated now or in the future were such as royal princes or persons in a position more or less equivalent to that of the governors of Northern Ireland and of the Free State they might possibly acquiesce, but of this he was doubtful. Sir John Anderson [Home Office] pointed out that of course no assurance of this nature could be given, and that any ascertainment of the views of the Free State would have to be made with great care and privacy. It would be out of the question to restrict the Order to within the borders of Northern Ireland, and any change in the Statutes should be in the direction of making it an Imperial Order.'[4]

This is the first indication of what to some was a failure of nerve and to others was prudent caution; the conflict of attitudes and advice within the civil service in London, towards the Order of St Patrick and towards the Irish Free State. Generally, ministers and civil servants at the Home Office adopted a robust attitude; reconstitute the Order and overrule any objections from the Irish Free State government. This attitude was counter-balanced (and eventually outweighed) by the sensitivity and cautiousness of the new Dominions Office. This department was created in 1925 specifically to conduct relations with the independent dominions of Canada, Australia, New Zealand, South Africa – and the newest dominion, the Irish Free State. Those who pressed for the revival of the Order throughout the 1920s were doubtless irritated by the attitude of the ministers and civil servants of the Dominions Office, but that department was only following its prime directive: to maintain and enhance cordial relations between the dominions, and that included relations between the United Kingdom and the Irish Free State. If responsibility for the loss of the Order of St Patrick can be said to lie anywhere, then it lies with the civil servants of the Dominions Office.

Throughout the period 1926–46, successive officials at the Dominions Office consistently held the view that the Order of St Patrick was simply not worth a fight with the Irish government, and by continuously advising caution and delay, they effectively killed the Order. In July 1926, Sir Charles Davis, Permanent Under Secretary for Dominions Affairs, delivered a frank and blunt assessment of an Order that was effectively moribund, and which, he believed, should be allowed to lapse. 'Candidates for the Order cannot in future be drawn from the class which has hitherto supplied all its members from outside the royal family – that is to say peers of Ireland or peers closely connected with and domiciled in Ireland. If therefore new appointments are to be made to the Order at all (other than members of the royal family) they must either be limited to persons who have rendered very distinguished service to the British government in Ireland (i.e. in effect to governors of Northern Ireland), or the connection between the Order and Ireland must be dropped altogether. As for the first of these alternatives, apart from the objections which I understand you feel to making the Order a Northern Irish preserve, we should certainly see considerable objection to a proposal which in effect would mean that every Governor of Northern Ireland would become a KP – whereas Governors-General are rarely if ever given anything higher than GCMG [Knight Grand Cross of the Order of St Michael and St George]. As for the second alternative, I am bound to say that I am at a loss to understand why the Order should be revived at all if its whole tradition and *raison d'être* is to be abandoned ... I feel strongly that it would be far better that no new appointments should be made to the Order at all unless and until a change of feeling arises in the Irish Free State which would enable appointments such as were formerly made to be made once more.'[5] That opinion effectively ended the debate in summer of 1926, and established the Dominions Office case against the Order from that date onwards.

The Dominions Office might have thought that it had buried the issue in 1926, but Lord Stamfordham was nothing if not tenacious, and he raised the future of the Order again with the Prime Minister, in February 1927. Lord Monteagle of Brandon, who had been appointed a Knight of St Patrick in 1885, died on Christmas Eve 1926, and his death raised the number of vacancies to seven. The diminishing number of Knights, and his perception of government inaction, underlay the note of urgency that was now evident in Stamfordham's letters. 'Can you tell me whether anything has been done, or is being done, with regard to the Order of St Patrick? ... I am continually being asked by members of the Order whether the King is going to make any new appointments, to which I can only reply that the matter is entirely in the hands of the Prime Minister.'[6] This disingenuous comment is not unlike that in Cromer's letter of March 1926, the mark of a good private secretary whose prime duty was to protect his employer. There is no evidence that Stamfordham was being 'continually asked' by the remaining members of the Order, and no one in the Government or the civil service doubted that Lord Stamfordham spoke with the full knowledge and support of King George V.

The proof of this assertion lies in the Dominions Office response to Stamfordham's letter. Geoffrey Whiskard, an Assistant Secretary in the Dominions Office noted that, 'the King has again raised the question of the Order of St Patrick and desires to appoint the Prince of Wales at an early date ... I should have thought that it was for Sir John Anderson [Permanent Under Secretary at the Home Office] to advise the Prime Minister to attempt to dissuade the King from his intention'.[7] But the Prime Minister now felt that he could no longer oppose the King's, 'reiterated desire to confer the Order of St Patrick on the Prince of Wales and possibly also the Duke of York',[8] and asked the Home and Dominions Offices to examine the problem once again, to see whether the Order could be given some future role in the new Ireland. Stamfordham received the reply that both he and the King had wanted. 'The Prime Minister sees no reason at all why His Majesty should refrain from conferring the Order upon the Prince of Wales, or the Duke of York, should he so wish; indeed to do so would seemingly relieve the situation.'[9] Stamfordham reported that the King was 'glad' to hear this news.[10]

At the apex of the Dominions Office and the Home Office, stood two different cabinet ministers. Leopold Amery, Secretary of State for the Colonies and the Dominions, echoed the cautious views of his civil servants. The attitude of Sir William Joynson-Hicks, the Home Secretary, was bombastic and pugnacious.

Amery's comments displayed sensitivity for Irish feeling and he constantly urged restraint to avoid provoking a dispute which might cause unnecessary damage to Anglo-Irish relations. The Cumann na nGaedheal government in the Irish Free State was facing the rising popularity of the nascent republican Fianna Fáil party of Eamon de Valera, and a general election was due in 1927.

Joynson-Hicks, 'Jix' as he was known to his friends, was all for bringing the Order over to England, reviving it, and ignoring any protestations from the Free State government. He could not or would not accept for one moment that the internal affairs of the Irish Free State might affect the future of the Order of St Patrick. The civil servants of his department argued that one or two appointments of members of the royal family would publicly indicate that the Order was still alive, and therefore it might be possible to defer the question of further Irish appointments for some years, although it was obvious that sooner or later that matter would have to be faced. 'Our view here is that it is very difficult to go on leaving the Order in suspense merely to avoid raising troublesome questions with the Free State ... and I think that Mr Amery will have to make up his mind now whether he desires to press the Prime Minister to urge upon the King a further postponement of the appointments which His Majesty has it in mind to make.'[11]

Amery agreed not to raise objection to the appointment of royal princes for the time being, but felt that there should be no revision of the Statutes until it could be effected with the concurrence of the Free State government on the basis that the Order was an 'all-Ireland Order'. If not it would certainly mean the severance of all connections between the Order and the Irish Free State, and was this really desirable? The Irish Free State was only five years old, and in a sense it was still stabilising, and assessing the nature of its relationship with the United Kingdom. A time might well arrive when the Free State would find a use for such an historic honour as the Order of St Patrick, so why upset its government at this stage? Amery also demonstrated that as no revision of the Statutes had been deemed necessary before the appointment of the Duke of Abercorn in December 1922, doubts might be raised as to the validity or propriety of that appointment if they were to be revised before the next appointment. He urged a delay in appointing Irish peers, until the Free State was prepared to take an active interest in the Order; to do otherwise would either give the Order an exclusive Northern Ireland association, or it would lose any connection with Ireland at all, and either prospect was to be deplored. 'You will appreciate that what Mr Amery has in mind is the hope (not, he believes, entirely vain) that the time may come when the Order may again be, in the fullest sense, an all Ireland Order centred in Dublin; and he feels ... that anything which may tend to prevent so desirable (if remote) a consummation should be avoided.'[12]

Sir John Anderson, Permanent Under Secretary at the Home Office, and with an eye to feelings in Northern Ireland, disagreed with Amery. 'You will see that while Mr Amery no longer desires to press his objection to the appointment of royal princes, he is still strongly opposed to any revision of the Statutes. My own view remains as stated in my letter to Whiskard of the 1st instant. The Statutes of the Order are obviously out of date and to leave them in that state would seem tantamount to declaring the Order to be dormant. I do not think that public opinion, either here or in Northern Ireland, would be easily reconciled to that state of things ... I should prefer to see the appointments made without any prior intimation to the Free State Government. I certainly would deprecate telling Mr Cosgrave [President of the Executive Council of the Irish Free State] ... that no appointments outside the royal circle are in contemplation. I would also suggest that without prejudice to the question of making further appointments, the revision of the Statutes should be quietly taken in hand upon the alternative bases that the headquarters of the Order remain in Dublin or are removed to Northern Ireland so that the way may be clear of technical obstacles ... it is time we had a definite decision.'[13] Anderson's comment was typical of the general attitude to the Order within the Home Office, an attitude that was governed by a desire to protect the interests of Northern Ireland, and therefore a tendency to be indifferent to the interests of the Irish Free State. His sweeping statement, that public opinion in Britain and Northern Ireland would not be reconciled to a dormant Order of St Patrick, need not be treated seriously.

In March 1927, the King brought another individual into the debate on the future of the Order. Lord Stamfordham and the Earl of Cromer, were now followed by the Earl of Granard. Stamfordham and Cromer had directed their enquiries or wishes to the office of the Prime Minister of the United Kingdom. Granard, like Cromer and Stamfordham a member of the royal household, was also a prominent figure in the Irish Free State, and he proved to be a key figure during 1927–8, acting as an emissary from the United Kingdom government to the Irish Free State government.

Bernard Arthur William Hastings Forbes, eighth Earl of Granard, had four principal qualifications for the task he was about to undertake. Firstly, he was an Irish Roman Catholic peer, and sufficiently eminent and popular to have been considered as a possible Governor-General of the Irish Free State in 1922; secondly, he held the honorific office of Master of the Horse in the royal household; thirdly, he was President of the Senate, the upper chamber of the Oireachtas (the Irish Free State parliament), to which he had been nominated by the Irish government in 1922; and fourthly, he was a Knight of St Patrick. He had access, at a uniquely high level, both to the King and to the Irish Free State government.

On 17 March 1927, the King met Granard and asked him, with deceptive innocence and nonchalance, the size of the establishment of the Order of St Patrick, and the number of vacancies. Granard, duly replied the next day to Stamfordham, informing him that there were now eight vacancies. He also told Stamfordham of his own, quite pragmatic feelings about the future of the Order. 'Many would regret the passing of this Irish Order, but I think that the general opinion would be that it would be better if it came to an end than its character should be changed and we, in the south, would greatly deplore if this great Order was conferred only on Irishmen resident in Northern Ireland.'[14] Stamfordham's reply showed no regard for pragmatism. 'I cannot help thinking that both Healy and Cosgrave, when the time comes, will not wish to debar the south of Ireland from membership. In any case I do not think His Majesty will allow the Order to die out ... Surely in the event of the Free State refusing to permit its citizens to accept the Order, its government would never consent to St Patrick's Hall being used for St Patrick's ceremonies, or for the housing of banners? And yet, I suppose, there would be a howl if the banners were transferred to Belfast?'[15]

Granard's pragmatism again showed clearly against Stamfordham's single-minded determination. If the King was to decide to maintain the Order, Granard suggested that its statutory maximum should be lowered to the pre-1833 figure of fifteen Knights. Life had changed in Ireland and many Irish peers had left the country for good. In 1927 peers were still considered to be the natural constituency from which to make appointments to the Order of St Patrick but there were, in 1927, only thirty-three peers resident in the Irish Free State; two others being represented by their eldest sons. Time was changing for the Irish peerage; it no longer commanded the authority that it had done in viceregal days, and there was no longer a viceregal court. The burning of so many of the great houses in the years 1921–3 had sent an ominous sign to the owners of the country estates, that a new Ireland was emerging.

It was an Ireland that, at least in part, cared very little for the landlords and their houses. Many peers had felt the wind of change blowing through Ireland and had moved to Britain. To select eight Knights of St Patrick from the thirty-three peers still resident in the Irish Free State, could only devalue the Order.

Granard himself did not believe that Cosgrave personally would wish to debar the appointment of Free State citizens to the Order, 'but he feels a certain difficulty in submitting names, as he would be liable to criticism from the Republican Party, which might be undesirable just before an election'. Granard reiterated his objection to transferring the Order to the north of Ireland, and if the banners were to be removed at all, it would be better to bring them over to Britain, and then reconsider the question of a chapel. 'I am crossing to Ireland on Tuesday night, and shall see Cosgrave on Wednesday morning about various questions, but I shall not raise the question of the Patrick, unless you think it would be desirable for me to find out what he thinks privately. He is quite frank with me and tells me everything that is going on.'[16] This was what Stamfordham wanted to hear. There was now a window of opportunity for him to make direct contact, through Granard, with the Irish Free State government. Stamfordham and Granard met and talked on 22 March 1927, and Granard saw Cosgrave in Dublin on 23 March.

The result was disappointing. Granard's positive view about Cosgrave's attitude towards reconstituting the Order, proved to be mistaken. He used the argument that the King was being pressed by peers resident in the north to keep the Order alive by making new appointments,[17] but it was to no avail. Cosgrave's position was clear and unmistakable; he told Granard that any move to revive the Order would be 'most undesirable'.[18] He did agree to take soundings and to prepare a memorandum in due course, but Granard was not very hopeful. 'He [Cosgrave], like most of our people, lives in the past, and he cannot get away from the view that the Order in question was instituted by King George III to bribe peers to vote for the Union.'[19] Cosgrave was mistaken in his belief about the origins of the Order, but his opinion probably represented a substantial section of opinion within the Irish government. The Order of St Patrick was a relic of the bad days, and it was quite beyond redemption. Stamfordham thanked Granard for the report of his encounter with Cosgrave, and blithely ignored the intimation of the serious problems that might lie ahead. 'I have spoken to Downing Street', he wrote to Granard, 'and I gather the matter is really getting a move on.'[20]

Granard and Cosgrave met again on 30 March 1927, and the peer was informed of something that he probably did not really wish to hear. Cosgrave told Granard that he had asked the Attorney-General to provide a legal opinion on the status of the Order, though there was no prospect of an opinion for another three weeks or more. In fact it took fourteen months, and the report was not delivered to the cabinet until May 1928. Granard then went to lunch with Timothy Healy, the Governor-General who took the view that it would be 'a great mistake' to request an answer from the Irish government at that time. As a barrister, Healy knew well that once a legal opinion had been given by so high an official as the Attorney-General, all future Irish governments would be bound by it, and he advised that no action should be taken for another year, until after the forthcoming Irish election. Granard conveyed the news back to Stamfordham. 'Will you let me have your views? I know that Cosgrave would like to postpone a decision, but perhaps the King may wish for an immediate decision.'[21] Stamfordham was inclined to accept Healy's advice, 'though I cannot see why if the King wishes to give say two Patricks to peers in the north of Ireland His Majesty should not do so'.[22] Granard thought of a very cogent reason. 'There will be some criticism in the south, and it will look as if the Order is to become an Orange one, especially as of the existing Knights, I am the only Catholic.' If the King was minded to follow Healy's advice, Granard was quite willing to tell Cosgrave to let the matter rest for the time being.[23]

At this point it becomes clear that Stamfordham and the King were pursuing an initiative with regard to the Order of St Patrick, independent of and unknown to the Prime Minister in London. By return of post Stamfordham sent a letter to Granard: 'You must not tell Cosgrave to let the matter drop for the present, because my correspondence with you has been private and unknown to the Prime Minister, who might accuse us of "queering the pitch". Would it not be well for you to let Baldwin know of your conversation with Cosgrave, or would you prefer my doing so?'[24] At Granard's request, Stamfordham duly forwarded their correspondence to Downing Street.

On 30 May Stamfordham was formally notified that the Prime Minister had reached a decision that the future of the Order should now be seriously considered, with a view to reconstituting it in one form or another. The King was delighted. 'His Majesty is very glad to think that steps are now being taken to alter the Statutes to meeting existing relations between England, Northern Ireland, and the Free State. His Majesty cannot help hoping that, after the elections in Ireland are over, Mr Cosgrave may perhaps be prepared to look at the whole question of the Order of St Patrick in a different light to what he has done hitherto. I have written a separate letter to the Prime Minister about now conferring the Order upon the Prince of Wales.'[25] Some time during May 1927, the King and the Prime Minister may have met to discuss the future of the Order of St Patrick, and during the course of that meeting, the King would have been told that there would be no government objection to the appointment of the Prince of Wales.

The long awaited event was revealed on 3 June 1927, when the appointment of the Prince of Wales as a Knight of St Patrick was published in the Birthday Honours List. The reaction of the press was generally one of astonishment since there was now a widespread belief that the Order was to be allowed to lapse, and the *Belfast News Letter* reported that the announcement had caused, 'a good deal of speculation'.[26] The appointment of the prince, the first in nearly five years, broke an important psychological barrier. As the Order was demonstrably alive, so it would now have to be formally reconstituted. A committee was established, consisting of representatives of the Dominions Office (Sir Charles Davis and Geoffrey Whiskard), the Home Office (Sir John Anderson and Harry Boyd), the Secretary of the Central Chancery of the Orders of Knighthood (Major Harry Stockley), and the Prime Minister's principal private secretary (Sir Ronald Waterhouse). Sir John Anderson was appointed chairman.

The first meeting of the committee was held on 5 July 1927, and concluded that if the Order was to be used again, it would have to be reconstituted; nothing would be achieved by endeavouring to amend the Statutes of 1905. The situation in Ireland had changed so drastically that nothing less than new Letters Patent and a completely new set of Statutes would suffice. Anderson noted that the existing Statutes provided for a maximum of ceremonial and an excessive number of Officers; more than any other Order. So the meeting agreed that the new Statutes should be as simple as possible, and provide for a minimum of ceremonial, giving the widest possible discretion to the Sovereign in ceremonial matters such as investitures. It was also agreed that the Irish character of the Order should be retained, not as formerly by the provision of an Irish habitat and by the Officers being holders of Irish official posts, but by the appointments themselves, which should be limited as before to persons having a close connection with Ireland. The large number of Officers should be reduced to six: a Grand Master, who should be a member of the royal family appointed by the Sovereign; a Chancellor, who should be a Knight of the Order, also nominated by the Sovereign; a King of Arms, a post to be filled by Ulster as before; a Registrar, who should be the Secretary of the Central Chancery of the Orders of Knighthood; a Secretary; and a Gentleman Usher of the Black Rod. Some discussion took place as to whether a Genealogist was strictly necessary, and it was resolved to investigate the reasons for the original appointment. Some thought was also given to

The insignia of the Prince of Wales, later King Edward VIII and Duke of Windsor (KP 1927). The collar and badge are of 18 carat gold and were made by West and Son of Dublin. They bear the Dublin hallmark of 1887-8, and the reverse of the badge is engraved *West and Son Dublin College Green*. The star is unmarked though probably from the period 1870-1890, and the reverse is engraved *West and Son Dublin*.

the colour of the Usher's Rod. 'It seems rather a pity that the Usher should be "of the Black Rod" as the title can be confused with *the* Usher of the Black Rod attached to the Order of the Garter. The colours green, scarlet, blue and purple are already allocated to other Orders and yellow would hardly be suitable, so there is no great choice. There would be many objections to making any change but it seems just worth mentioning.'[27] The Home Office was instructed to prepare the new Letters Patent, and Sir Nevile Wilkinson was charged with drafting the new Statutes.

At the second meeting of the committee, on 13 July 1927, Wilkinson was present by invitation, and put forward the idealistic and unworkable proposal that the office of Chancellor of the Order should be held jointly by the Governor-General of the Irish Free State and the Governor of Northern Ireland. The idea was overruled on the grounds that objections might be raised to mentioning the Irish Free State in the Letters Patent. It would also imply equality between the Governor-General and the Governor, and as the whole matter of the conferment of honours in the dominions was shortly to be raised, the adoption of Wilkinson's suggestion might raise an awkward precedent. Wilkinson recommended that although the functions of the Genealogist were obsolete, the post should be left alone during the lifetime of Sir

Henry Burke (he died in 1930). The statutory maximum number of Knights was to remain at twenty-two, although some members of the committee favoured a reduction to the original fifteen. The decision to remain at twenty-two was influenced by the thought that any reduction might lead to the undesirable inference that the reduction was a consequence of the Irish Free State having come into being. Wilkinson objected to the appointment of the Secretary of the Central Chancery as Registrar, on the grounds that it might offend national feeling in Ireland and lead to a general supposition that the administration of the Order was to be absorbed into the Central Chancery, and that it infringed his own rights as the executive officer of the Order; the latter point was probably uppermost in his mind. Furthermore, all the records were still at his office in Dublin, and it was inconvenient to remove them. Wilkinson's arguments were fallacious; the Central Chancery was already involved through the custody of the insignia (most of which had been transferred to London in the period 1923–6 in accordance with the King's wishes), and there was no intention to reduce Ulster's rights. But, in deference to Wilkinson's feelings, it was decided that all reference to a Registrar should be omitted, and the Central Chancery should keep only a register of appointments.

By the date of the third and final meeting of the committee on 19 July 1927, Wilkinson had drafted a new set of Statutes incorporating all the decisions of the first two meetings. The Statutes were, as desired, a model of simplicity, but they were vague in key areas, reflecting only the still unclear position and purpose of the Order. Statute XXVIII, for example, ordered Ulster King of Arms within a year from the investiture of each Knight to make an escutcheon of his armorial bearings on a plate of metal, and a banner, 'which shall be disposed as shall be directed by the Sovereign'.[28] Wilkinson copied this injunction directly from Statute XXXIV of the 1905 Statutes with the exception of the last phrase. As St Patrick's Hall was no longer available for the erection of banners and plates, the matter should be left entirely in the hands of the Sovereign. Given the situation in 1927, it was probably the best that Wilkinson could do, but the wording was unsatisfactory. The Grand Master was described as 'First or Principal Knight Companion', to end the strange anomaly begun in 1783 and confirmed in 1905, of the Grand Master not being a Knight of the Order. The insignia of the Order was to be deposited in a 'place of safety' rather than 'a steel safe in the strong room'. New Knights were to be invested 'at such time and in such place' as the King should direct, and it was decided not to particularise the source from which a new Knight received his insignia. Further debate in the autumn of 1927, agreed to the abolition of the offices of Registrar, Knight Attendant, Dublin Herald, Cork Herald, Athlone Pursuivant and Cork Pursuivant, though any existing holders of the appointments would continue to hold office until death or resignation. It would have been better to leave the drafting of the new Statutes until the final position of the Order had been established, but within its limitations, Wilkinson's draft represented a workable revision of the 1905 statutes, given that the Order was now without a home and in a state of limbo.

Meanwhile, the number of Knights continued to diminish; three more Knights died during 1927: Lord Oranmore and Browne in June, the Earl of Iveagh in October, and the Earl of Mayo in December, bringing the number of vacancies to ten. With the Order now nearly half vacant, it was obviously dormant, even if it was not yet moribund. The committee had done its work of reconstitution, and the new appearance of the Order was ready to be officially unveiled. All that remained was to secure the support of the Irish Free State. The next step was to present the result of the committee's work to the Free State government, and to hope for a favourable reaction.

CHAPTER NINE

FROM ACROSS THE WATER

The response of the Irish Free State

═══

We could not think of advising His Majesty to reconstitute the Order,
and of course without our advice and concurrence
no purely British peer could be made a Knight of St Patrick.
WILLIAM COSGRAVE, 21 May 1928

T HE 1927 INTER-DEPARTMENTAL COMMITTEE decided that the first approach to the Irish government should be by means of an informal talk between the two heads of government: Stanley Baldwin of the United Kingdom and William Cosgrave of the Irish Free State. Although the reconstitution of the Order was now agreed, there was not felt to be any urgency in taking the next step of an approach to the Irish government, and there was no reason why a discussion between the two heads of government should not wait until Cosgrave next visited London; it seems that there was no thought of Baldwin going to Dublin.

By the early months of 1928 nothing had happened, because neither Cosgrave nor any of his senior ministers had visited London, but something had to be done, because the vigilant Stamfordham was still pressing for action or at least news of developments.[1] So there was no choice but to send an emissary to Cosgrave in Dublin, and, once again, the Earl of Granard was the obvious candidate. Granard visited Cosgrave on 28 March 1928, with an *aide-mémoire* drafted by the Home Office, specifically to assess the reaction of the Irish government to a reconstituted Order of St Patrick. He was briefed to make it clear that, 'the King and the British Government intend that the Order should continue in being as a live Order, preserving a distinctive Irish character, but that the Government are anxious to proceed in the manner least likely to cause embarrassment to the Free State Government'.[2]

It was a kind thought, but it came five years too late. Had the United Kingdom government made appointments to the Order immediately after the creation of the Irish Free State in December 1922, the Order might have survived. But there had been five years of cautious hesitation, with no appointments outside the ranks of the royal family. Now the work of reconstitution was complete and the Irish government was to be asked for its opinion. Initiative and opportunity had been lost in 1922, and by 1927 there was little possibility that momentum could be regained. In 1922–3, the Cosgrave administration was facing a bitter civil war, and the future of the Order of St Patrick would not have been a major subject for debate. The situation in 1928 was such that Cosgrave could only say 'no'; any other reply would have jeopardised his political future. The Irish republican movement had fractured in May 1926, with the more moderate sections of Sinn Fein leaving to form a new political party known as Fianna Fáil, under the leadership of Eamon de Valera. The new party contested the general election in June 1927, and the result was a clear expression of the extent of support for an Irish republic. Cosgrave's Cumann na nGaedheal party won forty-six seats; de Valera's Fianna Fáil won forty-four seats, and Cosgrave, who was now in a minority, only held on to power by an alliance with the twenty-two seat Labour Party. As the Dáil was so evenly divided, a further general election was inevitable, and was called in December 1927. The result produced fifty-seven seats for de Valera and sixty-seven seats for Cosgrave, and thirteen seats for Labour; republicanism was a rising political force in the Irish Free State. Had Cosgrave and his government even been neutral in their attitude towards the reconstitution of the Order of St Patrick, it would have been politically embarrassing at a difficult time for his government, to do anything other than vigorously oppose the United Kingdom government. He had already made himself a hostage to fortune by agreeing that the Irish government would pay land annuities arising from the land legislation of the nineteenth and early twentieth centuries, and also take responsibility for the payment of pensions to certain former members of the Royal Irish Constabulary which had been disbanded in 1922; the total cost of these two commitments amounted to some five million pounds. Payment of the land annuities was an especially unpopular measure, and provided ammunition for the many opponents of the Government, who charged Cosgrave and his party with being too committed to the British Commonwealth.

This was the political setting in which Cosgrave was trying to operate. In alliance with the Labour party and a group of independents, he managed to govern for a further four and a half years, but his party was in a minority, and his hold on power was not certain by any means. The Labour party had no especial regard for the monarchy, and its members in the Dáil had refused to attend the joint sessions of the Oireachtas in 1922 and 1923 to hear a 'speech from the throne' by the Governor-General. The republican Fianna Fáil party looked for every opportunity to discredit Cumann na nGaedheal, and it would have had a field day with a reconstituted Order of St Patrick. Cosgrave probably cared little about the Order or its use; but he did care about his own position as President of the Executive Council of the Irish Free State, and he was not about to provide Fianna Fáil with further ammunition to use against him, by overtly or tacitly approving Britain's continued use and control of something that had once been such a prominent feature of the viceregal court. There was never any possibility that his government would acquiesce in the reconstitution of the Order; any attempt at reconstitution would have to be met with strong opposition.

By the beginning of May 1928 Granard had had several meetings with Cosgrave and, surprisingly, and naively, he still believed the outlook to be reasonably favourable. 'I am inclined to think that he will refuse to submit names, and that he will ask also that the headquarters of the Order be moved from Dublin. I think that he will probably say that he will not question the distinction being given to domiciled Irishmen for services rendered outside the jurisdiction of the Irish Free State, and this would seem to render eligible Irish peers holding English titles by virtue of which they sit in the British Parliament, practically all the present members of the Order fulfil these conditions.'[3] Granard either hoped or believed that Cosgrave would simply decline to have anything to do with the Order, but whether this was based on fact or on wishful thinking, his cautious hope or belief was again dashed. In March 1927, Cosgrave had commissioned John Costello, the Irish Attorney-General, to produce a full report on the Order and its history. He might have been more sympathetic then, but two general elections later, his position was a good deal less sure, and a further letter to the Attorney-General in April 1928, indicated exactly where his sympathies lay, and possibly also his attitude towards the use of the President of the Senate of the Irish Free State for such a purpose. 'I enclose a letter from Senator Lord Granard. We have a treachery ... There is one satisfaction in this business that the office of Ulster King of Arms will be finally disposed of, granted that some decision will be taken. I wonder why nobody raised that question up to this. The furniture and records of that institution constitute its most important asset.'[4] 'The President [Cosgrave] is very anxious to have the exam: of the question of the K. of St. P. completed as he understands that a despatch is coming on the matter. He suggests that we should examine the question of whether we can make any claim to exclusive right of the Order on the ground that in opting out under the Treaty, the Nrthrn: Govt: surrendered its claim to the right. Whether we could claim that no action should be taken towards the creating of new K's of St. P. pending consideration of the setting up of a separate Dominion Order for the I. F. State on the lines of the Order of the Buffalo in Canada.'[5] These documents prove that Granard's latest mission was destined to fail.

Comissioned in March 1927, the Attorney-General's lengthy fourteen-page report, was finally delivered to the Irish Cabinet in May 1928, and dated 18 May. The four-teen months delay was probably due to preoccupation with the two Irish general elections of June and December 1927, or perhaps an indication to Cosgrave in March 1927 that the issue was hardly an urgent one.

The Attorney-General reviewed the history of the Order, and then discussed the award of titles of honour by the Crown in countries of the British Empire with dominion status, paying particular attention to Canada, because it seemed to him to be, 'very relevant to and vital for the determination of the problems now presented in the case of the Order of St Patrick, that the principles at present governing the grant of such honours and dignities should be ascertained with some degree of precision'. The key to the argument that he presented to the Executive Council was contained in Article 5 of the constitution of the Irish Free State: 'No title of honour in respect of any service rendered to, or in relation to, the Irish Free State may be conferred on any citizen of the Irish Free State except with the approval of, or upon the advice of, the Executive Council of the State'. The wording was quite clear; the Executive Council had absolute authority to prevent any citizen of the Irish Free State from accepting any honour, including the Order of St Patrick. Armed with this weapon, the Attorney-General then began his discourse.

'The Order of KP is, in my opinion, clearly a 'title of honour' within the meaning of Article 5 of the Constitution. That Order cannot, therefore, be conferred on a citizen of the Irish Free State without the approval or advice of the Executive Council ... If the Order is granted in respect of services rendered in or in relation to the Irish Free State ... I would go further and say that the grant to a person not a citizen of the Free State but who was domiciled or ordinarily resident in the Free State would not be proper without the same approval or advice.' He declared the position of Northern Ireland to be irrelevant since neither its government nor its Parliament had any jurisdiction over titles of honour, and, having opted out of the Irish Free State, it should be regarded for those purposes as part of Great Britain. 'In fact everything connected with the Order, its further existence or non-existence, its reconstitution and all other matters connected with it would be for the Executive Council to decide and advise ... In all matters in reference to this Order the King would be bound to act on the advice of Irish Ministers without the intervention of any British Minister.'[6]

The Attorney-General had now gone much further than the prescription of Art-icle 5 of the Irish Free State constitution. He had claimed the Order of St Patrick as the property of the Irish Free State, based on a view that the Order, as a corporate entity, was ordinarily domiciled in the Free State. His point was well made, though arguable. The chancery of the Order was in the Bedford Tower of Dublin Castle, the banners and hatchments of the Knights were in St Patrick's Hall in the same castle, and probably about half the Knights of the Order still lived in Ireland. It could therefore be claimed that the Order was a part of the administrative, architectural, historical and social fabric of the Irish Free State, and it was not unreasonable for the Government of that state to claim to possess it as part of its own. The sadness of what subsequently transpired, lies in the fact that the Free State government laid claim to the Order of St Patrick, with the sole intention of destroying it.

The Attorney-General's report was discussed at a meeting of the Irish cabinet on 21 May 1928, and formally approved. 'It was decided that the Order being now moribund, should be allowed completely to disappear. The President was authorised to inform Lord Granard accordingly.'[7] Cosgrave gave a copy of the Attorney-General's memorandum to Granard, accompanied by a formal letter and an informal hand-written note. The formal letter was for wider distribution: 'We have formed the opinion that the Order of St Patrick in its origin and in its character was a purely Irish Order and still remains so in so far as it is still in existence. Consequently we are of the opinion that everything connected with the Order ... would be for the

Executive Council to decide and advise. The setting up of the government of Northern Ireland does not, in our view, alter the position. The government of Northern Ireland has not, nor has the Parliament of Northern Ireland any jurisdiction over dignities or titles of honour, and having opted out of the Irish Free State must be regarded for those purposes as part of Great Britain. In our view they cannot lay claim to participate in a purely Irish order. They have, of course, all other Orders of the British Empire open to them. We have formed a very strong view that in all the circumstances the most appropriate manner of dealing with the Order is that it should be allowed gradually to lapse. We could not think of advising His Majesty to reconstitute the Order, and of course without our advice and concurrence no purely British peer could be made a Knight of St Patrick.'[8] Cosgrave's hand-written letter to Granard contained a clear warning of what would lie ahead if the British government pressed ahead with its plans for the Order. He quoted the example of the Canadian House of Commons that, in 1919, had set up a select committee to consider the position of honours awarded to Canadian citizens. The result was an address to the King urging him, 'to refrain hereafter from conferring any title of honour or titular distinction on any of your subjects domiciled or ordinarily residing in Canada, save such appellations as are of a professional or vocational character or which appertain to an office'.[9] 'I apprehend', wrote Cosgrave, 'a motion in the Dail to set up a committee on the same lines as that which was appointed in Canada ... I feel sure also that the report of the committee would be couched in even stronger terms than the Canadian.'[10]

Granard reported the depressing news to Baldwin, taking Cosgrave's memorandum with him. His mission had been unsuccessful, and the situation was now worse than before. The Irish government had been alerted to the proposed reconstitution of the Order, and delivered its response in the clearest terms, by way of legal opinion. The Irish government had no real interest in the Order of St Patrick, except to ensure that it withered away. There was no question of them refusing to have anything to do with the Order of St Patrick; the Order was an Irish honour; it fell within their jurisdiction, it belonged to them, and it was at their disposal.

As ever, the Home Office and the Dominions Office were divided on how to proceed. Sir William Joynson-Hicks, the Home Secretary, described the memorandum as 'delightfully impertinent',[11] and took a typically 'Jixian' view that Cosgrave should be disregarded, the Order brought over to England, reconstituted, and any further objections ignored. 'It seems to be perfectly ridiculous that a good Order of this kind should be allowed to lapse, merely because Cosgrave and Co. have an objection to it.'[12] Other counsels to Stanley Baldwin were more cautious: 'Prime Minister ... I'm not at all so sure about this. No doubt it is a "good Order"; but is it "good enough" if it is a question of a row? Or is any Order good enough for that?'[13]

Granard tried to take a balanced view between Joynson-Hicks and Amery and aroused the annoyance of the former in no uncertain terms. Joynson-Hicks was convinced that Granard supported his position. 'When I last saw you I certainly understood you to say that you thought the best thing His Majesty's government could do, having heard Mr Cosgrave's views, would be to say, quite politely but firmly that we differ from them, and proceed, under royal prerogative, to reconstruct the Order in such a way as His Majesty might decide. You and I even discussed the kind of men who should be appointed to the Order, the number of the Order, and the position of a chapel for the Order in this country. Now I understand from my colleague, Amery, that you have told him exactly the opposite, and that you do not think any alterations should be made, but that the Order should be simply allowed to die out, with the exception of any royal appointments ... I should be glad if you could let me have a note as to what your real views are.'[14] On the same day, Joynson-Hicks wrote to Baldwin, urging that, 'something should be done without delay to controvert the line taken by Mr Cosgrave ... Unless we now make our position clear he will have some reason to assume that his views are accepted'.[15]

Granard replied that he saw no divergence. During their original discussion, he had proceeded along the line that the Order of St Patrick would be bestowed on the King's personal initiative, as in the case of the Royal Victorian Order, and on this ground, he could see no difficulty. But it was his understanding that the British government had receded from this position, and that appointments to the Order of St Patrick would be made as hitherto, by the King, but only on the recommendation of the United Kingdom government. 'I venture to think that great exception would be taken to such action in the dominions; and it would certainly place H.M.'s ministers in Ireland in a very difficult position. Let us assume that an appointment is made in this way. What answer can the Irish minister give when he is asked how the appointment has been made, and has to reply that it had been made on the advice of H.M.'s English ministers. The next question would be: Have the English ministers any right to advise the King on questions affecting persons domiciled within the area of jurisdiction of the Irish Free State, and is not such action at variance with the treaty?'[16] It was not only at variance with the terms of the 1922 treaty; it was also at variance with the spirit and the letter of the 1926 Imperial Conference. The position of the Irish Free State government had now been clearly stated: 'we could not think of advising His Majesty to reconstitute the Order'. The delegates to the 1926 conference had agreed that it would not be in accordance with constitutional practice for advice to be tendered to the King by the Government of the United Kingdom, in any matter appertaining to a dominion, against the views of the Government of that dominion. However much the King personally might want to keep the Order of St Patrick alive, he would be seen to be acting on the advice of his United Kingdom ministers against the advice of his Irish Free State ministers.

Granard was Irish, and his sensitivity to the position of the Irish Free State government was shared by Leopold Amery, who also took a cautious view: 'In view of the action we have already taken, it may be impossible to avoid proceeding to the extent indicated: if so, I am prepared to acquiesce, provided we go very slow. But personally, I should prefer the Order to remain for the time being with its Statutes unchanged, new appointments being restricted to the royal family, and, like appointments to the Victorian Order, being made by His Majesty without ministerial advice. If this were adopted, there is, in my opinion, just a chance that the Free State might come in later.'[17] The Government decided to adopt Amery's view, and Granard was then asked to inform Cosgrave that his views were not shared by the British government.

The further sequence of events then becomes unclear. Granard, who frequently travelled between London and Dublin, conveyed the British government's position informally to Cosgrave sometime in August 1928. He was supplied with a letter from the Prime Minister's office, dated 3 August, which stated that the views expressed in Cosgrave's letter were, 'in several of their main respects not shared by His Majesty's government in the Great Britain'.[18] Granard showed the letter to Cosgrave, who subsequently returned to Granard the original of the letter, without, at that point, making any comment.[19] But the comment was not long in coming, and took the form of a flanking action. On 1 September the Irish cabinet decided that the time had come to take control of the Office of Arms, as from 1 October, as a way of signalling their grave displeasure at the impending reconstitution of the Order. Seizing the Office of the Arms would preclude its use as the Chancery of the Order, and finally end the irritating presence of Crown officials paid by the United Kingdom Treasury, and occupying handsome offices in the Upper Castle Yard of Dublin Castle.

There was a short delay, and it was not until 10 November 1928 that the Irish Minister for External Affairs addressed a letter to the Dominions Secretary, announcing his government's intention of assuming control of the Office of Arms, 'at the earliest possible date ... They feel sure that His Majesty's government in Great Britain will assist them in expediting the matter and will issue any instructions that may be necessary for the formal transfer of the office.'[20] Opinion in the Dominions Office was certain that the Irish government had raised the status of the Office of Arms only because of the British government's declared position on the future of the Order of St Patrick.[21] It was a tit-for-tat reaction, and it worked. At first, the letter made no difference to the plan to reconstitute the Order. Joynson-Hicks directed the Clerk of the Crown in Chancery to prepare a warrant for the King's signature, causing Letters Patent to be passed under the Great Seal for reconstituting the Order, and this was certainly under way by 7 December 1928. But the Letters Patent, and the Statutes which had been drafted by Nevile Wilkinson in July 1927, were not published, and the Order was not reconstituted.

Something happened in early December 1928 to slow if not halt the process of reconstituting the Order of St Patrick. There is no evidence of what it might have been, except that on or about 3 December, William Joynson-Hicks and Leopold Amery met in the House of Commons. Amery asked that the documents should not be submitted to the King until after the settlement of a question affecting civil servants' pay, which was then under discussion with the Free State government. Joynson-Hicks agreed and Amery was relieved. 'I was very glad to hear from you in the House the other day that you propose to go slow as regards the Order of St Patrick ... It will be essential for some further explanation to be given to the Free State government as to our intentions, and the present moment, in view of the questions just now outstanding between our two governments, would be particularly inopportune for such an explanation.'[22] The only conclusions to be drawn from this letter are either that Joynson-Hicks had come to his senses of his own accord, or else that Amery had persuaded him to do so.

In December 1928 the Baldwin government decided not to proceed with reconstituting the Order, to avoid provoking a constitutional controversy with the Irish Free State Government on a matter closely affecting the prerogatives of the Crown, at a time when there were other areas of dispute between the United Kingdom and the Irish Free State.[23] King George V was the Sovereign of both kingdoms, and to exercise his power as the fount of honour in a way that was specifically objectionable to the Irish Free State government, was a grave risk. With substantial opposition to the monarchy in the Irish Free State, the reconstitution of the Order of St Patrick could only jeopardise the position of the King, if he were seen to be acting on the advice of his British ministers against the advice of his Irish ministers.

The future of the Order of St Patrick was put on hold in December 1928 and not resumed until September 1929; not only because of disputes between London and Dublin on other issues, but also because of the serious illness of the King, and then the approach of the general election in June 1929. The King developed acute septicaemia in November 1928, and was not able fully to resume his duties until September 1929. The result of the election was the defeat of the Conservative government of Stanley Baldwin, and its replacement by a Labour government headed by Ramsay MacDonald.

The status of the Office of Arms was still under consideration by the Irish government, and John Costello, the Irish Attorney-General who had reported on the Order of St Patrick in May 1928, produced a report on the Office of Arms in February 1929, and the report was circulated to members of the cabinet on 12 April. He found it demeaning, he wrote, that in any matter relating to the Office of Arms, the Irish government was obliged to use the good offices of the British government: 'That is contrary to our position and ought not to be tolerated ... I am clearly of the opinion that the Office of Arms ought to be taken over by the Irish government.'[24] It was not until August 1929, that the new Dominions Secretary, Lord Passfield, issued a formal reply to the Irish Minister for External Affairs on the subject of the future of Ulster King of Arms and his office in Dublin Castle. He stated that Ulster King of Arms was, like Garter King of Arms in London and Lyon King of Arms in Scotland, a servant of the Crown, and exercised his functions by Royal Warrant. In this sense, he was not under the control of the United Kingdom government and he could not therefore be 'transferred' to the Government of any other Dominion. The United Kingdom government had no objection to the Free State authorities being responsible for paying the salaries of the Office staff. 'It would not appear, however, that this would give to His Majesty's Government in the Irish Free State any greater control over Ulster that is at present or has in the past been exercised by His Majesty's Government in the United Kingdom.'[25] The despatch was passed to the Irish Minister of Finance who described it as an, 'official concoction which he [the Dominions Secretary] probably signed without reading. Its bamboozling tone is very objectionable'.[26] The policy of the Irish government was again delivered to the British government on 29 January 1930: 'The Office (of Arms) performs purely Irish functions and the performance of some of these functions involves the exercise of the Royal Prerogative. The performance of all such functions and the exercise, whenever necessary, of the Royal Prerogative in connection therewith are all matters which must be performed and exercised respectively under the direction and control of the Executive Council'.[27] This was followed by yet another despatch from another new Dominions Secretary, Mr J. H. Thomas, in July 1930: 'The functions of Ulster extend to the whole of Ireland and are not limited to the area of the Irish Free State. It would seem constitutionally proper that, in the exercise of Ulster's jurisdiction in relating to persons belonging to, and matters arising in Northern Ireland, any ministerial action should be taken by ministers in the United Kingdom and not by ministers in the Irish Free State'.[28] On that note, the matter was allowed to rest, the Dominions Office advising that it should not be raised again until Sir Nevile Wilkinson either retired or died. If the Irish Free State government wished to proceed further then the United Kingdom government would propose a conference between officials of the two governments. The matter was discussed at a meeting of the Irish cabinet on 13 June 1931, and was referred to a sub-committee consisting of the President of the Executive Council, the Vice-President, and the Attorney-General. Whether this relatively informal sub-committee ever met is doubtful; if it did, then it adopted a cautious policy of no action, because no reply had been sent to the United Kingdom government before the defeat of Cosgrave's government at the general election in March 1932, nor even by January 1935 as Irish officials subsequently noted.

Parley and agreement there seems to have been between the two governments on some issues, but there still remained one individual who was determined on action. The King was continuing to maintain an interest in developments, and to apply gentle pressure. 'It is clear from the correspondence on our files and from records of interviews with Lord Stamfordham that the King has maintained an interest in the proposed reconstitution of the Order and was impatient of the delay in arriving at a solution of the problems involved ... As the Prime Minister was unable to deal with the matter himself, he requested the Home Secretary to approach His Majesty on the subject. Sir William Joynson-Hicks ... dictated a memorandum reporting the gist of his conversation with His Majesty. From this memorandum it appears that His Majesty stated definitely that he did not propose that the Order should be allowed to die out; in His Majesty's view, the Order of St Patrick was an Order in his hands, and if the Free State did not desire to have any of their citizens appointed to the Order, His Majesty did not propose to appoint them to the Order. At that interview His Majesty approved the Home Secretary's proposal to proceed forthwith with the reconstitution of the Order.'[29] On 22 November 1928, Lord Stamfordham had met Harry Boyd, the Ceremonial Secretary at the Home Office, and asked for news of progress. 'He said that for more than 12 months he had inquired at intervals about the Order but that nothing ever seemed to happen. He said that the King had approved the action which S[ecretary]. of S[tate]. was taking and it was quite expected that H[ome] O[ffice] would proceed with the formal steps at once.'[30] Of course many things were happening and continued to happen, but it seems that nobody had thought to keep the King and Lord Stamfordham informed.

In August 1929, once again, the question of what to do with the Order of St Patrick was raised by Lord Stamfordham with the Prime Minister's private secretary. Ramsay MacDonald, the new Prime Minister, was due to visit the King at Balmoral, and was warned by C. P. Duff, his private secretary, that the King would wish to discuss the Order with him. 'I am afraid that the subject of ... the reconstitution of the Order of St Patrick will be raised ... I cannot feel that any good purpose could possibly be served by trying to reconstitute this Order at the present time.'[31] In the same month, J. H. Thomas, Lord Privy Seal and Minister of Employment, also visited Balmoral, only to find the King raising the Order of St Patrick with him during the course of their discussions.

Throughout the debates of 1926–30, the continued influence of King George V can be detected, but it was not until September 1930 that Lord Stamfordham gave the fullest exposition of the King's attitude towards the Order and the Irish Free State memorandum of May 1928. In a letter to C. P. Duff, Stamfordham indignantly rebuked the claim of the Cosgrave government to control the Order. 'Have the authorities at the D[ominions] O[ffice] read the Statutes of the Order of St Patrick – I have; and cannot find one word to justify Cosgrave's assumption that the Government of I[rish] F[ree] S[tate] have anything whatever to do with the Order except of course that it could not be conferred by the King on any citizen of the I. F. S. except with the sanction of that Government. The King can give it to anyone in Northern Ireland on the advice of the PM.'[32] Ten days later he wrote a longer letter to Duff in which he revealed that the King had taken 'the gravest exception' to the claim that the future of the Order was entirely a matter for the Irish Free State government to determine; nor could he agree with the view of the United Kingdom government that the Irish Free State could make out a strong claim for regarding the Order, 'as intimately and essentially within their own domain'. 'The King read the 2nd paragraph of Mr Cosgrave's minute with some astonishment for it practically declines to recognise Northern Ireland as being Irish ... As to the 3rd paragraph, the King is at a loss to understand what justification Mr Cosgrave has for concluding with the following: "And of course without our advice and concurrence no purely British Peer could be made a Knight of St Patrick" ... His Majesty does not admit that the conferring of the Order of St Patrick by the Sovereign upon anyone on the recommendation of the British Prime Minister is a "matter for appertaining to the Irish Free State"; unless the King proposed to grant the Order to a citizen of that State. This His Majesty would never contemplate, as the Government of the Irish Free State have passed resolutions debarring the acceptance of honours by its citizens ... The King, however, maintains that, with the concurrence of his Prime Minister, the Sovereign can confer the Order upon anyone he may select in Great Britain, Northern Ireland, or in any part of the Dominions, subject to the approval of their respective Prime Ministers.'[33] There was no escaping the fact that the King accorded the future of the Order of St Patrick a high priority, and something would have to be done to conclude the debate one way or another, if only to satisfy the King. 'It is quite clear that the King wishes to proceed in the matter, or else to be fully satisfied as to the reason why further action is undesirable ... In view of the King's interest in the matter, which Stamfordham will certainly not allow him to forget, will you treat this question as one of some urgency.'[34]

Towards the end of September 1930, a conference was held between representatives of the Home Office and the Dominions Office, and the meeting concluded in complete agreement. The British government could not accept the Irish government memorandum of May 1928; the Order was not an exclusively Irish Free State institution, although it was distinctively Irish and should remain so. All that remained was to issue the abortive Letters Patent of December 1928, and to publish revised Statutes. Both departments agreed that it would be a mistake to publish anything while the Imperial Conference was meeting in London (1 October to

14 November 1930). Cosgrave would be present at the conference, and any announcement might cause him public embarrassment. When the conference was concluded, and the delegates had departed, work could begin on publicising the reconstituted Order of St Patrick. C. P. Duff took the line that it would hardly be prudent to promise the King that action would be taken as soon as the Imperial Conference was concluded in case something else then occurred which would still make it inopportune to revive the Order. 'The answer might be to the effect that you agree with the King in disagreeing with Mr Cosgrave's view of the situation; that, at the same time, it would hardly be possible to proceed to reconstitute the Order without letting Mr Cosgrave know; that it would not be opportune in the middle of the Imperial Conference to announce this decision, against which we know Mr Cosgrave will protest.'[35]

The Imperial Conference began its sessions on 1 October 1930. Two days later, MacDonald addressed a letter to Lord Stamfordham in which he outlined his decision to accept the recommendations of the departmental meeting, but nevertheless still to be cautious. 'The Prime Minister feels that it would hardly be possible to proceed with the reconstitution of the Order without at least acquainting Mr Cosgrave of the intention to do so. Having regard to the views which the latter expressed in his unofficial minute, this intimation is not likely to be by any means agreeable to him: and, as there are already so many delicate and even controversial matters at issue in the course of the deliberations of the Imperial Conference, it would hardly be politic, in the Prime Minister's view, to throw a fresh apple of discord into the general arena at this moment. So soon, however, as the Imperial Conference is over and the path cleared of the thorny topics now outstanding, the Prime Minister would propose, if the considerations set out commend themselves to the King, that the Government should consider at once whether the time is not ripe for submitting to His Majesty that the steps necessary for the reconstitution of the Order should be taken forthwith.'[36]

Everything was now in place for a public announcement that new life was to be breathed into the dormant Order of St Patrick, but no announcement was made, and the sequence of events is unclear. Was Cosgrave informed of the proposal to reconstitute the Order? Were the 'thorny topics now outstanding' resolved? Why was nothing further done? Why were all the carefully laid plans of 1926–30 not implemented 'forthwith' after 14 November 1930? The answer is once again because of the inherent caution of the Dominions Office and its Secretary of State, J. H. Thomas. 'Having regard to the present situation *vis-à-vis* the Irish Free State Government on constitutional questions, it is practically certain that an intimation to Mr Cosgrave of the nature contemplated would arouse a controversy and, as the point at issue is the right of Irish Free State Ministers to advise the King on this matter, the whole question of advice to the King on Dominion matters would almost inevitably be raised ... Mr Thomas feels that it would be most unwise to precipitate a discussion, the outcome of which cannot be foreseen but which might well have most far-reaching and unfortunate consequences.'[37]

Duff reinforced the views of the Dominions Office with a piece of sound advice to his Prime Minister. 'I attach a letter from the Dominions Office giving their views on the question of reviving the Order of St Patrick. This, in effect, postpones the question till the Greek Kalends [a obsolete term meaning 'never']. You know the pressure which there is from the Palace for the revival of the Order. True, it is a good Order, but is any Order good *enough* for all the trouble this will cause?'[38] Duff's point was well made, but MacDonald rejected it. 'Northern Ireland still remains and has an immediate interest in the Order. The Prime Minister feels that all that would have to be done would be to inform Mr Cosgrave of the fact that the Order is to be reconstituted, telling him that of course no Irish Free State persons would be appointed to it without his prior consent; and that Mr Cosgrave cannot take any legitimate exception to that.'[39] So the argument was thrown back to the Dominions

Office who tossed it back to Duff with an equally valid argument. 'Mr Thomas asks me to say ... that he still feels that the present moment would be most inopportune for taking up this matter with the Irish Free State. He agrees that Mr Cosgrave is in error in holding that the interest of Northern Ireland can be ignored, but he is strongly of the opinion that it would be an even greater error, if we, on this side, were to ignore the very special interest of the Irish Free State.'[40] Duff duly reported back to MacDonald. 'There is no doubt that to tell Mr Cosgrave that we intend to revive this Order ... would be regarded by him as a slap in the face.'[41] Shortly afterwards MacDonald and Thomas met to discuss the Order, and agreed not to take the matter any further. As the Dominions Office had successfully halted the reconstitution of the Order in December 1928, so it did so again in December 1930.

Throughout the debates in this period, one underlying theme surfaced from time to time – the essential Irishness of the Order of St Patrick – and it was this consideration that effectively finished the Order. The Order was the national honour of Ireland, and its relationship was to the whole of Ireland. While there are references in some contemporary documents to the Order being reconstituted as an imperial Order, it would in practice have been restricted mostly to residents of Northern Ireland. It is possible that there was still a lingering hope on the part of the Dominions Office and others that the Irish Free State Government might, one day, be prepared to submit nominations, but there was no immediate prospect of that happening. On 19 March 1927, before any serious plans had been laid, Lord Granard had indicated his own feelings on the Irishness of the Order. 'I think that the general opinion would be that it would be better if it came to an end than its character should be changed and we, in the south, would greatly deplore if this great Order was conferred only on Irishmen resident in Northern Ireland.'[42] A memorandum of 1 September 1930 confirmed that such an opinion was held by others: 'The King could reconstitute the Order without the advice of any Ministers and appoint to it similarly, but the Free State reaction to this would be to prohibit the taking of any such honour by any of their citizens; and if the Order was thus confined to persons resident outside the Free State, it would change so much in character as practically to have come to an end'.[43]

Sections of opinion in government and civil service held the hope that the Irish Free State might come to regard the Order as part of its heritage, and agree to preserve it from oblivion. On this premise, it was far better to allow a period of continued dormancy, with the exception of the appointment of royal princes, and to re-examine the matter at a more propitious time. As time passed by, this prospect receded into the far distance. At the general election on 9 March 1932, the Cumann na nGaedheal party of William Cosgrave was defeated by the Fianna Fáil party led by Eamon de Valera. De Valera was, to his supporters, the living embodiment of Irish nationalism, and was intent on moving the Irish Free State towards republican status, and there was never the slightest chance that he would co-operate with the United Kingdom government over the future of the Order. Shortly after the Irish general election, Ramsay MacDonald again raised the question of the Order with J. H. Thomas. 'The Prime Minister now asks whether present circumstances do not make it advisable to look into this matter afresh so that if the time has come or is coming when we need not pay so much deference to Free State susceptibilities, we may be ready to proceed without further delay.'[44] The only further reference is to a proposal by Thomas for a meeting with MacDonald to discuss the Order once again. It is unlikely that Thomas, desirous of not offending the relatively moderate Cosgrave, would have adopted a different attitude towards his militant and hardline successor Eamon de Valera. A 1938 memorandum explicitly confirmed the agreement that must have been reached by MacDonald and Thomas in April 1932. 'It was felt that as the whole basis of the Order was its relation to Ireland it was undesirable that it should be allowed to become an Order solely connected with Northern Ireland. In the circumstances the question of reconstituting the Order has not been pressed. It seems reasonably clear that Mr de Valera's attitude in this matter would be the same as that of Mr Cosgrave.'[45]

After 1932 there were two further appointments to the Order of St Patrick, and one last serious debate about reconstituting the Order, but time was running out. The strenuous efforts of 1927–30 were not repeated until 1942–3 and, by that time, the two principal protagonists of the Order – King George V and Lord Stamfordham – were dead. Stamfordham died in March 1931, and when Sir Nevile Wilkinson heard the news, he was on tour in Argentina, exhibiting Titania's Palace, and wrote glumly to Sadleir in Dublin: 'I am very sorry to see Stamfordham's death, he was our most valuable champion, and I fear his successor may be a broken reed as far as we are concerned'.[46] Wilkinson's gloomy prognostication about Clive Wigram was not far wide of the mark. Whereas Stamfordham was a deeply entrenched conservative, Wigram was a reformer, with an eye to disarming republicanism by publicising the monarchy as an active, hard-working and contemporary institution. He would not have thought the Order of St Patrick worth a fight with the Irish government.

Less than five years later, Stamfordham was followed to the grave by King George V, in January 1936. In a way, that seemed to set the seal on the fate of the Order. The King had personally been invested as a Knight of St Patrick in Dublin Castle in 1897; he had attended the investiture of the Earl of Mayo in 1905, and he had invested two Knights in 1911, amid the splendour of St Patrick's Hall, Dublin Castle, and at Buckingham Palace, the four Knights appointed from 1917 to 1922. The new King, Edward VIII, had never been to Dublin, and therefore probably had little inclination to embrace a cause that was so dear to his father. The death of the King removed a powerful weapon from the armoury of those who desired to keep the Order of St Patrick alive.

As the 1930s lengthened and turned into the 1940s, the Order of St Patrick fell into a peaceful sleep. By 1938 the clouds of war were beginning to darken the horizon, and it was at the height of that war that a final attempt was made to awaken the sleeping Order.

The star of the Duke of Gloucester.
The reverse bears elements of a London hallmark
although there is no date letter.

CHAPTER TEN

THE LAST POST AT DUBLIN CASTLE

The passing of the Office of Arms

=====

It may be mentioned . . . that the Order continues to exist but with diminishing numbers and will tend to disappear as new members cannot be appointed except on the advice of the Executive Council of Saorstat Eireann, which advice will not be given.
Irish government memorandum, December 1936

THE POSITION OF ULSTER KING OF ARMS and the Office of Arms was the subject of periodic discussion between the London and Dublin governments in the years 1922–43. Sir Nevile Wilkinson himself believed, on the basis of no evidence whatever, that the Irish Free State government was anxious that his office should continue, hoping and believing that he would be able to exercise his duties in Dublin without protest, and with growing popular approval. The question mark hanging over Ulster was the same that hung over the Order of St Patrick of which he was the executive officer, and while there was any possibility of the Order being maintained, even in a modified form, nothing should be done to jeopardise the continued existence of the office of Ulster King of Arms. The Treasury was acutely conscious of the cost of maintaining the Office, and pointed to the substantially diminished duties of Ulster King of Arms. There was no longer any viceregal ceremony for Ulster to supervise, nor any connected with the Order, and there was a comparatively heavy deficit on the cost of the Office. In 1920–1 the receipts totalled £461, and the expenditure £1,998. In 1923–4 the expenditure fell to £1,610, and the receipts increased to £945, but the Treasury proposed that Ulster's salary should be reduced from the high figure of £600, to about £300–400. The Colonial Office agreed that for work done by Wilkinson himself, £600 was an over payment, but in view of their decision to maintain the Office, they recommended that nothing further should be done until Wilkinson's resignation or death. The Office of Arms was the only department left which served the whole of Ireland, and from this aspect alone its retention was desirable.

Life in the Office of Arms was not much disturbed by the change of government in 1922, although it was certainly more difficult for a period. The staff, under the jurisdiction of the diligent Thomas Sadleir, went about their business as usual, paid by the Treasury in London, though occupying premises in Dublin Castle, which now belonged to the government of the Irish Free State. Wilkinson left all routine matters of heraldry and genealogy to his deputies, George Burtchaell (until his death in 1921) and Thomas Sadleir (from 1921), preferring to spend most of his time at his London home at 6 Duchess Street, off Portland Place, much to the annoyance of the Treasury. During his tenure of the office of Ulster King of Arms, Wilkinson did most of his work in London, and there is evidence that he expressly stipulated that he should be allowed to do this before accepting the appointment in 1908.[1] He did not own a house in Dublin, and when there on business, he seems to have used a room at the Kildare Street Club. In September 1911 Wilkinson's predecessor, Sir Arthur Vicars, wrote to his friend James Fuller, official architect to the Church of Ireland. 'I know nothing about my old Office except that Wilkinson is never there & Burtchaell runs the whole show & has no time for anything.'[2]

During the difficult and violent months that preceded and succeeded the partition of Ireland in December 1922, Wilkinson did not visit Dublin at all. At least from April 1922 until July 1923 he remained mostly in London, pleading ill-health to the extent of having to go to Bath to 'take the waters'. One of Wilkinson's complaints during the period was that the Kildare Street Club had been occupied by 'irregulars' who had taken all his clothes.[3] During his absences, the Office of Arms continued under the supervision of his deputy, Thomas Sadleir, a hard-working and conscientious man who had succeeded George Burtchaell as Deputy Ulster, though not as Athlone Pursuivant on the latter's death in 1921. Thomas Sadleir was undoubtedly underpaid for his considerable workload. Sir Nevile received a salary of £600 p.a., and a clerical assistance allowance of £590 p.a. The latter sum was distributed between three officials: Thomas Sadleir received £300 p.a. as Registrar and Deputy Ulster; £170 p.a. went to a herald painter; and the sole secretary/typist received £120 p.a.

The Treasury tried to get rid of Wilkinson in 1925, but were dissuaded from doing so by the joint opinion of the Home Office and the Dominions Office that his Office, small though it was, did have the usefulness of being an all-Ireland institution; this was the only justification for retaining the Office. Of Wilkinson himself, there was nothing positive to be said, particularly with regard to his involvement in his own Office. Nobody in the civil service at the time thought very highly of him, and he was regarded as someone who took a salary for doing nothing. He seems to have thought of his office as little more than a ceremonial sinecure, as in many ways it was after 1922, except that there were no longer any ceremonies to supervise. He had, 'attempted to have his duties performed by deputy when he took up his residence in London ... it became necessary to summon Ulster to Dublin and insist on his spending a certain amount of time in Dublin each year ... I have some reason for thinking that the present Ulster avails himself of his social connections with a view to bringing influence to bear on the Earl Marshal ... and possibly also in higher quarters ... Sir Nevile Wilkinson might be persuaded to resign. A very good case could be made out for demanding his resignation, as he now has very little to do, and his salary is clearly excessive for the amount of time he is required to spend in the discharge of his duties. There can be no real urgency in regard to this matter, and it would be very much better to leave things as they are until a vacancy in the Office of Ulster occurs in the natural course of events.'[4]

Whatever his attitude to the office of Ulster King of Arms, and the opinions held of him, Major Sir Nevile Rodwell Wilkinson had an impressive appearance. Elizabeth, Countess of Fingall remembered him as, 'a superb figure with his height and extraordinary good looks ... and a tireless worker for the better treatment of children'.[5] One of his two daughters was mentally handicapped, and it may have been her disability that caused Wilkinson to spend fifteen years (1907–22) constructing the extraordinary sixteen-room model house called 'Titania's Palace', opened by Queen Mary in 1923. He took it abroad on several occasions in the 1920s and 1930s – the United States of America, Canada, Newfoundland, the Netherlands, Australia, New Zealand, Chile and Argentina (on that occasion taking care to learn Spanish) – exhibiting it to raise funds for disabled children. 'By 1926 it had raised £80,000 ... transported in its purpose-built, padded packing cases to 160 cities all over the world, admired by c.1,700,000 people.'[6] Wilkinson's surviving letters, written while away on tour, to Sadleir, display an almost childlike pleasure for the warm reception that the palace always received on its overseas tours; but his letters rarely offered any thanks to Sadleir for maintaining the daily running of the Office of Arms in Dublin.

Before each of his overseas tours, Wilkinson wrote punctiliously to the King, to the Governor-General of the Irish Free State, and to the Governor of Northern Ireland, asking for permission to go on leave of absence. These Titania's Palace tours were often quite lengthy and he was away from the United Kingdom for months at a time. In October 1925, he asked for 12–15 months leave, beginning in December 1926, to go to the United States. He spent four months in Argentina in 1931, and four months in Australia in 1934, and his letters to Sadleir are full of delight at the crowds of people who queued to see Titania's Palace. He was at his happiest in touring the world with his toy palace and seeing the pleasure that it gave to so many children. He loved living and working in the fantasy world of fairyland, which was so different from harsh realities of post-1922 Dublin. 'From 1922, his imaginative fantasy extended into make-believe tales for Yvette, an imaginary young critic and companion who shared his hopes, fears and dreams',[7] and they were published under the titles of *Yvette in Italy, Yvette in Venice, Yvette in Switzerland*, etc. In his entry in *Who's Who*, he gave his sole recreation as 'tinycraft', and Titania's Palace represented the apotheosis of his considerable artistic talent in decorative minutiae. This was the area in which he excelled, and his diminished ceremonial role in post-viceregal Ireland enabled him to indulge in this great passion for creating beauty in miniature.

Wilkinson may have been in his element in touring the world with his fairyland palace, but there were those who were less than impressed by his demonstrable lack of interest and involvement in the work of the Office of Arms. When he visited the United States in 1926, the Home Office floated the possibility that he might take unpaid leave. 'It is probable that you will not be able to cancel his appointment, which is for life by Letters Patent under the Great Seal of Ireland. There being no Great Seal now, I am not aware of any means short of an Act of Parliament by which the Patent could be revoked. It will therefore, be necessary for you to fall back on the special leave arrangement, with or without pay, and you will discover that Wilkinson has influential friends who will probably bring pressure to bear on you with a view to continuing his salary.'[8] Of Thomas Sadleir himself, the Home Office took a better view: 'Treat Sadleir as liberally as possible. He is an excellent little fellow who has always been underpaid, and it strikes me that the allowance of £100 a year is rather mean, especially if it is to be deducted from Wilkinson's pay. I think Sadleir ought to get at least £500 inclusive during Wilkinson's absence'.[9]

The Office of Arms functioned with a small staff that was below what was required to maintain efficiency, and the active and regular presence of Wilkinson would have made a considerable difference. His frequent and prolonged absences did not justify his salary, and staff who worked at the Office at the time, recalled that, even when in Dublin, he would take 'gentlemanly' week-ends off, sometimes Thursday evenings to Tuesday mornings. When the practical Edward MacLysaght took over the Office as Chief Genealogical Officer in 1943, he was appalled at the state of arrears, and Sadleir confessed that he had been too worried to ask for extra staff, in case the Office was closed down.

Although there were two Heralds attached to the Order of St Patrick: Major Guillamore O'Grady (Dublin Herald) and Captain Richard Alexander Lyonel Keith (Cork Herald), they had no duties or responsibilities within the Office of Arms at all, and their functions were entirely ceremonial. They were present at formal investitures of the Order, in attendance on Ulster King of Arms, and they made their appearance at other viceregal ceremonies, but no heraldic or genealogical work or knowledge was required of them. Major O'Grady, the son of a surgeon, lived in Dublin until his death in 1952, and those who worked in the Office of Arms before the Second World War had slight memories of him. A graduate of Trinity College, Dublin, and auditor of the college historical society, he was called to the Bar in 1903 and held a commission in the South of Ireland Yeomanry. On his appointment in 1908, he was described as, 'a gentleman of means, and a landowner in Co. Clare ... He takes an interest in heraldic and genealogical studies, and has completed indexes to marriage licence bonds of several Irish counties'.[10]

Captain Keith, known as 'Leo' to his friends, held a commission in the 3rd Battalion, Seaforth Highlanders, and was an aide-de-camp to the Countess of Aberdeen at the time of his appointment as Cork Herald 1910. He married in 1908, as her second husband, Mrs Olga Pim of Brennanstown House, Co. Dublin. Seriously injured in

1914 in the early months of the First World War, he seems to have spent the remainder of his life in England, retaining his nominal office until 1952, three years before his death. Unlike Ulster King of Arms and Dublin Herald, he was not present at the coronation of King George VI in 1937.

On 25 May 1920 Captain Gerald Burgoyne was appointed Deputy Cork Herald. On 3 June 1920 a writ was prepared for the King's signature by Wilkinson, allowing the appointment of a Junior Pursuivant to the Order, giving effect to the provisions of the 1905 statutes, and reinstating yet another office abolished by the Royal Warrant of 1871. No appointment of a Junior Pursuivant seems to have been made, but in 1921 Burgoyne was formally given the title of Cork Pursuivant, an office created by the terms of a revision of Statute XXIV, dated 1 March 1921. This unique appointment apparently arose because of the injuries sustained by Leo Keith in the First World War. The new Cork Pursuivant was, 'to perform such duties as the present Cork Herald, by reason of disabilities incurred in His Majesty's service, is unable to perform'.[11]

Burgoyne was typical of the type of person used to fill decorative sinecures of the time. A tall handsome moustachioed man, he was called to the Bar at Middle Temple, but never practised, and served as a regular in 3rd Dragoon Guards 1896–1910 and 4th Royal Irish Rifles 1910–20. For a while he had his own room in the Office of Arms, and may have undertaken a very limited amount of work in the Office. But he seems to have had virtually no heraldic knowledge, and the little work that he did was not enough to satisfy the conscientious Sadleir. Burgoyne married, for the second time, in 1922. Thereafter he left Ireland and lived mostly in Somerset. The volume of letters from Sadleir to Wilkinson in the period April 1922 to July 1923 indicates Sadleir's sometimes barely concealed irritation with Burgoyne's lack of commitment to what Sadleir perceived to be his duties. On 3 April 1922 Sadleir reported that, 'Burgoyne has returned from his rambles in Berkshire and Westmeath'.[12] In 19 May 1922, 'Major Burgoyne returned to-day; he expects to be over about three weeks'.[13] On 14 June Burgoyne, 'induced a man to apply for a Grant of a Badge, which is an item not contemplated in our scale of fees'.[14] On 16 June 1922, Sadleir reported that, because Burgoyne was no longer living in Dublin, 'I have to cope with almost everything single-handed'.[15] Five weeks later, any possibility of help ended. 'Major Burgoyne told me that he was going to marry an R[oman] C[atholic] widow; he would be much better employed in assisting me here.'[14] In August 1923, perhaps not realising that it would have incensed Sadleir, Wilkinson reported to his deputy that Cork Pursuivant and Dublin Herald were both racing at Cowes.[17] Burgoyne went to Ethiopia in 1936 at the outbreak of the war with Italy, and offered his services to Emperor Haile Sellassie. Given command of a Red Cross mule train, he was killed in March 1936 during an Italian bombing raid. No new Cork Pursuivant was appointed; it was clear by the time of Burgoyne's death that another one would never be needed.

On 21 March 1922, the Office of Arms received formal notification from the Irish Ministry of Home Affairs that the use of envelopes headed OHMS [On His Majesty's Service] was to be discontinued immediately, and replaced by those headed 'Rialtas Sealadach Na hEireann' [Provisional Government of Ireland].[18] It was the first indication for Ulster's little heraldic court that times had changed. Wilkinson himself was absent in London, and there he remained for some time. On 8 April 1922 a further letter from the Ministry of Home Affairs, addressed to Wilkinson at the Office, instructed him to transfer all documents and records relating to the office of Ulster King of Arms, to the Irish Public Record Office at the Four Courts in Dublin. 'You are directed to give effect to this arrangement at your earliest convenience.'[19] Sadleir reported to Wilkinson on 10 April that an official from the Public Record Office called at the Office, 'and took stock of our documents'.[20]

Wilkinson's response from London was to order Sadleir to close the Office, and to write immediately to the Lord Lieutenant. To Wilkinson's discredit, his main interest appears to have been concern for his salary rather than for the records of the Office of Arms. 'It is clearly impossible for the work of my office to be carried on without such records and documents: and Grants of Arms and such like, cannot be issued without the consent and approval of His Majesty. I presume therefore that it is the intention of the provisional government to abolish my office. If this is the case I hope Your Excellency will bring my claims favourably before the Lords Commissioners of H. M. Treasury, as I should be deprived of a life appointment.'[21]

It is a matter for thanksgiving that the records of Ulster's Office were never transferred to the Public Record Office, and the extent of the disturbed state of Dublin made such a move unlikely, as Sadleir reported to Wilkinson on 20 April. 'I do not think anything will be done for some time with regard to our records being transferred, the Record Office being in the hands of "irregulars". For several nights past there have been frequent & prolonged outbursts of firing, which is most alarming. I hope it may be quiet before your return.'[22] The Irish Free State was in the grip of a civil war between those who had accepted the treaty that had partitioned Ireland, and those who regarded it as an act of betrayal to accept anything less than a thirty-two county republic of Ireland. A group of republicans had seized the Four Courts building, and shortly afterwards it was gutted by fire. Countless historic and invaluable records were destroyed, and the records of the Office of Arms would have been lost in the conflagration had they been transferred to the Four Courts.

The issue was passed back and forth between Dublin and London in the period April to September 1922. The Irish government was in no doubt that the future of the records of the office had been settled. 'It was *expressly* agreed that all historical and genealogical and heraldic documents and records in the office of the Ulster King were to be forthwith handed over to the Irish government and were to be regarded as ours ... It was in pursuance of this agreement that the Government decided to transfer the records to the Record Office where it was contemplated that the genealogical and research work of the office hitherto carried on in Ulster's Office would be for the future continued possibly with some member or members of the existing staff in the Ulster King's office.'[23] This position was indignantly refuted by officials at the Irish Office in London, who denied that any such agreement had been made. That said, and not withstanding the destruction of the Four Courts, if the Irish government wished to take over any non-heraldic documents of general or public interest, they should be given the opportunity of examining any relevant documents. 'This seems to be a necessary preliminary to any transfer.'[24] No further action was taken by the Irish government at the time, partly because of the dispute as to what could be transferred, partly because the records could hardly be transferred to the burnt-out shell of the Four Courts, and partly because it was argued that the Office of Arms was part of the royal household, and therefore beyond the jurisdiction of the provisional government. 'It has been clearly ascertained that the office of Ulster King of Arms is an appanage of the King, and as such pertains to the Lord Lieutenant, but not at all to the provisional government. I know for this reason His Excellency would feel a responsibility and a certain anxiety about its treatment, and for that reason, I share Wilkinson's hope that you may be able to postpone any uprooting of it at any rate until he himself can get over to Dublin.'[25]

A letter from the principal law officer of the Irish provisional government to Sadleir, suggests that the latter may have had a hand in the proposal to transfer the records of the Office of Arms to the Four Courts, and with an eye to securing his own future. 'I had practically arranged to give effect to your suggestion about the Record Office and setting up a genealogical department there, when the war began and the Record Office went up in smoke. I think you said you would submit a memorandum on the possibilities of making a paying department of genealogical work in the Record Office.'[26]

Sadleir was not to be blamed; Ireland was changing dramatically, and he had to manage the Office of Arms virtually single-handed, and for a small salary. On 16 May he reported to Wilkinson that, 'in spite of all my efforts, I cannot keep down the arrears which now amount to sixty-eight enquiries'.[27] A letter of 22 June 1922 evokes Sadleir's exasperation. 'It is very unfortunate that Mr Moore is so deplorably slow, as it means that I have to be constantly finding fault with him, which he resents, & is extremely distasteful to me. He is really of no assistance whatever, and such things as the salary sheets I have to make out, simply because he would never have them ready in time. Now that Major Burgoyne is no longer living in Dublin, I find I have to cope with almost everything single-handed. Of course, as regards your work, I am only too glad to undertake it, but I get tired of doing the work of a man who is not ill, but merely indolent.'[28] The situation had not improved by February 1923, as Sadleir reported to Wilkinson. 'The accumulation of work in the Office quite depresses me. It is far more than I can cope with, and as the expense of paying Miss Elliott and Miss O'Rourke, really leaves so little out of my £300 p.a. that, unless you can induce the Treasury to raise my salary, I really cannot go on.'[29]

Outside the Office of Arms and Dublin Castle, any semblance of normal life in Dublin was rapidly disappearing. On 26 April 1922, Sadleir reported that, 'forcible seizure of the Masonic Hall had caused some alarm'.[30] On 1 May the situation was rapidly deteriorating. 'We seem to be on the verge of a crisis here. I had to give lunch to two members of the Kildare Street Club who had been unable to get in there, as it is closely barricaded. It seems that the secretary was notified that it would be required for Belfast refugees, and as the Free State authorities refused to supply protection, the only thing to do was to close the doors.'[31] On 24 May, 'we had a renewal of heavy firing last night.[32] On 23 June, 'Much shooting in the streets here all last night',[31] and on 28 June, 'A battle is raging here since 3am, the din being awful. It is said that the Four Courts are being attacked. I can see one of the guns operating from the windows, as it is front of the City Hall. It is a short, stumpy looking thing, & seems to fire up in the air'.[33] On 30 June, 'I carried on at the Office till 1.30 on Thursday, when the fighting spread all up Dame Street, & we were warned by the Provisional Government that we might have to leave at any moment. I therefore closed the Office & at some risk made my way, via Dame Lane and Nassau Street, to Westland Row, where I was able to get a train to Lansdowne Road, as no trams were running. The sound of firing still continues at intervals, but I do not know where it is taking place.'[35] Mr Moore was still proving to be a difficult employee. 'Now that I have to do Moore's work, my own is greatly in arrears.'[36] On 4 October, 'owing to the fighting at night I had to leave my house and move to Celbridge'.[37]

In October 1922, Sadleir was facing considerable personal difficulties. On 13 October, 'My house at Celbridge was raided on Thursday week by eleven "Irregulars", who got in through a window at 1 in the morning; last Wednesday my house in Dublin was raided by an armed and drunken man who called himself a "Free Stater". Fortunately I encountered the latter, but it was about two hours before I could get rid of him.'[38] On 23 October, 'Owing to a strike on the Kingsbridge line, I have been having great difficulty in getting in to the Office, and 13 miles is a long way to cycle daily. Last Monday, when the local butcher was killed, we had quite a panic at Celbridge, so I did not attempt the ride. The next day 20 armed men raided the Telephone Exchange there, and threw all the instruments into the river.'[39] In February 1923, Sadleir reported to Wilkinson that Dublin Castle had been attacked but not much damage was done apart from a few broken windows.[40] In June 1923, 'some sort of an attack appears to have been made on the Guard Room in the early hours of yesterday morning, with the result that the door leading into Burgoyne's room, from the Guard Room, was completely smashed in'.[41]

In view of all that Sadleir had done during a very difficult period, Wilkinson was sufficiently thoughtful enough to offer, in December 1922, to get Viscount FitzAlan to recommend Sadleir for an MVO; an offer which Sadleir gratefully but firmly declined. 'I am too poor a man to seek honours or decorations of any sort, and would rather that you took no steps in the matter.'[42] The only surprising element is that Wilkinson first asked Sadleir if he would like to see his name go forward; it would have been better if he had quietly and confidentially recommended Sadleir for an honour without informing him.

Little of note took place concerning the Order of St Patrick in those difficult months. With the departure in October 1922 of Sir Hamar Greenwood, the last Chief Secretary of Ireland, and the last Chancellor of the Order, the vigilant Sadleir enquired of Wilkinson whether Greenwood had surrendered his badge of office, 'as he did not leave it here'. Sadleir also asked in the same letter whether he should endeavour to recover the collar of the recently deceased Earl of Gosford.[43]

As early as March 1923, the government of Northern Ireland had begun to express an interest in the status of the Office of Arms; because the office was located in Dublin, it aroused the deep suspicion of the northern government. Discreet approaches were made by the Imperial Secretary's Department in Belfast to the Home Office in London, to establish the precise status of Ulster King of Arms and his office. 'Is Ulster being paid by the Imperial Government? Is his appointment a life appointment? What is the official theory of his relations to the Northern Government? I think I should be right in saying that if he is to continue to have his Office in Dublin, the Northern Government would like to be dealt with by the English College of Arms.'[44] The response was quick and firm. 'I hope that the Northern Ireland Government will not stir up this question – a difficult one over which we should walk very warily and take our time. I cannot say of course what view the King is likely to take about it, but I think that we certainly ought to assume that when the advice of the Government is being considered, His Majesty's personal views on this matter ought to be given the greatest possible weight'.[45]

The Office of Arms continued to be the subject of an intermittent three-way discussion throughout the 1920s and 30s. The governments in London, Dublin and Belfast all expressed an interest in its future, of one kind or another. The Dublin government, especially in 1928–30, expressed the strong view that the Office should be fully under their jurisdiction. The London government took the view that it should remain under their control because part of Ulster's jurisdiction covered Northern Ireland, which was part of the United Kingdom. Furthermore, Ulster King of Arms exercised the Royal Prerogative with regard to the grant of arms; all the more reason why his office should remain under the control of London, given the uncertain attitude of the Irish Free State towards the Sovereign. Whereas attitudes in London and Dublin remained fairly constant from 1922 until the death of Wilkinson in 1940, the attitude of the Belfast government changed over the years. After the partition of Ireland, the government in Belfast viewed anything in the south with deep suspicion, even the granting of armorial bearings by a King of Arms in Dublin. It may seem surprising that the Belfast government did not take a deeper interest in acquiring the records and staff of the Office of Arms, but it appears that the reason for not pressing a claim was based purely on concern that the cost of running the Office would have to be met by the Northern Ireland government. 'The matter as you know has been frequently raised, but the Prime Minister [Sir James Craig] has always demurred at having the Office transferred here in view of the expense. I believe something like £1,000 a year would have to be found for the upkeep of the Office.'[46]

As the 1930s progressed, a different attitude was discernible. Questions of cost were forgotten, and replaced by a sense of regret that in the maelstrom of 1921–3, the Belfast government had not seized the initiative and asked for the transfer of the Office of Arms to Northern Ireland. The matter was debated in Northern Ireland newspapers, and with the death of Sir Nevile Wilkinson in 1940, the Northern Ireland government renewed its interest in the Office and in the Order of St Patrick. In 1941, Archbishop Charles D'Arcy of Armagh, Primate of the Church of Ireland, suggested that the Office of Arms should be re-established at Armagh because it was the primatial city of Ireland.[47] The archbishop clearly had an agenda of his own, which hopefully was more altruistic than the aggrandisement of his own see and position; in 1924 he had called for the establishment of a chapel for the Order of St Patrick in his own cathedral church.

The continued presence of the Office of Arms had not been forgotten by the Irish government. After letting the matter lie dormant for six years, they raised the question again in the autumn of 1936, and an interesting reference to the Order appears in the lengthy memorandum detailing the duties of Ulster. 'It may be mentioned that the Ulster King of Arms is ex officio an officer of the Order of the Knights of St Patrick under the title of King of Arms, as well as Registrar. [The Order] continues to exist but with diminishing numbers, and will tend to disappear as new members cannot be appointed except on the advice of the Executive Council of Saorstat Eireann, which advice will not be given. This aspect of the matter is consequently of little live interest at the moment.'[48] This seems to indicate that the Irish government had no knowledge of the appointment of the Duke of Gloucester, and that of the Duke of York only months previously. The Dominions Office still insisted that nothing should be done until after the death of Sir Nevile Wilkinson, although he was, 'taking an unconscionable time to die ... To raise the question seriously now might bring a proposal for division of functions, and perhaps it would be better to leave it as it is until we make some further progress on the unity issue. It is, after all, a good thing to have at least one office in Dublin with functions for the whole of Ireland.'[49]

Wilkinson lingered for another two years, dying on the morning of Sunday, 29 December 1940. His mind had begun to fail and death must have come as a release both for himself and his family. In January 1939, he was seen walking along Whitehall by one of his cousins, who was shocked at the obvious deterioration in his health, and wrote to Sadleir in Dublin. 'I saw your chief ... walking in Whitehall two days ago and was surprised to observe he has suddenly become an old gentleman. What has happened? It is not surely his years which bear him down'.[50] At the beginning of the Second World War, in September 1939, he was reported to have had, 'a severe nervous breakdown, and though his health is better than it was, it seems unlikely ... that he will make a complete recovery ... From our point of view [the Treasury] we should be glad to see the Office, which costs about £3,000 a year, abolished, or transferred to Eire'.[51]

Nevile Wilkinson spent the last two years of his life mostly in a nursing home in Morehampton Road, Dublin, where his punctilious deputy would visit him once each week, presumably to inform him about the activities at the Office of Arms, that he was no longer able to understand. One of Wilkinson's last letters was a rather sad scribbled note dated 24 February 1940, addressed to Sadleir. 'I am a little better, but I don't think I shall be able to carry on. My memory is so bad except of intense pain that I cannot carry my mind back to the salary signature, and I fear it may have miscarried. I hope they will put you in my place and continue the office with a new registrar ... Have you somebody to help you during my very long absence. I am still writing from the nursing home.'[52]

If Wilkinson was ever aware of the political wrangling over the future of his Office, he gave no indication, believing to the end that the great majority of Irishmen were basically conservative at heart with a deep reverence for the institutions of the past, and therefore that his office would continue. In the days of the union, he had introduced the custom of hanging three coloured paintings, mounted on dark cloth, from the parapet of the balcony of the Office of Arms, on ceremonial occasions. The paintings depicted a badge and a star of the Order, hanging either side of a lozenge-shaped painting depicting the armorial bearings of the Office itself. In all probability they were the work of Sir Nevile himself. One of three paintings was seen by the author in 1982, and showed the badge of the Order beautifully executed on a canvas measuring 520mm by 470mm. With the disappearance of investitures, levees, drawing rooms, and the other ceremonial events of the viceregal court the paintings were put into store. There they remained until 1938 when, as a gesture of courtesy, Wilkinson had them hung out again for the inauguration of Dr Douglas Hyde, the first President of Ireland. No one could fault Ulster on courtesy, but the gesture was scarcely tactful; incensed officials of the republican government ordered him to remove them.

Little more than a month after Wilkinson's death, the question of the future of the Office was raised for the last time. Towards the end of January 1941, Dr Richard J. Hayes, Director of the National Library of Ireland wrote to the Secretary of the Department of Education, claiming the valuable collection of books and manuscripts held at the Office. But a period of more than two years elapsed between Wilkinson's death and the formal closure of the Office of Arms in April 1943. The delay was partly due to the Second World War, and partly to the decision of the Irish government not to force the closure of the Office as an urgent issue. 'I took the opportunity some fair time ago to have a word with the Taoiseach about this matter. I suggested, and he agreed, that the British attitude towards matters of this sort had been so clearly indicated to us, we should only risk another snub if we brought it up during the war period. Apart from not wanting to give us any concessions just now, the general British attitude with regard to outstanding anomalies is to let sleeping dogs lie. Moreover, we have so many important things to extract out of the British that I am afraid the introduction of the Office of Arms would give a wrong view of our sense of proportion. These arguments do not appear to be very cogent, and are not very unlike an excuse for laziness, but I am personally convinced that the moment is not propitious.'[53]

Debate on the future of the Office was taking place in London. The Dominions Office consulted Sir Alexander Hardinge, the King's Private Secretary, the Earl Marshal, and various other interested parties on the best way to proceed. Although Sadleir had himself asked to be appointed to the office of Ulster King of Arms, two days after the death of Wilkinson,[54] and received the written support of the Earl of Granard,[55] the conclusion was that it would be impossible to appoint a new King of Arms on the old basis, with jurisdiction relating to the whole of Ireland, given the present status of the Irish Free State. But in deference to the general feeling that the historic office should not be allowed to disappear completely, it was proposed that the office of Ulster should be amalgamated with one of the three existing Kings of Arms in London. The jurisdiction of the new combined office would then be extended to cover Northern Ireland. The Irish government would then be free to make what arrangements it pleased in relation to the continuance of the functions of the Dublin Office. 'I should add that Ulster King of Arms is, by virtue of his office, the Registrar of the Order of St Patrick. In view of the fact that since 1922 no appointments have been made to this Order apart from members of the royal family, it is not considered that any practical difficulties would arise as regards the Order.'[56]

The records of the Office initially presented something of a problem as those of the Irish Free State and Northern Ireland were inextricably mixed. On 30 December 1941, Sir John Maffey, the United Kingdom Representative in Dublin (the title of ambassador being considered inappropriate), wrote to the Department of the Taoiseach proposing the amalgamation plan, adding that the British government would expect all the records to be transferred to London. The request was greeted with disbelief by the Minister of External Affairs who described it as preposterous: 'If we acquiesced, there would be a clear implication that we accepted partition as permanent. Moreover the documents are undoubtedly ours, and the British have not a shadow of right to them. In fact the whole proposal is particularly audacious'.[57] There was concern that the United Kingdom government might begin to remove the records clandestinely, but de Valera decided that there was no urgency and the matter could safely be left until the war was over, on the strict understanding that no new Ulster should be appointed in the meantime.[58]

The decision to close the Office of Arms had been reached by December 1941, Thomas Sadleir was not formally notified of the decision until July 1942, although he had received unofficial intimations of the likely outcome as early as February 1941..[59] The Office of Arms was to be formally abolished, and the office of Ulster King of Arms was to be amalgamated with Norroy King of Arms, whose jurisdiction would be extended to cover Northern Ireland as well as the northern counties of England. At this date, in the summer of 1942, it was intended that provision should be made for Sadleir himself. 'The Home Secretary is anxious that the new arrangement shall not involve the loss of your help and experience ... use should be made of the valuable experience you have acquired and of your erudition in all matters relating to the exercise of the functions of Ulster ... At the present moment there is a vacancy amongst the Heralds, and the plan for the carrying on of Ulster's work by the College of Heralds would be greatly facilitated if you were to become a Herald and a Member of the College.'[60] The plan envisaged that Sadleir would effectively assist Norroy, and continue to reside in Ireland, if he so wished, for most of the year. 'The arrangement by which you have been paid from the Treasury as Deputy to Ulster was adopted as a temporary arrangement pending the settlement of the future position of the office; the arrangement cannot go on indefinitely and ought to be brought to an end at an early date.'[61]

By the beginning of 1943, the Dominions Office was adamant that the whole matter should be resolved without further delay. Thomas Sadleir, who continued to run the Office of Arms, derived any powers which he had from a delegation by Ulster, and with the death of Wilkinson, he no longer had any authority to carry out functions peculiar to a King of Arms. It was a very unsatisfactory position which had already lasted longer than it was easy to justify, and it was necessary to take some

The Office of Arms becomes the Genealogical Office. Eamon de Valera (left) and Thomas Sadleir (right) at the transfer of the Office to the Irish Government in April 1943.

definite step to regularise the position without further delay.[62] Maffey discussed the amalgamation proposal with de Valera, who accepted it with some reluctance, and 1 April 1943 was agreed as the date of the transfer of the Office to Irish control.

The last two months saw a hurried tidying up of loose ends. The Office of Arms had been understaffed for many years, and the Grant Books, for example were months in arrears, much to the wrath of Dr Edward MacLysaght, who was appointed to head the reconstituted Office. Confirmations and new grants of arms had to be entered and illustrated in the Grants Book as a record by Miss McGrane, the Office Painter. Her work was of the highest quality, and inevitably time-consuming. Pedigrees for clients were copied by hand, and arrears were almost certain to develop. The newspapers only made matters worse by using such headlines as 'Ulster King of Arms Ancient Office to be Wound-up' and 'Office of Arms Passes', or, slightly more emotive, 'Eire Takes Over Office of Arms'. When the *Irish Times* announced in late March that the Office of Arms was about to close, the shock waves spread throughout the Common-wealth and the Office was inundated with letters and telegrams from all over the world making last-minute requests to have heraldic or genealogical work done under the old regime. The last request for a grant of arms came from Australia, and the last request for a family tree came from a professor in the University of Allahabad in India. Thomas Sadleir was a conscientious man, and the situation clearly worried him: 'What bothers me most is that the Grant Book and Pedigree Register have yet to be brought up to date, since I feel we could not hand over imperfect records. The fact that poor Sir Nevile was nearly two years in a Mental Home caused arrears, and with a small staff it has been impossible to overtake them'.[63]

As the life of the Office drew to a close, Sadleir was visited on 19 March 1943 by the Deputy Keeper of Records from the Public Record Office of Northern Ireland. 'Mr Sadleir was very frank about all the prospective arrangements for the carrying on of his Office although he emphasised that no final arrangement has yet been reached. However, he understood that he was to vacate the premises by the 1st April next; the records were to remain where they were, he himself was to be regarded as a member of the English College of Arms and is to go over there periodically, (he mentioned once in 8 weeks or so) to discharge his duties. Apparently there had been some discussion with Mr de Valera about the continuance of the Office under Eire, and Mr Sadleir had raised the point that the King was the "Fount of Honour" and there would be difficulty about issuing grants under any other name. When the suggestion was put forward that the grants might be "in the name of the Irish People" Mr Sadleir expressed the opinion that such grants would possess practically no attraction for the kind of persons interested in Arms and Pedigrees ... Mr Sadleir said that it seemed anomalous that Ulster King's functions should now be exercised from outside Ireland and he said that he had at one time endeavoured to have transfer made to the North of Ireland (rather to Armagh than Belfast, as it was a more ancient city). I said I would mention the matter on my return to Belfast to the authorities who were considering the whole question. I gathered that it could be done by periodical visits and he said that all that he would want would be a "living wage" and there would also be some assignment of premises.'[64]

Sadleir's informal proposal for the continuation of Ulster as a separate King of Arms, based in Northern Ireland, but forming part of the College of Arms in London was vetoed by the Earl Marshal on the ground that a reconstituted Ulster King of Arms would have no salary and would only derive income from the grants of arms to Irishmen, issued jointly with Garter King of Arms. The produce of the fees would be so small that there might be difficulty in finding an individual to accept the office. Given Sadleir's financial situation, he would receive a better income as a Pursuivant. 'He has had very ungenerous treatment in the past. He has been in the Office for twenty-seven years and has been doing all the work himself for a considerable time. It might be embarrassing if the Eire authorities were to offer him more attractive terms.'[65]

Sadleir was an expert in heraldry and genealogy and undoubtedly the foremost Irish authority on both subjects in his time. He had worked at the Office of Arms since 1913, and the Irish government offered him the task of heading the reconstituted Office under a different title at the generous salary of £600 p.a., but he declined from sentimental loyalty to the Crown. In his place the Irish government appointed Dr Edward MacLysaght, the distinguished genealogist, to the new post of Chief Genealogical Officer, a title changed to Principal Herald in 1944, and then to Chief Herald of Ireland. MacLysaght arrived in the Office on 1 March to familiarise himself with the place before the formal transfer of responsibility on 1 April, but he might as well not have bothered. Sadleir duly installed him in Wilkinson's old office, but instead of coaching the Chief Genealogical Officer-designate, Sadleir merely produced one or two manuscripts each day for MacLysaght to look at. While the two men were personally friendly to each other, it was inevitable that the brisk and efficient MacLysaght would become impatient with the rather deliberate and conscientious Sadleir. To Mac-Lysaght, Sadleir was unco-operative, old-fashioned, and slightly cranky, a lingering relic of the authority of the Crown in Ireland when all else had been swept away. In his memoirs he described Sadleir as, 'an unrepentant Unionist in politics, having nothing but ascendancy contempt for the new regime, and he had a pseudo-English accent delivered invariably in a raucous bark not unlike that of a sea-lion'.[66] Sadleir understandably resented the fact that his place should be taken by a rebel, a Sinn Feiner, and a representative of the upstart republican government, who knew little and probably cared nothing for the intricate ways of heraldry and genealogy in which he had immersed himself for more than thirty years.

A slightly old-fashioned figure, Thomas Ulick Sadleir was the son of The Reverend Francis Sadleir, and the great-grandson of Provost Sadleir of Trinity College (1837–51). He was born in 1882 and, while an undergraduate at Trinity College, Dublin, developed an interest in heraldry through the study of old book plates. His first known contact with the Office of Arms was in December 1901 when he left his visiting card at 44 Wellington Road, Dublin, the home of Sir Arthur Vicars. Ulster King of Arms duly responded to the interest expressed by a nineteen-year-old undergraduate. 'If you have nothing else on, will you come & dine in a quiet way on Friday at 7.30 – don't dress, come as you are. You may like to see some of my books etc. that I have here, although most of my interesting things are at the Castle – I am always glad to encourage anyone interested in Heraldry.'[67]

Sadleir did occasional work at the Office of Arms in the following years. After graduation, he was trained as a barrister at King's Inns and was called to the Bar in 1906. He worked on the Leinster Circuit before entering the Office of Arms in 1913. George Dames Burtchaell, Athlone Pursuivant and Deputy Ulster King of Arms, appointed Sadleir Registrar of the Office in April 1915. On Burtchaell's death in 1921, Sadleir was appointed Deputy Ulster King of Arms in succession. Had times been other than they were, he might also have expected to succeed Burtchaell as Athlone Pursuivant. But the Government had already taken the first steps towards a transfer of power and the dismantling of their administration in Ireland, and the historic office of Athlone Pursuivant, dating from 1552, was left unfilled. Burtchaell died on 18 August 1921, and five days later, Wilkinson wrote to Sadleir asking him to take over the duties of Athlone, with the salary attached to it, 'until such time as I am able to appoint a successor'.[68] Sadleir's definitive reply is unknown, but his provisional draft response indicates a degree of irritation, perhaps on the part of one who had expected automatic succession. 'I am willing, in order to suit your personal convenience, to carry out temporarily the duties of Athlone Pursuivant, on the understanding that I am to be paid the full salary enjoyed by the late lamented Mr Burtchaell, and that I am . . . not to be put to the expense of buying any distinctive uniform.'[69]

Sadleir was always conscious of his status as a barrister and wore his gown over a suit at work, which lent him a rather schoolmasterly appearance. Underpaid by the

Treasury, he was often short of money, and his frugal lunch consisted of a pot of tea and a bun at Bewley's Oriental Cafe in Grafton Street. He had every right to feel aggrieved at the way Sir Nevile Wilkinson expected him to run the Office without commensurate pay, but he remained consistently loyal and made a point of visiting Wilkinson once a week when the latter was confined to a nursing home for the last two years of his life. Sadleir would visit the College of Arms in London from time to time, 'giving ample warning to all in the building because his laugh could be heard from one end to the other'.[70]

Sadleir was full of interesting stories and anecdotes, and his knowledge was encyclopaedic and legendary. Until his death he kept in touch with a wide range of correspondents in the Commonwealth and the United States. His colleagues and friends testify to his great courtesy and generosity and his unrivalled knowledge of Irish heraldry, and also to his willingness to teach others everything he knew. Had the two governments been able to agree on the course, he would certainly have succeeded Wilkinson as Ulster. As it was, his deeply ingrained loyalty to the Crown caused him to resign from a job that he loved, and an Office where he had worked for some thirty years, and it is difficult not to feel touched by the pathos of his last years. In July 1942, it was intimated to him that he might expect to receive the offer of a position in the College of Arms in London. He was formally offered the post of Rouge Dragon Pursuivant in March 1943, by the Earl Marshal,[71] but the offer proved to be still-born. On 3 May, Sadleir received an encouraging letter from Alfred Trego Butler at the College, assuring him that, 'we are only too anxious to help and for your appointment here to be fixed at the earliest possible date'.[72] The letter proved to be premature and, if the offer was not formally rescinded, Sadleir's lack of a private income was proving to be a considerable obstacle. Early in June, the Home Office warned the United Kingdom Representative in Dublin that the Letters Patent appointing Sadleir to the College of Arms could not be issued, since the College, 'have not been prepared to proceed with the appointment while there was this doubt about the situation'.[73]

A few months earlier, on 22 March, de Valera met with Sir John Maffey and asked whether there was likely to be any delay in handing over the records of the Office to Irish control on 1 April. 'With much difficulty he then told me that Sadleir's name had appeared in *Stubb's Gazette* and it became clear that there was a certain uneasiness ... as to whether any special risks were attached to a man financially embarrassed in control of valuable records.'[74] Sadleir was in debt to a bullion dealer for the purchase of items of jewellery. The dealer concerned was one Moses Joseph, a man of dubious reputation, who had on more than one occasion been prosecuted, without success, for receiving stolen goods. The sum claimed by Joseph was initially £310, but later reduced to £177. Whatever the truth of this incident, it is difficult to imagine that very correct Thomas Sadleir behaving with anything other than the utmost propriety. It seems that Sadleir was in such a serious financial plight that he was forced to sell the tabard of Ulster King of Arms, which he had inherited from Wilkinson.[75] He sold it to an antique dealer in Nassau Street, Dublin, from whence it was purchased by the Northern Ireland government and placed on display in the Parliament Building at Stormont.

It proved impossible for Sadleir to clear all the arrears of work by 1 April, and he was still working at the Office in early July. His financial difficulties were exacerbated when the Treasury refused to pay him a salary after 31 March, and he was forced to write letter after letter to try to obtain some recognition and compensation for his work after that date. For a man who was so loyal a unionist that he would rather leave the office where he had worked for thirty years, rather than run it under another government, his treatment was cold and ungenerous, and the sum of £250 that he eventually received, paltry and mean. A similar view was taken by Edward MacLysaght, the new Chief Herald of Ireland.[76]

Sadleir's letters to the Treasury in the weeks after the handover make sad reading: 'I am seriously worried at the turn of events, particularly as I have had no regular income since the 31 March, though I have continued to work daily at clearing the arrears of work ... I had been offered a post at the College of Arms, but Garter's objections to my lack of means are insurmountable so I must seek other employment. But after thirty years service, I do not think I should be left penniless.'[77] This letter, dated 3 July 1943 seems to indicate that, whether or not Garter King of Arms had formally rescinded the offer of a post at the College, Sadleir himself had realised that he was in no position to accept an unpaid position with an uncertain income. Sadleir's friend Anthony Wagner, a Pursuivant at the College, could not himself detect the real reason why the offered appointment was never taken up. 'It certainly is open to doubt whether a move to England would in the long run be economic for you. It always did seem doubtful to me in view of the higher cost of living here and particularly in London. But the pros and cons of that naturally depended on the details of your private affairs of which I had no knowledge. I don't quite gather whether your letter ... amounts to a withdrawal of your candidature for the College. You make it sound rather like that without saying so in terms.'[78] In February 1944 Sadleir again raised the question of a position at the College of Arms, but was informed by the Home Office that this was out of the question. 'I am afraid it is no use re-opening arrangements for absorbing you in the College of Arms which must be regarded as having definitely lapsed.'[79]

Eventually he was offered the subordinate and poorly-paid post of assistant librarian in the library of King's Inns. The librarian, a Miss Walsh, was a woman of pronounced republican sympathies who had little liking for anyone loyal to the Crown and she treated Sadleir with a discourtesy that was close to contempt. His salary of £250 p.a. was less than he had received at the Office of Arms, but after representations to the Home Office by his friends the earls of Shrewsbury and Wicklow, he was awarded a Civil List pension of £250 p.a. in February 1952, for services to scholarship. It was the largest Civil List pension since that awarded to Dr Johnson. Tom Sadleir died in 1957 at the age of seventy-five. A tablet in his memory was unveiled in Castleknock Church, Co. Dublin, where his grandfather had been incumbent for more than half a century. Tom Sadleir's wife, Norma, whom he had married in 1922, later moved to London, where she died in 1986.

CHAPTER ELEVEN

THE FINAL EFFORTS

Gloucester and York: Churchill and Attlee

———

I have discussed this matter several times with His Majesty and am very much inclined to the revival of the Patrick. Why should de Valera pig the whole of this famous Order.
WINSTON CHURCHILL, 16 April 1943

A T THE IRISH GENERAL ELECTION of March 1932, the Cumann na nGaedheal party of William Cosgrave, which had held power for ten years, was defeated by the Fianna Fáil party of Eamon de Valera. De Valera's attitude to the Order is not on record, but there is every reason to suppose that he would have been more intransigent than his predecessor. Violently opposed to the settlement of 1922, and strongly committed to a thirty-two county republic, he systematically dismantled the constitution that he had inherited, in the period 1932–6. In 1937, the Irish Free State became in effect what he wanted it to be, a republic, and the new constitution of that year replaced the name 'Irish Free State' with 'Ireland' or 'Eire', and the Governor-General with a President. If de Valera was even aware of the continued shadowy existence of the obsolescent Order of St Patrick, it would have scarcely concerned him. He had more important matters to attend to, and in any case, the Attorney-General's memorandum of May 1928 clearly stated government policy towards the Order. Only one appointment had been made in ten years, and there was no reason to suppose that the British government was doing anything other than respecting the Irish decision of 1928. In fact, he was so concerned with other issues, that neither he nor his government registered any protest (possibly because they had no objection) at the appointment of two new Knights of St Patrick: the Duke of Gloucester on 29 June 1934 and the Duke of York on 17 March 1936.

In May 1934, the Duke of Gloucester, third son of King George V, visited Northern Ireland; it was one of the few royal visits there since 1922. After the duke's departure, the Duke of Abercorn, wrote to the King on 31 May describing the tour as a 'triumphant success ... It would give extreme pleasure to all classes and creeds in Northern Ireland, if I may suggest that Your Majesty could see your way to confer upon the Duke of Gloucester the Knighthood of the Order of St Patrick as this would bind him still further to the territorial area of Ulster [the duke was also Earl of Ulster]', and that the appointment should be made 'upon the occasion of Your Majesty's birthday'. The duke informed the King that he had made this request with the full knowledge of the Prime Minister of Northern Ireland, Lord Craigavon, 'who strongly endorses it on behalf of his government'.[1] Abercorn was knocking on an open door, and probably knew that he was doing so; he may even have written to the King at the suggestion of the Northern Ireland Prime Minister.

Within a day or so, the King discussed the proposed appointment of the duke with Ramsay MacDonald, the Prime Minister, and found to his pleasure that MacDonald agreed with the proposal: 'He was glad to hear of the King's wish. It is the King's appointment, and the Prime Minister was glad to hear of a step which would keep the Order alive'.[2] Given that the proposed appointment might arouse a reaction in the Irish Free State, it was referred to the Dominions Office for an opinion. J. H. Thomas, the Secretary of State, raised no objection, but advised that the appointment should not be included in the forthcoming Birthday Honours List, since all appointments therein were made on ministerial recommendation. Should the duke's appointment appear in the list, it might be inferred that it had been made on the recommendation of the British government and not on the initiative of the King. 'The King readily accepts the Prime Minister's suggestion that the honour should not be gazetted until some time has elapsed since the Birthday Gazette, to avoid any misunderstanding that it was conferred on the recommendation of the Prime Minister, especially as there are two Thistles in the list.'[3]

Having secured the support of the Prime Minister and the Dominions Office, Sir Clive Wigram, the King's Private Secretary, replied to the Duke of Abercorn's letter, saying that, 'the idea certainly commends itself to His Majesty'. As the appointment of a royal prince was in prospect, it would be done on the initiative of the King, and not on that of the Prime Minister, therefore, 'it would be a mistake to include the honour among the Birthday Honours, which are made upon ministerial advice . . . I am sure you will agree therefore that the honour, if bestowed, should be given apart from the two half-yearly lists'.[4] Wigram's statement needs some qualification. In 1934, the Order of St Patrick was officially given, with the Orders of the Garter and the Thistle, on the initiative of the Prime Minister of the United Kingdom, though with the approval of the monarch. In practice, it had been given to no one outside the royal family for twelve years, and the appointment of a royal prince was within the personal jurisdiction of the sovereign. With the Dominions Office caveat, Abercorn's recommendation was accepted, and the appointment of the Duke of Gloucester was announced in the *London Gazette* on 29 June.

There seems to have been no negotiation or consultation with the Irish government on the duke's appointment, and there was no suggestion that it might have been prudent. The duke's appointment was in full accordance with the 1927 recommendations that no one but members of the royal family should be appointed for the time being, and everything possible was done to avoid causing any offence to the Irish Free State government. The appointment was linked to the duke's successful visit to Northern Ireland, and 'official authorities' stressed that it was being conferred upon him in his capacity as Earl of Ulster. The *Belfast News Letter* greeted the appointment with 'great satisfaction': 'Where, I wonder, will the Duke be invested? Circumstances seem to rule out Dublin Castle. It would create tremendous enthusiasm in the loyal province with which the Duke is so closely associated if the ceremony could take place here, and thus preserve the association of the Order with Ireland'.[5] In fact the duke was invested quietly and privately by the King at Buckingham Palace, probably on 30 June or shortly afterwards. Although the *Belfast News Letter* strongly advocated the association of the Order with Northern Ireland, and this was voiced on several occasions, particularly at the time of the passing of the Ireland Act in 1948–9, government policy of avoiding such a situation, was maintained. Only in the debates of 1943, by which time it was generally accepted in London that the partition of Ireland was permanent, was it accepted that the republic of Ireland would never participate in any plan to reconstitute the Order.

The appointment of the Duke of Gloucester in June 1934 was followed by the appointment of the Duke of York in March 1936. King George V died in January of that year, to be succeeded by his eldest son, as King Edward VIII. The new King was unmarried, and his brother, the Duke of York, now became heir presumptive to the throne. In such a situation, the King may have considered it anomalous that the heir to the throne should not possess the third of the three national Orders, which was already held by their younger brother, the Duke of Gloucester. There is no doubt that the Duke of York was appointed on the personal initiative of the new King, who discussed it with the Prime Minister, Stanley Baldwin, at an audience on 12 February 1936,[6] and Baldwin gladly concurred. No objections were raised by the Dominions Office or the Home Office and, by wish of the King,[7] the duke's appointment was gazetted on 17 March, St Patrick's Day, well clear of either the New Year or Birthday Honours Lists. As the gazetting of the Duke of Gloucester's appointment had included his subsidiary titles of *Earl of Ulster* and Baron Culloden, to draw attention to the Irish title, so the Duke of York was also gazetted as Earl of Inverness and *Baron Killarney*. There is no clear evidence of when the duke was invested. A set of insignia of the Order of St Patrick was sent to Buckingham Palace on 15 February, to be, 'at hand when His Majesty wants it',[8] and the duke probably received it on 17 March.

On hearing the news, Lord Craigavon promptly sent a telegram to the duke congratulating him on his appointment, and inviting him to revisit Northern Ireland. The appointment of the duke on St Patrick's Day added a note of irony, since no ceremony of the Order had been held on the feast day of its titular saint since the installation of the first fifteen Knights in 1783. The *Belfast News Letter* trumpeted the appointment as heralding a visit by the duke to Northern Ireland in the summer, and announced that the people of Northern Ireland would receive the news of a new Knight of St Patrick with feelings of 'deep satisfaction'. In an editorial, the *Belfast News Letter* pointed out that the appointment was a welcome announcement and that, 'for some years after the constitution of the Irish Free State many people thought that the Order was to be allowed to die out … The Order was complete with twenty-two Knights so lately as 1924, but as no successors were appointed on the deaths of Lords Enniskillen, Bandon, Listowel, Pirrie, Ypres, Dunraven and Montearl the opinion grew that there were to be no new Knights'.[9] The *Irish Independent* carried the investigation a stage further: 'The appointment of the Duke of York … indicates the King's intention to preserve this Order … His own appointment to the Order in 1927 came as a surprise, as it was believed that King George, in view of the changed status of Ireland, intended to let it lapse … Nor are any more appointments likely unless it were thought suitable to appoint a Knight whose connection was with Northern Ireland only. The Government is very anxious not to offend Free State susceptibilities in such matters'.[10] The paper was obviously mistaken about the King's intentions towards the future of the Order. Evidence has shown that he had no intention of allowing it to lapse.

There must have been a number of observers at the time, who thought that the appointments of the Duke of Gloucester in 1934 and the Duke of York in 1936, presaged the full reconstitution and revival of the Order. With full examination of all surviving contemporary documents, it is now clear that they were only isolated incidents, and not part of a strategic plan. The appointment of the Duke of Gloucester is consistent with what is known of the views of King George V and the Northern Ireland government of Lord Craigavon, and the appointment of the Duke of York indicates that the views of King Edward VIII were not dissimilar, though probably not as passionate as those of his father. If the King had not abdicated in December 1936, the Duke of Kent might have followed his brothers into the Order, but this is speculative. The Duke of York was the one hundred and forty-sixth and last Knight of the Order of St Patrick, and brought the total number of Knights to three royal and nine non-royal. The senior royal Knight was the Duke of Connaught, a son of Queen Victoria and the King's great-uncle, who had been appointed as far back as 1869. The senior non-royal Knight was Lord Castletown, appointed in 1908.

The lack of reaction on the part of the Irish government is not difficult to explain. Eamon de Valera did not, in principle, care anything about what the royal family did or called itself or awarded itself, as long as it had no role, formal or informal, in the Government of the Irish Free State. He was initially reluctant to secure the passage of an act by the Oireachtas, to recognise the abdication of King Edward VIII, because it would have been a public acknowledgement that there was a King in and of the Irish Free State. His principal aim was to remove the monarchy from the constitution of the Irish Free State, and until that process was complete, his policy was completely to ignore the King except when it was legally impossible to do so. The appointment of two royal princes as Knights of St Patrick would have been of trifling interest or concern to him. The appointment of an Irish peer, resident in Ireland, would have been a demonstration of royal authority in Ireland, and been the cause of a very strong reaction.

The appointment of the Duke of York seemed to re-awaken the interest of the Prime Minister, Stanley Baldwin. The arrival of St Patrick's Day 1937 caused him once again to consider briefly whether the time had not come to revive the Order. The Dominions Office was asked to answer three questions. Was it practicable to appoint new Knights of the Order? Was it politically undesirable to do so? If it was possible to proceed, what procedure should be adopted? The reply was the familiar note of caution. 'Owing to various anachronisms in the Letters Patent and Statutes resulting from the establishment of the Irish Free State, it is impossible, without entirely disregarding the provisions of the Statutes, to make any fresh appointments ... It would certainly still seem inadvisable that without the consent or at least the acquiescence of the Irish Free State Government (which would hardly be obtainable) any step should be taken to reconstitute the Order; in consequence it would appear impracticable that any appointment, other than one which could be regarded as made personally by the King without the advice of Ministers (e.g. the appointment of a member of the Royal Family) should be made to the Order.'[11] That was the end of Baldwin's role in the story of the declining and diminishing Order. He retired from office a little more than two months later, on 28 May 1937. The government of his successor, Neville Chamberlain, was preoccupied with the rapidly deteriorating situation in Europe, and there is no evidence of any government interest in the future of the Order in the period 1937–42.

One by one, the elderly Knights and Officers died. The offices of Grand Master and Chancellor had been vacant since partition in 1922, and the offices of Secretary, Genealogist and Usher were allowed to remain unfilled on the deaths of the holders in 1926, 1930 and 1933 respectively. Whatever limited functions they still possessed passed to Sir Nevile Wilkinson, who still operated as Ulster King of Arms in Dublin Castle. During a correspondence with the Treasury in 1938 regarding the cost of replacing a collar of the Order, Wilkinson ridiculously declared: 'I am making this suggestion direct because all the offices of the Order: Chancellor, Ulster King of Arms, Registrar, Knight Attendant, Genealogist, and Usher of the Black Rod, are at present held by me'.[12]

With Major Guillamore O'Grady, Dublin Herald, Wilkinson attended the coronation of King George VI in May 1937, and the Irish government apparently raised no objections. It was probably the last public ceremonial appearance of the last Ulster King of Arms, before increasing mental incapacity resulted in his confinement to a nursing home. His death in December 1940, and the closure of the Office of Arms in March 1943, drew a line under the Chancery of the Order of St Patrick in Bedford Tower of Dublin Castle.

In his memoirs, published in 1978 when he was ninety years old, Edward MacLysaght, the first Chief Herald of Ireland, recalled that he had been told by Eamon de Valera to continue all the activities of the Office of Arms, now renamed the Genealogical Office, *except* matters relating to the Order of St Patrick; this would continue to be under the direct authority of the Sovereign. The story sounds implausible, but even if MacLysaght's memory was correct, it is doubtful if de Valera would have issued this directive had he realised how widely MacLysaght would interpret it. Several items relating to the Order still remained in the Genealogical Office, and they were all removed by Thomas Sadleir and handed over to Sir John Maffey, the United Kingdom Representative in Dublin, without any interference by MacLysaght. The most important item, the Seal of the Order, was handed over on 9 April 1943, an event which was to cause annoyance five years later. The Seal was followed by two collars, two volumes of the register of the Order, a copy of the statutes bound in blue leather for the use of the Sovereign, a silver and enamel badge, and a miscellaneous collection of such peculiarities as a large blue 'state table cloth', described as mouldy and mildewed, used at investitures, a blue satin hassock, a red velvet cushion, and the collars of SS worn by Dublin Herald and Cork Herald.

There was no longer any base for the Order in Dublin, and it was clear that the Irish government would oppose any further appointments. The hope that Eire might eventually be persuaded to co-operate over the Order, which had governed the plans and decisions of 1927–30, was not going to materialise. With de Valera in power in Dublin, and Eire a republic in all but name, there cannot have been anybody of any influence left who still believed that any action should be deferred until the Dublin government was prepared to co-operate in maintaining the existence of the Order. If it was to survive, it would have to be transferred to England or to Northern Ireland. To transfer it to England and reconstitute it independently of Ireland with which it would cease to have any territorial connection, would make a nonsense of the history and ethos of the Order. There was of course the option of transferring it to Northern Ireland, but no one seemed to consider this either viable or desirable.

The death of Wilkinson and the abolition of the Office of Arms had in fact re-awakened Northern Ireland's interest in the Order, and a short correspondence took place between the private secretaries to the Governor and to the Prime Minister of Northern Ireland. 'Ulster is Registrar of the Order of St Patrick, and unless steps are taken to modify the existing statutes the disappearance of Ulster would mean the Order's death. The Prime Minister [James Miller Andrews] feels that this would be a great misfortune and he thinks that steps should be taken to save the Order so that distinction could be conferred in appropriate cases and thus keep in being the historic Order of St Patrick.'[13] If Northern Ireland could control the office of Ulster, the Order of St Patrick might well be brought within the orbit of influence of the Northern Ireland government. The next move was obvious; Northern Ireland must 'seize the initiative'. On 10 January 1941, Oscar Henderson, private secretary to the Duke of Abercorn, Governor of Northern Ireland, wrote to the Home Office in London, enquiring if the Governor should make a recommendation regarding the future of the Office of Arms. 'His Grace is at the moment considering certain suggestions made by the Government of Northern Ireland as to how this Office should be reconstituted in view of the political change in Ireland and we feel most strongly that Northern Ireland must be consulted in this matter before any appointment is made.'[14] The reply was very much of the 'we are taking care of this, there is no need for you to concern yourself' type. 'This is not an office on which it would be appropriate for the Governor of Northern Ireland to make a recommendation. The question of what the future arrangements should be raises a number of difficult problems which are at present being considered and we will certainly see that Northern Ireland is consulted.'[15] There was little that the Northern Ireland government could do, except frequently and firmly to state its conviction that the Order of St Patrick should be kept alive. On the eve of the dissolution of the Office of Arms (1 April 1943), Northern Ireland still kept a close eye on the future of the Order. 'As you know we have suggested that the new holder of the office [Norroy and Ulster King of Arms] should continue to be Registrar of the Order of St Patrick ... We do not intend to let this matter fall into abeyance and I am making further representations to the Home Office.'[16]

It was the outbreak of the Second World War in 1939 that caused the position of the Order to come under scrutiny yet again; this time on the initiative of Winston Churchill, the Prime Minister.

In May 1942 Churchill, possibly searching for ways to revive the dormant Order, asked that consideration be given to reconstituting the Order of St Patrick as a gallantry decoration, and sought the advice of the Dominions Secretary, Clement Attlee; the idea was given short shrift. 'Appointments to the Order have almost invariably been peers with large Irish estates. A reconstitution of the Order on this basis would not, therefore, afford any substantial means of rewarding Irishmen who performed distinguished and gallant services in the course of the war. On the other hand, to reconstitute the Order as a gallantry decoration, apart from the fact that it means a break with tradition, would surely be a retrograde step. In Mr Attlee's view gallantry decorations should be like the VC and George Cross, available to anyone whose conduct reaches the prescribed standard, and any idea of a territorial limitation seems quite inappropriate.'[17]

Winston Churchill was not easily daunted, and on 16 April 1943 he again raised the question of reviving the Order; on this occasion his language was choice and Churchillian. The desert war in Tunisia was drawing to a close and, should it end in victory, there would be the question of how to recognise the services of its two most successful commanders, General Sir Harold Alexander and General Sir Bernard Montgomery. 'I should think that General Montgomery should have the GCB. There is always a possibility of the King reviving the Patrick for General Alexander, pray examine this ... I have discussed this matter several times with His Majesty and am very much inclined to the revival of the Patrick. Why should de Valera pig the whole of this famous Order.'[18] The Committee on the Grant of Honours, Decorations and Medals in Time of War was duly asked to examine the possibility of recommending the revival of the Order, though the request was phrased in language that was slightly more sanitised. 'Mr Churchill does not see why Mr de Valera should monopolise the whole of this famous Order. The question has arisen because the Prime Minister has been considering what high honours might be recommended if the operation in Tunisia should end triumphantly. There is, therefore some urgency in the matter.'[19]

General the Honourable Sir Harold Alexander was an obvious candidate for the Order of St Patrick, as far as anyone was in 1943. Third son of the fourth Earl of Caledon, he was the scion of a family resident in County Tyrone since 1790. Although he was born in London in 1891, and his personal home was in Berkshire, there was no doubting that his ancestry was impeccably Irish. General Sir Bernard Montgomery's credentials were less certain, but at some point, someone discovered that he had Irish connections and might be a possible candidate for the Order of St Patrick. He had also been born in London, in 1887, and lived there until 1923 when his parents moved to County Donegal, where his mother was still living in 1943. He may have regarded Eire as his home from 1923 until his marriage in 1927, and possibly again after his wife's death in 1938. Beyond this slight connection, it was adduced as additional support that his grandfather, Robert Montgomery, was born and baptised at Templemore, Londonderry in 1809. Although Irish descent might therefore be claimed, Montgomery's personal connection with Ireland was, in the opinion of one observer, 'somewhat sketchy'.[20]

Once again, the question of reconstituting the Order of St Patrick was opened up for discussion; once again the views of the Home Office and the Dominions Office were sought; once again the two departments offered conflicting advice; and once again the exercise ended in failure. Sir Alexander Maxwell of the Home Office was the first to respond, and his bullish response was much like the standpoint taken by Sir William Joynson-Hicks in 1927. 'I think it is quite likely that after vigorous protests have been made, nevertheless any Irishman who receives the Order of St Patrick for services in the war will be welcomed in Dublin in a most friendly spirit. At some time or other, unless the Order of St Patrick is to perish entirely – and this would seem a pity – we shall have to face the possibility of protests from the Eire Government, and on the whole I am inclined to think that the present time is as suitable a time for facing and getting through these protests as we are likely to find. If the Order is revived, as the Prime Minister contemplates ... the conferment of those honours will be so popular that it will be extremely difficult for the Eire Government to make capital out of protests which will have to be based on abstract principles ... How far de Valera will feel it necessary to protest I do not know.'[21]

At this point, a correspondence, which appears to have been quite unofficial, took place between the Home Office and the Northern Ireland Cabinet Secretariat. L. S. P. Freer of the Home Office wrote a personal handwritten letter to Robert Gransden, the Northern Ireland Cabinet Secretary, informing him that, once again, there was a possibility of life for the Order. 'We should rather welcome an award of this kind . . . We should do what we can to revive the Order and I do not think that we need insist on the removal from St Patrick's Cathedral of the banners of the earlier Knights . . . Perhaps you would let me know what you think. I can then advise as to whether any representations should be made.'[22] With more than a hint of marshalling support, Gransden wrote to Oscar Henderson, private secretary to the Duke of Abercorn, enquiring about the duke's position on retaining the banners in St Patrick's Cathedral. It was hardly likely that Gransden was interested in seventy-year-old banners in a cathedral in Dublin. It was much more likely that he was using a fairly non-controversial item to elucidate the feelings of the duke on the future of the Order itself; he was not to be disappointed. 'The duke most strongly feels that it would be a great pity if this Order were allowed to die out as it is bound to do in that all the members except royal Knights are elderly. Do you think it would be possible to make discreet enquiries through the College of Heralds as to His Majesty's intention with regard to this Order.'[23] Gransden was delighted. 'I have conveyed the Governor's views to the Home Office, and both the Prime Minister and I have made the strongest representations that this Order should not be allowed to fall into abeyance.'[24] Strong as their representations might be, the fate of the Order of St Patrick was not something over which they had any real influence. There were other and wider considerations than the wishes of the Governor and the Prime Minister of Northern Ireland.

Sir Eric Machtig of the Dominions Office consulted Sir John Maffey, the United Kingdom Representative in Dublin, who opposed the plans as being prejudicial to Anglo-Irish relations; the time was not propitious for such a step. He thought that a time might come when it would be possible to revive the Order of St Patrick, as an award for men of Irish origin who had rendered service to the British Commonwealth. 'While the Eire Government could not very well raise objection to the award of British honours to Irishmen who had rendered valuable war service as members of the United Kingdom Forces, they would, in view of Eire's present position of neutrality, certainly resent the use for this purpose of an Order which in its origin and history, was essentially Irish. The revival of the Order as one for award to persons connected with Northern Ireland only would be unlikely to raise difficulty in relation to Eire, but he wondered whether such a limitation would not be likely to detract from the value of the Order in the eyes of possible recipients.'[25] At a meeting on 30 April 1943, representatives of various governments met to discuss the Order, and no one present was in any doubt that the revival of the Order as an award to persons connected solely with Northern Ireland was undesirable; it was still an all-Ireland Order, and therefore it was to be an all or nothing Order.[26]

The attitude of Sir Alexander Hardinge, the King's Private Secretary, was quite different from the attitude of Lord Stamfordham in 1927–30, but then King George V was dead, and King George VI was not as deeply concerned about the fate of the Order of St Patrick as his father had been. Hardinge, in a letter to Sir Robert Knox, Ceremonial Officer at the Treasury, thought the whole exercise was pointless. 'It does seem to me to be rather a waste of time . . . until the overriding and so far intractable political issues have been dealt with.'[27] Hardinge's attitude was not necessarily that of the King who, according to Churchill, was 'very favourable to the idea and has made some inquiries through his own staff'.[28]

The draft report of the Committee on the Grant of Honours, Decorations and Medals in Time of War, did no more than rehearse these conflicting arguments of its departmental members. 'It seems unlikely that we shall come to an agreement . . . The Dominions Office regard the political considerations as precluding any further appointments to the Order. The Home Office incline to the view that the political considerations are greatly exaggerated. They do not consider that such action would be likely to cause any appreciable irritation in Eire, and they consider that it would be better to use the Order and ensure its continued existence for a useful purpose than to allow the Eire Government to bring it to an end. We suggest that before action is taken the Prime Minister may care to refer the question to the ministers mainly concerned.'[29]

Debate continued at civil servant level within the Home Office, and especially the Dominions Office. Each letter, minute or memorandum emanating from the latter department reinforced the belief that the reconstitution of the Order of St Patrick was pointless, and would only upset the delicate relations between London and Dublin. Persons appointed to the Order were either Irish or they were not. If they were not, then there was no sense in appointing them to this Irish Order. If they were Irish, then their appointment to an Order, hitherto exclusively associated with Ireland and awarded for services in relation to Ireland, could only be interpreted as a recognition of services to Ireland; and this could only be accorded on the advice of the Government representing the greater part of Ireland, and not in the face of what would be the certain opposition of that government. This was the advice given by Sir Eric Machtig to Clement Attlee, Deputy Prime Minister and Secretary of State for Dominions Affairs. 'No one doubts that the United Kingdom Government could, if they chose, disregard the objections of the Eire Government and revive the Order for use in the manner proposed. The question is as to the wisdom of doing so. Without agreeing in the slightest degree with the Eire government's attitude towards the King, the British Empire and the war, one cannot but feel that there would be something anomalous in the revival of an Irish Order for conferment on Irishmen without the concurrence of the (main) Irish government. The Cosgrave government objected to this in the past, and the de Valera government would be bound to object all the more now, as the honour would be awarded for war service, whereas the Eire government professes to be neutral. The reconstituted Order would therefore become a "running sore" between us and the Eire government and Irishmen awarded it would be classed as "renegades" by the Eire Government. Is it really worthwhile to bring about such a situation like this on such an issue?'[30]

Consideration of the future of the Order now passed from the level of civil servants to that of senior members of the cabinet. Clement Attlee duly reflected the advice of his senior departmental officials and cautioned against use of the Order to recognise war services by Irishmen. 'It would . . . be regarded as a deliberate pinprick applied to Irish Nationalist opinion. We have enough real grievances against Mr de Valera without the need for using pinpricks. It has been suggested that if we fail now to revive the Order, there is a danger of it lapsing entirely. I see no sufficient ground for this view. The Order has admittedly lain dormant for the past twenty years . . . but there is no reason why it should not have been given to the retiring Prime Minister of Northern Ireland if that had otherwise been regarded as desirable. In short, I suggest that the best course is . . . to keep it alive by use when any appropriate circumstances arise for recognising services in Ireland (i.e. in relation to Northern Ireland at present) and to hope for the day when the people of Southern Ireland will take a more reasonable view of their association with the British Commonwealth than their government at present are prepared to take.'[31]

Attlee's position on the Order relating solely to Northern Ireland appears to have been motivated indirectly, and at least in part, by the views of one who could claim to have a very real interest in the future of the Order of St Patrick – Sir Basil Brooke, Prime Minister of Northern Ireland from 6 May 1943. On 14 May 1943, Brooke held a meeting with Herbert Morrison, the Home Secretary and, 'on his own initiative and without any knowledge that the matter had been discussed', raised the question of whether the Order might be conferred on Generals Alexander and Montgomery.[32] Morrison was convinced that Brooke's intervention at this stage was totally coincidental; but we cannot exclude the possibility that Brooke had prior knowledge of Churchill's initiative. In any case, Morrison fully supported Brooke. 'I believe that in the minds not only of Ulstermen but of many other Irishmen there would be a strong sentiment in favour of conferring on Irish generals an honour which is distinctively Irish.'[33] Morrison conveyed the essence of his meeting with Brooke in a letter to Attlee.

On 10 May 1943, a meeting took place between Attlee, Morrison and Sir John Anderson, who had been Permanent Under Secretary of State at the Home Office at the time of the abortive discussions in 1927–30. Anderson had entered Parliament in 1938 as Member of Parliament for the Scottish Universities, and was now a member of the war cabinet as Lord President of the Council. The three men agreed on three points: firstly, that there was nothing to prevent the King, on the recommendation of United Kingdom ministers, giving honours to generals who belong to the Dominions for services to the United Kingdom forces, though they acknowledged that the relevant Dominion government should be consulted in the case of an individual who had not severed his connection with the Dominion. Secondly, nothing should be done to imply that the King could not, on the advice of United Kingdom ministers, confer the Order of St Patrick on distinguished Irishmen. Thirdly, there was no objection to conferring the Order on Irishmen specifically for service to Northern Ireland. 'The general view was that the question whether the Patrick should be used for the purpose proposed by the Prime Minister was a question of expediency and not a constitutional question ... It was recognised on the one hand that Mr de Valera could, not unreasonably, say that to use an Order which is distinctively Irish in its association for decorating Irishmen for services in a war in which Eire is neutral is peculiarly inappropriate; and that on the other hand the fact that Eire is neutral and therefore repudiates interest in the war services rendered by Irishmen can be used as an argument for maintaining that the question on which United Kingdom Ministers can advise the King without reference to the Dominion government which has repudiated any interest in their service.'[34] On that concluding note, the three men resolved to send their conflicting views to the Honours Committee for its report to Churchill.

On 23 July 1943 Churchill, without responding to Attlee, referred the matter to Viscount Simon, former leader of the Liberal Party, and now the Lord Chancellor in the wartime coalition government. As John Costello, had given his legal opinion to the Irish government in May 1928, so now Lord Simon gave his legal opinion to the United Kingdom government in August 1943. After reviewing the history of the Order, Simon turned his attention to present practicalities. He was firmly of the opinion that there were no administrative or technical problems to prevent the appointment of new Knights. 'I am satisfied that if such appointments are constitutionally proper and politically wise, there is no obstacle that need arise from any want of power to make them. No new Letters Patent would seem to be required. The new appointments could be made by Warrant under the King's Sign Manual and sealed with the Seal of the Order. The Warrant of Appointment could direct that inasmuch as there is no Chancellor of the Order, the Seal should be affixed by Norroy and Ulster King of Arms. This is the official whom since April 1st last, has taken over the duties of Ulster King of Arms. These details can be worked out without troubling the Prime Minister. The Warrant would dispense with the ceremony of investiture as the new Knights are absent from the United Kingdom.' Simon then went on to the question of possible objections from the Irish Free State; here he found no constitutional difficulties. 'I think the answer to this is that it is not proposed to use this Order for the purpose of rewarding Irishmen in respect of services they have rendered to Eire, and that as it is only proposed to revive the Order for the purpose of conferring honours on Irishmen in respect of their services to the United Kingdom, this is not a matter "appertaining to the affairs of a Dominion".' The real difficulty was the very

Irishness of the Order. 'It is the association of St Patrick with Ireland and the undoubtedly Irish complexion of the Order which are likely to give rise to protest . . . Most important of all is the political question of whether it is wise to bring about another controversy with Eire by carrying through the proposal. Controversy with de Valera there certainly will be, and there is no method of avoiding it by relying upon reasonable and powerful argument to show that he is wrong. Moreover on this point, Cosgrave and his friends will support de Valera's view; it was they who objected to the suggestion made in 1928. I conceive that de Valera will be roused to protest more particularly because of the name of Saint Patrick and of the purely Irish associations which that name suggests . . . I anticipate . . . that the carrying out of this plan will produce a considerable sense of grievance and operate in a way which does not improve relations with the Eire government.'[35]

Simon concluded his memorandum by observing that there was no better moment than the present. 'If the Order of St Patrick is ever going to be revived, the present occasion is much the best for the purpose. The choice is really between letting the Order die out . . . and taking this opportunity of infusing fresh blood into the Order. I am inclined to think that if the Order is revived, as the Prime Minister contemplates, for Irishmen who have rendered distinguished service in the war, the conferment of these honours will be so popular that it will be difficult for the Eire Government to make capital out of protests which will have to be based on abstract propositions, most of which are unfounded in fact. The crucial consideration is whether, when a high honour connected with the name of St Patrick has been conferred on these Irishmen for their war services, this will not give so much general gratification that objections to using the Order on the recommendation of the British Prime Minister will lose their force.'[36]

Churchill himself recognised the difficulties involved and, with the Second World War in full swing, and far from won, he took the advice of Sir J. Grigg, the Secretary of State for War. 'I am hoping that the King will consent to revive the Patrick for both Generals Alexander and Montgomery, but I agree with you that the moment has not yet come. They have both received promotion and honours recently, and are engaged in most important operations.'[37] On that note, and once again, the Order of St Patrick was covered with dust sheets and put away.

CHAPTER TWELVE

FROM THE NORTH

Sir Basil Brooke and the Northern Ireland interest

=====

I can assure you that the revival of the Order would give the greatest possible pleasure in Northern Ireland.
SIR BASIL BROOKE, 20 March 1945.

THE 1920 GOVERNMENT OF IRELAND ACT partitioned Ireland into two sections: the twenty-six counties of the Irish Free State, known as Ireland or Eire from 1937; and the six counties of Northern Ireland, which remained a part of the United Kingdom. It proved impossible to implement the Government of Ireland Act 1920, in the south, and the Irish Free State was the result of the subsequent treaty between representatives of the United Kingdom government and Irish representatives. In the north, the provisions of the act were implemented, and Northern Ireland was given internal self-government, with its own Parliament, government and Prime Minister, and with the Sovereign represented by a ceremonial Governor. The parliament of Northern Ireland consisted of a Senate and a House of Commons. The House of Commons had fifty-two directly elected members, and the Senate had twenty-six members elected by the House of Commons. Although proportional representation was used in the elections of 1921 and 1925, from 1929 onwards election was by means of single-member constituencies. But whatever the method of election, the Parliament of Northern Ireland from 1922–72 was dominated by a unionist majority. At every election, unionists won between 33–40 of the House of Commons seats, with the nationalists winning most of the remainder, and so the unionists became an entrenched majority in the Government of Northern Ireland.

There is no evidence that the Northern Ireland government showed much interest in the fate of the Order of St Patrick, beyond Sir James Craig's letter of July 1924, until Sir Basil Brooke became Prime Minister of Northern Ireland in 1943. Brooke was Prime Minister for twenty years (1943–63), and a unionist of unshakeable convictions. He also developed an affection for the Order of St Patrick, and at one time there was a rumour in Northern Ireland that he would have much preferred it to the viscountcy that he received in 1952. He had begun his premiership in May 1943 with an appeal to Herbert Morrison, the Home Secretary, to confer the Order of St Patrick on Generals Alexander and Montgomery. Less than two years later, he wrote to Morrison again, in March 1945, with a general appeal for the Order to be revived. 'I think it would be very unfortunate if objections are raised to the revival of the Order on purely political grounds. The Governor, with whom I have already discussed the matter, is in full agreement with me that it would be a gracious gesture if steps could be taken to prevent this Order from falling into abeyance, and we all hope that you may be able to take such action as you consider appropriate for the renewal of the grant of this distinguished decoration ... I can assure you that the revival of the Order would give the greatest possible pleasure in Northern Ireland.'[1]

Brooke's letter caused a renewed flurry of activity between March and November 1945. Morrison sympathised with his request and replied that he would ensure that his observations 'were fully considered'.[2] He forwarded the letter to Clement Attlee, Deputy Prime Minister and Lord President of the Council, and voiced his own support. 'I am, of course, aware that at your instance this question was considered in 1943, but I hope you will not regard the decision then reached as final. The revival of the Order would, I am sure, give great satisfaction in this country as well as in

Northern Ireland, and the end of the European war might provide an appropriate occasion for this step. While I see the difficulties from the point of view of relations with Eire, their importance ... can easily be exaggerated.'[3]

Once again there were words of caution from Sir Charles Dixon at the Dominions Office, but more so. 'It is a pity that the Prime Minister of Northern Ireland should have taken this opportunity to revive a hare which was so peacefully sleeping. I should have thought that, in view of the development in the war situation since the question was last considered in 1943, there would be no difficulty in finding some other, and more suitable honour for the commanders concerned ... without having recourse to so dubious an expedient as the KP.'[4] Dixon at least regarded the Order of St Patrick as dead and buried.

There followed the usual consultations between civil servants in the Home and Dominions Offices, on this occasion with a unanimous and surprising conclusion; that there was no objection to using the Order to recognise distinguished service in Northern Ireland, nor even to it being used to recognise war service by eminent generals of Irish extraction. The following minute was drafted within the Home Office, but expressed the views of both departments. 'I think, therefore, we may take it that when a suitable occasion arises for conferring the Order on someone connected with Northern Ireland there will be no difficulty in doing so, and this, I assume, is the essential point to which Sir Basil attaches importance.'[5] The result of the debate was duly put to Clement Attlee, 'who is glad to learn that the Order may still be used at the appropriate time for recognising distinguished service'.[6] No further action was taken in March 1945, but Brooke had now acquired what he was seeking, government approval in principal for the use of the Order of St Patrick to recognise distinguished service that was, in some way, connected with Northern Ireland, and he was not long in putting forward a name.

In October 1945 Brooke visited Morrison's successor, James Chuter Ede, and again pressed the claim of Field Marshal the Honourable Sir Harold Alexander. 'His services during the war and his appointment as Governor-General of Canada would make it particularly appropriate to bestow this honour on so distinguished a son of Northern Ireland.'[7] Again the Dominions Secretary (Lord Addison, since the general election of July 1945), expressed caution. 'Such an appointment, however, would carry the risk of controversy with Mr de Valera, and from the Dominions Office point of view it would certainly be preferable that this issue should not be raised. But if it is desired to confer this distinction on Field Marshal Alexander I should not press this objection.'[8] Addison also observed that there were a number of customary distinctions given to Governor-Generals, including a peerage, appointment as a Knight Grand Cross in the Order on St Michael and St George, and membership of the Privy Council, and therefore perhaps it was unnecessary to raise the question of the Order of St Patrick for Alexander. Addison dispatched a copy of his response to Chuter Ede, whose reply was frank and unanswerable. 'If we were to refrain from recommending this honour on the present occasion because of the risk of controversy with the Eire Government, can any future case be imagined in which this risk will be less?'[9] Addison's efforts were supported by his civil servants, at least one of whom was not above sending messages of support to Belfast. In October 1945, Robert Gransden, the Northern Ireland Cabinet Secretary, received a note headed 'secret and personal' from A. J. Kelly in the Home Office in London. 'It is now in train for the final decision. I only hope the GCMG [Knight Grand Cross of the Order of St Michael and St George] does not win!! Somehow I don't think it will unless the original idea relating to it has gone too far.'[10] The Order of St Patrick still had its supporters.

The future of the Order was now in the hands of Clement Attlee, who had succeeded Winston Churchill as Prime Minister in July 1945. Attlee had before him, conflicting advice from two of his cabinet ministers, the Home Secretary and the Dominions Secretary, and the final decision was his to make; he was not long in making it. On 6 November, he replied to the Home Secretary rejecting the proposal to appoint Field Marshal Alexander to the Order of St Patrick. 'In the first place I agree with the Dominions Secretary that it would be preferable not to raise the issue at this time. I am considering the honours to be awarded to outstanding war leaders, and after full reflection I think that a peerage would be more suitable in this case than a KP. I am as anxious as anyone to keep this Order alive, and I suggest that the name of Field Marshal Alexander might come up for consideration in a few years' time when one may hope that the position will be easier than it is now.'[11]

Attlee was supported by King George VI, the two men having discussed the future of the Order at the end of 1944. 'His Majesty would like to have time before reviving the Order, when Eire's attitude is more in tune with ours.'[12] Attlee was still disposed to adhere to the views that he had expressed in 1943 against the reconstitution of the Order, and he had the backing of a more cautious and sensitive King. Brooke had been defeated by the combined opposition of the King, the Prime Minister and the Dominions Office, and in the opinion of the last, a risk of unnecessary controversy with the Government of the republic of Ireland had once again been precluded.

Brooke had no intention of giving up the struggle, and his recommendation of Field Marshal Alexander was rapidly followed by another recommendation for the Order – this time from Earl Granville, the Governor of Northern Ireland. The proposed name was another distinguished military son of Northern Ireland – Field Marshal Viscount Alanbrooke – and it now seems clear that discussions at various levels were taking place in the halls of Stormont Castle in 1945, with the purpose of preserving the Order of St Patrick from extinction and asserting the proprietorial claim of Northern Ireland to submit recommendations. In all probability, Granville knew what Brooke was doing and Brooke knew what Granville was doing, and even if they were not acting in concert or according to an arranged strategy, the harmony of timing is such as to leave the observer suspicious of any claim of coincidence.

On 6 November 1945, Attlee vetoed the appointment of Alexander, partly on the ground that he was about to receive a peerage, but did not close the door to his appointment to the Order of St Patrick at some future date. Nine days later, the Governor of Northern Ireland wrote to the Home Office recommending another distinguished soldier for the Order, and this time one upon whom a peerage had already been conferred. It is unlikely that the Governor would have made a recommendation without first consulting his Prime Minister, although he claimed that he did not. 'I have not consulted my Prime Minister in the matter as I feel Sir Basil would be diffident of making the suggestion as Lord Alanbrooke is his uncle.'[13] Yet he begins his letter, 'I have now had the opportunity of going fully into the correspondence which has gathered over a long period of years in the matter of the Order of St Patrick'.[14] That statement in itself begs the question, 'why?' Would Granville have concerned himself with the dormant Order, unless Brooke had asked him to do so? Granville was gently 'put down' by Sir Alexander Maxwell at the Home Office, who reminded the Governor that it was not within the functions of the Home Office or the Prime Minister of Northern Ireland, to make a recommendation for an honour to recognise services rendered outside Northern Ireland, which was certainly the case with Alanbrooke.[15]

Field Marshal Alexander had been vetoed on the ground that a peerage was about to be conferred on him. Field Marshal Alanbrooke, upon whom a peerage had already been conferred was vetoed because he had performed no services within Northern Ireland. The pro-Order lobby in Northern Ireland was undaunted, and there quickly came a third nomination of one who was performing services in Northern Ireland. Granville's recommendation of Alanbrooke was followed two days later by a letter recommending Granville himself – from his own private secretary, Oscar Henderson. On his appointment as Governor of Northern Ireland in 1922, the Duke of Abercorn had been immediately appointed to the Order on the recommendation of the outgoing Lord Lieutenant; in 1945, his successor was not. Earl Granville had in fact been appointed a KCVO (Knight Commander of the Royal Victorian Order) in 1945 on his departure from the Isle of Man, where he had been Lieutenant Governor from 1937. Oscar Henderson revealed that Granville had spoken to him of his recommendation of Lord Alanbrooke. 'I must tell you, privately, that in the circles in which I move there has been comment that Lord Granville was not given the KP on appointment as Governor of Northern Ireland. The "Thinkers" here (and there are a few!) feel it would be a very great pity if this Order is allowed to die out and so long as there is a government in the Northern part of Ireland, closely associated with Great Britain, it is felt that this Order of Knighthood gives Irishmen an equal standing with Englishmen and Scotsmen ... It seems to me – and this purely a personal opinion as this is a private letter – that it would be invidious if any appointments are made to this Order before it is received by Lord Granville, though I do not for a moment suggest that Lord Alanbrooke is other than most suitable to be honoured.'[16] It was a good try, but there was little chance that he would succeed. The Dominions Office would have raised the point that they had first made in July 1926. 'We should certainly see considerable objection to a proposal which in effect would mean that every Governor of Northern Ireland would become a KP – whereas Governor-Generals are rarely if ever given anything higher than GCMG.'[17] Granville was not appointed to the Order of St Patrick, and he retired from the governorship of Northern Ireland in December 1952, six months before his death, without receiving any further honour.

At some point before July 1946, King George VI informed Clement Attlee, that he would like to resume personal control of the Orders of the Garter, the Thistle, and the St Patrick; conferring them on his own authority, without any reference to the Prime Minister. The King felt that the three honours had been considerably devalued by being used for political patronage, an ironic comment when the origins of the Order of St Patrick are considered, and he was anxious to raise their status by assuming personal responsibility for appointments. Attlee raised no objection to the King's proposal, but there was the sensitive issue of the Order of St Patrick. A meeting was held at Buckingham Palace on 12 July 1946 to consider the form in which this new development could be announced to the public. Those present included the King's Private Secretary, Sir Alan Lascelles, Major Michael Adeane, Sir Edward Bridges, Sir Eric Machtig, Sir Robert Knox and T. L. Rowan. A draft announcement was prepared, to be made at the time that any appointments under the new procedure were announced. 'You will note that ... no reference is made to the Thistle and the Patrick ... The object of this procedure is to avoid the possibility of the Eire Government raising difficulties about the Patrick. If questions were asked about the Patrick, it would merely be said that the matter did not arise as no appointments were being made at the present moment.'[18] All options were still open on the Order of St Patrick, but nothing further was to be done for the present. Attlee consulted Churchill, reiterating that he proposed to do nothing with the Patrick for the time being. 'The Eire Government might raise objections in regard to the Patrick. I do not necessarily admit that these objections would have any sound basis but on the other hand, it would obviously be much better to avoid anything of this sort if possible.'[19] The King himself noted in his diary his feelings of delight at having the Garter and the Thistle returned to his personal control, but he made no reference to the Patrick, perhaps implicitly recognising that it was no longer a live issue.[20] The official line was maintained in June 1947, with the appointment of the first two Knights of the Thistle under the new procedure. 'If any questions are raised about the Patrick, we shall take the line which has been agreed by all concerned, namely that an announcement about this Order will if necessary be made when any appointment to it is announced.'[21]

So the Order of St Patrick was gradually passing into the shadows. With the exception of the Sovereign and the two royal dukes – Windsor and Gloucester – there were only seven Knights still alive: the Earl of Granard, the intermediary in the exchanges between London and Dublin in 1927–30; the Earl of Arran, the Liberal

philanthropist; the Earl of Shaftesbury, former Lord Mayor of Belfast and Lord Chamberlain to Queen Mary; the Earl of Donoughmore, the Conservative politician; Viscount Powerscourt, who had declined the lord lieutenancy in 1916; Field Marshal the Earl of Cavan; and the Duke of Abercorn, the first Governor of Northern Ireland. Powerscourt was the youngest, at sixty-six, and Cavan was the oldest, at eighty-one. The others were all in their seventies. The life clock of the Order of St Patrick was running down, and a series of deaths between August 1946 and October 1948 brought the Order to the brink of extinction. The deaths of the Earl of Cavan in August 1946, and Viscount Powerscourt in March 1947, removed two more Knights. The last Grand Master, Viscount FitzAlan of Derwent died in May 1947. Viscount Greenwood, the last Chancellor, died on 10 September 1947, on the same day as the Earl of Granard. Granard had become a distinguished and respected politician in the Irish Free State after partition. He had been appointed to the Irish Council of State and his funeral in Northern Ireland was attended by President Sean O'Kelly and Prime Minister Eamon de Valera. The death of the Earl of Donoughmore in October 1948 evoked a memory of the beginning of the Order. His ancestor, John Hely-Hutchinson, Prime Serjeant of Ireland, and later first Earl of Donoughmore, had read the Royal Warrant creating the Order to the assembled Knights in St Patrick's Hall on 11 March 1783.

Time was now running out for the Order of St Patrick. One by one, the elderly Knights died, and as the Order faded from living memory, so did the prospects of reconstitution and revival. The question of reconstituting the Order had exercised the minds of three government departments in the 1920s, but by 1948 there were few people left in office who could remember the great days of the Order before the First World War. There was nobody left to fight for the cause of an Order, whose shadowy existence was becoming something of an anachronistic relic of a vanished culture. The glittering social world of viceregal Dublin and the Anglo-Irish aristocracy, in which the Order had once figured so prominently, was drifting from memory to history; and it had become clear that the Order itself really had no future without a radical overhaul. The announcement in 1948 that southern Ireland intended to withdraw from membership of the Commonwealth, finally severed the last tenuous constitutional links binding it to the United Kingdom.

The withdrawal of Ireland from the Commonwealth in April 1949 produced the last flickering of light around the Order of St Patrick. Sir Basil Brooke again asked for the Statutes of the Order to be revised, and even that everything associated with the Order be removed from Dublin. Whether he ever received an answer is uncertain. The last document in the Home Office file relating to the Order contains the following draft reply to Brooke. 'The reason that the Order has not been used hitherto has been the attitude of the Free State, and subsequently the Eire, Government. Now that that Government is going out of the Commonwealth, their objections to the use of the Order will no longer have any force and we may now go ahead with the plan of 1928 for revising the statutes to bring them into line with the situation when the Republic of Ireland Bill becomes operative. One question which we shall later have to consider is whether the Order should remain an exclusively Northern Ireland Order in view of the smallness of Ulster, but that need not affect the decision, which can be taken now, that the Order shall not be allowed to lapse ... Sir Basil Brooke can be assured that the Order of St Patrick will not be allowed to lapse, that the revision of the statutes will be put in hand upon Eire leaving the Commonwealth.'[22] The paper is headed 'Draft note for the Prime Minister in response to a suggestion by Sir Basil Brooke'. There is no subsequent paper, and the only conclusion to be drawn is that Clement Attlee disagreed with its content, and chose not to use it.

The consequential silence and inactivity may have provoked the comment by Sir Hugh O'Neill (later Lord Rathcavan), Member for Antrim, in the House of Commons on 11 May 1949. The House was debating the second reading of the Ireland Bill, which gave recognition to southern Ireland's formal adoption of republican status, and its withdrawal from the Commonwealth. Beginning with a plea for the continued election of Irish representative peers to the House of Lords, O'Neill moved to the status of the Order: 'What is going to be the future of that great Order of Knighthood of St Patrick which ... has historic associations of the greatest importance? Is the Order of St Patrick to go on, or is it not? If it is to go on it seems to me that it should be transferred to the part of Ireland which remains within the United Kingdom, and I should have thought that was a natural thing to have brought about at this time'.[23] In view of his close friendship with Sir Basil Brooke, O'Neill's statement was to be expected. The Government returned no answer to his rhetorical question.

Notes of a meeting with the Governor of Northern Ireland in March 1950, indicate no more than the passing interest of historical record. 'Some years ago we took up the question of reviving the Order. It was then decided that the Order should not be allowed to lapse, but we understood that the revision of the Statutes would be put in hand after Eire left the Commonwealth ... The matter is one for the monarch, as appointments to the Order, like the Garter and the Thistle, are made by the King personally ... I think it would be open to the Governor, if he felt so disposed, to make a recommendation direct to the King.' This minute is accompanied by a hand-written note in the adjacent margin. 'The Governor made little comment. He will take an opportunity of raising the matter.'[24] Whether Granville ever discussed the Order with King George VI is unknown, but if he did so, it is quite probable that the King cautioned him against pursuing the matter further.

In 1957, the Northern Ireland government briefly tried another route to the Order. Sir Gerald Wollaston, Norroy and Ulster King of Arms from 1944, died in March 1957, and Sir Robert Gransden, secretary to the Northern Ireland cabinet, asked the Home Office in London to reconsider the position of the amalgamated office of Norroy and Ulster King of Arms. An internal Northern Ireland government memorandum from the Government Press Officer to the Ministry of Home Affairs suggested that the office of Ulster could be separated from Norroy and transferred to Northern Ireland. Although there would be a very limited heraldic role for the office in its new base, the title could possibly be combined either with the Serjeant of Arms or with the Gentleman Usher of the Black Rod, both officials of the Northern Ireland Parliament. 'If the appointment could be made in this way the Ulster King could fulfil a ceremonial role and also act as Herald or King of Arms for the Order of St Patrick ... when and if we get the Order revived. In that case the Great Hall of the Northern Ireland Parliament could become the Chancery of the Order. The banners of the Knights could hang there enhancing the dignity of the hall and avoiding the possible accusation of sectarianism which might arise if a chapel were created for the Order.'[25] What was possibly Gransden's last hope was immediately crushed by the Home Office in London. 'We don't like the suggestion ... we think the better course would be to continue the existing arrangement and ... we hope it won't be too long before the Earl Marshal submits to the Queen the name of a man eminent in heraldic matters for appointment as Sir Gerald Wollaston's successor.'[26] Gransden was clutching at straws in his attempt to repatriate the office of Ulster King of Arms. Twelve years had passed since the last serious debate on the future of the Order, and fourteen years since the amalgamation of the offices of Norroy and Ulster. In 1957 Gransden himself retired as Northern Ireland cabinet secretary to become the Northern Ireland Agent-General in London. He retired from that post in 1962 and died in 1972.

Basil Brooke was the last Prime Minister of Northern Ireland to take a serious interest in the Order of St Patrick, and there appears to be no surviving written evidence for his interest after 1948. There were those who put about the rumour that he himself had wanted to be appointed a Knight of St Patrick, but there is no evidence for this assertion, and he was to receive greater honours. He was created a viscount in 1952 and a Knight of the Garter in 1965. After twenty years in office he retired as Prime Minister of Northern Ireland in 1963 and died in 1973.

The story of Northern Ireland's attitude to the Order of St Patrick after 1948, is one of dwindling interest. By 1960, the Order had been consigned to the graveyard that it shares with hundreds of other defunct or dormant Orders of greater or lesser repute. Brooke's successor, Terence O'Neill, Prime Minister of Northern Ireland 1963–9, remembered being in favour of the continuation of the Order before he succeeded Brooke, feeling that it could be made into a symbol of unity if leading Catholics of the province could be persuaded to accept it; He was less interested in the question of the repatriation of Ulster King of Arms. 'This is not a matter on which I feel strongly or which I consider of any great importance. So far as I am concerned I am content to leave the matter where it rests.'[27] O'Neill raised the question of Irish peers being allowed to sit in the House of Lords with Jack Lynch (Prime Minister of Ireland, 1966–73 and 1977–9), who seemed quite uninterested in the whole matter. O'Neill was convinced that London would do nothing for the Irish peers without the consent of Dublin, and therefore they would do nothing for the Patrick. 'I think we must now realise that London never had any intention of keeping the Patrick alive – unless Dublin itself was keen, and this was obviously never on.'[28]

Apparently in these twilight years, the Church of Ireland again laid a claim to the spiritual side of the Order. O'Neill remembered that when plans were being laid for the completion of St Anne's Cathedral in Belfast, the cathedral authorities offered informally to build a special chapel to house the Order, on the lines of the Thistle Chapel attached to St Giles Cathedral in Edinburgh – if the Order was revived.[29] O'Neill's assertion is not supported by any evidence in the archives of St Anne's Cathedral, though he himself was convinced that the offer had been made; it can therefore only have been unofficial and probably verbal.

When Wollaston's successor, Aubrey Toppin, retired as Norroy and Ulster King of Arms in 1966, the Home Office courteously notified the Northern Ireland government of the appointment of his successor, and received a brief and courteous acknowledgement in reply. If the Order of St Patrick or the office of Ulster King of Arms were discussed at all in Northern Ireland government circles after 1963, such discussion would almost certainly have ended after 1968, when the advent of civil disturbances would have sharply lowered the priority of such matters. The process was completed by the abolition of the Northern Ireland Parliament and government in 1972.

The now long-forgotten honour was momentarily mentioned in the House of Commons in 1993, during a debate on the revision of the honours system. The Reverend Martyn Smyth, Member of Parliament for Belfast, South, welcomed the changes introduced by the Conservative government of John Major, and then concluded his speech: 'Has the right honourable Gentleman consulted his right honourable and learned Friend the Secretary of State for Northern Ireland with a view to restoring the Order of St Patrick?' The Prime Minister's response was brief and to the point: 'I have not consulted my right honourable and learned Friend on the matter'.[30]

CHAPTER THIRTEEN

INTO THE SHADOWS

The twilight years

====

In suggesting that the order of honour should be known as the Order of St Patrick, the Minister is aware that the British Order of chivalry, 'The Most Illustrious Order of St Patrick' is still in existence . . . The Minister does not regard the existence of this dying British Order as in any way an inhibiting factor in relation to the above proposal.
HUGH MCCANN, 9 April 1963

THE ORDER OF ST PATRICK lingered on after 1950, forgotten by most people, and with hardly any substance, and all but five of its Knights were dead; yet there remained the continued existence of two individuals, whose existence raised an issue for those preparing for the coronation of Queen Elizabeth II in June 1953. The two elderly heralds of the Order, Major Guillamore O'Grady, Dublin Herald, and Captain Richard Alexander Lyonal Keith, Cork Herald, had been appointed to their offices in 1908 and 1910 respectively at comparatively youthful ages and, more than forty years later, they were both still alive. Though their duties were non-existent, and had been since 1922, the appointments of these surviving relics from the zenith of the Order's history, had never been revoked. It is almost certain that the investiture of Earl Kitchener of Khartoum and the Earl of Shaftesbury in 1911 was their last ceremonial function with the Order of St Patrick. They played no role in the Office of Arms, and therefore they were not included in the metamorphosis of that Office in 1943. After the death of Sir Nevile Wilkinson in December 1940, it was noted that 'there are . . . one or two surviving Irish heralds, but they never come near the Office'.[1] They were inactive and of no consequence, and therefore they had been overlooked and forgotten. But they still had their rights; the English heralds from the College of Arms and the Scottish heralds from the Court of the Lord Lyon, would be summoned to attend the coronation. By right of history and precedent, should not the two Irish heralds, albeit representing a diminishing Order of Knighthood and abolished Office of Arms, also be present?

At the coronation of King George V in 1911, Dublin Herald and Cork Herald both presented claims to be present; their claims were allowed, but no duties were assigned. At the coronation of King George VI in 1937 the procedure was repeated, and Dublin Herald accompanied Ulster of Arms. Cork Herald was not present, probably because of serious injuries sustained in the First World War. But what was to happen in 1953? In 1937, Ireland was still a member of the Commonwealth, and an Ulster King of Arms still functioned in Dublin Castle, but the subsequent fifteen years had brought dramatic changes. Ireland was now a republic outside the Commonwealth, and the Office of Arms had ceased to exist in 1943. The presence of two heralds named 'Dublin' and 'Cork' at the coronation in 1953 might possibly cause the raising of eyebrows if not offence to the Irish delegation, and become an unnecessary irritant on an otherwise joyful occasion of national celebration.

In May 1952, Brigadier Ivan De la Bere, Secretary of the Central Chancery of the Orders of Knighthood, sent a proof copy of the list of members of the Order of St Patrick to Sir Gerald Wollaston, Garter King of Arms: 'Will you be good enough to notify me as soon as possible if you consider that any amendments are necessary'.[2] Wollaston was quick to reply: 'Discussed with him on tel. Dublin Herald again in view of the coronation and we agreed still better to leave him out'.[3] The name of Major O'Grady had, in fact, been omitted from the annual printed list of Knights and Officers of the Order after 1940, possibly due to his continued residence in Dublin. He died on 4 September 1952, at the age of seventy-three, and in 1956 his sister presented his tabard, badge and baton to the College of Arms in London. Cork Herald, however, was still alive at the age of sixty-eight. As far as the Irish heraldic establishment was concerned, Captain Richard Alexander Lyonel Keith had disappeared into obscurity after 1922, and in December 1950, Sir Gerald Wollaston wrote to Thomas Sadleir to enquire whether Keith was alive or dead, and if he was dead, when he had died.[4] Keith, unlike O'Grady, was never accorded an entry in *Who's Who*, and was less easily traced. He worked for Christopher's, a London wine merchant, until 1954, after which he lived in retirement at the Chequers Hotel at Newbury in Berkshire. After discussions between the Central Chancery and the College of Arms, Keith was approached and the tactful suggestion was made that he might care to relinquish the office of Cork Herald, which had been nothing more than a sinecure since 1922. Keith visited Garter King of Arms on 10 July 1952, 'and agreed that we should strike his name out of the list'.[5] Leo Keith was a handsome man with an indomitable spirit, a great sense of humour, a sociable love of parties, and a great capacity as a story teller. He was kind, thoughtful, and popular, and well-liked by all who knew him. It was quite in keeping with his character that he should have agreed to Garter's suggestion without fuss or objection.

By this time, the Order was little more than the shadow of a shade. The death of the Duke of Abercorn in 1953 reduced the number of Knights to four – the Dukes of Gloucester and Windsor, and the Earls of Arran and Shaftesbury. Although there remained a Norroy and Ulster King of Arms, who was officially King of Arms, Registrar and Knight Attendant of the Order of St Patrick, these latter offices were now devoid of meaning. Lord Arran died in December 1958 and Lord Shaftesbury in March 1961, both of them being ninety-one years of age. For a short while longer, the riband and star of the Order were still occasionally seen on the chest of the Duke of Gloucester. On a visit to army units in Kenya in 1962, the duke wore the star, riband and badge, with the tropical uniform of the Royal Inniskilling Fusiliers, of which he was colonel-in-chief. On 18 November 1962, when the colours of that regiment were laid up in St Macartin's Cathedral, Enniskillen, the duke attended the ceremony and service in the cathedral, and again wore the riband, star and badge of the Order. It was a statement of protocol and tradition, not one of provocation; it was natural for the colonel-in-chief of an Irish regiment, while in Ireland, to wear the insignia of the Irish Order to which he had been appointed, but it was a more memorable event than many might have realised at the time. It was probably the last occasion on which the insignia of the Order of St Patrick was worn in Ireland by the man who was to become the last Knight of St Patrick. In the summer of 1968 the duke suffered two strokes which prevented him from undertaking any further public engagements. With the death of the Duke of Windsor in May 1972, the Duke of Gloucester became the last Knight of St Patrick, and his death on 10 June 1974, nineteen days short of the fortieth anniversary of his appointment to the Order, marked the closure of the roll of the Knights Companions of the Most Illustrious Order of St Patrick.

After the exchanges between William Cosgrave and Lord Granard in the period 1927–30, successive Irish governments showed little interest in the Order of St Patrick. The Attorney-General's memorandum of May 1928 had made the Irish position quite clear, and because successive British Prime Ministers were alert to the delicate and sensitive state of relations between the United Kingdom and the Irish Free State, the fate of the Order was effectively sealed in 1928. There was never any hint of a change of mind or a willingness to negotiate; the memorandum of May 1928 remained the definitive response.

In May 1948, Dr Nicholas Nolan, an assistant secretary in the Department of the Taoiseach, was perusing a copy of *Thom's Directory*, which included a list of the remaining Knights of St Patrick. He noted that the list included the name of the Duke of Gloucester, and 1934, the year of his appointment, 'an interesting fact – not disclosed by the previous papers on this file'.[6] Nolan was correct; there was no note of the appointment of the duke, fourteen years earlier, even though it was widely reported in Dublin newspapers at the time; and he felt obliged to remedy the deficiency by inserting the details of the appointment as recorded in the *London Gazette*. Reading the Attorney-General's minute of May 1928, Nolan noticed firstly, that the appointment had breached Irish government policy and secondly, that appointments were made by warrant under the royal sign manual and the Seal of the Order. He concluded, somewhat pedantically, that if the Seal was still in the possession of the Genealogical Office in Dublin Castle, 'we would have in our hands an effective weapon with which to kill the Order . . . for, having the Seal under our control, we could decline to permit it to be used for the purpose of sealing the warrants of appointments of any further Knights'.[7] On making enquiries at the Genealogical Office, Nolan was informed by Edward MacLysaght, the Chief Herald, that the Seal had been handed over on request to a member of the staff of the British Representative in Dublin on 9 April 1943, five years earlier. Nolan's annoyance at having his plan ruined is barely concealed: 'It was, in my view, a mistake of the first magnitude for the Genealogical Office to part with this Seal in the cavalier fashion in which they evidently did . . . The question for us to consider now is: Can we do anything effective at this stage to remedy the damage that has been done by the surrender of this Seal? I am afraid not. Possession is nine points of the law, and it would, in my view, be quite futile for us to prevail on the British authorities to restore the Seal to us . . . As the result of the apparently thoughtless disposal of what was, in fact, Irish state property, a golden opportunity of implementing, by a process of attrition, the former Executive Council's decision of the 21st May 1928 that the Order of the Knights of St Patrick should be allowed completely to disappear, has been lost'.[8] Why Nolan should have pursued the matter of the Seal with such obsessive malevolence is puzzling, since the passage of fourteen years since the appointment of the Duke of Gloucester must surely have been sufficient evidence that the Order was being allowed to lapse. It is interesting to note that, despite his vigilance about the appointment of the Duke of Gloucester in 1934, he failed to notice and record the appointment of the Duke of York in 1936.

Nolan's declared intention, finally to destroy the Order of St Patrick, did not answer one pertinent question; namely, with what was it to be replaced in the republic of Ireland? The question has been considered by successive Irish governments from time to time in the years since 1928, but seemingly with a lack of commitment and enthusiasm, and consequently, with no result.

The first attempt to establish an honour for the Irish Free State occurred in the months between December 1929 and June 1930, towards the end of the United Kingdom government's first serious attempt to reconstitute the Order of St Patrick. A plan for a new 'State decoration', was prepared in the Department of External Affairs and circulated on 6 December 1929. It was to be styled the Cross of the Legion of St Patrick, and those upon whom it was to be conferred, were to be known collectively as the Legion of St Patrick. The Legion would be a three-class honour, consisting of commanders, officers and members. The Governor-General would be the head of the legion with the rank of commander. On ceasing to be Governor-General, he would retain the grade of commander in the Legion. All appointments would be made by the Governor-General on the advice of the Executive Council. Investitures would take place on 6 December each year (the date of the creation of the Irish Free State) and would be performed publicly by the Governor-General, or by his representative. On great and solemn occasions, the Governor-General would wear a collar and badge, and a star on the left side of his coat. Although the proposed Legion was a multi-class honour, and one without the category of knight, it clearly borrowed much from the Order that it was intended to replace.

A preliminary draft, prepared in the Department of External Affairs and modified by Ernest Blythe, Vice-President of the Executive Council and Minister of Finance, was submitted to a meeting of the council on 10 December 1929. The plan was referred back to the Ministers of Finance and External Affairs and the Attorney-General for further discussion of the details. On 17 June 1930, drafts of the letters patent and Statutes were circulated. The matter was discussed at a meeting of the Executive Council on 1 July 1930, and the council took the decision that it should be further discussed at an informal meeting of ministers.

At the informal meeting, held on 3 July, it was agreed that the arrangements for the new decoration of honour should be completed, 'but that care should be taken to avoid any suggestion that the establishment of a decoration was being considered on the basis of a political manoeuvre'.[9] A meeting of the full Executive Council, held on 8 July, decided that unofficial negotiations with the United Kingdom Government, 'should be initiated at the earliest possible opportunity, preferably verbally'.[10] The Minister of External Affairs undertook to 'bear this decision in mind for appropriate action at a suitable opportunity'.[11]

A suitable opportunity did not arise, and the defeat of the Cosgrave government at the General Election on 9 March 1932 ended any possibility that the Legion of St Patrick might ever leave the drawing board. The new president of the Executive Council, Eamon de Valera, was concerned with much weightier issues than a state decoration: the place of the Crown in the Irish constitution; the presence of the Governor-General at the Viceregal Lodge in Phoenix Park; the oath of allegiance; and payment of the land annuities. He would certainly have been opposed to securing the institution of a decoration by means of royal instruments. He would also have rejected the idea of holding public ceremonies on 6 December, a date linked with the treaty that he so much detested, and the allied concept of enhancing the status and authority of the Governor-General. The creation of an Irish State Order went into abeyance and was not raised again until 1941.

On 23 August 1941, Oscar Traynor, the Irish Minister of Defence, submitted a plan for a new Irish honour to de Valera. In the days of the civil war of 1922–3, Traynor had commanded the Dublin Brigade of the Irish Republican Army, and was a revered figure within the Fianna Fáil party. That said, his understanding of the intricacies of honours and decorations was limited, and his quaint and peculiar decoration combined a fascination for Irish antiquity, and an admiration for the French Legion of Honour. He proposed the creation of a new Order to be called 'The Order of the Lunulu', the name deriving from a crescent-shaped piece of gold dating from the great age of Irish Celtic culture, 'since it represents a period when this country led the world in the use of gold as an ornament'.[12] Traynor proposed that the Order should be divided into five classes or branches. First would come 'The Lunulu', limited to one recipient who in the opinion of the government had, 'done most for Ireland'; second, 'Champions of the Lunulu', for distinguished or meritorious service to the State; thirdly, 'Commanders of the Lunulu' for the field of letters and learning; fourth, 'Officers of the Lunulu' to be 'at the disposal of the Government'; and a fifth miscellaneous class called 'Members of the Lunulu'. The concept was fanciful and romantic, and originated from someone with no experience in the field of orders and decorations; it was quickly discarded by de Valera. 'While the Taoiseach does not regard this matter as one of any urgency, he thinks that it ought to be pursued as opportunity offers ... He is not disposed to approve of the suggestions of the department of Defence.'[13]

In 1963 the Fianna Fáil government of Sean Lemass (Taoiseach, 1959–66) briefly considered the creation of an Irish honour to be called 'The Order of St Patrick'. In October 1962, Mrs Isabelle MacKenzie Lester of County Antrim wrote to Lemass suggesting that the old Order of St Patrick should be revived and conferred on Eamon de Valera, president of Ireland from 1959. She felt it would be a very signal Irish honour conferred on a very celebrated personage in recognition of his life's work. She remembered being present in St Patrick's Hall at an investiture in, she thought, 1910 and, 'it was a most beautiful moving and colourful ceremony of which Irish men and women could be proud'.[14] There was no investiture in 1910, but she was probably present at the investiture of Lords Kitchener and Shaftesbury by King George V in 1911.

Lemass courteously replied that although the Irish government had no honours or decorations of any kind at its disposal, the need for one was becoming more generally recognised, 'and some consideration has been given to its institution'.[15] Nothing came of this brief correspondence until the matter was given a new impetus six months later with the impending visit of President John Kennedy of the United States of America. The Irish government realised, really too late, that the country had no honour to give this Irish-American president as a gesture of friendship and respect. The department of the Taoiseach initially suggested that the president should be made an honorary citizen of Ireland, until it was pointed out that by Article 9 of the Irish constitution, loyalty to the state was expected from all citizens. This could hardly be expected of a foreign head of state. Once again the institution of an honour was considered. Frank Aiken, Minister of External Affairs suggested that an honour, to be known as the Order of St Patrick, should be created to be conferred on foreign citizens. He added that he was aware of the existence of the 'dying British order',[16] of the same name, but did not regard it as an inhibiting factor. Aiken was another veteran republican and former chief of staff of the Irish Republican Army, and the surviving remnants of the Most Illustrious Order of St Patrick would not have concerned him in the slightest. His description of the Order of St Patrick as a 'British Order', was a notable departure from the policy outlined by the Executive Council in 1928, when the Irish Free State government was adamant that it was an Irish Order, and suggests that Aiken was completely unaware of the debates of 1927–30. Aiken requested the Irish ambassador in Washington to ascertain the American practice regarding the acceptance of foreign Orders, and submitted his plans to the Taoiseach's department.

Though undoubtedly well intentioned, Aiken like Traynor before him, had little knowledge of honours. He proposed that the new Order should be divided into four classes: members of the Supreme Cross (the title of 'knight' was unacceptable in a republic), members of the Grand Cross, members of the Cross, and members. Appointments to the Order were to be made by the president on the advice of the government, with the exception of the Supreme Cross to which appointments were only to be made after consultation with the Council of State. Recipients were to be persons who in the opinion of the government had, 'done honour to the State', and who were, 'citizens of states other than Ireland'.[17] To create an institution as intricate and important as an Order in so short a period, and solely to meet the need of one particular event in time, was questionable to say the least. The importance of the award, quite apart from the time and effort required to draft Statutes, and design and manufacture insignia, would have caused debate and work lasting several months.

There are isolated examples of honours created and used purely to honour foreign nationals, but such honours are arguably nonsensical. An honour which is not given to citizens of a state becomes something of an oddity when given to foreign nationals as a token of that state's esteem and regard. The proposal to confer the honour only on foreigners was presumably designed to be in accord with the article of the Irish constitution which prohibits the conferring of honours on Irish citizens. Aiken's use of the title 'Order of St Patrick' for his proposed honour was an additional puzzle. Why use the name of an existing Order which throughout its history was conferred on Irishmen or those intimately connected with Ireland? The plan was never implemented. The reply from Washington indicated that the president was not allowed to accept foreign decorations. The urgency had passed and so had the opportunity. The proposal got no further than a few pieces of paper, and 'the Order of St Patrick', joined 'the Order of the Lunulu', and 'the Cross of the Legion of St Patrick' as a might-have-been. Ireland still has no means of honouring its own citizens, or foreign nationals, other than the conferment of an honorary degree by Trinity College, Dublin, or by any of the other universities which have been created in Ireland in recent years.

The cataclysmic events of 1921–2 rendered the Order of St Patrick something of an anomaly in the new Ireland. The civil servants and politicians who argued for the retention and reconstitution of the Order between 1922 and 1948, failed to see that it had for too long been manifestly a part of the Anglo-Irish establishment. The Knights were, for the most part, the principal land-owning peers of Ireland. The investitures were a ceremonial feature of the viceregal court as much as the Garter ceremonies were a feature of the royal court. The Lord Lieutenant in Dublin, with his castle, his court and his household, and surrounded by the aristocracy, was in many ways a smaller-scale replica of the Sovereign and the royal court in London. His state entrance to the city at the beginning of his viceroyalty and his investiture with the Grand Master's insignia by the Lords Justices, was not unlike the inauguration of a head of state. His state exit at the end of his viceroyalty, along streets lined with troops, accompanied by the commander-in-chief of the army in Ireland, resembled the departure of a monarch.

It is against this background and within this context that the Order of St Patrick needs to be set, for a full understanding of why it failed to survive. The ceremonial aspects of British rule in Ireland disappeared in 1921–2, the status of the Anglo-Irish ascendancy in the new Ireland declined in the succeeding years, and the Order rapidly lost its *raison d'être*. Those who fought for its survival, did so mostly from a romantic affection for a chivalric artifice that was neither needed nor desired by the greater part of a nation with which it had been inextricably linked. The post-1922 proponents of the Order were destined never to win their case, because their arguments were based on nostalgia for the past, dislike of the present, and unreality about the future. They wanted to retain this great Irish Order, while palpably, almost wilfully refusing to accept the fact that the government of the Irish Free State did not. So there began the search for a new *raison d'être*, and with the passing of the years, successive attempts to reconstitute the Order of St Patrick grew progressively weaker, as successive Irish governments grew progressively more hostile. The discussions of 1927–30 constituted the only really serious attempt at reconstitution. After the delivery of the Irish Attorney-General's opinion and the warning of the Irish Executive Council, in May 1928, no subsequent United Kingdom government ever felt that the Order was, at the end of the day, worth saving. The appointments of the Duke of Gloucester in 1934 and the Duke of York in 1936 were within the limited circle of the royal family, and of no real significance to Anglo-Irish relations. There was no reason why the King of the Irish Free State should not appoint his sons to this Irish Order, but who else could be appointed? The discussions of 1942–3 effectively focused on the Order as a campaign honour, and signalled the extent to which the debate about its future had moved on to even more uncertain ground. In 1927–30, the Order was to be reconstituted as of right, without the need to identify a constituency of potential recipients. In 1942–3, two successful military commanders, one with very dubious Irish connections, were being used almost as an excuse for reconstitution. The efforts of the Northern Ireland government in 1945–9, only served to demonstrate the extent to which the Order of St Patrick was no longer of any importance.

The Order remains unsupplanted by a new Irish honour and theoretically continues to exist in the shadows, as the national honour of Ireland, but this is the consequence of a general policy decision not to declare the formal demise of any honour. In August 1947, India was partitioned, and the new independent states of India and Pakistan came into being and, overnight, a raft of honours specifically for service in the subcontinent, ceased to be used. The principal casualties were the Order of the Star of India, the Order of the Indian Empire and the Order of the Crown of India, and there were lesser honours including the Order of British India, the Indian Order of Merit and Kaiser-i-Hind Medal. The independence of India and Pakistan rendered these honours redundant, but no official announcement to that effect was ever made, and this was formally noted in relation to the Order of St

Patrick in May 1950. 'As a matter of policy, it has been agreed in connection with the change of status of India and Pakistan that there should be no pronouncement whatever that the King has decided that the Order of the Star of India and the Order of the Indian Empire have become defunct. This is the practice, for general reasons of policy, which has always been adhered to in relation to the Order of St Patrick.'[18] By 1950, it was accepted that the Order was finished.

The supporting cast disappeared in 1922, and for more than twenty years the Order languished in the wings, while various individuals endeavoured to find a new role that it could usefully play. If the United Kingdom government had seized the initiative in 1922, as it seemed to have done with the appointment of the Duke of Abercorn, and transferred the Order to Belfast almost as soon as partition had been accomplished, it might have survived. It would have been unwarrantably large for the few peers living in Northern Ireland, though the gradual democratisation of the Orders of the Garter and the Thistle to include the appointment of non-peers would have been followed in the case of the Order of St Patrick. But such a change in usage would have swept aside one hundred and forty years of history, and reduced the Order to a shadow of what it had once been.

Throughout the period 1922–1949 there existed a lingering but dwindling hope, that the government of southern Ireland would in time 'come to its senses' and accept the Order of St Patrick as a part of its heritage. By December 1948, that hope had mostly evaporated, and the milestones are not difficult to see: the opinion of the Attorney-General and the decision of the Executive Council in May 1928; the coming to power of the Fianna Fáil government of Eamon de Valera in March 1932; the removal of the King from any role in the government of the Irish Free State in December 1936; and the assumption of republican status and the withdrawal of southern Ireland from the Commonwealth in April 1949.

The present dormancy of the Order of St Patrick will probably still produce a feeling in certain quarters that here was a needless loss, if only for the aesthetic reason that its sky blue robes and insignia will probably never be worn again. But the principal reason for the existence of the Order of St Patrick departed with the partition of Ireland in 1922, and the very design of the insignia of the Order – the intertwining of rose and crown and harp and shamrock – clearly symbolised one specific aspect of eighteenth-century political triumphalism, asserting that two nations were in fact one, and should have and be seen to have 'but one mind'. *Quis separabit?* declared the Order of St Patrick – who shall separate? The history of Ireland in the twentieth century has delivered the answer to this once rhetorical question, and the Order, that from its inception was nailed firmly to the mast of unionism, has now become a concluded part of Irish history.

To those who might wistfully long for a revived Order of St Patrick, there is only one answer. A revived, reconstituted or renewed Order would need to have a very different appearance, to enable it to serve a very different purpose from its days as the principal honour of 'that part of Our United Kingdom called Ireland'. It can never be used now or in the future as though the events of 1922 had never taken place; to do so would be a denial of the reality of history, and a fairly pointless attempt to give substance to a spectre. It could, at best, only be a pale shadow of its former glory, and there is something pathetic about attempts to revive or preserve things which have long since lost meaning or *raison d'être*. The Order was the product of a particular period in Irish history. It was created because it was needed, and while the need continued, so did the Order, serving a purpose and playing a role. Purpose and role have both ceased to exist, but the Most Illustrious Order of St Patrick remains in a state of suspension. It has never been abolished, although it could be; it only lies in abeyance. But the termination of that period of abeyance is not in prospect at the present time. Whether it might have a role to play in an Ireland of the future, is for the proponent to argue, not for the historian to speculate.

CHAPTER FOURTEEN

THE AGE OF THE PEACOCK

The robes and insignia of the Order

———

Many ideas have been thrown out upon the colour of the riband.
The colours already occupied by the three Orders of Great Britain left little choice.
This circumstance ... determined me to recommend the colour sky blue
which forms the field of the Arms of Ireland.
EARL TEMPLE, 13 January 1783

THE DESIGN AND MANUFACTURE of the robes and insignia of the new Order in the early weeks of 1783 was undertaken with as much haste as the creation of the Order itself. There are few surviving documents on the subject, but enough to form a picture of how the crown, the shamrock, the rose, the harp, the red saltire and the sky blue riband were gathered together to form the visible emblems of the company of the Knights of the Most Illustrious Order of St Patrick.

There were two guiding principles: firstly, the robes and insignia were to be distinctively Irish, appropriate to the now 'independent' kingdom of Ireland; and secondly, they were to reflect the continuing and enduring bond between England and Ireland. It is difficult to identify the person who designed the insignia of the Order of St Patrick, if only because there is little about the design that is original. The shamrock, the harp, and the red saltire, the so-called cross of Saint Patrick, all familiar emblems of Ireland, were borrowed from the insignia of the Friendly Brothers of Saint Patrick, a quasi-masonic society founded in the early seventeenth century, during the reign of King James I, with the intention of preventing duelling. King James I had issued an edict in 1613 forbidding duelling, and some of the wording of the edict was identical to that included in the laws and constitutions of the Friendly Brothers. The Friendly Brothers were often referred to, especially in pre-1783 days as 'The Order of St Patrick', and a contemporary journal referred to the origins of the Order lying with the Friendly Brothers, 'many of whose symbols the new Order has adopted'.[1]

The Grand Benevolence (Grand Master) of the Friendly Brothers wore a collar of knots of gold ornamented with shamrocks. In 1786 it was reported that an ornament consisting of several hearts, surmounted by an eastern-style crown, and having an escrol over the hearts, with the motto QUIS SEPARABIT, was worn by all the Friendly Brothers, embroidered on a green ribbon between two button holes on their waistcoats. The 'more perfect brothers' wore a gold medal to one of the button holes. On one side was the group of hearts mentioned above, and on the other, the heart and crown again, surrounded by a collar composed of eight knots, and the motto FIDELIS ET CONSTANS. It seems clear that although the Order of St Patrick was a new honour in 1783, it was, ceremonially, a lineal descendant of the Friendly Brothers of Saint Patrick.

Although the motto of the new Order was also borrowed from the Friendly Brothers, the choice of QUIS SEPARABIT (who shall separate), was as much motivated by contemporary political developments. The new legislative independence of the Irish Parliament could become a prelude to the opening of a wider gulf between the kingdoms of Great Britain and Ireland, and this was one of Temple's concerns. 'The situation of the two kingdoms inseparably united, as I trust they ever will be, by the same spirit of loyalty to their sovereign, by reciprocal affection, and by a conviction of their common interest, suggested to me the propriety of recommending to His Majesty a motto which, I truly hope, speaks the sentiments of every subject of the empire.'[2] The imposition of a crown on each of the three leaves of the shamrock was adopted for much the same reason.

The motto QUIS SEPARABIT can also be traced beyond the insignia of the Friendly Brothers of Saint Patrick, to a medal struck in the reign of Queen Anne, in allusion to the declaration in her speech to Parliament on 9 November 1703, of her, 'earnest desires to see her subjects in perfect peace and union'. On one side is the Queen's head, crowned, with the usual inscription; and on the reverse is a collar of roses, each rose containing a heart, linked together with two chains, and surrounding the words QUIS SEPARABIT, under a heart, radiated and crowned. Around the collar is the inscription 'united by God in love and interest'.[3]

The earliest references to designs for the insignia occur in December 1782, when Grenville reported to his brother that the King was pleased with the motto QUIS SEPARABIT. 'To this would apply very well the collar which Hawkins told me had been thought of, trefoils and roses alternate. Townshend will write, or has wrote, to you, for a plan, which plan is meant to include badges, and all other playthings belonging to it'.[4] This letter implies that William Hawkins, Ulster King of Arms, may have had some role in devising the original design. But Temple's assessment of Hawkins was that the Irish King of Arms was simply not equal to the task, and contemporary correspondence between Temple and his brother, refers to the involvement of Joseph Edmondson, Mowbray Herald Extraordinary at the College of Arms in London. Edmondson was a coach painter by trade, and herald painter to the King. He had a considerable private practice, which aroused the jealousy of his fellow heralds at the College of Arms, who felt that it encroached on their own prerogatives. He was created Mowbray Herald Extraordinary in January 1764 and died in February 1786.

Edmondson's surviving papers[5] include sketches of the sceptre of Ulster King of Arms and the rod of the Gentleman Usher but if he had any involvement at all, it was limited. Temple sent a despatch to London on 17 January enclosing, 'drawings for our Order';[6] these were presumably drawn up by Hawkins, and he wrote to his brother on the same day, asking him to make contact with Edmondson, 'and know from him if he will undertake banners, spurs . . . and that he shall be paid if he will come over and superintend our nonsense, besides the usual sum for the banners, and know from him what it is, and what he will expect from us'.[7]

Relations between Edmondson and Temple were not smooth, principally it seems because of the heavy fees charged by the former. In addition to his fees for making the stall plates of the new Knights, Edmondson then proposed to charge twenty guineas per Knight, to superintend the inaugural ceremonies. By 31 January, Edmondson complained to Grenville that his bill for the stall plates had not been paid, and that in addition to the fee for superintending the ceremonies, he wished to make alterations to the already approved designs for the collars and badges.[8] At this point, Temple lost patience with Edmondson, and on 9 February he decided to abandon the idea of using his services. 'Edmondson makes so enormous a demand . . . You will therefore let Edmondson know that I am not at liberty to follow my inclination in bringing him here; and, as to his drawings, I have already had the former returned approved, and therefore cannot alter them.'[9] Edmondson's role in formulating the insignia and ceremonies of the Order of St Patrick ceased on 9 February.

The colour of the riband was probably Temple's personal choice. The colours of the three existing Orders in 1783, dark blue for the Garter, green for the Thistle, and scarlet for the Bath, restricted the choice for the new Irish Order. The colour orange was initially proposed for the riband and mantle, in honour of King William III and, 'the sense which this kingdom enjoys of the benefits she received from the glorious revolution and from that great prince whose name is so deservedly dear to them'.[10] It was rejected partly on the ground that it was the colour of the riband worn by the baronets of Nova Scotia and partly and more importantly, to avoid placing the Order on any sectarian footing by giving it a colour so indissolubly wedded to Irish

Protestantism. Temple wrote that there was a generally expressed wish to put an end to every appearance which could constitute a party distinction, and to begin the new Order by clothing the Knights in such an aggressively Protestant colour would hardly have augured well for its future. No Roman Catholic Knights were, in fact, appointed before the Earl of Fingall in 1821, but the point was well made. By 27 January 1783, Temple had settled on sky blue as the colour of the Order, being the colour of the field of the arms of Ireland. 'You will press the approbation of the Order, and I must wish the colour may not be altered, as the sky-blue so strongly differs from the Garter, and as it has been recommended by all those whom I have consulted.'[11]

Although the designation 'sky-blue' was officially adopted, it is not easy to define precisely what is or was meant by that description, as the definition of 'sky-blue' changed with the époque, and sometimes with the whim of individual Lord Lieutenants. A letter by Horace Walpole in February 1783, speaks of the King instituting a new Order of Knighthood in Ireland, and the Knights were to wear, 'a watered light blue ribbon'.[12] The word 'watered' can be dismissed immediately; there is no reference in the 1783 Statutes to Knights wearing ribands of 'watered' silk. Walpole's belief that the colour was 'light' blue is also a mystery, since a portrait of Lord Temple shows the peer attired in a mantle of a royal blue shade. This may have been an affectation on the part of Temple, to wear a different mantle from those of the Knights. In 1832, Sir William Betham discussed the colour of the ribbon with the Earl of Charlemont, who had been made a Knight of St Patrick in October 1831. 'My friend Mr Rock [Dublin Herald] leaves Dublin for London tomorrow by long sea voyage. I have given him a ribband of St Patrick of the dark colour for your lordship. The original ribband was much paler. Lord Wellesley when Grand Master [1821–8] caused the dark to be made, but very little was ordered, and it is now nearly expended, and I presume the modern motions of economy will prevent any more being made or ordered at the public expense ... I send your lordship by Mr Rock, a ribband of the pale colour.'[13] Wellesley was again Grand Master 1833–5, and possibly again reintroduced the darker shade. The royal blue shade was certainly in use in 1842, when Sir Harris Nicolas published his *History of the Orders of Knighthood of the British Empire*; in volume 4 he illustrates a ribbon of a shade much like that in the portrait of Lord Temple.

By the end of the nineteenth century, 'sky-blue' was interpreted as a very pale blue, and quite different from the deep blue of the earlier years. There is no documentary evidence to enable a date or a purpose to be fixed for the introduction of such a visible and significant change, and any thoughts must be speculative. One possible explanation might be the substantial enlargement of the Order of St Michael and St George in 1868. Founded in 1818, principally for the citizens of Malta and the Ionian Islands, the Order was enlarged in 1868 to become an honour for overseas service generally. Freed from its Mediterranean straightjacket, the ribbon of a Knight Grand Cross of the Order of St Michael and St George would have become a much more familiar sight after 1868. There may have been a conscious decision to lighten the shade of the royal blue of the Order of St Patrick, to avoid any confusion with the 'saxon-blue' of the Order of St Michael and St George. Alternatively, the creation of the Order of the Star of India in 1861, with its ribbon of 'light blue with white edges' might indicate that it was sufficiently similar to the 'sky blue' of the Order of St Patrick, to require the addition of white edges, to raise a distinction between the two ribbons.

The pale 'sky-blue' was certainly in use by 1886 when Sir Bernard Burke crossly ordered the ribbon makers not to include any other shade. 'The colour of the St Patrick's ribbon is sky blue ... The colour of the ribbon you supply [has] a tinge of green [which] is quite *incorrect* and cannot be used. You must supply another.'[14] When the makers of the ribbon remonstrated that Burke himself had authorised it, he replied with an indignant denial. 'I never gave directions to have the ribbon of St

Patrick tinted with green. It must be made in accordance with the established colour.'[15] What Burke rejected in 1886, Arthur Vicars allowed in 1895. 'This is the colour blue tinged with a green and is the same as that used for Lord Iveagh's mantle – to which I raised no objection.'[16] The shade of sky blue tinged with green that seems first to have appeared with Lord Iveagh in 1895, was formally confirmed by a sealed pattern dated 18 February 1903,[17] and this was the ribbon as last used. Some reference books have described the colour of the ribbon of the Order as 'St Patrick's blue', but there is no official authorisation for this nomenclature.

The mantle of a Knight was made of sky-blue satin, lined with white silk, with a vestigial and symbolic hood of the same colours and materials attached to the right shoulder. The mantle was fastened around the neck by a looped cordon (approximately 410cm in length) of interwoven blue silk and gold thread, with a large blue silk and gold tassel at each end. The mantle was the personal property of each Knight, and provided by each Knight at his own expense. In 1837 Earl Talbot wrote to Sir William Betham to enquire where he might procure a new mantle. 'I cannot find mine which I imagine have been either lost or cut up for masquerade dresses by my children who doubtless thought they were of no use to me when I left Ireland.'[18]

Temple wanted to use the occasion of the first installation as a demonstration of Irish manufacturing skills, guessing how popular such a move would be with the people of Dublin in providing them with work. The *Dublin Evening Post* reported that 2,000–3,000 yards of satin were used in the manufacture of the costumes of the Knights and Esquires, 'the produce of several looms . . . which incessantly worked day and night for these six weeks past to complete in time the extensive commission'.[19] The silk for the mantles was woven under the supervision of the Castle draper, Mr Magan of High Street, Dublin. It was originally intended that the mantles should be made of velvet, but as it was found impossible to procure the necessary quantity by 17 March, satin was adopted instead, 'and occasioned no small growling among the mercers that a woollen draper should presume to employ Irish artists on silk looms'.[20] The mantles were made by Mr Ray, a tailor, of 27 Stafford Street, who was obliged to place an advertisement in the *Dublin Evening Post* on 4 March addressed to the new Knights: 'Unless they forward their measures to him immediately to have their robes made, they will unavoidably be disappointed, as the time until the 17th inst is so very short, it will not admit of any delay'.[21] Evidently the response was not overwhelming and Mr Ray had to repeat his advertisement as late as 13 March. In the few days preceding the installation service, both Mr Ray, and Mr Clements, manufacturer of the collars and badges, obligingly opened their houses to allow the public to see the robes and insignia of the new Irish Order.

Successive Lord Lieutenants followed the directive in the Statutes of the Order about the use of Irish materials, and before the 1819 installation, Earl Talbot gave Sir William Betham strict instructions to ensure that the occasion was as beneficial as possible to the manufacturers of Dublin.[22] But despite the ruling of the Statutes, that the mantles should be of Irish manufacture, Sir Harris Nicolas reported in 1842 that they were invariably being made of French satin; and it was not until the lieutenancy of the Earl of Carlisle (1855–8 and 1859–64) that the use of Irish material was re-introduced. The practice was continued by the revised Statutes of 1905 which directed that the mantle was to be made of satin or silk 'wrought in Ireland'.

An embroidered form of the star was attached to the left side of the mantle. At some stage during the nineteenth century these embroidered stars were replaced by metal stars. They were certainly in use by 1890, when one was made by Robinson and Steel of 11 Dawson Street, Dublin, for the third Earl of Kilmorey. Contemporary photographs indicate that all subsequent mantle stars were of metal, though the eccentric Lord Castletown (KP 1907) may have worn an embroidered mantle star. The mantle stars were simpler enlargements of the much smaller breast star, measuring approximately 245mm square, with fluted rays. They were generally made of a base metal, possibly pewter, and the obverse was then coated with copper, and then silvered. Though their lifetime was probably longer than that of their embroidered predecessors, they were unwieldy and clumsy objects, and their sheer weight must have caused a certain amount of discomfort to the wearer. Robinson and Steele was still in existence in 1911, when its letter heading used the style, 'Robe Makers to the Most Illustrious Order of St Patrick'.

The only other items of dress specified for the Knights by the 1783 Statutes, were the shoes and the hats. The white leather shoes had knots of crimson riband, and survived until 1821 when King George IV order them to be replaced by boots of white kid leather, turned up with sky blue, with red heels and a bow of crimson riband on the in-step, attached to the spur leather, and gilt spurs.

The hat was of white satin lined with blue, turned up at the front with an embroidered star fixed to it. It also had a band of crimson satin embroidered with the design of the collar, and was surmounted by three falls of ostrich feathers coloured red, white and blue, This spectacular and gaudy headgear was apparently too much even for the extravagant sartorial tastes of King George IV, and in August 1821 he commanded that the hat should be changed to black velvet without the band, but retaining the feathers. The 1821 installation appears to have been the last occasion on which hats were worn. They would not have been worn at the simpler investitures in the Viceregal Lodge from the 1830s onwards, and contemporary engravings of the 1868 installation show the Knights bareheaded. It seems unlikely that hats were ever worn apart from the processions to and from the installations in the cathedral, with the exception of the installation dinners of 1783 and 1821, and that they fell into disuse after 1821.

Two other items of costume are not mentioned in the 1783 Statutes; the surcoat and the under-habit. The Knights were instructed to wear, beneath the mantle, a garment described as a surcoat. Like the mantle it was of sky-blue satin and lined with white silk. Essentially a coat for everyday wear, but in the materials and colours of the Order, it was worn by uninstalled Knights on their way to the cathedral, who were then robed with the mantle during the course of the ceremony. The surcoat was certainly worn by the Knights at the 1783 installation, but probably, like the hats, not used again after 1821.

Like the surcoat, the under-habit of a Knight is not prescribed in the 1783 Statutes and it is doubtful if one was worn before the 1821 installation, or at any subsequent date. King George IV, who had redesigned the hat, commanded the Knights to wear a doublet and trunk hose *a la Henri Quatre*, made with white satin trimmed with silver plate lace, and Vandyke fringe. They also wore white stockings with crimson knee rosettes. The sword belt, which was originally of crimson satin, was changed to crimson velvet. This elaborate costume, typical of the Regency, was a product of the wardrobe concerns of King George IV, and like the hat, the surcoat, and the boots, the under-habit was probably not worn again after 1821, if only because there was no opportunity for it to be worn. Those Knights of St Patrick who were present at the coronations of King William IV in 1831, Queen Victoria in 1838, King Edward VII in 1902 and King George V in 1911 were more probably attired as peers in coronation robes.

These colourful costumes lingered on in memory after 1821, and Sir Arthur Vicars was careful to include the hats, the surcoats, the under-habits and the boots more than eighty years after they were last worn, in the revised Statutes of 1905. Vicars may have desired to keep them as a sentimental relic of the installation ceremonies, or because they had never formally been abolished, and that they might just be needed again in the future. The brief description in Statute X simply states that the under-habits shall be, 'of white silk laced with gold'.

Until 1833, when the ceremony was effectively abolished, each Knight was required to appoint three Esquires to attend him at installations; at the installation of 1868, each of the Knights present had two Esquires in attendance. There being no provision for Esquires in the Garter, the arrangement was copied from the Order of the Bath. Temple wrote that it would contribute much to the splendour of the Order and, 'it is particularly recommended by the noblemen as a thing which will be highly acceptable to them'.[23] The ordinances of 28 February 1783 purport to relate to the habit of the Esquires, but they are not described there, nor are they mentioned in any subsequent statute. The dress eventually devised for them consisted of a white satin surcoat lined with blue silk, with an embroidered shield on the left breast depicting a red Cross of St Patrick on a silver background. Their under-habit was a vest with sleeves, of blue satin, trimmed with white silk lace; breeches of blue satin, slashed with white and edged with red; white silk stockings; white knee and shoe rosettes; blue satin shoes; a lace ruff and ruffles, and a blue satin bonnet; together with a Knight's sword, in a sheath of crimson velvet. The impracticability of this costume as a defence against inclement weather was recorded in his memoirs by Lord Frederic Hamilton, one of the Esquires present in April 1868 at the last installation. With the abolition of the installation services, the Esquires disappeared from the ceremonies of the Order, and they not mentioned in the 1905 Statutes.

The mantles of the Officers worn before the changes of 1833 were, with two exceptions, almost identical to those worn by the Knights. The anomalous position of the Grand Master becomes apparent almost immediately. During his term of office, the Grand Master was authorised to wear the mantle and collar of a Knight, and a distinctive badge surmounted by a crown worn pendant from the neck, but he was not entitled to wear the riband or badge of a Knight.

The inconsistency of a Grand Master presiding over an Order of which he was not himself a member has no parallel in any other Order. His mantle was the same as that of the Sovereign, 'save only those alterations which befit Our dignity'.[24] The Sovereign's mantle was identical to a Knight's mantle, but with the addition of a train. At the 1821 installation, four pages were needed to carry the train of the mantle of King George IV.

The mantles of the Prelate and the Chancellor were also identical to a Knight's mantle. In May 1833 a number of additional Statutes directed that the Officers should cease to wear the star of the Order on their mantles, and replace it with the badge of the Order, a red Cross of St Patrick on a silver field, surrounded by the motto and date of the Order, QUIS SEPARABIT, MDCCLXXXIII, and a wreath of shamrocks. The mantle of the Registrar was originally the same as that worn by the Chancellor and the Prelate, except that it was shorter. The same change from star to badge was made in May 1833. The mantles of the Secretary and the Genealogist were the same length as that of the Registrar, but when the stars were removed in 1833, they were replaced by a plain silver shield charged with a red saltire, but without the motto, date, or wreath of shamrocks.

The mantles of the two lowest Officers, the Usher of the Black Rod, and the Ulster King of Arms, were strikingly different from those of their fellow Officers. Instead of the familiar sky blue, the mantles of the King of Arms and the Usher were directed by the Statutes to be made of crimson satin lined with white silk, and shorter than those of the Secretary and Genealogist. Before the removal of the star from the left side in May 1833 and its replacement by the shield and cross, the two Officers must have presented an appearance similar to the Knights of the Bath.

When functioning as Ulster King of Arms, rather than as King of Arms of the Order of St Patrick, the holder of the office wore a tabard of velvet and cloth of gold, and a black velvet cap embroidered with a crowned harp badge. The two Heralds wore tabards of silk, with black velvet caps, and the four Pursuivants wore tabards of damask. When the office of Registrar was amalgamated with Ulster King of Arms in 1890, Ulster continued to use the crimson mantle of the King of Arms, rather than the longer sky-blue mantle of the Registrar.

The desire to make the Order a reflection of the link between England and Ireland

OPPOSITE:
(top left) King George IV's riband badge, formed of diamonds, rubies and emeralds, English, 1812.
(top right) Queen Victoria's riband badge, formed of diamonds, rubies and emeralds, English, 1812.
(bottom) King George V's diamond star, formed of diamonds, rubies, emeralds and enamel, English, c.1880–90. The reverse is engraved *George/ Prince of Wales/April 1910.*
(The Royal Collection © Her Majesty The Queen)

and at the same time do nothing to lessen its distinctive Irishness can clearly be seen in the design of the insignia. Collars, stars and badges are awash with harps and shamrocks on one hand, and roses and crowns on the other. The collar consists of enamelled roses and gold harps placed alternately and joined together with fourteen gold knots – symbolically tying together England and Ireland. The leaves of each rose were enamelled alternately red within white and white within red, and in the late Georgian collars, the roses were surrounded by a border of shamrocks. The central part of the collar from which the badge was suspended, consisted of an imperial crown above a harp, emphasising the central role of the Crown in Ireland.

This appears to have been the original design proposed by Joseph Edmondson, derived from the insignia of the Friendly Brothers of Saint Patrick, and approved by the King. At the end of January 1783, he proposed a number of alterations. 'The first is the knots in the collar. If they are gold, and the harp likewise, the whole will look, I think, too like a Lord Mayor's gold chain, and will make no show; nothing being more dull to the eye than plain gold. He wants to have them enamelled, so as to be like the strings and tassels of the mantle. He will also send a drawing of the badge, with the wreath of trefoil [shamrock] drawn in single leaves, instead of the full wreath, which looks, as he says truly, like a civic crown or oak garland.'[25] As the original design had already been approved, there was no question of altering the design, and Edmondson's proposals were rejected by Temple.[26]

Given that the collars were made in a hurry, in space of only a few weeks in February 1783, the quality was inevitably going to be poor. There is one collar in official custody, with thin hammered knots, and enamelled roses of eighteenth-century style, that may well be an original collar. It bears a strong resemblance to the collar worn in a portrait by the first Marquess of Waterford, one of the founder Knights. The original collars were made by Mr Clements of Parliament Street, Dublin. He appears to have had less than six weeks notice to make the collars and badges, being charged with the responsibility on or about 7 February 1783. The *Dublin Evening Post* records that he went to London on that day to prepare the collars and badges, 'which were found impracticable to procure here in proper time'.[27] This report is arguably suspect, and was probably more of a public relations exercise than a statement of fact, especially given Grenville's question to his brother. 'Is the jewellery – I mean collars and badges – to be done in Ireland? I believe there is no workmanship at all of that sort there.'[28] The *Post* also reported that the collars were worth £200 each, and the badges a further £100. There seems no reason to doubt this since, in an article on 22 February, the newspaper reported that each Knight had been required to deposit £500 guineas with the Usher to ensure that, 'no risque whatever may be incurred by any of the tradesmen employed in furnishing the robes, jewels, etc'.[29] The collars and badges were completed in the remarkably short period of four weeks, and sent across to Dublin on 9 March. They were exhibited a few days later at Mr Clements's house, shortly before the installation.

In 1804, Viscount Somerton (Archbishop of Dublin, and Chancellor of the Order, 1801–9) decided to lay claim to a perquisite similar to that enjoyed by the Chancellor of the Order of the Garter – claiming the collars of deceased Knights as an apanage of his office. He discussed the matter with Ulster King of Arms, who asked the College of Arms in London for its opinion on the subject. The reply was returned by Francis Townsend, Windsor Herald, that the collars of deceased Knights of the Garter had always been considered the perquisite of the Chancellor of that Order, and that he could find nothing in the Statutes of the Order of St Patrick to prevent the Chancellor of that Order from enjoying the same privilege. Somerton communicated his request to the Earl of Hardwicke (Grand Master, 1801–6). Apparently Hardwicke was reluctant to deal with such a difficult and possibly expensive subject, as the archbishop had received no reply by January 1806. By that time, the Duke of Leinster had died, and his collar was returned direct to the Grand Master by the duke's family. The archbishop was annoyed at this move. He had submitted a claim backed by precedent and authoritative support to which the Grand Master had not bothered to reply. Hardwicke appears to have been the kind of person who ignores problems in the fervent hope that they will go away; not so the archbishop. He called to see Hardwicke on 10 January 1806, and the Grand Master, feeling himself cornered, admitted the archbishop's claim and agreed to forward the Duke of Leinster's collar.

Two and a half months later, the archbishop had still not received the collar, and he called on the Grand Master again. Hardwicke expressed surprise, and informed him that he had issued instructions to a Mr Marsden, in whose custody it reposed, to pass it to the Chancellor. Pursuing the matter with the relentless intensity of a bloodhound, the archbishop then called on Mr Marsden, who denied receiving any such orders from Lord Hardwicke! The Grand Master was clearly saying one thing and doing something else. He was not really prepared to admit the archbishop's claim, but neither was he prepared to face him and say so. If Hardwicke had given a decisive 'no' to the archbishop's claim in November 1804, the matter might have been easily and swiftly disposed of, instead of drifting on for fifteen months. His continued evasiveness and inactivity served only to convince the archbishop that his claim was more justified than in fact it was. Seven vacancies had occurred during the time of Archbishop Fowler as Chancellor (1783–1801), but no claim was made and the collars were duly delivered to the new Knights. Considering that no similar privilege was enjoyed by any Officer of the Order of the Thistle or the Order of the Bath, the archbishop was on very uncertain ground in basing his claim solely on the practice of the Order of the Garter, and on an absence of any prohibition of such practice in the Statutes of the Order of St Patrick. In his final letter to the archbishop, Hardwicke explained what had worried him from the beginning. There was no fund available from which the expense of providing new collars could be defrayed. The sum allotted for the civil establishment in Ireland was strictly appropriated, and contained no miscellaneous head of accounts for incidental charges such as the provision of new collars for Knights of St Patrick. Therefore he felt that he could not sanction the archbishop's claim. 'I have no objection to bring the subject under the consideration of His Majesty as Sovereign of the Order, or to have a document in the office, by which it may appear that such a claim has been made by Your Grace.'[30] After further delay, a compromise was reached whereby the Chancellor was assigned the duty of reclaiming the collars and badges of deceased Knights, returning them to the Grand Master, and receiving a fee of £100 for every set so returned. This right was enshrined in an additional statute in June 1809.

The Chancellor's privilege of reclaiming the collars of deceased Knights did not survive the death of Archbishop Somerton in 1822. His successor, William Magee, objected to receiving a fee on such an occasion, conceiving it to be inconsistent with his dignity as an archbishop, and the grant was rescinded by warrant dated 17 May 1833. However, the claim surfaced again in December 1844, on this occasion not from the Archbishop of Dublin, but from the Dean of St Patrick's Cathedral. The Honourable Henry Pakenham was appointed dean in 1843, and took charge of a cathedral that was in a serious state of decay. He saw the restoration of the cathedral as his main task, but was seriously hampered by a lack of funds. Understandably, he was anxious to explore every avenue of raising money to restore the building and, at some point discovered the £100 fee formerly payable to the archbishops of Dublin. Seeing the chance of obtaining a fairly frequent if irregular source of income, the dean wrote to Sir Robert Peel, the Prime Minister, claiming the fee, and happily blackening Archbishop Magee's name in the process. The dean argued that the fee was of right given to the Archbishop of Dublin, not solely to Archbishop Magee who, though he may not have wished to receive it himself, had no right to surrender it for his successors. Archbishop Whateley, who had succeeded Magee in 1831, had not been informed of the termination of the fee in 1833. Furthermore, Magee's son and

OPPOSITE:
The Sovereign's mantle of His Majesty King George VI, illustrated by gracious permission of Her Majesty Queen Elizabeth II. The label on the mantle reads: *Wilkinson & Son late John Hunter, Tailors and Robe Makers to His Majesty, 34 & 36 Maddox Street, Hanover Square, London. H.M. The King.*

The collar, crown, harp and oval badge are unmarked; the collar may be from the eighteenth century. The round badge was made by West and Son of Dublin. It is made of 18 carat gold and bears the Dublin hallmark for 1880–1. The star has no marks, but the reverse is engraved *West and Son, Dublin.*

The collar and round badge were made by Brown of Dublin of 18 carat gold, and the badge bears the Dublin hallmark for 1821–2 and the maker's mark 'EM'. The reverse of the collar is engraved with the following names and dates: *Marquis of Headfort, invested 28th Nov. 1885; Earl of Cavan, investiture dispensed, 24 Oct. 1894; Baron Clonbrock, invested 29th Aug. 1900.*

The collar was made by West and Son, *c.*1830–7, and the reverse of the crown is engraved *9 Capel Street, Dublin, Fecerunt.* There are elements of a Dublin hallmark, but no date letter. The round badge was made of 18 carat gold by Clarke and West of Dublin, and bears the Dublin hallmark for 1818–19. The oval badge has no marks or inscriptions. The reverse of the collar is inscribed with the following names: *Edmund, Earl of Cork, 22 July 1835; Valentine, Earl of Kenmare, 1 June 1872; Reginald, Earl of Meath, 1905.*

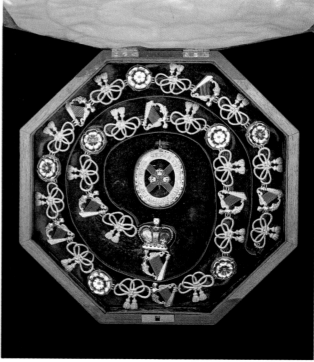

executor insisted that his father had received the fee and, 'it must be remembered that Archbishop Magee was greatly impaired in his faculties before his death'.[31] Archbishop Whateley had considered the ruinous state of the cathedral and was willing to surrender his claims to the dean. 'Allowing the claim would be an act of justice for a holy purpose. In the national expense it is nothing, to its peculiar object it is everything. The dean adds no more lest on the one hand he should seem to weaken his claim by putting former right on the footing of a mere favour, or on the other hand lest he should appear to be insensible to the favour, by which he hopes to obtain a dormant right.'[32] The reaction in London was predictable. 'To repair a Protestant Cathedral by such means, when the wealth of the Irish Church is remembered, would be degradation in the extreme and no one but a dean could contemplate such an arrangement.'[33] Sir Robert Peel duly replied to the dean, declining to revive the abolished allowance on the ground that it might cause 'much dissatisfaction'.

The story of the return, storage and supply of insignia at the beginning of the nineteenth century is one of confusion and inefficiency, and the story of the archbishop's fee sheds some light on an unsatisfactory state of affairs. Sir Chichester Fortescue, Ulster King of Arms 1788–1820, seems to have taken little care of the insignia. Until William Betham arrived at the Office of Arms in 1807, the story of insignia is one of misplaced collars and badges, and odd items turning up in offices all over Dublin Castle – anywhere, it seems except the Chancery of the Order in the Bermingham Tower. Lord Carysfort, who was appointed a Knight in 1784, did not receive a collar until May 1806. The collar of the Marquess of Waterford (KP 1783, died in 1800) was never apparently returned, and the fact was not noticed until six years after the death of the marquess, during the negotiations between Hardwicke and Somerton. The archbishop also told Hardwicke that the Duke of Portland had given him a collar, though he did not know by whom it had been worn and how it had come into the duke's possession. When the Marquess of Ely died in 1806, his collar was delivered to the Earl of Carysfort, who had been appointed in 1784 and installed in 1800, but the badge was kept for use at the investiture of the Marquess of Headfort, who filled the vacancy caused by the death of Ely. But four years later, in 1810, Headfort wrote to the Home Secretary complaining that he had still not received any insignia, and, at his installation in 1809, he had been the only Knight not to be invested with a collar. It seems that some of the insignia was kept at St Patrick's Cathedral, since Betham wrote to the dean in September 1814 asking him to return, 'as soon as convenient such collars and badges . . . as may at present be in your possession', together with the names of the Knights by whom they were worn.[34] Before the 1819 installation, Betham wrote to the Grand Master saying that he had an old collar and badge in his possession, but could not say by which deceased Knight it had formerly been worn. 'It was delivered to me by the late Mr Taylor of the Chief Secretary's Office in whose possession it had been for some years, and he had forgotten from whom he had received it.'[35]

When Betham took over effective control of the Office of Arms from Sir Chichester Fortescue in 1811, he adopted a conscientious approach to the custody and care of insignia of the Order. During his reign as King of Arms, the insignia was kept in an iron chest in the Office of Arms in Dublin Castle, and this was ordered by an additional statute in February 1814. When Betham was in London in October 1831, a letter arrived at his office in Dublin instructing him to bring four badges and ribands to London to enable King William IV to invest four new extra Knights of the Order. Betham apologised for the fact that the insignia could not be provided in his absence: 'they were deposited agreeably to the Statutes in an iron chest of which the key was in my custody'.[36] The Office of Arms was situated in the Bermingham Tower during the nineteenth century, and transferred to the Bedford Tower in 1903.

Betham's policy of discipline towards the return and storage of insignia, went as far as requiring the return of the collar worn by the Duke of Kent, after the duke's death in

A silver gilt collar, *c.* 1840. Each link is stamped with a lion passant. The harp and the knots are additionally engraved with the maker's mark 'JJE'.

1820. Colonel Frederick Wetherall, the duke's equerry replied, hoping that the duchess might be allowed to retain the collar. 'The collar now in possession of the Dowager Duchess of Kent, was that worn by the late King [George III], and appears to have been given ... by His late Majesty to the Duke of Kent, who not having been installed, had no other collar belonging to the Order. Under these circumstances, I am not aware that it would be [appropriate] to call for this collar, which may be considered a personal gift,

The star of the Duke of Kent (KP 1783), *c.* 1806–10, with eyelets for sewing. The reverse is engraved *Gilbert, Jewellers to Their Majesties*.

and therefore was of considerable value in the estimation of His late Royal Highness as also that of the duchess. However, if Your Lordship and Lord Talbot should be of a different opinion, I shall bring the matter before Her Royal Highness, who will, I have no doubt, direct the collar to be immediately given up.'[37] The matter was referred to King George IV, who decided, in view of the circumstances, that the duchess should be allowed to keep the collar.[38] Talbot issued a warning to Betham not to pursue the matter. 'Under the circumstances of their having been presented to His Royal Highness by the late King, it is not deemed advisable to press the Duchess of Kent to give up possession of these insignia.'[39]

The Earl of Arran (KP 1909).

RIGHT:
An Usher's badge in gold and enamel with stones set into the crown. The badge belonged to Viscount Charlemont (Usher 1879–1913).

BELOW:
The jewelled star of the Earl of Granard (KP 1909). There are no marks, but the reverse is engraved *West & Son College Green*.

BELOW:
(left) A Grand Master's badge worn by the Earl of Eglinton and Winton (Grand Master 1852, and 1858–9).
(centre) A Grand Master's badge worn by the Earl of Eglinton and Winton (Grand Master 1852 and 1858–9).
(right) A Grand Master's badge worn by Field Marshal the Earl of Ypres (Grand Master 1918–21), the reverse engraved *Presented to John Denton Pinkstone French, KP by Charles Stewart Henry, 7th Marquess of Londonderry, KG, 1921.*

Betham ordered new robes and insignia as and when required. Before the 1819 installation, he purchased three new collars, new robes for the Prelate and the Registrar, new badges for the Prelate and the Chancellor, three dresses and swords for the Grand Master's pages and Esquires, and shoes, swords and ruffs for the Officers. Before the 1821 installation, he ordered six new collars (for the six extra Knights). From contemporary post-instal-lation correspondence, the Dublin jewellers, West and Co., who made so much insignia for the Order during the nineteenth century, had made collars for the installation, convinced that they had been so authorised, and it was left to Betham rapidly to dash their expectations. 'I have only to state', wrote Betham to West and Co., 'that I gave you *no orders* to make any collars. I had some conversation with you on the subject and, when I found you intended to have the collars made in England, I could not consistently with my duty allow it to be done. I

The badge of the Duke of Kent (KP 1783). The reverse is engraved *The gift of HM King George III to Prince Edward, Duke of Kent, April 1804*. It is the oldest oval St Patrick badge known to exist.

must decline any further correspondence with you on the subject. If you have made collars without directions, it is your own affair. Mr Jacob West distinctly told me if he got the order he must do it in England, and I determined to have them made in Ireland agreeably to the Statutes if possible.'[40]

It seems that not all the collars were ready in time for the ceremony itself, and Betham was forced to borrow at least one collar with which to invest the Earl of Roden. The finer detail of the arrangement was lost on the peer, who protested when Betham asked for it to be returned after the installation service. 'There is no intention to deprive Your Lordship of the collar, but to have it finished, which it is not at present. New collars are preparing for all the new Knights. The collar was borrowed from Lord Meath to invest Your Lordship, as we had not more than four collars for the five knights. I pledge myself to Your Lordship to let you have the same collar again or one exactly like it in every respect.'[41]

The 1833 increase of the Order to twenty-two Knights created two additional vacancies, once the surviving extra Knights had been absorbed into the new statutory complement, and two additional collars had to be made for the Earls of Leitrim and Donoughmore, both appointed in April 1834. The Treasury authorised payment in December 1834,[42] and the new collars were made by West and Co. – presumably in Ireland.

The collars made for the 1821 installation are the finest examples of St Patrick collars, and were made by Brown, of 3 Fowne's Street, Dublin, at a cost of £250 each. The slightly crude workmanship of the eighteenth-century collars was replaced by a light and graceful appearance. The knots joining the roses and harps together, for example, resemble pieces of silk cord which have been carefully looped with all the appropriate curves and bends, and tied together with a faithful reproduction of an intricate knot. The knots on the original collars resemble lengths of cable bent into shape and held there by two semi-circular pieces representing a knot from which depend four tassels. The roses of the 1821 collars are encircled by rings of shamrocks which are not specified in the Statutes, nor do they appear on earlier, or the majority of later examples. Additional collars were ordered throughout the nineteenth century as required, but the later Victorian collars tend to be heavier in appearance. The knots resemble the gilded versions of the ropes and tassels that were used to loop back velvet curtains in Victorian sitting rooms. The number of tassels on each knot seems to have been reduced from four to two during the reign of King William IV.

Betham was proud of the new collars made in 1821, and he was utterly vigilant in securing their return. One of the six extra Knights created in 1821, the Earl of Courtown, died in 1835. Being in London, the new earl duly returned his father's collar to Garter King of Arms, asking that it be forwarded to Betham in Dublin. Betham was sufficiently observant to notice that the collar returned was not the same one that had been issued to the earl in 1821; it was furthermore, not gold but silver-gilt. It transpired that the deceased earl had lost the collar given to him at his installation, and had a replacement made by the London company of Storr and Mortimer, but in silver-gilt instead of gold. Betham objected to receiving this duplicate and insisted that the earl provide a gold collar, which he adamantly refused to do. 'I do not consider that I am bound to give a gold one; the more particularly as I have been informed that the lost collar was of less value than the one which I have returned.'[43] Betham regarded this as nothing short of a slur on his professional competence and upbraided the earl for making such an ill-informed comment. 'It was of pure gold, duly stamped, and cost the sum of £250 which I paid to the jeweller who made it . . . and I can take it upon myself to declare positively that not one [of the six 1821 collars] was of silver gilt . . . The order was made by the goldsmith to the Order under the supervision of Ulster King of Arms, who should be responsible for their weight and purity of gold, and duly stamped.'[44] Betham's indignation was to no avail; the earl refused to consider himself bound to return any collar other than which he had found on the death of his father,[45] and in December 1836, the Treasury formally authorised the purchase of a new collar to replace that lost by Courtown.[46]

Like the collar, the badge of the Order was officially provided by the Crown, but beyond that deceptively simple statement the history and development of badges of the Order of St Patrick is complex. Nothing is known of the earliest examples, other than that they were round. The design consisted of the so-called cross of St Patrick, a saltire gules, charged with a green shamrock bearing three crowns, one on each leaf, all mounted on a white enamel ground surrounded by the motto QUIS SEPARABIT MDCCLXXXIII in gold letters on a gold ground.

The linking of the red saltire with St Patrick is tenuous since it had nothing whatever to do with the saint. The harp and the shamrock are certainly closely associated with Patrick, the latter as the emblem of his trinitarian faith and preaching. But the cross, the symbol of martyrdom, could be thought of as singularly inappropriate for one who died peacefully in his bed. The red saltire was traditionally the badge of the Fitzgerald family, and is sometimes described as the 'Geraldine' cross. The description 'Cross of St Patrick' was used in the 1783 Statutes, and the usage was

(left), a badge, c. 1825–32; (centre) a badge, pre-1825; (right) a badge c. 1833–45.

OPPOSITE:

(top) A Grand Master's badge; there are no marks or inscriptions.

(first row, left to right) (1) The badge of the Prelate. Made of 18 carat gold by Clarke and West of Dublin, and bearing the Dublin hallmark for 1818–19; the mitre is set with small jewels. (2) The star of the Grand Master; late nineteenth century, no marks or inscriptions. (3) The badge of the Chancellor. Made by Clarke and West of Dublin, and bearing the Dublin hallmark for 1818–19.

(second row, left to right) (1) The badge of the Secretary, no marks or inscriptions. (2) The badge of the Registrar, no marks or inscriptions. (3) The badge of the Genealogist; the reverse is engraved *Genealogist.*

(third row, left to right)
(1) The badge of the King of Arms. Made by West and Son of Dublin, and bearing the Dublin hallmark for 1938. (2) The badge of Dublin Herald. No marks or inscriptions. (3) The badge of the Usher of the Black Rod. Made by West and Son of Dublin of 18 carat gold in the period 1838–41, and bearing the maker's mark 'E+JJ'. The reverse displays a miniature representation of the Usher's Rod set in a field of white enamel.

(below, left to right)
(1) The rod of Dublin Herald. No marks, but one of the caps is engraved *Dublin Herald of Arms.*
(2) The rod of Ulster King of Arms. Made by West and Son of Dublin, and bearing the Dublin hall mark for 1907–08.
(3) The collar of SS of Ulster King of Arms. Made by West and Son of Dublin, and bearing the Dublin hallmark for 1893–4.
(4) The crown of Ulster King of Arms. Made by West and Son of Dublin, and bearing the Dublin hallmark for 1911–12.
(5) The rod of the Usher of the Black Rod. No marks, but the shield held by the lion bears the inscription 'VR', *c.*1838.
(6) The rod of Athlone Pursuivant. Made by West and Son of Dublin, and bearing the Dublin hallmark for 1899–1900. One cap is engraved *Athlone Pursuivant of Arms.*

confirmed when the cross was incorporated into the Union Flag of 1801. It is possible that since so many members of the Fitzgerald family held high offices of state in Ireland up to the early sixteenth century, the use of their armorial bearings in such official contexts as the sealing of documents might have given the cross the status of a national emblem over a period of time. The powerful and influential head of the family, the Duke of Leinster, was one of the founder Knights of the Order.

There are indications that the red saltire was regarded as a national emblem much earlier than the late eighteenth century. The arms of Trinity College, Dublin, which were in use as early as 1612 show two flags flying from the turrets of the castle which forms the main part of the charge. One bears the cross of St George, and the other, the red saltire, doubtless representing Ireland. Irish soldiers stationed in England in 1628 wore a cross of red ribbon on St Patrick's Day. A contemporary picture map of the siege of Duncannon Fort, Co Wexford, in 1645 shows the attacking force marching under a saltire, and there are other examples that indicate the widespread use of the red saltire as a national emblem in pre-eighteenth century days.

By 1825 new oval badges were being made with the centres open or pierced and, after 1832, the motto was rendered in gold on a ground of sky-blue enamel. The 1783 Statutes directed that the badge should be removed from the collar and worn from the riband, when the collar was not worn. We may infer from this that the Knights were supplied with one detachable collar badge, and this is supported by the receipts signed by each new Knight from 1821 to 1845 which mention one collar and one badge appendant. The receipt signed by Earl O'Neill on 12 February 1814 mentions one collar and two badges, indicating that he may have been supplied with a separate riband badge.[47] Every other receipt signed during Betham's period of office mentions only a collar and badge, or a collar alone. The situation is further complicated by the fact that the additional Statute of June 1809, which made provision for fees payable to the Officers on the recovery of collars and badges, specifically mentions a collar and two badges.

The custom of having two badges seems to have been an early nineteenth century phenomenon, and had certainly lapsed by the end of that century, when the collar badge was to be removed and worn on a riband which each Knight had to provide at his own expense. The riband itself was of sky-blue silk, four inches in width and was worn over the right shoulder, the bow and badge resting on the left hip. On 19 July 1927, during the discussions on the proposed reconstitution of the Order, the committee considering the ceremonial aspects, recommended that the King should command the Knights of St Patrick to wear the riband over the left shoulder, in line with the Knights of the Garter and the Thistle. This was described as, 'a long-standing grievance of the Knights of St Patrick'.[48] As the Order was not reconstituted, the recommendation was never implemented.

The official badge presented something of a problem for the Knights, because of its size and weight. The collar badge measured as much as 65mm by 80mm and sometimes more, and while it might look magnificent suspended from a collar, it was awkward and uncomfortable to wear from a riband at the left hip. This situation led to the manufacturing of a number of small, privately commissioned badges during the first half of the nineteenth century, sometimes enamelled, but more often in plain gold. Before 1830

The badge of the Duke of Connaught (KP 1869). The reverse is engraved *West and Son, Dublin, Jewellers to the Order of St Patrick, 1871*. An unusually late example of a round badge, it may have been made to match an earlier collar.

they were generally round, and the earliest extant example bears a London hallmark of 1809. The differences between the original round badges, the privately manufactured plain gold badges, and the post-1825 oval badges inevitably led to a belief that the Order of St Patrick had separate collar and riband badges on the lines of the George and Lesser George of the Garter. This is not so; there was only one badge of the Order, and the changes in its style between the late eighteenth and mid-nineteenth centuries should not be taken to imply anything more.

The 1783 Statutes directed the Knights to wear on the left side of their outer garment, the badge 'encircled within rays in form of a star of silver'.[49] This is the only mention in the Statutes of what for many people is the most often seen and most familiar item of insignia – the star. The Knights of St Patrick were probably worse off in this area than the Knights of any other Order, as they were not officially provided with a star until 1916.[50] The other Orders were provided with official stars from the mid-nineteenth century onwards. Consequently, there are a large number of stars in existence, varying in style and quality from the standard star of enamel and silver, to a few magnificent jewelled pieces. Those stars differing in design generally date from the first half of the nineteenth century. After about 1880 they were of a standard design – with an occasional exception – and the majority were made by West and Son, the Dublin jewellers. The names of the following jewellers have been seen engraved on the backs of Patrick stars made at various points throughout the nineteenth century. 'Gilbert, Cockspur Street, London', 'Tnycross (sic) and Son, Dublin', 'Storr and Mortimer, London', 'Clarke and West', 'West and Son, Dublin', Kitching and Abud, London', 'Garrard, London', 'Hancock, London', 'Hunt and Roskill, London', 'Rundell, Bridge and Rundell, London', 'Brown, Dublin', and 'Hamlet, London'. At the installation of 1821, Brown, the jeweller of 3 Fowne's Street, Dame Street, Dublin, described themselves as 'Jewellers to the Most Illustrious Order of St Patrick' and declared that the collars and stars to be worn at the installation would be ready for inspection beforehand.[51]

A star of the sprung section type with tubular fittings on the reverse for pinning, and a slightly later brooch fitting, c.1810.

The Statutes prescribe that the rays of the star should be of silver, consisting of eight points, four greater and four lesser. This is the only regulation about the design of the star, apart from placing the badge at the centre, and the absence of any precise description gave full reign to the imagination and crafts-manship of London and Dublin jewellers. Even the regulations regarding the lengths of points were ignored in many cases. The rays of the star are faceted in the majority of surviving pieces, though there are a number of stars with fluted rays, particularly examples from the first half of the nineteenth century.

A star with eyelets for sewing, and a slightly later brooch fitting. The motto and date are inset with rose diamonds. The reverse is engraved. *Hamlet. Jeweller to Their Royal Highnesses the Princesses Augusta Elizabeth Mary and Sophia. Princes Street. Leicester Square, c.1825.*

There are no surviving eighteenth-century stars. In common with the other Orders, they would almost certainly have been embroidered; the wearing of a star worked in silver and enamel became fashionable only after 1800. The earliest known example of a metal St Patrick star is that worn by the second Earl of Arran (1783) which has the unique feature of fretwork gold lettering for the motto and date. The star of the Duke of Kent (1783), dated about 1805–10, has a tiny ring at the extremity of each of the eight points indicating that it was intended to be sewn to a coat in eighteenth century fashion. A few examples of jewelled stars are known. The first recorded example is one made for the Earl of Mornington, later Marquess Wellesley (1783). Wellesley was Governor-General of

The investiture of the
Earl of Mayo in St
Patrick's Hall, Dublin
Castle, 3 February
1905.

St Patrick's Hall,
Dublin Castle, c.1995.

Bengal in 1799 at the time of the subjugation of the rebel state of Mysore under Tippoo Sultan, and the army in gratitude for his leadership, 'caused a star and badge of the Order of St Patrick to be prepared, in which as many of the jewels as could be found suitable were taken from the Treasury of Tippoo'.[52] He initially refused it, but subsequently accepted it from the hands of the East India Company, and was delighted to have it. 'It is magnificently beautiful and of enormous value. I should think about 8 or 10,000 pounds sterling; it is the most superb decoration I have ever seen.'[53] After his resignation from the Order in 1810 to accept the Order of the Garter, he would not have been able to wear the star and badge of the Order of St Patrick again. What happened to the jewelled Patrick star and badge is unknown, but the marquess was in some financial difficulties in the last years of his life, and it may have been sold to pay his creditors, and even broken up, though his silver star and enamelled badge did survive. There appeared in *The Times* on 31 March 1885, the following article: 'There have been three Irishmen – namely, Lord Wellesley, Lord Mayo, and Lord Dufferin, who have been Governors-General of India and also Knights of St Patrick. When Lord Mayo went to India the star of the Order worn by Lord Wellesley was lent to him by Mr Alfred Montgomery, and he used it during the period of his viceroyalty. After his death Mr Montgomery presented the star to Lady Mayo and when Lord Dufferin went to India, she lent it to him and he now wears it.'[54] The badge and star still exist, and were auctioned at Sotheby's in London in 1995.

The jewelled star of the sixth Earl of Milltown (1889) is a fine example of a jewelled Knight's star. The rays, motto, date, field and crowns are composed wholly of diamonds, the shamrock of emeralds and the cross of four large rubies. Curiously, for a jewel on a silver base backed with a sheet of nine carat gold, it does not bear a hallmark. It was made by Garrard and Co, using the highest quality gems, for the sixth earl, who was appointed a Knight in September 1889. After enjoying the honour for little more than four months, he died in February 1890, and the star was presented to the National Gallery of Ireland by his widow in 1902. There are several diamond stars of the Order in existence, generally made for knights whose wealth or popularity was such that they or their friends could afford to have such costly pieces produced. One example of a star set with paste stones is known, but it presents a tawdry appearance.

Mantles, collars, stars and badges were the principal accoutrements of the Knights of St Patrick. They were also invested with a sword, which is described in the 1905 Statutes as having a belt and scabbard of crimson velvet and a gilt handle. The sword is described in Statute X of the 1905 edition, which deals with the insignia of each Knight. Whereas the mantle, star, collar, badge and ribbon are described together in the first paragraph of that statute, the sword appears in the second paragraph, accompanying the hat, the

boots, the surcoat and the under-habit. But unlike the hat, the boots, the surcoat and the under-habit, themselves vestigial relics of the days of the installation ceremonies, the girding of a new Knight with a sword remained a part of the investiture ceremony, up to and including the last ceremonial investiture, in 1911.

The anomalous position of the Grand Master was never satisfactorily resolved during the active period of the Order's existence, and nowhere is this more obvious than in his insignia. By the original Statutes, the Grand Master was permitted to wear the mantle and collar, and the Grand Master's badge. This was a small badge worn at the neck surmounted by a harp of gold and an enamelled imperial crown set with small stones. As he was not a member of the Order, it is questionable whether the Grand Master should ever have been allowed to wear the mantle and collar. He was not permitted to wear the badge of a Knight Companion, the star, or the riband, but according to Sir William Betham, this injunction was ignored by every Grand Masters in the period up to 1839, who regularly wore the star on their coat. The origin of this custom seems to lie with Earl Temple. On 6 April 1783, after his resignation as Lord Lieutenant, he sent a personal request to be allowed to continue to wear the badge of the Order. 'I will desire to have his permission to retain and wear that badge which I now wear as an honourable distinction to me as having been allowed to found it under his orders, and pressing for no further mark of his approbation, to fill circumstances, may enable him to think of me.'[55] Presumably the King granted his request and the practice was allowed to continue with all subsequent past Grand Masters.

King William IV added to the confusion by permitting ex-Grand Masters to wear a replica of the Grand Master's badge for the remainder of their lives. 'His late Majesty [King William IV] orally commanded that the past Grand Masters should continue during their lives to wear ribband and badge.'[56] This inconsistency was carried further by Queen Victoria who subsequently authorised former holders of the Office to wear the star as well. 'It is now proposed to add thereto the star, which suggestion arose very naturally out of the anomalous character in which these noblemen were placed, but it makes the matter still more inconsistent and anomalous, for if a person be not legally qualified to act as Grand Master, it would be out of all character that he should wear the ribband and star of the Order, not being a Knight ... I beg most respectfully to suggest that Her Majesty's gracious intentions would be best accomplished by declaring the noblemen who now fill, have filled, or may fill the office of Grand Master ... to be Extra Knights of the Order.'[57] According to the earliest regulations, the star could not be worn by any Knight, even though he may have been invested with the riband and the badge, until he had been installed or dispensed from installation.

The star is described in the Statutes as the 'Ensign' of the Order, and, apart from the colour of a riband, the most recognisable sign of membership of the Order. To allow it to be worn by several persons who had never been appointed Knights of the Order was strikingly incongruous, but Betham's opinion was not accepted. Since the office of Lord Lieutenant was a political appointment, and the holder changed with the government of the day, a new Grand Master was appointed on average about every four years. It was quite a common situation to find three or four living ex-Grand Masters at any particular time. When the Earl of Aberdeen assumed office in 1905, seven of his predecessors were still alive, making a total of eight individuals entitled to wear the insignia of the Grand Master, though only one of them actually held the office. It would be of interest to know whether all eight of them were ever present at the same function, wearing their insignia. During the course of the revision of the Statutes in 1903–05, Sir Arthur Vicars also proposed to clear up the anomalous position of the Grand Master, by making each Lord Lieutenant an extra Knight of the Order.[58] The proposal was firmly vetoed by the King.[59]

The most well-known insignia of the Grand Master was the diamond star, the diamond badge, and the jewelled badge, which have collectively entered history as

A Grand Master's badge, c.1850. (top) obverse (bottom) reverse.

the Irish Crown Jewels; the story of their fate is discussed in chapter six. The pieces were presented to the Order by King William IV to be worn by the Grand Master on formal occasions. Made by the London firm of Rundell, Bridge and Rundell, on Ludgate Hill, they were received at the Office of Arms by James Rock, Dublin Herald, in March 1831. The three pieces were contained in a mahogany brass bound case, with an inlaid plate on the cover, engraved with a list of its contents. The loss of these beautiful pieces in 1907 took place in an age before photography was as widespread as it is today, and only line drawings in the 1905 Statutes of the Order, indicate the glittering appearance of the originals. They were valued by West and Son of Dublin at £30,000 in August 1899.

The Officers' badges were, with slight modifications and two exceptions, variants of a Knight's badge. The badge of the Prelate, like the office itself, is not mentioned in the original Statutes of 28 February 1783, but is specifically dealt with in the additional Statute of 11 March of the same year. The badge is a circular one, typical of those issued to Knights until about 1825, surmounted by an archiepiscopal mitre with its lappets trailing down the edges of the badge. It was worn at the neck suspended from a sky-blue riband. After the death of Archbishop Marcus Beresford, the last Prelate, in 1885, the badge remained in the possession of the Beresford family until 1971, when it was purchased by the Ulster Museum in Belfast. Made of eighteen carat gold, it bears the Dublin hallmark for 1819 and was made by Clarke and West. There is a record of a further Prelate's badge being made by Rundell, Bridge and Rundell in 1835 at the command of King William IV for presentation to the Archbishop of Armagh, Lord John Beresford.

The badge of the Chancellor was of embossed gold, in the shape of a purse, with a circular badge on the obverse, without motto or date. It was worn at the neck from a sky-blue riband. The badge, together with the Chancellor's mantle, was retained for some time after his departure from Ireland by Sir Hamar Greenwood, the last Chancellor; the badge was given to the Central Chancery of the Orders of Knighthood in 1942 by the Countess of Wicklow. To the anomaly of the past Grand Masters of the Order wearing a Grand Master's badge, the 1905 Statutes added a further anomaly of past Chancellors being allowed to wear a miniature version of the Chancellor's badge, but only if they had been cabinet ministers.[60]

The badge of the Registrar was also of embossed gold, in the shape of a book, with the same circular device on the obverse as that of the Chancellor. After the death of the last clerical Registrar in 1890 and the amalgamation of the office with Ulster King of Arms, the badge was kept at St Patrick's Cathedral until 1895, when it was handed over to Ulster King of Arms. The badge came close to being the subject of a legal dispute in 1910 when Sir Arthur Vicars, removed as Ulster King of Arms in 1908, refused to return the badge to the Office of Arms. 'I . . . am rather bothered over a legal case that is coming on. The Irish Govt . . . are taking proceedings against me for an obsolete badge – not my Ulster one which I handed over – but another that I have an absolute right to. Its value is only nominal, but on principle I won't give it up . . . I have entered an appearance & intend to defend myself.'[61] Despite this display of bravado, Vicars had no stomach for a fight, and on 22 November he informed the Chief Crown Solicitor that he had despatched, 'the obsolete badge formerly worn by the Registrars' to the King.[62]

The badge of the Secretary is oval in shape, consisting of a cross and shamrock on a white enamel background surrounded by a wreath of shamrocks on gold. In his *History of the Orders of Knighthood of the British Empire*, published in 1842, Sir Harris Nicolas includes an illustration of the Secretary's badge surmounted by a crown. This is not directed by the Statutes, either of 1783 or of 1905, and there is no crown on the present surviving badge.

The badge of the Genealogist was identical to that of the Secretary and the above comments and descriptions apply.

A nineteenth-century Grand Master's badge.

The badges of the Usher and the King of Arms differ widely from those of the other Officers. The Usher's badge is circular in shape and overlaid with sky-blue enamel. The obverse displays a gold harp in the centre and is encircled with the motto and date. The reverse of the badge displays a representation of the Usher's rod set in a field of white enamel. The rod itself is an unremarkable slender wooden rod some three feet in length, with silver gilt caps at each end. The upper end is topped with a sphere surmounted by a lion sejant bearing a shield with the inscription 'VR'.

The badge of the King of Arms was designed to reflect his dual role as Ulster King of Arms and King of Arms (or Principal Herald) of the Order of St Patrick. The obverse bears a red saltire on a white field, impaled with a gold harp on a dark blue field, all encircled with the motto and date of the Order. The reverse contains the arms of the office of Ulster, *Or a Cross Gules on a Chief also Gules a Lion passant guardant between a harp and a Portcullis all Or*, encircled with the motto: VLSTER REX ARMOR: TOTIUS

Richard Chenevix Trench, Archbishop of Dublin 1863–84 and Chancellor of the Order of St Patrick 1863–84, wearing the Chancellor's badge.

HIBERNIAE. Alone of all the officers, Ulster wore his badge from a gold chain of three strands rather than a sky-blue riband. A badge was made for Sir Arthur Vicars in 1899 at a cost of £22, and it is recorded that Vicars was given leave to sell his old badge to the Lord Lieutenant for £10.[63] The present surviving badge was made by West and Son of Dublin, and bears the Dublin hallmark for 1938.

When functioning as Ulster King of Arms, rather than King of Arms of the Order of St Patrick, Ulster wore a collar of SS from the centre of which hung a harp. He also carried a silver gilt rod, the top of which was square in form, bearing on two faces the Royal Arms and the Cross of St Patrick, and on the other two, the badge of the Order. As with the English and Scottish Kings of Arms, Ulster possessed a crown which was worn only at coronations. There was nothing to distinguish it from the crowns of the other Kings of Arms. Sir Arthur Vicars had a crown made in May 1902 for the approaching coronation of King Edward VII. It was chased silver gilt with a satin cap, ermine border, and lined with silk. Together with a japanned tin case lined with satin, to hold the crown, the cost was £28. The present surviving crown of Ulster was made by West and Son of Dublin, for the coronation of King George V in 1911, and bears the Dublin hallmark for 1911–12.

The Heralds and Pursuivants each wore a badge containing the Cross of St Patrick on a white field surrounded by the motto and date, though the surviving badge of Dublin Herald is pierced. The two Heralds wore collars of SS and carried batons, and Athlone Pursuivant carried a baton. Each baton was eighteen and a half inches in length, and had silver caps at each end, one bearing a crown and the other a harp. Although only Officers of the Order, the two Heralds also wore tabards on ceremonial occasions. On his appointment as Cork Herald in 1829, the young Molyneux Betham was forced to write to the widow of his predecessor, Theobald O'Flaherty, asking her to return the tabard and badge of Cork Herald, 'as I shall have occasion to use those articles next week at the swearing-in of the new Lord Mayor.'[64] She responded, claiming them as the personal property of her late husband, so the elder Betham was forced to write a more stern letter. 'You are under a wrong impression ... they belong to the office and not to the individual ... I possess abundant evidence in Mr O'Flaherty's own handwriting that he never considered them his property.'[65]

There is no description of the Seal of the Order in the foundation Warrant; and the Statutes merely refer to, 'a Common Seal of the Arms of the Order'. In 1842 Sir Harris Nicolas described the Seal as the Cross of St Patrick on a field argent surcharged with a shamrock, and encircled with the inscription: THE SEAL OF THE MOST ILLUSTRIOUS ORDER OF SAINT PATRICK. However, the Seal as last used is much more elaborate. Set in a heavy iron stand, it bears the royal arms and the badge of the Order, and is encircled by the inscription in Latin: SIGILLUM ILLUSTRISSIMI ORDINIS DE SANCTO PATRICIO.

There is some information regarding the cost of insignia. Garrard, the Crown Jewellers in London, produced a gold and enamel badge in 1869 for £34, and a star for £16 10s 0d. In August 1916 King George V commanded that all future Knights be provided with a star at public expense,[66] and the fee required of each Knight was raised from £50 to £65 to cover the cost. The fee was formally incorporated into the Statutes in 1919,[67] but abolished in 1937 as part of the general abolition of fees for dignities.[68]

The star was the least expensive item of the insignia to produce and, as late as 1939, the estimated cost of manufacture was still put at only £16 10s 0d. The Knights of St Patrick were certainly at a disadvantage in having to procure their own stars, Knights of all the other Orders having been officially provided with them since about 1858. The situation, however, is far from clear, and there appears to have been a certain amount of confusion as to which stars were returnable and which were not. Of the eight Knights appointed between 1916 and 1922 inclusive, the stars of four were not returned, and there are examples of stars of Knights appointed before 1916 being returned and accepted with the other insignia.

From about the middle of the nineteenth century, most of the stars of the Order of St Patrick were manufactured by West and Son of Grafton Street, Dublin, and this continued almost to the end. Four days after the appointment of the Duke of Gloucester as a Knight of St Patrick on 29 June 1934, Sir George Crichton, Secretary of the Central Chancery of the Orders of Knighthood, wrote to Sir Nevile Wilkinson indicating that if he had to order a star from West and Son, there was no necessity for a leather case to be ordered as well, as the Chancery could probably provide one.[69] On 2 August, the Duke of Gloucester, who had already either acquired or been given a star, passed it to the Privy Purse Office, asking for repairs to be made to a defective piece of enamel.[70] The star was duly sent to Garrard's, who returned it to the Central Chancery a week later. Probably in the belief that Crichton was asking him to provide the duke with a star, Nevile Wilkinson did order one from West and Son, and this was delivered to the Central Chancery on 20 September 1934.[71] It was probably the last star and the last piece of insignia of the Order of St Patrick to be made by West and Son.

On the matter of a broad riband for the duke, Wilkinson was a little less than vigilant and the result was an understandable degree of embarrassment and annoyance. Wilkinson provided the duke with a riband made in Dublin. It could have been expected that his long experience as the executive officer of the Order of St Patrick would have trained him to recognise an incorrect riband, but not so. When the duke first tried to wear the riband in the presence of his father, 'the King pointed out that it was not only the wrong colour, but was a quarter of an inch too narrow. On reference to the Central Chancery, the Duke of Gloucester was informed that the King was perfectly right, and that it was not the same colour as the sealed pattern or the same width ... The matter is rather complicated by the fact that he received the riband from Dublin'.[72] Apologies were duly presented, and Wilkinson was summoned to the Central Chancery to explain his inefficiency.

The *Dublin Evening Post* reported in 1783 that the original collars and badges cost £300 each. The price of £250 charged by Brown for a collar and badge in 1821 remained fairly constant until the end of the active life of the Order. The cost of providing collars and badges for the Dukes of Connaught and Edinburgh in 1869 and 1880 respectively, was £262 10s on each occasion.[73] The Treasury paid £262 10s for a collar and badge in 1902. In 1911 West and Son estimated the cost of a collar and badge at £252 10s, and a London firm estimated £213. The last occasion on which the Treasury purchased insignia for the Order was in 1919 when £245 was paid for a collar alone. This was probably the collar presented to the Earl of Desart at his investiture in December 1919. The last official estimate for producing a collar and badge was made by West and Son on 7 June 1938, and proved that the stable prices of the nineteenth century had gone for ever.

Collar in 14 carat gold	£325	Collar in 18 carat gold	£375
Badge in 14 carat gold	£50	Badge in 18 carat gold	£60
Total	£375	Total	£435

The need for an estimate was occasioned by the death of Lord Castletown, in May 1937. His wife had died some ten years earlier, there was no heir to the title, and the residuary legatee, Colonel Geoffrey Fitzpatrick, died little more than a year after Castletown himself. In the resulting confusion, the staff at both Lord Castletown's homes were unable to trace his insignia for more than two years. Colonel Randal Skeffington-Smyth wrote to Sir Nevile Wilkinson in a state of anxiety. 'What are we to do? I found the star ... last September. But after much search I cannot find the collar.'[74] The matter came to the notice of the Treasury in 1938 when the cost of a replacement collar was being considered. Sir Nevile Wilkinson reported that there was no need to purchase an immediate replacement. The sum of £250 was a sufficient amount to claim from the executors of the estate, being slightly more than the original cost.

The unofficial response was one of deep suspicion. 'For all we know to the contrary, Lord Castletown may, for instance, have sold the collar without being entitled to do so, in response to an offer to purchase gold, and therefore why should his executors be allowed to pay anything less than the full market price? If Sir N. Wilkinson is unable to obtain payment of £435, we might then perhaps split the difference between that sum and £213–250, and be content with £320. Very possibly we shall be lucky if we obtain the £250 Ulster mentions, as he is doing the bargaining for us, but I cannot help thinking that he has been unnecessarily kind to the executors in selecting that figure.'[75] In any case, it was likely that a prudent recipient of an honour of this kind would have his insignia insured and revalued from time to time for that purpose. If the full replacement cost was charged to the executors, they could reclaim it from the insurance company. In August 1938, Nevile Wilkinson reported that he had heard from Castletown's solicitors to the effect that the collar and badge had not been insured, though they had not yet given up hope of tracing them, and had allowed them until 1 January 1939 to continue the search.[76]

The matter drifted on until March 1939 when a box containing a badge and star was discovered at his home, Grantstown Manor, though the collar was still missing. The star, for which Lord Castletown had paid £16 10s in 1907, was the personal property of his family, but the Treasury briefly considered the possibility of retaining it as part of the sum owed to them though its low value made such a course hardly worthwhile. The collar was eventually discovered at Lord Castletown's other home, Doneraile Court, in August 1939, prompting a rather cross remark from the Treasury: 'It would have saved us all a lot of trouble if the collar had been treated with the care which its value warranted, but we can at least be grateful that we have not had the unpleasant duty of extracting full compensation from the heirs of the estate.'[77] Lord Castletown's badge was eventually delivered to the Central Chancery of the Orders of Knighthood in August 1940, followed by his collar in the following month.

In some ways, the 1938–40 correspondence about Lord Castletown's insignia was entirely academic, because the fate of the Order was now becoming clear. There was really no need to extract money from the Castletown estate, or to purchase an additional collar. In addition to the Sovereign's collar, and that kept with the Crown Jewels at the Tower of London, each of the remaining eleven Knights possessed a collar, and there were a further twelve spare collars at the Central Chancery. The Chancery also possessed fifteen badges and five stars. 'It seems clear that the present stock of collars, etc. is ample. There have been no fresh appointments to the Order for the past ten years or so, and the stock is probably sufficient for all time.'[78]

The phrase 'sufficient for all time', redolent of security and eternity, soon fell victim to the mundane consideration of practicality. After the transformation of the Office of Arms into the Genealogical Office in 1943, the insignia of deceased Knights of St Patrick was forwarded directly to the Central Chancery of the Orders of Knighthood in London. The Earl of Granard died in September 1948, and his insignia was forwarded to the Chancery in November. The Earl of Donoughmore died in October 1948, and in December Brigadier Ivan De la Bere, Secretary of the Central Chancery, reported that his office held the badge and star of the Grand Master, the badges of the Chancellor, the Genealogist, the Secretary and the Usher, the crown of Ulster King of Arms, the collars of SS of Dublin Herald and Cork Herald, together with sixteen collars, six stars and twenty-one badges.[79]

By 1957, with all but four of the Knights of St Patrick now dead, the collection of St Patrick insignia at the Chancery had risen to nineteen collars, ten round badges, fifteen oval badges and six stars, and questions of storage and finance were raised by the Treasury Officer of Accounts. 'I have recently completed the annual check of the stock of insignia etc., held by the Central Chancery. While I was there, I was struck by the large number of pieces of Indian and St Patrick Orders which they hold, for which there is no foreseeable use. Most of it is in a poor condition and, being in large boxes, takes up an unreasonable amount of space in their better strong room. I feel we should seriously consider disposing of some of this old insignia.'[80] In the mind of the Treasury, it was unrealistic to retain so much St Patrick insignia, on the ground that it might be needed in the future. Sir Robert Knox of the Ceremonial Office concurred with the view of the Treasury that the time had come to dispose of at least a proportion of what could now be regarded as redundant insignia. 'I saw no objection … I explained that all arrangements relative to the Order of St Patrick had been, for many years, on a mark time basis.'[81] The die was cast and the process had begun, and although a large proportion of the insignia of the Order was disposed of on the grounds of practicality, it seemed to be a statement of a common belief that the Order of St Patrick was finished.

There was no intention to dispose of all the insignia of the Order; only to reduce the stock to a more realistic level, and the grounds for doing so were faultlessly logical. 'It would substantially reduce the problem of storage. Space would become available in the new strong room for some of the more valuable insignia at present stored elsewhere and the potential risk of loss by burglary, fire etc. would be correspondingly reduced. It would also save time spent in checking the stock of this insignia each quarter.'[82] Practical though the plan might have been, the fate of the disposed insignia was not altogether laudable. There were a number of possible options for disposing of the redundant insignia. It was now accepted, for reasons of practicality and finance, that the insignia could not be retained in perpetuity but sale to a dealer for subsequent re-sale to members of the public was deemed to be quite out of the question: 'It has for long been regarded as very undesirable that there should be a risk that collars of the Orders of Chivalry should find their way in to the market.'[83] Sets of insignia could perhaps be offered for display to various museums, but to which museums should they be allocated, and might such a policy stimulate requests from other museums; such requests having been consistently refused.[84]

The only remaining option was to dispatch the insignia to the Royal Mint for breaking up and for re-using whatever gold and silver could be retrieved. No one considered retaining the pieces for their history or artistry. Specimen examples of the redundant insignia were sent to the Royal Mint to see whether the break-up process was practicable and financially worthwhile. The result being satisfactory, thirteen collars, four round badges and nine oval badges of the Order of St Patrick were dispatched to the mint in the summer of 1958, and a residual stock of six collars, six round badges, six oval badges and six stars was retained against any future need.

What had been 'sufficient for all time' in 1938 had become quite definitely 'surplus to requirement' only twenty years later.

CHAPTER FIFTEEN

REMAINING FRAGMENTS

The residue of the Order

═══

The Banners of all the Knights, royal and otherwise, with the Sovereign,
are to be hung up again in St Patrick's Hall.
SIR NEVILE WILKINSON, 10 May 1932

T HE ORDER OF ST PATRICK may be described as presently dormant, but there are surviving fragments that serve as reminders of its existence. It may be mourned by some, despised by others, and forgotten by most, but some remnants of its former existence can still be seen in Ireland.

Despite officially shunning attempts to revive the Order of St Patrick, successive Irish governments have endeavoured to preserve and restore the ceremonial fragments of the Order that still remain in its possession. The Irish provisional government was given control of Dublin Castle in January 1922. St Patrick's Hall had not been used for any investitures since 1911 and it had functioned as a hospital during the First World War, but the banners, crests, helmets, swords and hatchments of the Knights were still in place. In July 1922, the Irish government requested that the banners be taken down. Thomas Sadleir, running the Office of Arms virtually single handed while Sir Nevile Wilkinson resided at his home in London, informed the provisional government that the banners were the property of the Order and could not be removed without the authority of Ulster King of Arms. In reply, the provisional government offered him facilities to remove them.[1] It is not clear what then happened, but Sadleir would have reported the episode to Wilkinson, who then thought it prudent to have the banners of at least the living Knights, removed from the hall and stored for safety in the Office of Arms, and there they remained for ten years.

On 9 March 1932, the Fianna Fáil party won the general election, defeating the Cumann na nGaedheal party of William T. Cosgrave, and Eamon de Valera took office as President of the Executive Council. De Valera's attitude to the Order of St Patrick is not on record, but he was fanatically obsessed with ridding the Irish Free State of any sign of monarchical authority, and any conferment of the Order of St Patrick on a citizen of the Irish Free State would have been regarded by him as an intrusion of the crown into the internal affairs of the Free State. Between 1932 and 1936, the provisions of the 1922 Treaty, in so far as they allowed the Crown a role in the government of the Irish Free State, were systematically abolished, and by December 1936, the Irish Free State was a republic in fact and in appearance, if perhaps not quite in theory. De Valera's attitude was one of unrelenting intent to erase any lingering sign of royal authority, but he appears to have showed a surprising degree of pragmatism towards the decoration of St Patrick's Hall, Dublin Castle.

At the time of Fianna Fáil's victory in the 1932 election, Dublin was preparing for a great Eucharistic Congress, to be held towards the end of June. The event was to be attended by a papal legate, Cardinal Lorenzo Lauri, and the Government decided to hold a reception for the cardinal, the delegates and other distinguished guests, in the state apartments of Dublin Castle. The Government wished St Patrick's Hall to look as impressive as possible for the occasion, and de Valera asked Wilkinson to re-hang the banners of the Knights of St Patrick.[2] Wilkinson, conscious that he was employed by the Crown, immediately conveyed the request to Sir Clive Wigram, the King's Private Secretary, but asked Sadleir to investigate the state and location of the surviving banners. 'The banners of all the Knights, royal and otherwise, with the

Sovereign, are to be hung up again in St Patrick's Hall ... Look out all the banners which are in the drawers of my big desk in my room, and see how many are available. In case we re-arrange the Hall, I think we should be able to replace all the (decrepit?) banners; they were left up because they were too dilapidated to take down. I think it will be possible to work down half way both sides with good condition banners and remove the fragments, leaving the three top cross standards under the gallery empty! There should be about a dozen.'[3] On 12 May, King George V discussed de Valera's request with Stanley Baldwin, the Prime Minister, and both men agreed that the banners could be re-erected for this occasion; there was, in fact, no other option. 'As the banners are in Ulster King of Arms' office in the Castle, all the Free State have to do is to go and take them, if we decline to give them.'[4]

Wilkinson, again resident in London, wrote to the ever-conscientious Sadleir in Dublin instructing him to undertake the work. 'I want you to go to Atkinson and get an estimate, at once please, for making the royal banner, the Prince of Wales and the Duke of Connaught. Also those of the present Knights whose banners are not yet carried out. I have undertaken that we will not spend more than £15 on any of them. I am assuming that the King's banner if it exists at all, is in bad condition, and it is important that it should look well. Powerscourt must return his banner to the office. I will write to him later. Meanwhile Miss McGrane should get out drawings for Cavan, Desart and Abercorn. If the estimate is below £15 for appliqué banners, as it should be if the cheaper fringe is used, please get him to start work on as many as possible at once, as they must be ready to be hung up for the Congress. Meanwhile you had better get the dilapidated relics of the deceased Knights taken down. I doubt if Castletown is fit to go up again. On the left (facing the royal banners) will come Castletown, Arran, Donoughmore, Midleton, Desart. On the other side Granard, Shaftesbury, Powerscourt, Cavan and Abercorn. Please see how many crests are available, as they may have to be restored also. The stall plates can wait until my return ... Let me know how you get on with Atkinson, and if the King's banner still exists. The Duke of Connaught's was taken down a long time ago, and the Prince of Wales has the arms of Saxony in pretence, so it isn't any use for the present man.'[5]

Although no new stall plates were erected, the ten banners were duly re-hung, and there most of them remained for the next thirty years. By the beginning of 1962 they were in a sorry state; nine banners were still hanging, and one dilapidated banner was in the store of the Office of Public Works. After a visit to the hall by representatives of the department of the Taoiseach and the commissioners of public works in January 1962, it was decided to restore the hall to the appearance that it had or should have had in December 1922. The surviving banners would be repaired and the missing banners replaced with replicas. Since the 1928 opinion of the Attorney-General that the Order was a purely Irish Order and everything connected with it was a matter for the Irish government, the banners could be regarded as the property of the Irish state. It was decided that the banners should be those of the Knights of St Patrick at the time of the establishment of the Irish Free State on 6 December 1922, and with the aid of the Genealogical Office, replicas of the missing banners were made and hung. The hall has been redecorated on a number of occasions since 1962, and since the last redecoration in 1996, the banners now hang in the following order:

Viscount Powerscourt (1916)	Earl of Mayo (1905)
Earl of Meath (1905)	Earl of Shaftesbury (1911)
Earl of Bandon (1900)	Earl of Granard (1909)
Viscount Pirrie (1909)	Lord Oranmore and Browne (1918)
Earl of Enniskillen (1902)	Royal Standard
Earl of Listowel (1873)	Earl of Ypres (1917)
Duke of Abercorn (1922)	Lord Monteagle of Brandon (1885)

Lord Castletown (1908) Earl of Arran (1909)
Earl of Dunraven and Mountearl (1876) Earl of Midleton (1916)
Earl of Cavan (1916) Earl of Donoughmore (1916)
Earl of Desart (1919) Earl of Iveagh (1896)
(main entrance from the Battle Axe Landing)

It can be seen that among the banners are the Royal Standard, and the banner of the Duke of Abercorn, appointed Governor of Northern Ireland, after the establishment of the Irish Free State. There are twenty-one Knights' banners, plus the Royal Standard, reflecting the fact that there was a vacancy at the time of the establishment of the Irish Free State in December 1922; the Earl of Gosford had died in April that year.

The cumulative hatchments are fixed to the walls below the banners, but bear no relation to the banners above, and appear in the following order:

Lord Inchiquin (1892) Earl of Cavan (1894)
Earl of Limerick (1892) Earl of Caledon (1897)
Earl of Kilmorey (1890) Earl Roberts (1897)
Earl of Rosse (1890) Earl of Arran (1898)
Earl of Milltown (1890) Earl of Lucan (1899)
Marquess of Ormonde (1888) Lord Clonbrock (1900)
Lord Monteagle of Brandon (1885) Earl of Bandon (1900)
Marquess of Headfort (1885) Earl of Enniskillen (1902)
Viscount Wolseley (1885) Marquess of Waterford (1902)
Lord Annaly (1885) Earl of Mayo (1905)
Earl of Howth (1884) Earl of Meath (1905)
Lord Carlingford (1882) Earl of Iveagh (1896)
Lord O'Hagan (1882) Lord Castletown (1908)
Earl of Portarlington (1879) Earl of Granard (1909)
Earl of Erne (1889) Viscount Pirrie (1909)
Duke of Manchester (1877) Earl of Arran (1909)
Earl of Carysfort (1874) Earl Kitchener of Khartoum (1911)
Marquess of Londonderry (1874) Earl of Shaftesbury (1911)
Earl of Kenmare (1872) Earl of Bessborough (1915)
Viscount Powerscourt (1871) Earl of Ypres (1917)
Earl of Cork (1835) Earl of Donoughmore (1916)
(main entrance from the Battle Axe Landing)

With the exception of the Earl of Cork (1835), the hatchments record most of the Knights appointed after the disestablishment of the Church of Ireland. The presence of a plate for the eighth Earl of Cork is an anomaly, as he was appointed to the Order in 1835, and died in 1856, long before the disestablishment of the Church of Ireland; it may have been presented by his son, the ninth earl, who was appointed a Knight in 1860, and died in 1904. The banner and plate of the ninth earl can still be seen in St Patrick's Cathedral. There are no plates in the hall for any of the following post-disestablishment Knights: Viscount Southwell (1871), Lord Carew (1872), the Earl of Dunraven and Mountearl (1872), the Earl of Listowel (1873), the Duke of Edinburgh (1880), the Duke of Clarence and Avondale (1887), Prince Edward of Saxe-Weimar (1890), the Duke of York (1897), the Earl of Longford (1901), Lord de Ros (1902), Viscount Powerscourt (1916), the Earl of Midleton (1916), the Earl of Cavan (1916), Lord Oranmore and Browne (1918), the Earl of Desart (1919), the Duke of Abercorn (1922), the Prince of Wales (1927), the Duke of Gloucester (1934), and the Duke of York (1936).

The absence of hatchments for Viscount Southwell and Lord Carew is explained by the fact that banners and hatchments were not erected in St Patrick's Hall until 1885. Southwell had died in 1878, and Carew in 1881. The absence of hatchments for the Earl of Dunraven and Mountearl (1872), the Earl of Listowel (1873), the Earl of Longford (1901) and Lord de Ros (1902), is difficult to explain, especially in the cases of Dunraven and Listowel, both of whom lived on into the 1920s. Unless the hatchments were removed on the deaths of those Knights, the only conclusion to be drawn is that they were never placed in the hall. These Knights were appointed before the promulgation of the 1905 Statutes, which ordered Ulster King of Arms to cause a plate to be erected within a year of the investiture of a new Knight, or of his dispensation from investiture. There are no hatchments for the royal Knights of St Patrick; presumably the consequence of a dispensation.

The absence of hatchments for six of the non-royal Knights appointed between 1916 and 1922, is more easily explained. The troubled state of Ireland after 1916, and the demands of the First World War, caused inevitable delays. Although there is a hatchment for the Earl of Ypres (1917), formerly Viscount French, it was probably hurried through when the field marshal arrived as Lord Lieutenant of Ireland in 1918. There are no plates for the other nine Knights appointed in 1916 and afterwards. Sir Nevile Wilkinson was engaged in correspondence as late as 1922 regarding the manufacture of hatchments for the Earl of Midleton (1916) and Viscount Powerscourt (1916). They were being made by John Smyth and Sons of 17 Wicklow Street, Dublin; but not without difficulty, as the company reported. 'After making a very nice job of the engraving of the Lord Midleton plate, it has, unfortunately, got completely spoiled in the enamelling, so badly spoiled, in fact, that we have put another one in the engravers hands to replace it. The heat required for enamelling twists and warps the plate and when we attempt to hammer the plate to set it flat, the enamel chips. The Powerscourt plate we have engraved but shall not attempt enamelling until we have an opportunity of consulting with you.'[6] The partition of Ireland and the creation of the Irish Free State in 1922 probably ended the Wilkinson–Smythe correspondence, and so concluded the heraldic gallery of the Knights of St Patrick in St Patrick's Hall.

There was a last brief echo in 1939, when Wilkinson met with a Treasury official on 26 June, and told him that he was anxious to erect a plate for Field Marshal the Earl of Cavan. Wilkinson was convinced that Cavan had been appointed a Knight in 1922 (in fact it was 1916), and that the field marshal had paid £20 for a plate to be manufactured. Wilkinson also asserted that Cavan was about to go on a visit to Dublin, and would want to see his plate in position in St Patrick's Hall. After a flurry of correspondence within the Treasury, it was established that Cavan had indeed paid £49 10s in 1916 for a banner and an escutcheon; and that only a banner had been erected; this was sufficient evidence for the Treasury to authorise expenditure. 'I think this is good enough to authorise Ulster to go ahead with the escutcheon on the understanding that it does not cost more than £22.'[7] In the summer of 1939, Wilkinson's mind was beginning to fail, and whether because of that, or because of an unsympathetic Irish government, or for any other reason, a hatchment for Lord Cavan was never placed in the hall.

St Patrick's Hall was originally constructed in 1746–7. It was re-roofed in 1769, and the present pilasters probably date from the time of Waldré's ceiling paintings, 1787–1802. The mirrors and cove decoration are late Victorian, and the niche and screen were erected in the 1840s.[8] The hall is an elegant and beautiful room and still presents the appearance of being the home of the Order of St Patrick. Twenty-two banners and forty-two hatchments are still in position, but the helmets, lambrequins and swords were removed in 1996 when the hall was redecorated. They were found to be decorated papier-mâché reproductions, and were in poor condition and in need of extensive cleaning. They are currently in store, pending completion of research into the best way to deal with them, and funds becoming available to carry out the work. At one end of the hall, above the gallery, two gilded allegorical figures support a representation of the star of the Order. Successive Irish governments have shown care to preserve the historic appearance of the hall, and the sense of history was enhanced when the ninth Earl of Granard presented his late father's star of the Order to the Irish government for permanent display in the hall in 1973.[9] As the star enshrines the memory of one who had acted as an intermediary between the United Kingdom and Irish Free State goverments in the 1920s, in an effort to preserve the Order, its place in St Patrick's Hall is a fitting tribute and an appropriate final resting place; it can be seen below the hatchment of the Earl of Meath.

Less than a mile from Dublin Castle stands the National Cathedral and Collegiate Church of St Patrick, spiritual home of the Order for the first eighty-eight years of its life. On the disestablishment of the Church of Ireland from 1 January 1871, the cathedral ceased to play any role in the life of the Order, but by special wish of Queen Victoria (who had opposed the disestablishment of the Church), the banners then hanging remained in position. The crests, helmets, lambrequins, swords, banners and hatchments can still be seen today. The crests, helmets, lambrequins and swords are made entirely of wood, and the swords in particular are poor quality objects that might have emerged from a theatrical costumier. On close exmination, it can be seen that the 'scabbards' are in fact no more than pieces of red velvet and blue silk wrapped around the 'blade' of the sword. The painted banners are still in good condition for their age, as are the painted hatchment plates below, although these are of variable quality. Each plate depicts the armorial bearings of the Knight, above a grand proclamation of his styles and titles; the Duke of Leinster (1783) for example is described as 'The High Puissant and Most Noble Prince'. The crests, banners and hatchments are arranged in the following order:

THE HIGH ALTAR

North side	*South side*
TWELFTH STALL	TWELFTH STALL
Crest	*Crest*
Earl of Gosford	Earl of Erne
Banner	*Banner*
Earl of Gosford	Earl of Erne
Hatchment	*Hatchment*
Earl of Gosford (186-)*	Earl of Erne (1869)
ELEVENTH STALL	ELEVENTH STALL
Crest	*Crest*
Earl of Mayo	Marquess of Clanricarde
Banner	*Banner*
Earl of Mayo	Marquess of Clanricarde
Hatchment	*Hatchment*
Earl of Mayo (no date)	Marquess of Clanricarde (1831)
TENTH STALL	TENTH STALL
Crest	*Crest*
Marquess of Waterford	Marquess of Dufferin and Ava
Banner	*Banner*
Marquess of Waterford	Marquess of Dufferin and Ava
Hatchments	*Hatchment*
Earl of Inchiquin (1783)	Viscount Massereene and Ferrard
Marquess of Waterford (1869)	(1851)

* The last digit on the Gosford plate is indistinct, but would have been an 'x', giving the date as 1869.

NINTH STALL

Crest
Earl of Dunraven and Mountearl
Banner
Earl of Dunraven and Mountearl
Hatchments
Earl of Donoughmore (1834)
Earl of Dunraven and Mountearl (1866)

NINTH STALL

Crest
Marquess of Donegall
Banner
Marquess of Donegall
Hatchment
Earl of Listowel (1839)

EIGHTH STALL

Crest
Lord Lurgan
Banner
Lord Lurgan
Hatchments
Earl of Fingall (1846)
Lord Lurgan (1864)

EIGHTH STALL

Crest
Earl of Charlemont
Banner
Earl of Charlemont
Hatchment
Earl of Charlemont (1833)
Earl of Charlemont (1865)

SEVENTH STALL

Crest
Earl of Cork and Orrery
Banner
Earl of Cork and Orrery
Hatchments
Earl of Cork and Orrery(1860)
Earl of Shannon (1809)

SEVENTH STALL

Crest
Earl of Arran
Banner
Earl of Arran
Hatchment
Earl of Arran (1783)

SIXTH STALL

Crest
Earl of Granard
Banner
Earl of Granard
Hatchments
Earl of Courtown (1821)
Earl of Granard (1857)

SIXTH STALL

Crest
Earl of Carysfort
Banner
Earl of Carysfort
Hatchment
Earl of Carysfort (1869)

FIFTH STALL

Crest
Lord Cremorne
Banner
Lord Cremorne
Hatchments
Earl of Mornington (1783)
Lord Cremorne (1855)

FIFTH STALL

Crest
Marquess Conyngham
Banner
Marquess Conyngham
Hatchment
Marquess Conyngham (1833)

FOURTH STALL

Crest
Marquess of Headfort
Banner
Marquess of Headfort
Hatchments
Marquess of Headfort (1809)
Marquess of Headfort (1885)

FOURTH STALL

Crest
Marquess of Londonderry
Banner
Marquess of Londonderry
Hatchment
Marquess of Downshire (1859)

THIRD STALL	THIRD STALL
Crest	*Crest*
Earl of Roden	Marquess of Drogheda
Banner	*Banner*
Earl of Roden	Marquess of Drogheda
Hatchments	*Hatchment*
Earl of Roden (1821)	Earl of Drogheda (1783)
Earl of Wicklow (1842)	
SECOND STALL	SECOND STALL
Crest	*Crest*
Royal Crest	Earl of Howth
Banner	*Banner*
Lord Farnham	Earl of Howth
Hatchments	*Hatchment*
Lord Farnham (1845)	Earl of Clanbrassil (1783)
Earl of Westmeath (1783)	
FIRST STALL	FIRST STALL
Crest	*Crest*
Duke of Connaught	Royal Crest
Banner	*Banner*
Duke of Connaught (old banner)	Duke of Cambridge
Hatchment	*Hatchments*
Duke of Leinster (1783)	Queen Victoria (1837)
	Prince Consort (1842)
THE PRECENTOR'S STALL	THE DEAN'S STALL
Banner	*Banner*
Duke of Connaught (new banner)	Royal Standard

The plates are not consistently dated. Sometimes the date given is that of nomination, sometimes investiture, sometimes installation, sometimes dispensation from installation. The most curious wording appears on the plate of the Marquess of Downshire, who was 'conceded July 1859'.

When the first stall plates were erected for the founder Knights, William Grenville expressed the hope that they, and the plates of succeeding Knights, would remain in position in perpetuity. 'In the chapel at Windsor [for the Knights Companions of the Order of the Garter] they are obliged now to put them up loose, in order to their being removed; the consequence is, that they are frequently lost. Besides, the plates of the first sixteen might then be fixed in the centre of each stall as mark of distinction for the founders ... I should think that the Grand Master at each installation might be allowed to put up his, as the banner must of course always be the Sovereign's.'[10] The desire was probably never a practicality. Each plate measures approximately 30cm x 36cm, and the size is almost certainly the reason for the absence of a cumulative collection of plates from the years 1783 to 1871. Only six of the founder Knights are still represented by their stall plates, although that for Lord Inchiquin (later Marquess of Thomond) is obviously a much later replacement. The attitude of the cathedral authorities was another factor. Lord Farnham, invested as a Knight in November 1845, complained in October 1846 that his hatchment had still not been erected. Betham duly apologised to the peer, citing an obstructive dean. 'The painter Mr Phillipps went to the cathedral to put them up, when he was stopped by the dean ... The dean I find objected to the shifting the plates from stall to stall, a matter which cannot be avoided. I must consult the architect of the Board of Works to settle some plan of shifting the plates without injury to the stalls which the dean objects to.'[11]

The presence of two banners for the Duke of Connaught and none for the Prince of Wales is something of a mystery. The prince was installed in April 1868, three years before the Church was disestablished, and his banner was still in position in 1939. This confusion probably dates from the results of a fire in the cathedral on Friday 22 March 1940. The fire was discovered by the cathedral verger shortly before 9.30am. It began on the south side of the chancel, owing to the fusing of electric light wires, a short circuit probably caused by a mouse, a dead mouse being discovered among the smouldering debris near the Dean's stall where the fire originated. On the south side, the dean's stall, with eight of the canons' stalls and the Knights' banners above, were completely destoyed; the banners on the north side were scorched. The stall plates blistered and buckled in the intense heat. New stalls were carved and erected, to match those on the north side, and the banners and hatchment plates were either reconditioned or replaced by a team under the supervision of Thomas Sadleir. Some of the plates still show signs of the effect of the fire, and that of the Prince Consort is so blackened that the design and the inscription are hardly discernable.

Sir John Maffey, the United Kingdom Representative in Dublin, expressed his concern and offered to have the damaged royal standards replaced, and it was probably at this stage that the mistake was made. While new standards for the Sovereign and the Duke of Cambridge were received, a second Connaught banner was sent, instead of a new one for the Prince of Wales. The prince, later King Edward VII, had died in 1910, but the Duke of Connaught, who had been made a Knight of St Patrick as far back as 1869, was still alive at the age of ninety. The two Connaught banners are basically the same, but one is obviously much older than the other. The labelling is the same (in the centre a cross gules and on each of the others a fleur-de-lis azure), but on the older banner is an inescutcheon with the arms of Saxony. The newer banner, received in 1942, omits the inescutcheon. The retention of the arms of Saxony would have been rendered anomalous by the loss of independence of that state. By the end of the First World War, Saxony, along with all the other German states, had been consigned to oblivion. The Dean and Chapter were still proud of their historic link with the Order and in February 1939, the Dean wrote to the Duke of Connaught congratulating him on the seventieth anniversary of his appointment to the Order. In reply the Dean was informed that, 'the Duke deeply appreciates the kind way in which you have referred to his long connection with the Order of St Patrick, of which he is so proud to be the Senior Knight'.[12]

During work on the organ in 1994, the banners on the north side of the chancel were removed to allow the erection of scaffolding. Some were washed and others were repainted. In a number of cases where the canvas sleeve holding the staff of the banner had begun to rot, new canvas sleeves were sewn on by hand. When the banners were re-hung, they were matched as near as possible to the appropriate hatchment beneath.[13] Further work was done in 1998 when the crests were rearranged, in an attempt to match them to the banners and hatchments. There are still a few anomalies, especially on the south side of the choir, but short of ordering new banners, plates and crests, there is no possibility that everything can be positioned in total harmony. The banners on the south side are in the same position as when erected in 1941. Those on the north side were re-arranged in 1994 and 1998, and there is now probably greater harmony in the arrangement than at any time since the fire of 1940.

The painted banners require little maintenance, being made of a fabric that needs no more than occasional dusting. In spite of all the vicissitudes in Anglo-Irish relations during the last one hundred years, there is something faintly nostalgic about the fact that in this one small corner of Dublin, the wishes of Queen Victoria are still faithfully observed. The symbolic swords and helmets are still fixed to the canopy of each stall below the banners, and the hatchment plates fastened to the backs of the stalls provide an heraldic record of thirty-four of the knights appointed between 1783 and 1871. The paucity of plates on the south side of the chancel is probably explained by the fire of 1940 which may have damaged others beyond repair.

The cathedral also houses another relic of the Order; the immaculately painted roll of the Knights of St Patrick. The work of Sir Nevile Wilkinson, it was formerly in the Kildare Street Club, and now hangs in the robing room of St Patrick's Cathedral. The roll is painted on an unpolished, waxed mahogany board in four sections with classical, scrolled embellishments and raised capital letters. The board itself was executed in the workshop of James Hicks in Lower Pembroke Street, and bears the names and armorial bearings of every Knight of St Patrick from 1783 to 1927. The work is thought to have been done about 1921. The name of the Prince of Wales (1927) is in poor condition and was added at the time of his appointment. The names of the last two Knights, the Dukes of Gloucester (1934) and York (1936) have never been

The roll of the Knights of St Patrick, formerly in the Kildare Street Club and now in St Patrick's Cathedral. The work of Sir Nevile Wilkinson, c.1921.

added. Wilkinson exhibited at least part of the roll, together with some Knights' banners that he had embroidered, at the sixth exhibition of the Arts and Crafts Society of Ireland which opened in September 1921.[14] The roll was kept in the Kildare Street Club until 1976 when it was presented to the cathedral.

Although the cathedral has not seen a procession of the Knights of St Patrick since April 1869, the present day visitor can still see a procession of figures clad in sky blue. By the early 1970s, the black cassocks worn by the cathedral choir were badly worn and in need of replacement. In 1971 they were replaced with sky-blue cassocks to commemorate the link between the cathedral and the Order. The dean and canons themselves wear a thin band of sky-blue material immediately below their clerical collars, and the colour of the Order of St Patrick has now become the colour of St Patrick's Cathedral.

In the summer of 1981, seven years after the death of the last Knight of St Patrick, the possibility was raised of marking the bicentenary of the foundation of the Order, in March 1983. At the suggestion of the dean, it was decided that the occasion should be marked and used to commemorate something which had been the national honour of Ireland for nearly 140 years. It was also felt that the 146 Knights of the Order should be remembered, and thanks given to God for their life and work. The matter was discussed at a number of meetings during the winter of 1982–3 by a steering committee, and the decision was taken to hold a service of thanksgiving in St Patrick's Cathedral on Sunday, 13 March 1983, followed by a reception in the deanery. Invitations were issued to as many descendants of Knights of the Order as could be traced, together with representatives of a number of related societies and organisations, and a congregation of more than 500 people, headed by the Lord Mayor of Dublin, gathered in the cathedral on Sunday, 13 March at 3.15pm.

The service began with an anthem specially composed by the cathedral organist, a setting of the biblical text: *Quis separabit nos a caritate dei quae est in Christo Jesu Domino Nostro?*. (Who shall separate us from the love of God which is in Christ Jesus our Lord?) The service was conducted by the Dean, Dr Victor Griffin, seven of whose predecessors had held the office of Registrar of the Order, from 1783 to 1890. The first lesson was read by the Earl of Rosse, a descendant of two Knights of St Patrick, and the second lesson was read by Bishop George Simms, former Archbishop of Armagh, whose predecessors had held the office of Prelate of the Order from 1783 to 1885. After the singing of the anthem, Sir Hubert Parry's setting of Psalm 122: *I was glad when they said unto me, we will go into the house of the Lord*, an address was delivered by the author, and the service concluded with the singing of the Te Deum – preserving a tradition from the installation services begun 200 years earlier. The event was reported with interest in the (Dublin) *Evening Press*. 'Two hundred years ago this week the first Knights of The Most Illustrious Order of St Patrick were installed in the cathedral in a display of pomp and pageantry ... There were only 146 knights in all ... The last of them, the Duke of Gloucester, died in 1974. It is practically certain there will never be another.'[15]

The bicentenary service of the Order in 1983 was entirely unofficial, although the Lord Mayor of Dublin, the British ambassador, and a number of the descendants of Knights were present. Looking back, across the years that have passed since it took place, the service seems with hindsight to have been an extraordinary thing to have done at the time; to have celebrated in Dublin, in Ireland, the two hundredth anniversary of the foundation of an Order, to which successive Irish governments had been decidedly antipathetic. There was some criticism on the ground that the service was unofficial and unauthorised; others thought it was pointless and unnecessary; one derided it as a misguided attempt to breathe life into something that was dead. The response to these criticisms was that the service was never intended to be anything other than unofficial, though it originated with the proposal of the Dean to hold such a service in his own cathedral. As to being unnecessary and misguided, that was not the experience of those who were present. There was no indulgence in wishful thinking, no thought that the Order should be revived, and certainly no desire to turn back the clock to an age that had passed. But there was a feeling, a strong feeling, that instead of allowing the Order simply to dribble away, the two hundredth anniversary should be marked by a service that would partly be an occasion to draw a line under the Order, to acknowledge the fact that its day was over, that it was 'finished', but simultaneously to commemorate and celebrate its role and the place of its Knights in the history of Ireland.

Apart from the historic temporal and spiritual homes of the Order, there are a few other visible relics of the Order. The mantle of the Earl of Donoughmore (1916) can be seen on display in the Genealogical Office, which moved out of the Bedford Tower of Dublin Castle several years ago, and now occupies part of the former Kildare Street Club at 2 Kildare Street. A few hundred yards further along Kildare Street is the National Museum of Ireland, among the exhibits in which can be seen the mantle of Lord Clonbrock (1900). It was purchased by the museum from the sale of the contents of Clonbrock House, County Galway, in 1971. In Northern Ireland, the mantle, collar, star and badge of the Earl of Shaftesbury (1911) are at the Ulster Museum in Belfast, as is the Grand Master's mantle of the Marquess of Londonderry (1886–9), and Viscount Charlemont's badge as Usher of the Black Rod (1878–1913).

The badge of the Earl of Shaftesbury (KP 1911), made by West and Son of Dublin.

On 1 April 1900, the regiment of the Irish Guards was formed by command of Queen Victoria to commemorate the bravery of the Irish troops who fought in the Boer War. The first recruit enlisted on 21 April, and many more Irishmen already serving in regiments of the Brigade of Guards and Regiments of the Line took the opportunity of transferring. The star of the Order was taken as the cap badge and it remains so to this day. The star is also the badge of the Irish Guards Association, and attractive miniature stars can be seen gracing the wives of members of the association.

Occasionally elements of the design of the insignia are worn as decorative jewellery. The brooches of the wives of members of the Irish Guards Association are a case in point. Florence, Viscountess Massereene and Ferrard (d.1929), wife of the eleventh viscount and daughter-in-law of the tenth viscount, KP, had a replica of the star, minus the rays, made in jewels for use as a brooch. Wearing it one night at a ball, she attracted the attention of King Edward VII, who expressed his surprise that ladies were now eligible for admission to the Order of St Patrick. The viscountess pointed to the fact that the brooch was not an exact copy of the star, and the King was appeased![16]

That the Order should have survived 1922 in a familiar and enduring comic opera is perhaps more surprising. On 25 November 1882 the Savoy Theatre in London witnessed the opening night of a new two-act opera by William Gilbert and Arthur Sullivan. It was entitled *Iolanthe, or The Peer and the Peri*, and the rather superficial plot disguises a humorous and witty piece of satire on the peerage and the House of Lords. The opera is still a favourite among devotees of the famous partnership. The supporting cast consists in part of a chorus of sixteen peers who wear differing coronets according to their rank. But instead of the traditional scarlet parliamentary robes, the peers make their spectacular entrance attired in the mantles and collars of the four senior Orders of Knighthood: the Garter, the Thistle, the St Patrick, and the Bath. The D'Oyly Carte Opera Company, set up to continue performing the operas in the manner faithful to the wishes of author and composer, adhered strictly to the costume directions of the original production. The events of 1922 which ended the active existence of the Order made no difference to the stage Knights who continued to be received with great applause by audiences, until the demise of the company in the spring of 1982.

The Order of St Patrick is still survived by its ceremonial parent, the Friendly Brothers of Saint Patrick, which is now little more than a dining club, divided into regional 'knots'. The badge of its 'perfect brothers' still bears the symbols once borrowed by the Order: the shamrock, the interlaced knots, and the motto, QUIS SEPARABIT?

Though the Order of St Patrick is commonly thought of as no longer being in existence, it has never been formally abolished; it is still an extant though non-functioning part of the honours system of the United Kingdom, and new Knights Companions could still be appointed. The death of the Duke of Gloucester in June 1974 did, in a sense, mark the end of the Order, in that he was the last surviving Knight of St Patrick; and there is now no one who can use the postnominal letters 'KP' to indicate membership of the Order. But there are still two individuals who are entitled to wear robes or insignia that indicate association with the Order of St Patrick. The Sovereign is Sovereign of all the Orders of Knighthood, and therefore still Sovereign of the Order of St Patrick, and at liberty to wear the mantle, collar, star and badge of the Order should an appropriate occasion present itself. In addition to its Sovereign, the Order still has one remaining Officer, in the shape of Norroy and Ulster King of Arms, who is still its King of Arms, Registrar and Knight Attendant, and may still of right wear the badge and scarlet mantle of the King of Arms.

It is all very well to declare here what may be theory and what may be done or worn of right, but the practicability of these rights is quite another matter, and it has to be admitted that the possibility of the robes or insignia of the Order ever being worn again, is remote.

CHAPTER SIXTEEN

ILLUSTRISSIMI

The Knights of St Patrick

===

No blot upon its escutcheon, no failure in its duty,
and no declension of its untarnished fame.
LORD O'HAGAN, 18 January 1882

ON HIS APPOINTMENT as a Knight of St Patrick, the distinguished Irish jurist, Lord O'Hagan, recorded his pride at being associated with an Order founded at the brightest period of the chequered history of Ireland. There had been, he said, 'no blot upon its escutcheon, no failure in its duty, and no declension of its untarnished fame'.[1] It had never been associated with any political faction, or with sectarian intolerance, and in its spirit and action it was a national Order. Thomas O'Hagan was the son of a trader from Belfast, and rose to be the first Roman Catholic Lord Chancellor of Ireland, and one of the few Roman Catholic Knights of St Patrick. This was a considerable achievement in the mid-nineteenth century, but O'Hagan's delight at receiving the Order, coupled with a meagre knowledge of its earliest history, probably clouded his usual judicial perspicacity, and caused him to deliver this faintly ridiculous piece of flattering hyperbole.

The active history of the Order stretched over a period of one hundred and forty years and, inevitably, the criteria for appointment to the Order in the early twentieth century were different from those governing appointments in the late eighteenth century. Different governments in different ages used the Order for different purposes, and it would be wrong to make any generalised assessment of the worth of those appointed to the Order. It makes no sense to judge the character and ability of an eighteenth-century Knight of St Patrick by the meritocratic principles of the present age. Few of the early Knights would have qualified for the honour, if assessed by contemporary standards of deserving merit, and most of them have long been forgotten by all except historians of the period. But they were 'important' people in their day, and there is no reason to doubt that they were believed to be so by their contemporaries. It would be best simply to state that the general uniting principle of 'Irishness' governed appointments to the Order. Closer examination reveals that the Knights of St Patrick were a very diverse collection of individuals, and it is impossible to do justice to the lives of each of them in the space of one chapter.

A collected biography of the one hundred and forty-six Knights would fill another volume, and this work is primarily a history of the Order as an institution, rather than an account of the lives of the individual Knights. But as the period since 1922 has demonstrated, without the Knights there is effectively no Order, and the lives of the Knights do shed some light on the changing way in which the Order was used by successive governments. The following section is not a detailed account of the reason for every appointment to the Order, nor does it pretend to include every Knight; it only attempts to trace some themes, and open windows on some colourful personalities.

The Most Illustrious Order of St Patrick, in its origin, was much like other honours of the time, 'not merely intended *honoris causa*; but . . . a subtle engine of Government wherewith to secure the interest of some leading men . . . It is a fact too often experienced that the offer of a glittering bauble for personal ornament, has greater influence . . . than any lucrative temptation'.[2]

In the period up to the dissolution of the Irish Parliament in 1801, party politics were to an extent irrelevant, since party majorities could vanish overnight on some issues. The most powerful and influential peers, whatever their politics, found the Order offered to them, either as a reward for past service, or as an inducement to render future service. They were prominent and influential lords of the land of Ireland, whose votes in the Irish Parliament could mean the difference between victory and defeat for the government. These men were typical of the world of eighteenth-century politics, and formed the obvious constituency from which to make the first appointments to the Order of St Patrick.

The twenty-one 'Irish Parliament Knights', appointed between 1783 and 1801 were marked by their political power and influence. They knew the extent of their power, and many of them were openly ambitious, either to be appointed to the Order, or (an easier task) to be promoted in the peerage, or both. According to Lord Temple, the Duke of Leinster (1783) wanted to be assured that the Order of St Patrick would not be his final reward. 'The Duke of Leinster was restive about the Order being given to him as a full compensation for his services. However, I have talked him into good humour, but he specifically bargains that this shall not prejudice his claims upon the Garter, which I have as gravely agreed to.'[3] Temple later said that the Prince of Wales had promised the Garter to the duke in 1789, but Leinster never received it, and died in 1804 at the age of fifty-five, still only a Knight of St Patrick.

The prominence of the Earl of Clanricarde was indicated when, in 1789, he was created Marquess of Clanricarde. Apart from the marquessate of Kildare (a subsidiary title of the Duke of Leinster), there were no other marquesses in Ireland. But the honour lasted for only eight years. When Clanricarde died in 1797 at the age of fifty-four, the marquessate became extinct.

As a young man, the Earl of Westmeath is said to have served with distinction in the French army. His first wife brought him a considerable estate on their marriage in 1731. In 1787 he obtained a pension of £800 p.a., and died in 1792 at the age of seventy-eight.

The Earl of Inchiquin was created Marquess of Thomond in 1800 and, to enable him to sit in his own right in the House of Lords at Westminster, Baron Thomond of Taplow in 1801. His 'open and cheerful manner ... banishes reserve and makes every Society into which he goes pleasant'.[4] In the estimation of his second wife, 'there is not such another man in the world: He is the best man in it. In trifles he is irritable in the extreme; but in everything of moment calm and firm; bearing what happens with fortitude'.[5]

The Earl of Drogheda was described as, 'a very eccentric character, passionately fond of play, to which he was a victim all his life, and subjected to great pecuniary embarrassments. In his later years his estates were put out to nurse, and a moderate pension was allowed to him by his creditors'.[6] He had long wanted to be given a marquessate, and in 1776, King George III wrote to Lord Bute. 'I cannot but express my astonishment at Lord Harcourt's presumption in telling Lord Drogheda that there would be no difficulty in making him a marquess ... I desire to hear no more of Irish marquesses. I feel for English earls and do not choose to disgust them.'[7] Drogheda was given his heart's desire in 1795, when he was created Marquess of Drogheda. He was created Baron Moore of Moore Place in 1801, because he was the oldest marquess, and to give Lord Cornwallis room to manoeuvre. 'He is perfectly insignificant in respect to weight and interest in the country, and I only recommended him as being the oldest marquess in order to assist me in providing room for friends in the representative peerage.'[8] Drogheda had pursued a career in the army, though he never saw active service, and rose to the rank of field marshal in 1821. He died in December of the same year at the age of ninety-one.

The Earl of Tyrone was created Baron Tyrone of Haverfordwest in the peerage of Great Britain in 1786. 'I prefer Baron Tyrone, that I may write my name the same way in both kingdoms ... [but if] necessary to be Baron Tyrone of some place [in England] ... I should choose to be Baron Tyrone of Haverfordwest, ... of St Davids, or Hubberston, these places being all opposite to the coast of this country.'[9] Waterford was a considerable power in the land. 'This nobleman is the leader of the aristocratic party in Ireland, and has so much weight, that the English government, it is said, do nothing without him. He, it was who, with his brother commissioner, had sufficient power to throw out Lord Fitzwilliam, and upset his administration altogether. Lord Fitzwilliam declared, in the English House of Lords, that it was impossible for him to effect any good in that kingdom, unless he could destroy the power of the Beresfords.'[10] He was created Marquess of Waterford in 1789, and died in 1800 at the age of sixty-five.

The Earl of Shannon rose no higher than an earl, but was given a barony in the peerage of Great Britain in 1786, becoming Baron Carleton. 'Before the Union, no man possessed greater parliamentary interest than the Earl of Shannon; insomuch that no vice-regent felt easy on his throne, until he had secured his lordship's friendship, who was considered a sound politician but no orator.'[11] He died in 1807 at the age of seventy-nine.

The Earl of Clanbrassil similarly was given no promotion in the peerage. In 1774 he was described as, 'old of his age (having lost all his fore teeth), but he is tall, genteel and very well bred'.[12] He was the second and last Earl of Clanbrassil. At his death in 1798, at the age of sixty-seven, all his peerages became extinct.

The Earl of Mornington established a certain pre-eminence among the founder Knights by his distinguished career as Governor-General of India, though his connections with Ireland were tenuous by the end of the eighteenth century. His Irish estate was described as, 'a very small one, and the mansion house upon it going to ruin'.[13] He was created Baron Wellesley of Wellesley, in the peerage of Great Britain in 1797, and Marquess Wellesley of Norragh in the peerage of Ireland in 1799. Only twenty-two at the time of his appointment to the Order of St Patrick, he resigned the Order in 1810 on his appointment as a Knight of the Garter, and personally surrendered his insignia of the Order of St Patrick to King George III on the day of the chapter in which he was invested with the Order of the Garter. He was later twice Lord Lieutenant of Ireland (in 1821–8 and 1833–4) and became the only person to be Grand Master of the Order of which he had once been a Knight. His appointment as Lord Lieutenant in 1833 brought forth a waspish assessment from the Clerk to the Privy Council. 'Once very brilliant, probably never very efficient, he is now worn out and effete. It is astonishing that they should send such a man, and one does not see why, because it is difficult to find a good man, they should select one of the very worst they could hit upon. It is a ridiculous appointment.'[14] Within a short time Greville came to rue his words. 'Since he has been in Ireland, [he] has astonished everybody by his activity and assiduity in business. He appeared, before he went, in the last stages of decrepitude, and they had no idea the energy was in him.'[15] For all his abilities – which were considerable – Wellesley was nakedly ambitious. He wrote to Lord Grenville in May 1799. 'You will gain much credit by conferring some high and brilliant honour upon me immediately. The Garter would be much more acceptable to me than any additional title, nor would any title be an object which should not raise me to the same rank which was given to Lord Cornwallis.'[16] Mornington was given an Irish marquessate, and was intensely annoyed that it was Irish and not British. On his retirement from public life, he is alleged to have said to Lord Broughton, 'You got £20,000 for me from the Court of Directors [of the East India Company]; you ought now to get a dukedom for me from the Queen'.[17] He was never given a dukedom (unlike his brother, the Duke of Wellington), and he died without legitimate issue, in 1842, when the barony and marquessate died with him. He was the last survivor of the founder Knights.

The Earl of Arran enjoyed an unremarkable career, and died in 1809 at the age of seventy-five. He was, however, remembered as, 'a nobleman of the mildest disposition, and most elegant manners'.[18]

At the time of his appointment to the Order, the Earl of Courtown was Lord of the

ILLUSTRISSIMI · 215

The Earl of Inchiquin
(KP 1783)

Bedchamber to the Prince of Wales, which may well have been among the criteria for his appointment. 'He has no earthly influence in Parliament, and indecently enough, through some connections he has in England, got himself named of the [Privy] Council here, without any application to Lord Harcourt.'[19] He was created Baron Saltersford in the peerage of Great Britain in 1796, and died in 1810 at the age of seventy-eight.

The Earl of Charlemont, whom Temple had been so careful to consult in 1783, was a fierce opponent of the union, and its approach is said to have hastened his death in 1799 at the age of seventy. In 1775 he was described thus: 'In private life amiable and respectable. In public, violent, petulant and waspish'.[20] Edmund Burke called him, 'the most public-spirited, and at the same time the best natured and best bred man in Ireland'.[21]

The Earl of Bective enjoyed rapid promotion in the peerage. He succeeded his

father as a baronet in 1757, becoming Sir Thomas Taylour. He became Baron
Headfort in 1760, Viscount Headfort in 1762, and Earl of Bective in 1766, dying in
1795 at the age of seventy.

The Earl of Ely was the shortest-lived of the founder Knights, dying on 8 May
1783 at the age of seventy-three, when his peerages became extinct.

Lord Carysfort (1784) was the first Knight to be appointed after the founder
Knights, and this despite the fact that he had supported Henry Grattan's agitation for
a fully independent Irish Parliament. The Lord Lieutenant had no hesitation in
recommending his appointment. 'No man stands as forward in my opinion as Lord
Carysfort to whose exertions and steady support in parliament my administration
has been under great obligation. Although not in any official situation, he has had
the confidence of the government, and has borne a great share in the support of its
measures in a manly, spirited and noble manner.'[22] The view was not entirely shared
by other contemporaries. 'Esteemed a good and elegant scholar. His temper had yet
more goodness and elegance to boast of ... [as a public speaker] his utterance is
disagreeably slow, tedious and hesitating, perpetually interrupted by the interjections
Ah! Ah! Ah! Ah! ... He votes with the administration and is in favour of the Union.'[23]
He was created Earl of Carysfort in 1789, and Baron Carysfort of the hundred of
Norman Cross (in the peerage of Great Britain) in 1801. He died in 1828 at the age
of seventy-six.

The premature death of the Earl of Ely in 1783 was followed by the appointment of
his nephew to the Order in 1794. The new Knight was described as 'greedy and
shameless'. At the time of the Act of Union, he received £45,000 for loss of his six
boroughs. But before he would agree to vote for the legislation, he insisted on an
Irish marquessate and a United Kingdom barony. He began his life in 1738 as
Charles Tottenham. In 1785 he was created Baron Loftus of Loftus Hall; in 1786 he
succeeded to his father's baronetcy; in 1789 he was created Viscount Loftus of Ely; in
1794, Earl of Ely; and in 1801, Marquess of Ely and Baron Loftus of Long Loftus. He
died in 1806 at the age of sixty-eight, having risen from a commoner to a marquess
in sixteen years. His family motto *Prends moi tel que je suis* (Take me for what I am)
was either entirely appropriate, or singularly inappropriate, according to opinion.

The Earl of Clermont (1795) was a friend of the Prince of Wales, and another
Knight who was typical of the age, as Lord Temple indicated to Lord Grenville in
1806. 'Lord Clermont desires you will not conceive Fortescue, the Irish member, his
nephew, to be in opposition. This he has thought it necessary to explain as Fortescue
has been making as if he was in opposition the whole session; but Lord Clermont has
sworn, and Fortescue has sworn too, that his wish and intention is to support your
government. I take it for granted that this is preparatory to some attempt at a job.'[24]
Born William Henry Fortescue, he was created Baron Clermont in 1770, Viscount
and Baron Clermont in 1776, and Earl of Clermont in 1777. He died in 1806 at the
age of eighty-four when the earldom became extinct.

The Earl of Ormonde and Ossory (1798) was head of the historic Anglo-Norman
Butler family of Kilkenny. In 1801 he was created Baron Butler of Lanthony in the
peerage of the United Kingdom, and in 1816, Marquess of Ormonde. 'He is a young
man of an aspiring disposition, and is believed, from his uniform support of
government, in legislative union, and its other measures, to have in view a new
creation, if not restoration of the old title Duke of Ormond.'[25] In 1811 parliament
granted him £216,000 as compensation for the resumption by the Crown of the
hereditary prisage of wines in Ireland, granted to his ancestor in 1327. He died in
1820 at the age of fifty when the barony and marquessate became extinct.

Viscount Dillon (1798) was described as possessing, 'considerable property, power,
and influence, which he exerts in favour of the Union'.[26] In Dillon's case, the Lord
Lieutenant, Earl Camden, wrote to the Duke of Portland telling him quite definitely
that intimations had been made to Dillon that he might expect to be appointed to the

Order. 'Lord Dillon's exertions both inside and outside parliament have been used . . . with great effect, in support of His Majesty and his government in this kingdom. I think it therefore to be a justice due to Lord Dillon to state these services.'[27] He died in 1813 at the age of sixty-eight.

The Earl of Altamont (1800) was described as having, 'a full, strong, and distinct voice; his language is neither elegant nor animated; little adapted to command attention, conciliate the regard, or invigorate the minds of his hearers; and is alike deficient in philosophical clearness and grammatical precision; he, for the most part, expresses himself in a peremptory magisterial tone, and is abundant without selection, flowing without energy; his delivery is at times so rapid, as to embarrass his pronunciation; and destroy all propriety of emphasis; his manner is vehement and overbearing, and his action ungraceful, belabouring the air without mercy'.[28] Whatever the deficiencies of his powers of communication, Altamont was a strenuous supporter of the Union and was rewarded not only with the Order of St Patrick, to which he had pressed his claim in 1783, but also by being created Marquess of Sligo in 1800. He was given an United Kingdom peerage as Baron Monteagle of Westport in 1806. 'Lord Altamount (sic) had from the first declared himself in its favour [the Union], and the tone of his whole correspondence with the Government indicates a man of real public spirit, yet he bargained for and obtained a marquessate.'[29] 'He had, no doubt, received his riband as a reward for his parliamentary votes, and especially in the matter of the Union; yet, from all his conversation upon that question, and from the general conscientiousness of his private life, I am convinced that he acted all along upon patriotic motives.'[30] He died in 1809 at the age of fifty-two.

Earl Conyngham (1801) was also a consistent supporter of the Union, and received the Order of St Patrick as a reward. 'His manner is warm and spirited, but too much marked with the remains of soldier-like importance and military insolence; his action is strong, forcible, and energetic, pointedly conveying his sentiments, and evidently the effusion of the moment, not the studied exhibition of the day . . . In his political capacity, he has ever been a steady supporter of administration, and has always deserved the thanks of the minister, though, perhaps, not always those of his country.'[31] His promotions in the peerage – Viscount Slane, Earl of Mount Charles and Marquess Conyngham in 1816, and Baron Minster of Minster Abbey in 1821 – may perhaps have been due more to his wife's liaison with King George IV. He died in 1832 at the age of sixty-six.

The appointments of Lords Sligo in 1800 and Conyngham in 1801 were the last of the 'Irish Parliament Knights'. With the abolition of that parliament in 1801, a slightly different breed of Knight began to emerge. The Irish peers were no longer such a force to be reckoned with; their political influence, although not extinguished, was now subsumed within the United Kingdom Parliament, and their power was reduced accordingly; but they were still prominent landowners in a country dominated by landlords.

As 'achievement' or lack of it was not a bar to admission to the Order in those early days, so neither was age. Of the 146 Knights, more than a third were aged thirty-nine or under at the time of their appointment. The Earl of Mornington (later Marquess Wellesley) was only twenty-two at the time of his investiture as one of the first Knights in 1783. The Earl of Ormonde was twenty-eight at the time of his appointment in 1798. The Earl of Granard (1857) was twenty-three, and the fifth Marquess of Waterford (1868) was twenty-four. The Earl of Gosford (1869) was twenty-eight. The sixth Marquess of Waterford was appointed in 1902 at the age of twenty-six. As late as 1916, Viscount Powerscourt was appointed at the age of thirty-five. The youngest of the Knights was Prince Edward, later Duke of Kent and Strathearn, who was appointed a founder Knight in 1783 at the age of fifteen. In 1869, Prince Arthur, later Duke of Connaught and Strathearn, was appointed at the age of eighteen. If members of the royal family are discounted as 'special cases', the youngest Knight on appointment was the second Marquess of Sligo, who was appointed in March 1810, ten months after his twenty-first birthday.

Age of Knights at the time of appointment

19 or under	20–29	30–39	40–49	50–59	60–69	70–79
2	10	34	33	43	19	5

The oldest Knight at the time of appointment to the Order was the twenty-fourth Baron de Ros (1902) who was seventy-five. The oldest Knight at the time of death was the Duke of Connaught, who was four months short of his ninety-second birthday. Three other Knights – the Marquess of Drogheda (1783), the Earl of Listowel (1873), and the Earl of Shaftesbury (1911) also lived to be ninety-one.

Age of Knights at the time of death

20–29	30–39	40–49	50–59	60–69	70–79	80–89	90–99
1	1	6	24	34	45	30	5

Two Knights enjoyed the honour for less than a year; the Earl of Ely (1783) for four months; and the Earl of Milltown (1889) for eight months. The longest holder of the honour was the Duke of Connaught; he was appointed in March 1869 and died in January 1942 having been a Knight of St Patrick for more than seventy-two years. Another member of the royal family, the Duke of Cambridge (1851) was a Knight for fifty-two years. Excluding these royal dukes, three Knights held the honour for more than fifty years: the Earl of Gosford (1869) for fifty-two years, the Earl of Listowel (1873) for fifty-one years, and the Earl of Dunraven and Mountearl (1876) for fifty years.

The practice of appointing to the Order successive heads of the same family, was not dissimilar to the practice with other Orders. As there were 'Garter families' in England and 'Thistle families' in Scotland, so there were 'Patrick families' in Ireland. The second Marquess of Waterford (1806), the first Marquess of Headfort (1806) and the third Earl of Shannon (1808) were sons of founder Knights, and the practice of handing the Order out to successive heads of the same family or bearers of the same title continued well into the nineteenth century. The second (1783), fourth (1841), fifth (1898), and sixth (1909) earls of Arran; the second (1821) and fourth (1896) Earls of Caledon; the first (1851) and second (1872) barons Carew; the first (1784), fourth (1869), and fifth (1874) earls of Carysfort; the ninth (1894) and tenth (1916) earls of Cavan; the first (1783), second (1831), and third (1865) earls of Charlemont; the twelfth Earl (1783) and the first Marquess (1831) of Clanricarde; the first (1801) and second (1833) marquesses Conyngham; the eighth (1835) and ninth (1860) earls of Cork; the second (1783) and third (1821) earls of Courtown; the second (1821) and third marquesses (1857) of Donegall; the third (1834) and sixth (1916) earls of Donoughmore; the third (1831) and fourth (1859) marquesses of Downshire; the first (1783) and third (1868) marquesses of Drogheda; the third (1866) and fourth (1872) earls of Dunraven and Mountearl; the third (1783) Earl, and the first (1794) and second (1807) marquesses of Ely; the second (1810) and fourth (1902) earls of Enniskillen; the third (1868) and fourth (1889) earls of Erne; the eighth (1821) and ninth (1846) earls of Fingall; the third (1855) and fourth (1869) earls of Gosford; the seventh (1857) and eighth (1909) earls of Granard; the first (1806), second (1839) and third (1885) marquesses of Headfort; the third (1835) and fourth (1884) earls of Howth; the second (1839) and third (1873) earls of Listowel; the fourth (1856) and fifth (1874) marquesses of Londonderry; the second (1813) and fifth (1901) earls of Longford; the sixth (1869) and seventh (1905) earls of Mayo; the tenth (1821) and twelfth (1905) earls of Meath; the fourth (1841) and sixth (1890) earls of Milltown; the eighteenth Earl (1798) and the first (1821), second (1845), and third (1888) marquesses of Ormonde; the seventh (1871) and eighth (1916) viscounts Powerscourt; the second (1806) and third (1821) earls of Roden; the third

(1845) and fourth (1890) earls of Rosse; the second (1783) and third (1808) earls of Shannon; the first (1800) and second (1810) marquesses of Sligo; the third (1837) and fourth (1871) viscounts Southwell; the first (1783) and second (1809) marquesses of Thomond. The Beresford family was the most highly favoured of all: the first (1783), second (1806), third (1845), fifth (1868) and sixth (1902) marquesses of Waterford were all appointed at comparatively youthful ages. Whether the fourth marquess would have been appointed had he lived long enough is debatable. He was an ordained priest of the Church of Ireland, and was rector of Mullaghbrack when he died in 1866.

After the formal development of political parties in the nineteenth century, appointments to the Order remained very much the prerogative of the party in power, despite Lord O'Hagan's claim that it stood above party strife. Apart from a few distinguished exceptions, the politics of the new Knight, were invariably those of the government of the day, and so it remained almost until the end. For the most part, the Knights were wealthy land-owning peers with firm political affiliations. The concept of meritocracy in the award of honours is a twentieth-century phenomenon, but there is evidence that the Order of St Patrick was not given out indiscriminately, and there is a discernible change in the criteria for appointment during the one hundred and forty years of the Order's existence.

Politics remained a fairly constant factor in the choice of a Knight, the government of the day naturally using the fount of honour to quench the thirst of its supporters. While briefly Prime Minister in 1868, Benjamin Disraeli appointed three Conservative peers to the Order, the Marquess of Waterford, the Earl of Erne and the Earl of Mayo. 'I think there will be a great rumpus ... if Waterford does not get it. He was sulky some time ago, but during the last session has attended much more in the House [of Lords]. No doubt Erne has stronger claims ... but there is no one who in position, rank or property can compare with Waterford. Personally your choice is a matter of perfect indifference to me – I merely write to you on Party grounds.'[32] Mayo, who had been Chief Secretary of Ireland, was appointed an extra Knight of St Patrick on leaving to be Viceroy of India. Again, in his second term as Prime Minister, from 1874 to 1880, Disraeli appointed a further three Conservative peers, the Marquess of Londonderry (1874), the Duke of Manchester (1877), and the Earl of Portarlington (1879). The apparent anomaly of an English duke being appointed to the Order of St Patrick is explained by the fact that the Mandeville dukes of Manchester owned an estate in County Armagh.

In his first two terms as Prime Minister, William Gladstone appointed a total of fifteen peers to the Order. Excluding the Duke of Connaught, the Queen's second son, who might reasonably be expected to stand above party politics, and Field Marshal Viscount Wolseley because of his distinguished military career, the remaining thirteen were all Liberal peers. The long period of Conservative rule stretching with few interruptions from 1885 to 1905, under the Marquess of Salisbury and then Arthur Balfour, saw the appointment of twenty Conservative peers to the Order. An echo of an eighteenth-century principle emerged in 1888 on the death of Lord Annaly. Four days after the early death of Annaly, who had been a Knight for only three years, the Earl of Kilmorey wrote to the Prince of Wales to press his claims. 'May I venture to ask Your Royal Highness to use your powerful influence ... in securing for me the vacancy in the Order of St Patrick ... I have consistently supported my party for 20 years in both Houses [he was MP for Newry 1871–4, and elected a representative peer for Ireland in 1881]. I am the holder of an Irish title, dating from the time of Charles II. I am one of the largest landed proprietors in Ireland, and Your Royal Highness knows an active member of society on both sides of the channel. This is the only distinction I can aspire to.'[33] There was little the Prince could do except to pass the letter on to the Prime Minister, saying that he had known Kilmorey for twenty-eight years, and asking for his name to be taken into consideration. The peer achieved his desired honour, but not until 1890, four vacancies later.

The line of Conservative peers appointed by Salisbury and Balfour was punctuated only by a solitary Liberal, the ninth Earl of Cavan, appointed during the brief Liberal administration of Lord Rosebery in 1894. As a peer of Ireland, Cavan had no right to sit in the House of Lords unless elected as an Irish representative peer, but he was able to sit in the House of Commons as member for South Somerset 1885–92. His principal pastime was lawn tennis, and in his entry in *Who's Who*, he proudly declared that his estate at Wheathampstead boasted the largest covered lawn tennis court in England.

With a seat in the House of Lords guaranteed by birth and death, governments could not always be sure that the politics of a peer would remain constant. Earl O'Neill (1809) was an Irish representative peer for forty years until his death in 1841, but his political allegiance was less easy to determine. 'Lord O'Niell (*sic*) is a man likely to take his own course in politics, and we have no means of establishing a communication with him.'[34]

A number of Knights were appointed, not only because of their political allegiance, but because of their political service, and a number of them had been members of the House of Commons for varying periods. The Earl of Cork and Orrery (1860) was Liberal MP for Frome 1854–6, and held a number of political royal household appointments including Master of the Buckhounds and Master of the Horse. He was one of the few Liberal peers who supported the home rule policy of William Gladstone after 1886. The Earl of Kenmare (1872) had been Liberal MP for County Kerry, from 1852 until the death of his father in 1871. Although never a member of the cabinet, he held a number of political royal household appointments between 1856 and 1886, usually Vice-Chamberlain of the household. He parted company with Gladstone over home rule in 1886 and became a Liberal Unionist. Lord Carlingford (1882), born at his family home in County Louth, was a career politician, and held a succession of cabinet offices during Gladstone's first and second ministries. At the time of his appointment to the Order, he was Lord Privy Seal. Although an Irish landlord, his life came to centre in his political activities at Westminster, and in the care of his English estates. His father had been MP for Hillsborough in the last Irish Parliament before the union, and Carlingford himself had served as chief secretary of Ireland 1865–6 and 1868–71. The Earl of Howth (1884) was Liberal MP for Galway 1868–74; the Earl of Kilmorey (1890) was MP for Newry 1871–4; the Earl of Lucan (1898), Conservative MP for Mayo 1865–74; the Earl of Enniskillen (1902), Conservative MP for Enniskillen 1868–80 and Fermanagh 1880–5, and a Conservative Whip 1874–85. The Earl of Donoughmore (1916), Chairman of Committees in the House of Lords, had been a junior minister in the Conservative government of Arthur Balfour (1902–5).

Viscount Midleton (1916) was a former Secretary of State for War and for India (1900–05) in the Conservative governments of Lord Salisbury and Arthur Balfour. The Brodrick family were prominent in Surrey, but had settled in Ireland in 1641. Midleton's principal residence was at Peper Harrow, Godalming, but the greater part of his estates were in County Cork, and he had a residence at The Grange, Midleton. Midleton had been a Conservative MP for Surrey constituencies 1880–1905 and became leader of the Irish peers in 1908. He presented the southern unionist case against home rule for Ireland, but when it became clear that southern unionism was a lost cause, he began to work for some form of home rule. He played a principal role in the establishment of a second chamber in the Irish Free State Parliament, but refused to serve in it, because of its restricted powers.

Although political allegiance was a factor in the selection of a peer for the Order, the character and public service of the peer gradually was recognised as an additional qualification. The Earl of Enniskillen (1810) was described by Daniel O'Connell as, 'one of the finest looking Irish gentlemen' and, 'that rare good thing in Ireland, a resident nobleman, spending his income amongst his own tenantry'.[35] The Earl of Fingall (1821), was the first Roman Catholic peer appointed to the Order, and led the campaign for Catholic Emancipation. The Earl of Roden (1821) 'morally no less than physically ... was one of the noblest among many noble specimens of the Irish aristocracy; his lofty stature, stalwart frame, and countenance beaming with honesty, courage and generosity, rather than with intellectual power, marking him out for influential if not commanding ascendancy ... But nowhere was he more at home, – for both he and his excellent lady had become very religious, – than when presiding at his chapel and teaching in his Sunday school'.[36] Fingall was followed by a few other Roman Catholic Knights: Viscount Southwell (1837), the Earl of Fingall (1846), the Earl of Granard (1857), the Earl of Dunraven and Mountearl (1866), Viscount Southwell (1871), the Earl of Kenmare (1872), Lord O'Hagan (1882), and the Earl of Granard (1909). The smallness of the numbers did not indicate a bias towards the Protestant peers, only the fact that there were very few Roman Catholic peers.

The Earl of Leitrim (1834), 'displayed liberal tendencies distinctly in advance of his time, showing his strong disapproval of the many sinecure offices then conferred on prominent politicians, by resigning the post of Searcher, Packer, and Gauger when it devolved upon him in 1828 on the death of his brother'.[37] The Earl of Dartrey (1855) was known to be, 'a model landlord and country gentleman, as also one of the best amateur chess players'.[38] The Earl of Kenmare (1872) was extremely popular with his tenants, and it was said that if a man was a tenant of the earl, it was as good as a dowry for his daughter.[39] Viscount Powerscourt (1871) was, 'generally esteemed as a liberal patron of the fine arts, and an excellent landlord'.[40] The Earl of Portarlington (1879) was praised for his decision to sell his English estates, inherited from the Earl of Dorchester, to clear the debts on his Irish estates and, 'discharging the duties which belong to his rank as a resident proprietor'.[41] The Marquess of Ormonde (1888) had the reputation for being an excellent landlord and remained on friendly terms with all his tenants until his death in 1919, despite living through some of the more difficult periods of Irish history.

Not all the Knights were so honourable. The Marquess of Drogheda (1783) has already been referred to. The Marquess of Sligo (1810) was convicted at the Old Bailey on 16 December 1812 of having persuaded some sailors aboard Royal Navy ships in the Mediterranean to navigate his yacht to England; he was sentenced to pay a fine of £5,000 and to be imprisoned in Newgate for four months.[42] 'The men were discovered in his vessel after his solemn declaration that they were not there.'[43] The Marquess of Clanricarde (1831) enjoyed the dubious honour of being Lord Privy Seal for three weeks in 1858. Lord Palmerston the Prime Minister of the day had defied public opinion by appointing him to the cabinet position despite the fact that Clanricarde had recently been revealed as the father of an illegitimate child. The peer's appointment to the office contributed to the fall of the Government. He was described in 1847 as, 'a tall, thin, aristocratic man, bald and bland, wearing ... tight pantaloons, striped silk socks and pumps'.[44] The Earl of Landaff (1831) was a gambler and a personal enemy of King George IV. At the trial of Queen Caroline in 1821, he and his wife had testified in favour of the proprietary behaviour of the Queen at the court of Naples. Despite his Welsh title, with its English phonetic spelling, the Mathew earls of Landaff were an old Irish family with an estate in County Tipperary. The Marquess of Headfort (1839) was described in 1837 as, 'a chattering, capering, spindleshanked gaby'.[45] The Marquess of Londonderry (1856) was long remembered for taking part in a duel. In June 1838, he was shot through the wrist at Wormwood Scrubs by Monsieur Gerard de Melcy, husband of the opera singer Grisi, to whom, without having received any encouragement, he had addressed a declaration of love. He died in 1872, 'after long seclusion in consequence of mental disease'.[46] The Marquess of Donegall (1857) was described as, 'a typical easy going

Irishman, always in debt'. He and his hot-tempered wife were known as 'Bel and the Dragon'.[47] The Duke of Manchester (1877) was described by Disraeli as 'silly but not dull', and by another as, 'a curious mixture of good nature and oddity, he was continually airing some extraordinary theory or complaining of some hitherto unknown ailment . . . and was a well intentioned bore'.[48]

The Earl of Gosford (1869) was made a Knight of St Patrick at the age of twenty-seven. He was a friend of the Prince of Wales (later King Edward VII) and was Vice-Chamberlain to Queen Alexandra from 1901 until his death. He was never especially prominent in politics, although he was a Liberal until the question of home rule split the party in 1886. Those who knew Gosford, spoke warmly of his old-fashioned, highly-bred courtesy and charm as a companion and his reputation as a raconteur. 'It would be hard to believe that throughout his long life in the changing world of society and sport, he ever made an enemy.'[49] Unfortunately, some early successes made him a devoted follower of the turf. In the eighteen-eighties he sold the library of Gosford Castle, a library collected by his father and grandfather, to pay a racing debt. In 1921 the remaining contents of the castle had to be sold. The loss of his ancestral home perhaps contributed to his death at the age of eighty in April 1922.

Although not financially ruined, the marquesses of Waterford, who numbered five Knights of St Patrick in their ranks, were particularly smitten by tragedy. The second marquess (1806) died of the good old eighteenth-century complaint of gout, at the age of fifty-four. The third marquess (1845) was notoriously and sometimes violently eccentric in his youth. 'He painted the Melton toll bar a bright red, put aniseed on the hoofs of a parson's horse, and hunted the terrified divine with bloodhounds. On another occasion he put a donkey into the bed of a stranger at an inn. He took a hunting box in the shires, and amused himself with shooting out the eyes of the family portraits with a pistol. He smashed a valuable French clock on the stairway at Crockford's with a blow of his fist, and solemnly proposed to one of the first railway companies in Ireland to start two engines in opposite directions on the same line in order that he might witness the smash, for which he proposed to pay.'[50] But he matured with age, and by the time of his death, he was, 'one of the best landlords and most improving cultivators [in Ireland] and had become universally popular and respected'.[51] He died in a riding accident while jumping hurdles outside the courtyard of his house. The fifth marquess (1868) had, 'a thoroughly able, direct, frank, masculine mind, and with a good deal of liberality and breadth of apprehension. They say he is of a dictatorial turn . . . It does not prevent him from being a man of strong, clear sense, and of hearty straight ways'.[52] He committed suicide in 1895 by shooting himself; the verdict was temporary insanity. For many years he had been partially paralysed, caused by a fall from his horse while hunting, in consequence of which he was allowed to remain seated when addressing the House of Lords. The sixth marquess (1902) was drowned in 1911 on a dark December night in the small river which flowed between his house and the kennels. He had been walking home from Kilmacthomas Lodge, where timber was being cut down, along a path which passed along the edge of the Clodagh River. It was believed that he had tripped over a branch and fallen face down into the river. The fourth marquess died of gastric fever in 1866 at the age of fifty-two, and the seventh marquess died in a shooting accident in 1934 at the age of thirty-three.

The Waterfords were not alone among the Knights in their catalogue of tragic deaths. The Marquess of Thomond (1783) died after a fall from his horse. The Earl of Bective (1783) died of paralysis. The Marquess of Ely (1807) died from cholera. Lord Farnham (1845) and his wife, were burned to death in a railway accident in North Wales in 1868. Viscount Massereene (1851) died from the effects of a fall from a terrace in his garden while uprooting a shrub which gave way, suddenly, with him. Lord Lurgan (1864) died at the age of fifty after seven years of paralysis. The Earl of Mayo (1869), Viceroy of India 1868–72, was assassinated in office while on a visit to the Andaman Islands, by an Afghan convict. The Duke of Edinburgh (1880) died from cancer of the larynx. The Earl of Longford (1901), a quiet and self-effacing country squire who was at his happiest when among his soldiers, or shooting, hunting and overseeing his estate, was killed in action at Gallipoli in 1915, one of thousands who died in that disastrous campaign. At the outbreak of the war he had told his son that he would give ten years of his life to take part in a charge.[53] Given his wish, he was killed at Scimitar Hill and his body was never found. Another victim of the First World War was Earl Kitchener of Khartoum (1911) who was drowned at sea when his ship was torpedoed in 1916.

The Order was not without its genial eccentrics; of whom Lord Castletown (1908) was a celebrated figure in his day. The only son of the first Lord Castletown, illegitimate son and heir of the last Earl of Upper Ossory, Castletown was an ardent Irish nationalist, a supporter of the Celtic revival, believed in fairies, and changed his politics as frequently as some people change their minds. While Member of Parliament for Portarlington (1880–1883), he was the only member of the House to sit as a Liberal Conservative. Castletown had founded the Celtic Association as a forum for bringing together the Celts of Ireland, Scotland, Wales, Cornwall, the Isle of Man, and Brittany. In recognition of his service in this area, the Welsh made him a druid. 'Barnie' Castletown, as he was known, was nominated a Knight of St Patrick during his tenure of the office of Chancellor of the Royal University of Ireland in 1907. It was intended that he should be invested in the summer of 1907 during the visit of King Edward VII, but the investiture was postponed because of the theft of the Crown Jewels. In his memoirs Castletown seemed oblivious of the fact. 'The ceremony took place some time after [my appointment], and was rather embarrassing for me, especially as I had to make a speech at the banquet which Lord Aberdeen ... gave to other Knights, officials and friends. I was told by my dear old friend [the Marquess of] Ormonde that I had acquitted myself well, and we passed on to the ceremony, which was in St Patrick's Hall. The other Knights sat at a table, and I was introduced, took the oath, and was duly knighted by the Lord Lieutenant. I remember I had two esquires carrying my helmet and sword, my banner was unfurled, and I took my seat at the table with the other members of the Order. It was all very quaint and medieval, and I felt much flattered by the honour.'[54]

The Earl of Portarlington (1879) inserted a peculiar clause in his will, that he should be buried with all the rings he usually wore on his fingers; that his jewelled badge of the Order of St Patrick should be returned to the Queen, with his prayer that she will ordain that no Knight of the Order should wear the badge, unless surmounted by the harp and crown, as on this one and certain others.

The Order of St Patrick was never intended to recognise scholarship, and few of the Knights qualified for appointment for their contribution to any field of learning. One of them was the Earl of Dunraven and Mountearl (1866), who was deeply knowledgeable about the literature and archaeology of Ireland. His Celtic and medieval learning, and antiquarian studies were widely known and appreciated.

The two most notable Knights in the category of learning, were the third (1845) and fourth (1890) earls of Rosse, both of whom were distinguished astronomers. William, third Earl of Rosse (1845) was one of the well-known astronomers of his age. He began by constructing a telescope with a reflecting speculum in the grounds of his castle at Birr in County Offaly. He did everything himself as there were no telescopes like this to be bought, or, indeed, other astronomers to help him. He started with the aid of a carpenter, a blacksmith, and some unskilled labourers, whom he trained. He experimented with all kinds of alloys to see which would be best for the speculum, even soldering plates of fine metal to the back of brass, before finally selecting an alloy of copper and tin. Still not satisfied with the results of his three-foot telescope, he constructed one twice that size when his father died and he inherited the estate in 1841. The result was the famous Leviathan of Parsonstown, the greatest telescope for over three-quarters of a century. It proved capable of gathering more light and seeing further into space than any telescope had ever been able to do before. Lord Rosse saw objects more than ten million light years away in space, and discerned their spiral nature as galaxies. His castle became a place of pilgrimage for all interested in astronomy, because it was the only place on earth from which such distant galaxies could be seen. His scientific eminence was recognised in 1849, when he was elected president of the Royal Society. He also deserves mention for his generosity towards the tenantry of his estate, a quality not displayed by many other nineteenth-century Irish landlords, when he devoted all the revenue from his estates to relieve the distress caused by the great famine of 1845–8.

On his death in 1867 he was succeeded by his eldest son, Lawrence, who had already learnt much from his father. The fourth earl was acclaimed for measuring the heat of the moon, designing and making an instrument on which a telescope could focus the lunar radiation. He made observations of Jupiter, measured the position of the satellites of Uranus, and confirmed the existence of the smaller ones of Mars. He counted the meteors which formed the shower ending of Beila's Comet and his last assistant devoted five years to drawing a map of the Milky Way. On his death in 1908, the astronomical work at Birr Castle came to a close, and the reflector of the famous Leviathan telescope was moved to the Science Museum in London.

A number of high-ranking army officers appear on the roll of Knights, including one of the founder Knights, Field Marshal the Marquess of Drogheda (1783), although he never saw active service. Field Marshal Viscount Gough (1857) came from an old Limerick family, that included a seventeenth century bishop of Limerick among his ancestors. Gough himself lived near Booterstown, Co. Dublin. He had fought in the Peninsular War under the Duke of Wellington, and led a British force up the Yangtze River in China, during the first Opium War 1840–2.

The name and title of Field Marshal Prince Edward of Saxe-Weimar (1890) seems, at first sight, a curious intrusion into a register of Irish Knights, and some Irishmen thought so as well. The prince's mother was a sister to Queen Adelaide, wife of King William IV. He was brought up mostly in England and, when they were both children, he was a playmate of his cousin Queen Victoria. The prince pursued a career in the army, and was Commander-in-Chief of the forces in Ireland 1885–90. Although he was thoroughly anglicised, his title did not endear him to Irish nationalists. The, Marquess of Londonderry, (Lord Lieutenant 1886–9), summoned a meeting of the Irish Privy Council for the purpose of proclaiming the Irish Land League to be a dangerous organisation. The marquess had strongly requested all the members of the council to be present, and all came with the exception of Prince Edward. 'On meeting His Highness, Lord Londonderry expressed surprise and regret at his failure to attend. The prince, in reply, pulled out of his pocket a copy of *United Ireland*, and read out something to the following effect. "Who are these men who are trampling on Irish freedom – the wicked Marquess of Londonderry? Well, he is an Irishman and Lord Lieutenant. Mr Arthur Balfour, the tiger-lily? Well, he is a Scotchman and Chief Secretary. But who have we next? His Serene Highness Prince Edward of Saxe-Weimar. What brings this bloodthirsty, cut-throat Hessian from foreign parts to strangle Irish liberty?" "After that," said the commander of the forces, "don't ask me to attend any more of your Privy Councils".'[55]

Field Marshal Viscount Wolseley (1885), who was Commander-in-Chief, Ireland, 1890–5, came from an old Staffordshire family on his father's side. His mother was born in Dublin and, after her husband's death when their son was eight, she took him back to Dublin where the future soldier was raised and educated. Wolseley was appointed to the Order on his return from the Sudan, where he had failed to arrive in time to relieve Khartoum and General Gordon. The failure was ascribed not to Wolseley but to Gladstone and his cabinet.

Field Marshal Earl Roberts (1897), came from a family long-established in County

LEFT:
Field Marshal the Earl
of Cavan (KP 1916).
RIGHT:
Field Marshal the Earl
of Ypres (KP 1917).

Waterford, and was Commander-in-Chief, Ireland, 1895–9. Field Marshal Earl Kitchener of Khartoum (1911) had a very tenuous connection with Ireland. He was born in County Kerry, only because his father, who had a house in Leicestershire, had taken a lease on a house there. At the age of thirteen, his parents moved to Switzerland for his mother's health and never returned. At the banquet after his investiture, Viscount Pirrie, attempted a joke with the field marshal. 'My friends tell me you're an Irishmen', said Pirrie. 'Friends don't always tell the truth', was the withering reply.[56] There was nothing especially Irish about Field Marshal the Earl of Cavan (1916). Although belonging to the historically Irish Lambart family of County Meath, he was born in Hertfordshire and had no connection with Ireland beyond his Irish peerages. The same was true of his father, also a Knight of St Patrick, who had been born in Hampshire. The family had been resident in England since the mid-eighteenth century. Field Marshal the Earl of Ypres (1917), better known as Viscount French, was Lord Lieutenant 1918–21. The French family had owned an estate in County Roscommon at least since the eighteenth century. General the Earl of Cork (1835) belonged to the Anglo-Irish Boyle family, and had long been resident in England. Brigadier General the Earl of Longford (1901) belonged to the Pakenham family, originally from Suffolk and resident in County Westmeath since the seventeenth century. Lieutenant General Lord de Ros (1902) was descended from Charlotte, Baroness de Ros in her own right, who married a younger son of the first Duke of Leinster in 1791. De Ros had been an equerry to the Prince Consort, and a lord-in-waiting to Queen Victoria, and lived at Old Court, Strangford, County Down.

Whereas Field Marshal Lord Cavan had an Irish title, but no real Irish interests, the Earl of Shaftesbury (1911), with a very English title, a residence at Wimborne in Dorset, and his position as Lord Chamberlain to Queen Mary, had very strong Irish connections. He had inherited the Belfast estates of the Marquess of Donegall, including Belfast Castle. Shaftesbury was also Lieutenant for the City of Belfast 1904–11 and for

County Antrim 1911–16, Lord Mayor of Belfast in 1907, Chancellor of Queen's University, Belfast 1909–23, and a Commissioner of the Congested Districts Board for Ireland 1902–14.

There were three governors-general or viceroys of India among the Knights of St Patrick: Marquess Wellesley (1783) in 1797–1805; the assassinated Earl of Mayo (1869) in 1868–72, and the Marquess of Dufferin and Ava (1864) in 1884–8. Mayo had been a career politician, serving as chief secretary for Ireland in 1852, 1858–9 and 1866–8. Dufferin, 'had all the best qualities of an Irishman, and as a companion there was no one like him. He had read enormously, and his knowledge of books, pictures, and music was unbounded, while no one was too insignificant, or too humble for him to be kind to'.[57] Lesser colonial administrators included the Marquess of Sligo (1810), Captain General of Jamaica 1833–6, and the second Earl of Clare (1845), Governor of Bombay 1830–4. The Marquess of Clanricarde (1831) was Under Secretary for Foreign Affairs 1826–7, Ambassador in St Petersburg 1838–41, before moving to the cabinet as Postmaster-General 1846–52. The Earl of Arran (1841) held posts in the diplomatic service in Stockholm, Paris, Lisbon and Buenos Aires 1820–37. His son, the fifth earl (1898), also served in the diplomatic service 1859–64. The seventh Earl of Granard (1857) served as an attaché at Dresden 1852–4. The twelfth Earl of Meath (1905) entered the diplomatic service in 1866 at the age of twenty-five, and held positions at Frankfurt, Berlin, The Hague and Athens, before leaving the service in 1873.

Only two Knights qualify in the category of distinguished jurists. Lord O'Hagan (1882) was called to the Bar in 1836 and rose to be Solicitor-General in 1860, Attorney-General in 1861, and finally Lord Chancellor of Ireland in 1868, the first Roman Catholic to hold the office since the Act of Settlement in 1701. He had been a nationalist in his younger days, and joined the Repeal Association in 1845, but when high office came his way, he found himself at odds with those he had once supported. 'He was thus invested with the responsibilities of office, and experienced some of its troubles. The tide of popularity was checked, and his duty having obliged him to prosecute some of the people whose cause under other circumstances he had advocated so warmly, a feeling of resentment was excited against him.'[58]

The Earl of Desart (1919) was a prominent southern unionist by the time of his appointment to the Order, but he had enjoyed a distinguished career as Solicitor to the Treasury, Director of Public Prosecutions, and finally a Judge of the Permanent International Court of Arbitration at the Hague. 'Throughout the public service, Lord Desart was recognised as an official of strong character and great ability, in whom the legal affairs of the Departments were safe, and who, in matters that came before him for advice ... could always be trusted to take a broad and statesmanlike view.'[59]

Businessmen were not a natural field from which to select Patrick Knights, but there were at least two and possibly three who might qualify for that category: the Earl of Iveagh (1895), was head of the Guinness brewing family. The Earl of Bessborough (1915), a barrister by profession, and secretary to the Speaker of the House of Commons 1884–95, had many interests in the world of business and finance, including being chairman of the London, Brighton and South Coast Railway Company, and of Guest, Keen and Nettlefolds.

Probably the most prominent businessman to enter the ranks of the Order was Viscount Pirrie (1909), the Belfast shipyard owner. Pirrie was a good example of a self-made, although well-connected man, and quite unlike the possessors of historic peerages who formerly filled the ranks of the Knights. 'A man of boundless energy, strong and well knit in frame, his bright bead-like eyes shone over cheeks which glowed with the clear colour which tells of mental activity allied with an iron constitution. His short iron-grey beard framed a sensitive mouth whose lines told of great kindliness, and from his lips the oft-repeated "What's tha-at" came with a soft burr which told of his northern origin.'[60] Educated at the Royal Belfast Academical

Institution (from which Queen's University developed), Pirrie went to the shipyard to work as an apprentice. His apprenticeship was of a technical kind and accompanied by academic study. He was distantly related to the Blackwoods (the marquesses of Dufferin and Ava), and the dukes of Hamilton and Abercorn, and regarded Lords Cadogan and Aberdeen as particular friends. Although he came from a solidly presbyterian unionist family, Pirrie was perceptive enough to realise that rigid northern Irish unionism would not prevent Home Rule, and that in the end the nationalist majority would win. He financed two Unionist candidates in Scotland at the general election of 1895, and was treasurer of the Ulster Defence Union, but in the new century he transferred his allegiance to nationalism, 'and by so doing, estranged from himself the political support of many of those who had been his best friends'.[61] In 1907 Lord Aberdeen appointed him Comptroller of the Household at Dublin Castle in succession to Viscount Powerscourt, at a salary of £300p.a. He was created a viscount in 1921 and died, childless, in 1924.

One Knight who was recognised not for his politics, but for his contribution to the cultural life of Ireland, was the Earl of Mayo (1905). In 1894, Mayo had founded the Arts and Crafts Society for Ireland, and his wife, Geraldine, revived the Royal Irish School of Art Needlework. Mayo was neither an artist nor a craftsman, but he had a general interest in Irish art and industrial and cultural affairs, and in 1891, his interest in history and antiquities had led him to establish the County Kildare Archaeological Society. In April 1894 Mayo sent out a circular letter in which he recommended the formation of a society with two principal objects: to improve the craftsman and attempt to raise the artistic level of his work; and to make the workman less of a machine producing many objects from one pattern. He also proposed to hold an exhibition of Irish arts and crafts in Dublin during the autumn of 1895. 'It was clear that Lord Mayo's proposed arts and crafts exhibition was being arranged with the intention not so much to gather up a miscellaneous display that might appeal to popular taste, but more to provide some sort of object lesson for native manufacturers and craftsmen. Drawing attention to the fact that good work could be done in Ireland, Mayo rounded off his articles in the *New Ireland Review* on an optimistic, even idealistic, note: "A beginning has, at any rate been made; fresh ground has been broken, and we have a work in which all our party-loving country can join and help one another. Arts and Crafts may be the means of leading us to a peaceful and friendly understanding of one another".'[62]

Mayo's influence was crucial in forming and guiding the arts and crafts movement in Ireland for more than thirty years, and its seventh and last exhibition was held in 1925. Mayo with so many other Irish peers had seen his house burnt in 1923, during the course of the civil war in southern Ireland, but, unlike others, he moved into the servants' wing, and declared that he would not be driven out of his own country. He died on the last day of 1927, in a London nursing home at the age of seventy-six. Palmerston, his Queen Anne revival house in County Kildare was filled with antiquarian books and a collection of Irish art and craft, and its destruction was an especially distressing loss to Irish culture. With his death came the demise of the Arts and Crafts Society of Ireland. 'His enthusiasm and energy had made him the society's figurehead for over thirty years. He had been the main link with the "Morris movement" in England in the 1890s and had been the strongest advocate of Irish arts and crafts in the years that followed. He was a prominent public figure in the 1920s, and even if others had taken over most of the executive running of the Arts and Crafts Society by that time, he must still have been an influential member. That we hear no more of the society after his death, apart from references to its demise, surely confirms the crucial role he played in its fortunes.'[63]

Among the philanthropic members of the Order was the Earl of Meath (1905), who gave up a promising career in the Diplomatic Service in 1873, when he and his wife decided to devote themselves to the, 'consideration of social problems and the

Lord Monteagle of
Brandon (KP 1885)

relief of human suffering'. He founded the Hospital Saturday Fund Committee in
1874, and the Dublin Hospital Sunday movement, both to raise money for hospitals.
In 1879 he founded the Young Men's Friendly Society which was later to develop
into the Church of England Men's Society. He also founded the Metropolitan Public
Gardens Association, and was the first chairman of the Parks Committee of the
London County Council. London owes the preservation of many of its open spaces,
and the formation of parks, gardens and playgrounds covering thousands of acres to
his energy and inspiration. After a long campaign, he succeeded in persuading the
government to institute Empire Day, celebrated annually on 24 May, the birthday of
Queen Victoria. Meath was something of a forbidding figure with his stern emphasis
on discipline, service and citizenship – he was Chief Scout Commissioner for Ireland
– but he had a dry humour, and an unquenchable enthusiasm and a practical
knowledge of the world and its ways, which ensured that he always found friends
and helpers for whatever scheme he embarked upon.

Meath told an amusing story at the time of his appointment as a Knight of St

The Earl of Meath
(KP 1905) with his star

Patrick. After the public announcement, he was walking down the front avenue at his country house, and noticed the wife of the gate keeper waiting for him. When he came within speaking distance, she threw up her arms and said to him, 'I always knew your lordship was such a saint that I was sure they would canonise you'. The peer was taken aback by this and replied that he had no idea what she meant. Whereupon the woman wittily replied, 'Sure, your lordship is a saint. An't yer a Saint of Saint Pathrick'.[64] Meath later repeated the story during an after-dinner speech given by the Lord Lieutenant in St Patrick's Hall.

A different kind of career was pursued by the Earl of Dunraven and Mountearl (1872), who was thirty-one years old, at the time of his appointment. Dunraven was a genuinely philanthropic and kind-hearted individual, although he lacked the kind of single-minded dedication that would have secured him greater things. He came to be respected warmly as, 'a sincere patriot and a consistent pursuer of national unity. It was not his fate to make any definite or outstanding contribution to an Irish settlement, but he smoothed many paths towards settlement notably in regard to the problems of the land and university education'.[65] In 1902 he initiated and presided at a conference that recommended a general policy of land purchase and became the basis of the Land Act of 1903. 'Few men in his day brought more intelligent good will to the service of Ireland, and few Irish politicians have done so little mischief to offset their work for good.'[66] Although a mild unionist for many years, he became a convinced supporter of the principle of dominion status for Ireland. The electorate of his neighbourhood returned him as the only unionist on the first county council of County Limerick: after his change of heart he was duly condemned as a disloyal Home Ruler by unionists. He loved outdoor sport, but his chief passion was sailing, and during the First World War, he bought and fitted yachts as hospitals, and paid their running costs from his own pocket. Another Knight addicted to the sea was the Marquess of Ormonde (1888) who was a noted yachtsman, and succeeded King Edward VII as Commodore of the Royal Yacht Squadron in 1901.

Lord Monteagle of Brandon (1885) was another moderate unionist who was converted to the concept of home rule for Ireland as something essential to the contentment and prosperity of Ireland. He actively sympathised with the aims of the Gaelic League, to make Ireland thoroughly Irish, by keeping alive, and spreading, its language, music, literature and customs. When he sold his estates to his tenants under the terms of the 1903 Land Act, he said that he could now live among them and help them without the suspicion of an ulterior motive. During the lord lieutenancy of Viscount French (1918–21), Monteagle wrote to *The Times*, publicly protesting at the wholesale arrests of nationalists that were taking place in Ireland, and in the summer of 1920 he introduced in the House of Lords a Bill for conferring dominion status on Ireland, with defence reserved. It failed to achieve support in the House at the time, but his action certainly influenced the government-sponsored Government of Ireland Act which became law in the same year. Monteagle was one of the Knights of St Patrick who might be described as conscientious but unspectacular. He was a resident landlord of the best type, who quietly and unobtrusively looked after his tenants, but said little about it. 'Highly cultivated and most attractive, a man of singular modesty and nobility of life ... If St Patrick takes any interest in his Knights, the last of whom will soon pass on, none will be more welcome to him than the gentle Knight who laboured and loved on the Shannon shore.'[67]

The partition of Ireland effectively began the disintegration and exile of the landed aristocracy of Ireland, not least because of the senseless destruction of so many of the great country houses in 1921–3. Castle Gore in County Mayo, the home of the Earl of Arran (1909), was burnt in 1922; it was never rebuilt, and the earl moved to England. The Earl of Bandon (1900) was forced to watch his house set on fire in June 1921, and was held hostage for about three weeks before being released. Broken by the loss of his home, he and his wife left for England, where he died in May 1924. The sadness of the Bandon case was that the earl had been a unionist and staunch conservative, and president of the County and City of Cork Unionist Association, but in August 1920, he called a meeting of the deputy lieutenants of County Cork to consider the future administration of Ireland, and the meeting unanimously condemned the British government for its failure to secure the observance of law, and having lost the confidence of all classes, and concluded by calling for dominion status for Ireland. The Earl of Bessborough (1915) died in 1920 at the age of sixty-nine, and was spared the sight of his house being burned in 1923. Although it was rebuilt, the family never went back to it, and it was sold in 1944.

Another ill-used Knight was the Earl of Desart (1919). He succeeded his brother in the peerage in 1886 and came to live at Desart Court, the ancestral home in County Kilkenny. As a lawyer, Desart had a talent for compromise and conciliation and, at the Irish Convention of 1917, he put forward a scheme for a wide measure of self-government for Ireland. His nationalist sympathies did not, however, prevent the burning of Desart Court in February 1923, principally because his sister-in-law, the Dowager Countess of Desart, was a member of the new Irish senate. Although the house was rebuilt in 1926 (it was demolished again in 1937), Lord Desart never went back to live in Ireland; he died in 1934 at the age of eighty-six. One Knight who refused to leave was the Earl of Mayo (1905) whose house Palmerston, near Straffan in County Kildare, was burnt in 1923. Mayo was conservative in politics but had strong nationalist sympathies, which had bred in him a loyalty to Ireland. Asked whether he would now go and live in England, he replied, 'I will not be driven from my own country'.[68] He and his wife settled into the servants' wing which had survived the fire, while the main house was rebuilt. The Earl of Granard's home, Castle Forbes, was damaged by a land mine on 26 February 1922; another mine failed to explode.

Some peers survived for a while in the new and changing Ireland. Eight of the Knights were elected either by the Privy Council or by their fellow peers to the senate of the stillborn legislature of Southern Ireland, envisaged by the Government of Ireland Act 1920: the earls of Desart (1919), Donoughmore (1916), Dunraven and Mountearl (1872), Granard (1909), Mayo (1905), Meath (1905) and Midleton (1916), and Lord Oranmore and Browne (1918). When the constitution of Southern Ireland was finalised in 1923, and the nation was transformed into the Irish Free State, three Knights were nominated by William Cosgrave to serve as members of Seanad Eireann, the upper house: the Earl of Dunraven and Mountearl (1923–6), the defiant Earl of Mayo (1923–7), and the Earl of Granard (1923–34). There could have been more: the earls of Desart, Donoughmore, Iveagh and Midleton refused to serve in the senate, which they regarded as a puppet assembly. Dunraven and Mayo had both been members of the Irish Landlords' Convention of 1903, which had paved the way for legislation in relation to the purchase of land by tenants. Granard had never been a unionist, and was a lifelong supporter of the Home Rule movement. He served as president of Seanad Eireann for several years and enjoyed the trust of both the Irish and British governments. He was eventually appointed to the Irish Council of State, a body of distinguished advisers to the president of Ireland.

Of the twenty-one Knights of St Patrick at the beginning of 1922, the majority either stayed in Ireland or divided their time between England and Ireland after partition. The exceptions were as follows: the Earl of Gosford had sold Gosford Castle in 1921 to pay his gambling debts, and moved to England. The earls of Arran, Bandon, Desart and Listowel saw their houses burnt, and also moved to England. After his resignation as Lord Lieutenant, the Earl of Ypres (Viscount French) left Ireland and lived mainly in Paris. In August 1923 he was appointed Captain of Deal Castle, and lived there until his death in May 1925. The Earl of Cavan had always lived mostly in England. The earls of Midleton and Shaftesbury moved to England at later dates. Shaftesbury presented Belfast Castle, with two hundred acres of land, to the city of Belfast in 1934.

The Earl of Arran (who died in 1958) and the Earl of Shaftesbury (who died in 1961), both Knights of St Patrick for forty-nine years, were the last two surviving non-royal Knights. Arran was also the last surviving member of the Privy Council of Ireland, to which no appointments were made after 1921.

Another category deserves to be mentioned; those who have refused the offer of the Order of St Patrick. Although a few names are known, this is not a well-documented area, and the following list should not be taken as exhaustive.

The cases of the sixth Earl of Antrim (1749–91), Earl Nugent (c.1702–88) and the first Earl of Hillsborough (1718–93), all proposed as founder Knights, are noted in chapter one. The second Earl of Rosse (1758–1841) is said to have been offered the Order, perhaps at the time of the Union which he vigorously opposed. The pleasant and respected third Duke of Leinster (1791–1874), first president of the Irish Education Board refused the Order in 1831, despite his name having been proposed by King William IV himself.[69] The sixth Earl of Granard (1760–1837) also refused the Order. The most prominent refusal was that of the second Viscount Lismore (1815–98), who was named a Knight on 14 September 1864, but subsequently declined the nomination because of the expense of becoming a Knight. Lismore, the second of the title, lived in Shanbally Castle at Clogheen in County Tipperary, designed for his father in c.1812 by John Nash. Beyond being Lord Lieutenant of County Tipperary 1857–85, he had no other qualification for being a Knight of St Patrick. It was said that, 'he showed a keen appreciation of the pleasures of the table'.[70] The eleventh Earl of Fingall (1859–1929) was said to have refused the Order on three occasions, the first being in 1888. On each occasion his refusal was for the same reason; he felt that he had not personally earned it.[71] In 1915, the Lord Lieutenant proposed conferring the Order on Lord Frederick Fitzgerald (1857–1924), Commissioner of National Education in Ireland, and the King gave his informal approval.[72] Fitzgerald was the younger brother of the fifth Duke of Leinster (1851–93) and uncle of the sixth duke (1887–1922). That effectively made him head of the Fitzgerald family, because the sixth duke was afflicted with a brain tumour and took no role in public life, or in the management of the family estates. If Lord Frederick had accepted the honour, he would have been the first and only non-peer to be appointed to the Order.

When the Order of St Patrick passed into abeyance after 1922, there remained the question of an alternative honour for Irish peers who would once have received the Patrick. The field was much reduced since there was now little likelihood of any British government honouring Irish peers living in the Irish Free State, but what of Irish peers living in Northern Ireland or in England? As the Order of St Patrick was now in abeyance, the choice lay between the Order of the Garter and the Order of Thistle. Of the two, the latter is emphatically Scottish in every aspect of its constitution and, excluding members of the Royal Family, only one non-Scotsman – King Olav V of Norway – has ever been appointed a Knight of the Thistle. The Order of the Garter on the other hand has never been strictly an English Order. Its conferment has always been wider than the boundaries of England, and two of the earlier Knights of St Patrick, Earl Talbot and Marquess Wellesley, resigned the Order of St Patrick on being appointed to the Order of the Garter. Excluding the twelve royal princes who were appointed both to the Patrick and the Garter, only three Knights of St Patrick have been additionally (and later) appointed Knights of the Garter:

Field Marshal Earl Roberts (KP 1897, KG 1901)
Field Marshal Earl Kitchener of Khartoum (KP 1911, KG 1915)
Duke of Abercorn (KP 1922, KG 1928)

In accordance with tradition, the twelve royal Knights of St Patrick, with the exception of Prince Edward, Duke of Kent, have first been appointed to the Order of the Garter.

Duke of Kent and Strathearn (KG 1786, KP 1783)
Duke of Cumberland (KG 1783, KP 1821)
Prince Consort (KG 1839, KP 1842)
Duke of Cambridge (KG 1835, KP 1851)
Prince of Wales (KG 1841, KP 1868)
Duke of Connaught (KG 1867, KP 1869)
Duke of Edinburgh (KG 1863, KP 1880)
Duke of Clarence and Avondale (KG 1883, KP 1887)
Duke of York (KG 1884, KP 1897)
Prince of Wales (KG 1910, KP 1927)
Duke of Gloucester (KG 1921, KP 1934)
Duke of York (KG 1916, KP 1936)

In 1783 the Order of St Patrick effectively supplanted the Order of the Garter as the customary honour for Irish peers; from 1922, the situation has reverted to the pre-1783 practice. Irish peers, peers with Irish titles, or peers having some other connection with Ireland, whose eminence was sufficient to qualify them for the Order of St Patrick before 1922, are now once more, mostly appointed to the Order of the Garter.

Viscount FitzAlan of Derwent (Lord Lieutenant 1921–22) (KG 1925)
Earl of Athlone (KG 1928)
Viscount Alanbrooke (KG 1946)

Viscount Alexander of Tunis (KG 1946)
Viscount Montgomery of Alamein (KG 1946)
Earl of Iveagh (KG 1955)
Lord Wakehurst (Governor of Northern Ireland 1952–64) (KG 1962)
Viscount Brookeborough (Prime Minister of Northern Ireland 1943–63) (KG 1965)
Earl of Longford (KG 1971)
Earl of Drogheda (KG 1972)

The exception to this rule is General Sir Richard O'Connor, a former Lord High Commissioner to the General Assembly of the Church of Scotland. who was appointed to the Order of the Thistle in 1971. Although domiciled in Scotland, his name and ancestry were unmistakably Irish.

The few remaining Irish peers whose service is sufficiently eminent to justify the conferment of a high honour, are to be included in the ranks of the Knights of the Garter, and this could also well apply to those residents of Northern Ireland who are not peers.

The image of a settled, landed and hereditary aristocracy in Ireland has all but disappeared in the years since 1922, and the fate of the descendants of the founder Knights is an illustration of the fate of the Irish aristocracy in general. Of the fifteen powerful Irish peers, appointed Knights of St Patrick in 1783, the descendant of one (the Earl of Tyrone), and the collateral descendant of another (the Earl of Inchiquin) are the only ones still resident in Ireland.

Prince Edward was fifteen at the time of his appointment as a Knight of St Patrick in 1783. One of the many sons of King George III, he was created Duke of Kent and Strathearn in 1799. He is now a forgotten historical figure, except for the fact that he married in July 1818, and fathered a daughter before his premature death in January 1820 at the age of fifty-two. The daughter succeeded to the throne in 1837 as Queen Victoria, and her father became the ancestor of the present royal family.

The descendants of the prickly and arrogant William Fitzgerald, 2nd Duke of Leinster prospered until the early twentieth century, when the seventh Duke (1892–1976) ran up enormous debts and sold his rights to the Leinster estates for his life time. Carton House was sold in 1951, and Kilkea Castle in 1960, and the eighth Duke (b.1914) now lives in Oxfordshire. Leinster House, in Kildare Street, Dublin, was sold in 1814 and, since 1924, has been the home of the Oireachtas (the Irish Parliament).

Henry de Burgh, twelfth Earl of Clanricarde, was created Marquess of Clanricarde in 1789. He was married, but had no children. On his death in 1797, the marquessate became extinct, and the earldom passed to a cousin. The male line of Thomas Nugent, sixth Earl of Westmeath, became extinct on the death of the eighth Earl in 1871, when the title passed to a distant cousin. The thirteenth Earl (b.1928), lives in Berkshire. The male line of Murrough O'Brien, fifth Earl of Inchiquin, and first Marquess of Thomond from 1800, became extinct on the death of the 3rd Marquess in 1855. The older title of Baron Inchiquin passed to a distant cousin, Sir Lucius O'Brien, who became the thirteenth Baron. The eighteenth Baron (b.1943), lives in Co. Clare. There are no living descendants of Charles Moore, sixth Earl of Drogheda, and first Marquess of Drogheda from 1795. His line died out in 1892 with the death of his grandson, the third Marquess, when the marquessate became extinct. The earldom passed to a cousin, and the twelfth Earl (b.1937) lives in London. George De la Poer Beresford, second Earl of Tyrone, and first Marquess of Waterford from 1789, died in 1800. The eighth Marquess (b.1933) still lives in the ancestral home at Portlaw in Co. Waterford. Richard Boyle, second Earl of Shannon is represented by his descendant, the ninth Earl (b.1924) who lives in Berkshire. James Hamilton, second Earl of Clanbrassil, married but had no children. On his death in 1798, his peerages became extinct. Richard Wellesley, second Earl of Mornington (Marquess Wellesley from 1799), married but had no children. On his death in 1842, the marquessate became extinct, and the earldom of Mornington passed to his brother. On the death of the fifth Earl in 1863, the title passed to his cousin, the second Duke of Wellington. Arthur Saunders Gore, second Earl of Arran is represented by his descendant, the ninth Earl (b.1938) who lives in England. James Stopford, second Earl of Courtown is represented by the ninth Earl (b.1954) who lives in England. The male line of James Caulfeild, fourth Viscount Charlemont and first Earl of Charlemont, became extinct on the death of the third Earl in 1892. The older title of Viscount Charlemont passed to a cousin, and the fourteenth Viscount (b.1934), a second-generation Canadian, lives in Ontario. The son of Thomas Taylour, first Earl of Bective, was created Marquess of Headfort in 1800. The family home of Headfort in County Meath was sold by the sixth Marquess (b.1932) in 1982. He lives in the Far East, while his heir, Lord Bective (b.1959), lives in London. Henry Loftus, third Earl of Ely is represented by his descendant, the eighth Marquess of Ely (b.1913). He and his son, Viscount Loftus (b.1943), both live in Canada.

Perhaps a day may come when the Order of St Patrick could be revived but, until a new, appropriate and acceptable constituency can be discerned, this seems unlikely in the foreseeable future.

The Sovereigns of the Order

════

HM King George III   (1783–1820)

Born:	*4 June 1748*
Sovereign:	*5 February 1783*
Esquires in March 1783:	
	Viscount Jocelyn
	Viscount Sudley
	Lord Robert Fitzgerald
Esquires in June 1809:	
	Earl of March
	Earl of Mountcharles
	The Honourable Richard Wingfield
Died:	*29 January 1820*

HM King George IV   (1820–1830)

Born:	*12 August 1762*
Sovereign:	*29 January 1820*
Esquires in August 1821:	
	Earl of Clanricarde
	Earl of Bective
	Earl of Mountcharles
Died:	*26 June 1830*

HM King William IV   (1830–1837)

Born:	*21 August 1765*
Sovereign:	*26 June 1830*
Died:	*20 June 1837*

HM Queen Victoria   (1837–1901)

Born:	*24 May 1819*
Sovereign:	*20 June 1837*
Died:	*22 January 1901*

HM King Edward VII   (1901–1910)

Born:	*9 November 1841*
Knight of St Patrick:	*18 March 1868*
Sovereign:	*22 January 1901*
Died:	*6 May 1910*

HM King George V   (1910–1936)

Born:	*3 June 1865*
Knight of St Patrick:	*6 July 1897*
Sovereign:	*6 May 1910*
Died:	*20 January 1936*

HM King Edward VIII   (1936)

Born:	*23 June 1894*
Knight of St Patrick:	*3 June 1927*
Sovereign:	*20 January to 11 December 1936*
Died:	*28 May 1972*

HM King George VI   (1936–1952)

Born:	*14 December 1895*
Knight of St Patrick:	*17 March 1936*
Sovereign:	*11 December 1936*
Died:	*6 February 1952*

HM Queen Elizabeth II   (1952–)

Born:	*21 April 1926*
Sovereign:	*6 February 1952*

APPENDIX TWO

The Grand Masters of the Order

1. **George Nugent-Temple-Grenville,** (1783)
   3rd Earl Temple (later 1st Marquess of Buckingham)
   Born: 18 June 1753
   Invested: 11 March 1783
   Died: 11 February 1813

2. **Robert Henley, 2nd Earl of Northington** (1783–1784)
   Born: 3 January 1747
   Invested: 3 June 1783
   Died: 5 July 1786

3. **Charles Manners, 4th Duke of Rutland** (1784–1787)
   Born: 15 March 1754
   Invested: 24 February 1784
   Died: 24 October 1787

4. **George Nugent-Temple-Grenville,** (1787–1790)
   1st Marquess of Buckingham
   Born and died: (as for number 1)
   Invested: 16 December 1787

5. **John Fane, 10th Earl of Westmorland** (1790–1795)
   Born: 1 June 1759
   Invested: 5 January 1790
   Died: 15 December 1841

6. **William Fitzwilliam, 4th Earl Fitzwilliam** (1795)
   Born: 30 May 1748
   Invested: 4 January 1795
   Died: 8 February 1833

7. **John Jeffreys Pratt, 2nd Earl Camden** (1795–1798)
   (later 1st Marquess Camden)
   Born: 11 February 1759
   Invested: 31 March 1795
   Died: 8 October 1840

8. **Charles Cornwallis, 1st Marquess Cornwallis** (1798–1801)
   Born: 31 December 1738
   Invested: 20 June 1798
   Died: 5 October 1805

9. **Philip Yorke, 3rd Earl of Hardwicke** (1801–1806)
   Born: 31 May 1757
   Invested: 25 May 1801
   Died: 18 November 1834

10. **John Russell, 6th Duke of Bedford** (1806–1807)
    Born: 6 July 1766
    Invested: 28 March 1806
    Died: 20 October 1839

11. **Charles Lennox, 4th Duke of Richmond** (1807–1813)
    Born: 9 December 1764
    Invested: 19 April 1807
    Died: 28 August 1819

12. **Charles Whitworth, 1st Earl Whitworth** (1813–1817)
    Born: 29 May 1752
    Invested: 26 August 1813
    Died: 13 May 1825

13. **Charles Chetwynd Chetwynd-Talbot,** (1817–1821)
    2nd Earl Talbot
    Born: 25 April 1777
    Invested: 9 October 1817
    Died: 10 January 1849

14. **Richard Wellesley, Marquess Wellesley** (1821–1828)
    Born: 20 June 1760
    Invested: 29 December 1821
    Died: 26 September 1842

15. **Henry William Paget, 1st Marquess of Anglesey** (1828–1829)
    Born: 17 May 1768
    Invested: 1 March 1828
    Died: 29 April 1854

16. **Hugh Percy, 3rd Duke of Northumberland** (1829–1830)
    Born: 20 April 1795
    Invested: 6 March 1829
    Died: 11 February 1847

17. **Henry William Paget, 1st Marquess** (1830–1833)
    of Anglesey
    Born and died: (as for number 15)
    Invested: 23 December 1830

18. **Richard Wellesley, Marquess Wellesley** (1833–1835)
    Born and died: (as for number 14)
    Invested: 6 September 1833

19. **Thomas Hamilton, 9th Earl of Haddington** (1835)
    Born: 21 June 1780
    Invested: 6 January 1835
    Died: 1 December 1858

20. **Constantine Henry Phipps, 2nd Earl of** (1835–1839)
    Mulgrave (later 1st Marquess of Normanby)
    Born: 15 May 1797
    Invested: 11 May 1835
    Died: 28 July 1863

21. **Hugh Fortescue, Viscount Ebrington** (1839–1841)
    (later 2nd Earl Fortescue)
    Born: 13 February 1783
    Invested: 3 April 1839
    Died: 14 September 1861

22. **Thomas Philip de Grey, 2nd Earl de Grey** (1841–1844)
    Born: 8 December 1781
    Invested: 15 September 1841
    Died: 14 November 1859

23. **William a'Court, 1st Baron Heytesbury** (1844–1846)
    Born: 11 July 1779
    Invested: 26 July 1844
    Died: 31 May 1860

24. **John William Ponsonby,** (1846–1847)
    4th Earl of Bessborough
    Born: 31 August 1781
    Invested: 11 July 1846
    Died: 16 May 1847

25. George William Frederick Villiers, (1847–1852)
4th Earl of Clarendon
    Born: 26 January 1800
    Invested: 26 May 1847
    Died: 27 June 1870

26. Archibald William Montgomerie, (1852)
13th Earl of Eglinton and 6th Earl of Winton
    Born: 29 September 1812
    Invested: 10 March 1852
    Died: 4 October 1861

27. Edward Granville Eliot, 3rd Earl of St Germans (1853–1855)
    Born: 29 August 1798
    Invested: 6 January 1853
    Died: 7 October 1877

28. George William Frederick Howard, (1855–1858)
7th Earl of Carlisle
    Born: 18 April 1802
    Invested: 13 March 1855
    Died: 5 December 1864

29. Archibald William Montgomerie, (1858–1859)
13th Earl of Eglinton and 6th Earl of Winton
    Born and died: (as for number 26)
    Invested: 12 March 1858

30. George William Frederick Howard, (1859–1864)
7th Earl of Carlisle
    Born and died: (as for number 28)
    Invested: 18 June 1859

31. John Wodehouse, 3rd Baron Wodehouse (1864–1866)
(later 1st Earl of Kimberley)
    Born: 7 November 1826
    Invested: 8 November 1864
    Died: 8 April 1902

32. James Hamilton, 2nd Marquess of Abercorn (1866–1868)
(later 1st Duke of Abercorn)
    Born: 21 January 1811
    Invested: 20 July 1866
    Died: 31 October 1885

33. John Poyntz Spencer, 5th Earl Spencer (1868–1874)
    Born: 27 October 1835
    Invested: 23 December 1868
    Died: 13 August 1910

34. James Hamilton, 1st Duke of Abercorn (1874–1876)
    Born and died: (as for number 32)
    Invested: 2 March 1874

35. John Winston Spencer-Churchill, (1876–1880)
7th Duke of Marlborough
    Born: 2 June 1822
    Invested: 12 December 1876
    Died: 5 July 1883

36. Francis Thomas de Grey Cowper, (1880–1882)
7th Earl Cowper
    Born: 11 June 1834
    Invested: 5 May 1880
    Died: 19 July 1905

37. John Poyntz Spencer, 5th Earl Spencer (1882–1885)
    Born and died: (as for number 33)
    Invested: 6 May 1882

38. Henry Howard Molyneux Herbert, (1885–1886)
4th Earl of Carnarvon
    Born: 24 June 1831
    Invested: 30 June 1885
    Died: 28 June 1890

39. John Campbell Hamilton-Gordon, 7th Earl of (1886)
Aberdeen (later 1st Marquess of Aberdeen and Temair)
    Born: 3 August 1847
    Invested: 10 February 1886
    Died: 7 March 1934

40. Charles Stewart Vane-Tempest-Stewart, (1886–1889)
6th Marquess of Londonderry
    Born: 16 July 1852
    Invested: 5 August 1886
    Died: 8 February 1915

41. Lawrence Dundas, 3rd Earl of Zetland (1889–1892)
(later 1st Marquess of Zetland)
    Born: 16 August 1844
    Invested: 5 October 1889
    Died: 11 March 1929

42. Robert Offley Ashburton Crewe-Milnes, (1892–1895)
2nd Baron Houghton (later 1st Marquess of Crewe)
    Born: 12 January 1858
    Invested: 22 August 1892
    Died: 20 June 1945

43. George Henry Cadogan, 5th Earl Cadogan (1895–1902)
    Born: 12 May 1840
    Invested: 8 July 1895
    Died: 6 March 1915

44. William Humble Ward, 2nd Earl of Dudley (1902–1905)
    Born: 25 May 1867
    Invested: 16 August 1902
    Died: 29 June 1932

45. John Campbell Hamilton-Gordon, 7th Earl (1905–1915)
of Aberdeen (later 1st Marquess of Aberdeen and Temair)
    Born and died: (as for number 39)
    Invested: 14 December 1905

46. Ivor Churchill Guest, 2nd Baron Wimborne (1915–1918)
(later 1st Viscount Wimborne)
    Born: 16 January 1873
    Invested: 18 February 1915
    Died: 14 June 1939

47. John Denton Pinkstone French, 1st Viscount (1918–1921)
French of Ypres (later 1st Earl of Ypres)
    Born: 28 September 1852
    Invested: 11 May 1918
    Died: 22 May 1925

48.* Edmund Bernard Fitzalan-Howard, (1921–1922)
1st Viscount FitzAlan of Derwent
    Born: 1 June 1855
    Invested: 2 May 1921
    Died: 18 May 1947

* Forty individuals held the office of Grand Master. Eight held the office twice.

The Knights Companions of the Order

1. **HRH Prince Edward Augustus (Duke of Kent and Strathearn from 1799)**

Born:	*2 November 1767*
Nominated:	*5 February 1783 (a founder Knight)*
Invested:	*16 March 1783*
(invested in Dublin by proxy – 11 March)	
Installed:	*17 March 1783 (by proxy)*
Esquires:	*The Honourable William Gore*
	The Honourable Robert Jocelyn
	The Honourable Charles Jones
Died:	*23 January 1820*

2. **William Robert FitzGerald, 2nd Duke of Leinster**

Born:	*13 March 1749*
Nominated:	*5 February 1783 (a founder Knight)*
Invested:	*11 March 1783*
Installed:	*17 March 1783*
Esquires:	*Captain Thomas Burgh*
	Richard Neville
	Robert Rochford
Died:	*20 October 1804*

3. **Henry de Burgh, 12th Earl of Clanricarde (Marquess of Clanricarde from 1789)**

Born:	*8 January 1743*
Nominated:	*5 February 1783 (a founder Knight)*
Invested:	*11 March 1783*
Installed:	*17 March 1783*
Esquires:	*Dennis Kelly*
	Richard Talbot
	Robert Dillon
Died:	*8 December 1797*

   Randall William Macdonnel, 6th Earl of Antrim (Marquess of Antrim from 1789)

Born:	*4 November 1749*
Nominated:	*5 February 1783 (a founder Knight)*
	(Lord Antrim refused the honour as he did not wish to relinquish the Order of the Bath)
Died:	*29 July 1791*

4. **Thomas Nugent, 6th Earl of Westmeath**

Born:	*? (baptised 18 April 1714)*
Nominated:	*5 February 1783 (a founder Knight)*
Invested:	*11 March 1783*
Installed:	*17 March 1783*
Esquires:	*Edward Hamilton*
	Thomas Nugent
	Oliver Nugent
Died:	*7 September 1792*

5. **Murrough O'Brien, 5th Earl of Inchiquin (1st Marquess of Thomond from 1800)**

Born:	*1726*
Nominated:	*5 February 1783 (a founder Knight)*
Invested:	*11 March 1783*
Installed:	*17 March 1783*
Esquires:	*Captain .... Sandford*
	Allan Bellingham
	Captain .... O'Brien
Died:	*10 February 1808*

6. **Charles Moore, 6th Earl of Drogheda (1st Marquess of Drogheda from 1795)**

Born:	*29 June 1730*
Nominated:	*5 February 1783 (a founder Knight)*
Invested:	*11 March 1783*
Installed:	*17 March 1783*
Esquires:	*John Moore*
	Ponsonby Moore
	Captain .... Vesey
Died:	*22 December 1821*

7. **George De la Poer Beresford, 2nd Earl of Tyrone (1st Marquess of Waterford from 1789)**

Born:	*8 January 1735*
Nominated:	*5 February 1783 (a founder Knight)*
Invested:	*11 March 1783*
Installed:	*17 March 1783*
Esquires:	*The Honourable J. Beresford*
	Marcus Beresford
	Theophilus Clements
Died:	*3 December 1800*

8. **Richard Boyle, 2nd Earl of Shannon**

Born:	*30 January 1727*
Nominated:	*5 February 1783 (a founder Knight)*
Invested:	*11 March 1783*
Installed:	*17 March 1783*
Esquires:	*The Right Honourable Thomas Connolly*
	Ralph Ward
	Lodge Morres
Died:	*20 May 1807*

9. **James Hamilton, 2nd Earl of Clanbrassil**

Born:	*23 August 1730*
Nominated:	*5 February 1783 (a founder Knight)*
Invested:	*11 March 1783*
Installed:	*17 March 1783*
Esquires:	*............... Rice*
	The Honourable John Jocelyn
	William Calbeck
Died:	*6 February 1798*

10. **Richard Wellesley, 2nd Earl of Mornington (Marquess Wellesley from 1799)**
    Born: 20 June 1760
    Nominated: 5 February 1783 (a founder Knight)
    Invested: 11 March 1783
    Installed: 17 March 1783
    Esquires: Gerald Fortescue
    Captain .... Fortescue
    Richard St George
    Resigned: 3 March 1810 (on appointment as a Knight of the Garter)
    Died: 26 September 1842

11. **Arthur Saunders Gore, 2nd Earl of Arran**
    Born: 25 July 1734
    Nominated: 8 March 1783 (a founder Knight)
    Invested: 11 March 1783
    Installed: 17 March 1783
    Esquires: Francis Gore
    Charles Cobbe
    Carnet Yelverton
    Died: 8 October 1809

12. **James Stopford, 2nd Earl of Courtown**
    Born: 28 May 1731
    Nominated: 5 February 1783 (a founder Knight)
    Invested: 11 March 1783
    Installed: 17 March 1783
    Esquires: Edward Smyth
    Francis Mathew
    Captain Walter Hone
    Died: 30 March 1810

13. **James Caulfeild, 1st Earl of Charlemont**
    Born: 18 August 1728
    Nominated: 5 February 1783 (a founder Knight)
    Invested: 11 March 1783
    Installed: 17 March 1783
    Esquires: Charles Stewart
    Richard Fitzgerald
    James Stewart
    Died: 4 August 1799

14. **Thomas Taylour, 1st Earl of Bective**
    Born: 20 October 1724
    Nominated: 5 February 1783 (a founder Knight)
    Invested: 11 March 1783
    Installed: 17 March 1783
    Esquires: The Honourable Robert Taylour
    Thomas Peppard
    .... Rowley
    Died: 14 February 1795

15. **Henry Loftus, 3rd Earl of Ely**
    Born: 18 November 1709
    Nominated: 5 February 1783 (a founder Knight)
    Invested: (The Earl of Ely died abroad before being invested or installed)
    Installed: (as above)
    Died: 8 May 1783

16. **Joshua Proby, 2nd Baron Carysfort (1st Earl of Carysfort from 1789)**
    Born: 12 August 1751
    Nominated: 5 February 1784 (in place of No 15)
    Invested: 5 February 1784
    Installed: 11 August 1800 (by proxy)
    Esquires: (unknown)
    Died: 7 April 1828

17. **Charles Tottenham Loftus, 4th Earl of Ely (1st Marquess of Ely from 1801)**
    Born: 23 January 1738
    Nominated: 12 December 1794 (in place of No 4)
    Invested: 12 December 1794
    Installed: 11 August 1800
    Esquires: (unknown)
    Died: 22 March 1806

18. **William Henry Fortescue, 1st Earl of Clermont**
    Born: 5 August 1722
    Nominated: 30 March 1795 (in place of No 14)
    Invested: (date unknown, but probably soon after nomination)
    Installed: 11 August 1800
    Esquires: (unknown)
    Died: 30 September 1806

19. **Walter Butler, 18th Earl of Ormonde (Marquess of Ormonde from 1816)**
    Born: 5 February 1770
    Nominated: 19 March 1798 (in place of No 3)
    Invested: 19 March 1798
    Installed: 11 August 1800
    Esquires: (unknown)
    Died: 10 August 1820

20. **Charles Lee Dillon, 12th Viscount Dillon**
    Born: 6 November 1745
    Nominated: 19 March 1798 (in place of No 9)
    Invested: 19 March 1798
    Installed: 11 August 1800
    Esquires: (unknown)
    Died: 9 November 1813

21. **John Denis Browne, 3rd Earl of Altamont (1st Marquess of Sligo from 1800)**
    Born: 11 June 1756
    Nominated: 5 August 1800 (in place of No 13)
    Invested: 5 August 1800
    Installed: 11 August 1800
    Esquires: (unknown)
    Died: 2 January 1809

22. **Henry Conyngham, 1st Earl Conyngham (1st Marquess Conyngham from 1816)**
    Born: 26 December 1766
    Nominated: 22 January 1801 (in place of No 7)
    Invested: 22 January 1801
    Installed: 29 June 1809
    Esquires: Gustavus Lambart
    Lieutenant Colonel Augustus Fitzgerald
    Colonel Henry John Clements
    Esquires in August 1821:
    Major General Augustus Fitzgerald
    James Arthur Douglas Bloomfield
    Edward Hamilton
    Died: 28 December 1832

23. **Henry De la Poer Beresford, 2nd Marquess of Waterford**

Born:	23 May 1772
Nominated:	14 March 1806 (in place of No 2)
Invested:	14 March 1806
Installed:	29 June 1809
Esquires:	Thomas King
	Charles Cobbe
	Lorenzo Hickey Jephson
Died:	16 July 1826

24. **Thomas Taylour, 1st Marquess of Headfort**

Born:	18 November 1757
Nominated:	15 May 1806 (in place of No 17)
Invested:	? (soon after nomination)
Installed:	29 June 1809
Esquires:	Lieutenant Colonel Thomas Pepper
	Richard Pepper
	George Pepper
Esquires in August 1821:	
	The Honourable Edward Anthony George Preston
	Colonel Thomas Pepper
	C. B. Ponsonby
Died:	24 October 1829

25. **Robert Jocelyn, 2nd Earl of Roden**

Born:	26 October 1756
Nominated:	13 November 1806 (in place of No 18)
Invested:	13 November 1806
Installed:	29 June 1809
Esquires:	The Honourable Price Blackwood
	George Walker
	Henry Straton
Died:	29 June 1820

26. **John Loftus, 2nd Marquess of Ely**

Born:	15 February 1770
Nominated:	3 November 1807 (in place of No 8)
Invested:	3 November 1807
Installed:	29 June 1809
Esquires:	P. O. Mitchell
	William Congreve Alcock
	W. B. F. Loftus
Died	26 September 1845

27. **Henry Boyle, 3rd Earl of Shannon**

Born	8 August 1771
Nominated:	5 April 1808 (in place of No 5)
Invested:	5 April 1808
Installed:	29 June 1809
Esquires:	Colonel William Stewart
	John Hyde
	Joseph Deane Freeman
Died:	22 April 1842

28. **Charles Henry St John O'Neill, 1st Earl O'Neill**

Born:	22 January 1779
Nominated:	13 February 1809 (in place of No 21)
Invested:	13 February 1809
Installed:	29 June 1809
Esquires:	Lieutenant Colonel George Jackson
	Archibald E. Obins
	George Stinton
Esquires in August 1821:	
	The Honourable John O'Neill
	P. O. Mitchell
	Colonel .... Clements
Died:	25 March 1841

29. **William O'Brien, 2nd Marquess of Thomond**

Born:	c.1765
Nominated:	11 November 1809 (in place of No 11)
Invested:	11 November 1809
Installed:	27 May 1819
Esquires:	Lord Edward O'Brien
	James Saurin
	M. A. Saurin
Esquires in August 1821:	
	James Saurin
	M. A. Saurin
	J. Smith Barry
Died:	21 August 1846

30. **Howe Peter Browne, 2nd Marquess of Sligo**

Born:	18 May 1788
Nominated:	24 March 1810 (in place of No 10)
Invested:	11 June 1811 (invested at Malta by dispensation)
Installed:	27 May 1819
Esquires:	Sir John Bourke
	James Browne
	Robert Browne
Died:	26 January 1845

31. **John Willoughby Cole, 2nd Earl of Enniskillen**

Born:	23 March 1768
Nominated:	27 April 1810 (in place of No 12)
Invested:	27 April 1810
Installed:	27 May 1819
Esquires:	Richard Magenis
	Richard Rochfort
	Arthur Magenis
Esquires in August 1821:	
	Richard Rochfort
	William Rochfort
	Arthur Magenis
Died	31 March 1840

32. **Thomas Pakenham, 2nd Earl of Longford**

Born:	14 May 1774
Nominated:	17 December 1813 (in place of No 20)
Invested:	17 December 1813
Installed:	27 May 1819
Esquires:	Charles Levinge
	William Pakenham
	William Ponsonby
Died:	24 May 1835

33. **HRH Prince Ernest Augustus, 1st Duke of Cumberland and Teviotdale (HM the King of Hanover from 1837)**

Born:	5 June 1771
Nominated:	12 February 1821 (in place of No 1)
Invested:	20 August 1821 (by proxy)
Installed:	28 August 1821 (by proxy)
Esquires:	John Hamilton
	Colonel the Honourable .... Stanhope
	William Balfour
Died:	18 November 1851

34. **George Augustus Chichester, 2nd Marquess of Donegall**

Born:	13 August 1769
Nominated:	12 February 1821 (in place of No 25)
Invested:	20 August 1821
Installed:	28 August 1821
Esquires:	Lord Edward Chichester
	Sir Stephen May
	Thomas Verner
Died:	5 October 1844

35. **Du Pre Alexander, 2nd Earl of Caledon**

Born:	14 December 1777
Nominated:	12 February 1821 (in place of No 19)
Invested:	20 August 1821
Installed:	28 August 1821
Esquires:	Henry Alexander
	Henry Lidsay
	The Honourable Cadwallader Blayney
Died:	8 April 1839

36. **Charles Chetwynd Chetwynd-Talbot, 2nd Earl Talbot**

Born:	25 April 1777
Nominated an extra Knight:	19 July 1821
Invested:	20 August 1821
Installed:	28 August 1821
Esquires:	The Honourable George Anson
	Lord Arthur Hill
	The Honourable Arthur F. De Roos
Became an ordinary Knight:	22 December 1821 (in place of No 6)
Resigned:	11 October 1844 (on being appointed a Knight of the Garter)
Died:	10 January 1849

37. **James Butler, 19th Earl of Ormonde (1st Marquess of Ormonde from 1825)**

Born:	15 July 1777
Nominated an extra Knight:	19 July 1821
Invested:	20 August 1821
Installed:	28 August 1821
Esquires:	Richard Rothe
	Humphry Butler
	William Bayly
Became an ordinary Knight:	16 July 1826 (in place of No 23)
Died:	18 May 1838

38. **John Chambre Brabazon, 10th Earl of Meath**

Born:	9 April 1772
Nominated an extra Knight:	19 July 1821
Invested:	20 August 1821
Installed:	28 August 1821
Esquires:	The Honourable Orlando Bridgman
	The Honourable William Wingfield
	Charles Hamilton
Became an ordinary Knight:	7 April 1828 (in place of No 16)
Died:	15 March 1851

39. **Arthur James Plunkett, 8th Earl of Fingall**

Born:	9 September 1759
Nominated an extra Knight:	19 July 1821
Invested:	20 August 1821
Installed:	28 August 1821
Esquires:	Lord Killeen
	Patrick Bellew
	Gerard Dease
Became an ordinary Knight:	23 October 1829 (in place of No 24)
Died:	30 July 1836

40. **James George Stopford, 3rd Earl of Courtown**

Born:	15 August 1765
Nominated an extra Knight:	19 July 1821
Invested:	20 August 1821
Installed:	28 August 1821
Esquires:	Captain John Phillimore
	The Honourable Montague Stopford
	Hamilton Grogan
Became an ordinary Knight:	28 December 1832 (in place of No 22)
Died:	15 June 1835

41. **Robert Jocelyn, 3rd Earl of Roden**

Born:	27 October 1788
Nominated an extra Knight:	19 July 1821
Invested:	20 August 1821
Installed:	28 August 1821
Esquires:	Ralph Howard
	Frederick Shaw
	Walter Newton
Became an ordinary Knight:	24 January 1833 (by the increase of the Order under the Statute of 24 January 1833)
Died:	20 March 1870

42. **Arthur Blundell Sandys Trumbell Hill, 3rd Marquess of Downshire**

Born:	8 October 1788
Nominated an extra Knight:	8 September 1831
Invested:	24 November 1831
Became an ordinary Knight:	24 January 1833 (by the increase of the Order under the Statute of 24 January 1833)
Installed:	30 January 1833 (by dispensation)
Died:	12 April 1845

43. **Ulick John de Burgh, 1st Marquess of Clanricarde**

Born:	20 December 1802
Nominated an extra Knight:	8 September 1831
Invested:	19 October 1831
Became an ordinary Knight:	24 January 1833 (by the increase of the Order under the Statute of 24 January 1833)
Installed:	30 January 1833 (by dispensation)
Esquires in April 1868:	Captain Oliver Martyn
	Richard Lynch-Staunton
Died:	10 April 1874

44. Francis William Caulfeild, 2nd Earl of Charlemont

Born:	*3 January 1775*
Nominated an extra Knight: 8 September 1831	
Invested:	*19 October 1831*
Became an ordinary Knight: 24 January 1833 (by the increase of the Order under the Statute of 24 January 1833)	
Installed:	*30 January 1833 (by dispensation)*
Died:	*26 December 1863*

45. Francis James Mathew, 2nd Earl of Landaff

Born:	*2 or 20 January 1768*
Nominated an extra Knight: 8 September 1831	
Invested:	*24 November 1831*
Became an ordinary Knight: 24 January 1833 (by the increase of the Order under the Statute of 24 January 1833)	
Installed:	*30 January 1833 (by dispensation)*
Died:	*12 March 1833*

46. Francis Nathaniel Conyngham, 2nd Marquess Conyngham

Born:	*11 June 1797*
Nominated:	*27 March 1833 (by the increase of the Order under the Statute of 24 January 1833)*
Invested:	*27 March 1833*
Installed:	*3 April 1833 (by dispensation)*
Esquires in April 1868:	
	Colonel the Earl of Mountcharles
	Captain .... Greville-Nugent
Died:	*17 July 1876*

47. Nathaniel Clements, 2nd Earl of Leitrim

Born:	*9 May 1768*
Nominated:	*8 April 1834 (by the increase of the Order under the Statute of 24 January 1833)*
Invested:	*8 April 1834*
Installed:	*31 May 1834 (by dispensation)*
Died:	*31 December 1854*

48. John Hely-Hutchinson, 3rd Earl of Donoughmore

Born:	*1787*
Nominated:	*8 April 1834 (in place of No 45)*
Invested:	*8 April 1834*
Installed:	*31 May 1834 (by dispensation)*
Died:	*14 September 1851*

49. Edmund Boyle, 8th Earl of Cork and Orrery

Born:	*21 October 1767*
Nominated:	*22 July 1835 (in place of No 32)*
Invested:	*22 July 1835*
Installed:	*22 July 1835 (by dispensation)*
Died:	*29 June 1856*

50. Thomas St Lawrence, 3rd Earl of Howth

Born:	*16 August 1803*
Nominated:	*22 July 1835 (in place of No 40)*
Invested:	*22 July 1835*
Installed:	*22 July 1835 (by dispensation)*
Esquires in April 1868:	
	Captain Williams Bulkeley
	Captain H. A. Candy
Died:	*4 February 1874*

51. Thomas Anthony Southwell, 3rd Viscount Southwell

Born:	*25 February 1777*
Nominated:	*12 September 1837 (in place of No 39)*
Invested:	*12 September 1837*
Installed:	*20 September 1837 (by dispensation)*
Died:	*29 February 1860*

52. Thomas Taylour, 2nd Marquess of Headfort

Born:	*4 May 1787*
Nominated:	*15 April 1839 (in place of No 37)*
Invested:	*15 April 1839*
Installed:	*18 April 1839 (by dispensation)*
Esquires in April 1868:	
	The Earl of Bective
	Lord John Taylour
Died:	*6 December 1870*

53. William Hare, 2nd Earl of Listowel

Born:	*22 September 1801*
Nominated:	*29 April 1839 (in place of No 35)*
Invested:	*29 April 1839*
Installed:	*7 May 1839 (by dispensation)*
Died:	*4 February 1856*

54. Joseph Leeson, 4th Earl of Milltown

Born:	*11 February 1799*
Nominated:	*13 March 1841 (in place of No 31)*
Invested:	*13 March 1841*
Installed:	*21 March 1841 (by dispensation)*
Died:	*31 January 1866*

55. Philip Yorke Gore, 4th Earl of Arran

Born:	*23 November 1801*
Nominated:	*6 May 1841 (in place of No 28)*
Invested:	*6 May 1841*
Installed:	*19 July 1841 (by dispensation)*
Esquires in April 1868:	
	Lord Brabazon
	Viscount Sudeley
Died:	*25 June 1884*

56. HRH Prince Francis Albert Augustus Charles Emanuel, Duke of Saxony, Prince of Saxe-Coburg and Gotha (The Prince Consort from 1857)

Born:	*26 August 1819*
Nominated an extra Knight: 20 January 1842	
Invested:	*20 January 1842 (by dispensation)*
Installed:	*20 January 1842 (by dispensation)*
Died:	*14 December 1861*

57. William Forward Howard, 4th Earl of Wicklow

Born:	*13 February 1788*
Nominated:	*5 June 1842 (in place of No 27)*
Invested:	*15 June 1842*
Installed:	*5 November 1842 (by dispensation)*
Died:	*22 March 1869*

58. William Parsons, 3rd Earl of Rosse

Born:	*17 June 1800*
Nominated:	*(in place of No 34)*
Invested:	*4 January 1845*
Installed:	*9 January 1845 (by dispensation)*
Died:	*31 October 1867*

59. **Henry De la Poer Beresford, 3rd Marquess of Waterford**
     Born: *26 April 1811*
     Nominated: *(in place of No 36)*
     Invested: *4 January 1845*
     Installed: *9 January 1845 (by dispensation)*
     Died: *29 March 1859*

60. **John Fitzgibbon, 2nd Earl of Clare**
     Born: *10 June 1792*
     Nominated: *17 September 1845 (in place of No 30)*
     Invested: *20 September 1845*
     Installed: *20 September 1845 (by dispensation)*
     Died: *18 August 1851*

61. **John Butler, 2nd Marquess of Ormonde**
     Born: *24 August 1808*
     Nominated: *17 September 1845 (in place of No 42)*
     Invested: *20 September 1845*
     Installed: *20 September 1845 (by dispensation)*
     Died: *25 September 1854*

62. **Henry Maxwell, 7th Baron Farnham**
     Born: *9 August 1799*
     Nominated: *12 November 1845 (in place of No 26)*
     Invested: *14 November 1845*
     Installed: *14 November 1845 (by dispensation)*
     Esquires in April 1868:
                    The Honourable Richard Maxwell
                    Colonel H. T. Clements
     Died: *20 August 1868*

63. **Arthur James Plunkett, 9th Earl of Fingall**
     Born: *29 March 1791*
     Nominated: *9 October 1846 (in place of No 29)*
     Invested: *21 October 1846*
     Installed: *21 October 1846 (by dispensation)*
     Died: *22 April 1869*

64. **John Foster-Skeffington, 10th Viscount Massereene
     and 3rd Viscount Ferrard**
     Born: *30 November 1812*
     Nominated: *3 July 1851 (in place of No 38)*
     Invested: *3 July 1851*
     Installed: *3 July 1851*
     Died: *28 April 1863*

65. **HRH Prince George William Frederick Charles,
     2nd Duke of Cambridge**
     Born: *26 March 1819*
     Nominated: *17 November 1851 (in place of No 60)*
     Invested: *17 November 1851*
     Installed: *17 November 1851 (by dispensation)*
     Esquires in April 1868:
                    Captain Arthur E. A. Ellis
                    Captain Alexander Fletcher
     Died: *17 March 1904*

66. **Robert Shapland Carew, 1st Baron Carew**
     Born: *9 March 1787*
     Nominated: *(in place of No 48)*
     Invested: *18 November 1851*
     Installed: *18 November 1851 (by dispensation)*
     Died: *2 June 1856*

67. **Richard Dawson, 3rd Baron Cremorne
     (1st Earl of Dartrey from 1866)**
     Born: *7 September 1817*
     Nominated: *(in place of No 61)*
     Invested: *22 February 1855*
     Installed: *21 April 1855 (by dispensation)*
     Esquires in April 1868:
                    Captain the Honourable Robert Dawson
                    Captain the Honourable Lewis P. Dawnay
     Died: *12 May 1897*

68. **Archibald Acheson, 3rd Earl of Gosford**
     Born: *20 August 1806*
     Nominated: *(in place of No 47)*
     Invested: *22 February 1855*
     Installed: *21 April 1855 (by dispensation)*
     Died: *15 June 1864*

69. **Frederick William Robert Stewart, 4th Marquess
     of Londonderry**
     Born: *7 July 1805*
     Nominated: *(in place of No 53)*
     Invested: *28 August 1856*
     Installed: *23 December 1856 (by dispensation)*
     Died: *25 November 1872*

70. **George Arthur Hastings Forbes, 7th Earl of Granard**
     Born: *5 August 1833*
     Nominated: *(in place of No 66)*
     Invested: *30 January 1857*
     Installed: *10 March 1857 (by dispensation)*
     Esquires in April 1868:
                    Captain Richard Reynolds Peyton
                    Auchmuty Musters
     Died: *25 August 1889*

71. **Hugh Gough, 1st Viscount Gough**
     Born: *3 November 1779*
     Nominated: *(in place of No 49)*
     Invested: *20 January 1857*
     Installed: *10 March 1857 (by dispensation)*
     Died: *2 March 1869*

72. **George Hamilton Chichester, 3rd Marquess of Donegall**
     Born: *10 February 1797*
     Nominated: *(in place of No 33)*
     Invested: *(not invested but permitted to wear the
                    insignia by warrant of the Grand Master,
                    28 January 1857; insignia delivered to him
                    3 February 1857))*
     Installed: *10 March 1857 (by dispensation)*
     Died: *20 October 1883*

73. **Arthur Wills Blundell Sandys Trumbull Windsor Hill,
     4th Marquess of Downshire**
     Born: *6 August 1812*
     Nominated: *(in place of No 59)*
     Invested: *24 May 1859*
     Installed: *2 July 1859 (by dispensation)*
     Esquires in April 1868:
                    The Earl of Hillsborough
                    Lord Arthur Hill
     Died: *6 August 1868*

74. **Richard Edmund St Lawrence Boyle, 9th Earl of Cork and Orrery**
    Born: 19 April 1829
    Nominated: (in place of No 51)
    Invested: 13 June 1860
    Installed: 20 June 1860 (by dispensation)
    Esquires in April 1868:
      Lord Richard Grosvenor
      Arthur Smith Barry
    Died: 22 June 1904

75. **Frederick Temple Hamilton-Temple-Blackwood, 5th Baron Dufferin and Claneboye and 1st Baron Clandeboye (1st Marquess of Dufferin and Ava from 1888)**
    Born: 21 June 1826
    Nominated: (in place of No 64)
    Invested: 28 January 1864
    Installed: 11 February 1864 (by dispensation)
    Esquires in April 1868:
      Gawen Hamilton
      John Perceval Maxwell
    Died: 12 February 1902

76. **Charles Brownlow, 2nd Baron Lurgan**
    Born: 10 April 1831
    Nominated: 31 March 1864 (in place of No 44)
    Invested: 31 March 1864
    Installed: 12 April 1864 (by dispensation)
    Esquires in April 1868:
      Captain Francis Brownlow
      Thomas B. Urquhart
    Died: 16 January 1882

    George Ponsonby O'Callaghan, 2nd Viscount Lismore
    Born: 16 March 1815
    Nominated: 14 September 1864 (in place of No 68)
      (Lord Lismore subsequently refused the honour)
    Died: 29 October 1898

77. **James Molyneux Caulfeild, 3rd Earl of Charlemont**
    Born: 6 October 1820
    Nominated: (in place of No 68)
    Invested: 28 December 1865
    Installed: 26 February 1866 (by dispensation)
    Esquires in April 1868:
      The Honourable Edward A. B. Acheson
      The Honourable George Villiers
    Died: 12 January 1892

78. **Edwin Richard Windham Wyndham-Quin, 3rd Earl of Dunraven and Mountearl**
    Born: 19 May 1812
    Nominated: (in place of No 54)
    Invested: 13 March 1866
    Installed: 31 March 1866 (by dispensation)
    Esquires in April 1868:
      The Honourable Henry Crichton
      R. Spencer Liddell
    Died: 6 October 1871

79. **Henry Francis Seymour Moore, 3rd Marquess of Drogheda**
    Born: 14 August 1825
    Nominated: (in place of No 58)
    Invested: 7 February 1868
    Installed: 20 February 1868 (by dispensation)
    Esquires in April 1868:
      Captain H. E. Moore
      Walter Bulwer
    Died: 29 June 1892

80. **HRH The Prince of Wales (HM King Edward VII from 1901)**
    Born: 9 November 1841
    Nominated an extra Knight:
    Invested: 18 March 1868
    Installed: 18 April 1868
    Esquires: Captain the Honourable Charles F. Crichton
      Captain the Honourable C. C. Molyneux
    Sovereign of the Order: 22 January 1901
    Died: 6 May 1910

81. **John Henry De la Poer Beresford, 5th Marquess of Waterford**
    Born: 21 May 1844
    Nominated: (in place of No 73)
    Invested: 17 November 1868
    Installed: 16 January 1869 (by dispensation)
    Died: 23 October 1895

82. **John Crichton, 3rd Earl of Erne**
    Born: 30 July 1802
    Nominated: (in place of No 62)
    Invested: 17 November 1868
    Installed: 16 January 1869 (by dispensation)
    Died: 3 October 1885

83. **Richard Southwell Bourke, 6th Earl of Mayo**
    Born: 21 February 1822
    Nominated an extra Knight: 11 November 1868
    Invested: (at Calcutta) 18 January 1869
    Became an ordinary Knight: 2 March 1869 (in place of No 71)
    Installed: 12 April 1869 (by dispensation)
    Died: 8 February 1872

84. **HRH Prince Arthur William Patrick Albert (1st Duke of Connaught and Strathearn from 1874)**
    Born: 1 May 1850
    Nominated an extra Knight:
    Invested: 30 March 1869
    Installed: 1 May 1869 (by dispensation)
    Died: 16 January 1942

85. **Granville Leveson Proby, 4th Earl of Carysfort**
    Born: 14 September 1825
    Nominated: (in place of No 57)
    Invested: 2 June 1869
    Installed: 12 June 1869 (by dispensation)
    Died: 18 May 1872

86. **Archibald Brabazon Sparrow Acheson, 4th Earl of Gosford**
    Born: 19 August 1841
    Nominated: (in place of No 63)
    Invested: 2 June 1869
    Installed: 12 June 1869 (by dispensation)
    Died: 11 April 1922

87. **Mervyn Edward Wingfield, 7th Viscount Powerscourt**
    Born: *13 October 1836*
    Nominated: *(in place of No 41)*
    Invested: *2 August 1871*
    Died: *5 June 1904*

88. **Thomas Arthur Joseph Southwell, 4th Viscount Southwell**
    Born: *6 April 1836*
    Nominated: *(in place of No 52)*
    Invested: *2 August 1871*
    Died: *26 April 1878*

89. **Robert Shapland Carew, 2nd Baron Carew**
    Born: *28 January 1818*
    Nominated: *(in place of No 78)*
    Invested: *29 February 1872*
    Died: *8 September 1881*

90. **Valentine Augustus Browne, 4th Earl of Kenmare**
    Born: *16 May 1825*
    Nominated: *1 June 1872 (in place of No 83)*
    Invested: *3 June 1872*
    Died: *9 February 1905*

91. **William Hare, 3rd Earl of Listowel**
    Born: *29 May 1833*
    Nominated: *(in place of No 69)*
    Invested: *20 February 1873*
    Died: *5 June 1924*

92. **William Proby, 5th Earl of Carysfort**
    Born: *18 January 1836*
    Nominated: *(in place of No 50)*
    Invested: *31 August 1874*
    Died: *4 September 1909*

93. **George Henry Robert Charles William Vane-Tempest, 5th Marquess of Londonderry**
    Born: *26 April 1821*
    Nominated: *23 April 1874 (in place of No 43)*
    Invested: *31 August 1874*
    Died: *6 November 1884*

94. **Windham Thomas Wyndham-Quin, 4th Earl of Dunraven and Mountearl**
    Born: *12 February 1841*
    Nominated: *7 August 1872 (in place of No 85)*
    Invested: *13 May 1876*
    Died: *14 June 1926*

95. **William Drogo Montagu, 7th Duke of Manchester**
    Born: *15 October 1823*
    Nominated: *(in place of No 46)*
    Invested: *3 March 1877*
    Died: *22 March 1890*

96. **Henry John Reuben Dawson-Damer, 3rd Earl of Portarlington**
    Born: *5 September 1822*
    Nominated: *(in place of No 88)*
    Invested: *8 February 1879*
    Died: *1 March 1889*

97. **HRH Prince Alfred Ernest Albert, Duke of Edinburgh, Duke of Saxony, Prince of Saxe-Coburg and Gotha**
    Born: *6 August 1844*
    Nominated an extra Knight:
    Invested: *14 May 1880*
    Died: *30 July 1900*

98. **Thomas O'Hagan, 1st Baron O'Hagan**
    Born: *29 May 1812*
    Nominated: *17 January 1882 (in place of No 89)*
    Invested: *17 January 1882*
    Died: *1 February 1885*

99. **Chichester Samuel Parkinson-Fortescue, Baron Carlingford (2nd Baron Clermont from 1887)**
    Born: *18 January 1823*
    Nominated: *9 February 1882 (in place of No 76)*
    Invested: *11 April 1882*
    Died: *30 January 1898*

100. **William Ulick Tristram St Lawrence, 4th Earl of Howth**
    Born: *25 June 1827*
    Nominated: *(in place of No 72)*
    Invested: *8 May 1884*
    Died: *9 March 1909*

101. **Luke White, 2nd Baron Annaly**
    Born: *26 September 1829*
    Nominated: *1 January 1885 (in place of No 55)*
    Invested: *9 February 1885*
    Died: *17 March 1888*

102. **Thomas Spring Rice, 2nd Baron Monteagle of Brandon**
    Born: *31 May 1849*
    Nominated: *1 January 1885 (in place of No 93)*
    Invested: *9 February 1885*
    Died: *24 December 1926*

103. **Garnet Joseph Wolseley, Viscount Wolseley**
    Born: *4 June 1833*
    Nominated: *(in place of No 98)*
    Invested: *28 November 1885*
    Died: *26 March 1913*

104. **Thomas Taylour, 3rd Marquess of Headfort**
    Born   *1 November 1822*
    Nominated: *28 November 1885 (in place of No 82)*
    Invested: *28 November 1885*
    Died: *22 July 1894*

105. **HRH Prince Albert Victor Christian Edward of Wales (Duke of Clarence and Avondale from 1890)**
    Born: *8 January 1864*
    Nominated an extra Knight:
    Invested: *28 June 1887*
    Died: *14 January 1892*

106. **James Edward William Theobald Butler, 3rd Marquess of Ormonde**
    Born: *5 October 1844*
    Nominated: *(in place of No 101)*
    Invested: *26 April 1888*
    Died: *26 October 1919*

107. **John Henry Crichton, 4th Earl of Erne**
    Born: *16 October 1839*
    Nominated: *(in place of No 96)*
    Invested: *4 April 1889*
    Died: *2 December 1914*

108. **Edward Nugent Leeson, 6th Earl of Milltown**
    Born: *9 October 1835*
    Nominated: *26 September 1889 (in place of No 70)*
    Invested: *7 February 1890*
    Died: *30 May 1890*

109. Francis Charles Needham, 3rd Earl of Kilmorey

Born:	*2 August 1842*
Nominated:	*22 April 1890 (in place of No 95)*
Invested:	*24 May 1890*
Died:	*28 July 1915*

110. Lawrence Parsons, 4th Earl of Rosse

Born:	*17 November 1840*
Nominated:	*7 July 1890 (in place of No 108)*
Invested:	*29 August 1890*
Died:	*29 August 1908*

111. HH Prince William Augustus Edward of Saxe-Weimar

Born:	*11 October 1823*
Nominated an extra Knight:	*30 September 1890*
Invested:	*24 November 1890 (at Windsor); 18 December 1890 (at Dublin)*
Died:	*16 November 1902*

112. William Hale John Charles Pery, 3rd Earl of Limerick

Born:	*17 January 1840*
Nominated:	*8 February 1892 (in place of No 77)*
Invested:	*18 March 1892*
Died:	*8 August 1896*

113. Edward Donough O'Brien, 14th Baron Inchiquin

Born:	*14 May 1839*
Nominated:	*(in place of No 79)*
Invested:	*5 August 1892*
Died:	*9 April 1900*

114. Frederick Edward Gould Lambart, 9th Earl of Cavan

Born:	*21 October 1839*
Nominated:	*25 September 1894 (in place of No 104)*
Invested:	*3 November 1894*
Died:	*14 July 1900*

115. Edward Cecil Guinness, 1st Baron Iveagh (1st Viscount Iveagh from 1905, 1st Earl of Iveagh from 1919)

Born:	*10 November 1847*
Nominated:	*27 November 1895 (in place of No 81)*
Invested:	*25 February 1896*
Died:	*7 October 1927*

116. James Alexander, 4th Earl of Caledon

Born:	*11 July 1846*
Nominated:	*14 November 1896 (in place of No 112)*
Invested:	*11 February 1897*
Died:	*27 April 1898*

117. HRH Prince George, Duke of York (HRH the Prince of Wales 1901–1910; HM King George V from 1910)

Born:	*3 June 1865*
Nominated an extra Knight:	*6 July 1897*
Invested:	*20 August 1897*
Sovereign of the Order:	*6 May 1910*
Died:	*20 January 1936*

118. Frederick Sleigh Roberts, 1st Baron Roberts (1st Earl Roberts from 1901)

Born:	*30 September 1832*
Nominated:	*4 June 1897 (in place of No 67)*
Invested:	*20 August 1897*
Died:	*14 November 1914*

119. Arthur Saunders William Charles Fox Gore, 5th Earl of Arran

Born:	*6 January 1839*
Nominated:	*9 March 1898 (in place of No 99)*
Invested:	*15 March 1898*
Died:	*14 March 1901*

120. George Bingham, 4th Earl of Lucan

Born:	*8 May 1830*
Nominated:	*8 May 1898 (in place of No 116)*
Invested:	*2 March 1899*
Died:	*5 June 1914*

121. James Francis Bernard, 4th Earl of Bandon

Born:	*12 September 1850*
Nominated:	*24 April 1900 (in place of No 113)*
Invested:	*29 August 1900*
Died:	*18 May 1924*

122. Luke Gerald Dillon, 4th Baron Clonbrock

Born:	*10 March 1834*
Nominated:	*2 August 1900 (in place of No 114)*
Invested:	*29 August 1900*
Died:	*12 May 1917*

123. Thomas Pakenham, 5th Earl of Longford

Born:	*19 October 1864*
Nominated:	*15 May 1901 (in place of No 119)*
Invested:	*10 June 1901*
Died:	*21 August 1915*

124. Henry De la Poer Beresford, 6th Marquess of Waterford

Born:	*28 April 1875*
Nominated:	*(in place of No 75)*
Invested:	*15 March 1902*
Died:	*1 December 1911*

125. Lowry Egerton Cole, 4th Earl of Enniskillen

Born:	*21 December 1845*
Nominated an extra Knight:	*11 August 1902*
Invested:	*11 August 1902*
Became an ordinary Knight:	*17 March 1904 (in place of No 65)*
Died:	*28 April 1924*

126. Dudley Charles FitzGerald De Ros, 24th Baron De Ros

Born:	*11 March 1827*
Nominated an extra Knight:	*11 August 1902*
Invested:	*11 August 1902*
Became an ordinary Knight:	*5 June 1904 (in place of No 87)*
Died:	*29 April 1907*

127. Dermot Robert Wyndham Bourke, 7th Earl of Mayo

Born:	*2 July 1851*
Nominated:	*1904 (in place of No 74)*
Invested:	*3 February 1905*
Died:	*31 December 1927*

128. Reginald Brabazon, 12th Earl of Meath

Born:	*31 July 1841*
Nominated:	*(in place of No 90)*
Invested:	*13 April 1905*
Died:	*11 October 1929*

129. **Bernard Edward Barnaby Fitzpatrick,**
2nd Baron Castletown
  Born: *29 July 1849*
  Nominated: *(in place of No 126)*
  Invested: *29 February 1908*
  Died: *29 May 1937*

130. **William James Pirrie, Baron Pirrie (Viscount Pirrie**
from 1921)
  Born: *31 May 1847*
  Nominated: *(in place of No 110)*
  Invested: *4 February 1909*
  Died: *6 June 1924*

131. **Bernard Arthur William Patrick Hastings Forbes,**
8th Earl of Granard
  Born: *17 September 1874*
  Nominated: *(in place of No 100)*
  Invested: *21 May 1909*
  Died: *10 September 1948*

132. **Arthur Jocelyn Charles Gore, 6th Earl of Arran**
  Born: *14 September 1868*
  Nominated: *(in place of No 92)*
  Invested: *13 December 1909*
  Died: *19 December 1958*

133. **Anthony Ashley-Cooper, 9th Earl of Shaftesbury**
  Born: *31 August 1869*
  Nominated an extra Knight: 19 June 1911
  Invested: *10 July 1911*
  Became an ordinary Knight: 26 March 1913 (in place of
             No 124)
  Died: *25 March 1961*

134. **Horatio Herbert Kitchener, 1st Viscount Kitchener of**
Khartoum (1st Earl Kitchener of Khartoum from 1914)
  Born: *24 June 1850*
  Nominated an extra Knight: 19 June 1911
  Invested: *10 July 1911*
  Became an ordinary Knight: 1 December 1911 (in place of
             No 103)
  Died: *5 June 1916*

135. **Edward Ponsonby, 8th Earl of Bessborough**
  Born: *1 March 1851*
  Nominated: *(in place of No 120)*
  Invested: *28 May 1915*
  Died: *1 December 1920*

136. **Richard Walter John Hely-Hutchinson, 6th Earl of**
Donoughmore
  Born: *2 March 1875*
  Nominated: *(in place of No 118)*
  Invested: *18 April 1916*
  Died: *19 October 1948*

137. **Mervyn Richard Wingfield, 8th Viscount Powerscourt**
  Born: *16 July 1880*
  Nominated: *(in place of No 107)*
  Invested: *18 April 1916*
  Died: *21 March 1947*

138. **William St John Fremantle Brodrick, 9th Viscount Midleton**
(1st Earl of Midleton from 1920)
  Born: *14 December 1856*
  Nominated: *(in place of No 109)*
  Invested: *18 April 1916*
  Died: *13 February 1942*

139. **Frederick Rudolph Lambart, 10th Earl of Cavan**
  Born: *16 October 1865*
  Nominated: *(in place of No 123)*
  Invested: *18 November 1916*
  Died: *28 August 1946*

140. **John Denton Pinkstone French, 1st Viscount French**
(1st Earl of Ypres from 1922)
  Born: *28 September 1852*
  Nominated: *4 June 1917 (in place of No 133)*
  Invested: *6 June 1917*
  Died: *22 May 1925*

141. **Geoffrey Henry Browne, 3rd Baron Oranmore and Browne**
  Born: *6 January 1861*
  Nominated: *3 June 1918 (in place of No 122)*
  Invested: *22 June 1918*
  Died: *30 June 1927*

142. **Hamilton John Agmondesham Cuffe, 5th Earl of Desart**
  Born: *30 August 1848*
  Nominated: *(in place of No 106)*
  Invested: *18 December 1919*
  Died: *4 November 1934*

143. **James Albert Edward Hamilton, 3rd Duke of Abercorn**
  Born: *30 November 1869*
  Nominated: *15 December 1922 (in place of No 135)*
  Invested: *21 December 1922*
  Died: *12 September 1953*

144. **HRH The Prince of Wales (HM King Edward VIII 1936;**
HRH the Duke of Windsor 1936–1972)
  Born: *23 June 1894*
  Nominated an extra Knight: 3 June 1927
  Invested: *3 June 1927*
  Sovereign of the Order: 20 January to 10 December 1936
  Died: *28 May 1972*

145. **HRH Prince Henry, 1st Duke of Gloucester**
  Born: *31 March 1900*
  Nominated an extra Knight: 29 June 1934
  Invested: *? (the insignia was sent to Buckingham Palace*
             on 30 June 1934)
  Died: *10 June 1974*

146. **HRH Prince George, Duke of York (King George VI**
from 1936)
  Born: *14 December 1895*
  Nominated an extra Knight: 17 March 1936
  Invested: *? (the insignia was sent to Buckingham Palace*
             on 14 February 1936)
  Sovereign of the Order: from 10 December 1936
  Died: *6 February 1952*

ALPHABETICAL INDEX

The Officers of the Order

I. PRELATES

*This office was held ex-officio by the (Church of Ireland)
Archbishop of Armagh 1783–1885.*

**The Most Reverend and Right Honourable
Richard Robinson (1st Lord Rokeby from 1777)** (1783–1794)

Born:	1708*
Nominated:	11 March 1783
Invested:	21 May 1783
Died:	11 October 1794

**The Most Reverend and Right Honourable
William Newcome** (1795–1800)

Born:	10 April 1729
Invested:	29 January 1795
Died:	11 January 1800

**The Most Reverend, Right Honourable and
Honourable William Stewart** (1800–1822)

Born:	March 1755
Invested:	16 December 1800
Died:	6 May 1822

**The Most Reverend and Right Honourable
Lord John George De La Poer Beresford** (1822–1862)

Born:	22 November 1773
Invested:	27 July 1822
Died:	18 July 1862

**The Most Reverend and Right Honourable
Marcus Gervais Beresford** (1862–1885)

Born:	14 February 1801
Invested:	4 November 1862
Died:	26 December 1885

*The office of Prelate was abolished in 1885 on the death of Archbishop
Beresford, in accordance with the Royal Warrant of 1871.*

** The date of Lord Rokeby's birth is uncertain. See the article in The
Complete Peerage.*

II. CHANCELLORS

*This office was held ex-officio by the (Church of Ireland) Archbishop of Dublin
1783–1884; by Archbishop Chenevix Trench in a personal capacity 1884–6,
and by the Chief Secretary of Ireland 1886–1922.*

**The Most Reverend and Right Honourable
Robert Fowler** (1783–1801)

Born:	1726?
Nominated:	5 February 1783
Invested:	11 March 1783
Died:	10 October 1801

**The Most Reverend and Right Honourable
Charles Agar, 1st Viscount Somerton (1st Earl of
Normanton from 1806)** (1801–1809)

Born:	22 December 1736
Invested:	15 December 1801
Died:	14 July 1809

**The Most Reverend and Right Honourable
Euseby Cleaver** (1809–1819)

Born:	1746
Invested:	17 October 1809
Died:	10 December 1819

**The Most Reverend and Right Honourable
Lord John George De La Poer Beresford** (1820–1822)

Born:	22 November 1773
Invested:	16 May 1820
Resigned:	(on appointment as Archbishop of Armagh)
Died:	18 July 1862

**The Most Reverend and Right Honourable
William Magee** (1822–1831)

Born:	18 March 1766
Invested:	29 July 1822
Died:	18 August 1831

**The Most Reverend and Right Honourable
Richard Whateley** (1831–1863)

Born:	1 February 1787
Invested:	24 November 1831
Died:	8 October 1863

**The Most Reverend and Right Honourable
Richard Chevenix Trench** (1863–1886)

Born:	9 September 1807
Invested:	28 June 1864
Died:	27 March 1886

**The Right Honourable Sir Michael Edward
Hicks-Beach (later 1st Earl St Aldwyn)** (1886–1887)

Born:	23 October 1837
Invested:	7 January 1887
Died:	30 April 1916

The Right Honourable Arthur James Balfour (1887–1891)
(later 1st Earl of Balfour)
    Born: 25 July 1848
    Invested: 18 March 1887
    Died: 19 March 1930

The Right Honourable William Lawies Jackson (1891–1892)
(later 1st Lord Allerton)
    Born: 16 February 1840
    Invested: ?
    Died: 4 April 1917

The Right Honourable John Morley (1892–1895)
(later 1st Viscount Morley of Blackburn)
    Born: 24 December 1848
    Invested: 10 September 1892
    Died: 23 September 1923

The Right Honourable Gerald William Balfour (1895–1900)
(later 2nd Earl of Balfour)
    Born: 9 April 1853
    Invested: 16 July 1895
    Died: 14 January 1945

The Right Honourable George Wyndham (1900–1905)
    Born: 19 August 1863
    Invested: 24 November 1900
    Died: 8 June 1913

The Right Honourable Walter Hume Long (1905)
(later 1st Viscount Long of Wraxall)
    Born: 13 July 1854
    Invested: 14 April 1905
    Died: 26 September 1924

The Right Honourable James Bryce (1905–1907)
(later 1st Viscount Bryce)
    Born: 10 May 1838
    Invested: (never invested, but sworn 14 December 1905)
    Died: 22 January 1922

The Right Honourable Augustine Birrell (1907–1916)
    Born: 19 January 1850
    Invested: 29 January 1907
    Died: 20 November 1933

The Right Honourable Henry Edward Duke (1916–1918)
(later 1st Lord Merrivale)
    Born: 5 November 1855
    Invested: 11 August 1916
    Died: 20 May 1939

The Right Honourable Edward Shortt (1918–1919)
    Born: 10 March 1862
    Invested: 11 May 1918
    Died: 10 November 1935

The Right Honourable Ian Macpherson (1919–1920)
(later 1st Lord Strathcarron)
    Born: 14 May 1880
    Invested: 2 June 1919
    Died: 14 August 1937

The Right Honourable Sir Hamar Greenwood (1920–1922)
(later 1st Viscount Greenwood)
    Born: 7 February 1870
    Invested: 19 June 1920
    Died: 10 September 1948

The office of Chancellor has been vacant since 19 October 1922; the office of Chief Secretary of Ireland was abolished on 6 December 1922.

III. REGISTRARS

This office was held ex-officio by the Dean of Saint Patrick's Cathedral 1783–1890,
by Dean West in a personal capacity 1886–1890, by Ulster King of Arms 1890–1943,
and by Norroy and Ulster King of Arms since 1943.

The Very Reverend William Cradock (1783–1793)
    Born: 1741
    Invested: 11 March 1783
    Died: 1 September 1793

The Very Reverend Robert Fowler (1793–1794)
    Born: ?
    Appointed: October 1793
    Invested: ?
    Resigned: April 1794 (on appointment as Archdeacon of Dublin)
    Died: December 1841

The Very Reverend James Verschoyle (1794–1810)
    Born: 1750
    Invested: 18 March 1798
    Died: 13 April 1834

The Very Reverend John William Keatinge (1810–1817)
    Born: 18 May 1769
    Invested: 19 March 1798
    Died: 6 May 1817

The Very Reverend and Honourable (1817–1828)
Richard Ponsonby
    Born: 1772
    Invested: 13 July 1818
    Resigned: (on appointment as Bishop of Killaloe and Kilfenora)
    Died: 27 October 1853

The Very Reverend Henry Richard Dawson (1828–1840)
    Born: 1792?
    Invested: 24 March 1828
    Died: 24 October 1840

The office of Registrar was vacant 1840–1842. Robert Daly was declared Dean of Saint Patrick's Cathedral in 1842, by the court of delegates appointed to investigate the validity of the election held on 8 December 1840. The other candidate in the election was James Wilson, subsequently Bishop of Cork, Cloyne and Ross.

The Very Reverend Robert Daly (1842–1843)
Born: 8 June 1783
Invested: (never invested)
Resigned: (on appointment as Bishop of Cashel, Emly,
Waterford and Lismore, 12 January 1843)
Died: 16 February 1872

**The Very Reverend and Honourable
Henry Pakenham** (1843–1863)
Born: 24 August 1787
Invested: 1843
Died: 25 December 1863

The Very Reverend John West (1864–1890)
Born: 1806
Invested: 31 March 1864
Died: 5 July 1890

IV. KINGS OF ARMS

*This office was held ex-officio by Ulster King of Arms 1783–1943, and by Norroy and
Ulster King of Arms since 1943. The first King of Arms,
Sir William Hawkins, was appointed Ulster King of Arms in 1765.*

Sir William Hawkins (1783–1787)
Born: 16 March 1730
Appointed: 5 February 1783
Invested: 11 March 1783
Died: 27 March 1787

Gerald Fortescue (1787)
Born: 15 November 1751
Appointed: ?
Invested: 9 April 1787
Died: 27 October 1787

Rear-Admiral Sir Chichester Fortescue (1788–1820)
Born: 7 June 1750
Appointed: 31 January 1788
Invested: 21 February 1788
Died: 22 March 1820

Sir William Betham (1820–1853)
Born: 22 May 1779
Appointed: 18 April 1820
Invested: 25 April 1820
Died: 26 October 1853

Sir John Bernard Burke (1853–1892)
Born: 5 January 1814
Appointed: 18 November 1853
Invested: ?
Died: 12 December 1892

Sir Arthur Edward Vicars (1893–1908)
Born: 27 July 1864
Appointed: 23 February 1893
Invested: 7 March 1893
Removed: 30 January 1908
Died: 14 April 1921

Sir Nevile Rodwell Wilkinson (1908–1940)
Born: 26 October 1869
Appointed: 30 January 1908
Invested: 4 February 1909
Died: 22 December 1940

Thomas Ulick Sadleir (acting) (1940–1943)
Born: 15 September 1882
Died: 21 December 1957

Sir Algar Howard (1943–1944)
Born: 7 August 1880
Appointed: 5 April 1943
Resigned: 2 June 1944 (on appointment as Garter
Principal King of Arms)
Died: 14 February 1970

Sir Gerald Woods Wollaston (1944–1957)
Born: 2 June 1874
Appointed: 2 June 1944
Died: 4 March 1957

Aubrey John Toppin (1957–1966)
Born: 1881
Appointed: 20 July 1957
Resigned: 13 October 1966
Died: 7 March 1969

Richard Preston Graham-Vivian (1966–1971)
Born: 10 August 1896
Appointed: 10 November 1966
Resigned: 10 August 1971
Died: 30 September 1979

Walter John George Verco (1971–1980)
Born: 18 January 1907
Appointed: 8 September 1971
Resigned: 30 June 1980

John Phillip Brooke Brooke-Little (1980–1995)
Born: 6 April 1927
Appointed: 7 July 1980
Resigned: (on appointment as Clarenceux King of Arms)

David Hubert Boothby Chesshyre (1995–1997)
Born: 22 June 1940
Appointed: 22 June 1995
Resigned: (on appointment as Clarenceux King of Arms)

Thomas Woodcock (1997–)
Born: 20 May 1951
Appointed: 17 April 1997

DEPUTY ULSTER KINGS OF ARMS

The following list is not complete, and only includes known appointments made after the institution of the Order of Saint Patrick in 1783.

William Bryan	1788–1793
William Betham	1807–1820

Molyneux Cecil John Betham	1839–1853
Sir Henry Farnham Burke	1889–1893
George Dames Burtchaell	1910–1911 and 1915–1921
Thomas Ulick Sadleir	1921–1943

V. SECRETARIES

George Frederick Nugent, Viscount Delvin (1783–1792)
(later Earl of Westmeath)

Born:	*18 November 1760*
Appointed:	*5 February 1783*
Invested:	*11 March 1783*
Resigned:	*1792 (on succession as Earl of Westmeath)*
Died:	*30 December 1814*

Sir Richard Bligh St George, Bt (1793–1800)

Born:	*5 June 1765*
Appointed:	*16 November 1792*
Invested:	*15 February 1793*
Resigned:	*1800*
Died:	*29 December 1851*

Sir Frederick John Falkiner, Bt (1800–1815)

Born:	*1768*
Appointed:	*?*
Invested:	*?*
Died:	*1815 (listed in the Royal Kalendar as being alive in 1823)*

(The office of Secretary was vacant 1815–1828)

Major-General George John Forbes, (1828–1836)
commonly called **Viscount Forbes**

Born:	*3 May 1785*
Appointed:	*?*
Invested:	*28 March 1828*
Died:	*13 November 1836*

The Honourable Robert Edward Boyle (1837–1853)

Born:	*March 1809*
Appointed:	*?*
Invested:	*12 September 1837*
Resigned:	*28 February 1853*
Died:	*3 September 1854*

Lowry Vesey Townley Balfour (1853–1878)

Born:	*1819*
Appointed:	*18 April 1853*
Invested:	*22 February 1855*
Died:	*11 February 1878*

Gustavus William Lambart (1878–1886)

Born:	*7 August 1814*
Appointed:	*10 March 1878*
Invested:	*8 February 1879*
Died:	*1 November 1886*

Sir Gustavus Francis William Lambart (1886–1926)

Born:	*25 March 1848*
Appointed:	*3 December 1886*
Invested:	*26 April 1887*
Died:	*16 June 1926*

The office of Secretary has been vacant since 1926.

VI. GENEALOGISTS

Charles Henry Coote (2nd Lord Castle Coote (1783–1804)
from 1 March 1802)

Born:	*25 August 1754*
Appointed:	*5 February 1783*
Invested:	*11 March 1783*
Resigned:	*1804*
Died:	*22 January 1823*

Sir Stewart Bruce (1804–1841)

Born:	*?*
Appointed:	*?*
Invested:	*18 December 1804*
Died:	*19 March 1841*

Sir William Edward Leeson (1841–1885)

Born:	*February 1801*
Appointed:	*?*
Invested:	*6 May 1841*
Died:	*21 April 1885*

The office of Genealogist was abolished in 1885 on the death of Sir William Leeson, in accordance with the Royal Warrant of 1871, and reinstated in 1889.

Sir Henry Farnham Burke (1889–1930)

Born:	*12 June 1859*
Appointed:	*16 August 1889*
Invested:	*7 February 1890*
Died:	*21 August 1930*

The office of Genealogist has been vacant since 1930.

VII. USHERS OF THE BLACK ROD

John Freemantle   (1783)
Born: ?
Appointed: 5 February 1783
Invested: 11 March 1783
Died: ?

Sir Willoughby Aston   (1783–1784)
Born: c.1748
Appointed: ?
Invested: 13 October 1783
Died: ?

Colonel Andrew Barnard   (1784–1790)
Born: ?
Appointed: ?
Invested: 26 February 1784
Died: ?

The Honourable Henry Fane   (1790–1796)
Born: 4 May 1739
Appointed: ?
Invested: 20 January 1790
Died: 4 June 1802

Nicholas Price   (1796–1799)
Born: ?
Appointed: ?
Invested: ?
Died: ?

Thomas Lindsay   (1799–1806)
Born: ?
Appointed: ?
Invested: ?
Died: ?

Sir Charles Hawley Vernon   (1806–1835)
Born: 22 July 1766
Appointed: ?
Invested: 14 March 1806
Died: 24 June 1835

Major the Honourable Sir Francis Charles Stanhope (1835–1838)
Born: 29 September 1788
Appointed: ?
Invested: 22 July 1835
Removed: 1838
Died: 9 October 1862

Sir William Edward Leeson   (1838–1841)
Born: February 1801
Appointed: 8 May 1838
Invested: 15 April 1839
Resigned: (on appointment as Genealogist of the Order)
Died: 21 April 1885

Lieutenant Colonel Sir George Morris   (1841–1858)
Born: 1774
Appointed: ?
Invested: 6 May 1841
Died: May 1858

Sir George Burdett L'Estrange   (1858–1878)
Born: 1796
Appointed: 10 June 1858
Invested: 24 May 1859
Died: 5 February 1878

**Colonel James Alfred Caulfeild,
7th Viscount Charlemont**   (1879–1913)
Born: 20 March 1830
Appointed: 1 February 1879
Invested: 8 February 1879
Died: 4 July 1913

Sir John Olphert   (1915–1917)
Born: 2 September 1863
Appointed: 15 May 1915
Invested: (never invested)
Died: 11 March 1917

Sir Samuel Murray Power   (1918–1933)
Born: 29 September 1863
Appointed: 29 October 1918
Invested: ?
Died: 17 March 1933

The office of Usher of the Black Rod has been vacant since 1933.

VIII. CORK HERALDS

William Bryan   (1783–1796)
Born: ?
Appointed: 15 March 1783
Died: ?

Solomon Delane   (1796–1813)
Born: ?
Appointed: 11 January 1796
Died: ?

Theobald Richard O'Flaherty   (1813–1829)
Born: ?
Appointed: 1813
Died: 1829

Molyneux Cecil John Betham   (1829–1880)
Born: 14 August 1813
Appointed: 29 September 1829
Died: 31 January 1880

The office of Cork Herald was abolished in 1880 on the death of Molyneux Betham, in accordance with the Royal Warrant of 1871, and reinstated by the revised Statutes of 1905.

Peirce Gun Mahony   (1905–1910)

Born:	30 March 1878
Appointed:	25 September 1905
Resigned:	1910
Died:	26 July 1914

Captain Richard Alexander Lyonal Keith   (1910–1952)

Born:	10 August 1883
Appointed:	8 December 1910
Removed:	24 July 1952
Died:	6 November 1955

The office of Cork Herald has been vacant since 1952.

IX. DUBLIN HERALDS

Thomas Meredyth Winstanley   (1783–1827)

Born:	?
Appointed:	24 February 1783
Died:	?

James Rock   (1827–1833)

Born:	c.1786
Appointed:	31 March 1827
Died:	18 May 1833

Captain Sheffield Philip Fiennes Betham   (1834–1890)

Born:	15 April 1817
Appointed:	1834
Died:	2 July 1890

The office of Dublin Herald was abolished in 1890 on the death of Sheffield Betham, in accordance with the Royal Warrant of 1871, and reinstated by the revised Statutes of 1905.

Francis Richard Shackleton   (1905–1907)

Born:	19 September 1876
Appointed:	25 September 1905
Resigned:	November 1907
Died:	24 June 1941

Major Guillamore O'Grady   (1908–1952)

Born:	1879
Appointed:	18 June 1908
Invested:	4 February 1909
Died:	4 September 1952

The office of Dublin Herald has been vacant since 1952.

X. ATHLONE PURSUIVANTS

The office of Athlone Pursuivant was created in 1552.
The following list only includes those attached to the Order of Saint Patrick from 1783.

Thomas Meredyth Winstanley   (1780–1783)

Born:	?
Appointed:	19 December 1780
Removed:	1 May 1783 (having been apppointed Dublin Herald on 24 February 1783)
Died:	?

George Twisleton Ridsdale   (1783–1807)

Born:	?
Appointed:	27 May 1783
Died:	?

William Betham   (1807–1820)

Born:	22 May 1779
Appointed:	7 November 1807
Resigned:	18 April 1820 (on appointment as Ulster King of Arms)
Died:	26 October 1853

James Rock   (1820–1827)

Born:	c.1786
Appointed:	2 May 1820
Resigned:	31 March 1827 (on appointment as Dublin Herald)
Died:	18 May 1833

Molyneux Cecil John Betham   (1827–1829)

Born:	14 August 1813
Appointed:	12 February 1827
Resigned:	29 September 1829 (on appointment as Cork Herald)
Died:	31 January 1880

William Crawford   (1829–1865)

Born:	?
Appointed:	29 September 1829
Died:	15 November 1865

Captain Robert Smith   (1865–1882)

Born:	14 September 1792
Appointed:	10 March 1865
Died:	26 November 1882

Bernard Louis Burke   (1883–1892)

Born:	17 May 1861
Appointed:	13 January 1883
Died:	5 July 1892

John Edward Burke   (1892–1899)

Born:	19 March 1868
Appointed:	27 July 1892
Removed:	13 May 1899
Died:	9 March 1909

Henry Claude Blake (1899–1907)

Born: 5 December 1874
Appointed: 13 May 1899
Resigned: 7 February 1907
Died: ? (still alive in 1932?)

Francis Bennett-Goldney (1907)

Born: 1865
Appointed: 14 February 1907
Resigned: November 1907
Died: 27 July 1918

George Dames Burtchaell (1908–1921)

Born: 12 June 1853
Appointed: 18 June 1908
Invested: 4 February 1909
Died: 18 August 1921

The office of Athlone Pursuivant has been vacant since 1921.

DEPUTY ATHLONE PURSUIVANTS

*The following list is not complete, and only includes known appointments made after
the institution of the Order of Saint Patrick in 1783.*

Joseph Nugent Lentaigne (1874–1882)

Born: ?
Appointed: 12 June 1874
Resigned: 1882
Died: ?

Bernard Louis Burke (1882–1883)

Born: 17 May 1861
Appointed: 11 February 1882
Resigned: 13 January 1883 (on appointment as Athlone Pursuivant)
Died: 5 July 1892

XI. JUNIOR PURSUIVANTS

*The following list of Junior Pursuivants is taken mostly from the 1905 revised Statutes of the Order.
The incomplete nature of the list suggests that a full list of appointments was unobtainable even then.*

Coote Carroll (1765–alive in 1831)

Appointed: 18 April 1765

Thomas Croker (1783–?)

Henry (or Humphry) Minchin (1783–?)

Bryan Connor (1795–1813)

Major George Twisleton Ridsdale (1796–1809)

William Baker (1796–?)

Theobald Richard O'Flaherty (1803–1813)

Resigned: 1813 (on appointment as Cork Herald)

Patrick Kennedy (1803–before 1813)

Charles Wilson

John O'Flaherty (1813–1823)

Appointed: 30 April 1813
Removed: 1823 (having taken Holy Orders)

James Rock (1813–1820)

Born: c.1786
Resigned: 1820 (on appointment as Athlone Pursuivant)
Died: 18 May 1833

Patrick L. Mahony (1819–?)

Molyneux Cecil John Betham (1820–1827)

Born: 14 August 1813
Resigned: 1827 (on appointment as Athlone Pursuivant)
Died: 31 January 1880

James Daws (1823–alive in 1831)

Appointed: 10 October 1823

Alfred Betham (1825–1841)

Appointed: 14 June 1825
Died: 1841

Sheffield Philip Fiennes Betham (1825–1834)

Born: 15 April 1817
Resigned: (on appointment as Dublin Herald)
Died: 2 July 1890

James Jackson (1826–alive in 1831)

Appointed: 30 September 1826

William Crawford (1827–1829)

Resigned: 1829 (on appointment as Athlone Pursuivant)

William Heron (1829–before 1836)

Appointed: 29 September 1829

Joseph Cooper/Cotton Walker (1830–c.1837)

William Skeys (afterwards Skey) (1839–1847)

Appointed: 29 September 1839
Removed: 1848

Captain Robert Smith   (1840–1865)
> *Born:* 14 September 1792
> *Appointed:* 14 June 1840
> *Resigned:* 10 March 1865 (on appointment as Athlone
>   Pursuivant)
> *Died:* 26 November 1882

Francis Beetham (afterwards Betham)   1841–1853
> *Appointed:* 22 June 1841

Charles Patrick MacDonnell   (1850–1870)
> *Died:* 1870

Columbus Patrick Drake   (1854–1889)
> *Appointed:* 28 January 1854
> *Died:* 1889

George Frith Barry   (1865–1891)
> *Appointed:* 21 March 1865
> *Died:* 14 February 1891

The office of Junior Pursuivant ceased to exist on the death of George Frith Barry in 1891, having been abolished in accordance with the Royal Warrant of 1871. It was possibly reinstated by the terms of the revised statutes of 1905.

XII. CORK PURSUIVANT

The office of Cork Pursuivant was established by additional statute on 1 March 1921.

Major Gerald Achilles Burgoyne   (1921–1936)
> *Born:* 1874
> *Died:* March 1936

The office of Cork Pursuivant has been vacant since 1936.

Letters Patent, Statutes, Warrants, Ordinances and other documents

═══

WARRANT 5 FEBRUARY 1783

GEORGE R.

Right trusty and right well-beloved Cousin and Councillor, We greet you well. Whereas it hath been the custom of wise and beneficent Princes in all ages to distinguish the virtue and loyalty of their subjects by marks of honor, to be a testimony of their dignity, and of their excellency in all qualifications which render them worthy of the favor of their Sovereign, and the respect of their fellow-subjects; that so their eminent merits may stand acknowledged to the world, and create a virtuous emulation in others to deserve such honorable distinction. And whereas Our loving subjects of Our Kingdom of Ireland have approved themselves steadily attached to Our Royal Person and Government, and affectionately disposed to maintain and promote the welfare and prosperity of the whole empire; and We being willing to confer upon Our subjects of Our said Kingdom a testimony of Our sincere love and affectionate regard, by creating an Order of Knighthood in our said Kingdom, with Constitutions, Ordinances, Customs, and Ceremonies similar to those observed in the most dignified institutions of the same nature; and whereas you have humbly represented unto Us, that such a testimony of Our Royal Favor will be highly acceptable to Our people of Our said Kingdom of Ireland; it is Our Royal will and pleasure, and We do hereby authorize and require you upon receipt thereof, forthwith to cause Letters Patent to be passed under the Great Seal of Our said Kingdom of Ireland, for creating a Society or Brotherhood, to be called Knights of the Most Illustrious Order of Saint Patrick, to consist of the Sovereign and Fifteen Knights Companions, and for constituting and appointing Our dearly-beloved fourth Son Prince Edward; Our right trusty and right entirely Cousin and Councillor, William Robert, Duke of Leinster; Our right trusty and right well beloved Cousin and Councillor, Henry, Earl of Clanricarde; Our right trusty and right well beloved Cousin, Randal William, Earl of Antrim; Our right trusty and right well beloved Cousin and Councillor, Thomas, Earl of Westmeath; Our right trusty and right well beloved Cousin and Councillor, Murrough, Earl of Inchiquin; Our right trusty and right well beloved Cousin and Councillor, Charles, Earl of Drogheda; Our right trusty and right well beloved Cousin and Councillor, George de la Poer, Earl of Tyrone; Our right trusty and right well beloved Cousin and Councillor, Richard, Earl of Shannon; Our right trusty and right well beloved Cousin and Councillor, James, Earl of Clanbrassil; Our right trusty and right well beloved Cousin, Richard, Earl of Mornington; Our right trusty and right well beloved Cousin and Councillor, James, Earl of Courtown; Our right trusty and right well beloved Cousin, James, Earl of Charlemont; Our right trusty and right well beloved Cousin, Thomas, Earl of Bective; and Our right trusty and right well beloved Cousin and Councillor, Henry, Earl of Ely, to be Knights Companions of the Most Illustrious Order of Saint Patrick, of which Order We Ourselves, Our Heirs and Successors, shall perpetually be Sovereign, and of which Our Lord Lieutenant General and General Governor of Ireland or Our Lord Deputy, or Deputies of Our said Kingdom, or Our Lords Justices, or other Chief Governor or Governors of Our said Kingdom for the time being shall officiate as Grand Masters. And it is Our further will and pleasure, that the said Society or Brotherhood of the Knights of the Most Illustrious Order of Saint Patrick shall have a Common Seal, and shall have a Chancellor, Register, Secretary, Genealogist, Usher, King of Arms, Heralds, Pursuivants, and such other Officers as We from time to time shall think fit to appoint, under Our sign manual, and that they shall observe all such Constitutions, Ordinances, Customs, and Ceremonies, as shall be enjoined them under Our sign manual. And it is further Our will and pleasure, that the said Knights, being Commoners, shall have rank and precedency in all places immediately after Barons' eldest Sons, and that the Wives of the said Knights Companions shall, in like manner, have rank and precedency immediately after the Wives of Barons' eldest Sons, and before all other inferior ranks. And it is Our further will and pleasure, that upon any vacancy happening in the said Society or Brotherhood, by death or resignation of any of the Knights, a successor shall be elected by the other Knights in manner as shall be directed by the Constitutions and Ordinances to be established under Our sign manual as beforementioned. And in the said Letters Patent you are to cause to be inserted all such clauses as shall be necessary to make the same most full, valid, and effectual. And for so doing this shall be as well unto you as unto all other Our officers and ministers concerned herein, a sufficient warrant. And so We bid you heartily farewell.

Given at Our Court of St James's, the Fifth day of February, 1783, in the 23rd year of Our Reign.

By His Majesty's Command.

THOMAS TOWNSHEND

To Our right trusty and right well beloved Cousin and Councillor, George, Earl Temple, Our Lieutenant General and General Governor of Our Kingdom of Ireland, or to Our Lieutenant Deputy, Justices, or other Chief Governor or Governors of Our said Kingdom for the time being.

STATUTES AND ORDINANCES 28 FEBRUARY 1783

GEORGE R.

George the Third, by the Grace of God, of Great Britain, France, and Ireland, King, Defender of the Faith, &c. To all to whom these presents shall come, greeting. Whereas We have thought fit, for the dignity and honor of Our Realm of Ireland, to ordain, establish, create and found a Company of Sixteen noble and worthy Knights for to be of the Most Illustrious Order of St Patrick; and, whereas for the honorable continuance, augmentation, and maintenance of the same, it is fitting that Statutes and Ordinances should be observed and kept by the Common Brethren, Knights, and Companions of the said Most Illustrious Order; Know ye therefore, that We, the most High, most Excellent, and most Puissant Prince, George the Third, by the Grace of God, of Great Britain, France, and Ireland, King, Defender of the Faith, and so forth, and Sovereign of the Most Illustrious Order of St Patrick, for the right singular love and entire affection which We bear to the said Most Illustrious Order, and for the honourable continuance and increasing of the same, do make, ordain, constitute and declare the Statutes and Ordinances which shall be from henceforth observed, kept, and ensued by the Sovereign and the Knights Companions of the said Most Illustrious Order, in manner and form following:

FIRST, It is ordained and accorded, that the King, His Heirs, and Successors, shall be for evermore Sovereigns of the said Most Illustrious Order of St Patrick, to which Sovereign, and to his Heirs and Successors, shall appertain the declaration, solution, determination, interpretation, reformation and disposition of all causes concerning and touching anything of obscurity or doubt contained in the Statutes of the said Most Illustrious Order.

SECONDLY, That whenever the said Sovereign cannot, by reason of his absence without the said Realm of Ireland, hold the Chapters, or do, or perform such things as by the Statutes shall appertain to him to do, touching the said Most Illustrious Order, his Lord Lieutenant General and General Governor of this his realm, or his Lord Deputy, or Lord Justices for the time being, shall be, and are hereby declared, Grand Masters of the said Most Illustrious Order, and shall do all things, and enjoy all privileges, rights, and prerogatives, and do all manner of things touching the said Most Illustrious Order, in as ample a manner as We ourselves could have done as Sovereign of the said Most Illustrious Order, if We ourselves had been present within the said Realm.

THIRDLY, It is ordained that none shall be elected or chosen to be Fellow or Companion of the said Most Illustrious Order, except he be a Gentleman of Blood, and that he be a Knight, and without reproach; and as touching the declaration of a Gentleman of Blood, it is declared that he shall be descended of three descents of Noblesse, that is to say, of name and of arms, both of his father's side and of his mother's side, a certificate of which, signed by Our Principal King at Arms within Our said Realm of Ireland, shall be delivered by each Knight immediately after his election, and before his investiture, and shall be deposited with Our Genealogist or Registrar of Our said Most Illustrious Order.*

FOURTHLY, That the Sovereign shall, whenever it seemeth meet unto him, by summons under the Seal of the Order, direct a Chapter to be holden at such place within this Realm of Ireland as he shall appoint, and that all the Knights of the said Order shall then and there be present in the full habits of the said Most Illustrious Order, which they shall always wear in Chapters, except by dispensation from the Sovereign; and if they come not at the time assigned, without having a just and reasonable excuse which may be acceptable to the said Sovereign, or without being otherwise pardoned by the said Sovereign for his absence, by special letters of

---

* The certificate of noblesse was worded as follows: To All and Singular to whom these presents shall come, I N., Ulster King of Arms and Principal Herald of All Ireland, Knight Attendant of the Most Illustrious Order of St Patrick, do hereby certify and declare that I have examined the descents of N. and find them in conformity to the Statutes of the Most Illustrious Order of St Patrick. In witness whereof I hereunto subscribe my name and title, and affix my official seal.

excuse, by which letters their names and causes shall be written, he shall be reprimanded at the next Chapter for the first offence, and for the second offence he shall lose the rank which he hath in the said Order, and placed below all the other Knights and Companions of the said Order; and for the third offence he shall be punished in such manner as to the said Chapter shall seem meet.

FIFTHLY, It is ordained that all and every Knight of the said Company shall wear on the great and solemn Feasts to be appointed by the Sovereign, the collar of the said Order, and at all other times shall wear the Badge of the said Order, pendant from a sky-blue Ribband over the right shoulder, and as soon as they shall be installed shall wear the Device of the Order on the left side of their outer garment, in such manner as shall be directed by the Sovereign. And if any Knight of the Company be found to appear without the said Collar, Badge and Device, at such time as by these Statutes he is directed to wear the same, that he pay, immediately after the challenge shall be made to him by any of the six Officers of the Order, the sum of twenty shillings; and if he do enter the said Chapter without the Collar, Badge and Device, and without the said Habits, except when they be dispensed with by the Sovereign, he shall forfeit the sum of five pounds to whomsoever of the said Officers shall challenge him.

SIXTHLY, It is ordained that the Knights of the said Most Illustrious Order, always and as often as they shall wear their Mantles, shall go before the Sovereign, every of them with his Fellow that is fore-against him, ordinarily as they be set in their Stalls; and the Officers of the said Order shall immediately precede the Sovereign; and the said Knights shall sit at the table according to their Stalls, except children or brethren of Kings and Princes strangers, the which shall keep their places after their estates.

SEVENTHLY, It is ordained that all strangers that shall be elected Fellows of the said Order, shall be certified by Letters of the Sovereign of their election the which Letters Certification, with the Statutes of the said Order, under the common Seal, shall be sent unto them at the cost of the said Sovereign, in all diligence, and at the farthest they shall be certified of this in four months after the said election, to the end the said elect may advise them by the Statutes if they will receive the said Order or no. But if the said Sovereign have great and high lets and business, that then he may defer the certification of the said election at his good pleasure unto the time of opportunity and conveniency. After the certification shall have been delivered, and that the Sovereign shall be certified that the said elect will receive the said Order, then the Sovereign shall send unto the said elect by his Ambassador, his whole Habit, with the Ribband and Collar; and that all such strangers of what estate, dignity, or condition that they be of, shall send within seven months after the reception of the said Ribband, Collar, and Habit and that he have certified the Sovereign to have received those things by a sufficient Deputy after the estate of his Lord and Master, so that he be a Knight without reproach to be stalled in his place, the which shall bring with him a Mantle of sky-blue satin of the order of that which he shall send him, and also his Banner, Sword, Helmet and Crest, for to be and abide in the Cathedral Church of St Patrick, in Dublin, during his life, and that the Mantle in the time that the said Deputy shall be stalled by the said Sovereign or his Deputy shall be put upon his right arm, for to hold the said Mantle upon his arm, and shall be accompanied and led by two of the Knights of the said Order from the door of the Chapter unto the Stall, and there being shall make his oath, and shall be stalled for and in the name of the said Lord and Master. And the Mantle aforesaid, the said Deputy shall bear it upon his right arm during Divine Service, being set in the state of his Lord and Master, without bearing of it any time after, and to have no manner of voice in the Chapter, or to come in it in the absence of him that hath sent him; and if he send not his Deputy within seven months aforesaid, without having a reasonable excuse, which shall be acceptable to the Sovereign or his Deputy, the election shall be void of him, except that the said Knight be prevented by great affairs, then he may send his excuse to the said Sovereign or to his Deputy within a month after; and after, as his excuse is, the Sovereign or his Deputy will allow or accept it, that then the said Sovereign may give unto him four months more of respite; and if he come not, or send not his Deputy before the time of the four months be finished, that then in this case the election shall be wholly void from him from that time.

EIGHTHLY, It is ordained that if any of the said Company die, the Sovereign or his Deputy after that they shall have certification of his death, shall be bound for to send and give notice by their letters to all the Fellows of the said Most Illustrious Order, being within Ireland, for to come and be with the said Sovereign or his Deputy, in which place so-ever it be, where it shall please him to assign conveniently, within six weeks after the certification of the death of the said Knight, the which also assembled, or at the least six with the Sovereign, or his Deputy aforesaid, every of them that there shall be present and come to the election, shall name nine of the worthiest and sufficient Knights without reproach that he shall know, subjects of the said Sovereign, or others so to be, that they hold no contrary party, or be against him, that is, to wit; Three Dukes, Marquisses, Earls of greater Estate, three Barons or Bannerets, and three Bachelor Knights, the which denominations the Chancellor of the same Order shall write; that is, to wit, the Archbishop of Dublin, for the time being, or in his absence, the Registrar that is to wit, the Dean of the Cathedral Church of St Patrick, in Dublin, for the time being, or the most ancient, of the said Company in their absence, and the denominations so done by all or six of the least by him that hath written, shall be showed to the said Sovereign, or his Deputy, that then shall choose of them that be named he that shall have the most voices, and also he that the Sovereign shall esteem to be the most honorable to the said Order and most profitable to his Crown and to his Realm; and if there be any Knights of the said Order that shall fail to come to the said election, if he be not prevented by a just cause and that the said cause of his excuse showed under his seal of arms, be found by the Sovereign or his Deputy, to be just and reasonable, and his excuse to be acceptable and allowed, and that if his cause be not just, and that he come not to the Ceremonies above named, it is ordained that he shall be reprimanded at the next Chapter for the first offence, and for the second offence he shall lose the rank which he hath in the said Order, and be placed below all other Knights and Companions of the said Order, and for the third offence he shall be punished in such manner as to the said Chapter shall seem meet.

NINTHLY, It is ordained that if any Knight of the said Company should depart, another is chosen and elect, he shall have soon after his election receive the Ribband in signification that he is one of the Knights and Fellows of the Order of St Patrick, and his Robe and Hood shall be delivered him in the Cathedral Church of St Patrick, in Dublin, where the publick stallation of the said Knights shall be always held immediately after his Commission has been read before the Sovereign, or his Deputy, and the Company, and after that shall be led by two Knights of the said Order, accompanied with the other Noblemen, and Officers of the Order shall also be present, and his Mantle shall be borne before him by one of the Knights of the said Order, the which Mantle shall be delivered to him for his Habit, after that he shall have made his oath before his Stall, and not before, and this done he shall return into the Chapter House, where he shall receive by the Sovereign or his Deputy, the Collar, and so he shall have the full possession of his Habit wholly, except great Princes, strangers, the which may receive their Habits wholly within the Chapter House, and if he die before he have received the Habit, he shall not be named one of the Founders, seeing he has not had full possession of his estate, but he shall have the one part of the Divine Service above-named for the delivery of the Ribband, and none other things above it; And if he so chosen come not in all good diligence after the reception of the Ribband in the said place for to be stalled, and especially within the year of his election, and if he be a Knight dwelling within the Realm, and hath no reasonable excuse, then the election shall be void of him, and another new election shall be made, and neither the Banner, the Sword, nor the Helmet, nor the Crest of him so chosen shall be put upon his Stall before his coming, to the end that if he come not, his said Hatchments be not taken down, or availed, but honestly put out of the Chair and the Crest and other things shall abide to the profit and use of the said Order.

TENTHLY, It is ordained that whosoever shall be chosen to this degree of honor, shall be installed in the lowest Stall according to his election except Kings and Princes of a foreign nation.

ELEVENTHLY, It is ordained if there be any Stall or place void, the Sovereign at his pleasure may advance and translate by his special licence any Knights of the said Company in the said Stall, if so be that it be higher than the Stall that he was in before, Also the Sovereign may once in his life, if it please him, make a general translation of all the Stalls at his pleasure, except Emperors, Kings, and Princes, the which shall always keep their Places and Stalls, unless that they be translated into a higher Stall, in the which translation the long continuance in the Order, and the praiseworthiness and merits of the Knights ought to be considered and remembered, the which Knights from henceforth in going and sitting at all times, that they shall wear their Mantles, shall keep their Places after the order of their Stalls, and not after their Estates, as is aforesaid.

TWELFTHLY, It is ordained, that every Knight within the year of his stallation, shall cause to be made an Escutcheon of his Arms and Hatchments in a plate of metal such as shall please him, and that it be surely set upon the back of his Stall, and the other that shall come after shall have their Escutcheons and Hatchments in like manner: but their plates of metal nor their Hatchments shall not be so large nor so great as those of the first Founders were.

THIRTEENTHLY, It is ordained that no Knight chosen and elected to be Fellow of the said Illustrious Order shall be stalled by procurement or Deputy, except he be a stranger, and may not well come hither in his proper person to be stalled, or other that is busied without the Realm for the affairs of his Sovereign, or by his commandment and licence as is above directed.*

FOURTEENTHLY, It is ordained that every Knight entering the said Order shall promise and swear faithfully the oath, that is to say 'I Sir A. B. promise and swear to my true power during my life, and during the time that I shall be Fellow of the Most Illustrious Order of St Patrick, to keep, defend and sustain the honors, rights and privileges of the Sovereign of the said Order, and well and truly I will accomplish all the Statutes, Points and Ordinances of the said Order, as though they were read to me from Point to Point, and from Article to Article, and that wittingly and willingly I will not break any statutes of the said Order, or any Article in them contained, except in such as I shall have received a dispensation from the Sovereign, So help me God and the contents of this Book.' This done the said Knight shall, with due reverence and kneeling, receive the Badge, the which the Sovereign, shall put over his right shoulder, saying these words 'Sir the loving Company of the Order of St Patrick hath received you their Brother, Lover, and Fellow, and in token and knowledge of this, they give you and present you this present Badge, the which God will that you receive and wear from henceforth to His praise and pleasure, and to the exaltation and honor of the said Illustrious Order and yourself.'

FIFTEENTHLY, And it is further ordained, that the following admonitions shall be read by the Chancellor or Registrar of the said Order, to every Knight at his first admission to the said Illustrious Order, that is to say,

Upon putting on the Collar,
'Sir, the loving Company of the Order of St Patrick hath received you their Brother, Lover, and Fellow, and in token and knowledge of this they give you and present you this present Badge, the which God will that you receive and wear from henceforth to his praise and pleasure, and to the exaltation and honor of the said Illustrious Order and yourself.'

Upon putting on the Sword,
'Take this sword, to the increase of your honour; and in token and sign of the Most Illustrious Order, which you have received, wherewith you being defended may be bold strongly to fight in the defence of those rights and ordinances to which you be engaged, and to the just and necessary defence of those who be oppressed and needy.'

Upon putting on the Mantle,
'Receive this Robe and Livery of this Most Illustrious Order, in augmentation of thine honour, and wear it with the firm and steady resolution, that by your character, conduct, and demeanour, you may approve yourself a true servant of Almighty God, and a worthy Brother and Knight Companion of this Illustrious Order.'

SIXTEENTHLY, It is ordained that every Knight, as soon as he shall be summoned to his stallation shall appoint three sober, discreet, and sufficient Esquires of the Body, who shall be Gentlemen of Blood and without reproach; and as touching the Declaration of Gentlemen of Blood, it is declared that they shall be descended of three descents of Noblesse, that is to say of name and of arms, both of the father's side and of the mother's side, a certificate of which, signed by Our Principal King at Arms within Our said Realm shall be delivered by each Knight fourteen days before his stallation, and shall be deposited with Our Genealogist of Our said Most Illustrious Order, which Esquires shall be duly ministering to the said Knight during the time of his stallation, and at all and every other time when they shall be duly summoned to do their service to the said Knight, and shall be habited according to the Ordinance of the Sovereign, in such Habit as shall befit their situation as Esquires of the Body to the Knights of Our said Most Illustrious Order.

SEVENTEENTHLY, It is ordained that there shall be six officers appertaining to the said Order, that is to say, Chancellor, Secretary, Registrar, Genealogist, Usher at Arms, named the Black Rod, and King at Arms named Ulster, the which shall be received and sworn to be of the Council of the said Order and shall have such Charges and Privileges as are expressly declared in the Ordinances of the Sovereign, and shall wear for a Cognizance about their necks such Badge as shall be assigned to them by the Sovereign.

EIGHTEENTHLY, It is ordained that a Common Seal of the Arms of the Order be made, the which shall rest in the custody and keeping of the Chancellor of the Order, and if he should depart or go forth twenty miles far from

*The Deputy must be a Knight.

the Sovereign he shall then deliver the Seal to the Registrar, Secretary or Genealogist, or to any other Person that it shall please the Sovereign to ordain or appoint.

ORDINANCES touching the Badges, Devices, and Habits of Our Knights Companions of Our Most Illustrious Order of St Patrick; the Habits of their Esquires, and the Badges and Habits of the Officers of Our said Order.

FIRST, We do ordain that Our Lord Lieutenant General and General Governor of Our Realm of Ireland shall wear at all Chapters and Installations at which We Ourselves cannot be present, the same Habits and Robes which We Ourselves should wear, and which are to be of the same materials and fashion as those of Our Knights, save only those alterations which befit Our dignity; and he shall wear Our Collar on all solemn Feasts as hereinafter described, and at all other times he shall wear pendant at his neck, from a sky-blue ribband, the Badge of Our said Order, surmounted by a harp crowned with an Imperial Crown.

And as touching the Habits of the Knights Companions of Our Most Illustrious Order, the Mantles shall be of sky-blue satin, lined with a white silk; having on the left shoulder a hood of blue satin, lined also with white silk; and the said Mantle shall be tied with two strings of blue silk, mixed with gold; their Shoes shall be of white leather with knots of crimson ribband; the belt of their sword shall be of crimson satin, and they shall have a handle gilt, and a scabbard of crimson velvet.

And Our said Knights Companions shall each of them wear a round Hat covered with white satin and lined with blue, the front of which shall be turned back, and the same device, encircled with rays affixed thereto, as We shall direct to be worn on the left side of their outer garment; and the said Hat shall be surmounted with three falls of ostrich feathers, which shall be red, blue, and white, and round the Hat shall be a band of crimson satin, embroidered after the fashion of the great Collar of the Order, which We shall hereafter describe.

The Collar of Our Most Illustrious Order shall be of Gold, and it shall be composed of Roses and of Harps alternate, tied together with a knot of Gold, and the said Roses shall be enamelled alternately white leaves within red, and red leaves within white; and in the centre of the said Collar shall be an Imperial Crown, surmounting a Harp of Gold, from which shall hang the Badge of Our said Order; and the said Badge shall be of Gold, surmounted with a wreath of Shamrock, or Trefoil, within which shall be a Circle of Gold containing the Motto of Our said Order in Letters of Gold, viz., QUIS SEPARABIT; together with the date 1783, being the year in which Our said Order was founded, and encircling the Cross of St Patrick, gules, surmounted with a trefoil vert, each of its leaves charged with an imperial Crown or, upon a field argent. And this Badge We ordain shall be worn pendant from a sky-blue ribband over the right shoulder, at all times when Our said Knights shall not wear the Collar of the Order, and We further ordain, that Our said Knights Companions shall wear the said Badge, encircled within rays in form of a Star of Silver consisting of eight points, that is to say, four greater and four lesser, on the left side of their outer garment.

And We further ordain that Our said Knights shall, in all Armorial Bearings, use the said Collar encircling their Coats Armorial.

And We ordain that the Chancellor of Our said Most Illustrious Order shall wear the same Mantle as Our said Knights, and shall wear a Badge of Gold, pendant at his neck from a sky-blue ribband, which shall be of a square form, representing a Purse, and charged with the same Cross, gules, surmounted as before on a field argent, and encircled with a Wreath of Shamrocks.

And the Registrar of Our said Order shall wear the same Mantle as before described, but it shall be shorter, and he shall wear a Badge of Gold pendant at his neck from a sky-blue Ribband, in the shape of a Book, charged with the same Device as that of Our Chancellor of Our said Most Illustrious Order.

And Our Secretary and Genealogist shall each of them wear a Mantle of the same length as that of Our Registrar, with a Surcoat of white silk, and shall wear, pendant at their necks from a sky-blue ribband, the same Badge as that of Our Knights, excepting only the Circlet of Gold with the Motto.

And the Usher of Our said Order shall wear a crimson satin Mantle, but shorter, and Habit the same as Our said Secretary and Genealogist; and shall wear a Badge, pendant at his neck by a sky-blue ribband which Badge shall bear the harp of gold upon a field azure, encircled with the motto as before. And the King of Arms of Our said Order shall wear the same Habit and Mantle as our Usher, and a Badge, pendant at his neck by a sky-blue ribband containing the Cross, gules, of Our said Order, upon a field argent, impailed with the Arms of Our said Realm of Ireland, and both encircled with the Motto above mentioned.

And that these several Devices may more plainly appear, We have directed them to be properly depicted and emblazoned in their proper colours.

And lastly, We will and direct that the Mantles, Habits, and Vestments above-ordained, shall be of those manufactures known by the description of Satins and Silks wrought within Our Realm of Ireland.

Given at Our Court at St James's, the 28th day of February 1783, in the 23rd year of Our Reign.
G. R.

ORDINANCE REGARDING THE FEES OF THE OFFICERS

GEORGE R.

ORDINANCE touching the Fees to be demanded and taken of Our Knights Companions of the Most Illustrious Order of St Patrick, which We will to be taken at the times and in the manner following from each of Our said Knights Companions:

The Fees of Honor upon Knighthood, to be paid to such persons as usually receive the same according to the custom observed within Our Realm of Ireland.

	£	s	d
To Our Secretary of Our said Order,	25	0	0
To Our Genealogist of Our said Order,	25	0	0
To Our Usher of Our said Order,	20	0	0
To Our King at Arms of *ditto*,	15	0	0
To Our two Heralds, each £10,	20	0	0
To Our four Pursuivants, each £5,	20	0	0

And the said Fees shall be again demanded and paid by the said Knights at the times of their Installation, and an allowance shall then be made to Our Officers of Arms who shall prepare the Banner, Sword, and Helmet of each Knight, which shall be affixed over their respective Stalls.
G. R.

WARRANT 7 MARCH 1783

GEORGE R.

Right trusty and right well-beloved Cousin and Councillor, We greet you well: Whereas We did by Warrant under Our Royal Sign Manual, bearing date the Fifth day of February last, authorise and require you, upon receipt thereof, to cause Letters Patent to be passed under the Great Seal of Our Kingdom of Ireland, for creating a Society or Brotherhood to be called Knights of the Most Illustrious Order of St Patrick, to consist of the Sovereign and Fifteen Knights Companions therein mentioned, and among others, Our right trusty and right well-beloved Cousin, Randal William, Earl of Antrim; and the said Earl of Antrim being desirous to relinquish the acceptance of the Stall intended for him, because he cannot be allowed to retain the Military Order of the Bath with which he has already been invested, Our will and pleasure is, that you forthwith cause Letters Patent to be passed under the Great Seal of Our said Kingdom of Ireland, for creating Our right trusty and well-beloved Cousin, Arthur, Earl of Arran, one of the original Knights of the said Most Illustrious Order of St Patrick; and you will cause to be inserted in our said Letters Patent a clause revoking so much of Our aforesaid Letters Patent, whereby We appoint Our said right trusty and right well-beloved Cousin, Randal William, Earl of Antrim, and for so doing this shall be as well unto you, as unto all other Our officers and ministers herein concerned, a sufficient Warrant. And so we bid you heartily farewell.

Given at Our Court at St James's, the 7th day of March, 1783, in the 23rd year of Our Reign.
SIDNEY

To Our right trusty and right well-beloved Cousin and Councillor, George, Earl Temple, Our Lieutenant General and General Governor of Our Kingdom of Ireland, or to Our Lieutenant Deputy, Justices, or other Chief Governor or Governors for the time being.

WARRANT II MARCH 1783

By the Lord Lieutenant General and General Governor of Ireland, Grand Master of the Most Illustrious Order of St Patrick.

NUGENT TEMPLE

Whereas His Majesty hath been pleased to signify his royal pleasure for the Investiture in England of His Royal Highness Prince Edward, as one of the Knights of the Most Illustrious Order of Saint Patrick, and for His Royal Highness's Installation by proxy in the Cathedral Church of St Patrick, Dublin; We, George Grenville Nugent Temple, Earl Temple, Lord Lieutenant General and General Governor of Ireland, and Grand Master of the Order of St Patrick, by virtue of the powers vested in Us by the Statutes and Ordinances of the said Order, do hereby, in pursuance of His Majesty's pleasure as aforesaid, dispense with the Investiture of His Royal Highness Prince Edward in this Kingdom, and do direct that the Investiture of His Royal Highness by His Majesty shall be entered in the Register of the said Most Illustrious Order.

By command of His Excellency the Grand Master,

R. DUBLIN, *Chancellor*

ADDITIONAL STATUTE II MARCH 1783

By the Lord Lieutenant General and General Governor of Ireland, Grand Master of the Most Illustrious Order of St Patrick.

NUGENT TEMPLE

Whereas by the Second Article of the Statutes and Ordinances of the Most Illustrious Order of St Patrick, under His Majesty's Sign Manual, dated at His Majesty's Court at St James's, the 28th day of February 1783, in the 23rd year of his Reign, it is ordained that whenever the Sovereign cannot, by reason of his absence without the Realm of Ireland, hold the Chapters, or do, or perform such things as by the Statutes shall appertain to him to do touching the said Most Illustrious Order, his Lord Lieutenant General and General Governor of this his Realm of Ireland, or his Lord Deputy, or Lords Justices, for the time being, shall be and are thereby declared Grand Masters of the said Most Illustrious Order, and shall do all things, and enjoy all privileges, rights and prerogatives, and do all manner of things touching the said Most Illustrious Order, in as ample a manner as His Majesty could have done as Sovereign of the said Most Illustrious Order if His Majesty had been present within the said Realm: And whereas We, George Grenville Nugent Temple, Earl Temple, Lord Lieutenant General and General Governor of this His Majesty's Kingdom of Ireland, and, in his absence, Grand Master of the said Most Illustrious Order, have received the signification of His Majesty's pleasure that a Prelate be appointed to the said Order, and that his Grace the Lord Archbishop of Armagh, Primate and Metropolitan of all Ireland for the time being, shall be Prelate of the said Most Illustrious Order:

We, therefore, by virtue of the powers vested in Us by the Ordinance aforesaid, at this first Chapter of the said Most Illustrious Order, now holden this 11th day of March 1783, do declare, appoint, and direct, that the Lord Archbishop of Armagh, Primate and Metropolitan of all Ireland, be the Prelate of the said Most Illustrious Order of St Patrick; and that he shall be received and sworn to be of the Council of the said Order, and shall have such charges and privileges as are expressly declared in the Ordinances hereinafter mentioned, and shall wear, as a Cognizance about his neck, such Badge as shall be hereinafter assigned to him.

And as touching the duty of the said Prelate, it is hereby ordained that the Oath prescribed by the Fourteenth Article of the said Statutes to be taken by every Knight entering the said Order, shall be administered to such Knight by the Prelate, or in his absence by the Chancellor of the said Most Illustrious Order, or in the absence of the Chancellor, by the Registrar of the said Order. Also, that when each Knight shall have received the Badge, the which the Sovereign shall have put over his right shoulder, the Prelate shall, at the command of the Sovereign, pronounce the Admonition directed by the said Fourteenth Article to be delivered to the Knight at such time.

And touching the Habit and Badge of the said Prelate of the said Most Illustrious Order, We do hereby ordain that he shall wear the same Mantle in colour, form, and substance, as is appointed to be worn by the Knights of the said Order, and shall wear a Badge of Gold, pendant at his neck from a sky-blue ribband, which shall be the like Badge as is appointed to be worn by the said Knights, surmounted with an Archiepiscopal Mitre.

By command of His Excellency the Grand Master.

R. DUBLIN, *Chancellor*

PROCLAMATION

By the Lord Lieutenant General and General Governor of Ireland, Grand Master of the Most Illustrious Order of St Patrick.

A PROCLAMATION

Whereas His Majesty hath signified his royal pleasure, that the Great Ball-room in His Majesty's Castle, in which the Ceremony of the Investiture of the Knights of the Most Illustrious Order of St Patrick shall be performed, shall receive from thenceforward the honorable denomination of the Hall of St Patrick, and shall always be distinguished by that name; and that in the said Hall the Chapters of the said Most Illustrious Order shall at all times be held, except when it is otherwise ordered by the Sovereign:

We do therefore hereby direct and proclaim, that this Hall be hereafter called the Hall of St Patrick. Whereof Our Officers of State, and all other Persons whatsoever are to take Notice.

GOD SAVE THE KING

ADDITIONAL STATUTE 8 JUNE 1809

GEORGE R.

Right trusty and right entirely beloved Cousin and Councillor, We greet you well: Whereas, for divers reasons, Us thereunto moving, We have thought fit to ordain and command that the Collars and Badges of all Knights Companions of Our Most Illustrious Order of Saint Patrick who shall hereafter decease, shall be returned to the Grand Master of the said Order, and that after the decease of each such Knight, the Chancellor of the said Order of Saint Patrick for the time being, shall be intituled to the Sum of One hundred Pounds upon the Collar and two Badges of each such deceased Knight being delivered to the said Grand Master; and whereas We have also thought fit to ordain and command, that the Registrar of Our said Most Illustrious Order for the time being shall, upon the Investiture of every Knight Companion of the said Most Illustrious Order, be intituled to ask, demand, and receive from each Knight the Fee of Twenty-five Pounds, and that the like fee of Twenty-five Pounds shall be again demanded and taken of the said Knight Companion at the time of his Installation by Our Registrar aforesaid, in like manner as the said sum of Twenty-five Pounds is and has been accustomed to be demanded and taken by Our Secretary and Genealogist of the said Order, as already set forth in the Statutes:

We therefore do by these Presents, out of Our mere motion, grace, and bounty, give and grant unto Our right trusty and right well-beloved Cousin and Councillor, the Right Honorable and Most Reverend Father in God, Charles, Earl of Normanton, Archbishop of Dublin, and Primate of Ireland, Chancellor of Our said Most Illustrious Order of Saint Patrick, during the time that he, the said Archbishop of Dublin, shall continue to enjoy the said Office of Chancellor, and to all future Chancellors of the said Order for the time being, the Sum of One hundred Pounds for each Knight Companion of the said Order who shall decease during his and their respective Chancellorships, to have and convert the same to his and their own personal use, profit, and advantage, without rendering any account of the same to Us, Our Heirs or Successors; provided nevertheless, that the said Sum shall not be paid to the said Chancellor until the Collar and Badges have been delivered to the Grand Master as aforesaid.

And therefore We do hereby intimate Our royal will and pleasure to the heirs, executors, and administrators of all such Knights Companions of the said Most Illustrious Order of Saint Patrick as shall hereafter decease, that within three months after the decease of any such Knight they shall deliver the before-mentioned Collars and Badges to the Grand Master of Our said Order of Saint Patrick.

And We do further ordain that Our very Reverend James Verschoyle, Doctor of Laws, Dean of the Collegiate Church of Saint Patrick, Dublin, Registrar of Our said Most Illustrious Order of Saint Patrick, during the time that he the said Dean of Saint Patrick shall continue to enjoy the said Office of Registrar, and that all future Registrars of the said Order for the time being shall, upon the Investiture of every Knight Companion of the said Order, ask, demand and receive from the Knight Companion so invested, the Fee of Twenty-five Pounds; and that the like Fee of Twenty-five Pounds shall again be demanded and taken of the said Knight Companion at the time of his Installation by Our Registrar aforesaid, in like manner as the said Sum of Twenty-five Pounds is and has been demanded and taken by Our Secretary and Genealogist, as already set forth in the Statutes of the said Most Illustrious Order of Saint Patrick.

And We do hereby command that this Our intimation and direction be henceforward considered as an addition, and be annexed to the Statutes of the said Order; and for all these purposes these presents shall be a sufficient warrant and discharge; and so We bid you very heartily farewell.

Given at Our Court of St James's, this 8th day of June, in the Forty-ninth year of Our reign.
By His Majesty's special command,
LIVERPOOL

To Our right trusty and right entirely beloved Cousin and Councillor, Charles, Duke of Richmond, Our Lieutenant General and General Governor of that part of Our United Kingdom called Ireland, or to Our Lieutenant Deputy, Justices, or other Chief Governor or Governors there for the time being.

WARRANT 8 SEPTEMBER 1810

By the Lord Lieutenant General and General Governor of Ireland, Grand Master of the Most Illustrious Order of St Patrick.

RICHMOND

Whereas His Majesty hath been graciously pleased to signify his royal pleasure for the Investiture of the Most Honorable Howe Peter, Marquess of Sligo, with the Ensigns of the Most Illustrious Order of St Patrick at Malta: We therefore by virtue of the powers vested in Us by the Statutes and Ordinances of the said Most Illustrious Order of St Patrick, do hereby dispense with the Knighthood and other Ceremonies usually observed in conferring the said Order, and We authorise and permit the said Marquess of Sligo to wear the Ribband and Badge, and during his absence in Foreign Parts, and previous to his Installation, to wear the other Insignia of the said Most Illustrious Order; and We do hereby authorize and require you, in pursuance of His Majesty's pleasure to deliver to the said Marquess of Sligo, the Ribband and Badge of the said Most Illustrious Order, which are herewith transmitted to you; for which this shall be your warrant.

Given at His Majesty's Castle of Dublin, this 8th day of September, 1810.
By His Grace's command,
W. W. POLE

To Major-General Hildebrand Oakes, His Majesty's Commissioner for the Civil Affairs of Malta, or His Majesty's Principal Officer there.

ADDITIONAL STATUTE 12 FEBRUARY 1814

By His Excellency Charles Viscount Whitworth, KB, Lord Lieutenant General and General Governor of that part of the United Kingdom of Great Britain and Ireland called Ireland, Grand Master of the Most Illustrious Order of Saint Patrick.

WHITWORTH

Whereas, by the Additional Statute of the Most Illustrious Order of Saint Patrick, dated at the Court of St James's, the eighth day of June, in the Forty-ninth Year of the Reign of Our Most Gracious Sovereign, His Majesty was pleased to order and direct that the heirs, executors, and administrators of all such Knights Companions of the said Most Illustrious Order of Saint Patrick as should thereafter decease, should, within three months after such decease, deliver the Collar and two Badges to the Grand Master of the said Order: and whereas, there has not hitherto been assigned to any Officer of the said Most Illustrious Order, or other Person, the duty of applying for, and demanding, and receiving in the name of the Grand Master, and of safe keeping of the said Collars and Badges, until they shall be disposed of according to the Order and Command of the Grand Master for the time being; by which means much inconvenience and delay has arisen in the returning of the said Collars and Badges. It is therefore the pleasure and command of Us, the Grand Master of the said Most Illustrious Order, that the Ulster King of Arms and Knight Attendant of the said Most Illustrious Order, and his Successors in the said Office, or his or their Deputy, shall have full power in the name of the Grand Master, to apply to the heirs, executors, or administrators of such deceased Knights for the Collars and Badges aforesaid; and having obtained them shall notify the same to the Grand Master, and to the Chancellor of the Order; upon which the Sum of One hundred Pounds shall be paid to the Chancellor, according to the direction and command in the aforesaid additional Statute.

We are also pleased to direct and command that an iron chest, with a sufficient lock, shall be supplied to the said Ulster King of Arms, or his Deputy, and fixed in a safe room in the Office of Arms, in which the said Collars and Badges shall be deposited for safe keeping, until they be disposed of by the Grand Master; and when the said Badges or Collars are delivered to any Knight by order of the Grand Master, he shall give a receipt for the same to the said Ulster King of Arms, or to his Deputy, in the following terms:

"I Sir A. B., Knight Companion of the Most Illustrious Order of Saint Patrick, do hereby acknowledge to have received from C. D., Ulster King of Arms (or his Deputy, as the case may be), one Collar (or Badge) of the said Most Illustrious Order, which I promise for myself, my heirs, executors, and administrators, shall be safely delivered and returned to Ulster King of Arms, or his Deputy, for the Grand Master of the said Most Illustrious Order, within three months after my resignation of the said Most Illustrious Order, or of my decease, agreeable to an additional Statute of the said Order, dated the eighth day of June in the Forty-ninth year of the Reign of His Most Excellent Majesty King George the Third, and to an Order of His Excellency Charles, Viscount Whitworth, Lord Lieutenant General and General Governor of Ireland, Grand Master of the said Most Illustrious Order, dated at Dublin Castle, the twelfth day of February 1814. In witness whereof I have hereunto set my hand this —— day of ————————."

We are also pleased to direct that the said Ulster King of Arms, and Knight Attendant for the time being, or his Deputy, shall be empowered to cause to be repaired such Collars or Badges as may stand in need thereof, as well as those of the Knights as of the Officers of the Order, and that the expense attending such repairs, as also the expense of postage and carriage of the Collars and Badges, shall be allowed and paid to the said Ulster King of Arms (or his Deputy) on his certificate upon his honor of the same being true and correct, and truly and correctly done and performed. The said Ulster King of Arms, (or his Deputy), shall also be authorized to procure to be made such ribband as may be necessary for the Investiture of the Knights, or the use of the Officers of the said Most Illustrious Order, the expense of which he shall also be paid on his said certificate.

Given at His Majesty's Castle of Dublin, this 12th day of February 1814.
By His Excellency's command,
R. PEEL

ADDITIONAL STATUTE 20 FEBRUARY 1830

GEORGE R.
Right trusty and right entirely beloved Cousin and Councillor, We greet you well:

Whereas in and by the Warrant under the Royal Signet and Sign Manual of Our Royal Father of Blessed Memory, for the creation of the Most Illustrious Order of Saint Patrick, bearing date the Fifth day of February, 1783, it is, amongst other things, ordained and provided, that the said Order shall consist of the Sovereign and Fifteen Knights Companions: and whereas We were graciously pleased in the year 1821, in virtue of the powers inherent in Us, as Sovereign, and in contemplation of the solemnity of Our Royal Coronation, to dispense, on that happy occasion, with the aforesaid Ordinance and Regulation, and to declare that Our right trusty and right well-beloved Cousin and Councillor, Charles Chetwynd, Earl Talbot, Our right trusty and right well-beloved Cousins, James, Earl of Ormonde and Ossory (now Marquess of Ormonde), John Chambre, Earl of Meath, Arthur James, Earl of Fingall, and Our right trusty and right well-beloved Cousins and Councillors James George, Earl of Courtown, and Robert, Earl of Roden, should be Extra Knights of Our said Most Illustrious Order, and should hold and enjoy all, singular the titles, privileges, immunities, rights, and advantages which the Knights of Our said Most Illustrious Order might lawfully hold and enjoy: and whereas, in pursuance of such Our Royal Dispensation, Our said loving subjects severally received from Us the honor of Knighthood, were invested with the Ensigns of Our said Order, and were subsequently, on the Twenty-eighth day of August in the same Year, solemnly installed in Our Royal presence, in the Cathedral Church of Saint Patrick, as Extra Knights Companions of Our said Most Illustrious Order; We, therefore, taking the same into Our Royal consideration, are graciously pleased to ordain and declare that the said Extra Knights Companions shall, in all Chapters of the Order, and other Solemnities, rank next to and immediately after the regular Knights Companions now existing, and before any Knights Companions hereafter to be made, and that they shall, amongst themselves, rank in the order in which their names are hereinbefore enumerated; and We do hereby further determine, ordain, and declare, that on the decease of a regular Knight Companion of Our said Most Illustrious Order, the senior Extra Knight Companion thereof for the time being shall succeed, and be entitled to the Stall in Our said Order which shall become vacant by the decease of such Knight Companion; and We do hereby command that this Our intention and direction be henceforth considered as an addition, and be annexed to the Statutes of the said Order, and for all these purposes these presents shall be a sufficient warrant and discharge; and so We bid you very heartily farewell.

Given at Our Court at Windsor, the 20th day of February, 1830, in the Eleventh year of Our reign.
By His Majesty's command,
ROB. PEEL

To Our right trusty and right entirely beloved Cousin and Councillor, Hugh, Duke of Northumberland, KG, Our Lieutenant General and General Governor of that part of Our United Kingdom of Great Britain and Ireland, called Ireland; or to Our Lieutenant Deputy, Justices, or other Chief Governor or Governors there for the time being.

DOCUMENTS RELATING TO THE GRAND MASTER'S INSIGNIA, MARCH 1831

On the 15th of March, 1831, the Earl of Erroll, hereditary High Constable of Scotland, and Master of the Horse to His Majesty King William the Fourth, by His Majesty's command, arrived in Dublin, delivered to Ulster King of Arms a Mahogany brass-bound Case, with an inlaid plate on the cover, engraved with a list of its contents, together with a Manuscript description of its Contents, with Drawings representing the size and appearance of the Star and Badges therein contained, of which the following is a copy:

'A description of the Jewels of the Order of St Patrick, made by command of His Majesty King William the Fourth, for the use of the Lord Lieutenant, and which are Crown Jewels.

A large Star of the Order of St Patrick, composed of fine Brilliant Rays and Circles, and Emerald Shamrock on a Ruby Cross; in the centre the Motto of the Order in Diamonds on blue enamelled ground, the size expressed in the Margin.

A large Badge of the Order of St Patrick, surmounted with the Crown, all composed of fine Brilliants, with Emerald Shamrock, Ruby Cross, etc., as expressed in the Margin No. 1.

A Gold Badge of the Order of St Patrick, richly enamelled with Emeralds and Rubies, as expressed in the Margin No. 2..

The whole of the above, contained in a Mahogany brass-bound Case, with an inlaid Plate on the Cover, engraved with a list of its contents,

RUNDELL, BRIDGE & CO.,
Jewellers to their Majesties.

To which is added, in the handwriting of His Majesty, the following:

St James's Palace, March 7, 1831.
These Jewels are to be handed over by each Lord Lieutenant to his Successor, with the Sword of State.
WILLIAM R.

ADDITIONAL STATUTE 18 NOVEMBER 1831

WILLIAM R.
Right trusty and entirely beloved Cousin and Councillor, We greet you well: Whereas, in and by the Warrant under the Royal Signet and Sign Manual of Our late Father of blessed memory, for the creation of the Most Illustrious Order of Saint Patrick, bearing date the Fifth day of February 1783, it is, amongst other things, ordained and provided, that the said Order shall consist of the Sovereign and Fifteen Knights Companions; and whereas We have been graciously pleased, in virtue of the powers inherent in Us, as Sovereign, upon the solemn occasion of the Coronation of Us and Our most dearly beloved Consort, the Queen, to dispense with the aforesaid Ordinance and Regulation, and to declare that Our right trusty and entirely beloved Cousin, Arthur Blundell Sandys Trumbull, Marquess of Downshire, Our right trusty and entirely beloved Cousin and Councillor, Ulick John, Marquess of Clanricarde, Our right trusty and right well-beloved Cousin and Councillor, Francis William, Earl of Charlemont, and Our right trusty and right well-beloved Cousin, Francis James, Earl of Llandaff *(sic)*, should be Extra Knights of Our said Most Illustrious Order, and should hold and enjoy all and singular the titles, privileges, immunities, rights and advantages which the Knights Companions of Our said Order might lawfully hold and enjoy: We, therefore, taking the same into Our Royal consideration,

are graciously pleased to ordain and declare, that the said Extra Knights Companions shall, in all Chapters of the Order, and other Solemnities, rank next to and immediately after the regular Knights Companions and Extra Knights now existing, and before any Knights Companions hereafter to be made, and that they shall, amongst themselves, rank in the order in which their names are hereinbefore enumerated; and We do hereby further determine, ordain, and declare, that on the decease of a regular Knight Companion of Our said Most Illustrious Order, the Senior Extra Knight Companion thereof for the time being shall succeed, and be entitled to the Stall in Our said Order which shall become vacant by the decease of such Knight Companion; and We do hereby command that this Our intention and direction be henceforth considered as an addition, and be annexed to the Statutes of the said Order, and for all these purposes, these presents shall be a sufficient warrant and discharge; and so We bid you heartily farewell.

Given at Our Court at St James's, the 18th day of November, 1831, in the Second year of Our reign.
By His Majesty's command,
MELBOURNE

To Our right trusty and entirely beloved Cousin and Councillor, Henry William, Marquess of Anglesey, KG, Our Lieutenant General and General Governor of that part of Our United Kingdom called Ireland; or to Our Lieutenant, Deputy, Justices, or other Chief Governor or Governors for the time being.

ADDITIONAL STATUTE   24 JANUARY 1833

WILLIAM R.
Right trusty and right entirely beloved Cousin and Councillor, We greet you well: Whereas in and by the Warrant under the Sign Manual of Our late Royal Father, King George the Third, of Blessed Memory, for the creation of the Most Illustrious Order of Saint Patrick, bearing date the Fifth day of February 1783, it is, among other things, ordained and provided, that the said Order shall consist of the Sovereign and Fifteen Knights Companion, and whereas for divers reasons, Us thereunto especially moving, We are graciously pleased to augment the Number of the Knights Companions of the said Most Illustrious Order; We do therefore hereby ordain, command, and declare, that the said Most Illustrious Order shall henceforward consist of the Sovereign and Twenty-two Knights Companions, and that the present existing Extra Knights Companions shall be considered and deemed Regular Knights Companions of the said Most Illustrious Order. And We do further, in virtue of the power in Us, as Sovereign of the said Most Illustrious Order of Saint Patrick, ordain, command and declare, for Us, Our Heirs and Successors, Sovereigns of the said Most Illustrious Order, that it may and shall be lawful for Us, Our Heirs and Successors, Sovereigns of the said Order, by Warrant under the Royal Sign Manual, to dispense with the Installation of the present Uninstalled Knights Companions, or of those who may be hereafter appointed by Us, Our Heirs and Successors, and to confer upon the said Knights Companions, whose Installations may be so dispensed with, all the Rights, Privileges, Advantages and Immunities which should have been enjoyed by them if formally installed, as prescribed by the Statutes of the said Most Illustrious Order. Provided nevertheless, and it is Our Royal Will and Pleasure, that all the accustomed Fees which would have been due and payable to the Officers of Our said Order in case the said Knights Companions had been formally installed, shall be paid to the Officers of Our said Most Illustrious Order by the Knights Companions who shall hereafter receive such Dispensation as aforesaid. And We do hereby command and ordain that this Our intention and Direction be henceforward considered as an Addition, and be annexed unto the Statutes of the said Most Illustrious Order. To which these Presents shall be your sufficient Warrant; and so We bid you heartily farewell.

Give at Our Court at St James's this 24th day of January, 1833, in the Third Year of Our reign.
By His Majesty's command,
MELBOURNE

To Our right trusty and entirely beloved Cousin and Councillor, Henry William. Marquess of Anglesey, KG, Our Lieutenant General and General Governor of that part of Our United Kingdom called Ireland, or to Our Lieutenant, Deputy, Justices, or other Chief Governor or Governors there for the time being.

ADDITIONAL STATUTE 30 JANUARY 1833

WILLIAM R.

Right trusty and entirely beloved Cousin and Councillor, We greet you well: Whereas We, as Sovereign of the Most Illustrious Order of Saint Patrick, have full power to dispense with all the Statutes, Ordinances, and Regulations required to be observed in conferring the said Order: and whereas, since the last Installation of Our said Most Illustrious Order, We have, in consideration of the highly distinguished and meritorious services of Our right trusty and entirely beloved Cousin, Arthur Blundell Sandys Trumbull, Marquess of Downshire, Our right trusty and entirely beloved Cousin and Councillor, Ulick John, Marquess of Clanricarde, Our right trusty and right well-beloved Cousin and Councillor, Francis William, Earl of Charlemont, and Our right trusty and right well-beloved Cousin, Francis James, Earl of Llandaff (sic), been graciously pleased to nominate them to be Knights Companions of Our said Most Illustrious Order. We, therefore, for divers reason Us thereunto especially moving, do hereby dispense with all the aforesaid Statutes, Ordinances, and Regulations, and do give and grant unto them the said Marquess of Downshire, the Marquess of Clanricarde, the Earl of Charlemont, and the Earl of Llandaff (sic), full power and authority to wear and use the Collar and all other Ornaments appertaining to Our said Most Illustrious Order, and to sit in the Stalls which shall be assigned to them respectively in Our Cathedral Church of Saint Patrick; and also to have, hold, and enjoy all and singular the rights, privileges, and advantages belonging to Knights Companions of Our said Order, in as full and ample a manner as if they had been formally Installed, any Decree, Rule, or Usage to the contrary notwithstanding, and for these purposes, these presents shall be a sufficient warrant and discharge; and so We bid you heartily farewell.

Given at Our Court at St James's, the 30th day of January, 1833, in the Third year of Our reign.
By His Majesty's command,
MELBOURNE

To Our right trusty and entirely beloved Cousin and Councillor, Henry William, Marquess of Anglesey, KG, Our Lieutenant General and General Governor of that part of Our United Kingdom called Ireland; or to Our Lieutenant, Deputy, Justices, or other Chief Governor or Governors there for the time being*.'

ADDITIONAL STATUTES 17 MAY 1833

WILLIAM R.

Right trusty and entirely beloved Cousin and Councillor, We greet you well: Whereas for reasons Us thereunto specially moving. We are pleased to revise and make certain alterations in the Statutes of Our Most Illustrious Order of Saint Patrick, which time and circumstances have rendered necessary, We do therefore hereby direct and command, that the Second, Third, Fourth, Fifth and Eighth Statutes of the said Most Illustrious Order, and the Ordinances touching the Badges, Devices and Habits of the said Most Illustrious Order, be altered and stand as follows, that is to say:

SECONDLY, That whenever the said Sovereign shall be pleased to direct Chapters to be held in that part of this Realm called Ireland, or do or perform such things as by the Statutes shall appertain to do, touching the said Most Illustrious Order, His Lord Lieutenant General and General Governor of Ireland, or His Lord Deputy, or Lords Justices for the time being, Grand Masters of the said Most Illustrious Order, shall do all things and enjoy all privileges, rights and prerogatives, and do all manner of things touching the said Most Illustrious Order, in as ample a manner as We Ourselves could have done as Sovereign of the said Most Illustrious Order, if We Ourselves had been present in Ireland.

THIRDLY, It is ordained that none shall be elected or chosen to be Fellow, or Companion, of the said Most Illustrious Order, except he be a Gentleman of Blood, and that he be a Knight, and without reproach; and as touching the declaration of a Gentleman of Blood, it is declared that he shall be descended of three descents of Noblesse; that is to say, of name and of arms, both of his father's side, and of his mother's side, a certificate of which, signed by Our principal King of Arms of Ireland, shall be delivered by each Knight immediately after his election, and before his investiture, and shall be deposited among the archives of Our said Order.

FOURTHLY, That the Sovereign shall, whenever to Him it seemeth meet, direct a Chapter to be holden at such

* A similar royal letter was issued under the Signet and Sign Manual dispensing with the installation of all succeeding Knights until the abolition of the ceremony in 1871.

place as He shall appoint, and that all the Knights of the said Order shall then and there be present in such of the Habits of the said Most Illustrious Order, as the Sovereign shall direct; and if they come not at the time assigned, without having a just and reasonable excuse which may be acceptable to the said Sovereign, or without being otherwise pardoned by the said Sovereign for their absence, by special letters of excuse, by which letters their names and causes shall be written, they shall be reprimanded at the next Chapter for the first offence, and for the second offence they shall lose the rank which they have in the said Order, and be placed below all the other Knights Companions of the said Order; and for the third offence they shall be punished in such manner as to the said Chapter shall seem meet.

FIFTHLY, It is ordained that all and every Knight of the said Company shall wear, on the great and solemn Feasts to be appointed by the Sovereign, the Collar of the said Order, and at all other times shall wear the Badge of the said Order, pendant from a sky-blue Ribband over the right shoulder, and as soon as they shall be installed, or have a dispensation of their Installation from the Sovereign, shall wear the Star of the Order on the left side of their outer garment, in such manner as shall be directed by the Sovereign. And if any Knight of the Company be found to appear without the said Collar, Badge, and Star, at such time as by these Statutes he is directed to wear the same, that he pay, immediately after the challenge shall be made to him by any of the seven Officers of the Order, the sum of twenty shillings; and if he do enter the Chapter without the said Collar, Badge, and Star, and without the said Habits, except when they be dispensed with by the Sovereign, he shall forfeit the sum of five pounds to whomsoever of the said Officers who shall challenge him.

EIGHTHLY, It is ordained that if any of the said Company die, the Sovereign, or his Deputy, after that they shall have certification of his death, shall be bound to send and give notice by their letters to all the Fellows of the said Most Illustrious Order, to come and be with the said Sovereign, or his Deputy, in which place soever it be, where it shall please him to assign conveniently, within six weeks after the certification of the death of the said Knight, the which also assembled, or at the least the six with the Sovereign, or his Deputy above-said, every of them that there shall be present and come to the election shall name nine of the worthiest and sufficient Knights, without reproach, that he shall know, subjects of the said Sovereign, or others, so to be that they hold no contrary party, or be again him, that is, to wit, three Dukes, Marquesses, Earls of greater estate; three Barons, or Bannerets; and three Bachelor Knights, the which denominations the Chancellor of the same Order shall write, that is, to wit, the Archbishop of Dublin, for the time being, or in his absence, the Registrar, that is, to wit, the Dean of the Cathedral Church of Saint Patrick, in Dublin, for the time being, or the most ancient Resident of the said Company in their absence, or such of the seven Officers as the Sovereign shall command, and the denominations so done by all or six of the least by him that hath written, shall be showed to the said Sovereign, or his Deputy, that then shall choose of them that be named him that shall have the most voices, or him that the Sovereign shall nominate and esteem to be the most honorable to the said Order, and most profitable to his Crown and to his Realm; and if there be any Knights of the said Order that shall fail to come to the said election, if he be not prevented by a just cause, and that the said cause of his excuse, showed under his seal of arms, be found by the Sovereign, or his Deputy, to be just and reasonable, and his excuse to be acceptable and allowed, and that if his cause be not just, and he come not to the Ceremonies abovenamed, it is ordained that he shall be reprimanded at the next Chapter for the first offence, and for the second offence he shall lose the rank which he hath in the said Order, and be placed below all other the Knights Companions of the said Order, and for the third offence he shall be punished in such manner as to the said Chapter shall seem meet.

And whereas, by the Act of Union, Ireland became part and parcel of Our United Kingdom, and Our King of Arms of all Ireland has not had, since that event, any specific place or precedence assigned to him among Our Kings of Arms by special Ordinance or Royal Authority, We do hereby direct and command, that in all Ceremonials and Assemblies Ulster King of Arms shall have place immediately after the Lord Lyon King of Arms of Scotland.

And, as touching the Habits of the Knights Companions, of Our Most Illustrious Order, the Mantles shall be of sky-blue satin, lined with a white silk, having on the right shoulder a hood of blue satin, lined also with white silk; and the said Mantle shall be fastened by a cordon of blue silk and gold, having a pair of tassels of the same materials; their Boots shall be of white leather, turned up with sky-blue; and their Spurs shall be gilt; the belt and scabbard of their sword shall be of crimson velvet, and the handle gilt.

And Our said Knights Companions shall each of them wear a round Hat, of black velvet, the front of which shall be turned back, and the Star of the Order shall be affixed thereon, and the said Hat shall be surmounted with three falls of ostrich feathers, which shall be red, blue, and white.

The Collar of Our said Most Illustrious Order shall be of Gold, and it shall be composed of Roses and of Harps alternate, tied together with a knot of Gold, and the said Roses shall be enamelled alternately white leaves within red, and red leaves within white; and in the centre of the said Collar shall be an Imperial Crown; surmounting a Harp of Gold; from which shall hang the Badge of Our said Order; and the said Badge shall be of Gold surmounted with a Wreath of Shamrock, or Trefoil, within which shall be a Circle of Blue Enamel, containing the Motto of Our said Order in Letters of Gold, viz.., QUIS SEPARABIT; together with the date MDCCLXXXIII., being the year in which Our said Order was founded, and encircling the Cross of Saint Patrick, gules, surmounted with a trefoil vert, each of its leaves charged with an Imperial Crown, or, upon a field argent.

And this Badge We ordain shall be worn pendant from a sky-blue ribband over the right shoulder, at all times when Our said Knights shall not wear the Collar of the Order, and We further ordain, that Our said Knights Companions shall wear the same Badge, encircled within rays in form of a Star of Silver consisting of eight points, that is to say, four greater and four lesser, on the left side of their outer garment.

And We further ordain that Our said Knights shall, in all Armorial Bearings, use the said Collar encircling their Coats Armorial.

And We ordain that the Prelate and Chancellor of Our said Most Illustrious Order shall wear the same Mantle as Our said Knights, having on the right side, instead of the Star, the Badge of the order, viz.: the Cross of St Patrick on a field argent, surrounded by the Motto and Date of the Order, QUIS SEPARABIT, MDCCLXXXIII., and the Wreath of Shamrocks; and the Prelate shall wear the Badge assigned to him by the Statute, dated the Eleventh of March, one thousand seven hundred and eighty-three, that is to say, the like Badge worn by Our Knights, surmounted with an Archiepiscopal Mitre; and the Chancellor shall wear a Badge of Gold, pendant at his neck from a sky-blue ribband, which shall be of a square form, representing a Purse, and charged with the same Cross, gules, surmounted as before on a field argent, and encircled with a Wreath of Shamrocks.

And the Registrar of Our said Order shall wear the same Mantle as Our Prelate and Chancellor, but it shall be shorter, and he shall wear a Badge of Gold, pendant at his neck from a sky-blue ribband, in the shape of a Book, charged with the same Device as that of Our Chancellor of Our said Most Illustrious Order.

And Our Secretary, Genealogist, Usher, and King of Arms shall wear upon the left side of the Mantles appointed by the Statutes to be worn by them respectively, the Cross of St Patrick on a field argent, but without the Motto.

And whereas, by Warrant, under his Royal Signet and Sign Manual, His late Majesty, King George the Third, Our Royal Father, of blessed Memory, dated at St James's, the Eighth day of June, in the Forty-ninth Year of His Reign, His Majesty was pleased was pleased to direct that the Chancellor of the said Order of St Patrick 'shall be entitled to the sum of one hundred pounds upon the Collar and two Badges of each deceased Knight being delivered to the Grand Master;' And whereas the Chancellor, the late Archbishop of Dublin objected to receive the said hundred pounds, conceiving it to be inconsistent with the dignity of the Archbishop to receive fees on such occasion; We, therefore, cancel and repeal so much of the said Warrant as concerns the said grant of one hundred pounds to the said Chancellor, and declare the same to be null and void for ever hereafter.

And We do hereby command and ordain that this out intention and direction be henceforward considered as part and parcel of the statutes of the said Most Illustrious Order, to which these presents shall be your sufficient Warrant; and so We bid you heartily farewell.

Given at our Palace of St James's, this 17th day of May, 1833, in the Third Year of Our Reign.
By His Majesty's command,
MELBOURNE

To Our right trusty and entirely beloved Cousin and Councillor, Henry William, Marquess of Anglesey, KG, Our Lieutenant General and General Governor of that part of Our United Kingdom called Ireland; or to Our Lieutenant, Deputy, Justices, or other Chief Governor or Governors there for the time being.

ORDINANCE 17 MAY 1833

ORDINANCE touching the Fees to be demanded and taken of Our Knights Companions of the Most Illustrious Order of St Patrick, which We will to be taken at the times and in the manner following from each of Our said Knights Companions:

(The Fees of Honour upon being made Knights Bachelor, to be shared with Our household by Our Officers of Arms in Ireland.)

	£	s	d
To Our Registrar of Our said Order	25	0	0
To Our Secretary of Our said Order	25	0	0
To Our Genealogist of Our said Order	25	0	0
To Our Usher of Our said Order	20	0	0
To Our King of Arms of Our said Order	25	0	0
To Our Herald (sic) of Our said Order	10	0	0
To Our Four Pursuivants, each £5	20	0	0

And the said Fees shall be again demanded and paid by the said Knights at the time of their Installation or dispensation from that Ceremony, and an allowance shall then be made to Our Officers of Arms, who shall prepare the Banner, Sword, and Helmet of each Knight, which shall be affixed over their respective Stalls, and the Plate of their Armorial Bearings, which shall be affixed in their said Stalls, in Our Cathedral Church of St Patrick, Dublin.

Given at Our Palace of St James's, this 17th day of May, 1833, in the Third Year of Our Reign.
By His Majesty's command,
MELBOURNE

To Our right trusty and entirely beloved Cousin and Councillor, Henry William, Marquess of Anglesey, KG, Our Lieutenant General and General Governor of that part of Our United Kingdom called Ireland, or to Our Lieutenant Deputy, Justices, or other Chief Governor or Governors there for the time being.

WARRANT 23 APRIL 1839

VICTORIA R.
Right trusty and well-beloved Councillor, We greet you well: Whereas it is Our will and pleasure that a Chapter of the Most Illustrious Order of St Patrick should be holden for the purpose of investing Our right trusty and right well beloved Cousin, William, Earl of Listowell (sic), with the Insignia of a Knight Companion of the said Order, We do hereby, pursuant to the second clause of His late Majesty's Warrant, bearing the date the 17th day of May, 1833, for revising and making certain alterations in the Statutes of the said Most Illustrious Order, authorize and direct you to hold a Chapter of the said Most Illustrious Order in Dublin Castle (three or more Knights being present) on Monday the Twentieth-ninth day of April instant, or on any such subsequent day as you shall appoint, for the purpose aforesaid, and to do all such things, and enjoy all such privileges, rights, and prerogatives, and to do all manner of things, touching the said Most Illustrious Order, in as ample a manner as We Ourselves could have done as Sovereign of the said Most Illustrious Order, if We Ourselves had been present in Ireland, for which these presents shall be your sufficient warrant; and so we bid you heartily farewell.

Given at Our Court at St James's, the 23rd day of April, 1839, in the Second Year of Our Reign.

By Her Majesty's command,
J. RUSSELL

To Our right trusty and entirely beloved Cousin and Councillor, Hugh, Baron Fortescue (commonly called Viscount Ebrington), Our Lieutenant General and General Governor of that part of Our United Kingdom called Ireland, or to Our Lieutenant Deputy, Justices, or other Chief Governor or Governors for the time being.

WARRANT 25 AUGUST 1837

VICTORIA R.
Right trusty and right well-beloved Cousin and Councillor, We greet you well: Whereas We, for divers reasons Us thereunto especially moving, are pleased to revise and make certain alterations in the Statutes of Our Most Illustrious Order of Saint Patrick, We do therefore hereby direct and command that the 14th Article of the

Statutes of Our said Order be altered, in as far as regards the Oath heretofore enjoined to be taken, and shall henceforth stand as follows, that is to say: FOURTEENTHLY, It is ordained that every Knight admitted into Our said Order shall make and subscribe the following declaration: 'I declare upon my honor, that during the time I shall be a Fellow of this Most Illustrious Order of Saint Patrick, I will keep, defend, and sustain the honors, rights, and privileges of the Sovereign of the said Order, and well and truly accomplish all the statutes, points, and ordinances of the said Order, as though they were read to me from point to point, and article to article, and that wittingly and willingly I will not break any statutes of the said Order, or any article in them contained, excepting such as I shall have received a dispensation from the Sovereign.' This done, the said Knight shall, with due reverence and kneeling, receive the Badge, the which the Sovereign shall put over his right shoulder, saying these words: 'Sir, the loving Company of the Order of Saint Patrick hath received you their Brother, Lover, and Fellow, and in token and knowledge of this they give you, and present you this present Badge, the which God will that you receive and wear from henceforth to His praise and pleasure, and to the exaltation and honor of the said Illustrious Order and yourself. And it is Our further will and pleasure that the 17th Article of the aforesaid statutes shall also be altered, and stand as follows: 'SEVENTEENTHLY, It is ordained that there shall be seven Officers appertaining to the said Order, that is to say, a Prelate, Chancellor, Secretary, Registrar, Genealogist, Usher at Arms, named the Black Rod, and King of Arms, named Ulster, all which shall have and enjoy such charges and privileges as are expressly declared in the ordinances of the Sovereign, and shall wear respectively the Mantles and Badges appointed by the former statutes of Our said Order: and the persons who may hereafter be admitted as Officers of Our said Most Illustrious Order shall, at their admission into their respective offices, in lieu of the oath or oaths heretofore taken by the Officers, severally make and subscribe a declaration* that they will, during the time they shall hold their respective offices, faithfully discharge the duties thereof, and diligently and duly observe and execute all the commands of the Sovereign, in as far as to their respective offices appertains. And We further will and command, that the several declarations so ordained to be made and subscribed by Our Knights of Our said Order, who may be elected into Our said Order from and after the date of these presents, and the declaration herein ordained to be made by the persons who may hereafter be appointed to any office in Our said Order, shall be deposited in the care and custody of Our Ulster King of Arms for the time being, to be preserved by him amongst the Archives of Our said Order. And it is Our will and pleasure that this Our intention and direction be henceforth considered as part and parcel of the statutes of Our Most Illustrious Order, and for all these purposes these presents shall be your sufficient warrant; and so We bid you heartily farewell.

Given at Our Court at St James's, this twenty-fifth day of August, One thousand eight hundred and thirty-seven, in the First Year of Our reign.
By Her Majesty's command,
J. RUSSELL.

To Our right trusty and right well beloved Cousin and Councillor, Constantine Henry, Earl of Mulgrave, Our Lieutenant General and General Governor of that part of Our United Kingdom called Ireland, or to Our Lieutenant, Deputy, Justices, or other Chief Governor or Governors there for the time being.

The Prelate and the Chancellor

I promise to my true power, during my life, and during the time that I shall be [Prelate][Chancellor] of the Most Illustrious Order of St Patrick, to be of Council, and keep and accomplish all the Statutes, Points and Ordinances of the said Order, so far as they regard the Office of [Prelate][Chancellor] of the said Most Illustrious Order, except in such as I shall have received a dispensation from the Sovereign.

The Registrar, the Secretary and the Genealogist

I promise to my true power, during my life, and during the time that I shall be [Registrar] [Secretary] [Genealogist] of the Most Illustrious Order of St Patrick, to be of Council, and to keep all the secrets of the said Order, and that all things which appertain to the Office of [Registrar][Secretary][Genealogist] I will duly observe, and obey all things which I shall receive in command from the Sovereign.

The King of Arms and the Gentleman Usher of the Black Rod

I promise and swear to my true power, during my life and during the time that I shall be [King of Arms][Usher] of the Most Illustrious Order of St Patrick, diligently and duly observe and execute all things

---

* This declaration replaced the following oaths previously sworn by the Officers.

which shall be commanded by the Sovereign, and which it is my duty to perform as [King of Arms][Usher] of the said Most Illustrious Order.

(The Genealogist's oath was restored on the appointment of Henry Farnham Burke on 16 August 1889.)

WARRANT 9 JULY 1839

VICTORIA R.

Right trusty and well-beloved Councillor, We greet you well: Whereas it hath been represented to Us that His late Majesty King William the Fourth, Our Royal Uncle and Predecessor of Blessed Memory, was pleased to command, as Sovereign of the Most Illustrious Order of Saint Patrick, that the Lords Lieutenant General and General Governors of that part of Our United Kingdom of Great Britain and Ireland called Ireland, Grand Masters of the said Most Illustrious Order, should on all occasions wear the Star of the said Most Illustrious Order, on the left side of their outer garment; and whereas His said late Majesty was further pleased to command that the Noblemen who had filled heretofore, or should hereafter fill the high and distinguished office of Lord Lieutenant General and General Governor of Ireland, and Grand Master of the said Most Illustrious Order, should during their natural lives wear the Badge of the Grand Master, pendant round their neck, from the Ribband of the Order, in the same manner as they wore them during the period they held the Office as Grand Master, And whereas no statute has hitherto passed for carrying the said Royal commands into effect, We do hereby order, direct, and command, as Sovereign of the said Most Illustrious Order, that the Grand Masters of the said Most Illustrious Order shall wear on the left side of their outer garment the Star of the said Most Illustrious Order; and also, that the Noblemen who have heretofore filled, or shall hereafter fill, the high and distinguished office of Grand Master of the said Most Illustrious Order, shall henceforward be, and they are hereby authorized to wear the Badge and Ribband of Grand Master, and to wear the Star of the said Most Illustrious Order during their natural lives; and We do hereby command and ordain, that this Our intention and direction be henceforward considered as part and parcel of the statutes of Our said Most Illustrious Order, for which these presents shall be your sufficient warrant; and so We bid you heartily farewell.

Given at Our Court of St James's, the ninth day of July, in the Third Year of Our reign.
By Her Majesty's command,
J. RUSSELL.

To Our right trusty and well-beloved Councillor, Hugh, Baron Fortescue (commonly called Viscount Ebrington), Our Lieutenant General and General Governor of that part of Our United Kingdom called Ireland, or to Our Lieutenant Deputy, Justices, or other Chief Governor or Governors there, for the time being.

WARRANT 20 JANUARY 1842

VICTORIA R.

Right trusty and right well-beloved Cousin and Councillor, We greet you well: Whereas by the Statutes of Our Most Illustrious Order of St Patrick, the number of Knights Companions is limited to twenty-two, and We the Sovereign of the said Order, being desirous of evincing in an especial manner Our Royal regard for Our dearly beloved Consort, His Royal Highness Francis Albert Augustus Charles Emanuel, Duke of Saxony, Prince of Saxe Coburg and Gotha, Knight Companion of Our Most Noble Order of the Garter, and Knight Grand Cross of Our Most Honorable Military Order of the Bath, We do hereby, in virtue of the power inherent in Us as Sovereign, dispense with the statute whereby the number of Knights Companions thereof is limited as aforesaid, in so far as may be required for the especial purpose of admitting Our said dearly beloved Consort a Knight Companion of Our said Most Illustrious Order; and We do hereby accordingly ordain and declare Our said dearly beloved Consort a Knight of Our said Most Illustrious Order of St Patrick; and We do hereby also declare Our Royal will and pleasure that except for the express purpose and occasion before mentioned, and during the life of His Royal Highness, it is not Our Royal intention that the number of Knights Companions should extend beyond the number of twenty-two, and we do further ordain and declare by this statute that Our said dearly beloved Consort, His Royal Highness, Francis Albert Augustus Charles Emanuel, Duke of Saxony, Prince of Saxe Coburg and Gotha, shall take place and precedence of all other Knights Companions of Our said Most Illustrious Order, any statute, decree or usage to the contrary notwithstanding.

Given at Our Court at Our Castle of Windsor, under the Seal of Our said Order, this twentieth day of January, 1842, in the Fifth Year of Our Reign.

By the Sovereign's especial command,

JAMES GRAHAM

To Our right trusty and well-beloved Cousin and Councillor, Thomas Philip, Earl de Grey, Our Lieutenant General and General Governor of that part of Our United Kingdom called Ireland, or to Our Lieutenant Deputy, Justices, or other Chief Governor or Governors there, for the time being.

WARRANT 20 JANUARY 1842

VICTORIA R.

Right trusty and right well beloved Cousin and Councillor, We greet you well: Whereas by a Statute of the Most Illustrious Order of St Patrick, bearing date the seventeenth day of May, 1833, it is directed that the form of admitting Knights Companions thereof should be by election in a Chapter of the Knights, nevertheless We, having this day been pleased to declare Our dearly-beloved Consort, His Royal Highness Francis Albert Augustus Charles Emanuel, Duke of Saxony, Prince of Saxe Coburg and Gotha, Knight Companion of Our Most Noble Order of the Garter, and Knight Grand Cross of Our Most Honorable Military Order of the Bath, to be a Knight Companion of Our said Most Illustrious Order of St Patrick, are further pleased, by virtue of the power inherent in Us as Sovereign, to dispense with the aforesaid statute and We do further dispense with the accustomed ceremony of Investiture, and do give and grant unto His Royal Highness Francis Albert Augustus Charles Emanuel, Duke of Saxony, Prince of Saxe Coburg and Gotha, full power and authority to wear and use the Ribband and Badge appertaining unto Our said Order, and to have, hold and enjoy all and singular the rights, privileges, and advantages belonging to a Knight of Our said Most Illustrious Order of St Patrick, in as full and ample a manner as if His Royal Highness had been formally invested by Us, any statute or usage to the contrary notwithstanding.

Given at Our Court at St James's, the twentieth day of January, 1842, in the Fifth Year of Our Reign.

By Her Majesty's command,

JAMES GRAHAM

WARRANT 22 JANUARY 1842

VICTORIA R.

Right trusty and well-beloved Cousin and Councillor, We greet you well: Whereas We, as Sovereign of the Most Illustrious Order of St Patrick, have full power to dispense with all the statutes, ordinances, and regulations required to be observed in conferring the said Order, and whereas since the last Installation of the Our said Most Illustrious Order, We have been graciously pleased to nominate Our dearly-beloved Consort, His Royal Highness Francis Albert Augustus Charles Emanuel, Duke of Saxony, Prince of Saxe Coburg and Gotha, Knight Companion of Our Most Noble Order of the Garter, and Knight Grand Cross of Our Most Honorable Military Order of the Bath, to be a Knight Companion of Our said Most Illustrious Order of St Patrick, We therefore, for divers reasons Us thereunto especially moving, do hereby dispense with all the aforesaid statutes, ordinances, and regulations, and do give and grant unto Our said dearly-beloved Consort full power and authority to wear and use the Collar and all other ornaments appertaining to Our said Most Illustrious Order, and to sit in the Stall which shall be assigned to him in Our Cathedral Church of St Patrick, and also to have, hold, and enjoy all and singular the rights, privileges and advantages belonging to a Knight Companion of Our said Order in as full and ample a manner as if he had been formally installed, any decree, rule, or usage to the contrary notwithstanding; and for these purposes these presents shall be a sufficient warrant and discharge.

Given at Our Court of St James's, the 22nd day of January, 1842, in the Fifth Year of Our Reign.

By Her Majesty's command,

JAMES GRAHAM

WARRANT 14 JULY 1871

VICTORIA R.

Right trusty and right well-beloved Cousin and Councillor, We greet you well: Whereas We, for divers reasons Us thereunto specially moving, are pleased to revise and make certain alterations in the Statutes and Ordinances of Our Most Illustrious Order of Saint Patrick, which time, circumstances and Parliamentary enactment have rendered necessary. We do therefore hereby abrogate and repeal all every the said Statutes and Ordinances so far as they in anywise refer to, concern or require the ceremonial of Installation and the said Statutes and Ordinances are in this respect hereby abrogated and repealed accordingly. And We do hereby declare, direct and command that all Knights of our said Most Illustrious Order to be henceforth created shall have and enjoy all the rank, privileges, distinctions, immunities, and advantages of Installed Knights. Further, We do hereby direct and command that after the death or resignation of each of the present holders of the following offices of the said Most Illustrious Order, viz., those of Prelate, Registrar, Genealogist, Cork Herald, Dublin Herald and Junior Pursuivant, the place of such officer of the Order, who shall happen to resign or die, shall not be filled up, and that the permanent officers of the said Most Illustrious Order shall be the following only, viz: Chancellor (a Layman), Secretary, Usher, Ulster King of Arms (being also Registrar and Keeper of the records of the Order), and Athlone Pursuivant of Arms. And further we do hereby abrogate and repeal all and every the said Statutes and Ordinances so far as they refer to or require payment of Fees or charges to be demanded or taken of Our Knights Companions of the said Most Illustrious Order henceforward to be created; and in lieu thereof We do hereby direct, ordain, and command that a sum not exceeding £300 shall be demanded and taken of every Knight Companion hereafter to be admitted the said Most Illustrious Order by Our King of Arms of Ireland to be so dealt with by him as shall be directed by the Commissioners of Our Treasury. And We do hereby command and ordain that this Our intention and direction of the Statutes of the said Most Illustrious Order, to which these presents shall be your sufficient Warrant, and so We bid you heartily farewell.

Given at Our Court at St James's, the Fourteenth day of July 1871, in the thirty-fifth year of Our reign.
By Her Majesty's command.

H. A. BRUCE

LETTERS PATENT 28 JULY 1905

Edward the Seventh, by the Grace of God, of the United Kingdom of Great Britain and Ireland and of the British Dominions beyond the Seas, King, Defender of the Faith, Emperor of India, and Sovereign of the Most Illustrious Order of Saint Patrick, to all to whom these Presents shall come, Greeting!

Whereas Our Royal Progenitor and Predecessor King George the Third did, by Warrant under His Royal Sign Manual given at the Court of Saint James's, on the Fifth day of February in the year of Our Lord One Thousand Seven Hundred and Eighty-three, in the Twenty-third year of His reign, authorise and require that Letters Patent should be passed for creating a Society or Brotherhood to be called Knights of the Most Illustrious Order of Saint Patrick, of which Order His said late Majesty, His Heirs and Successors, should perpetually be Sovereigns; and it was thereby declared and provided that, in addition to the Sovereign, the said Order should consist of fifteen Knights; and further, that the Lords Lieutenant-General and General Governor of Ireland or other Chief Governor or Governors thereof for the time being should officiate as Grand Masters, and also, that upon any vacancy happening in the said Society or Brotherhood, by death or resignation of any of the Knights, a successor should be selected by the other Knights; and it was thereby further provided that the said Order should be governed by such constitutions, ordinances, customs and ceremonies as should be enjoined under the Royal Sign Manual, and further, that the Order should have a Common Seal and a Chancellor, Registrar, Secretary, Genealogist, Usher, King of Arms, Heralds, Pursuivants and such other Officers as should from time to time be appointed under the Royal Sign Manual.

And Whereas divers Statutes, Ordinances and other Instruments have from time to time been made, ordained, passed and declared touching the said Order by which Statutes or some of them, the number of the Knights of the said Order hath been increased from fifteen to twenty-two.

And Whereas it is expedient that certain further changes should be made in the constitution of the said Order: Now therefore Know ye, that We, by these Our Letters Patent, do hereby ordain and direct that the said

Order shall as heretofore be known and described by the style and designation of the Most Illustrious Order of Saint Patrick.

And We do further ordain, direct and appoint, that the said Order shall consist of the Sovereign and a Grand Master and of twenty-two Knights Companions.

And We do hereby ordain, direct and appoint, that We, Our Heirs and Successors, Kings or Queens Regnant of the United Kingdom aforesaid, shall be Sovereigns of the said Order.

And We do hereby ordain, direct and appoint, that Our Lord Lieutenant-General and General Governor of that part of Our United Kingdom called Ireland, for the time being, shall be Grand Master of the said Order.

And We further ordain, direct and appoint, that the number of Knights Companions to which the Order is limited shall not restrict Us, Our Heirs and Successors, from appointing at Our pleasure any Foreign Princes as Honorary Knights Companions and any Princes of the Blood Royal, being descendants of His late Majesty King George the First, as Extra Knights Companions, and that if at any time hereafter any occasion should arise rendering it expedient to increase the number of Knights Companions of the said Order, it shall be competent to Us, Our Heirs and Successors, by any Statute or Statutes to be hereafter made, to authorise any such increase of the number of Knights Companions notwithstanding the present limitation of the number of such Knights Companions to twenty-two.

And We do further ordain, direct and appoint, that when and so often as any person shall hereafter be appointed to be a Member of the said Order, such appointment shall be made by a Warrant under the Sign Manual of Us, or Our Heirs and Successors, and sealed with the Seal of the Order.

And We do hereby ordain, direct and appoint, that Statutes shall be made from time to time and so often as may be necessary for the government and regulation of the Order. Each and every Statute so made shall, unless and until it is repealed or amended, have the same force and effect as if made under Letters Patent. Provided always that no such Statute or Statutes shall contain any matter repugnant to these Our Letters Patent, or shall have any force or authority unless before the actual making and promulgation thereof, We, or Our Heirs and Successors, shall have signified by a Warrant under Our Sign Manual, Our pleasure that the same should be so made and promulgated.

And We do hereby ordain, direct and appoint, that the said Order shall have a Chancellor, who shall be the person holding the Office of Chief Secretary to the Lord Lieutenant-General and General Governor of Ireland for the time being, a King of Arms, who shall be the person holding the Office of Ulster King of Arms and Principal Herald of All Ireland, and who shall also be Registrar of the Order, a Secretary, a Genealogist, a Gentleman Usher of the Black Rod, Heralds and Pursuivants of Arms; and any person hereafter to be appointed to any of the said Offices, save to the Offices of Chancellor and King of Arms, shall be appointed by a Warrant under the Sign Manual of Us, or Our Heirs and Successors. In Witness whereof We have caused these Our Letters to be made Patent.

Witness Ourself at Westminster, the Twenty-eighth day of July, in the Fifth Year of Our Reign.
By Warrant under the King's Sign Manual.
MUIR MACKENZIE.

STATUTES 29 JULY 1905

WARRANT repealing all existing Statutes and Ordinances of the Most Illustrious Order of Saint Patrick, and enacting other Statutes and Ordinances in lieu thereof.

EDWARD R. & I.
Edward the Seventh, by the Grace of God, of the United Kingdom of Great Britain and Ireland and of the British Dominions beyond the Seas, King, Defender of the Faith, Emperor of India, and Sovereign of the Most Illustrious Order of Saint Patrick: To all to whom these Presents shall come, Greeting!

WHEREAS Our Royal Progenitor and Predecessor, King George the Third, by Warrant under His Royal Signet and Sign Manual, bearing date at Saint James's the fifth day of February, one thousand seven hundred and eighty-three, authorized the creation of a Society or Brotherhood to be called Knights of the Most Illustrious Order of Saint Patrick.

And whereas divers Statutes, Ordinances and other Instruments have from time to time been made, ordained, passed and declared touching the said Order.

And whereas by Letters Patent under the Great Seal of the United Kingdom of Great Britain and Ireland, bearing date at Westminster the twenty-eighth day of July, one thousand nine hundred and five, in the fifth year of Our reign, We have thought fit to make certain changes in the constitution of the said Order.

And whereas certain alterations and modifications in, and additions to, the existing Statutes and Ordinances of the said Order have been rendered necessary by time, circumstances and Parliamentary enactment.

And whereas, in order more conveniently to effect the same, We deem it expedient that all the existing Statutes and Ordinances now in force affecting the said Order should be repealed and other Statutes and Ordinances enacted, ordained and declared in lieu thereof for the government and regulation of the said Order.

Now know ye that, in exercise of the power inherent in Us as Sovereign of the said Most Illustrious Order, and in pursuance of the said Letters Patent of the twenty-eighth day of July, one thousand nine hundred and five, We do hereby annul, abrogate and repeal all and every the said Statutes and Ordinances, and that We have made, ordained and established, and by these Presents sealed with the Seal of the Order, do make, ordain and establish the following Statutes and Ordinances, which shall from henceforth be inviolably observed and kept within the said Order in manner and form following, that is to say:

I. It is ordained that this Order of Knighthood shall as heretofore be styled and designated in all acts, proceedings and pleadings as "The Most Illustrious Order of Saint Patrick," and by no other designation.

II. It is ordained that the said Most Illustrious Order shall consist of the Sovereign, the Grand Master and twenty-two Knights Companions, with such Extra Knights Companions of the Order as may be appointed in manner hereinafter, as in Our said Letters Patent is provided.

III. It is ordained that We, Our Heirs and Successors, Kings or Queens Regnant of the United Kingdom, are and for ever shall be Sovereigns of this Most Illustrious Order, to whom doth and shall belong all power of annulling, interpreting, explaining or augmenting these and every part of these Statutes.

IV. It is ordained that Our Lord Lieutenant General and General Governor of that part of Our United Kingdom called Ireland for the time being shall, as heretofore, hold and enjoy the Office of Grand Master of this Most Illustrious Order, and shall in Our absence proceed, in Our Name and on Our behalf, to do all things and shall enjoy all privileges, rights and prerogatives touching the said Order, in as ample a manner as We Ourselves could have done as Sovereign of the said Order, if We Ourselves had been present in Ireland; And it is further ordained that it shall be the especial duty of the said Grand Master to enforce the due observance of the Statutes and Ordinances of this Order, and that he shall likewise direct the issue of all Letters of Summons whenever the Sovereign shall be pleased to command an Investiture of the said Most Illustrious Order.

V. It is ordained that the Honorary Knights Companions shall consist of foreign Princes upon whom We may think fit to confer the Honour of being received into this Order, and that the number of such Honorary Members may consist of as many foreign Princes as We, Our Heirs and Successors, shall think fit to appoint.

VI. It is ordained that it shall be competent for Us, Our Heirs and Successors, to appoint at Our Pleasure any Princes of the Blood Royal, being descendants of His late Majesty King George the First, as Extra Knights Companions of this Order.

VII. It is ordained that, although We have deemed it expedient in the foregoing Statutes to prescribe and limit the number which shall constitute this Most Illustrious Order, it shall, nevertheless, be lawful for Us, Our Heirs and Successors, by virtue of the powers to Us and them reserved in and by Our said Letters Patent of the twenty-eighth day of July, one thousand nine hundred and five, to increase the number of Members, and to assign a place to any person whom We may think fit to admit into the same.

VIII. It is ordained that when We, Our Heirs and Successors, shall be pleased to nominate and appoint any person to be a Member of this Order, such appointment shall be made by Warrant under Our Sign Manual and sealed with the Seal of the Order

IX. It is ordained that in all solemn ceremonials and in all other places and assemblies whatsoever the Knights Companions of this Order, if and when Commoners, shall have rank and precedency after Barons' eldest sons, that is to say, immediately after Knights Companions of the Most Noble Order of the Garter and the Most Antient and Most Noble Order of the Thistle, and that the wives of the said Knights Companions shall, in like manner, have rank and precedency after the wives of Barons' eldest sons; And it is further ordained, that (with the exception of the Members of the Royal Family) the Knights Companions of this Order, shall take rank among each other according to the dates of their respective nominations to this Order.

X. It is ordained that Our Habits and Robes, as Sovereign of this Most Illustrious Order, shall be of the same material and fashion as are hereinafter appointed for the Knights Companions, save only with those alterations which may befit and distinguish Our Royal Dignity; And it is further ordained that the Grand Master for the time being and the Knights Companions shall at all Investitures of the Order, and upon all great and solemn occasions to be appointed, wear mantles of sky-blue satin or silk wrought in Ireland, lined with white silk, having on the right shoulder a hood of the same material, and the said Mantles shall be fastened by a cordon of blue silk and gold, having two blue silk and gold tassels attached thereto, on the left side of which Mantles shall be embroidered a representation of the Star of a Knight Companion, which shall be composed of silver, consisting of eight points, that is to say, four greater and four lesser, issuing from a centre enclosing a representation of the Badge of the Order, but without the wreath of trefoils as hereinafter described. And We do command that the Grand Master for the time being and the Knights Companions shall wear the said Star of the Order in silver upon the left side of their Coats or outer garments, and that they shall wear at Investitures of the Order, as well as on all days usually termed "Collar Days," a Collar of gold composed of Roses and Harps alternately, tied together with knots of gold, and the said Roses shall be enamelled alternately white leaves within red and red leaves within white; and in the centre of the said Collar shall be an Imperial jewelled Crown surmounting a Harp of Gold, from which shall hang the Badge of the Order, which shall be composed of gold as follows: the Cross of Saint Patrick gules, on a field argent, surmounted by a trefoil slipped vert, each leaf charged with an Imperial Crown or; all within a circle of sky-blue enamel with the motto of Our said Order, "QUIS SEPARABIT, MDCCLXXXIII," thereon in letters of gold, the whole enclosed by a wreath of trefoils vert, on a gold ground and enamelled in their proper colours, in form and arrangement as in the representation thereof annexed to these Our Statutes. Further, it is ordained that, upon all other occasions appointed, the said Knights Companions shall wear the said Badge pendent from a sky-blue ribbon of four inches in width over the right shoulder.

And Our said Knights Companions shall each of them wear a round hat of black velvet, the front of which shall be turned back, and the Star of the Order shall be affixed thereon, and the said hat shall be surmounted with three falls of ostrich feathers, which shall be red, blue and white; their boots shall be of white leather turned up with sky-blue, and their spurs shall be gilt, the belt and scabbard of their sword shall be of crimson velvet with the handle gilt. The Surcoats shall be of sky-blue satin lined with white silk, and the Under-habits of white silk laced with gold.

XI. And it is further ordained that upon all other occasions, except as hereinbefore provided, the Grand Master for the time being shall wear around his neck, pendent from a sky-blue ribbon of two inches in width, the Badge of Our said Order, surmounted by a Harp crowned with an Imperial Crown.

XII. And it is ordained that, in pursuance of the Royal Ordinance of Our Royal Predecessor, King William the Fourth, bearing date the seventh day of March, one thousand eight hundred and thirty-one, the jewelled Insignia of the Grand Master made by Command of His said late Majesty for the use of the Grand Master of the said Most Illustrious Order, of which a description and representation is hereunto annexed, and which are Crown Jewels, shall be handed over by each Lord Lieutenant General and General Governor of Ireland, Grand Master of the said Most Illustrious Order, to his successor at such time as the Sword of State is delivered over, and shall be deposited by Our Ulster King of Arms in the Chancery of the Order along with the other Insignia of the Order.

(1) A Large Star composed of fine Brilliant Rays and Circles with Emerald Shamrock on a Ruby Cross; in the centre the Motto of the Order in Diamonds on blue enamelled ground.

(2) A Large Badge of the Order of Saint Patrick, pendent from a representation of a Harp ensigned with the Imperial Crown, all composed of fine Brilliants with Emerald Shamrock on a Ruby Cross; in the centre the Motto of the Order in Diamonds on blue enamelled ground, surrounded by a Wreath of Shamrocks in emeralds, the whole enclosed by a Circle surmounted by the Harp and Crown in Brilliants.

(3) A Gold Badge of the Order of Saint Patrick, pendent from a representation of a Harp ensigned with the Imperial Crown richly enamelled and jewelled with Emeralds and Rubies.

XIII. It is ordained that every Nobleman who has heretofore filled or shall hereafter have filled the high and distinguished Office of Grand Master of the said Order shall be and is hereby authorized to wear a Badge similar to that worn by the Grand Master as hereinbefore described, pendent from the neck by a sky-blue ribbon of two inches in width.

XIV. It is ordained that whenever the Sovereign shall be pleased to command a Chapter to be held for the purpose of investing a Knight Companion of this Most Illustrious Order, that there shall be three Knights Companions at least present besides the Sovereign or the Grand Master, to constitute the Chapter, unless the Sovereign or the Grand Master be pleased to grant a dispensation therefrom under the Seal of the Order, that the Knights Companions having assembled, wearing their Mantles, Stars and Collars, and being attended by the Officers of the Order, shall proceed into the presence of the Sovereign or Grand Master, in the Chapter Room, and take their respective seats at the Chapter Table, according to their seniority, and the Roll of the Knights shall then be called over by Ulster King of Arms. The Sovereign or Grand Master having been pleased to declare the cause of holding the Chapter, shall then declare the name, style and title of the Knight-Elect nominated to be a Knight Companion of the said Most Illustrious Order, and command the two Junior Knights present to receive the Knight-Elect at the door of the Chapter Room and conduct him to the right of the Chair of State with his Mantle, Banner, Sword, Helm and Crest borne before him, and immediately preceded by Ulster King of Arms bearing the Insignia of the Order on a cushion. The Usher of the Black Rod shall then present the Knight-Elect, who kneeling shall receive the honour of Knighthood, unless he shall have previously received that honour. The Declaration shall then be read by the Chancellor of the Order to the Knight-Elect, who shall sign the said Declaration, which shall be placed by the Secretary in the Register of the Order. The Knight shall then kneel, and the Sovereign or Grand Master, assisted by the two Senior Knights Companions present, will place the Ribbon with the Badge over the Knight's right shoulder, passing it obliquely to the left and pronouncing the Admonition, and gird him with the Sword and robe him with the Mantle, while the Chancellor reads the prescribed Admonitions. His Banner shall then be unfurled and his titles proclaimed by Ulster King of Arms. The Proclamation being ended, the newly invested Knight, having received the congratulations of the assembled Knights Companions, shall be conducted to his seat at the Chapter Table by Ulster King of Arms. The Chapter being ended, the Names, Styles and Titles of the Knights Companions present shall be proclaimed by the King of Arms, and they shall withdraw from the presence of the Sovereign or Grand Master, with the usual reverences, attended by the Officers of the Order.

XV. It is ordained that every Knight admitted into the said Order shall make and subscribe the following Declaration: "I declare upon my honour that during the time I shall be a Knight Companion of this Most Illustrious Order of Saint Patrick, I will keep, defend and sustain the honours, rights and privileges of the Sovereign of the said Order, and well and truly accomplish all the Statutes, points and ordinances of the said Order, as though they were read to me from point to point, and article to article, and that wittingly and willingly I will not break any Statutes of the said Order, or any article in them contained, excepting those from which I shall have received a dispensation from the Sovereign."

XVI. And it is ordained that the following Admonition shall be read by the Sovereign or Grand Master to every Knight on investing him with the Ribbon and Badge of the said Order: "Sir, the loving Company of the Order of Saint Patrick hath received you their Brother, Lover and Fellow, and in token and knowledge of this We give you and present you this Badge, the which God will that you receive and wear from henceforth to His praise and pleasure, and to the exaltation and honour of the said Most Illustrious Order and yourself."

XVII. And it is further ordained that the following Admonitions shall be read by the Chancellor, or in his absence by some other Officer of the said Order who shall be appointed by the Sovereign or Grand Master, to every Knight at his Investiture into the said Order, that is to say, upon putting on the Sword: "Take this Sword to the increase of your honour and in token and sign of your Membership of this Most Illustrious Order wherewith you being defended may be bold strongly to fight in the defence of those Rights and Ordinances to which you may be engaged, and to the just and necessary defence of those that be oppressed and needy." Upon putting on the Mantle: "Receive this Robe and Livery of this Most Illustrious Order in augmentation of thine honour, and wear it with a firm and steady resolution that by your character, conduct and demeanour you may approve yourself a true Servant of Almighty God, and a worthy Brother and Knight Companion of this Most Illustrious Order."

XVIII. It is ordained that if any person, nominated and appointed a Knight Companion of this Most Illustrious Order, shall, at the time of such nomination and appointment as aforesaid, be absent from our United Kingdom, it shall be competent for Us, Our Heirs and Successors, to dispense with the Ceremony of his Investiture, or to authorize by a Warrant under Our Sign Manual, and sealed with the Seal of this Order, to wholly dispense with the Ceremony of Investiture, and the said Warrant shall fully permit and authorize the person so nominated to wear the Insignia of a Knight Companion of the said Most Illustrious Order, in as full and ample a manner as if he had been invested by Us, Our Heirs or Successors; And We do hereby admit such Knight Companion to the rights, privileges and precedency belonging to a Knight Companion, including among such rights and privileges the use and enjoyment of the distinctive appellation of a Knight Bachelor of these Realms, until it shall be convenient for the Sovereign or Grand Master to confer that honour, or to grant it by Letters Patent under the Great Seal: Provided, nevertheless, that nothing herein contained shall be construed or interpreted to authorize the assumption of the distinctive appellation appertaining to a Knight Bachelor of these Realms, by a Knight Companion of this Most Illustrious Order, until either after he has been invested by the Sovereign or Grand Master, or otherwise, according to the foregoing provisions of this present Statute.

XIX. It is ordained that on the decease of each and every Knight Companion of this Most Illustrious Order, the heirs, executors and administrators of all such Knights Companions shall, within three months after the decease of any such Knight, deliver the before-mentioned Collars and Badges to the Sovereign or the Grand Master, for the service of the Order. And Ulster King of Arms, or his Deputy, shall have full power in the name of the Grand Master to apply to the heirs, executors or administrators of such deceased Knights for the Collars and Badges aforesaid.

XX. And it is further ordained that the said Collars and Badges shall be deposited for safe keeping in a steel safe in the strong room in the Chancery of the Order in the Office of Arms in Ireland until they be disposed of by the Grand Master. And when the said Badges or Collars are delivered to any Knight by order of the Grand Master, he shall give a receipt for the same to Ulster King of Arms, or to his Deputy, as hereinafter set out:: "I, Sir A. B., Knight Companion of the Most Illustrious Order of Saint Patrick, do hereby acknowledge to have received from C. D., Ulster King of Arms [or his Deputy, as the case may be], one Collar and one Badge of the said Most Illustrious Order, which I promise for myself, my heirs, executors and administrators, shall be safely delivered and returned to Ulster King of Arms, or his Deputy, for the Grand Master of the said Most Illustrious Order within three months after my resignation of the said Most Illustrious Order, or of my decease, agreeable to the Statutes of the said Order. In Witness whereof I have hereunto set my hand this —— day of ——————".

XXI. It is ordained that for the greater splendour and dignity of this Most Illustrious Order, it shall be lawful for the Knights Companions, in conformity with antient usage, upon all occasions to bear and use Supporters to their Arms; And we do by these presents direct and command Our Ulster King of Arms for the time being to grant Supporters to such Knights Companions as shall not be entitled otherwise thereto. It shall likewise be lawful for all Knights Companions to surround their Armorial Ensigns with a representation of the Collar, Circle and Motto of this Order, with the Badge pendent thereto.

XXII. It is ordained that the Seal of the Order shall consist of the Arms following, to be engraven thereon, viz., Argent, a saltire gules, over all a trefoil slipped vert, charged with three crowns or, impaling Our Royal Arms, with this circumscription, "Sigillum Illustrissimi Ordinis de Sancto Patricio"; And Our Royal Will and Pleasure is that the said Seal shall for ever hereafter be the Seal of the said Order of Saint Patrick; and that the Statutes, to be perpetually and inviolably observed within the said Order, shall be established and sealed by and with the same Seal; And We do hereby for Us, Our Heirs and Successors, declare and ordain that the said Statutes so to be given by Us, Our Heirs and Successors, to which the said Seal shall be affixed, shall be of the same force and validity as if the same Statutes had been verbatim recited in Our said Letters Patent of the twenty-eighth day of July, one thousand nine hundred and five, and had been passed under the Great Seal of Our said United Kingdom. And the custody of the said Seal shall be committed to Ulster King of Arms, to be kept by him in Our Office of Arms, in Our Castle of Dublin, where the Chancery of the Order shall be established.

XXIII. In order to make such additional provisions as shall effectually preserve pure this Most Illustrious Order, it is ordained that if any Knight Companion of this Order be convicted of treason, cowardice, felony, or of any crime derogatory to his honour as a Knight or a Gentleman, or if he be accused of any such offence, and doth not, after a reasonable time, surrender himself to be tried for the same, he shall forthwith be degraded from the Order by an especial Ordinance issued for that purpose, signed by the Sovereign, and sealed with the Seal of this Order. It is hereby further declared, that We, Our Heirs and Successors, Sovereigns of this Order, are and for ever shall be sole judges of the circumstances demanding such degradation and expulsion. Moreover, the Sovereign shall at all times have power to restore to this Most Illustrious Order such Members thereof as may at any time have been expelled.

XXIV. It is ordained that there shall be the following Officers attached to this Most Illustrious Order, that is to say, a Chancellor (who shall be the Chief Secretary to Our Lord Lieutenant General and General Governor of Ireland during the time he shall hold such Office), a King of Arms, Knight Attendant on the Order, who shall be the person holding the Office of Ulster King of Arms (Registrar and Keeper of the Records of the Order), a Secretary, a Genealogist, and Gentleman Usher of the Black Rod, Dublin and Cork Heralds and Athlone Pursuivant of Arms, and We are pleased to declare and command that the present holders of any of the said Offices shall continue to hold them in conformity with the provisions of these Statutes; and that the said Officers, collectively and individually, shall exercise and enjoy all the rights and privileges appertaining to the same, and We do further hereby direct and command that such Mantles and Insignia as in these Statutes they are directed to wear shall be prepared as heretofore at the charge of the State; moreover, the said Officers of this Order, who attend within Our Royal Palace for the service of the Order, shall continually remain under the protection of the Sovereign, and are hereby declared to be servants of Our Royal Household. Further, we are pleased to declare and command that the Officers of this Order shall take rank and precedence amongst themselves as follows: The Chancellor, The King of Arms (being also Registrar), The Secretary, The Genealogist, The Gentleman Usher, The Heralds and The Pursuivants. And it is hereby declared that the said Offices of King of Arms, Secretary, Genealogist, Gentleman Usher, Heralds and Pursuivants shall be holden during good behaviour.

XXV. It is ordained that the persons who are admitted as Officers of the said Order shall, at their admission into their respective Offices, severally make and subscribe the following Declaration that they will, during the time they shall hold their respective Offices, faithfully discharge the duties thereof in as far as to their respective Offices appertain: "I promise to my true power, during my life, or during the time that I shall be [Chancellor] of the Most Illustrious Order of Saint Patrick, diligently and duly to observe and execute all things which shall be commanded by the Sovereign, or by the Grand Master, and which it is my duty to perform as [Chancellor] of the said Most Illustrious Order."

XXVI. It is ordained that the Chief Secretary for the time being to Our Lord Lieutenant General and General Governor of Ireland shall be the Chancellor of this Most Illustrious Order during the time he shall hold such Office of Chief Secretary, and that in all Ceremonies of the Order he shall wear, over a surcoat of white silk, the same Mantle as Our said Knights Companions, having on the right side instead of the Star a representation of the Badge of the Order, namely, the Cross of Saint Patrick on a field argent, surrounded by the Motto and Date of the Order, "QUIS SEPARABIT, MDCCLXXXIII," and the Wreath of trefoils. He shall wear around his neck, pendent from a sky-blue ribbon two inches in width, a Badge of Gold, which shall be in the form of a Purse and charged with a representation of the Badge of the Order enamelled in the proper colours. And every person who has heretofore filled, or shall hereafter have filled, the Office of Chancellor of the said Most Illustrious Order and at the same time be a Cabinet Minister, shall, upon ceasing to hold the said Office, be entitled to and they are each hereby authorized to wear during their natural lives a miniature of the Badge of one-half the dimensions of the Badge of Office formerly worn by them as Chancellors of the Order. The Chancellor shall affix, or cause to be affixed, the Seal of the said Most Illustrious Order to all Statutes and other instruments and writings of the said Order which require to be passed under the said Seal. He shall, moreover, sedulously attend to the service of the said Order, and perform such other duties as he may be directed by these Statutes or by the Sovereign or Grand Master.

XXVII. It is ordained that Our Ulster King of Arms for the time being shall be the King of Arms, Knight Attendant on the Order, and shall have the custody of the Seal and of the Archives of the Order and the jewelled Insignia of the Grand Master. He shall attend to the service of the Order generally, and shall obey and execute such commands and directions as he may receive from the Sovereign or the Grand Master relating to the same. He shall prepare and engross all Warrants and instruments which shall require to be sealed with the Seal of the

Order. He shall carefully record in the Register all nominations to the Order and the proceedings thereunto relating, and on the decease of a Knight Companion of the Order, he shall obtain possession of the Insignia worn by such deceased Knight, and deposit the same for safe custody in the Chancery of the Order as in the Statutes is directed. As executive Officer he shall summon the Knights Companions to all Chapters of the Order, and shall attend all Investitures of the Order, and shall carry out all requirements touching the Ceremonial of an Investiture of Knight Companion of the Order. And further it is ordained that in all Ceremonials of the Order he shall wear, over a surcoat of white silk, a Mantle of crimson satin, but shorter in proportion than the Chancellor's, lined with white satin and tied with a cordon of crimson silk and gold, having two crimson silk and gold tassels attached thereto, on the left side of which Mantle shall be embroidered a shield bearing the Cross of Saint Patrick gules, on a field argent; and he shall wear around his neck, pendent from a sky-blue ribbon of two inches in width, a Badge of Gold containing the Cross Gules of Our said Order upon a field argent, impaled with the Arms of Ireland, both encircled with the Motto of the Order and surmounted with an Imperial Crown; on the reverse shall be displayed on a ground of green enamel the Official Arms of Ulster King of Arms ensigned with his Crown encircled by the Wreath of trefoils, and the whole enamelled in their proper colours. The said Badge to be worn pendent from a gold Chain of three strands upon Collar days, Investitures of the Order and public occasions. And in all Ceremonials and Assemblies whatsoever, Ulster King of Arms shall have place and precedence among Our Kings of Arms, as heretofore, immediately after Lyon King of Arms, who shall have place, as heretofore, immediately after Garter Principal King of Arms.

XXVIII. It is ordained that the Secretary and Genealogist shall be appointed by Us, Our Heirs and Successors, that in all Ceremonies of the Order they shall wear over surcoats of white silk, Mantles like unto that appointed for the Chancellor of the Order, but shorter in proportion, on the left side of which Mantles shall be embroidered the same device as borne by the King of Arms of this Order, and shall each of them wear around their necks, pendent from a sky-blue ribbon of two inches in width, the same Badge as Our Knights Companions, only without the Motto. They shall sedulously attend to the service of the said Order, and perform such other duties as they have heretofore performed, and as they may be directed by these Statutes or by the Sovereign or Grand Master.

XXIX. It is ordained that the Gentleman Usher of the Black Rod of this Most Illustrious Order shall be appointed by Us, Our Heirs and Successors; that in all Ceremonies of the Order he shall wear, over a surcoat of white silk, a Mantle like unto that appointed for the King of Arms, but shorter in proportion, and wear around his neck, pendent from a sky-blue ribbon of two inches in width, a Badge of Gold, containing the Arms of Ireland enamelled in their proper colours and encircled with the Motto of the Order as before, and that he shall carry the Black Rod of this Order ensigned with a lion sejant in gold. He shall introduce into the presence of the Sovereign or Grand Master, prior to their Investiture, those persons to be knighted or to be invested, and shall sedulously attend to the service of the said Order and perform such other duties as he may be directed by these Statutes or by the Sovereign or Grand Master.

XXX. It is ordained that the Heralds and the Pursuivants of Arms shall be appointed by Us, Our Heirs and Successors, that in all Ceremonies of the Order they shall wear the usual habit of a Herald and Pursuivant respectively, and shall each of them wear around their necks, pendent from a sky-blue ribbon of two inches in width, a Badge containing the Cross of Saint Patrick gules, on a field argent, encircled with the Motto of the Order, the whole enamelled in their proper colours. They shall assist in all Ceremonies and sedulously attend to the service of the said Order, and assist Ulster King of Arms in all preliminary work in connection with the Ceremonies of the Order, and perform such other duties as may be directed by these Statutes or by the Sovereign or the Grand Master.

XXXI. It is ordained that on the resignation or decease of an Officer of the Order, his Badge of Office shall be returned to Ulster King of Arms for the service of the Order.

XXXII. It is ordained that the Seventeenth day of March in every year, being Saint Patrick's Day, shall henceforth be taken and deemed to be the Anniversary of the Institution of this Order.

XXXIII. It is ordained that the Great Ballroom in Our Castle of Dublin, in which the Ceremony of the public Investiture of the Knights of the Order shall be performed, shall always be distinguished by the honourable denomination of "The Hall of Saint Patrick," and in the said Hall the Chapters of the Order shall at all times be held, except when it is otherwise ordered by the Sovereign or Grand Master.

XXXIV. It is ordained that Ulster King of Arms shall, within a year after the Investiture of every Knight of the Order or of his dispensation therefrom, cause to be made an escocheon of his Arms and Hatchments in a plate of metal, which shall be put up in the Hall of Saint Patrick in Our Castle of Dublin, together with his Banner, Sword, Helm and Crest as heretofore.

XXXV. It is ordained that Ulster King of Arms and Knight Attendant for the time being, or his Deputy, shall, as heretofore, be empowered to cause to be repaired such Insignia of the Order as may stand in need thereof, and that the expense attending such repairs, as also the expense of carriage of the Collars and Badges, shall be allowed and credited to Ulster King of Arms, or his Deputy, on his certificate upon his honour of the same being true and correct and truly and correctly done and performed. The said Ulster King of Arms, or his Deputy, shall also be authorized to procure to be made such things as may be necessary for the investiture of the Knights, or the use of the Officers of the said Order, the expense of which he shall also be paid on his said certificate. And that the several Insignia of the Knights Companions and Officers of the Order may more plainly appear, We have directed them to be properly depicted and emblazoned in their proper colours.

XXXVI. It is ordained that a sum not exceeding fifty pounds shall be demanded and taken by Ulster King of Arms from every Knight Companion to be admitted to the said Most Illustrious Order, to be so dealt with by him as the Commissioners of Our Treasury shall from time to time direct.

XXXVII. We are further pleased to ordain that the Chancery of the said Most Illustrious Order, wherein a record of all proceedings connected therewith shall be carefully deposited and preserved, shall be in the Office of Arms in Our Castle of Dublin.

XXXVIII. And lastly, We do hereby command and enjoin that these Statutes and every article thereof, shall be inviolably kept and observed within Our said Order, reserving to Ourselves, Our Heirs and Successors, the power of annulling, altering, abrogating, augmenting, interpreting, or dispensing with, the same or any portion thereof, by a notification sealed with the Seal of the Order, which alterations, abrogations, augmentations, interpretations or dispensations, shall be taken and received as part and parcel of these Statutes.

Given under the Seal of the said Order at Our Court at Saint James's this twenty-ninth day of July, one thousand nine hundred and five in the Fifth year of Our Reign.
By His Majesty's Command,
A. AKERS DOUGLAS.

REVISION OF STATUTES XII, XIX, XX AND XXXVI 8 MARCH 1919

GEORGE R. I.
Right trusty and well-beloved Cousin and Councillor, We greet you well! Whereas We for divers reasons Us thereunto specially moving are pleased to revise and make certain alterations in the Statutes and Ordinances of Our Most Illustrious Order of Saint Patrick which time and circumstance have rendered necessary, We do therefore hereby direct and command that Statutes XII, XIX, XX and XXXVI of Our said Most Illustrious Order be altered and stand as follows, that is to say:

XII. And it is ordained that on the resignation, removal or decease of every Grand Master of the said Most Illustrious Order, the Insignia of the Grand Master shall be delivered to Ulster King of Arms or his Deputy and deposited in the Chancery of the Order to be handed over to the next succeeding Lord Lieutenant General and General Governor of Ireland, as soon as he is sworn and the Sword of State is delivered to him.

XIX. It is ordained that on the decease of each and every Knight Companion of this Most Illustrious Order, the heirs, executors and administrators of all such Knights Companions shall within three months of the decease of any such Knight deliver the beforementioned Collars, Badges and Stars to the Sovereign or the Grand Master for the Service of the Order. And Ulster King of Arms or his Deputy shall have full power in the name of the Grand Master to apply to the heirs, executors or administrators of such deceased Knights for the Collars, Badges and Stars aforesaid.

XX. And it is further ordained that the said Collars, Badges and Stars shall be deposited for safe keeping in a steel safe in the strong room in the Chancery of the Order in the Office of Arms in Ireland until they be disposed of by the Grand Master. And when the said Collars, Badges and Stars are delivered to any Knight by order of the Grand Master or Sovereign, he shall give a receipt for the same to Ulster King of Arms or to his Deputy as hereinafter set out:

I, Sir A. B., Knight Companion of the Most Illustrious Order of Saint Patrick do hereby acknowledge to have received from C. D., Ulster King of Arms (or his Deputy as the case may be) one Collar, one Badge and one Star of the said Most Illustrious Order, which I promise for myself, my heirs, executors and administrators shall be safely delivered and returned to Ulster King of Arms or his Deputy for the Grand Master of the said Most Illustrious Order within three months after my resignation of the said Most Illustrious Order or of my decease agreeably to the Statutes of the said Order. In witness whereof I have hereunto set my hand this —— day of ———— .

XXXVI. It is ordained that a sum not exceeding sixty five pounds shall be demanded and taken by Ulster King of Arms, or his Deputy from every Knight Companion to be admitted to the said Most Illustrious Order to be so dealt with by him as the Commissioners of Our Treasury shall from time to time direct.

And it is Our Will and Pleasure that this our intention and direction be henceforth considered as part and parcel of the Statutes of Our said Most Illustrious Order, for which purposes these Presents shall be your sufficient Warrant. And so we bid you heartily farewell!

Given at our Court at Saint James's, the eighth day of March, 1919, in the ninth year of Our Reign;
By His Majesty's command.
EDWARD SHORTT

To Our right trusty and well-beloved Cousin and Councillor, John Denton Pinkstone, Viscount French of Ypres, KP, GCB, OM, GCVO, KCMG, Our Lord Lieutenant General and General Governor of that part of Our United Kingdom of Great Britain and Ireland called Ireland, or to Our Lieutenant, Deputy, Justices or other Chief Governor or Governors there for the time being.

REVISION OF STATUTE XXIV 1 MARCH 1921

GEORGE R. I.

Right trusty and well-beloved Cousin and Councillor, We greet you well! Whereas We for divers reasons Us thereunto specially moving are pleased to revise and make certain alterations in the Statutes and Ordinances of Our Most Illustrious Order of Saint Patrick which time and circumstance have rendered necessary, We do therefore hereby direct and command that Statute XXIV of Our said Most Illustrious Order be altered and stand as follows, that is to say:

XXIV. It is ordained that there shall be the following Officers attached to this Most Illustrious Order, that is to say a Chancellor (who shall be the Chief Secretary to Our Lord Lieutenant General and General Governor of Ireland during the time that he shall hold such office) a King of Arms, Knight Attendant on the Order who shall be the person holding the office of Ulster King of Arms (Registrar and Keeper of the Records of the Order), a Secretary, a Genealogist, and Gentleman Usher of the Black Rod, Dublin and Cork Heralds and Athlone and Cork Pursuivants of Arms, and We are pleased to declare and command that the present holders of any of the said offices shall continue to hold them in conformity with the provision of these Statutes; and that the said Officers, collectively and individually, shall exercised and enjoy all the rights and privileges appertaining to the same, and We do further hereby direct and command that such Mantles and Insignia as in these Statutes they are directed to wear shall be prepared as heretofore at the charge of the State; moreover, the said Officers of this Order who attend within Our Royal Palace for the Service of the Order, shall continually remain under the protection of the Sovereign, and are hereby declared to be servants of Our Royal Household. Further, We are pleased to declare and command that the Officers of the this Order shall take rank and precedence amongst themselves as follows:- The Chancellor, The King of Arms (being also Registrar), The Secretary, The Genealogist, The Gentleman Usher of the Black Rod, The Heralds and Pursuivants. And it is hereby declared that the said Offices of King of Arms, Secretary, Genealogist, Gentleman Usher, Heralds and Pursuivants shall be holden during good behaviour.

And it is Our Will and Pleasure that this Our intention and direction be henceforth considered as part and parcel of the Statutes of Our said Most Illustrious Order, for which purpose these Presents shall be your sufficient Warrant.

And so we bid you heartily farewell!

Given at Our Court at Saint James's, the first day of March 1921, in the eleventh year of Our Reign.
By His Majesty's command.
E. SHORTT

To Our right trusty and right well-beloved Cousin and Councillor, John Denton Pinkstone, Viscount French of Ypres, KP, GCB, OM, GCVO, KCMG, Field Marshal of Our Forces, Our Lord Lieutenant General and General Governor of that part of Our United Kingdom of Great Britain and Ireland called Ireland or to Our Lieutenant, Deputy, Justices or other Chief Governor or Governors there for the time being.

DRAFT LETTERS PATENT AND STATUTES 1927-8

Draft of new Letters Patent for reconstituting the Order of Saint Patrick, prepared in Home Office, July 1927.

Well beloved Counsellor Douglas McGarel, Baron Hailsham   July 1927/December 1928

GEORGE THE FIFTH, by the Grace of God, of Great Britain, Ireland and the British Dominions beyond the Seas, King, Defender of the Faith, Emperor of India, To all to whom these Presents shall come, Greeting:

Whereas, Our Royal Progenitor and Predecessor King George the Third did, by Warrant under His Royal Sign Manual given at the Court of Saint James's, on the Fifth day of February, one thousand, seven hundred and eighty-three, in the Twenty-third year of His reign, authorize the creation of a Society or Brotherhood to be called Knights of the Most Illustrious Order of Saint Patrick, of which Order His said late Majesty, His Heirs and Successors, should perpetually be Sovereigns.

And whereas certain Letters Patent, Statutes, Ordinances and other Instruments have from time to time been made, ordained, passed and declared touching the said Order.

And whereas certain changes in the constitution of the said Order have been rendered necessary by time, circumstances and Parliamentary enactment.

And whereas it is expedient that all the said Instruments now in force affecting the said Order should be repealed and other Instruments made, ordained, passed and declared in lieu thereof.

Now therefore know ye that We of Our special grace, certain knowledge and mere motion, have revoked and abrogated, and do hereby revoke and abrogate, all such Letters Patent, Statutes, Ordinances and other Instruments as aforesaid.

And know ye that We by these Our Letters Patent do hereby ordain and direct that the said Order shall as heretofore be known, styled and designated in all acts, proceedings and pleadings as the Most Illustrious Order of Saint Patrick.

And we do further ordain, direct and appoint, that Statutes shall be made from time to time and so often as may be necessary for the government and regulation of the Order and of the Ceremonial connected therewith. Each and every Statute so made shall, unless and until it is repealed or amended have the same force and effect as if made by Letters Patent. Provided always that no such Statute or Statutes shall contain any matter repugnant to these Our Letters Patent or shall have any force or authority unless before the actual making and promulgation thereof, We, or Our Heirs and Successors, shall have signified by a Warrant under Our Sign Manual, Our pleasure that the same should be so made and promulgated.

And We do hereby ordain, direct and appoint that the said Order shall consist of a Sovereign and a Grand Master and of twenty-two Knights Companions.

And We do hereby ordain, direct and appoint that We, Our Heirs and Successors, shall be Sovereigns of the said Order.

And We do hereby ordain, direct and appoint that a Prince of the Blood Royal or such other exalted personage, as We, Our Heirs and Successors shall hereafter appoint, shall be Grand Master of the said Order and, he shall be the First or Principal Knight Companion of the same.

And We do further ordain, direct and appoint, that the number of Knights Companions to which the Order is limited shall not restrict Us, Our Heirs and Successors, from appointing at Our pleasure any Foreign Princes as Honorary Knights Companions and any Princes of the Blood Royal as Extra Knights Companions, and that if at any time hereafter any occasion should arise rendering it expedient to increase the number of Knights Companions of the said Order, it shall be competent to Us, Our Heirs and Successors, by any Statute or Statutes to be hereafter made, to authorise any such increase of the number of Knights Companions notwithstanding the present limitation of the number of such Knights Companions to twenty-two.

And We do further ordain, direct and appoint that the said Order shall have a Common Seal.

And We do further ordain, direct and appoint, that when and so often as any person shall hereafter be appointed to be a Member of the said Order, such appointment shall be made by a Warrant under the Sign Manual of Us, or Our Heirs and Successors, and sealed with the Seal of the Order.

And We do hereby ordain, direct and appoint that the said Order shall have a Chancellor who shall be a Knight Companion of the said Order appointed by Us, or Our Heirs and Successors, a King of Arms, who shall be the person holding the Office of Ulster King of Arms, a Secretary and a Gentleman Usher of the Black Rod; and any person hereafter to be appointed to any of the said Offices save to the Offices of Chancellor and King of Arms, shall be appointed by a Warrant under the Sign Manual of Us, or Our Heirs and Successors.

And We do further ordain, direct and appoint that it shall be competent for Us, Our Heirs and Successors by a Warrant as aforesaid to appoint such other Officers for the service of the said Order, as We, Our Heirs and Successors shall deem fit.

And lastly We do hereby ordain, direct and appoint that nothing in these Our Letters Patent shall affect the continuity of the said Order or the rights and privileges of the existing Knights Companions and Officers thereof.

In witness whereof We have caused these Our Letters to be made Patent*.

Draft of new Statutes prepared by Ulster King of Arms as amended by the Conference held at the Home Office on July 19th 1927.

Warrant repealing all existing Statutes and ordinances of the Most Illustrious Order of Saint Patrick, and enacting other Statutes and Ordinances in lieu thereof.

GEORGE THE FIFTH, by the Grace of God, of Great Britain, Ireland and the British Dominions beyond the Seas, King, Defender of the Faith, Emperor of India, and Sovereign of the Most Illustrious Order of Saint Patrick: To all to whom these Presents shall come, Greeting:

Whereas, Our Royal Progenitor and Predecessor, King George the Third did, by Warrant under His Royal Sign Manual given at the Court of Saint James's, on the Fifth day of February, one thousand, seven hundred and eighty-three, in the Twenty-third year of His reign, authorize the creation of a Society or Brotherhood to be called Knights of the Most Illustrious Order of Saint Patrick, of which Order His said late Majesty, His Heirs and Successors, should perpetually be Sovereigns.

And whereas certain Letters Patent, Statutes, Ordinances and other Instruments have from time to time been made, ordained, passed and declared touching the said Order.

And whereas certain changes in the constitution of the said Order have been rendered necessary by time, circumstances and Parliamentary enactment.

And whereas by Letters Patent under the Great Seal of the Realm bearing date at Westminster the ____ day of ____ , one thousand, nine hundred and twenty-seven in the eighteenth year of Our Reign, We have thought fit to make certain changes in the constitution of the said Order.

And whereas, in order more conveniently to effect the same, We deem it expedient that all the existing Statutes and Ordinances now in force affecting the said Order should be repealed and other Statutes and Ordinances enacted, ordained and declared in lieu thereof for the government and regulation of the said Order and of the Ceremonial connected therewith.

Now know ye that, in exercise of the power inherent in Us as Sovereign of the said Most Illustrious Order, and in pursuance of the said Letters Patent of the _____ day of ____ , one thousand, nine hundred and twenty-seven, We do hereby annul, abrogate and repeal all and every the said existing Statutes and Ordinances, and that We have made, ordained and established, and by these Presents sealed with the Seal of the Order, do make, ordain and establish the following Statutes and Ordinances, which shall from henceforth be inviolably observed and kept within the said Order in manner and form following, that is to say:

I. It is ordained that this Order of Knighthood shall as heretofore be styled and designated in all acts, proceedings and pleadings as "The Most Illustrious Order of Saint Patrick", and by no other designation.

II. It is ordained that the said Most Illustrious Order shall consist of the Sovereign, the Grand Master and

• There is a note on the first page of file LCO6/953: 'This Patent was not proceeded with and never passed the Great Seal'. L. C. Ridley 29th July 1943.

twenty-two Knights Companions, with such Extra and Honorary Knights Companions of the Order as may be appointed in manner hereinafter, as in Our Letters Patent provided.

III. It is ordained that We, Our Heirs and Successors, are and for ever shall be Sovereigns of this Most Illustrious Order, to whom doth and shall belong all power of annulling, interpreting, explaining or augmenting these and every part of these Statutes.

IV. It is ordained that a Prince of the Blood Royal or such other exalted personage as We, Our Heirs and Successors shall hereafter appoint shall be Grand Master of the said Order and that he shall be the First or Principal Knight Companion of the same; And it is further ordained that it shall be the especial duty of the said Grand Master to enforce the due observance of the Statutes and Ordinances of this Order, and that he shall likewise direct the issue of all Letters of Summons whenever the Sovereign shall be pleased to command an Investiture of the said Most Illustrious Order.

V. It is ordained that it shall be competent for Us, Our Heirs and Successors, to appoint at Our Pleasure any Princes of the Blood Royal as Extra Knights Companions of this Order.

VI. It is ordained that Honorary Knights Companions shall consist of foreign Princes upon whom We may think fit to confer the Honour of being received into this Order, and that the number of such Honorary Members may consist of as many foreign Princes as We, Our Heirs and Successors, shall think fit to appoint.

VII. It is ordained that, although We have deemed it expedient in the foregoing Statutes to prescribe and limit the number which shall constitute this Most Illustrious Order, it shall, nevertheless, be lawful for Us, Our Heirs and Successors, by virtue of the powers to Us and them reserved in and by Our said Letters Patent of the day of _____ , one thousand, nine hundred and twenty-seven, to increase the number of Members, and to assign a place to any person whom We may think fit to admit into the same.

VIII. It is ordained that when We, Our Heirs and Successors, shall be pleased to nominate and appoint any person to be a Member of the Order, such appointment shall be made by Warrant under Our Sign Manual and sealed with the Seal of the Order.

IX. It is ordained that in all solemn ceremonials and in all other places and assemblies whatsoever the Knights Companions of this Order, if and when Commoners, shall have rank and precedency immediately after Knights Companions of the Most Noble Order of the Garter and the Most Antient and Most Noble Order of the Thistle, and that the wives of the said Knights Companions shall, in like manner, have rank and precedency after the wives of the Knights Companions of the said Orders.

X. It is ordained that Our Habits and Robes, as Sovereign of this Most Illustrious Order, shall be of the same material and fashion as are hereinafter appointed for the Knights Companions, save only with those alterations which may befit and distinguish Our Royal Dignity; And it is further ordained that the Grand Master for the time being and the Knights Companions shall at all Investitures of the Order, and upon all great and solemn occasions to be appointed, wear Mantles of sky-blue satin, silk or poplin [wrought in Ireland] lined with white silk or poplin, having on the right shoulder a hood of the same material, and the said Mantles shall be fastened by a cordon of blue silk and gold, having two blue silk and gold tassels attached thereto, on the left side of which Mantles shall be worn a representation of the Star of a Knight Companion, which shall be composed of silver, consisting of eight points, that is to say, four greater and four lesser, issuing from a centre enclosing a representation of the Badge of the Order, but without the wreath of trefoils as hereinafter described. And we do command that the Grand Master for the time being and the Knights Companions shall wear the said Star of the Order in silver upon the left side of their Coats or outer garments, and that they shall wear at Investitures of the Order, as well as on all days usually termed "Collar Days", a Collar of gold composed of Roses and Harps alternately, tied together with knots of gold, and the said roses shall be enamelled alternately white leaves within red and red leaves within white; and in the centre of the said Collar shall be an Imperial jewelled Crown surmounting a Harp of Gold, from which shall hang the Badge of the Order, which shall be composed of gold as follows: the Cross of Saint Patrick gules, on a field argent, surmounted by a trefoil slipped vert, each leaf charged with an Imperial Crown or; all within a circle of sky-blue enamel with the motto of Our said Order "QUIS SEPARABIT, MDCCLXXXIII", thereon in letters of gold, the whole enclosed by a wreath of trefoils vert, on a gold ground and enamelled in their proper colours.

Further, it is ordained that, upon all other occasions appointed, the said Knights Companions shall wear the said Badge pendent from a sky-blue ribbon of four inches in width over the left shoulder.

XI. And it is further ordained that upon all other occasions, except as hereinbefore provided, the Grand Master for the time being shall wear around his neck, pendent from a sky-blue ribbon of two inches in width, the Badge of Our said Order, surmounted by a Harp crowned with an Imperial Crown.

XII. And it is ordained that on the resignation or decease of the Grand Master of the said Order the Insignia of the Grand Master shall be delivered to Our [Ulster] King of Arms to be deposited in such place of safety as shall from time to time be determined by Us, Our Heirs and Successors, until it be delivered to a new Grand Master on his appointment by the Sovereign of the said Order.

XIII. And We do further ordain, direct and appoint that upon the nomination of any person to be a Knight Companion of the said Order he shall be invested with the Insignia thereof by Us, Our Heirs or Successors, in such manner and at such time and place as We, Our Heirs or Successors shall direct, but it shall be competent for Us, Our Heirs or Successors by Warrant under Our Sign Manual and sealed with the Seal of the Order to dispense with the ceremony of his investiture or to authorise the Grand Master of the said Order or other Knight Companion to perform in Our name and on Our behalf the said ceremony.

XIV. It is ordained that every Knight admitted into the said Order shall make and subscribe the following Declaration:

"I declare upon my honour that during the time I shall be a Knight Companion of this Most Illustrious Order of Saint Patrick, I will keep, defend and sustain the honours, rights and privileges of the Sovereign of the said Order, and well and truly accomplish all the Statutes, points and ordinances of the said Order, as though they were read to me from point to point, and article to article, and that wittingly and willingly I will not break any Statutes of the said Order, or any article in them contained, excepting those from which I shall have received a dispensation from the Sovereign."

XV. It is ordained that on the decease of each and every Knight Companion of this Most Illustrious Order, the heirs, executors and administrators of all such Knights Companions shall, within three months after the decease of any such Knight, deliver the before-mentioned Stars, Collars and Badges to the Sovereign or the Grand Master, for the service of the Order. And Ulster King of Arms, or his Deputy, shall have full power in the name of the Grand Master to apply to the heirs, executors or administrators of such deceased Knights for the Stars, Collars and Badges aforesaid.

XVI. And it is further ordained that the said Stars, Collars and Badges shall be deposited with Ulster King of Arms for safe keeping until they be disposed of by the Sovereign or by the Grand Master. And when the said Stars, Collars and Badges are delivered to any Knight by order of the Grand Master, he shall give a receipt for the same to Ulster King of Arms, or to his Deputy, as hereinafter set out:

"I, Sir A. B. Knight Companion of the Most Illustrious Order of Saint Patrick, do hereby acknowledge to have received one Star, one Collar and one Badge of the said Most Illustrious Order, which I promise for myself, my heirs, executors and administrators, shall be safely delivered and returned to Ulster King of Arms, or his Deputy, for the Grand Master of the said Most Illustrious Order within three months after my resignation of the said Most Illustrious Order, or of my decease, agreeable to the Statutes of the said Order. In Witness whereof I have hereunto set my hand this _____ day of _____ , ____ ".

XVII. It is ordained that for the greater splendour and dignity of this Most Illustrious Order, it shall be lawful for the Knights Companions, in conformity with antient usage upon all occasions to bear and use Supporters to their Arms; And We do by these presents direct and command Our Ulster King of Arms for the time being to grant Supporters to such Knights Companions as shall not be entitled otherwise thereto. It shall likewise be lawful for all Knights Companions to surround their Armorial Ensigns with a representation of the Collar, Circle and Motto of this Order, with the Badge pendent thereto.

XVIII. It is ordained that the Seal of the Order shall consist of the Arms following, to be engraven thereon, viz., Argent, a saltire gules over all a trefoil slipped vert, charged with three crowns or, impaling Our Royal Arms, with this circumscription, "Sigillum Illustrissimi Ordinis de Sancto Patricio"; And Our Royal Will and Pleasure is that the said Seal shall for ever hereafter be the Seal of the said Order of Saint Patrick, and that the Statutes, to be perpetually and inviolably observed within the said Order, shall be established and sealed by and with the same Seal; And We do hereby for Us, Our Heirs and Successors, declare and ordain that the said Statutes so to be given by Us, Our Heirs and Successors, to which the said Seal shall be affixed, shall be of the same force and validity as if the same Statutes had been verbatim recited in Our said Letters Patent of the day of _____ , one thousand nine hundred and twenty-seven, and had been passed under the Great Seal of the Realm. And the custody of the said Seal shall be committed to Ulster King of Arms.

XIX. In order to make such additional provisions as shall effectively preserve pure this Most Illustrious Order, it is ordained that if any Knight Companion of this Order be convicted of treason, cowardice, felony, or of any crime derogatory to his honour as a Knight or a Gentleman, or if he be accused of any such offence, and doth not, after a reasonable time, surrender himself to be tried for the same, he shall forthwith be degraded and expelled from the Order by an especial Ordinance issued for that purpose, signed by the Sovereign, and sealed with the Seal of this Order. It is hereby further declared, that We, Our Heirs and Successors, Sovereigns of this Order, are and for ever shall be the sole judges of the circumstances demanding such degradation and expulsion. Moreover, the Sovereign shall at all times have power to restore to this Most Illustrious Order, such Members thereof as may at any time have been degraded and expelled.

XX. It is ordained that there shall be the following Officers attached to this Most Illustrious Order, that is to say, a Chancellor, who shall be a Knight Companion of the said Order appointed by Us, or Our Heirs and Successors, a King of Arms who shall be the person holding the office of Ulster King of Arms, a Secretary, and a Gentleman Usher of the Black Rod, and We do further hereby direct and command that such Mantles and Insignia as in these Statutes the said Officers are directed to wear shall be prepared as heretofore at the charge of the State; moreover, the said Officers of this Order, who attend within our Royal Palace for the service of the Order, shall continually remain under the protection of the Sovereign, and are hereby declared to be servants of Our Royal Household. Further, we are pleased to declare and command that the Officers of this Order shall take rank and precedence among themselves as follows:- The Chancellor, The King of Arms, The Secretary and The Gentleman Usher. And it is hereby declared that the said Offices of King of Arms, Secretary and Gentleman Usher shall be holden during good behaviour.

XXI. It is ordained that the persons who are admitted as Officers of the said Order shall, at their admission into their respective Offices, severally make and subscribe the following Declaration that they will, during the time they shall hold their respective Offices, faithfully discharge the duties thereof in as far as to their respective Offices appertain:

"I promise to my true power, during my life, or during the time that I shall be [Chancellor] of the Most Illustrious Order of Saint Patrick, diligently and duly to observe and execute all things which shall be commanded by the Sovereign, or by the Grand Master, and which it is my duty to perform as [Chancellor] of the said Most Illustrious Order."

XXII. It is ordained that the Chancellor of the said Order shall wear the same Mantle as Our said Knights Companions, having embroidered on the right side a representation of the Badge of the Order, namely, the Cross of Saint Patrick on a field argent, surrounded by the Motto and Date of the Order, "QUIS SEPARABIT, MDCCLXXXIII," and the wreath of trefoils, he shall wear around his neck pendent from a sky-blue ribbon two inches in width, a Badge of Gold, which shall be in the form of a Purse and charged with a representation of the Badge of the Order enamelled in proper colours. The Chancellor shall affix, or cause to be affixed, the Seal of the said Most Illustrious Order to all Statutes and other Instruments and writings of the said Order which require to be passed under the said Seal. He shall, moreover, sedulously attend to the service of the said Order, and perform such other duties as he may be directed by these Statutes or by the Sovereign or Grand Master.

XXIII. It is ordained that Our Ulster King of Arms for the time being shall be the King of Arms, and shall have the custody of the Seal and of the Archives of the Order. He shall attend to the service of the Order generally, and shall obey and execute such commands and directions as he may receive from the Sovereign or the Grand Master relating to the same. He shall prepare and engross all Warrants and instruments which shall require to be sealed with the Seal of the Order. He shall carefully record in the Register all nominations to the Order and the proceedings thereunto relating. As executive Officer he shall summon the Knights Companions to all Chapters of the Order, and shall attend all Chapters of the Order, and shall carry out all requirements touching the Ceremonials of an Investiture of a Knight Companion of the Order. And further it is ordained that in all Ceremonials of the Order he shall wear, over a surcoat of white silk, a Mantle of crimson satin, but shorter in proportion than the Chancellor's, lined with white satin and tied with a cordon of crimson silk and gold, having two crimson silk and gold tassels attached thereto, on the left side of which Mantle shall be embroidered a shield bearing the Cross of Saint Patrick gules, on a field argent; and he shall wear around his neck, pendent from a sky-blue ribbon of two inches in width, a Badge of Gold containing the Cross Gules of Our said Order upon a field argent, encircled with the Motto of the Order and surmounted with an Imperial Crown; on the reverse shall be displayed on a ground of green enamel the Official Arms of Ulster King of Arms ensigned with his Crown encircled by the wreath of trefoils, and the whole enamelled in their proper colours. The said Badge to be worn pendent from a Gold Chain of three strands upon Collar days, Investitures of the Order and public occasions. And in all Ceremonials and Assemblies whatsoever, Ulster King of Arms shall have place and precedence among Our Kings of Arms, as heretofore, immediately after Lyon King of Arms.

XXIV. It is ordained that the Secretary shall be appointed by Us, Our Heirs and Successors, that in all Ceremonies of the Order, he shall wear a Mantle like unto that appointed for the Chancellor of the Order, but shorter in proportion, on the left side of which Mantle shall be embroidered the same device as borne by the King of Arms of this Order, and shall wear around his neck, pendent from a sky-blue ribbon of two inches in width, the same Badge as our Knights Companions only without the Motto. He shall sedulously attend to the service of the said Order, and perform such other duties as he has heretofore performed and as he may be directed by these Statutes or by the Sovereign or Grand Master.

XXV. It is ordained that the Gentleman Usher of the Black Rod of this Most Illustrious Order shall be appointed by Us, Our Heirs and Successors; that in all Ceremonies of the Order, he shall wear a Mantle like unto that appointed for the King of Arms, but shorter in proportion, and wear around his neck, pendent from a sky-blue ribbon of two inches in width, a Badge of Gold containing the Cross Gules of Our said Order, upon a field argent encircled with the Motto of the Order and that he shall carry the Black Rod of this Order ensigned with a lion sejant in gold. He shall introduce into the presence of the Sovereign or Grand Master, prior to their Investiture, those persons to be knighted or to be invested, and shall sedulously attend to the service of the said Order and perform such other duties as he may be directed by these Statutes or by the Sovereign or Grand Master.

XXVI. It is ordained that on the resignation or decease of an Officer of the Order, his Badge of Office shall be returned to Ulster King of Arms for the service of the Order.

XXVII. It is ordained that the Seventeenth day of March in every year, being Saint Patrick's Day, shall henceforth be taken and deemed to be the Anniversary of the Institution of this Order.

XXVIII. It is ordained that Ulster King of Arms shall, within a year after the Investiture of every Knight of the Order, or at his dispensation therefrom, cause to be made an escocheon of his Armorial Bearings in a plate of metal and a Banner which shall be disposed of as shall be directed by the Sovereign of the Order.

XXIX. It is ordained that Ulster King of Arms for the time being, or his Deputy, shall as heretofore, be empowered to cause to be repaired such Insignia of the Order as may stand in need thereof, and that the expense attending such repairs, as also the expense of carriage of the Collars and Badges, shall be allowed and credited to Ulster King of Arms, or his Deputy, on his certificate upon his honour of the same being true and correct and truly and correctly done and performed. The said Ulster King of Arms, or his Deputy, shall also be authorised to procure to be made such things as may be necessary for the Investiture of the Knights, or the use of the Officers of the said Order, the expense of which he shall also be paid on his said certificate.

XXX. It is ordained that a sum not exceeding sixty-five pounds shall be demanded and taken by Ulster King of Arms from every Knight Companion to be admitted to the said Most Illustrious Order, to be so dealt with by him as the Commissioners of Our Treasury shall from time to time direct.

XXXI. We are further pleased to ordain that a duplicate Register of the Knights Companions of the said Most Illustrious Order shall be maintained in the Central Chancery of the Order of Knighthood.

XXXII. And lastly, We do hereby command and enjoin, that these Statutes and every article thereof, shall be inviolably kept and observed within Our said Order, reserving to Ourselves, Our Heirs and Successors, the power of annulling, altering, abrogating, augmenting, interpreting, or dispensing with, the same or any portion thereof, by a notification sealed with the Seal of the Order, which alterations, abrogations, augmentations, interpretations or dispensations shall be taken and received as part and parcel of these Statutes.

Given under the Seal of the said Order at Our Court at Saint James's this _____ day of _____ one thousand, nine hundred and twenty-seven in the eighteenth year of Our Reign.

APPENDIX: CEREMONIAL AT INVESTITURE AND ADMONITIONS

Whenever the Sovereign shall be pleased to command a Chapter to be held for the purpose of investing a Knight Companion of this Most Illustrious Order, there shall be three Knights Companions at least present besides the Sovereign or the Grand Master, to constitute the Chapter, unless the Sovereign or Grand Master be pleased to grant a dispensation therefrom under the Seal of the Order. The Knights Companions having assembled, wearing their Mantles, Stars and Collars, and being attended by the Officers of the Order, shall proceed into the presence of the Sovereign or Grand Master, in the Chapter Room, and take their respective seats at the Chapter Table, according to their seniority, and the Roll of the Knights shall then be called over by Ulster King of Arms. The Sovereign or Grand Master having been pleased to declare the cause of holding the Chapter, shall then declare the name, style and title of the Knight-Elect nominated to be a Knight Companion of the said Most Illustrious Order, and command the two Junior Knights present to receive the Knight-Elect at the door of the Chapter Room and conduct him to the right of the Chair of State with his Mantle, Banner, Sword, Helm and Crest borne before him, and immediately preceded by Ulster King of Arms bearing the Insignia of the Order on a cushion. The Usher of the Black Rod shall then present the Knight-Elect, who kneeling shall receive the honour of Knighthood, unless he shall have previously received that honour. The Declaration shall then be read by the Chancellor of the Order to the Knight-Elect, who shall sign the said Declaration, which shall be placed by the Secretary in the Register of the Order. The Knight shall then kneel, and the Sovereign or Grand Master, assisted by the two Senior Knights Companions present, will place the Ribbon with the Badge over the Knight's left shoulder, passing it obliquely to the right and pronouncing the Admonition, and gird him with the Sword and robe him with the Mantle, while the Chancellor reads the prescribed Admonitions. His Banner shall then be unfurled and his titles proclaimed by Ulster King of Arms. The Proclamation being ended, the newly invested Knight, having received the congratulations of the assembled Knights Companions, shall be conducted to his seat at the Chapter Table by Ulster King of Arms. The Chapter being ended, the Names, Styles and Titles of the Knights Companions present shall be proclaimed by the King of Arms, and they shall withdraw from the presence of the Sovereign or Grand Master, with the usual reverences, attended by the Officers of the Order.

The following Admonition shall be read by the Sovereign or Grand Master to every Knight on investing him with the Ribbon and Badge of the said Order:

'Sir, the loving Company of the Order of Saint Patrick hath received you their Brother, Lover and Fellow, and in token and knowledge of this We give and present you this Badge, the which God will that you receive and wear from henceforth to His praise and pleasure, and to the exaltation and honour of the said Most Illustrious Order and yourself.'

The following Admonitions shall be read by the Chancellor, or in his absence by some other Officer of the said Order who shall be appointed by the Sovereign or Grand Master, to every Knight at his Investiture into the said Order, that is to say,

Upon putting on the Sword:
'Take this Sword to the increase of your honour and in token and sign of your Membership of this Most Illustrious Order wherewith you being defended may be bold strongly to fight in the defence of those Rights and Ordinances to which you may be engaged, and to the just and necessary defence of those that be oppressed.'

Upon putting on the Mantle:
'Receive this Robe and Livery of this Most Illustrious Order in augmentation of thine honour, and wear it with a firm and steady resolution that by your character, conduct and demeanour you may approve yourself a true Servant of Almighty God, and a worthy brother and Knight Companion of this Most Illustrious Order.'

Bibliography

Aberdeen, John Campbell, Marquess of, and Ishbel, Marchioness of,
  – 'We Twa', 2 volumes, (London, 1925).
  – More Cracks with 'We Twa' (London, 1929).
Allen, Gregory, 'The Great Jewel Mystery', Garda Review, (August 1976).
The annual register.
Anon., Kings, courts and society, (London, 1930).
Anon., The Order of Saint Patrick: An Ode, (1783).
Anson, Lady Clodagh, Victorian days, (London, 1957).
Aspinall, Arthur, The later correspondence of King George III, 5 volumes, (1962–70).
Bamford, Francis, and Bankes, Viola, Vicious Circle: The Case of the Missing Irish Crown
  Jewels, (London, 1965).
Bence-Jones, Mark, Twilight of the ascendancy, (London, 1982).
Benson, A. C., Esher, Viscount, and Buckle, G. E., Letters of Queen Victoria, 3 volumes,
  (London, 1926–8).
Blake, Robert, Disraeli, (London, 1966).
Bond, M and Beamish, D, The Gentleman Usher of the Black Rod, (London, 1976).
Bowe, Nicola Gordon and, Cuming, Elizabeth, The arts and crafts movement in Dublin
  and Edinburgh, (Dublin, 1998).
Brynn, Edward, Crown and castle, (Dublin, 1978).
Buckingham and Chandos, Duke of, Memoirs of the courts and cabinets of George the
  third, 4 volumes, (London, 1853).
Buckland, Patrick, Irish unionism 1: The Anglo-Irish and the new Ireland 1885–1922,
  (Dublin, 1972).
Butler, Iris, The eldest brother, (London, 1973).
Castletown, Lord, Ego, (London, 1923).
Cokayne, George Edward, and others, The complete peerage, 13 volumes, (London,
  1910–64).
Cornwallis, Charles, Correspondence of Charles, 1st Marquess Cornwallis, ed. Charles
  Ross, 3 volumes, (London, 1859).
De Quincey, Thomas, De Quincey's works, 15 volumes, (London, 1862–71).
Duff, David, Alexandra. Princess and queen, (London, 1980).
Dunraven and Mountearl, Earl of, Past times and pastimes, 2 volumes, (London, 1922).
Farington, Joseph, The Farington diary, 8 volumes, (London, 1922–8).
Fingall, Elizabeth, Countess of, Seventy years young. Memories of Elizabeth, Countess of
  Fingall told to Pamela Hinkson, (London, 1937).
Frankland, Noble, Prince Henry, Duke of Gloucester, (London, 1979).
Freer, Stephen, 'Arms and the Flag: St Patrick's Cross', The Coat of Arms, (Spring
  1977).
French, Doris, Ishbel and the empire. A biography of Lady Aberdeen, (Reading, 1988).
Gaughan, J. Anthony, Listowel and its vicinity, second edition, (Cork, 1974).
Gilbert, Sir John Thomas, History of the viceroys of Ireland (1865).
Gilmartin, John
  – 'Markievicz and the Knights of St Patrick', Irish Arts Review, Yearbook 1995,
    Volume 11, pp. 177–9.
  – 'Vincent Waldre's Ceiling Paintings in Dublin Castle', Apollo, January 1972, pp.
    42–7.
Glover, Richard, Memoirs of a celebrated political and literary character, (London, 1814).
Greville, Charles F., The Greville memoirs. A journal of the reigns of King George IV and
  King William IV, ed. Henry Reeve, 3 volumes, (London, 1874).

Hamilton, Lord Frederic, *The days before yesterday*, (London, 1920).

Hardy, Francis, *Memoirs of the political and private life of J. Caulfeild, Earl of Charlemont*, 2 volumes, second edition, (London, 1812).

Hayes-McCoy, Gerald Anthony, *History of Irish flags*, (1979).

Headlam, Maurice, *Irish reminiscences*, (London, 1947).

Healy, Timothy, *Letters and leaders of my day*, 2 volumes, (London, 1928).

Hobson, Bulmer, *Ireland, yesterday and tomorrow*, (Tralee, 1968).

Huntly, The Marquess of, *Milestones*, third edition, (London, 1926).

Jackson, Victor, *St Patrick's Cathedral, Dublin*, (Dublin, 1976).

Jefferson, Herbert, *Viscount Pirrie of Belfast*, (Belfast, 1948).

Johnston, Edith, *Great Britain and Ireland 1760–1800: A study in political administration*, (London, 1963).

Jones, Thomas, *Whitehall diary*, ed. Keith Middlemas, 2 volumes, (London, 1969).

Larmour, Paul, *The arts and crafts movement in Ireland*, (Belfast, 1992).

Lecky, William Edward Hartpole, *A history of Ireland in the eighteenth century*, 5 volumes, (London, 1892).

Lee, Sir Sidney, *King Edward VII: a biography*, 2 volumes, (London, 1925–7).

Lyons, Francis Stewart Leland, *Ireland since the famine*, (London, 1973).

MacCarthy Mor, The, *Ulster's Office 1552–1800*, (Little Rock, 1996).

MacDonagh, Michael, *The viceroy's post bag*, (London, 1904).

Macdougall, Henry, *Sketches of Irish political characters of the present day*, (London, 1799).

McDowell, Robert Brendan,
   – *Irish Public Opinion, 1750–1800*, (London, 1944)
   – *The Irish Administration, 1801–1914* (London, 1964).

MacLysaght, Edward, *Changing Times – Ireland since 1898*, (Gerrards Cross, 1978).

Malcomson, A. P. W., *Eighteenth century Irish papers in Great Britain*, volume 2, (Belfast, 1990)

Malloch, Russell J., 'The Missing Regalia of the Grand Master of the Order of Saint Patrick', *Orders and Medals*, (Autumn 1977).

Meath, Reginald, Earl of, *Memories of the nineteenth century*, (London, 1923).

Midleton, Earl of, *Records and reactions 1856–1939*, London, 1939.

Nevill, Ralph, *Sporting days and sporting ways*, (London, 1910).

Newman, Peter W., *Companion to Irish history. From the submission of Tyrone to Partition 1603–1921*, (Oxford, 1991).

Nicholson, Sir Harold, *King George V*, (London, 1952).

Nicolas, Sir Nicholas Harris, *History of the Orders of Knighthood of the British Empire*, 4 volumes, (London, 1842).

Nugent, Claud, *The memoir of Robert, Earl Nugent*, (London, 1898).

O'Dwyer, Frederick, 'The ballroom at Dublin Castle. The origins of St Patrick's Hall', in *Decantations. A tribute to Maurice Craig*, ed. Agnes Bernelle, (Dublin, 1992), p. 164.

O'Sullivan, Donal, *The Irish Free State and its senate*, (London, 1940).

Portlock, Ronald E., *The ancient and benevolent Order of the Friendly Brothers of St Patrick. History of the London Knots 1775–1973*, (London, 1973).

Raikes, Thomas, *A portion of the journal of Thomas Raikes Esq. from 1831 to 1847*, 4 volumes, (London, 1857).

Risk, James Charles, 'The Insignia of the Order of Saint Patrick', *Orders and Medals*, (Winter 1976).

Robinson, Henry, *Memories: wise and otherwise*, (London, 1923).

Ross of Bladensburg, John, *The years of my pilgrimage*, (London, 1924).

Rosse, William Brendan, Earl of, *Birr Castle*, (Dublin, 1982).

Sexton, Brendan, *Ireland and the crown 1922–1936. The governor-generalship of the Irish Free State*, (Dublin, 1989).

Sheppard, Edgar, *George, Duke of Cambridge. A memoir of his private life*, 2 volumes, (London, 1906).

Stanley, Lady Augusta, *Later letters of Augusta Stanley 1864–1876*, ed. Dean Stanley and Hector Bolitho, (London, 1929).

Teignmouth, Lord, *Reminiscences of many years*, 2 volumes, (Edinburgh, 1878).

Thackeray, William Makepeace, *The Irish sketch book*, 2 volumes, (London, 1843).

Wagner, Sir Anthony, *A herald's world*, (London, 1988).

Wake, Jehanne, *Princess Louise*, (London, 1988).

Walpole, Horace,
- *The last journals of Horace Walpole during the reign of George III from 1771–1783*, 2 volumes, (London, 1910).
- *The letters of Horace Walpole, fourth Earl of Orford*, (London, 1891).

Webb, Alfred, *A compendium of Irish biography*, (Dublin, 1878).

Wheeler-Bennett, John, *King George VI. His life and reign*, (London, 1958).

Wilkinson, Sir Nevile Rodwell, *To all and singular*, (London, 1922).

Wynne, Michael, 'A Replica Crown Jewel', *Apollo*, February 1982.

Yates, Edmond Hodgson, *Edmund Yates: his recollections and experiences*, 2 volumes, (London, 1884).

Ziegler, Philip, *King William IV*, (London, 1973).

References

<hr>

ARCHIVE SOURCES

BL Add MS	British Library, Department of Manuscripts (London)
COCB	Cabinet Office Ceremonial Branch (London)
CCOK	Central Chancery of the Orders of Knighthood (London)
GO	Genealogical Office (Dublin)
NA	National Archives (Dublin)
PRO	Public Record Office (London)
PRONI	Public Record Office of Northern Ireland (Belfast)
RA	Royal Archives (Windsor)
RCHM	Royal Commission on Historical Manuscripts (published reports)
Sadleir Papers	Correspondence of Thomas Ulick Sadleir, in the possession of Mr Randal Sadleir
SP	Salisbury Papers, Hatfield House
SPC (CM)	Saint Patrick's Cathedral (Chapter Minutes) (Dublin)

Preface

1   Joseph Cooper Walker, *An historical essay on the dress of the ancient and modern Irish . . . to which is subjoined a memoir on the armour and weapons of the Irish*, (Dublin, 1788).
2   RCHM, Charlemont MSS, 2 volumes, (London, 1891–4), volume 2 (1894), pp.74–5, Joseph Cooper Walker to Earl of Charlemont, 5 May 1788.

Chapter One: The politics of an honour. The eighteenth-century origins of the Order

1   CCOK, *Register of the Order of St Patrick*, volume 1, royal warrant, 5 February 1783.
2   PRO, SP/63/430, Viscount Townshend to Viscount Weymouth, 17 August 1769.
3   Horace Walpole, *The last journals of Horace Walpole during the reign of George III from 1771–1783*, 2 volumes, (London, 1910), volume 1, p.563.
4   PRONI, T3429/1/9, Earl of Buckinghamshire to Hotham Thompson, 9 April 1777.
5   PRO, SP/63/442, Lord Harcourt to Lord Rochford, 6 March 1774.
6   BL, Add MS 58,874, f. 20, Earl Temple to William Grenville, 21 December 1782.
7   RCHM, Rutland MSS, 4 volumes, (London, 1888–1905), volume 3 (1894), p.94, Duke of Rutland to Lord Sydney, 8 May 1784.
8   PRO, HO/100/3, Earl Temple to Viscount Townshend, 16 November 1782.
9   BL, Add MS 40,177, f. 134, Earl Temple to Viscount Townshend, November 1782.
10 BL, Add MS 58,874, f. 20, Earl Temple to William Grenville, 21 December 1782.
11 PRO, HO/100/3, Viscount Townshend to Earl Temple, 21 December 1783.
12 BL, Add MS 58,874, f. 23, Earl Temple to William Grenville, 25 December 1782.
13 Richard Glover, *Memoirs of a celebrated political and literary character*, (London, 1814), p.64.
14 Duke of Buckingham and Chandos, *Memoirs of the courts and cabinets of George the third*, 4 volumes, (London, 1853), volume 1, pp.105–6, William Grenville to Earl Temple, 28 December 1782.
15 ibid., p.116, William Grenville to Earl Temple, 7 January 1783.
16 ibid.
17 PRONI, D607/B/115, Earl Temple to Earl of Hillsborough, 6 January 1783.
18 RCHM, Fortescue MSS, 10 volumes, (London, 1892–1927), volume 1 (1892), p.183, Earl Temple to William Grenville, 17 January 1783.
19 Duke of Buckingham and Chandos, *Memoirs of the courts and cabinets of George the third*, 4 volumes, (London, 1853), volume 1, p.106, William Grenville to Earl Temple, 28 December 1782.
20 PRO, HO/100/200, Royal warrant, 7 March 1783.
21 RCHM, Fortescue MSS, volume 1 (1892), p.177, Earl Temple to William Grenville, 2 January 1783.
22 Claud Nugent, *The memoir of Robert, Earl Nugent*, (London, 1898), p.27.
23 ibid., p.29.
24 Duke of Buckingham and Chandos, *Memoirs of the courts and cabinets of George the third*, 4 volumes, (London, 1853), volume 1, p.117, William Grenville to Earl Temple, 7 January 1783.
25 PRO, HO/100/8, Earl Temple to Viscount Townshend, 17 January 1783.
26 BL, Add MS 40,177, Earl Temple to Viscount Townshend, 17 January 1783.
27 PRONI, Leinster Papers, D3078/3/4/5, Duke of Leinster to Earl Temple, 15 January 1783.
28 RCHM, Fortescue MSS, volume 1 (1892), p.199, Earl Temple to William Grenville, 1 March 1783.
29 PRO, HO/100/8, Earl Temple to Viscount Townshend, 13 January 1783.
30 RCHM, Lothian MSS, (London, 1905), p.419, Earl of Altamont to Earl of Buckinghamshire, 6 June 1783.
31 James C. Risk, *The history of the Order of the Bath and its insignia*, (London, 1972), p.3.
32 RCHM, Fortescue MSS, volume 1 (1892), p.190, Earl Temple to William Grenville, 9 February 1783.
33 Duke of Buckingham and Chandos, *Memoirs of the courts and cabinets of George the third*, 4 volumes (London, 1853), volume 1, p.152, William Grenville to Earl Temple, 15 January 1783.
34 ibid., p.192, William Grenville to Earl Temple, 17 March 1783.
35 ibid., p.135, William Grenville to Earl Temple, 25 January 1783.
36 ibid., p.138, William Temple to Earl Temple, 31 January 1783.
37 RCHM, Fortescue MSS, volume 1 (1892), p.190, Earl Temple to William Grenville, 9 February 1783.
38 ibid., p.196, Earl Temple to William Grenville, 16 February 1783.
39 PRO, HO/100/8, Earl Temple to Viscount Townshend, 13 January 1783.
40 Anon., *The Order of Saint Patrick: An Ode*, (London, 1783), stanza XIV.

41 RCHM, Charlemont MSS, 2 volumes, (London, 1891–4), volume 1 (1891), Lord Charlemont's memoirs of his political life 1755–1783, pp.152ff.

42 ibid., p.182, Earl Temple to William Grenville, 15 January 1783.

43 ibid., p.186, Earl Temple to William Grenville, 25 January 1783.

44 ibid., p.182, Earl Temple to William Grenville, 15 January 1783.

45 RCHM, Charlemont MSS, volume 1 (1891), Lord Charlemont's memoirs of his political life 1755–1783, p.156.

46 Duke of Buckingham and Chandos, *Memoirs of the courts and cabinets of George the third*, 4 volumes, (London, 1853), volume 1, p.140, William Grenville to Earl Temple, 31 January 1783.

47 RCHM, Fortescue MSS, volume 1 (1892), p.184, Earl Temple to William Grenville, 22 January 1783.

48 ibid., p.189, Earl Temple to William Grenville, 5 February 1783.

49 Duke of Buckingham and Chandos, *Memoirs of the courts and cabinets of George the third*, 4 volumes, (London, 1853), volume 1, p.139, William Grenville to Earl Temple, 31 January 1783.

50 RCHM, Fortescue MSS, volume 1 (1892), p.190, Earl Temple to William Grenville, 9 February 1783.

51 ibid., pp.195–6, Earl Temple to William Grenville, 16 February 1783.

52 *Dublin Evening Post*, 25 January 1783.

53 *Dublin Evening Post*, 27 February 1783.

54 ibid., 15 March 1783.

55 *Dublin Evening Post*, 25 March 1783.

Chapter Two: Constitutional and ceremonial. The Statutes, the Officers and the inaugural ceremonies

1 PRO, HO/100/8, Earl Temple to Viscount Townshend, 13 January 1783.

2 RCHM, Fortescue MSS, 10 volumes, (London, 1892–1927), volume 1 (1892), p.180, Earl Temple to William Grenville, 13 January 1783.

3 ibid., p.183, Earl Temple to William Grenville, 17 January 1783.

4 ibid., p.199, Earl Temple to William Grenville, 1 March 1783.

5 PRO, HO/100/52, Earl of Westmorland to Duke of Portland, 12 December 1794.

6 Arthur Aspinall, *The later correspondence of George III*, 5 volumes, (Cambridge, 1962–70), volume 2 (1962), p.306, Duke of Portland to King George III, 21 February 1795.

7 PRO, HO/100/8, Earl Temple to Viscount Townshend, 13 January 1783.

8 RCHM, Fortescue MSS, volume 1 (1892), p.177, Earl Temple to William Grenville, 2 January 1783.

9 *Dublin Evening Post*, 18 January 1783.

10 *Dublin Evening Post*, 21 January 1783.

11 CCOK, *Register of the Order of St Patrick*, volume 1, 'Statutes of the Most Illustrious Order of St Patrick', 1783, Statute II.

12 PRO, HO/100/8, Earl Temple to Viscount Townshend, 1 March 1783.

13 Duke of Buckingham and Chandos, *Memoirs of the courts and cabinets of George the third*, 4 volumes, (London, 1853), volume 1, p.148, William Grenville to Earl Temple, 8 February 1783.

14 RCHM, Fortescue MSS, volume 1 (1892), p.193, Earl Temple to William Grenville, 11 February 1783.

15 ibid., p.201, Earl Temple to William Grenville, 7 March 1783.

16 RCHM, Rutland MSS, 4 volumes, (London, 1888–1905), volume 3 (1894), p.78, Duke of Rutland to Earl Temple, 8 March 1784.

17 Duke of Buckingham and Chandos, *Memoirs of the courts and cabinets of George the third*, 4 volumes, (London, 1853), volume 1, p.106, William Grenville to Earl Temple, 28 December 1782.

18 RCHM, Fortescue MSS, volume 1 (1892), p.177, Earl Temple to William Grenville, 2 January 1783.

19 PRO, HO/100/240, Sir William Betham to Sir William Gosset, 13 October 1831.

20 RCHM, Fortescue MSS, volume 1 (1892), p.183, Earl Temple to William Grenville, 17 January 1783.

21 ibid., p.190, Earl Temple to William Grenville, 9 February 1783.

22 The MacCarthy Mor, *Ulster's Office 1552–1800*, (Little Rock, 1996), p.201.

23 ibid., p.206.

24 GO, MS 150, f. 26, Warrant of the Lord Lieutenant [Earl Camden], 19 March 1798.

25 CCOK, *Register of the Order of St Patrick*, volume 1, 'Statutes of the Most Illustrious Order of St Patrick', 1783, Sir Chichester Fortescue to the Lord Lieutenant, 19 March 1798.

26 RCHM, Fortescue MSS, volume 1 (1892), p.190, Earl Temple to William Grenville, 1 March 1783.

27 BL, Add MS 40,856, f. 78, Earl of Clanricarde to Earl Temple, 15 February 1783.

28 PRO, HO/100/8, Earl Temple to Lord Sydney, 2 April 1783.

29 RCHM, Fortescue MSS, volume 1 (1892), p.199, Earl Temple to William Grenville, 1 March 1783.

30 *London Gazette*, 11 March 1783.

31 *Dublin Evening Post*, 21 January 1783.

32 SPC (CM), volume 1764–92, 8 February 1783.

33 ibid., 22 February 1783.

34 ibid., 4 March 1783.

35 *Dublin Evening Post*, 27 February 1783.

36 *Dublin Evening Post*, 18 March 1783.

37 *The Times*, 22 March 1792.

38 RCHM, Charlemont MSS, volume 2 (1894), p.30, Earl of Orford to Earl of Charlemont, 23 November 1785.

39 BL, Add MS 58,874, f.41, Earl Temple to William Grenville, 15 January 1783.

40 Francis Hardy, *Memoirs of the political and private life of J. Caulfeild, Earl of Charlemont*, 2 volumes, second edition, (London, 1812), volume 2, p.67, Earl Temple to Earl of Charlemont, 6 January 1783.

41 RCHM, Fortescue MSS, volume 1 (1892), p.197, Earl Temple to William Grenville, 20 February 1783.

42 BL, Add MS 58,874, f.80, Earl Temple to William Grenville, 20 March 1783.

43 RCHM, Fortescue MSS, volume 1 (1892), p.190, Earl Temple to William Grenville, 9 February 1783.

44 BL, Add MS 58,874, f. 97, Earl Temple to William Grenville, 6 April 1783.

45 PRONI, Drennan Papers, D591/75, W. Drennan to Mrs M. McIver, June 1783.

46 *Dublin Evening Post*, 25 March 1783.

Chapter Three: The union and after. The Order in the early nineteenth century

1 PRO, HO/100/12, Earl of Northington to Lord North, 23 December 1783.
2 ibid.
3 Arthur Aspinall, *The later correspondence of George III*, 5 volumes, (Cambridge, 1962–70), volume 1 (1962), p.25, King George III to Lord Sydney, 18 January 1784.
4 ibid., Lord Sydney to King George III, 17 January 1784.
5 RCHM, Rutland MSS, volume 3 (1894), p.383, Earl of Mornington to Duke of Rutland, 17 April 1787.
6 ibid., p.365, 16 January 1787
7 Marquess Cornwallis, *Correspondence of Charles, 1st Marquis Cornwallis*, ed. Charles Ross, 3 volumes, (London, 1859), volume 3, p.100, Marquess Cornwallis to Ross, 20 May 1799.
8 George Edward Cokayne and others, *The complete peerage*, volume 3 (1913), p.456.
9 *Dublin Evening Post*, 18 March 1783.
10 Michael MacDonagh, *The viceroy's post-bag*, (London, 1904), pp.208–209, Earl of Roden to   Earl of Hardwicke, 1 July 1801.
11 ibid., p.209, Earl of Hardwicke to Earl of Roden.
12 ibid., p.209, Earl of Hardwicke to Earl of Roden, 8 November 1804.
13 ibid., p.210, Earl of Roden to Earl of Hardwicke, 10 November 1804.
14 ibid., p.214, Earl of Roden to Earl of Hardwicke, February 1805.
15 ibid., p.214, Earl of Hardwicke to Earl of Roden, 12 February 1805.
16 ibid., p.216, Earl of Hardwicke to Earl Spencer, 26 February 1806.
17 ibid., p.217, Earl Spencer to Earl of Hardwicke.
18 ibid., p.217, Marquess of Waterford to Earl of Hardwicke, 12 March 1806.
19 A. P. W. Malcomson, *Eighteenth century Irish papers in Great Britain*, (Belfast, 1990), volume 2, pp.83–4, Duke of Richmond to the Honourable Richard Ryder, 4 December 1809.
20 ibid., the Honourable Richard Ryder to Duke of Richmond, 8–9 December 1809.
21 ibid., p.137, Earl of Liverpool to Spencer Perceval, 5 July 1810.
22 SPC (CM), volume 1793–1819, 29 July 1800.
23 *Saunder's News Letter and Daily Advertiser*, 12 August 1800.
24 *Dublin Evening Post*, 4 July 1809.
25 GO, MS 308, Earl Talbot to Sir William Betham, 23 February 1819.
26 SPC (CM), volume 1793–1819, 4 August 1809.
27 Alfred Webb, *A compendium of Irish biography*, (Dublin, 1878), p.21.
28 *Irish Times*, 29 August 1821.
29 PRO, HO/100/200, Sir William Betham to Earl Talbot, 15 June 1821.
30 PRO, HO/100/199, Earl of Courtown to Earl Talbot, 23 December 1820.
31 ibid., Earl Talbot to Viscount Sidmouth, 25 December 1820.
32 PRO, HO/100/200, Earl Talbot to Viscount Sidmouth, 3 January 1821.
33 ibid., Viscount Sidmouth to Earl Talbot, 9 February 1821.
34 GO, MS 308, f.8, Chapter of the Order of Saint Patrick, 15 February 1821.
35 PRONI, D/4100/3/11, Earl Talbot to William Gregory, 27 June 1821.
36 PRO, HO/100/200, Earl Talbot to Viscount Sidmouth, 15 July 1821.
37 BL, Add MS 40,327, f.88, Sir William Betham to Archdeacon Singleton, 15 January 1830.
38 PRO, HO/100/200, Earl Talbot to Viscount Sidmouth, 25 February 1821.
39 Sir Nicholas Harris Nicolas, *History of the Orders of Knighthood*, 4 volumes, (London, 1842), volume 4, appendix, p.xii.
40 An unpublished article by the late Mrs P. B. Phair, based on the letter books of Sir William Betham and used here with her permission (no pagination).
41 *Dublin Freeman's Journal*, 7 September 1821.
42 GO, MS 365, ff.193–6, Report of Chief Constable Michael Farrell, 30 August 1821.
43 ibid., Sir William Betham to the Lord Lieutenant, 1 August 1821 [ff.167–8] and 7 August 1821 [f.173].
44 *Irish Times*, 29 August 1821.
45 ibid.
46 ibid.
47 Sir Nicholas Harris Nicolas, *History of the Orders of Knighthood*, 4 volumes, (London, 1842), volume 4, p.40.
48 *Irish Times*, 29 August 1821.
49 *Dublin Evening Post*, 18 August 1821.
50 GO, MS 365, ff.189–92, Alderman Frederick Darnley to Sir William Betham, 1 September 1821.
51 ibid., ff.193–6, Report of Chief Constable Michael Farrell, 30 August 1821.
52 ibid., ff.188–9, Sir William Betham to Alderman Frederick Darnley, 29 August 1821.
53 ibid., ff.193–6, Report of Chief Constable Michael Farrell, 30 August 1821.
54 *Irish Times*, 29 August 1821.
55 Five further extra knights (excluding members of the royal family) were appointed: Earl of Mayo, 1868; Earl of Enniskillen and Baron de Ros, 1902; Earl of Shaftesbury and Field Marshal Viscount Kitchener of Khartoum, 1911.
56 PRONI, Anglesey Papers, D619/28G, p.123/69, Earl Grey to Marquess of Anglesey, 22 August 1831.
57 Philip Ziegler, *King William IV*, (London, 1973), p.153.
58 GO, MS 380, ff.502–03, J. Shiffner or Skiffner to Viscount Melbourne, 4 January 1833.
59 *Report from the select committee on civil government charges*. H.C. 1831 (337), iv.
60 William Makepeace Thackeray, *The Irish sketch book*, 2 volumes (London, 1843), volume 2, p.312.
61 GO, MS 374, ff.270–1, Sir William Betham to Thomas Drummond, 27 November 1838.
62 GO, MS 380, ff.516–7, Viscount Melbourne's secretary to Sir William Betham, 11 February 1833.
63 PRONI, Anglesey Papers, D619/28G, p.267/142, Earl Grey to Marquess of Anglesey, 23 March 1833.
64 *The Times*, 19 September 1845.
65 PRO, PRO/30/3B, Letter 265, Archbishop of Dublin to Lord John Russell, 28 August 1837.
66 GO, MS 375, f.54, William Skeys to Sir William Betham, 11 October 1839.
67 GO, MS 377, ff.190–1, Sir William Betham to the Reverend Roger Dawson, 10 August 1847.
68 ibid., f.357, Sir William Betham to W. Knox Orme, 21 October 1848.

69 GO, MS 378, ff.269–71, Sir William Betham to Mr De la Bateman, 15 July 1852.
70 GO, MS 374, ff.124–6, drafts of a warrant [by Sir William Betham] for the Lord Lieutenant [Earl of Mulgrave], no date.
71 ibid., f.146, Sir William Betham to Sir William Leeson, 4 June 1838.
72 GO, MS 381, f..477, The Lord Lieutenant [Earl of Mulgrave] to Sir William Betham, 9 October 1838.
73 GO, MS 378, ff.356–7, Sheffield Betham to H. Millar, 7 November 1853. Molyneux Betham to John Gibbs, 7 November 1853.

Chapter Four: The new look. Farewell to the Church of Ireland

1 GO, MS 153, f.125, letter signed by Captain Robert Smith, 11 June 1874, and counter-signed by Marquess of Abercorn on 12 June 1874.
2 Robert Blake, *Disraeli*, (London, 1969), p.179.
3 Lady Augusta Stanley, *Later letters of Augusta Stanley 1864–1876*, ed. Dean Stanley and Hector Bolitho, (London, 1929), p.111.
4 PRONI, T2541, VR 85/59, Marquess of Abercorn to Earl of Mayo, 4 March 1868.
5 PRONI, T2541, VR 85/63, Marquess of Abercorn to Earl of Mayo, 6 March 1868.
6 A. C. Benson, Viscount Esher and G. E. Buckle, (editors), *Letters of Queen Victoria*, 3 volumes, (London, 1926–8), volume 1 (1926), pp.512–3, Benjamin Disraeli to Queen Victoria, 6 March 1868.
7 ibid., Queen Victoria to General Grey, 7 March 1868, pp.513–4.
8 ibid., Queen Victoria to Prince of Wales, 9 March 1868, pp.514–5.
9 PRONI, T2541, VR 85/64, Marquess of Abercorn to Earl of Mayo, 7 March 1868.
10 *The Clerical Journal*, 16 April 1868.
11 *The Daily Telegraph*, 20 April 1868.
12 *The Morning Star*, 20 April 1868.
13 *The Times*, 27 November 1872.
14 Lord Frederic Hamilton, *The days before yesterday*, (London, 1920), pp.91–2.
15 A. C. Benson, etc., *Letters of Queen Victoria 1862–1885*, 3 volumes, (London, 1926–8), volume 1 (1926), pp.522–3, Prince of Wales to Queen Victoria, 18 April 1868.
16 Edgar Sheppard, *George, Duke of Cambridge. A memoir of his private life*, 2 volumes, (London, 1906), volume 1, pp.276–277.
17 *Nation*, 18 April 1868, p.552.
18 Roger Fulford (ed) *Your dear letter. Private correspondence of Queen Victoria and the German crown princess 1865–1871*, (London, 1981), p.185.
19 RA, D27/83, Earl Spencer to William Gladstone, 1 July 1871.
20 PRO, HO/23524/109512/1, William Gladstone to Earl Spencer, 10 July 1871.
21 NA, CSORP/1891/8317, Sir Bernard Burke to John Mulhall, 5 March 1891.
22 GO, MS 322, ff.192–3, Sir Bernard Burke to the Lord Lieutenant, 11 December 1865
23 PRO, HO/45/9811/B7021, Marquess of Londonderry to Henry Matthews, 24 July 1889.
24 RA, D27/82, William Gladstone to Queen Victoria, 7 July 1871.
25 RA, A33/83, Viscount Palmerston to Queen Victoria, 26 September 1865.
26 *The Times*, 4 August 1871.
27 GO, MS 325, f.203, Sir Bernard Burke to John Mulhall, 21 March 1888.
28 GO, MS 324, ff.144–6, Sir Bernard Burke to T. H. Burke, 20 August 1881.
29 ibid., f.174, Sir Bernard Burke to ?[no name], 19 November 1881.
30 *Hansard*, House of Commons, 7 June 1883, columns 1904–05.
31 *The Irish Times*, 10 February 1885.
32 Sir Henry Robinson, *Memories: wise and otherwise*, (London, 1923), p.107.
33 ibid., p.137.
34 ibid., p.148.
35 RA, GVD, 3 February 1905.

Chapter Five: A new broom. The arrival of Arthur Vicars

1 GO, MS 325, f.277, Marquess of Drogheda to Marquess of Zetland, 28 February 1890.
2 ibid., f.278, Sir Bernard Burke to the Marquess of Zetland, 4 March 1890.
3 ibid., f.337, Memorandum by Sir Bernard Burke, no date.
4 Arthur Vicars, *An account of the antiseptic vaults beneath St Michan's Church, Dublin*, (Dublin, 1888).
5 NA, CSORP/1890/11178, Arthur Vicars to John Mulhall, 10 July 1890.
6 ibid., Arthur Vicars to Arthur Balfour, 12 July 1890.
7 ibid., Arthur Vicars to John Mulhall, 21 July 1890.
8 ibid., John Mulhall to Arthur Vicars, 23 July 1890.
9 NA, CSORP/1891/8317, Arthur Vicars to Arthur Balfour, 4 March 1891.
10 ibid., Arthur Vicars to Marquess of Zetland, 17 March 1891.
11 ibid., Arthur Vicars to John Mulhall, 18 March 1891.
12 ibid., Arthur Vicars to Sir West Ridgway, 26 March 1891.
13 PRO, HO/45/9860/B12823, Earl Cadogan to Sir Matthew White Ridley, 28 April 1899.
14 RA, Z477/252, Marquess of Salisbury to Queen Victoria, 3 July 1897.
15 RA, GV AA 12/61, Duke of York to Queen Victoria, 3 July 1897.
16 RA, GV AA 12/63, Duke of York to Queen Victoria, 25 August 1897.
17 RA, GVD, 20 August 1897.
18 *The Times*, 21 August 1897.
19 RA, Z477/261, Earl Cadogan to Queen Victoria, 1 September 1897.
20 Sir Harold Nicholson, *King George V*, (London, 1952), p.57.
21 PRO, HO/45/23524/109512/5, J. B. Dougherty to Under Secretary of State, Home Office, 28 October 1903.
22 PRO, HO/45/23524/109512/16, Sir Arthur Vicars to W. P. Byrne, 21 December 1904.
23 PRO, HO/45/23524/109512/4, 'The Memorial of Knights Companions of the Most Illustrious Order of Saint Patrick', June 1903.

24 PRO, HO/45/23524/109512/8, Memorandum by Garter King of Arms, 6 November 1903.
25 ibid., Memorandum by Ulster King of Arms, 15 January 1904.
26 PRO, HO/45/23524/109512/14, Viscount Knollys to Sir Douglas Dawson, 2 August 1904.
27 Statutes of the Order of St Patrick, (1905), Statute XXIII.
28 PRO, HO/45/23524/109512/14, E. W. Hamilton to Under Secretary, Dublin Castle, 5 May 1904.
29 The fee remained until the general abolition of fees for dignities in 1937.
30 PRO, HO/45/23524/109512/8, Memorandum by Ulster King of Arms, 15 January 1904.
31 PRO, BS/22/5, Evidence of Francis Richard Shackleton to the viceregal commission of enquiry, January 1908.
32 PRO, BS/22/4, Statements of Francis Richard Shackleton and Peirce Gun Mahony, 12 July 1907.

Chapter Six: Mysterious, detestable and disastrous. The theft of the Irish Crown Jewels

1   Anon., Kings, courts and society, (London, 1930), p.227.
2   Sir Henry Robinson, Memories: wise and otherwise, (London, 1923), p.221.
3   The Times, 9 July 1907.
4   Marquess and Marchioness of Aberdeen, More cracks with 'we twa', (London, 1929), p.142.
5   ibid., p.143.
6   Sir Sidney Lee, King Edward VII, 2 volumes, (London, 1925–7), volume 2 (1927), p.474.
7   Anon., Kings, courts and society, (London, 1930), pp.221–2.
8   David Duff, Alexandra. Princess and queen, (London, 1980), p.229.
9   Francis Bamford and Viola Bankes, Vicious circle, (London, 1965), p.63.
10 Jehanne Wake, Princess Louise, (London, 1988), p.378.
11 Francis Bamford and Viola Bankes, Vicious circle, (London, 1965), p.94.
12 Sir Sidney Lee, King Edward VII, (London, 1925–7), volume 2 (1927), p.474.
13 Francis Bamford and Viola Bankes, Vicious circle, (London, 1965), p.95.
14 RA, X13/4, Viscount Knollys to Earl of Aberdeen, 26 August 1907.
15 Sir Sidney Lee, King Edward VII, (London, 1925–7), volume 2 (1927), p.474.
16 Anon., Kings, courts and society, (London, 1930), p.232.
17 RA, W75/42A, Earl of Aberdeen to King Edward VII, 14 October 1907.
18 Francis Bamford and Viola Bankes, Vicious circle, (London, 1965), p.95.
19 Sir Sidney Lee, King Edward VII, (London, 1925–7), volume 2 (1927), p.474.
20 Bulmer Hobson, Ireland, yesterday and tomorrow, (Tralee, 1968), p.88.
21 ibid., pp.85–90.
22 PRO, CO/904/221, James Shaw to C. J. Beard, 5 February 1908.
23 BL, Add MS 46,065, ff. 66–75, November 1907.
24 ibid.
25 ibid.
26 PRO, CO/904/221, James Shaw to C. J. Beard, 5 February 1908.
27 Sir Sidney Lee, King Edward VII, (London, 1925–7), volume 2 (1927), p.474.
28 BL, Add MS 46,065, f.82, Herbert Gladstone to Augustine Birrell, 13 January 1908.
29 ibid.
30 RA, W75/54, Viscount Knollys to Earl of Aberdeen, 15 January 1908.
31 PRO, CO/904/221, Sir James Dougherty to Earl of Aberdeen, 7 February 1908.
32 'Circumstances of the Loss of the Regalia of the Order of St Patrick', Command No. 3936, Report of the Viceregal Commission, section 23; 23 January 1908.
33 Francis Bamford and Viola Bankes, Vicious circle, (London, 1965), p.187.
34 ibid., p.189.
35 J. Anthony Gaughan, Listowel and its vicinity, second edition, (Cork, 1974), p.322.
36 There are always two sides to a story. In their book Vicious circle, (London, 1965), Francis Bamford and Viola Bankes present a sympathetic portrait of a man unjustly murdered. The other side of the story is presented in J. Anthony Gaughan's book, Listowel and its vicinity, (Cork, 1974).
37 Francis Bamford and Viola Bankes, Vicious circle, (London, 1965), p.205.
38 PRO, CO/904/221, C. J. Beard to Assistant Under Secretary, 6 February 1908.
39 Sir Henry Robinson, Memories: wise and otherwise, (London, 1923), p.222.
40 NA, DT/S3926, Memorandum, 1 June 1927.
41 The Daily Telegraph, 2 November 1983.
42 PRO, HO/45/23524/109512/26, Formal submission by Edward Shortt to the King, 3 March 1919.
43 PRO, CO/904/221, Henry Claud Blake to Sir James Dougherty, 17 December 1907.
44 ibid., Henry Claud Blake to Francis Richard Shackleton, 12 September 1907.
45 Francis Bamford and Viola Bankes, Vicious circle, (London, 1965), p.146.
46 Sir Nevile Wilkinson, To all and singular, (London, 1925), p.171.
47 PRO, HO/45/10327/132452, unsigned note, 11 June 1908.
48 Sir Sidney Lee, King Edward VII, (London, 1925–7), volume 2 (1927), p.451, Viscount Knollys to Prime Minister.
49 RA, R27/67, Viscount Knollys to Sir Henry Campbell-Bannerman, 17 June 1906.
50 RA, X13/18, Earl of Aberdeen to Viscount Knollys, 22 January 1909.
51 Sir Sidney Lee, King Edward VII, (London, 1925–7), volume 2 (1927), p.52.
52 Sir Nevile Wilkinson, To all and singular, (London, 1925), p.174.
53 RA, GV 2057/2, Augustine Birrell to Viscount Knollys, 3 July 1911.
54 Sir Nevile Wilkinson, To all and singular, (London, 1925), p.203.
55 Elisabeth, Countess of Fingall, Seventy years young. Memories of Elisabeth, Countess of Fingall told to Pamela Hinkson, (London, 1937), p.336.

Chapter Seven: Unquiet times. The partition of Ireland

1   Sir Henry Robinson, Memories: wise and otherwise, (London, 1923), p.224.
2   ibid., p.228.

3 ibid., p.229
4 ibid., pp.229–3.
5 Maurice Headlam, *Irish reminiscences*, (London, 1947), p.73.
6 Mark Bence-Jones, *The twilight of the ascendancy*, (London, 1987), p.169.
7 RA, GV O537/54, Lord Wimborne to Lord Stamfordham, 14 May 1915.
8 ibid.
9 ibid., Lord Stamfordham to Lord Wimborne, 15 May 1915.
10 ibid., Lord Wimborne to Lord Stamfordham, 14 May 1915.
11 ibid., Lord Stamfordham to Lord Wimborne, 15 May 1915.
12 NA, CSORP/1920/2439, Lord Stamfordham to Herbert Samuel, 17 February 1916.
13 Maurice Headlam, *Irish reminiscences*, (London, 1923), p.74.
14 NA, CSORP/1920/2439, George Burtchaell to Samuel Power, 12 May 1917.
15 ibid., Minute signed 'W.D.', 2 July 1918.
16 F. S. L. Lyons, *Ireland since the famine*, (London, 1973), pp.370–1.
17 PRO, HO/45/16444, Lord Stamfordham to G. G. Whiskard, 6 January 1920.
18 PRO, PRO/30/59/4, f. 51, Diary of Sir Mark Grant-Sturgis, 2 April 1921.
19 *The Times*, 19 May 1947.
20 PRO, PRO/30/59/4, f. 79, Diary of Sir Mark Grant-Sturgis, 30 April 1921.
21 Thomas Jones, *Whitehall diary*, ed. Keith Middlemas, 2 volumes, (London, 1969), volume 1 1916–1925, p.223.
22 PRO, PRO/30/59/4, f. 48, Diary of Sir Mark Grant-Sturgis, 29 March 1921.
23 Timothy M. Healy, *Letters and leaders of my day*, 2 volumes, (London, 1928), volume 2, p.650.
24 PRO, HO/267/46, Viscount FitzAlan of Derwent to Ulster King of Arms, 16 September 1922.
25 CCOK, 3/22, Sir Nevile Wilkinson to Colonel George Crichton, 10 January 1922.
26 PRO, PREM/2/75, Extract from secretary's note taken at meeting of conference on Ireland with Irish ministers held on Saturday 10 June 1922 at 3pm.
27 PRO, HO/267/46, Sir Nevile Wilkinson to S. G. Tallents, 11 September 1922.
28 ibid., Viscount FitzAlan of Derwent to Ulster King of Arms, 16 September 1922.
29 PRO, CAB/43/1, Notes of a meeting of the British signatories to the treaty with Ireland, 10 June 1922.
30 ibid., Notes of a meeting 15 June 1922.
31 COCB, H57, William Cosgrave to David Lloyd George, 28 October 1922.
32 ibid., William Cosgrave to Duke of Devonshire, 30 November 1922.
33 COCB, H57, Viscount FitzAlan of Derwent to Andrew Bonar Law, 12 December 1922.
34 *The Times*, 6 December 1922.
35 PRO, CO/739/21, Geoffrey Buckland to Sir Mark Grant-Sturgis, 6 April 1923.
36 Sadleir Papers, Thomas Sadleir to Sir Nevile Wilkinson, 21 February 1923.
37 ibid., Thomas Sadleir to Sir Nevile Wilkinson, 27 February 1923.
38 PRO, CO/739/21, Sir Nevile Wilkinson to Sir Mark Grant-Sturgis, 23 April 1923.
39 ibid., Geoffrey Buckland to Sir Mark Grant-Sturgis, 6 April 1923.
40 ibid., Minutes of a meeting, 30 April 1923.
41 Sadleir Papers, Thomas Sadleir to Sir Nevile Wilkinson, 3 May 1923.
42 PRO, CO/739/21, Sir Mark Grant-Sturgis to Sir John Anderson, 5 May 1923.
43 ibid.
44 PRO, HO/45/23524/109512/29, G. G. Whiskard to Sir John Anderson, 19 March 1926.
45 ibid., Sir John Anderson to Sir Ronald Waterhouse, 8 April 1926.
46 PRO, PREM/2/75, Sir James Craig to Ramsay Macdonald, 10 July 1924.
47 PRO, HO/267/10, Archbishop of Armagh to S. G. Tallents, 28 February 1923.
48 ibid., S. G. Tallents to Sir Mark Grant-Sturgis, 1 March 1923.
49 ibid., Sir Ronald Waterhouse to Lord Stamfordham, 14 July 1924.

Chapter Eight: Diverging opinions. The King, the Home Office and the Dominions Office

1 PRO, HO/45/23524/109512/30, Note for the record by H. R. Boyd, 22 July 1926.
2 PRO, PREM/2/75, Earl of Cromer to Sir Ronald Waterhouse, 19 March 1926.
3 ibid., Lord Stamfordham to Prime Minister, 21 June 1926.
4 PRO, HO/45/23524/109512/30, Note for the record by H. R. Boyd, 19 July 1926.
5 PRO, HO/45/23525/109512/31, Sir Charles Davis to Sir John Anderson, 30 July 1926.
6 PRO, PREM/2/75, Lord Stamfordham to Sir Ronald Waterhouse, 11 February 1927.
7 COCB, H57, Minute by G. G. Whiskard, 24 February 1927.
8 PRO, DO/35/35, Sir John Anderson to G. G. Whiskard, 1 March 1927.
9 PRO, PREM/2/75, Sir Ronald Waterhouse to Lord Stamfordham, 19 February 1927.
10 ibid., Lord Stamfordham to Sir Ronald Waterhouse, 22 February 1927.
11 PRO, DO/35/35, Sir John Anderson to G. G. Whiskard, 1 March 1927.
12 PRO, HO/45/23525/109512/31, Sir Charles Davis to Sir John Anderson, 17 March 1927.
13 ibid., Sir John Anderson to Sir Ronald Waterhouse, 22 March 1927.
14 PRO, DO/35/14, Earl of Granard to Lord Stamfordham, 18 March 1927.
15 PRO, PREM/2/75, Lord Stamfordham to Earl of Granard, 18 March 1927.
16 ibid., Earl of Granard to Lord Stamfordham, 19 March 1927.
17 NA, DT/S3926, Memorandum by William Cosgrave, 23 March 1927.
18 PRO, PREM/2/75, Earl of Granard to Lord Stamfordham, 28 March 1927.
19 NA, DT/S5708, Note for the record by William Cosgrave, 23 March 1927.
20 PRO, PREM/2/75, Lord Stamfordham to Earl of Granard, 30 March 1927.
21 ibid., Earl of Granard to Lord Stamfordham, 1 April 1927.
22 ibid., Lord Stamfordham to Earl of Granard, 2 April 1927.
23 ibid., Earl of Granard to Lord Stamfordham, 4 April 1927.
24 ibid., Lord Stamfordham to Earl of Granard, 5 April 1927.
25 ibid., Lord Stamfordham to Sir Ronald Waterhouse, 31 May 1927.
26 *Belfast News Letter*, 9 June 1927.

27   PRO, HO/45/23525/109512/35, File note by H. R. Boyd, 14 July 1927.
28   PRO, DO/35/35, Statutes of . . . Order of St Patrick, Statute 28 (1927).

Chapter Nine: From across the water. The response of the Irish Free State

1   PRO, PREM/2/75, Note for the record by C. P. Duff, no date.
2   ibid., Order of Saint Patrick. Note for Lord Granard, 14 March 1928.
3   PRO, PREM/2/75, Earl of Granard to R. G. Vansittart, 2 May 1928.
4   NA, DT/S3926, William Cosgrave to John Costello, 2 April 1928.
5   ibid., undated and unsigned memorandum.
6   ibid., DT/S5708, John Costello to William Cosgrave, 18 May 1928.
7   ibid., Minute of a decision of the Irish cabinet, 21 May 1928.
8   PRO, PREM/2/75, Memorandum by William Cosgrave, 21 May 1928.
9   COCB, H57, Memorandum by Sir Oscar Dowson, Legal Adviser to the Home Office, 6 May 1943.
10   PRO, PREM/2/75, William Cosgrave to Earl of Granard, 21 May 1928.
11   ibid., Sir William Joynson-Hicks to Stanley Baldwin, 25 May 1928.
12   ibid., Sir William Joynson-Hicks to Stanley Baldwin, 19 June 1928.
13   ibid., unsigned memorandum to Stanley Baldwin, 19 June 1928.
14   PRO, HO/45/23525/109512/40, Sir William Joynson-Hicks to Earl of Granard, 30 July 1928.
15   ibid., Sir William Joynson-Hicks to Stanley Baldwin, 30 July 1928.
16   ibid., Earl of Granard to Sir William Joynson-Hicks, 3 August 1928.
17   PRO, DO/117/108, Leopold Amery to Stanley Baldwin, 23 July 1928.
18   NA, DT/S5708, Minute, department of the Taoiseach, 31 Bealtaine [May]1948.
19   ibid., William Cosgrave to Earl of Granard, 17 August 1928.
20   PRO, DO/35/51, Patrick McGilligan to Secretary of State for Dominions Affairs, 10 November 1928.
21   ibid., Memorandum by J. Stephenson, 17 December 1928.
22   PRO, PREM/2/75, Leopold Amery to Sir William Joynson-Hicks, 5 December 1928.
23   PRO, HO/45/23525/109512/45, Minute by H. R. Boyd to J. A. Thomas, 3 September 1930.
24   NA, DT/S3926, Report by Attorney-General [John Costello] to Cabinet, 1 February 1929.
25   ibid., Lord Passfield to Patrick McGilligan, 19 August 1929.
26   ibid., Memorandum from Minister of Finance, 19 October 1929.
27   ibid., Patrick McGilligan to Lord Passfield, 29 January 1930.
28   NA, DT/S5965, J. T. Thomas to Minister for External Affairs, 4 July 1930.
29   PRO, HO/45/23525/109512/45, F. A. Newsam to C. P. Duff, 18 September 1930.
30   PRO, HO/45/23525/109512/41, File note by H. R. Boyd, 24 November 1928.
31   PRO, PREM/2/75, C. P. Duff to Ramsay Macdonald, 1 September 1930.
32   PRO, HO/45/23525/109512/45, Lord Stamfordham to C. P. Duff, 7 September 1930.
33   ibid., Lord Stamfordham to C. P. Duff, 17 September 1930.
34   ibid., G. G. Whiskard to H. R. Boyd, 18 September 1930.
35   PRO, PREM/2/75, C. P. Duff to Ramsay Macdonald, 2 October 1930.
36   PRO, HO 45/23525/109512/45, Draft of a letter by C. P. Duff to Lord Stamfordham, 6 October 1930.
37   PRO, PREM/2/75, Sir Edward Harding to C. P. Duff, 24 November 1930.
38   ibid., C. P. Duff to Ramsay Macdonald, 24 November 1930.
39   ibid., C. P. Duff to Sir Edward Harding, 27 November 1930.
40   ibid., Sir Edward Harding to C. P. Duff, 6 December 1930.
41   ibid., C. P. Duff to Ramsay Macdonald, 6 December 1930.
42   PRO, DO/35/14, Earl of Granard to Lord Stamfordham, 18 March 1927.
43   PRO, PREM/2/75, Memorandum by C. P. Duff, 1 September 1930.
44   ibid., Sir Patrick Duff to J. H. Thomas, 1 April 1932.
45   PRO, HO/45/23525/109512/47, Memorandum headed *Order of St Patrick*, 10 January 1938.
46   Sadleir Papers, Sir Nevile Wilkinson to Thomas Sadleir, 7 April 1931.

Chapter Ten: The last post at Dublin Castle. The passing of the Office of Arms

1   COCB, H57, Geoffrey Buckland to S. G. Tallents, 10 March 1923.
2   Francis Bamford and Viola Bankes, *Vicious Circle*, (London, 1965), p.189, Arthur Vicars to James Fuller, 12 September 1911.
3   PRO, HO/267/46, Sir Nevile Wilkinson to S. G. Tallents, 11 September 1922.
4   PRO, HO/45/25901, Note for the record, 30 August 1927.
5   Elisabeth, Countess of Fingall, *Seventy years young. Memories of Elisabeth, Countess of Fingall told to Pamela Hinkson*, (London, 1937), p.334.
6   Nicola Gordon Bowe and Elizabeth Cumming, *The arts and crafts movement in Dublin and Edinburgh 1885–1925*, (Dublin, 1998), p.204.
7   ibid.
8   PRO, DO/35/14, C. M. Martin-Jones to James Rae, 12 February 1926.
9   ibid.
10   PRO, HO/45/10327/132452, Memorandum by Earl of Aberdeen, 11 June 1908.
11   PRO, HO/45/23524/109512/27, Viscount French to Home Secretary, 18 February 1921.
12   Sadleir Papers, Thomas Sadleir to Sir Nevile Wilkinson, 3 April 1922.
13   ibid., Thomas Sadleir to Lady Beatrix Wilkinson, 19 May 1922.
14   ibid., Thomas Sadleir, to Sir Nevile Wilkinson, 14 June 1922.
15   ibid., 16 June 1922.
16   ibid., 27 July 1922.
17   ibid., Sir Nevile Wilkinson to Thomas Sadleir, 4 August 1923.
18   ibid., Donal Sullivan to Ulster King of Arms, 21 March 1922.
19   PRO, HO/267/46, W. Swoarn (Ministry of Home Affairs) to Ulster King of Arms, 8 April 1922.
20   Sadleir Papers, Thomas Sadleir to Sir Nevile Wilkinson, 10 April 1922.
21   PRO, HO/267/46, Sir Nevile Wilkinson to Viscount FitzAlan of Derwent, 11 April 1922.

22 Sadleir Papers, Thomas Sadleir to Sir Nevile Wilkinson, 20 April 1922.
23 PRO, CO/739/2, Telegram received in the Irish Office, Alfred Cope to Lionel Curtis, 4 September 1922.
24 ibid., Greer to Antrobus, 20 September 1922.
25 PRO, HO/267/46, S. G. Tallents to A. W. Cope, 18 July 1922.
26 Sadleir Papers, Hugh Kennedy to Thomas Sadleir, 20 November 1922.
27 ibid., Thomas Sadleir, to Sir Nevile Wilkinson, 16 May 1922.
28 ibid., 22 June 1922.
29 ibid., 21 February 1923.
30 ibid., 26 April 1922.
31 ibid., 1 May 1922.
32 ibid., 24 May 1922.
33 ibid., 23 June 1922.
34 ibid., 25 June 1922.
35 ibid., 30 June 1922.
36 ibid., 27 July 1922.
37 ibid., 4 October 1922.
38 ibid., 13 October 1922.
39 ibid., 23 October 1922.
40 ibid., 23 February 1923.
41 ibid., 6 June 1923.
42 ibid., 9 December 1922.
43 ibid., 1 December 1922.
44 COCB, H57, S. G. Tallents to Geoffrey Buckland, 9 March 1923.
45 ibid., Geoffrey Buckland to S. G. Tallents, 10 March 1923.
46 PRONI, CAB/9R/52/1, C. H. Blackmore to Oscar Henderson, 3 February 1930.
47 ibid., Oscar Henderson to Robert Gransden, 2 January 1941.
48 NA, DT/S3926, Memorandum, 31 December 1936.
49 ibid., Joseph P. Walshe to Michael McDunphy, 4 Samhain [November] 1938.
50 Sadleir Papers, Lady Leconfield to Thomas Sadleir, 17 January 1939.
51 PRO, HO/45/25901, A. F. James to C. G. Markbreiter, 7 October 1940.
52 Sadleir Papers, Sir Nevile Wilkinson to Thomas Sadleir, 24 February 1940.
53 NA, DT/S3926, Joseph P. Walshe to P. Kennedy, 7 Bealtaine [May] 1941.
54 Sadleir Papers, Thomas Sadleir to ?, 31 December 1940.
55 ibid., Earl of Granard to Thomas Sadleir, 7 January 1941.
56 PRO, DO/35/1132/H616, J. J. S. Garner to Sir Alexander Hardinge, 17 December 1941.
57 NA, DT/S3926, Joseph P. Walshe to Maurice Moynihan, 16 January 1942.
58 ibid., M. O. Muimhneachain [Maurice Moynihan] to Joseph P. Walshe, 5 Feabhra [February] 1942.
59 Sadleir Papers, A. R. Wagner to Thomas Sadleir, 16 February 1941.
60 ibid., C. G. Markbreiter to Thomas Sadleir, 29 July 1942.
61 ibid.
62 PRO, DO/130/37, Sir Eric Machtig to Sir John Maffey, 7 January 1943.
63 PRO, DO/35/1132/H616, Thomas Sadleir to Garter Principal King of Arms, 15 February 1943.
64 PRONI, CAB/9R/52/1, Note of an interview with Mr Sadleir by D. A. Chart, 19 March 1943.
65 PRONI, CAB/9R/52/1, L. S. P. Freer to Robert Gransden, 27 March 1943.
66 Edward MacLysaght, *Changing Times: Ireland since 1898*, (Gerrards Cross, 1978), pp.182–3.
67 Sadleir Papers, Sir Arthur Vicars to Thomas Sadleir, 18 December 1901.
68 ibid., Sir Nevile Wilkinson to Thomas Sadleir, 23 August 1921.
69 ibid., draft letter, Thomas Sadleir to Sir Nevile Wilkinson, 23 August 1921.
70 Sir Anthony Wagner, *A herald's world*, (London, 1988), p.71.
71 PRO, DO/130/37, Duke of Norfolk to Thomas Sadleir, 26 March 1943.
72 Sadleir Papers, A. T. Butler to Thomas Sadleir, 3 May [1943].
73 PRO, DO/35/1132/H616, Sir Charles Dixon to Sir John Maffey, 9 June 1943.
74 PRO, DO/35/1132/H616, Sir John Maffey to Stephenson, 23 March 1943.
75 PRONI, CAB/9R/52/1, Wolf Cherrick to J. A. Stendall, 2 December 1943.
76 Sadleir Papers, Edward MacLysaght to Thomas Sadleir, 22 December 1944.
77 PRO, DO/130/37, Thomas Sadleir to C. G. Markbreiter, 3 July 1943.
78 Sadleir Papers, A. R. Wagner to Thomas Sadleir, 3 August 1943.
79 ibid., C. G. Markbreiter to Thomas Sadleir, 25 February 1944.

Chapter Eleven: The final efforts. Gloucester and York : Churchill and Attlee

1 RA, GV J2412/1, Duke of Abercorn to King George V, 31 May 1934.
2 COCB, H57, Note for the record by H. G. Vincent, 1 June 1934.
3 ibid., H57, Sir Clive Wigram to J. A. Barlow, 2 June 1934.
4 RA, GV J2412/2, Lord Wigram to Duke of Abercorn 2 June 1934.
5 *Belfast News Letter*, 30 June 1934.
6 COCB, H57, Lord Wigram to H. G. Vincent, 13 February 1936.
7 RA, PS GVI, PS 208/07, Lord Wigram to Major Harry Stockley, 19 February 1936.
8 RA, PS GVI, PS 208/03, Lord Wigram to Major Harry Stockley, 14 February 1936.
9 *Belfast News Letter*, 18 March 1936.
10 *Irish Independent*, 18 March 1936.
11 COCB, H57, Memorandum by W. C. Hankinson, 23 March 1937.
12 PRO, T/160/997/F1391/3, Sir Nevile Wilkinson to E. A. Bates, 11 July 1938.
13 PRONI, CAB/9R/52/1, Robert Gransden to Oscar Henderson, 9 January 1941.
14 ibid., Oscar Henderson to C. G. Markbreiter, 10 January 1941.
15 ibid., C. G. Markbreiter to Oscar Henderson, no date.
16 ibid., Robert Gransden to Oscar Henderson, 31 March 1943.
17 COCB, H57, J. J. S. Garner to J. M. Martin, 12 May 1942.

18 COCB, H57, Personal minute by Winston Churchill to Sir A. Cadogan and Sir Richard Hopkins, 16 April 1943.
19 PRO, HO/45/23525/109512/49, HW(P)1, Committee on the grant of honours, decorations and medals in time of war 1939–1943, Committee paper by Sir Robert Knox, 19 April 1943.
20 PRO, HO/45/23525/109512/50, Minute by Sir Eric Machtig to Viscount Simon, 4 August 1943.
21 PRO, HO/45/23525/109512/49, Note for the record by Sir Alexander Maxwell, 1 May 1943.
22 PRONI, CAB/9R/51/1, L. S. P. Freer to Robert Gransden, 22 April 1943.
23 ibid., Oscar Henderson to Robert Gransden, 20 May 1943.
24 ibid., Robert Gransden to Oscar Henderson, 12 June 1943.
25 PRO, DO/35/1126/H422/2, Minute by Sir Charles Dixon, 28 April 1943.
26 COCB, H57, Minute by Sir Charles Dixon, 30 April 1943.
27 COCB, H57, Sir Alexander Hardinge to Sir Robert Knox, 29 April 1943.
28 COCB, H57, Winston Churchill to Viscount Simon, 23 July 1943.
29 PRO, HO/45/23525/109512/49, HW(P)4, Committee on the grant of honours, decorations and medals in time of war 1939–1943. Provisional outline of a draft report by Sir Robert Knox, Order of Saint Patrick, 5 May 1943.
30 COCB, H57, Minute by Sir Eric Machtig to Clement Attlee, 5 May 1943.
31 PRO, HO/45/23524/109512/49, Minute by Clement Attlee to Winston Churchill, 25 May 1943.
32 ibid., Herbert Morrison to Clement Attlee, 14 May 1943.
33 ibid.
34 PRO, HO/45/23524/109512/49, Note of meeting, 10 May 1943.
35 COCB, H57, Memorandum by Viscount Simon, 5 August 1943.
36 ibid.
37 COCB, H57, Committee on the grant of honours, decorations and medals in time of war. Order of Saint Patrick. Extract from a minute by Winston Churchill, dated 19 July 1943.

Chapter Twelve: From the north. Sir Basil Brooke and the Northern Ireland interest

1 PRO, HO/45/23525/109512/51, Sir Basil Brooke to Herbert Morrison, 20 March 1945.
2 ibid., Herbert Morrison to Sir Basil Brooke, 23 March 1945.
3 ibid., Herbert Morrison to Winston Churchill, 26 March 1945.
4 COCB, H57, Minute by Sir Charles Dixon, 28 March 1945.
5 PRO, HO/45/23525/109512/51, Sir Alexander Maxwell to Robert Gransden, 24 May 1945.
6 ibid., Robert Gransden to Sir Alexander Maxwell, 14 June 1945.
7 PRO, HO/45/23525/109512/53, Minute by J. Chuter Ede to Clement Attlee, 22 October 1945.
8 ibid., Lord Addison to Clement Attlee, 27 October 1945.
9 ibid., J. Chuter Ede to Clement Attlee, 3 November 1945.
10 PRONI, CAB/9R/52/1, A. J. Kelly to Robert Gransden, 25 October 1945.
11 PRO, HO/45/23525/109512/53, Minute by Clement Attlee to J. Chuter Ede, 6 November 1945.
12 COCB, H57, Leslie Rowan to G. W. Tory, 25 October 1945.
13 PRO, HO/45/23525/109512/54, Earl Granville to Sir Alexander Maxwell, 15 November 1945.
14 ibid.
15 ibid., Sir Alexander Maxwell to Earl Granville, 19 November 1945.
16 ibid., Oscar Henderson to Sir Alexander Maxwell, 17 November 1945.
17 PRO, HO/45/23525/109512/31, Sir Charles Davis to Sir John Anderson, 30 July 1926.
18 PRO, HO/45/20289, Leslie Rowan to Arthur Peterson, 15 July 1946.
19 COCB, H57, Clement Attlee to Winston Churchill, 17 July 1946.
20 John Wheeler-Bennett, *King George VI. His life and reign.* (London, 1958), p.757.
21 COCB, H57, Leslie Rowan to Sir Eric Machtig, 13 June 1947.
22 PRO, HO/45/23525/109512/54, Draft note for the Prime Minister in response to a suggestion by Sir Basil Brooke, 24 November 1948.
23 *Hansard*, House of Commons, 11 May 1949, column 1877.
24 PRONI, CAB/9R/52/1, Note for P.M., Interview with Governor to-day, 24 March 1950.
25 ibid., Eric Montgomery to A. Robinson, 18 March 1957.
26 ibid., Sir Austin Strutt to Sir Robert Gransden, 4 April 1957.
27 ibid., Terence O'Neill to Sir Robert Gransden, 12 April 1957.
28 Letter to the author from Lord O'Neill of the Maine, 30 March 1981.
29 ibid., and another letter to the author, 18 June 1981.
30 *Hansard*, House of Commons, 4 March 1993, column 458.

Chapter Thirteen: Into the shadows. The twilight years

1 PRO, HO/45/25901, A. R. Wagner to C. G. Markbreiter, 31 December 1940.
2 CCOK, 1/5/52, Sir Ivan De la Bere to Sir Gerald Wollaston, 20 May 1952.
3 College of Arms, Printed and bound register of members of the Orders of the Garter, the Thistle and Saint Patrick, pencil note by Sir Gerald Wollaston.
4 Sadleir Papers, Sir Gerald Wollaston to Thomas Sadleir, 20 December 1950.
5 College of Arms, Printed and bound register of members of the Orders of the Garter, the Thistle and Saint Patrick, pencil note by Sir Gerald Wollaston.
6 NA (SPO), S5708, Memorandum by N. S. O'Nuallain [Nicholas Nolan], 7 May 1948.
7 ibid.
8 ibid., Memorandum by N. S. O'Nuallain [Nicholas Nolan], 26 May 1948.
9 NA, DT/S5965, Memorandum by Michael McDunphy, 4 July 1930.
10 NA, CAB 5/14, item No. 3, (8 July 1930).
11 NA, DT/S5965, Note by Michael McDunphy, 8 July 1930.
12 ibid., Oscar Traynor to Eamon de Valera, 23 August 1941.
13 ibid., M. O. Muimhneachain [Maurice Moynihan] to Roinn Gnothai Eachtracha [Department of External Affairs], 1 Mean Foir [September] 1941.

14 ibid., Isabelle Lester to Sean Lemass, 15 October 1962.
15 ibid., Sean Lemass to Isabelle Lester, 17 October 1962.
16 ibid., Hugh McCann to Department of the Taoiseach, 9 April 1963.
17 ibid., 'Draft heads of a Bill to establish an Honour to be known as the Order of St Patrick' (typed sheet, no indication of authorship).

Chapter Fourteen: The age of the peacock. The robes and insignia of the Order

1   *The gentleman's magazine*, volume LVI (1786), p.298.
2   PRO, HO/100/8, Earl Temple to Viscount Townshend, 13 January 1783.
3   Abel Boyer, *History of the life and reign of Queen Anne*, (London, 1722), pp.720–2.
4   Duke of Buckingham and Chandos, *Memoirs of the courts and cabinets of George the third*, 4 volumes, (London, 1853), volume 1, p.106, William Grenville to Earl Temple, 28 December 1782.
5   BL, Add MS 14,410
6   BL, Add MS 40,177, Earl Temple to Viscount Townshend, 17 January 1783.
7   ibid., p.183, Earl Temple to William Grenville, 17 January 1783.
8   Duke of Buckingham and Chandos, *Memoirs of the courts and cabinets of George the third*, 4 volumes, (London, 1853), volume 1, p.139, William Grenville to Earl Temple, 31 January 1783.
9   RCHM, Fortescue MSS, 10 volumes, (London, 1892–1927), volume 1 (1892), p.190, Earl Temple to William Grenville, 9 February 1783.
10 PRO, HO/100/8, Earl Temple to Viscount Townshend, 13 January 1783.
11 RCHM, Fortescue MSS, volume 1 (1892), Earl Temple to William Grenville, 27 January 1783.
12 Horace Walpole, *The letters of Horace Walpole, fourth Earl of Orford*, (London, 1891), ed. Peter Cunningham, volume 8, p.330.
13 GO, MS 371, f.45, Sir William Betham to Earl of Charlemont, 24 April 1832.
14 GO, MS 326, f.51, Sir Bernard Burke to Messrs Atkinson, 12 March 1886.
15 ibid., f.53, 13 March 1886.
16 ibid., f.54, Memorandum by Sir Arthur Vicars, no date.
17 ibid., f.55, sealed pattern, 18 February 1903.
18 GO, MS 312, ff.77–8, Earl Talbot to Sir William Betham, 29 July 1837.
19 *Dublin Evening Post*, 18 March 1783.
20 ibid., 22 February 1783.
21 ibid., 4 March 1783.
22 GO, MS 308, f.1, Earl Talbot to Sir William Betham, 23 February 1819.
23 PRO, HO/100/8, Earl Temple to Viscount Townshend, 13 January 1783.
24 CCOK, *Register of the Order of Saint Patrick*, volume 1, 'Ordinances touching the Badges, Devices and Habits of Our Knights Companions of our Most Illustrious Order of St Patrick; the Habits of their Esquires, and the Badges and Habits of the Officers of the said Order', 28 February 1783.
25 Duke of Buckingham and Chandos, *Memoirs of the courts and cabinets of George the third*, 4 volumes, (London, 1853), volume 1, p.139, William Grenville to Earl Temple, 31 January 1783.
26 RCHM, Fortescue MSS, 10 volumes, (London, 1892–1927), volume 1 (1892), p.190, Earl Temple to William Grenville, 9 February 1783.
27 *Dublin Evening Post*, 8 February 1783.
28 Duke of Buckingham and Chandos, *Memoirs of the courts and cabinets of George the third*, 4 volumes, (London, 1853), volume 1, p.140, William Grenville to Earl Temple, 31 January 1783.
29 ibid., 22 February 1783.
30 PRO, HO/100/137, Earl of Harwicke to Archbishop of Dublin, 27 March 1806.
31 BL, Add MS 40,555, ff. 61–7, Henry Pakenham to Sir Robert Peel, 4 December 1844.
32 ibid.
33 BL, Add MS 40,555, ? to Sir Robert Peel, 9 December 1844.
34 GO, MS 308, Sir William Betham to the Dean of St Patrick's Cathedral, 21 September 1814.
35 GO, MS 312, f. 13, Memorandum by Sir William Betham [probably to the lord lieutenant], no date.
36 PRO, HO/100/240, Sir William Betham to Sir William Gosset(?), 13 October 1831.
37 PRO, HO/44/2, f. 25, Lieutenant General Frederick Wetherall to Viscount Sidmouth, 21 May 1820.
38 GO, MS 365, f. 158, Sir William Betham to Mr Gregory, 4 July 1821.
39 GO, MS 150, f. 283, Earl Talbot to Sir William Betham, 26 December 1820.
40 ibid., f. 187, Sir William Betham to West & Co., 1 September 1821.
41 GO, MS 365, f.186, Sir William Betham to Earl of Roden, 30 August 1821.
42 GO, MS 381, f.191, J. Stewart to Sir William Betham, 2 December 1834.
43 ibid., ff.295–7, Earl of Courtown to Sir William Betham, 28 March 1836.
44 ibid., ff.271–2, Sir William Betham to Earl of Courtown, 30 March 1836.
45 ibid., ff.277–9, Earl of Courtown to Sir William Betham, 5 April 1836.
46 ibid., f.317, Mr Morpeth to Sir William Betham, 13 December 1836.
47 GO, MS 308, f.1, Receipt signed by Earl O'Neill, 19 February 1814.
48 COCB, H57, Major Harry Stockley to Sir Robert Knox, 4 May 1943.
49 CCOK, *Register of the Order of Saint Patrick*, volume 1, 'Ordinances touching the Badges, Devices and Habits of Our Knights Companions of our Most Illustrious Order of St Patrick; the Habits of their Esquires, and the Badges and Habits of the Officers of the said Order', 28 February 1783.
50 PRO, HO/45/23524/109512/25, R. W. Vernon to G. G. Whiskard, 12 September 1918.
51 *Dublin Evening Post*, 16 August 1821.
52 RCHM, Fortescue MSS, volume 6 (1908), p.51, Major General John Floyd to Major General George Harris, 9 November 1799.
53 Iris Butler, *The eldest brother*, (London, 1973), p.286.
54 *The Times*, 31 March 1885.
55 BL, Add MS, 58,874, f.97, Earl Temple to William Grenville, 6 April 1783.
56 PRO, HO/100/244, Sir William Betham to Alexander Macdonnell, 25 June 1839.
57 ibid.
58 PRO, HO/45/23524/109512/17, Sir Arthur Vicars to Earl of Dudley, 15 August 1904.

59 ibid., Viscount Knollys to M. L. Waller, 1 April 1905.
60 PRO, HO/45/23524/109512/6, Earl of Dudley to A. Akers Douglas, 20 October 1903.
61 Francis Bamford and Viola Bankes, *Vicious Circle*, (London, 1965), p.187, Sir Arthur Vicars to James Fuller, 9 October 1910.
62 PRO, HO/144/1648/156/610/9, Sir Arthur Vicars to Malachy Kelly, 22 November 1910.
63 GO, MS 327, f.188, Francis Mowatt to Sir Arthur Vicars, 29 April 1899.
64 GO, MS 369, f.288, Molyneux Betham to Mrs Mary O'Flaherty, 24 September 1829.
65 ibid., f.289, Sir William Betham to Mrs Mary O'Flaherty, 26 September 1829.
66 PRO, HO/45/23524/109512/25, R. V. Vernon to G. G. Whiskard, 12 September 1918.
67 PRO, HO/45/23524/109512/26, Formal submission by Edward Shortt to King George V, 3 March 1919.
68 PRO, HO/45/23525/109512/46, J. A. Barlow to Sir Nevile Wilkinson, 28 May 1937.
69 CCOK, 3/34, Colonel the Honourable Sir George Crichton to Sir Nevile Wilkinson, 3 July 1934.
70 ibid, Memorandum from the Privy Purse Office to Secretary of the Central Chancery of the Orders of Knighthood, 2 August 1934.
71 ibid., West and Son to Colonel the Honourable Sir George Crichton, 19 September 1934.
72 CCOK, 3.35, Keeper of the Privy Purse to Secretary of the Central Chancery of the Orders of Knighthood, 9 July 1935.
73 GO, MS 324, f. 70, Sir Bernard Burke to T. H. Burke, 27 November 1880.
74 PRO, T/160/997/F1391/3, Colonel Randal Skeffington-Smyth to Sir Nevile Wilkinson, 31 May 1938.
75 ibid., Sir Robert Knox to S. A. Sydney-Turner, 25 July 1938.
76 COCB, H57, Sir Nevile Wilkinson to E. A. Bates, 31 August 1938.
77 PRO, T/160/997/F1391/3, M. T. Flett to Sir Nevile Wilkinson, 15 August 1939.
78 ibid., Memorandum by F. Beaumont, 20 July 1938.
79 COCB, H57, Brigadier Ivan De la Bere to Sir Robert Knox, 10 December 1948.
80 COCB, H77/B/Part 3, L.J. Taylor to Sir Robert Knox, 11 October 1957.
81 ibid., Note for the record by Sir Robert Knox, 18 October 1957
82 ibid., L.J. Taylor to Brigadier Ivan De la Bere, 25 October 1957
83 ibid., R.R. Sedgwick to Lieutenant General Sir Archibald Nye, 18 May 1950
84 ibid., L.J. Taylor to Sir Robert Knox, 18 October 1957

Chapter Fifteen: Remaining fragments. The residue of the Order

1 NA, S5965, H. J. Mundow to N. S. O'Nuallain [Nicholas Nolan], 19 Eanair [January] 1962.
2 COCB, H57, Note for the record by C. P. Duff, 12 May 1932.
3 Sadleir Papers, Sir Nevile Wilkinson to Thomas Sadleir, 10 May 1932.
4 COCB, H57, Note for the record by C. P. Duff, 12 May 1932.
5 Sadleir Papers, Sir Nevile Wilkinson to Thomas Sadleir, 10 May 1932.
6 ibid., John Smyth & Sons to Sir Nevile Wilkinson, 12 April 1922.
7 COCB, H57, M. T. Flett to Sir Robert Knox, 28 July 1939.
8 Frederick O'Dwyer, 'The ballroom at Dublin Castle. The origins of St Patrick's Hall', in *Decantations. A tribute to Maurice Craig*, ed. Agnes Bernelle, (Dublin, 1992), p.164.
9 Letter to the author from Earl of Granard, 18 April 1981.
10 Duke of Buckingham and Chandos, *Memoirs of the courts and cabinets of George the third*, 4 volumes, (London, 1853), volume 1, p.140, William Grenville to Earl Temple, 31 January 1783.
11 GO, MS 377, f.125, Sir William Betham to Lord Farnham, 14 October 1846.
12 SPC, Captain Herbert Fitzroy Fyers to Dean of St. Patrick's Cathedral, 27 February 1939
13 Letter to the author from Charles Reede, 12 January 1998.
14 Paul Larmour, *The arts and crafts movement in Ireland*, (Belfast, 1992), p.196.
15 *The* [Dublin] *Evening Press*, 14 March 1983.
16 Letters to the author from Viscount Massereene and Ferrard, 12 November 1982 and 17 December 1982.

Chapter Sixteen: Illustrissimi. The Knights of St Patrick

1 *The Times*, 18 January 1882.
2 *Dublin Evening Post*, 25 January 1783.
3 RCHM, Fortescue MSS, 10 volumes, (London, 1892–1927), volume 1 (1892), p.182, Earl Temple to William Grenville, 15 January 1783.
4 Joseph Farington, *The Farington diary*, ed. by James Greig, 8 volumes, (London, 1922–8), volume 4 (1924), p.17.
5 ibid., p.189.
6 Thomas Raikes, *A portion of the journal of Thomas Raikes Esq. from 1831 to 1847*, 4 volumes, (London, 1857), volume 3, p.115.
7 George Edward Cokayne, and others, *The complete peerage*, 13 volumes, (London, 1910–64), volume 4 (1914), p.466.
8 Charles Ross (editor), *Correspondence of Charles, 1st Marquess Cornwallis*, 3 volumes, (London, 1859), volume 3, p.269.
9 RCHM, Rutland MSS, 4 volumes, (London 1888–1905), volume 3 (1894), p.292, Earl of Tyrone to Duke of Rutland, 19 April 1786.
10 Henry Macdougall, *Sketches of Irish political characters of the present day*, (London, 1799), p.22.
11 *The annual register 1807*, (London, 1809), p.577.
12 George Edward Cokayne, and others, *The complete peerage*, volume 3 (1912), p.213, Mrs Delaney, 5 April 1774.
13 Henry Macdougall, *Sketches of Irish political characters of the present day*, (London, 1799), p.13.
14 Charles F. Greville, *The Greville memoirs. A journal of the reigns of King George IV and King William IV*, ed. Henry Reeve, 3 volumes, (London, 1874), volume 3, p.31.
15 ibid., p.36.
16 RCHM, Fortescue MSS, volume 5 (1906), p.49, Earl of Mornington to Lord Grenville, 12 May 1799.
17 George Edward Cokayne, and others, *The complete peerage*, volume 9 (1936), p.237.

18 George Edward Cokayne, and others, *The complete peerage*, volume 1 (1910), p.228.
19 ibid., volume 3 (1913), p.469.
20 ibid., p.137.
21 ibid. Edmund Burke, 7 August 1785.
22 PRO, HO/100/12, Earl of Northington to Lord North, 23 December 1783.
23 Henry Macdougall, *Sketches of Irish political characters of the present day*, (London, 1799), pp.53–4.
24 George Edward Cokayne, and others, *The complete peerage*, volume 3 (1913), p.277.
25 Henry Macdougall, *Sketches of Irish political characters of the present day*, (London, 1799), pp.26–7.
26 ibid., p.77
27 PRO, HO/100/80, Marquess Camden to Duke of Portland, 21 January 1798.
28 Henry Macdougall, *Sketches of Irish political characters of the present day*, (London, 1799), pp.43–4.
29 W. E. H. Lecky, *A history of Ireland in the eighteenth century*, 5 volumes, (London, 1892), volume 5, pp.293–4.
30 Thomas De Quincey, *De Quincey's works*, 15 volumes, (London, 1862–71), volume 14, p.224.
31 Henry Macdougall, *Sketches of Irish political characters of the present day*, (London, 1799), p.56.
32 PRONI, T2541/V.R.236, Lord Colville to Marquess of Abercorn, 26 August 1868.
33 SP, Earl of Kilmorey to Prince of Wales, 1888
34 RCHM, Fortescue MSS, volume 8 (1912), p.157, W. Elliott to Lord Grenville, 26 May 1806.
35 George Edward Cokayne, and others, *The complete peerage*, volume 5 (1926), p.83.
36 Lord Teignmouth. *Reminiscences of many years*, 2 volumes, (Edinburgh, 1878), volume 1, pp.174–5.
37 George Edward Cokayne and others, *The complete peerage*, volume 7 (1929), p.581.
38 *Morning Post*, 14 May 1897.
39 Mark Bence-Jones, *The twilight of the ascendancy*, (London, 1987), p.24.
40 *The Times*, 19 July 1871.
41 *The Times*, 10 February 1879.
42 *The gentleman's magazine*, volume 82, part 2, p.668.
43 RCHM, Fortescue MSS, 10 volumes, (London, 1892–1927), volume 10 (1927), p.185 Lord Auckland to Lord Grenville, 16 December 1811.
44 Edmund Hodgson Yates, *Edmund Yates: his recollections and experiences*, 2 volumes, (London, 1884), volume 1, p.82.
45 ibid.
46 *The Times*, 27 November 1872.
47 George Edward Cokayne and others, *The complete peerage*, volume 4 (1916), p.392.
48 Marquess of Huntly, *Milestones*, third edition, (London, 1926), p.194.
49 *The Times*, 12 April 1922.
50 Ralph Nevill, *Sporting days and sporting ways*, (London, 1910), pp.7–8.
51 *The annual register 1859*, (London, 1860), p.494.
52 George Edward Cokayne, and others, *The complete peerage*, volume 12 (1959), p.424.
53 Peter Stanford, *Lord Longford. A life*, (London, 1994), p.18
54 Lord Castletown, *Ego*, (London, 1923), p.213.
55 Sir John Ross of Bladensburg, *The years of my pilgrimage*, (London, 1924), p.107.
56 Sir Nevile Wilkinson, *To all and singular*, (London, 1925), p.203.
57 George Edward Cokayne, and others, *The complete peerage*, volume 4 (1916), p.495.
58 *The annual register 1885*, (London, 1886), p.142.
59 *The Times*, 5 November 1934.
60 Sir Nevile Wilkinson, *To all and singular*, (London, 1922), pp.203–4.
61 Herbert Jefferson, *Viscount Pirrie of Belfast*, (Belfast, 1948), p.135.
62 Paul Larmour, *The arts and crafts movement in Ireland*, (Belfast, 1992), p.58.
63 ibid., p.216.
64 Earl of Meath, *Memories of the nineteenth century*, (London, 1923), p.87.
65 *The Times*, 16 June 1926.
66 *Dictionary of national biography 1922–1930*, (London, 1937), p.701.
67 *The Times*, 28 December 1926.
68 Mark Bence-Jones, *The twilight of the ascendancy*, p.233.
69 PRONI, D619/28G, p.123/69, Earl Grey to Marquess of Anglesey, 22 August 1831.
70 George Edward Cokayne and others, *The complete peerage*, volume 3 (1932), p.82.
71 Elisabeth, Countess of Fingall, *Seventy years young. Memories of Elisabeth, Countess of Fingall told to Pamela Hinkson*, (London, 1937), p.77.
72 RA, GV O537/54, Lord Wimborne to Lord Stamfordham, 14 May 1915.

INDEX